Privacy and Human Rights 2002

An International Survey of
Privacy Laws and Developments

Electronic Privacy Information Center
Washington, DC, USA

Privacy International
London, United Kingdom

First edition 2002
Printed in the United States of America
All Rights Reserved

ISBN: 1-893044-16-5

About the Electronic Privacy Information Center

The Electronic Privacy Information Center (EPIC) is a public interest research center in Washington, D.C. It was established in 1994 to focus public attention on emerging civil liberties issues and to protect privacy, the First Amendment, and constitutional values. EPIC is a project of the Fund for Constitutional Government. EPIC is a member of the Transatlantic Consumer Dialog, Global Internet Liberty Campaign, the Internet Free Expression Alliance and the Internet Privacy Coalition.

The EPIC Bookstore provides a comprehensive selection of books and reports on computer security, cryptography, the First Amendment and free speech, open government, and privacy. Visit the EPIC Bookstore at www.epic.org/bookstore/.

About Privacy International

Privacy International (PI) is a human rights group formed in 1990 as a watchdog on surveillance by governments and corporations. PI is based in London, England, and has an office in Washington, D.C. PI has conducted campaigns throughout the world on issues ranging from wiretapping and national security activities, to ID cards, video surveillance, data matching, police information systems, and medical privacy.

An electronic version of this report and updates is available from the Privacy International web page at http://www.privacyinternational.org/

EPIC Staff

Marc Rotenberg, Executive Director
David L. Sobel, General Counsel
Sarah Andrews, Research Director
Chris Hoofnagle, Legislative Counsel
Mikal Condon, Staff Counsel
Kate Rears, Editorial Director
Cedric Laurant, Policy Fellow
Mihir Kshirsagar, Policy Analyst
Wayne Madsen, Senior Fellow

Acknowledgments

This study was first written by David Banisar, Deputy Director of Privacy International in 1997 and has been updated on an annual basis since then. The 2002 updates were conducted by Sarah Andrews, Research Director at EPIC, and Gus Hosein, Senior Fellow at Privacy International. Substantial writing and research for this edition was provided by EPIC staff, and the law students who participated in the EPIC 2002 Internet Public Interest Opportunities Program (IPIOP): Nicole Anastasopoulos, Will DeVries, Marcia Hofmann, Dwayne Nelson, Carla Meninsky, Greg Pemberton, Sara Rose and Jason Young.

To gather information for this study and previous editions, knowledgeable individuals from academia, government, human rights groups and other fields were asked to submit reports and information. Their reports were supplemented with information gathered from Constitutions, laws, international and national government documents, news reports, human rights reports and other sources.

EPIC and Privacy International would like to thank the following people for providing invaluable reports, information and advice: Jason Abrams, EPIC; Andrzej Adamski, Nicolas Copernicus University, Poland; Yaman Akdeniz, Cyber-Rights & Cyber-Liberties; Andrej D. Bartosiewicz, Citizen's Initiative for a Good Law on Access To Information, Slovakia; Diana Alonso Blas, Registratiekamer, Netherlands; Joze Bogataj, Data Protection Inspector, Republic of Slovenia; Mads Bryde Andersen, University of Copenhagen, Denmark; Jacques Berleur, Facultes Universitaires N.D. de la Paix, Belgium; Colin Bennett, University of Victoria, Canada; Mark Berthold, Office of the Ombudsman, New Zealand; Ian Brown, University of London; Herbert Burkert,

GMD, Germany; Heiner Busch, Switzerland; Lee Bygrave, Norwegian Research Centre for Computers & Law; Rafael Fernandez Calvo, CLI, Spain; Anne Carblanc, OECD, France; Pavel Cerny, EPS, Czech Republic; David Casacuberta, Spain; Dmitry Chereshkin, Russian Academy of Natural Sciences; Tyng-Ruey Chuang, Taiwan Association of Human Rights; Kira Kolby Christensen. Legal Adviser, Datatilsynet, Denmark; Dr. Richard Claude, Washington, D.C.; Tracy Cohen, Link Centre, University of the Witwatersrand, South Africa; Ulrich Dammann, Bundesbeauftragte für den Datenschutz, Germany; Ravi Dhar, India; Alexander Dix, Commissioner for Data Protection and Access to Information, Brandenburg, Germany; Ronnie Downes, Irish Data Protection Agency; Bo Elkjaer, Denmark; Jón Erlendsson, Iceland; Emilio Aced Félez, Agencia De Protección De Datos, Spain; William G. Ferroggiard, National Security Archive, USA; Anne-Marije Fontein, College bescherming persoonsgegevens, Netherlands; Maurice Frankel, Campaign for Freedom of Information, United Kingdom; Miguel Angel Garcia, Estudios de Consumo, Spain; Marie Georges, CNIL, France; Rishab Aiyer Ghosh, India; Ann Goldsmith Office of the Privacy Commissioner, Canada; Eric Goldstein, Human Rights Watch Middle East/North Africa; Graham Greenleaf, University of New South Wales, Australia; Marina Gromova, Russia; Alex Hamilton, Liberty, United Kingdom; Pétur Hauksson, Mannvernd, Iceland; Hordur Helgi Helgason, Deputy Commissioner, Icelandic Data Protection Authority (Persónuvernd); Bénédicte Havelange, Commission de la Protection de la Vie Privée, Belgium; Helmut. Heil, Bundesbeauftragte für den Datenschutz, Germany; Jan Holvast, Holvast and Partners, Netherlands; Deborah Hurley, Harvard Information Infrastructure Project; Pavol Husar, Commissioner for the Protection of Personal Data in Information Systems, Slovak Republic; Joichi Ito, Japan; Joel Jaakkola, Finland; Ms. Ona Jakstaite, State Data Protection Inspection, Lithuania; Sigrún Jóhannesdóttir, The Icelandic Data Protection Commission; Barbara Jurgeleviciene, Senior inspector, State Data Protection Inspectorate of the Republic of Lithuania; Marina Karakonova, Access to Information Programme, Bulgaria; Alexander Kashamov, Access to Information Programme, Bulgaria; Michael Kassner, EPIC; Yeoh Beng Keat, Ministry of Energy, Communications and Multimedia, Malaysia; Maija Kleemola, Office of Data Protection Ombudsman, Finland; Igor Kowalewski, The Bureau of the Inspector General of Poland for Personal Data Protection; Natalia Krajcovicova, Head of Commissioner's Secretariat, Inspection Unit for the Protection of Personal Data, Slovak Republic; Dieter Kronegger, Arge Daten, Austria; Jorma Kuopus, Office of the Parliamentary Ombudsman, Finland; Margarita Lacabe, Derechos Human Rights; Anne-Christine Lacoste, Belgian Privacy Data Protection Commission; Steven Lau, Hong Kong Privacy Commissioner; Pippa Lawson, Public Interest Advocacy Centre, Canada; Georg Lechner, Austrian Data Protection

Commission; Anatoly Levenchuk, Russia; Vaida Linartaite, Chief Inspector, State Data Protection Inspectorate, Lithuania; László Majtényi, Hungarian Information and Privacy Commissioner; Veni Markovski, Internet Society Bulgaria; Joe Meade, Data Protection Commissioner, Ireland; Meryem.Marzouki, IRIS, France; Viktor Mayer-Schönberger, Harvard University; Robin McLeish, Hong Kong; Erich Moechel, Quintessenz, Austria; Andrea Monti, Studio Legale Monti, Italy; Dinesh Nair; Victor Naumov, St.Petersburg Institute for Informatics, Russia; Dr. Karel Neuwirt, Office for Personal Data Protection, Czech Republic; Detlef Nogala, Max-Planck-Institut, Germany; Nelly Ognyanova, Bulgarian Institute for Legal Development; Toshimaru Ogura, Professor of Toyama University, Japan; Kaidi Oone, Estonian State Chancellery, Department of State Information Systems; Maxim Otstavnov, Computerra, Russia; Pablo A. Palazzi, Argentina; Hugues Parasie, Commission de la Protection de la Vie Privée, Belgium; Stephanie Perrin, Zero Knowledge Systems, Canada; Alberto Escudero-Pascual, Royal Institute of Technology, Sweden; Andriy Pazyuk, Privacy Ukraine; Charlotte Edholm Petersen, Datatilsynet, Denmark; Signe Plumina, Director of State Data Inspection, Latvia; Erki Podra, Data Protection Inspectorate, Ukraine; Yves Poullet, Centre de Recherches Informatique et Droit, Belgium; Andrei Pribylov, Human Rights Network, Russia; Felix Rauch, President, Swiss Internet User Group; Joel Reidenberg, Fordham University Law School, USA; Katitza Rodriguez, Director, Privaterra, Peru; Dovota Rowicka, Bureau of Inspector General for the Protection of Personal Data, Poland; Felipe Rodriquez, Electronic Frontiers Australia; Roman Romanov, Sebastopol Group for Human Rights Protection, Ukraine; Anneliese Roos, University of South Africa; Dr Paul Roth, University of Otago, New Zealand; Dag Wiese Schartum, University of Oslo, Norway; Anat Scolnicov, Association for Civil Rights in Israel; Jin Wan Seo, Department of Public Administration, University of Inchon, South Korea; Per Helge Sørensen, Digital Rights, Denmark; Antonino Serra Cambaceres, Consumers International; Justyna Seweryoska, Bureau of the Inspector General for the Protection of Personal Data, Poland; Bernard Silva, Office of the Federal Privacy Commissioner, Australia; Sergei Smirnov, Human Rights Network, Russia; Robert Ellis Smith, Privacy Journal; Christoph Sobotta, University of Frankfurt, Germany; Per Helge Sørensen, Digital Rights, Denmark; Barry Steinhardt, ACLU; Blair Stewart, New Zealand Privacy Commission; Bettina Stomper, Quintessenz, Austria; Ivan Szekely, Central European University, Hungary; Jerome Thorel, France; Kosmas Tsiraktsopulos, Swiss Data Protection Commission; Marie Vallée, Videotron, Canada; Shauna Van Dongen, Privacy Journal, USA; Geetha Veloo Malaysia; Nigel Waters, Australia; Raymond Wacks, The University of Hong Kong; Elisabeth Wallin, The Data Inspection Board, Sweden; Elizabeth Jane Walsh, University College Cork, Ireland;

Maurice Wessling, Bits of Freedom, Netherlands; Ingrid Wilson; Australian Privacy Commission; Niti Wirudchawong, Official Information Commission, Thailand; Bobson Wong, Digital Freedom Network; Ko Youngkyoung, Social Information Networking Group, South Korea.

Financial assistance was provided by the Open Society Institute and the EPIC Trust.

Foreword

The events of September 11, 2001 brought new challenges to the protection of privacy in the modern era. In the rush to strengthen national security and to reduce the risk of future terrorist acts, governments around the world turned to legal authority and new technology to extend control over individuals. Many of these proposals have had far-reaching consequences for the protection of privacy.

But many of these same proposals were not new. Prior to September 11, law enforcement agencies sought expanded communications surveillance authority. Trade groups for the entertainment industry urged national governments to create new categories of computer crime that included copyright infringements. Sellers of computer database systems had pressed governments to buy more database systems. Developers of identification technologies had pushed for increased use of their own identification techniques. Pundits had called for greater transparency about private life. All of them found support in the events of September 11 to argue for greater surveillance of people who had committed no crime.

Still, September 11 has not yet signaled the end of privacy. Constitutional authority remained in place as a barrier against the proposals that most threatened democratic self-governance. Government institutions established to safeguard privacy turned their attention to the challenges posed by the response to September 11. Political leaders spoke out against the most egregious plans. Technical experts found flaws in facial recognition systems and constitutional scholars excised provisions in legislative proposals introduced in national parliaments. NGOs around the world rallied in support of campaigns to block and even repeal invasive proposals. In Great Britain, privacy advocates pushed back the expansive and unjustified Regulation of Investigatory Powers Act. Big Brother is not yet welcome in most countries.

The annual Privacy and Human Rights survey continues to document the ebb and flow of efforts to safeguard privacy in the modern era. EPIC Research Director Sarah Andrews edited the 2002 edition of Privacy and Human Rights, building on the earlier work of Simon Davies and David Banisar. Gus Hosein provided his expertise for several critical sections. The students participating in the EPIC Internet Public Interest Opportunities Program (IPIOP), national data protection authorities, and more than one hundred experts, scholars, and advocates have all lent their support to this effort.

It continues to be our hope that a careful examination of how countries around the world respond to new challenges, even those as horrific as September 11, will enable the safeguarding of privacy in the years ahead.

Marc Rotenberg
Executive Director
EPIC
July 2002

Privacy and Human Rights 2002

Executive Summary

This annual report by EPIC and Privacy International reviews the state of privacy in over fifty countries around the world. It outlines legal protections for privacy, and summarizes important issues and events relating to privacy and surveillance.

A major focus of the 2002 report has been to document the effects of September 11, 2001 on privacy and civil liberties. In response to the events of that day, specific anti-terrorism measures have been introduced in Australia, Austria, Canada, Denmark, France, Germany, India, Singapore, Sweden, the United Kingdom and the United States. Another significant development was the adoption, in June 2002, of the European Union's Electronic Communications Privacy Directive. This Directive allows European Union member states to enact laws requiring Internet Service Providers, and other telecommunications operators, to retain the traffic and location data of all people using mobile phones, text messaging, land-line telephones, faxes, e-mails, chatrooms, the Internet, or any other electronic communication devices, to communicate. Such data retention schemes are already in place in Belgium, France, Spain and the United Kingdom and have been proposed in the Netherlands. In New Zealand a law granting significant new interception authority to law enforcement is also pending. Among all of these measures, it is possible to identify a number of trends including: increased communications surveillance and search and seizure powers; weakening of data protection regimes; increased data sharing; and increased profiling and identification. While none of the above trends are necessarily new; the novelty is the speed in which these policies gained acceptance, and in many cases, became law.

On the other hand, the report finds that efforts to pass new data protection laws or to strengthen existing laws are continuing in Eastern Europe, Asia and Latin America. In August 2001, Peru enacted a data protection law covering credit reporting agencies and, in March 2002, created a Commission to draft a more comprehensive law. In Bulgaria, a new Personal Data Protection Act came into effect in January 2002. In Estonia, the Government is currently working on an amendment bill to the Data Protection Act to bring it into full compliance with the 1995 European Union Data Protection Directive. Poland ratified the Convention for the Protection of Individuals with Regard to Automatic

Processing of Personal Data (ETS No. 108) in May 2002. In Slovakia, an amended data protection law has been introduced and is expected to take place in September 2002. In 2001, Slovenia amended its Data Protection Act in order to establish an independent supervisory authority. A Personal Data Protection Act is pending in Malaysia. In Japan, two new anti-spam laws were adopted in 2002. In Singapore a National Internet Advisory Committee issued a Model Data Protection Code for the Private Sector in February 2002.

In addition, laws or codes to protect privacy in the workplace are gaining more prominence. In Finland, a new law on Data Protection in Working Life entered into force in October 2001. In December 2001, the President of the Russian Federation, signed into law the new Labor Code which includes protection of personal data. The United Kingdom Privacy Commissioner has drafted a four-part code on data protection in the workplace. The first of these, relating to privacy in the recruitment and selection process was issued in March 2002. The second, on employee monitoring, was released for public comment in April 2002. In Sweden, a national committee issued a proposal in March 2002 recommending specific legislation to protect the personal information of current employees, former employees and employment applicants in both the private and public sectors. In May 2002, the European Union Article 29 Data Protection Working Party issued a working paper on monitoring and surveillance of electronic communications in the workplace. In June 2002, the Hong Kong Data Protection Commission issued a draft a code of practice on workplace for public consultation. The new European Union Electronic Communications Directive, while leaving open the possibility of data retention in the members states, has also established important safeguards for information transmitted across the Internet. It prohibits unsolicited commercial marketing by e-mail (spam) without consent, and protects mobile phone users from precise location tracking and surveillance.

During the year new Freedom of Information Laws were passed in Peru and Mexico and went into effect in Poland.

Table of Contents

Overview

Privacy is a fundamental human right. It underpins human dignity and other values such as freedom of association and freedom of speech. It has become one of the most important human rights of the modern age.

Privacy is recognized around the world in diverse regions and cultures. It is protected in the Universal Declaration of Human Rights, the International Covenant on Civil and Political Rights, and in many other international and regional human rights treaties. Nearly every country in the world includes a right of privacy in its constitution. At a minimum, these provisions include rights of inviolability of the home and secrecy of communications. Most recently written constitutions include specific rights to access and control one's personal information. In many of the countries where privacy is not explicitly recognized in the constitution, the courts have found that right in other provisions. In many countries, international agreements that recognize privacy rights such as the International Covenant on Civil and Political Rights or the European Convention on Human Rights have been adopted into law.

Defining Privacy

Of all the human rights in the international catalogue, privacy is perhaps the most difficult to define.[1] Definitions of privacy vary widely according to context and environment. In many countries, the concept has been fused with data protection, which interprets privacy in terms of management of personal information.

Outside this rather strict context, privacy protection is frequently seen as a way of drawing the line at how far society can intrude into a person's affairs.[2] The lack of a single definition should not imply that the issue lacks importance. As one writer observed, "in one sense, all human rights are aspects of the right to privacy."[3]

Some viewpoints on privacy:

---

[1] James Michael, Privacy and Human Rights 1 (UNESCO 1994).

[2] Simon Davies, Big Brother: Britain's Web of Surveillance and the New Technological Order 23 (Pan 1996).

[3] Volio, Fernando, "Legal personality, privacy and the family" in Henkin (ed), The International Bill of Rights (Columbia University Press 1981).

In the 1890s, future United States Supreme Court Justice Louis Brandeis articulated a concept of privacy that urged that it was the individual's "right to be left alone." Brandeis argued that privacy was the most cherished of freedoms in a democracy, and he was concerned that it should be reflected in the Constitution.[4]

Robert Ellis Smith, editor of the *Privacy Journal*, defined privacy as "the desire by each of us for physical space where we can be free of interruption, intrusion, embarrassment, or accountability and the attempt to control the time and manner of disclosures of personal information about ourselves."[5]

According to Edward Bloustein, privacy is an interest of the human personality. It protects the inviolate personality, the individual's independence, dignity and integrity.[6]

According to Ruth Gavison, there are three elements in privacy: secrecy, anonymity and solitude. It is a state which can be lost, whether through the choice of the person in that state or through the action of another person.[7]

The Calcutt Committee in the United Kingdom said that, "nowhere have we found a wholly satisfactory statutory definition of privacy." But the committee was satisfied that it would be possible to define it legally and adopted this definition in its first report on privacy:

> The right of the individual to be protected against intrusion into his personal life or affairs, or those of his family, by direct physical means or by publication of information.[8]

The Preamble to the Australian Privacy Charter provides that, "A free and democratic society requires respect for the autonomy of individuals, and limits on the power of both state and private organizations to intrude on that autonomy . . . Privacy is a key value which underpins human dignity and other key values such

---

[4] Samuel Warren and Louis Brandeis, "The Right to Privacy," 4 Harvard Law Review 193–220 (1890).

[5] Robert Ellis Smith, Ben Franklin's Web Site 6 (Sheridan Books 2000).

[6] "Privacy as an Aspect of Human Dignity," 39 New York University Law Review 971 (1964).

[7] "Privacy and the Limits of Law," 89 Yale Law Journal 421, 428 (1980).

[8] Report of the Committee on Privacy and Related Matters, Chairman David Calcutt QC, 1990, Cmnd. 1102, London: HMSO, page 7.

as freedom of association and freedom of speech. . . . Privacy is a basic human right and the reasonable expectation of every person."[9]

Aspects of Privacy

Privacy can be divided into the following separate but related concepts:

Information privacy, which involves the establishment of rules governing the collection and handling of personal data such as credit information, and medical and government records. It is also known as "data protection";

Bodily privacy, which concerns the protection of people's physical selves against invasive procedures such as genetic tests, drug testing and cavity searches;

Privacy of communications, which covers the security and privacy of mail, telephones, e-mail and other forms of communication; and

Territorial privacy, which concerns the setting of limits on intrusion into the domestic and other environments such as the workplace or public space. This includes searches, video surveillance and ID checks.

Models of Privacy Protection

There are four major models for privacy protection. Depending on their application, these models can be complementary or contradictory. In most countries reviewed in the survey, several are used simultaneously. In the countries that protect privacy most effectively, all of the models are used together to ensure privacy protection.

Comprehensive laws

In many countries around the world, there is a general law that governs the collection, use and dissemination of personal information by both the public and

---

[9] "The Australian Privacy Charter," published by the Australian Privacy Charter Group, Law School, University of New South Wales, Sydney 1994.

private sectors. An oversight body then ensures compliance. This is the preferred model for most countries adopting data protection laws and was adopted by the European Union to ensure compliance with its data protection regime. A variation of these laws, which is described as a *co-regulatory model*, was adopted in Canada and Australia. Under this approach, industry develops rules for the protection of privacy that are enforced by the industry and overseen by the privacy agency.

Sectoral Laws

Some countries, such as the United States, have avoided enacting general data protection rules in favor of specific sectoral laws governing, for example, video rental records and financial privacy. In such cases, enforcement is achieved through a range of mechanisms. A major drawback with this approach is that it requires that new legislation be introduced with each new technology so protections frequently lag behind. The lack of legal protections for individual's privacy on the Internet in the United States is a striking example of its limitations. There is also the problem of a lack of an oversight agency. In many countries, sectoral laws are used to complement comprehensive legislation by providing more detailed protections for certain categories of information, such as telecommunications, police files or consumer credit records.

Self-Regulation

Data protection can also be achieved - at least in theory - through various forms of self-regulation, in which companies and industry bodies establish codes of practice and engage in self-policing. However, in many countries, especially the United States, these efforts have been disappointing, with little evidence that the aims of the codes are regularly fulfilled. Adequacy and enforcement are the major problem with these approaches. Industry codes in many countries have tended to provide only weak protections and lack enforcement. This is currently the policy promoted by the governments of the United States and Singapore.

Technologies of Privacy

With the recent development of commercially available technology-based systems, privacy protection has also moved into the hands of individual users. Users of the Internet and of some physical applications can employ a range of programs and systems that provide varying degrees of privacy and security of

---

communications. These include encryption, anonymous remailers, proxy servers and digital cash.[10] Users should be aware that not all tools are effective of protecting privacy. Some are poorly designed while others may be designed to facilitate law enforcement access. (For more discussion of this subject see the section on *Privacy Enhancing Techniques* at 64).

The Right to Privacy

The recognition of privacy is deeply rooted in history. There is recognition of privacy in the Qur'an[11] and in the sayings of Mohammed.[12] The Bible has numerous references to privacy.[13] Jewish law has long recognized the concept of being free from being watched.[14] There were also protections in Classical Greece and ancient China.[15]

Legal protections have existed in Western countries for hundreds of years. In 1361, the Justices of the Peace Act in England provided for the arrest of peeping toms and eavesdroppers.[16] In 1765, British Lord Camden, striking down a warrant to enter a house and seize papers wrote, "We can safely say there is no law in this country to justify the defendants in what they have done; if there was, it would destroy all the comforts of society, for papers are often the dearest property any man can have."[17] Parliamentarian William Pitt wrote, "The poorest man may in his cottage bid defiance to all the force of the Crown. It may be frail; its roof may shake; the wind may blow though it; the storms may enter; the rain may enter – but the King of England cannot enter; all his forces dare not cross the threshold of the ruined tenement."[18]

Various countries developed specific protections for privacy in the centuries that followed. In 1776, the Swedish Parliament enacted the Access to Public Records Act that required that all government-held information be used for legitimate

---

[10] EPIC maintains a list of privacy tools at <http://www.epic.org/privacy/tools.htm>.

[11] an-Noor 24:27-28 (Yusufali); al-Hujraat 49:11-12 (Yusufali).

[12] Volume 1, Book 10, Number 509 (Sahih Bukhari); Book 020, Number 4727 (Sahih Muslim); Book 31, Number 4003 (Sunan Abu Dawud).

[13] Richard Hixson, Privacy in a Public Society: Human Rights in Conflict 3 (1987). See also, Barrington Moore, Privacy: Studies in Social and Cultural History (1984).

[14] See Jeffrey Rosen, The Unwanted Gaze (Random House 2000).

[15] Id. at 5.

[16] James Michael, supra n.1, at. 15. Justices of the Peace Act, 1361 (Eng.), 34 Edw. 3, c. 1.

[17] Entick v. Carrington, 1558-1774 All E.R. Rep. 45.

[18] Speech on the Excise Bill, 1763.

purposes. France prohibited the publication of private facts and set stiff fines for violators in 1858.[19] The Norwegian criminal code prohibited the publication of information relating to "personal or domestic affairs" in 1889.[20]

In 1890, American lawyers Samuel Warren and Louis Brandeis wrote a seminal piece on the right to privacy as a tort action, describing privacy as "the right to be left alone."[21] Following the publication, this concept of the privacy tort was gradually picked up across the United States as part of the common law.

The modern privacy benchmark at an international level can be found in the 1948 Universal Declaration of Human Rights, which specifically protects territorial and communications privacy.[22] Article 12 states:

> No one should be subjected to arbitrary interference with his privacy, family, home or correspondence, nor to attacks on his honour or reputation. Everyone has the right to the protection of the law against such interferences or attacks.

Numerous international human rights treaties specifically recognize privacy as a right.[23] The International Covenant on Civil and Political Rights (ICCPR), Article 17,[24] the UN Convention on Migrant Workers, Article 14,[25] and the UN Convention on Protection of the Child, Article 16[26] adopt the same language.

---

[19] The Rachel affaire. Judgment of June 16, 1858, Trib. pr. inst. de la Seine, 1858 D.P. III 62. See Jeanne M. Hauch, Protecting Private Facts in France: The Warren & Brandeis Tort is Alive and Well and Flourishing in Paris, 68 Tulane Law Review 1219 (May 1994).

[20] See Prof. Dr. Juris Jon Bing, Data Protection in Norway, 1996, available at <http://www.jus.uio.no/iri/rettsinfo/lib/papers/dp_norway/dp_norway.html>.

[21] Warren and Brandeis, supra n.4.

[22] Universal Declaration of Human Rights, adopted and proclaimed by General Assembly resolution 217 A (III) of December 10, 1948, available at <http://www.un.org/Overview/rights.html>.

[23] See generally, Marc Rotenberg, ed., The Privacy Law Sourcebook: United States Law, International Law and Recent Developments (EPIC 2001).

[24] International Covenant on Civil and Political Rights, adopted and opened for signature, ratification and accession by General Assembly resolution 2200A (XXI) of December 16, 1966, entry into force March 23 1976, available at <http://www.unhchr.ch/html/menu3/b/a_ccpr.htm>.

[25] International Convention on the Protection of the Rights of All Migrant Workers and Members of Their Families, adopted by General Assembly resolution 45/158 of December 18, 1990, available at <http://www.unhchr.ch/html/menu3/b/m_mwctoc.htm>.

[26] Convention on the Rights of the Child, adopted and opened for signature, ratification and accession by General Assembly resolution 44/25 of November 20, 1989, entry into force September 2, 1990, available at <http://www.unhchr.ch/html/menu3/b/k2crc.htm>.

On the regional level, various treaties make these rights legally enforceable. Article 8 of the European Convention for the Protection of Human Rights and Fundamental Freedoms 1950[27] states:

> (1) Everyone has the right to respect for his private and family life, his home and his correspondence. (2) There shall be no interference by a public authority with the exercise of this right except as in accordance with the law and is necessary in a democratic society in the interests of national security, public safety or the economic well-being of the country, for the prevention of disorder or crime, for the protection of health of morals, or for the protection of the rights and freedoms of others.

The Convention created the European Commission of Human Rights and the European Court of Human Rights to oversee enforcement. Both have been active in the enforcement of privacy rights and have consistently viewed Article 8's protections expansively and interpreted the restrictions narrowly.[28] The Commission found in 1976:

> For numerous Anglo-Saxon and French authors, the right to respect "private life" is the right to privacy, the right to live, as far as one wishes, protected from publicity . . . In the opinion of the Commission, however, the right to respect for private life does not end there. It comprises also, to a certain degree, the right to establish and develop relationships with other human beings, especially in the emotional field for the development and fulfillment of one's own personality.[29]

The Court has reviewed member states' laws and imposed sanctions on numerous countries for failing to regulate wiretapping by governments and private individuals.[30] It has also reviewed cases of individuals' access to their personal information in government files to ensure that adequate procedures exist.[31] It has expanded the protections of Article 8 beyond government actions

---

[27] Council of Europe, Convention for the Protection of Human Rights and Fundamental Freedoms, (ETS no: 005) open for signature November 4, 1950, entry into force September 3, 1950, available at <http://conventions.coe.int/Treaty/EN/cadreprincipal.htm>.

[28] Nadine Strossen, Recent United States and Intl. Judicial Protection of Individual Rights: A comparative Legal Process Analysis and Proposed Synthesis, 41 Hastings Law Journal 805 (1990).

[29] X v. Iceland, 5 Eur. Comm'n H.R. 86.87 (1976).

[30] European Court of Human Rights, Case of Klass and Others: Judgement of 6 September 1978, Series A No. 28 (1979). Malone v. Commissioner of Police, 2 All E.R. 620 (1979). See Note, Secret Surveillance and the European Convention on Human Rights, 33 Stanford Law Review 1113, 1122 (1981).

[31] Judgement of 26 March 1987 (Leander Case).

to those of private persons where it appears that the government should have prohibited those actions.[32]

Other regional treaties are also beginning to be used to protect privacy. Article 11 of the American Convention on Human Rights sets out the right to privacy in terms similar to the Universal Declaration.[33] In 1965, the Organization of American States proclaimed the American Declaration of the Rights and Duties of Man, which called for the protection of numerous human rights, including privacy.[34] The Inter-American Court of Human Rights has begun to address privacy issues in its cases.

The Evolution of Data Protection

Interest in the right of privacy increased in the 1960s and 1970s with the advent of information technology. The surveillance potential of powerful computer systems prompted demands for specific rules governing the collection and handling of personal information. The genesis of modern legislation in this area can be traced to the first data protection law in the world enacted in the Land of Hesse in Germany in 1970. This was followed by national laws in Sweden (1973), the United States (1974), Germany (1977), and France (1978).[35]

Two crucial international instruments evolved from these laws. The Council of Europe's 1981 Convention for the Protection of Individuals with regard to the Automatic Processing of Personal Data[36] and the Organization for Economic Cooperation and Development's (OECD) Guidelines Governing the Protection of Privacy and Transborder Data Flows of Personal Data[37] set out specific rules covering the handling of electronic data. These rules describe personal information as data that are afforded protection at every step from collection to storage and dissemination.

---

[32] Id. at 848-49.

[33] Signed November 22, 1969, entered into force July 18, 1978, O.A.S. Treaty Series No. 36, at 1, O.A.S. Off. Rec. OEA/Ser. L/V/II.23 dec rev. 2, available at <http://www.oas.org/juridico/english/Treaties/b-32.htm>.

[34] O.A.S. Res XXX, adopted by the Ninth Conference of American States, 1948 OEA/Ser/. L./V/I.4 Rev (1965).

[35] An excellent analysis of these laws is found in David Flaherty, Protecting Privacy in Surveillance Societies (University of North Carolina Press 1989).

[36] Convention for the Protection of Individuals with regard to the Automatic Processing of Personal Data Convention, ETS No. 108, Strasbourg, 1981, available at <http://www.coe.fr/eng/legaltxt/108e.htm>.

[37] OECD, "Guidelines Governing the Protection of Privacy and Transborder Data Flows of Personal Data" Paris, 1981, available at <http://www.oecd.org/dsti/sti/it/secur/prod/PRIV-EN.HTM>.

The expression of data protection in various declarations and laws varies. All require that personal information must be:

- obtained fairly and lawfully;
- used only for the original specified purpose;
- adequate, relevant and not excessive to purpose;
- accurate and up to date;
- accessible to the subject;
- kept secure; and
- destroyed after its purpose is completed.

These two agreements have had a profound effect on the enactment of laws around the world. Nearly thirty countries have signed the COE convention and several others are planning to do so shortly. The OECD guidelines have also been widely used in national legislation, even outside the OECD member countries.

Rationales for Adopting Comprehensive Laws

There are three major reasons for the movement towards comprehensive privacy and data protection laws. Many countries are adopting these laws for one or more reasons.

To remedy past injustices. Many countries, especially in Central Europe, South America and South Africa, are adopting laws to remedy privacy violations that occurred under previous authoritarian regimes.

To promote electronic commerce. Many countries, especially in Asia, have developed or are currently developing laws in an effort to promote electronic commerce. These countries recognize that consumers are uneasy with the increased availability of their personal data, particularly with new means of identification and forms of transactions. These countries recognize consumers are uneasy with their personal information being sent worldwide. Privacy laws are being introduced as part of a package of laws intended to facilitate electronic commerce by setting up uniform rules.

To ensure laws are consistent with Pan-European laws. Most countries in Central and Eastern Europe are adopting new laws based on the Council of Europe Convention and the European Union Data

Protection Directive. Many of these countries hope to join the European Union in the near future. Countries in other regions are adopting new laws or updating older laws to ensure that trade will not be affected by the requirements of the European Union Directive.

The European Union Data Protection Directives

In 1995, the European Union enacted the Data Protection Directive in order to harmonize member states' laws in providing consistent levels of protections for citizens and ensuring the free flow of personal data within the European Union. The directive sets a baseline common level of privacy that not only reinforces current data protection law, but also establishes a range of new rights. It applies to the processing of personal information in electronic and manual files.[38]

A key concept in the European data protection model is "enforceability." Data subjects have rights established in explicit rules. Every European Union country has a data protection commissioner or agency that enforces the rules. It is expected that the countries with which Europe does business will need to provide a similar level of oversight.

The basic principles established by the Directive are: the right to know where the data originated; the right to have inaccurate data rectified; a right of recourse in the event of unlawful processing; and the right to withhold permission to use data in some circumstances. For example, individuals have the right to opt-out free of charge from being sent direct marketing material. The Directive contains strengthened protections over the use of sensitive personal data relating, for example, to health, sex life or religious or philosophical beliefs. In the future, the commercial and government use of such information will generally require "explicit and unambiguous" consent of the data subject.

The 1995 Directive imposes an obligation on member states to ensure that the personal information relating to European citizens has the same level of protection when it is exported to, and processed in, countries outside the European Union. This requirement has resulted in growing pressure outside Europe for the passage of privacy laws. Those countries that refuse to adopt adequate privacy laws may find themselves unable to conduct certain types of

---

[38] Directive 95/46/EC of the European Parliament and of the Council of 24 October 1995 on the Protection of Individuals with Regard to the Processing of Personal Data and on the Free Movement of such Data, available at <http://europa.eu.int/comm/internal_market/en/media/dataprot/law/index.htm>.

information flows with Europe, particularly if they involve sensitive data. (See below.)

In 1997, the European Union supplemented the 1995 directive by introducing the Telecommunications Privacy Directive.[39] This directive established specific protections covering telephone, digital television, mobile networks and other telecommunications systems.[40]. It imposed wide-ranging obligations on carriers and service providers to ensure the privacy of users' communications, including Internet-related activities. It covered areas that, until then, had fallen between the cracks of data protection laws. Access to billing data was severely restricted, as was marketing activity. Caller ID technology was required to incorporate an option for per-line blocking of number transmission. Information collected in the delivery of a communication was required to be purged once the call is completed.

In July 2000, the European Commission issued a proposal for a new directive on privacy in the electronic communications sector.[41] The proposal was introduced as a part of a larger package of telecommunications directives aimed at strengthening competition within the European electronic communications markets. As originally proposed, the new directive would have strengthened privacy rights for individuals by extending the protections that were already in place for telecommunications to a broader, more technology-neutral category of "electronic communications." During the process, however, the Council of Ministers began to push for the inclusion of data retention provisions, requiring Internet Service Providers and telecommunications operators to store logs of all telephone calls, e-mails, faxes, and Internet activity for law enforcement purposes. These proposals were strongly opposed by most members of the Parliament. In July 2001, the European Parliament's Civil Liberties Committee approved the draft directive without data retention stating:

> The Civil Liberties Committee ("LIBE Committee") expressed itself in favour of a strict regulation of law enforcement authorities' access to personal data of citizens, such as communication traffic and location data. This decision is fundamental because in this way the EP blocks

---

[39] Directive 97/66/EC of the European Parliament and of the Council of 15 December 1997 on the Processing of Personal Data and the Protection of Privacy in the Telecommunications Sector (Directive), available at <http://www.ispo.cec.be/legal/en/dataprot/protection.html>.

[40] European Union member countries were required to enact implementing legislation by October 1998. As of the summer 2002, however, several are still pending.

[41] European Commission, Proposal for a directive of the European Parliament and of the Council Concerning the Processing of Personal Data and the Protection of Privacy in the Electronic Communications Sector , available at <http://europa.eu.int/comm/information_society/policy/framework/pdf/com2000385_en.pdf>.

European Union States' efforts underway in the Council to put their citizens under generalised and pervasive surveillance, following the Echelon model.

Following the events of September 11, however, the political climate changed and the Parliament came under increasing pressure from member states to adopt the Council's proposal for data retention. The United Kingdom and the Netherlands, in particular, questioned whether the proposed privacy rules still struck "the right balance between privacy and the needs of the law enforcement agencies in the light of the battle against terrorism."[42] The Parliament stood firm and up to a few weeks before the final vote on May 30, 2002, the majority of MEPs opposed any form of data retention. Finally, after much pressure by the European Council and European Union governments, and well organized lobbying by two Spanish MEPs,[43] the two main political parties (PPE and PSE, the center-left and center-right parties) reached a deal to vote in favor of the Council's position.

On June 25, 2002 the European Union Council adopted the new Electronic Communications Privacy Directive as voted in the Parliament.[44] Under the terms of the new Directive member states may now pass laws mandating the retention of the traffic and location data of all communications taking place over mobile phones, SMS, landline telephones, faxes, e-mails, chatrooms, the Internet, or any other electronic communication device. Such requirements can be implemented for purposes varying from national security to the prevention, investigation and prosecution of criminal offences.

In other areas, the Electronic Communications Privacy Directive had a more favorable outcome. For example, it adds new definitions and protections for "calls," "communications," "traffic data" and "location data" in order to enhance the consumer's right to privacy and control in all kinds of data processing. These new provisions ensure the protection of all information ("traffic") transmitted across the Internet, prohibit unsolicited commercial marketing by e-mail (spam) without consent, and protect mobile phone users from precise location tracking and surveillance. The directive also gives subscribers to all electronic

---

[42] Jelle van Buuren, "Telecommunication Council Wants New Investigation Into Privacy Rules," Heise Online, October 17, 2001.

[43] Respectively, MEPs Ana Palacio Vallelersundi and Elena Paciotti, members of the PPE (European Peoples' Party/Christian Democrats) and PSE (Social Democrats) political parties.

[44] 2439th Council meeting, Luxembourg, June 25, 2002. Transcripts of proceedings available at <http://europa.eu.int/rapid/start/cgi/guesten.ksh?p_action.gettxt=gt&doc=PRES/02/180|0|AGED&lg=EN>.

communications services (such as GSM and e-mail) the right to choose whether they are listed in a public directory.

The Directive will enter into force from data of publication in the official journal. After that time member states will have fifteen months to implement its provisions.

Oversight and Privacy and Data Protection Commissioners

An essential aspect of any privacy protection regime is oversight. In most countries with an omnibus data protection or privacy act, there is an official or agency that oversees enforcement of the act. The powers of these officials - Commissioner, Ombudsman or Registrar - vary widely by country. A number of countries including Germany and Canada also have officials or offices on a state or provincial level.

Under Article 28 of the European Union Data Protection Directive, all European Union countries must have an independent enforcement body. Under the Directive, these agencies are given considerable power: governments must consult the body when the government draws up legislation relating to the processing of personal information; the bodies also have the power to conduct investigations and have a right to access information relevant to their investigations; impose remedies such as ordering the destruction of information or ban processing, and start legal proceedings, hear complaints and issue reports. The official is also generally responsible for public education and international liaison in data protection and data transfer. Many authorities also maintain the register of data controllers and databases. They must approve licensing for data controllers.

A number of countries that do not have a comprehensive act still have a commissioner. A major power of these officials is to focus public attention on problem areas, even when they do not have any authority to fix the problem. They can do this by promoting codes of practice and encouraging industry associations to adopt them. They also can use their annual reports to point out problems. For example, in Canada, the Federal Privacy Commissioner announced in his 2000 report the existence of an extensive database maintained by the federal government. Once the issue became public, the Ministry disbanded the database.

In a number of countries, this official also serves as the enforcer of the jurisdiction's Freedom of Information Act. These include Hungary, Estonia, Thailand and the United Kingdom On the sub-national level, many of the German Lund Commissioners have recently been given the power of information commissioner, and most of the Canadian provincial agencies handle both data protection and freedom of information.

A major problem with many agencies around the world is a lack of resources to adequately conduct oversight and enforcement. Many are burdened with licensing systems, which use much of their resources. Others have large backlogs of complaints or are unable to conduct significant number of investigations. Many that started out with adequate funding find their budgets cut a few years later.

Independence is also a problem. In many countries, the agency is under the control of the political arm of the government or part of the Ministry of Justice and lacks the power or will to advance privacy or criticize privacy invasive proposals. In Japan and Thailand, the oversight agency is under the control of the Prime Ministers Office. In Thailand, the director was transferred in 2000 after conflicts with the Prime Ministers' Office. In 2001, Slovenia amended its Data Protection Act in order to establish an independent supervisory authority and thereby ensure compliance with the Data Protection Directive. This was previously the responsibility of the Ministry of Justice.

Finally, in some countries that do not have a separate office, the role of investigating and enforcing the laws is done by a human rights ombudsman or by a parliamentary official.

Transborder Data Flows and Data Havens

The ease with which electronic data flows across borders leads to a concern that data protection laws could be circumvented by simply transferring personal information to third countries, where the national law of the country of origin doesn't apply. This data could then be processed in those countries, frequently called a "data havens," without any limitations.

For this reason, most data protection laws include restrictions on the transfer of information to third countries unless the information is protected in the destination country. For example, Article 12 of the Council of Europe's 1981

Convention places restrictions on the transborder flows of personal data.[45] Similarly, Article 25 of the European Directive imposes an obligation on member States to ensure that any personal information relating to European citizens is protected by law when it is exported to, and processed in, countries outside Europe. It states:

> The Member States shall provide that the transfer to a third country of personal data which are undergoing processing or are intended for processing after transfer may take place only if the third country in question ensures an adequate level of protection.

This requirement has resulted in growing pressure outside Europe for the passage of strong data protection laws. Those countries that refuse to adopt meaningful privacy laws may find themselves unable to conduct certain types of information flows with Europe, particularly if they involve sensitive data. Determination of a third country's system for protecting privacy is made by the European Commission. The overarching principle in this determination process is that the level of protection in the receiving country must be "adequate" rather than "equivalent." Therefore, a reasonably high standard of protection is expected from the third party, although the precise dictates of the Directive need not be followed.

On July 26, 2000 the European Commission ruled that both Switzerland and Hungary provide "adequate" protection for personal information and therefore that all transfers of personal data to these countries could continue. [46] In January 2002, the European Commission recognized that the Canadian Personal Information Protection and Electronic Documents Act (PIPEDA) provides adequate protection for certain personal data transferred from the European Union to Canada. The Commission's decision of adequacy does not cover any personal data held by federal sector or provincial bodies or information held by personal organizations and used for non-commercial purposes, such as data handled by charities or collected in the context of an employment relationship.[47] The Commission is currently looking into the privacy protection schemes in

---

[45] Council of Europe, Convention for the Protection of Individuals with regard to the Automatic Processing of Personal Data, 1981, available at <http://www.coe.fr/eng/legaltxt/108e.htm>.

[46] See European Commission Press Release, "Data protection: Commission adopts decisions recognising adequacy of regimes in United States, Switzerland and Hungary," July 27, 2000, available at <http://europa.eu.int/comm/internal_market/en/media/dataprot/news/safeharbor.htm>.

[47] Commission Decision of December 20, 2001, Official Journal of the European Communities L 2/13, available at <http://www.europa.eu.int/comm/internal_market/dataprot/adequacy/canada-faq_en.htm>

several other non-European Union countries, including New Zealand, Australia, and Hong-Kong.

Another possible way to protect the privacy of information transferred to countries that do not provide "adequate protection" is to rely on a private contract containing standard data protection clauses. This kind of contract would bind the data processor to respect fair information practices such as the right to notice, consent, access and legal remedies. In the case of data transferred from the European Union, the contract would have to meet the standard "adequacy" test, in order to satisfy the Data Protection Directive.[48] A number of model clauses that could be included in such a contract were outlined in a 1992 joint study by the Council of Europe, the European Commission and the International Chamber of Commerce.[49] In a June 2000 report (see below), the European Parliament accused the European Commission of a "serious omission" in failing to draft standard contractual clauses that European citizens could invoke in the courts of third countries before the Data Directive came into force.[50] It recommended that they do so before September 30, 2000.[51] In July 2001, the Commission issued a final decision approving the standard contractual clauses.[52] During the drafting process, the United States criticized the standard contacts as "unduly burdensome" and "incompatible with real world operations."[53]

European Union-United States "Safe Harbor" Agreement

Although the Commission never issued a formal opinion on the adequacy of privacy protection in the United States, there were serious doubts whether the

---

[48] See European Union, Internal Market Directorate, Background Information: Transfer of data to non-European Union countries – FAQ, available at
<http://europa.eu.int/comm/internal_market/en/media/dataprot/backinfo/info.htm>.

[49] Joint Study of the Council of Europe and the Commission of the European Communities (1992), available at
<http://www.coe.fr/dataprotection/Etudes_Rapports/ectype.htm>.

[50] European Parliament Resolution on the Draft Commission Decision on the Adequacy of the Protection Provided by the Safe Harbour Privacy Principles and related Frequently Asked Questions issued by the United States Department of Commerce, available at
<http://www.epic.org/privacy/intl/EP_SH_resolution_0700.html>.

[51] For general guidance on the role of contracts see European Union Article 29 Data Protection Working Group, "Transfers of personal data to third countries: Applying Articles 25 and 26 of the European Union data protection directive," July 24, 1998, available at
<http://europa.eu.int/comm/internal_market/en/media/dataprot/wpdocs/wp12en.htm>.

[52] Commission Approves Standard Contractual Clauses For Data Transfers To Non-European Union Countries, Press Release of the Internal Market Directorate, July 18, 2001, available at
<http://europa.eu.int/comm/internal_market/en/dataprot/news/clauses2.htm>.

[53] "Bush Administration Criticizes European Union Privacy Rules," EPIC Alert 8.06, March 29, 2001
<http://www.epic.org/alert/EPIC_Alert_8.06.html>.

United States' sectoral and self-regulatory approach to privacy protection would pass the adequacy standard set out in the Directive. The European Union commissioned two prominent United States law professors, who wrote a detailed report on the state of United States privacy protections and pointed out the many gaps in United States protection.[54]

The United States strongly lobbied the European Union and its member countries to find the United States system adequate. In 1998, the United States began negotiating a "Safe Harbor" agreement with the European Union in order to ensure the continued transborder flows of personal data. The idea of the "Safe Harbor" was that United States companies would voluntarily self-certify to adhere to a set of privacy principles worked out by the United States Department of Commerce and the Internal Market Directorate of the European Commission. These companies would then have a presumption of adequacy and they could continue to receive personal data from the European Union. Negotiations on the drafting of the principles lasted nearly two years and were the subject of bitter criticism by privacy and consumer advocates.[55] In early July, the European Parliament approved a forceful resolution that the agreement needed to be re-negotiated in order to provide adequate protection.[56]

On July 26, 2000, the Commission approved the agreement.[57] The Commission did, however, promise to re-open negotiations on the arrangement if the remedies available to European citizens prove inadequate. European Union member states were given 90 days to put the Commission's decision into effect and United States companies began joining Safe Harbor in November 2000. There is an open-ended grace period for United States signatory companies to implement the principles.

The principles require all signatory organizations to provide individuals with "clear and conspicuous" notice of the kind of information they collect, the purposes for which it may be used, and any third parties to whom it may be disclosed. This notice must be given at the time of the collection of any personal information or "as soon thereafter as is practicable." Individuals must be given the ability to choose (opt-out of) the collection of data where the information is

---

[54] Paul M. Schwartz and Joel R. Reidenberg, Data Privacy Law (Michie 1996).

[55] See e.g., Public Comments Received by the United States Department of Commerce in Response to the Safe Harbor Documents April 5, 2000, available at
<http://www.ita.doc.gov/td/ecom/Comments400/publiccomments0400.html>.

[56] European Parliament Resolution, supra, n.50.

[57] Commission Decision on the adequacy of the protection provided by the Safe Harbour Privacy Principles and related Frequently Asked Questions issued by the United States Department of Commerce, available at
<http://europa.eu.int/comm/internal_market/en/media/dataprot/news/decision.pdf>.

either going to be disclosed to a third party or used for an incompatible purpose. In the case of sensitive information, individuals must expressly consent (opt-in) to the collection. Organizations wishing to transfer data to a third party may do so if the third party subscribes to Safe Harbor or if that third party signs an agreement to protect the data. Organizations must take reasonable precautions to protect the security of information against loss, misuse and unauthorized access, disclosure, alteration and destruction. Organizations must provide individuals with access to any personal information held about them, and with the opportunity to correct, amend, or delete that information where it is inaccurate. This right is to be granted only if the burden or expense of providing access would not be disproportionate to the risks to the individual's privacy or where the rights of persons other than the individual would not be violated. In terms of enforcement, organizations must provide access to readily available and affordable independent recourse mechanisms that may investigate complaints and award damages. They must issue follow up compliance procedures and must adhere to sanctions for failing to comply with the Principles.

Privacy advocates and consumer groups both in the United States and Europe are highly critical of the European Commission's decision to approve the agreement, which they say will fail to provide European citizens with adequate protection for their personal data.[58] The agreement rests on a self-regulatory system whereby companies merely promise not to violate their declared privacy practices. There is little enforcement or systematic review of compliance. The Safe Harbor status is granted at the time of self-certification. There is no individual right to appeal or right to compensation for privacy infringements. There is an open-ended grace period for United States signatory companies to implement the principles. The agreement will only apply to companies overseen by the Federal Trade Commission and Department of Transportation (excluding the financial and telecommunications sectors) and there are special exceptions granted for public records information protected by European Union law.

In February 2002, the European Commission issued a report on the practical operation of the European Union-United States Safe Harbor Agreement.[59] This was the first report to evaluate the success of the agreement. It concluded that all the essential elements of the agreement are in place and that a structure exists for individuals to lodge complaints if they feel their rights have been infringed. It did

---

[58] See, e.g.the earlier Statement of the Transatlantic Consumer Protection Dialogue on United States Department of Commerce Draft International Safe Harbor Privacy Principles and FAQs March 30, 2000, available at <http://www.tacd.org/ecommercef.html#usdraft>.

[59] European Commission Staff Working Paper, February 2002, available at <http://europa.eu.int/comm/internal_market/en/dataprot/news/02-196_en.pdf>

find, however, that there is not sufficient transparency among the organizations that have signed up to Safe Harbor and that not all dispute resolution providers relied on to enforce Safe Harbor actually comply with the privacy principles in the agreement itself. The Commission will issue a full evaluation of the agreement in 2003.

In July 2002, the Article 29 Data Protection Working Party issued a working paper on the functioning of the agreement. In it, the Working Party expressed its intention to study the agreement in further detail with particular regard to "possible gaps between the principles...and the implementing practices" and also "the transparency requirements to be met by organizations." The Working Party called on all authorities, organizations and companies concerned to enhance compliance and awareness of the Agreement.[60]

---

[60] "Working Document on the Functioning of the Safe Harbor Agreement," Article 29 Data Protection Working Party, 11194/02/EN, July 2, 2002, available at
<http://europa.eu.int/comm/internal_market/en/dataprot/wpdocs/wp62_en.pdf>

Threats to Privacy

The Response to September 11, 2001

Even with the adoption of legal and other protections, violations of privacy remain a concern. In many countries, laws have not kept up with the technology, leaving significant gaps in protections. In other countries, law enforcement and intelligence agencies have been given significant exemptions. Without adequate oversight and enforcement, the mere presence of a law may not provide adequate protection. Finally, with recent transformations to data protection regimes, further gaps, exemptions, and inadequacies are arising.

It may take some years to fully evaluate the effects of September 11th 2001 on privacy and civil liberties. Shortly after the events of that day, previous proposals were re-introduced, and new policies with similar objectives were drafted to extend police surveillance authority.

The policy changes were not limited to the United States, as a large number of countries responded to the threat of terrorism. The country reports in this survey outline, in more detail, the many legislative shifts that took place around the world.

It was a time of fear, flux and uncertainty. The United Nations responded with Resolution 1368 calling on increased cooperation between countries to prevent and suppress terrorism.[61] NATO invoked Article 5, claiming an attack on any NATO member country is an attack on all of NATO; legislatures responded accordingly. The Council of Europe condemned the attacks, called for solidarity, and also called for increased cooperation in criminal matters.[62] Later the Council of Europe Parliamentary Assembly called on countries to ratify conventions combating terrorism, lift any reservations in these agreements, extend the mandate of police working groups to include "terrorist messages and the

---

[61] United Nations Resolution 1368 (2001), adopted by the Security Council at its 4370th meeting, September 12, 2001.

[62] Council of Europe Committee of Ministers, Declaration of the Committee of Ministers on the fight against international terrorism, adopted by the Committee of Ministers at the 763rd meeting of the Ministers' Deputies, September 12, 2001.

decoding thereof."[63]   The European Union responded similarly, pushing for a European arrest warrant, common legislative frameworks for terrorism, increasing intelligence and police cooperation, freezing assets and ensuring passage of the Money Laundering Directive.[64] The OECD furthered its support for the Financial Action Task Force on Money Laundering and, along with the G-7[65] and the European Commission, called for the extension of its mandate to combat terrorist financing.[66]   These calls for international cooperation were perceived by many as impetus to create new laws.

The European Commission considered requiring every member state of the European Union to make cyber-attacks punishable as a terrorist offence. New Zealand minimized public consultation on a proposed law to freeze the financial assets of suspected terrorists because the government felt it was bound by United Nations Security Council resolutions. France expanded police powers to search private property without warrants. Germany reduced authorization restraints on interception of communications, and increased data sharing between law enforcement and national security agencies.

Australia and Canada both introduced laws to redefine *terrorist activity* and to grant powers of surveillance to national security agencies (*ASIO* and *CSIS* respectively) for domestic purposes if terrorist activity or a terrorist affiliation is suspected. India passed a law to allow authorities to detain suspects without trial, conduct increased wiretapping, and seize funds and property.   The United Kingdom passed a law permitting the retention of data for law enforcement purposes in contravention to existing data protection rules. The United States passed a number of laws, including the USA-PATRIOT Act, which increases surveillance powers and minimizes oversight and due process requirements.

The above list of international and national initiatives is not exhaustive. New policies are being proposed every week with the goal of investigating, preventing, and suppressing terrorist activity. However, within this deluge of new policy proposals, a number of trends may be identified.

---

[63] Council of Europe Parliamentary Assembly, Recommendation 1534 (2001), Democracies Facing Terrorism, September 26, 2001 (28th Sitting), available at <http://assembly.coe.int/>.

[64] Commission of the European Communities, Brussels, Report From The Commission, Overview of European Union action in response to the events of the 11 September and assessment of their likely economic impact, 17.10.2001, COM(2001) 611 final.

[65] Statement of G-7 Finance Ministers and Central Bank Governors, Action Plan to Combat the Financing of Terrorism, October 6, 2001.

[66] See generally, <http://www1.oecd.org/fatf/>.

Increased Communications Surveillance and Search and Seizure Powers

Almost every country that changed its laws to reflect the environment following September 2001 increased the ability of law enforcement and national security agencies to perform interception of communications, and transformed the powers of search and seizure, and an increase in the type of data that can be accessed.

The novelty in these initiatives tends to arise in the reduced authorization requirements and oversight. This includes initiatives to weaken due process requirements; as occurred in Canada where the first anti-terrorism bill proposed that law enforcement agencies will no longer be required to justify the need for the wiretap. That is, in existing law, the judge authorizing the interception would need to be satisfied that "other investigative procedures have been tried and have failed, other investigative procedures are unlikely to succeed or the urgency of the matter is such that it would be impractical to carry out the investigation of the offence using only other investigative procedures."[67] In the law, an exception is established for all offences that fall under the broad category of "terrorist activity." Other parts of the law allow for interception authorization by the Minister of Defence instead of requiring judicial authorization.

There is also a general increase in the breadth of application of these powers, by incorporating and including new technologies and communications infrastructures, permitting additional government agencies to use these powers, and formalize roving powers. The USA-PATRIOT Act codified the use of Carnivore-style Internet surveillance technology, granting access to sensitive traffic data with only a court order rather than a judicial warrant. Moreover, the reporting regime in the United States was weakened with amendments to the Foreign Intelligence Surveillance Act so that fewer warrants would have to be requested and reported because the expiration time period was increased, and 'generic' orders could be requested allowing one warrant to be served on multiple service providers.

Attempts to differentiate the authorization and oversight requirements based on the communications-technology also occurred. The Australian government proposed in its Telecommunications Interception Legislation Amendment Bill 2002 to grant powers to intercept and read email, SMS and voice mail messages without a warrant because these communications were considered access to 'stored' data rather than 'intercepted' in real-time. This proposed act was

---

[67] Criminal Code of Canada, (CC 186(1b)), 2000.

rejected in the Senate in June 2002;[68] however, the Government claims that it "remains of the view that the approach adopted in the bill with respect to stored information is appropriate. However, to avoid holding up this important package of legislation, the government has agreed to remove these provisions from the bill and to deal with the issue at a later date." [69]

Weakening of Data Protection Regimes

In 2000, the United Kingdom proposed a policy to require the retention of communications traffic data for up to 7 years by a central government authority.[70] While the proposal faced significant resistance in the public discourse at that time, in December 2001 a similar policy was introduced and passed under the United Kingdom's anti-terrorism law in response to the events of September 2001. The new European Union directive on data protection in electronic services also supports the creation of such data retention laws within the European community and is consistent with international pressure to weaken data protection. In October 2001, President Bush sent a letter to the President of the European Commission requesting that the European Union "[c]onsider data protection issues in the context of law enforcement and counterterrorism imperatives," and as a result to "[r]evise draft privacy directives that call for mandatory destruction to permit the retention of critical data for a reasonable period."[71] Building from previously articulated concerns that "[d]ata protection procedures in the sharing of law enforcement information must be formulated in ways that do not undercut international cooperation,"[72] the United States Department of Justice submitted a number of recommendations to the European Commission working group on cybercrime, including the recommendation that

> Any data protection regime should strike an appropriate balance between the protection of personal privacy, the legitimate needs of service

---

[68] Electronic Frontiers Australia, Media Release: Senate Rejects Email Snooping Law - Victory For Online Privacy, June 28, 2002.

[69] Statement of Senator Ellison, Minister of Justice and Customs, Senate Official Hansard No.6 2002, June 27, 2002, available at <http://www.aph.gov.au/hansard/senate/dailys/ds270602.pdf>.

[70] Roger Gaspar (NCIS), "Looking to the Future : Clarity on Communications Data Retention Law," August 21, 2000, ACPO, ACPO(S), HM Customs & Excise, Security Service, Secret Intelligence Service, and GCHQ,.

[71] Letter from President George W. Bush to Mr Romano Prodi, President, Commission of the European Communities, Brussels, October 16, 2001, forwarded by the Deputy Chief of Mission, United States Mission to the European Union, available at < http://www.statewatchapterorg/news/2001/nov/06Ausalet.htm>

[72] Comments of the United States Government on the European Commission Communication on Combating Computer Crime, December 2001, available at
<http://www.cybercrime.gov/intl/USComments_CyberCom_final.pdf>.

providers to secure their networks and prevent fraud, and the promotion of public safety.[73]

This perspective was reiterated in May 2002, this time by the Group of 8 Justice and Interior Ministers, requesting that countries

> Ensure data protection legislation, as implemented, takes into account public safety and other social values, in particular by allowing retention and preservation of data important for network security requirements or law enforcement investigations or prosecutions, and particularly with respect to the Internet and other emerging technologies.[74]

Further discussion regarding the reduction of the protections of privacy afforded by data protection law will likely arise in September when the European Commission continues discussion of the implementation of the 1995 directive (95/46/EC).

Individuals and citizens are at the same time losing subject access rights under data protection and freedom of information regimes. In the interests of critical infrastructure protection, access to information is being reduced, limiting government accountability. Meanwhile, in order to protect sensitive investigative and intelligence data, subject access requests are restricted as some data banks are being exempted from both data protection and freedom of information laws.

Increased Data Sharing

A number of policies were introduced to enable and promote increased data sharing, both within and across government agencies, and with the private sector. The sharing of data between agencies introduces purpose-creep where data collected for one purpose is used for another, but also introduces highly sensitive data to arms of government that can not be expected to protect the data adequately.

---

[73] Prepared statement of the United States of America, presented at European Union Forum on Cybercrime, Brussels, 27 November 2001, available at <http://www.cybercrime.gov/intl/MMR_Nov01_Forum.doc>.

[74] Statement of the G8 Justice and Interior Ministers: Recommendations for Tracing Networked Communications Across National Borders in Terrorist and Criminal Investigations, May 14 2002, Mont Tremblant, Quebec, available at <http://www.g8j-i.ca/english/doc2.html>.

There are significant shifts in the policies and practices in the United States with changes to the Attorney General Guidelines regulating the actions and capabilities of the Department of Justice and FBI, increased sharing of information between the FBI and CIA supported by the USA-PATRIOT Act, and proposed policies to increase sharing with local law enforcement agencies. The United States is not alone in introducing such policies. The United Kingdom is proposing "joined-up government" within its consultation paper on modernizing government and public services[75] to create "data-sharing gateways" and provide "seamless" services. It also tried unsuccessfully to allow practically any government agency to gain access to the traffic data of individuals under the Regulation of Investigatory Powers Act, including local councils and parishes.[76]

The increased flow of data is also coming from the private sector. The United Kingdom and Canada proposed laws to grant law enforcement agencies access to travelers' information. The United Kingdom Home Office has recommended that it gain access to information from every passenger before international flights.[77]   The Canadian policy proposes to grant both the federal law enforcement and the intelligence agencies access to air passenger information, regardless of domestic or international travel, and to match this data with other personal information,[78] for a wide number of purposes and investigations, not limited only to terrorism.[79]

Similarly, the European Union is considering granting Europol access to the Schengen Information System, including privileges to change the information held on travelers.[80]   Germany has recommended to the European Union the creation of a database of "known trouble-makers," to be used "for criminal prosecution purposes and in order to avert dangers constitute a proper and necessary tool in the fight against international terrorism. However, in view of the fact that members and supporters of terrorist groups are known to roam

---

[75] The Performance and Innovation Unit of the Cabinet Office, "Privacy and data-sharing: The way forward for public services," April 2002, available at <http://www.cabinet-office.gov.uk/innovation/2002/privacy/report/>.

[76] "FIPR appalled by Huge Increase in Government Snooping," Foundation for Information Policy Research Press Release, June 10, 2002, available at <http://www.fipr.org/press/020610snooping.html>.

[77] "'Chaos' warning over airport security plan," BBC News Online, July 6, 2002, available at <http://news.bbc.co.uk/hi/english/uk/newsid_2104000/2104280.stm>.

[78] Solicitor General of Canada, RCMP and CSIS Access to Airline Passenger Information, available at <http://www.sgc.gc.ca/EPub/Pol/eAirPassInfo.htm>.

[79] Letter to Honourable David Collenette, Minister of Transport, on the subject of Bill C-55, from the Privacy Commissioner of Canada, George Radwanski, June 18, 2002. available at <http://www.privcom.gc.ca/media/nr-c/02_05_b_020618_e.asp>.

[80] "Europol to be given access to the S.I.S., then custody?" Statewatch, March 27, 2002.

---

across Europe, the measure would be much more effective if it were applied by all European Union Member States."

Data sharing between financial institutions and with government agencies has also increased. New money laundering agreements and regulations have been introduced to increase surveillance of transactions, and even expanded to include hedge funds and money transfer firms.[81] Donations to charities are receiving further scrutiny as both the charities and the donors are monitored to investigate links with terrorist groups.[82] Some financial institutions are also sharing personal information between themselves in order to minimize risk of clients being terrorists, or "undesirables."[83]

Increased Profiling and Identification

Following from data sharing, there are a number of proposals to create profiles or increase the existing profiles of individuals. This occurs in a number of ways; the most immediate appears to be the profile of travelers. There are proposals for a *next generation* computer-assisted passenger prescreening system that will bring in data from credit-reporting agencies and other companies,[84] and even previous flights and registries, set for data mining.[85] Other proposals include trusted-traveler programs involving biometrics in both the United States and Germany,[86] similar to schemes used at Ben Gurion Airport in Tel Aviv.[87] Some airports have also installed face-recognition technologies, while similar technologies are being implemented at national monuments, and even beaches.

In the longer term there are a number of proposals to increase profiling of citizens and non-citizens. These proposals are typically enhanced and complemented by national identification schemes, enhanced with biometrics.

---

[81] Glenn R. Simpson and Jathon Sapsford, "New Rules for Money-Laundering," The Wall Street Journal, April 23, 2002.

[82] "Financial Action Task Force on Money Laundering Special Recommendations on Terrorist Financing," available at <http://www.fatf-gafi.org/SRecsTF_en.htm>.

[83] Robert O'Harrow Jr., "Financial Database To Screen Accounts: Joint Effort Targets Suspicious Activities," Washington Post, May 30, 2002; at E01.

[84] "Special Report: New Threats To Privacy: The Intensifying Scrutiny at Airports," Business Week, June 5, 2002.

[85] Robert O'Harrow Jr., "Intricate Screening Of Fliers In Works -- Database Raises Privacy Concerns," Washington Post, February 1, 2002, at A01.

[86] "Iris Scans Take off at Airports," ComputerWorld, July 17, 2002.

[87] Ricardo Alonso-Zaldivar, "'Trusted' Air Travelers Would Minimize Wait Security: Passengers who Voluntarily Agree to a Background Check Could be Issued a Special Credential," Los Angeles Times, February 5, 2002.

There was considerable discussion in the United States in introducing such a national ID card scheme but no formal policy was introduced. Meanwhile non-citizens may already be tracked at border entry points and as they move within the country. A system called **Student and Exchange Visitor Information System** keeps track of foreign students to ensure that they are still registered and maintains a log of their addresses.

The United Kingdom is proposing the implementation of 'entitlement cards' in an effort to deal with immigration and illegal work, identity theft, but also supported by the fight against terrorism. Similarly, Hong Kong is planning to introduce a biometric chip identity card to verify fingerprints to authenticate travelers into China.

None of the above trends are necessarily new; the novelty is the speed in which these policies gained acceptance, and in many cases, became law.

Identity systems

Identity (ID) cards

Identity (ID) cards are in use in one form or another in virtually all countries of the world. The type of card, its functions, and integrity vary enormously. While a number of countries have official, compulsory, national ID cards that are used for a variety of purposes, many countries do not. These include Australia, Canada, India, Ireland, New Zealand, the United States and the Nordic countries. Those that do have such a card include Belgium, Egypt, France, Germany, Greece, Hong Kong, Malaysia, and South Africa.

Nationwide ID systems are established for a variety of reasons. Race, politics and religion often drive the deployment of ID cards.[88] The fear of insurgence, religious differences, immigration, or political extremism have been all too common motivators for the establishment of ID systems that aim to force undesirables in a State to register with the government, or make them vulnerable in the open without proper documents.

---

[88] Richard Sobel, *The Degradation of Political Identity Under a National Identification System*, 8 B.U. J. Sci. & Techapter L. 37, 48 (2002). See also National Research Council, "IDs -- Not That Easy: Questions About Nationwide Identity Systems," 2002, available at
<http://www.nap.edu/catalog/10346.html?opi_newsdoc041102>.

In recent years technology has rapidly evolved to enable electronic record creation and the construction of large commercial and state databases. A national identifier contained in an ID card enables disparate information about a person that is stored in different databases to be easily linked and analyzed through data mining techniques. ID cards are also becoming "smarter" - the technology to build microprocessors the size of postage stamps and put them on wallet sized cards has become more affordable. This technology enables multiple applications such as a credit card, library card, health care card, driver's license and government benefit program information to be all stored on the same national ID along with a password or a biometric identifier. Governments in Finland, Malaysia, and Singapore have experimented with such "Smart" ID cards. In July 2002, the Labor government in the United Kingdom launched a six-month public consultation process on whether the United Kingdom should adopt an "entitlement card" with similar features.[89] Critics contend that such cards, especially when combined with information contained in databases, enable intrusive profiling of individuals and create a misplaced reliance on a single document, which enables precisely the type of fraud the cards are meant to eliminate.[90]

In a number of countries, these systems have been successfully challenged on constitutional privacy grounds. In 1998, the Philippine Supreme Court ruled that a national ID system violated the constitutional right to privacy.[91] In 1991, the Hungarian Constitutional Court ruled that a law creating a multi-use personal identification number violated the constitutional right of privacy.[92] The 1997 Portuguese Constitution states "Citizens shall not be given an all-purpose national identity number." [93]

In other countries, opposition to the cards combined with the high economic cost and other logistical difficulties of implementing the systems has led to their withdrawal. Massive protests against the Australia Card in 1987 resulted in the near collapse of the government. Card projects in South Korea and Taiwan were

---

[89] "Entitlement Cards and Identity Fraud: A Consultation Paper," Presented to the Parliament by the Secretary of State for the Home Department, July 2002, available at
<http://www.homeoffice.gov.uk/cpd/entitlement_cards.pdf>.

[90] Simon Davies. "The Id Card Is The Fraudster's Friend," The Sunday Telegraph, July 7, 2002. See also, Oscar H. Gandy, Jr., The Panoptic Sort: A Political Economy of Personal Information (Westview Press 1993).

[91] Philippine Supreme Court Decision of the National ID System, July 23, 1998, G.R. 127685, available at <http://bknet.org/laws/nationalid.html>.

[92] Constitutional Court Decision No. 15-AB of 13 April 1991, available at
<http://www.privacy.org/pi/countries/hungary/hungarian_id_decision_1991.html>.

[93] Article 35 (5), Constitution Of The Portuguese Republic 1976 (as amended), available at
<http://www.parlamento.pt/leis/constituicao_ingles/crp_uk.htm#article_35>.

also stopped after widespread protests. In the United States plans to convert the state driver's license into a nationwide system of identification have stalled because of the stiff resistance from a broad coalition of civil society groups.[94]

Biometrics

Biometrics is the identification or verification of someone's identity on the basis of physiological or behavioral characteristics. Biometrics involves comparing a previously captured unique characteristic of a person to a new sample provided by the person. This information is used to authenticate or verify that a person is who they said they were (a one-to-one match) by comparing the previously stored characteristic to the fresh characteristic provided. It can also be used for identification purposes where the fresh characteristic is compared against all the stored characteristics (a one-to-many match). New biometric technology attempts to automate the identification or verification process by converting the provided biometric into an algorithm, which is then used for matching purposes. The computer matching technique necessarily produces either false positives, where a person is incorrectly identified as someone else, or false negatives, where a person who is meant to be identified by the system is not correctly identified. The two error rates are dependent, so for example reducing the number of false positives increases the number of false negatives. The tolerance level is adjusted depending on the need for security in the application.

The most popular forms of biometric ID are fingerprints, retina/iris scans, hand geometry, voice recognition, and digitized (electronically stored) images. The technology is gaining interest from governments and companies because, unlike other forms of ID such as cards or papers, it can be more difficult to alter or tamper with one's own physical or behavior characteristics. Important questions remain, however, about the effectiveness of the automated biometric matching techniques, particularly for large-scale applications.[95] Critics also argue that widespread deployment of biometric identification technology could remove the veil of anonymity or pseudo-anonymity in most daily transactions through the creation an electronic trail of people's movements and habits.[96]

---

[94] See generally EPIC's National ID Pages <http://www.epic.org/privacy/id_cards/>.

[95] Deutsche Bank Research, "Biometrics – Hype and Reality," May 22, 2002, available at <http://www.dbresearchaptercom/PROD/999/PROD0000000000043270.pdf>

[96] Roger Clarke, "Biometrics and Privacy," April 15, 2001, available at <http://www.anu.edu.au/people/Roger.Clarke/DV/Biometrics.html>.

Biometrics schemes are being implemented across the world. The technology is widely used in small settings for access control to secure locations such a nuclear facility or bank vault. It is increasingly being used for broader applications such as retail outlets, government agencies, childcare centers, police forces and automated-teller machines. Spain has commenced a national fingerprint system for unemployment benefits and healthcare entitlements. Russia has announced plans for a national electronic fingerprint system for banks. Jamaicans are required to scan their thumbs into a database before qualifying to vote in elections. In France and Germany, tests are under way with equipment that puts fingerprint information onto credit cards. Many computer manufacturers are considering including biometric readers on their systems for security purposes.

The most controversial form of biometrics – DNA identification – is benefiting from new scanning technology that can automatically match DNA samples against a large database in minutes. Police forces in several countries including Canada, Germany, and the United States have created national DNA databases. Samples are being routinely taken from a larger group of people. Initially, it was only individuals convicted of sexual crimes. Then it was expanded to people convicted of other violent crimes and then to arrests. Now, many jurisdictions are collecting samples from all individuals arrested, even for the most minor offenses. Former New York City Mayor Rudolf Giuliani even proposed that all children have a DNA sample collected at birth. In Australia, the United Kingdom, and the United States, police have been demanding that all individuals in a particular area voluntarily provide samples or face being considered a suspect. United States Attorney General Ashcroft has testified that he has asked the FBI to increase the capacity of its database from 1.5 million to 50 million profiles.[97]

At the same time, DNA data has been used as exculpatory evidence in many criminal trials. (For more discussion of this subject see the section on *Genetic Identification* at 78)

Surveillance of Communications

Most countries around the world regulate the interception of communications by governments and private individuals and organizations. These controls typically

---

[97] Attorney General Transcript, News Conference - DNA Initiatives, Monday, March 4, 2002, DOJ Conference Center.

take the form of constitutional provisions protecting the privacy of communications and laws and regulations that implement those requirements.

There has been great pressure on countries to adopt wiretapping laws to address new technologies. These laws are also in response to law enforcement and intelligence agencies pressure to increase surveillance capabilities. In Japan, wiretapping was only approved as a legal method of investigation in 1999. Other countries such as Australia, Germany, New Zealand, South Africa and the United Kingdom have all updated their laws to facilitate surveillance of new technologies.

The United States government has been at the forefront of promoting greater use of electronic surveillance. Former FBI Director Louis Freeh traveled extensively around the world, promoting the use of wiretapping in newly democratic countries such as Hungary and the Czech Republic. At the same time, the United States has led world efforts to ensure that all communications technologies have built in surveillance capabilities and to prohibit the manufacture and use of equipment that cannot be eavesdropped upon. The United States has also been working through international organizations such as the OECD, G-8 and the Council of Europe to promote surveillance.

Legal Protections and Human Rights

It is recognized worldwide that wiretapping and electronic surveillance is a highly intrusive form of investigation that should only be used in limited and unusual circumstances. Nearly all major international agreements on human rights protect the right of individuals from unwarranted invasive surveillance.

Nearly every country in the world has enacted laws on the interception of oral, telephone, fax and telex communications. In most democratic countries, intercepts are initiated by law enforcement or intelligence agencies only after it has been approved by an judge or some other kind of independent magistrate or high level official and generally only for serious crimes. Frequently, it must be shown that other types of investigation were attempted and were not successful There is some divergence on what constitutes a 'serious crime', and appropriate approval.

A number of countries including France and the United Kingdom have created special commissions that review wiretap usage and monitor for abuses. These bodies have developed an expertise in the area that most judges who authorize surveillance do not have, while they also have the ability to conduct follow up investigations once a case is complete. In other countries, the Privacy Commission or Data Protection Commission has some ability to conduct oversight of electronic surveillance.

An important oversight measure that many countries employ is the requiring of annual public reporting of information about the use of electronic surveillance by government departments. These reports typically provide summary details about the number of uses of electronic surveillance, the types of crimes that they are authorized for, their duration and other information. This is a common feature of wiretap laws in English-speaking countries and many others in Europe. Countries that issue annual reports on the use of surveillance include Australia, Canada, France, New Zealand, Sweden, the United Kingdom, and the United States.

These countries recognize that it is necessary to allow for people outside governments to know about its uses to limit abuses. They are widely used in many countries by the Parliaments for oversight and also by journalists, NGOs and others to examine the activities of law enforcement. The reports have shown an increase in the use of surveillance in many countries including the United States and the United Kingdom while others such as Canada have remained steady.

These laws are designed to ensure that legitimate and normal activities in a democracy such as journalism, civic protests, trade union organizing or political opposition are free from being subjected to unwarranted surveillance because they have different interests and goals than those in power. It also ensures that relatively minor crimes, especially those that would not generally involve telecommunications for facilitation, are not used as a pretext to conduct intrusive surveillance for political or other reasons.

However, wiretapping abuses have been revealed in most countries, sometimes occurring on a vast scale involving thousands of illegal taps. The abuses invariably affect anyone "of interest" to a government. Targets include political opponents, student leaders and human rights workers.[98] This can occur even in the most democratic of countries such as Denmark and Sweden, where it was recently disclosed that intelligence agencies were conducting surveillance of thousands of left-leaning activists for nearly 40 years.

---

[98] United States Department of State, Country Report on Human Rights Practices 1997, January 30, 1998.

The U.N. Commissioner on Human Rights in 1988 made clear that human rights protections on the secrecy of communications broadly covers all forms of communications:

> Compliance with Article 17 requires that the integrity and confidentiality of correspondence should be guaranteed de jure and de facto. Correspondence should be delivered to the addressee without interception and without being opened or otherwise read. Surveillance, whether electronic or otherwise, interceptions of telephonic, telegraphic and other forms of communication, wire-tapping and recording of conversations should be prohibited.[99]

The need for greater protection is recognized by many democratic countries around the world. Increasingly new standards, technologies and new policies are complicating the situation.

Legal and Technical Standards for Surveillance: Building in Big Brother

In the past 15 years, the United States government has led a worldwide effort to limit individual privacy and enhance the capability of its police and intelligence services to eavesdrop on personal conversations. This campaign had two strategies. The first is to promote laws that make it mandatory for all companies that develop digital telephone switches, cellular and satellite phones and all developing communication technologies to build in surveillance capabilities; the second is to seek limits on the development and dissemination of products, both in hardware and software, that provide encryption, a technique that allows people to scramble their communications and files to prevent others from reading them.[100]

Law enforcement agencies have traditionally worked closely with telecommunications companies to formulate arrangements that would make phone systems "wiretap friendly." These agreements range from allowing police physical access to telephone exchanges, to installing equipment to automate the interception. Because most telecommunications operators were either monopolies or operated by government telecommunications agencies, this process was generally hidden from public view.

---

[99] United Nations Human Rights Commissioner, The right to respect of privacy, family, home and correspondence, and protection of honour and reputation (Article 17), CCPR General Comment 16, April 8, 1988.

[100] See David Banisar and Simon Davies, "The Code War," Index on Censorship, January 1998.

Following deregulation and new entries into telecommunications in the United States in the early 1990s, law enforcement agencies, led by the FBI, began demanding that all current and future telecommunications systems be designed to ensure that they would be able to conduct wiretaps. After several years of lobbying, the United States Congress approved the Communications Assistance for Law Enforcement Act (CALEA) in 1994.[101] The act sets out legal requirements for telecommunications providers and equipment manufacturers on the surveillance capabilities that must be built into all telephone systems used in the United States. In 1999, at the request of the Federal Bureau of Investigation, an order was issued under CALEA requiring carriers to make available the physical location of the antenna tower that a mobile phone uses to connect at the beginning and end of a call.[102]

Due to heavy lobbying, the Internet Service Providers in the United States have so far been exempted from implementing these technical requirements. In other countries the computer industries have not been so fortunate. In Australia the Telecommunications Act 1997 places obligations on telecommunications operators to positively assist law enforcement in the performance of their duties and to provide an interception capability. The costs of these obligations are borne by the operators themselves.[103] Furthermore, the 2001 Cybercrime Act allows executing officers to require a "specified person" with "knowledge of a computer or a computer system" to provide assistance in accessing, copying or converting data held on or accessible from that computer. Failing to provide this assistance is an offence punishable by six months imprisonment.[104]

In the United Kingdom the Regulation of Investigatory Powers Act 2000 requires that telecommunications operators maintain a "reasonable interception capability" in their systems and be able to provide on notice certain "traffic data."[105] It also imposes on obligation on third parties to hand over encryption keys. These requirements were recently clarified in the Regulation of Investigatory Powers (Maintenance of Interception Capability) Order 2002.

---

[101] See EPIC Wiretap Pages <http://www.epic.org/privacy/wiretap/>.

[102] Third Report and Order adopted by the Federal Communications Commission, In the Matter of Communications Assistance for Law Enforcement Act, CC Docket No. 97-213, FCC 99-230 (1999) (the "Order"). The Order was released on August 31, 1999. A summary of the Order was published in the Federal Register on September 24, 1999. See 64 Fed. Reg. 51710.

[103] Telecommunications Act 1997, Parts 14 and 15.

[104] Cybercrime Act 2001, No. 161, 2001, inserting sections 3LA and 201A in the Crimes Act 1914, available at <http://scaleplus.law.gov.au/html/pasteact/3/3486/pdf/161of2001.pdf>.

[105] Regulation of Investigatory Powers Act 2000, sections 12 (1) and 22 (4) respectively, available at <http://www.hmso.gov.uk/acts/acts2000/20000023.htm>.

In the Netherlands, a new Telecommunications Act was approved in December 1998 that required that Internet Service Providers have the capability by August 2000 to intercept all traffic with a court order and maintain users logs for three months.[106] The law was enacted after XS4ALL, a Dutch ISP, refused to conduct a broad wiretap of electronic communications of one of its subscribers. In New Zealand, the Telecommunications (Residual Powers) Act 1987 requires network operators to assist in the operation of a call data warrant (equivalent to the United States trap and trace or pen register warrant).[107] An obligation to assist in the operation of a full interception warrant is now also being considered in New Zealand. The Telecommunications (Interception Capabilities) Bill currently being drafted by the Government would require all Internet Service Providers and telephone companies to upgrade their systems so that they are able to assist the police and intelligence agencies intercept communications. It would also require a telecommunications operator to decrypt the communications of a customer if that operator had provided the encryption facility.[108]

In January 2002, a new Law on the surveillance of mail and telecommunications entered into force in Switzerland, requiring ISPs to take all necessary measures to allow for interception.[109]

International cooperation played a significant role in the development of these standards. In 1993, the FBI began hosting meetings at its research facility in Quantico, Virginia called the "International Law Enforcement Telecommunications Seminar" (ILETS). The meetings included representatives from Canada, Hong Kong, Australia and the European Union. At these meetings, an international technical standard for surveillance, based on the FBI's CALEA demands, was adopted as the "International Requirements for Interception." In January 1995, the Council of the European Union approved a secret resolution adopting the ILETS standards.[110] Following this, many countries adopted the resolution into their domestic laws without revealing the role of the FBI in developing the standard. Following the adoption, the European Union and the

---

[106] Telecommunications Act 1998. Rules pertaining to Telecommunications (Telecommunications Act), December 1998.

[107] Telecommunications (Residual Powers) Act 1987, section 10D.

[108] "Interception Capability – Government Decisions," New Zealand Government Executive Press Release, March 21, 2002, available at <http://www.executive.govt.nz/speechaptercfm?speechralph=37658&SR=0>.

[109] Loi fédérale sur la surveillance de la correspondance postale et des télécommunications, (www.admin.ch/ch/f/rs/c780_1.html) and the respective new decree (www.admin.ch/ch/f/rs/c780_11.html)

[110] Council Resolution of 17 January 1995 on the lawful interception of telecommunications, Official Journal of the European Communities November 4, 1996, available at <http://europa.eu.int/eur-lex/en/lif/dat/1996/en_496Y1104_01.html>.

United States offered a Memorandum of Understanding (MOU) for other countries to sign to commit to the standards. A number of countries including Canada and Australia immediately signed the MOU. Others were encouraged to adopt the standards to ensure trade. International standards organizations, including the International Telecommunications Union and the European Telecommunication Standardisation Institute (ETSI), were then successfully approached to adopt the standards.

The ILETS group continued to meet. A number of committees were formed and developed a more detailed standard extending the scope of the interception standards. The new standards were designed to apply to a wide range of communications technologies, including the Internet and satellite communications. It also set more detailed criteria for surveillance across all technologies. The result was a 42-page document called ENFOPOL 98 (the European Union designation for documents created by the European Union Police Cooperation Working Group).[111]

In 1998, the document became public and generated considerable criticism. The committees responded by removing most of the controversial details and putting them into a secret operations manual that has not been made publicly available. The new document, now called ENFOPOL 19, expanded the type of surveillance to include "IP address (electronic address assigned to a party connected to the Internet), credit card number and E-mail address."[112] In April 1999, the Council proposed the new draft council resolution to adopt the ENFOPOL 19 standards into law in the European Union. The Council of Ministers revised the document and, in June 2000, approved a resolution calling for countries:

> to ensure that, in the development and implementation – in cooperation with communication service providers – of any measures which may have a bearing on the carrying out of legally authorised forms of interception of telecommunications, the law enforcement operational needs... are duly taken into account [113]

---

[111] ENFOPOL 98, September 1998, available (in German) at
<http://www.heise.de/tp/deutsch/special/enfo/6326/1.html>. See also Duncan Campbell, "Special Investigation: ILETS and the ENFOPOL 98 Affair," Heise Online, April 29, 1999, available at
<http://www.heise.de/tp/english/special/enfo/6398/1.html>.

[112] Draft Council Resolution on the Lawful Interception of Telecommunications in Relation to New Technologies ENFOPOL 19, March 15, 1999.

[113] Council of the European Union, Council Resolution on law enforcement operational needs with respect to public telecommunication networks and services, 9194/01, ENFOPOL 55, June 20, 2001.

The annex for the document sets out detailed guidelines for interception requirements for "all telecommunications services, circuit and packet switched, fixed and mobile networks and services." It expands the coverage of the original International User Requirements (IURs) to now include networking technologies, without acknowledging that technologies such as computer networking generate more and greater details of information including web browsing and mobile location information and thus applying traditional surveillance analogies result in more intrusive surveillance.

Internet Surveillance: Black Boxes and Key Loggers

A related development has been the use of "black boxes" on ISP networks to monitor user traffic. The actual workings of these black boxes are unknown to the public. What little information has been made public reveals that many of the systems are based on "packet sniffers" typically employed by computer network operators for security and maintenance purposes. These are specialized software programs running in a computer that is hooked into the network at a location where it can monitor traffic flowing in and out of systems. These sniffers can monitor the entire data stream searching for key words, phrases or strings such as net addresses or e-mail accounts. It can then record or retransmit for further review anything that fits its search criteria. In many of the systems, the boxes are connected to government agencies by high speed connections.

The April 2000, it was publicly revealed that the FBI had developed and was using an Internet monitoring system called "Carnivore" (now called DCS 1000).[114] The system places a PC running Windows NT at an Internet Service Provider's offices and can monitor all traffic about a user including e-mail and browsing. Carnivore "can scan millions of e-mails a second" and "would give the government, at least theoretically, the ability to eavesdrop on all customers' digital communications, from e-mail to online banking and Web surfing."[115] In response to the public uproar over Carnivore, Attorney General Janet Reno announced that the technical specifications of the system would be disclosed to a "group of experts" to allay public concerns.[116] In the fall of 2000, the Justice Department commissioned a team of experts at the IIT Research Institute and the Illinois Institute of Technology Chicago-Kent College of Law (IITRI) to

---

114 Testimony of Robert Corn-Revere, before the Subcommittee on the Constitution of the Committee on the Judiciary, United States House of Representatives, The Fourth Amendment and the Internet, April 6, 2000, available at <http://www.house.gov/judiciary/corn0406.htm>.

115 "FBI's System to Covertly Search E-Mail Raises Privacy," Wall Street Journal, July 11, 2000.

116 "Reno to double-check Carnivore's bite," Reuters, July 13, 2000.

undertake an independent review of the carnivore system. The IITRI group issued its final report on Carnivore in December 2000 and made several recommendations for changes to the system.[117]

In some countries, there have been laws or decrees enacted to require the systems to build in these boxes. Russia was the first country where this requirement was made public, and according to Russian computer experts, the United States government advised them on implementation. In 1998, the Russian Federal Security Service (FSB) issued a decree on the System for Operational Research Actions on the Documentary Telecommunication Networks (SORM-2) that would require Internet Service Providers to install surveillance devices and high speed links to the FSB which would allow the FSB direct access to the communications of Internet users without a warrant.[118] ISPs are required to pay for the costs of installing and maintaining the devices. When an ISP based in Volgograd challenged FSB's demand to install the system, the local FSB and Ministry of Communication attempted to have its license revoked. The agencies were forced to back off after the ISP challenged the decision in court. In a separate case, the Supreme Court ruled in May 2000 that SORM-2 was not a valid ministerial act because it failed several procedural requirements.

Following the Russian lead, in September 1999, Ukrainian President Leonid Kuchma proposed requiring that Internet Service Providers install surveillance devices on their systems based on the Russian SORM system. The rules and a subsequent bill were attacked by the Parliament and withdrawn. However, in August 1999, the security service visited a number of the large ISPs who were reported to have installed the boxes.

In the Netherlands, following the passage of the 1998 Telecommunications Act (see above), the Dutch Forensics Institute[119] developed a "black-box" for ISPs to install on their networks. The black box would be under control of the ISP and turned on after receiving a court order. The box would look at authentication traffic of the person to wiretap and divert the person's traffic to law enforcement if the person is online. Due to the inability of ISPs to adopt the requirements of the law, however, its implementation has been delayed.

---

[117] IITRI, Independent Technical Review of the Carnivore System, Final Report, December 8, 2000, available at <http://www.epic.org/privacy/carnivore/carniv_final.pdf>.

[118] "Russia Prepares To Police Internet," The Moscow Times, July 29, 1998. More information in English and Russian is available from the Moscow Libertarium Forum <http://www.libertarium.ru/libertarium/sorm/>.

[119] See Dutch Forensics Institute Homepage <http://www.holmes.nl/>.

In China, a system know as the "Great Firewall" routes all international connections through proxy servers at official gateways, where Ministry for Public Security (MPS) officials identify individual users and content, define rights, and carefully monitor network traffic into and out of the country. At a recent security industry conference, the government announced an ambitious successor project known as "Golden Shield." Rather than relying solely on a national intranet, separated from the global Internet by a massive firewall, China will now build surveillance intelligence into the network, allowing it to "see", "hear" and "think." [120] Content-filtration will shift from the national level to millions of digital information and communications devices in public places and people's homes.[121] The technology behind Golden Shield is incredibly complex and is based on research developed largely by Western technology firms, including Nortel Networks, Sun Microsystems and others. The Golden Shield efforts do not signal an abandonment of other avenues of access and content control. For example, details are only beginning to emerge about a new "black box" device, derived from technology previously used in airline cockpit data recorders, and broadly similar to the Carnivore system. Chinese Internet police would use the black box technology to monitor dissidents and collect evidence on illegal activities.[122]

New methods of surveillance, and in particular those capable of circumventing encryption, are also being developed. One such technological device is a "key logger" system. A key logger system records the keystrokes an individual enters on a computer's keyboard. Keystroke loggers can be employed to capture every key pressed on a computer keyboard, including information that is typed and then deleted. Such devices can be manually placed by law enforcement agents on a suspect's computer, or installed "remotely" by placing a virus on the suspect's computer that will disclose private encryption keys.

The question of such surreptitious police decryption methods arose in the case of *United States v Scarfo*.[123] There, the FBI manually installed a key logger device on the defendant's computer in order to capture his PGP encryption password. Once they discovered the password, the files were decrypted, and incriminatory

---

[120] G. Walton, China's Golden Shield: Corporations and the Development of Surveillance Technology in the People's Republic of China, (Rights and Democracy, 2001) at 9
<http://serveur.ichrdd.ca/english/commdoc/publications/globalization/goldenShieldEng.html>.

[121] B. Rappert, "Assessing the Technologies of Political Control" (1999) 36(6) J. of Peace Research 741. The Golden Shield Project contemplates automated voice recognition through digital signal processing; distributed, network video surveillance; and, content-filtration of the Internet.

[122] See *e.g.* L. Weijun, "China Plans to Build Internet Monitoring System," China News Daily, March 20, 2001 <http://www.cnd.org/Global/01/03/20/010320-3.html>.

[123] *United States v. Scarfo*, 180 F. Supp. 2d 572 (D.N.J. 2001)

---

evidence was found. In December 2001, the United States FBI confirmed the existence of a similar technique called "Magic Lantern."[124] This device would reportedly allow the agency to plant a Trojan horse keystroke logger on a target's computer by sending a computer virus over the Internet; rather than require physical access to the computer as is now the case. The new Danish Anti-Terrorism law, enacted in June 2002, appears to give law enforcement the power to secretly install this kind of snooping software on the computers of criminal suspects.[125]

Transactional and Location Data: Surveillance and New Communications Technologies

As new telecommunications technologies emerge, many countries are adapting existing surveillance laws to address the interception of networked and mobile communications. These updated laws pose new threats to privacy in many countries because the governments often simply apply old standards to new technologies without analyzing how the technology has changed the nature and sensitivity of the information. It is crucial for the protection of privacy and human rights that transactional data created by new technologies is given greater protection under law than traditional telephone calling records and other transactional information found in older systems.

In the traditional telephone system, transactional data usually takes the form of telephone numbers or telephone identifiers, the call metrics (e.g. length of call, time and date), countries involved, and types of services used. This data is usually collected and processed by telephone companies for billing and network efficiency (e.g. fault correction) purposes. While this data is stored by telephone companies, it is available to law enforcement authorities. Communications content, i.e. conversations, are not stored routinely. As a result, the obstacles to law enforcement access to this data were minimal: traffic data was available, legally less sensitive, and so accessible with lower authorization and oversight requirements. The content of communications was treated as more sensitive, and more invasive, and more difficult to collect, thus typically requiring greater authorization and oversight mechanisms.

Different communications infrastructures give rise to different forms of transactional data, however. When surfing the net, a user can visit dozens of

---

[124] Elinor Mills Abreu, "FBI Confirms 'Magic Lantern' Project Exists," Reuters, December 12, 2001.
[125] Law No. 378, June 6, 2002.

---

sites in just a few minutes and reveal a great deal about their personal situation and interests. This can include medical, financial, social interests and other highly personal information. As the Council of Europe acknowledges in the Explanatory Report of the Convention on Cybercrime,

> The collection of this data may, in some situations, permit the compilation of a profile of a person's interests, associates and social context. Accordingly Parties should bear such considerations in mind when establishing the appropriate safeguards and legal prerequisites for undertaking such measures. [126]

The detailed and potentially sensitive nature of the data makes it more similar to content of communications than telephone records.

Similarly, location information generated by mobile communications infrastructure, such as mobile phones and mobile IP, is more sensitive than the mere location of a fixed telephony communication. Mobile communications location information can provide details of an individual's movements and activities and whom they have met with. This location information may be combined with other transactional information such as websites visited using the mobile device, individuals called, search engine requests; all used to create a considerable profile. This affects a wide variety of human rights beyond the right of privacy including the rights of free speech and assembly.

Moreover, newer mobile communications protocols are becoming increasingly specific about location data, and the availability of this information is becoming part of the actual communications protocol. That is, the means of identifying the location of a device is becoming more precision-based, and this location information is communicated to a number of parties, not necessarily only between the device and the mobile communications operator. As a result, the location of the device can be more easily discerned, not necessarily requiring access to the data held by the operator.

In addition to this data that naturally arises the functioning of a wireless network, there are other initiatives driving the development of technologies that build in location-tracking capabilities. For example, in the United States, the Federal Communications Commission (FCC) directed wireless telephone service providers to begin implementing Automatic Location Identification (ALI) for emergency (911) calls by October 1, 2001. The ALI "accuracy standards" require

---

[126] Council of Europe Convention on Cybercrime (ETS no: 185), opened for signature on November 8, 2001.

providers to develop capabilities that will permit the location of users with the following degrees of precision: for handset-based solutions – 50 meters for 67 percent of calls, 150 meters for 95 percent of calls; for network-based solutions – 100 meters for 67 percent of calls, 300 meters for 95 percent of calls.[127] Other wireless devices and services increasingly are coming into use, including wireless personal digital assistants (PDAs), wireless Internet access, and automotive navigation and assistance services (telematics), which when combined with Global Positioning Satellite capabilities, can determine the physical locations of users very precisely.

While there is likely to be strong commercial and law enforcement demand for the collection and use of the location data generated by these services, a legal framework to protect privacy specifically with respect to location information has not yet been implemented. In the absence of legal clarity, some operators have been keeping this kind of data indefinitely. In October 2001, British mobile operator Virgin Mobile revealed that that it had retained all call records since it was created in 1999. Similarly, in November 2001, it was reported that Irish operators, Eircell and Digifone, were holding customer records for more than six years. In both cases, the operators, stated that they believed they were required to keep these records under the law. [128]

The level of legal protection afforded to other traffic data is similarly unclear. Policies generally treat all of this transactional data as 'traffic data'; this data then bears the protections afforded under the traditional telephone system. The United Kingdom in its Regulation of Investigatory Powers Act 2000 accepted, after an extensive debate, that there are varying levels of sensitivity to this data, and separates 'traffic data' (source and destination of a transaction used for routing within a network) from the more sensitive 'communications data' that includes URLs, domain names, etc. The latter requires greater authorization and oversight procedures. Not all countries have pursued this line of reasoning.

Previous United States policy differentiated between traffic data on cable and telephone communications. The Cable Act traditionally protected traffic data to a greater degree than telephone traffic data. Now that cable infrastructure is used for internet communications (which were previously used over telephone lines, and thus traditional laws applied), successive White House administrations worked to erase this distinction, finally succeeding with the USA-PATRIOT Act.

---

[127] See generally <http://www.fcc.gov/e911/>.

[128] "Telecom Companies Stored Information for Over Six Years," BNA World Data Protection Report, Volume 1, Issue 12, December 2001.

Rather than deal with the specifics of digital communications media and services, the changes in United States law reduces the protections of traffic data for all communications to what had previously existed for telephone communications data. This was clearly intended, under the guise of technological neutrality. According to Attorney General Ashcroft:

> Agents will be directed to take advantage of new, technologically neutral standards for intelligence gathering. (...) Investigators will be directed to pursue aggressively terrorists on the internet. New authority in the legislation permits the use of devices that capture senders and receivers addresses associated with communications on the Internet.[129]

Retention of Traffic and Location Data[130]

On May 30, 2002, the European Parliament voted on the new European Union Telecommunications Privacy Directive. [131] In a remarkable reversal of their original opposition to data retention, the members voted to allow each European Union government to enact laws to retain the traffic and location data of all people using mobile phones, SMS, landline telephones, faxes, e-mails, chatrooms, the Internet, or any other electronic communication devices, to communicate. The new Directive reverses the 1997 Telecommunications Privacy Directive by explicitly allowing European Union countries to compel Internet service providers and telecommunications companies to record, index, and store their subscribers' communications data.[132] The data that can be retained includes all data generated by the conveyance of communications on an electronic communications network ("traffic data") as well as the data indicating the geographic position of a mobile phone user ("location data").[133] The contents of communications are not covered by the data retention measures. These requirements can be implemented for purposes varying from national security to criminal investigations and prevention, and prosecution of criminal offences, all without specific judicial authorization.

---

[129] Testimony of the Attorney General to the Senate Committee on the Judiciary, Washington DC, September 25, 2001.

[130] See EPIC's Data Retention Page <http://www.epic.org/privacy/intl/data_retention.html>.

[131] Directive 2002/_/EC of the European Parliament and of the Council concerning the processing of personal data and the protection of privacy in the electronic communications sector (still unpublished). An unofficial consolidated version is available at <http://www.gilc.org/as_voted_2nd_read.html>.

[132] Article 15(1), id.

[133] Article 2(b) and (c), id.

Although this data retention provision is supposed to constitute an exception to the general regime of data protection established by the directive, the ability of governments to compel Internet service providers and telecommunications companies to store all data about all of their subscribers can hardly be construed as an exception to be narrowly interpreted. The practical result is that all users of new communications technologies are now considered worthy of scrutiny and surveillance in a generalized and preventive fashion for periods of time that States' legislatures or governments have the discretion to determine. Furthermore, because of the cross-border nature of Internet communications, this Directive is likely to have negative repercussions for citizens of other countries. There is a significant risk that non-European Union law enforcement agencies will seek data held in Europe that it can not obtain at home, either because it was not retained or because their national law would not permit this kind of access.

During the debates on the Directive, many members of the European Parliament, and the European Union privacy commissioners consistently opposed data retention, arguing that, these policies are in contravention of data protection practices of deletion of data once it is no longer required for the purpose for which it was collected; and also in contravention of proportionality principles in accordance with constitutional laws and jurisprudence. Similarly, the Global Internet Liberty Campaign, a coalition of 60 civil liberties groups organized a campaign and drafted an open letter to oppose data retention. The letter was sent to all European Parliament members and heads of European Union institutions after more than 16,000 individuals from 73 countries endorsed it in less than a week.[134] The letter asserted that data retention (for reasons other than billing purposes) is contrary to well-established international human rights conventions and case law.

While a few other countries have already established data retention schemes (Belgium, France, Spain and the United Kingdom) the implementation phase of the Directive's data retention provision may be bumpy in other Member States. The Directive may be seen as being in conflict with the constitutions of some European Union countries, with respect to fundamental rights such as the presumption of innocence, the right to privacy, the secrecy of communications, or freedom of expression.[135]

---

[134] Open Letter to Mr. Pat Cox, President, European Parliament, from the Global Internet Liberty Campaign, May 2002, at <http://gilc.org/cox_en.html>.

[135] This is the case in Spain where the recent law allowing data retention for a year has been challenged as being in direct opposition to the Spanish Constitution. For more details see <http://www.kriptopolis.com/net/tc.php>.

A related effort for enhancing government control of the Internet and promoting surveillance is also being conducted in the name of preventing "cyber-crime," "information warfare" or protecting "critical infrastructures." Under these efforts, proposals to increase surveillance of the communications and activities of Internet users are being introduced as a way to prevent computer intruders from attacking systems and to stop other crimes such as intellectual property violations.

The lead bodies internationally are the Council of Europe and the G-8, while there has also been some activity within the European Union.[136] The United States has been active behind the scenes in developing and promoting these efforts.[137] After meeting behind closed doors for years, these organizations finally, in 2000, made public proposals that would place restrictions on online privacy and anonymity in the name of preventing cyber-crime.

Council of Europe

The Council of Europe is an intergovernmental organization formed in 1949 by West European countries. There are now 43 member countries. Its main role is "to strengthen democracy, human rights and the rule of law throughout its member states." Its description also notes that "it acts as a forum for examining a whole range of social problems, such as social exclusion, intolerance, the integration of migrants, the threat to private life posed by new technology, bioethical issues, terrorism, drug trafficking and criminal activities."

On September 8, 1995, the Council of Europe approved a recommendation to enhance law enforcement access to computers in member states. The Recommendation of the Committee of Ministers to Member States Concerning Problems of Criminal Procedure Law Connected with Information states:

> Subject to legal privileges or protection, investigating authorities should have the power to order persons who have data in a computer system under their control to provide all necessary information to enable access to a computer system and the data therein. Criminal procedure law should ensure that a similar order can be given to other persons who have

---

[136] Dr Paul Norman, "Policing 'high tech crime' in the global context: the role of transnational policy networks," available at <http://www.bileta.ac.uk/99papers/norman.htm>.

[137] For details see <http://www.privacyinternational.org/issues/cybercrime/>.

knowledge about the functioning of the computer system or measures applied to secure the data therein.

Specific obligations should be imposed on operators of public and private networks that offer telecommunications services to the public to avail themselves of all necessary technical measures that enable the interception of telecommunications by the investigating authorities.

Measures should be considered to minimize the negative effects of the use of cryptography on the investigation of criminal offenses, without affecting its legitimate use more than is strictly necessary.

In 1997, the Council of Europe formed a Committee of Experts on Crime in Cyber-space (PC-CY). The group met in secret for several years drafting an international treaty and in April 2000, released the "Draft Convention on Cyber-crime, version 19." A number of subsequent versions were released until version 27 was released in June 2001.

The convention has three parts. Part I proposes the criminalization of on-line activities such as data and system interference, the circumvention of copyright, the distribution of child pornography, and computer fraud. Part II requires ratifying states to pass laws to increase their domestic surveillance capabilities to cater for new technologies. This includes the power to intercept internet communications, gain access to traffic data in real-time or through preservation orders to ISPs, and access to secured or "protected" data. The final part of the treaty requires all states to cooperate in criminal investigations. So, for example, country A can request country B to utilize any of the aforementioned investigative powers within country B for a crime that is being investigated in country A. There is no requirement for the crime in country A to actually qualify as a crime in country B, i.e. no requirement for dual-criminality. In this sense, the convention is the largest mutual legal assistance regime in criminal matters ever created.

The draft convention text was strongly criticized by a wide variety of interested parties including privacy and civil liberties groups for its promotion of surveillance and lack of controls such as authorization requirements and dual criminality;[138] prominent security experts for previously articulated limitations

---

[138] See, for example, Global Internet Liberty Campaign Member Letter on Council of Europe Convention on Cyber-Crime, October 18, 2000 at <http://www.gilc.org/privacy/coe-letter-1000.html>; and Global Internet Liberty Campaign Member Letter on Council of Europe Convention on Cyber-Crime Version 24.2, December 12, 2000 at <http://www.gilc.org/privacy/coe-letter-1200.html>.

on security software;[139] and industry for the costs of implementing the requirements, and the challenges involved in responding to requests from 43 different countries. The European Union's Data Protection Working Group has expressed concern regarding the convention's implications upon privacy and human rights, concluding that:

> The Working Party therefore sees a need for clarification of the text of the articles of the draft convention because their wording is often too vague and confusing and may not qualify as a sufficient basis for relevant laws and mandatory measures that are intended to lawfully limit fundamental rights and freedoms.[140]

The convention text was finalized in September 2001. After the terrorist attacks on the United States, the convention was positioned as a means of combating terrorism. A signing ceremony took place in November where it was signed by thirty countries, and later signed by another four. Only one country, Albania, has ratified the convention at the time of publication of this report. The Convention is open to the members of the Council of Europe and to countries that were involved in the development, which includes the United States, Canada, Japan and South Africa. All members of the latter group have signed on.

The convention will come in to force once ratified by five signatories states, of which three must be members of the Council of Europe. Once it is in force, other non-COE countries like China and Singapore can also ask to join. The Australian government announced in July 2001 that its bill on computer crime, which requires users to provide encryption keys, is based on the Convention.[141]

A draft protocol on Racism and Xenophobia is currently under consideration. This protocol apparently will require the criminalization of certain forms of Internet speech that some might find offensive.[142] There was some discussion of a second protocol on "terrorist messages and the decoding thereof," however discussion on this matter has not advanced publicly.[143]

---

[139] Statement of Concerns, July 20, 2000. <http://www.cerias.purdue.edu/homes/spaf/coe/index.html>.

[140] European Union Article 29 Data Protection Working Group, Opinion 4/2001On the Council of Europe's Draft Convention on Cyber-crime, March 22, 2001

[141] Cybercrime Bill 2001 Second Reading Speech by the Attorney General, The Parliament of the Commonwealth of Australia.

[142] See, e.g., Global Internet Liberty Campaign, Member Letter to Council of Europe Secretary-General Walter Schwimmer, February 6, 2002, <http://www.gilc.org/speech/coe_hatespeech_letter.html>.

[143] See, e.g., Global Internet Liberty Campaign, Member Letter to Council of Europe Secretary-General Walter Schwimmer, February 28, 2002, <http://www.gilc.org/speech/coe_hatespeech_2.html>.

G-8

The Group of 8 (G-8) is made up of the heads of state of eight industrialized countries in the world (Canada, France, Germany, Italy, Japan, Russia, the United Kingdom, and the United States. The European Commission participates as an observer). The leaders have been meeting annually since 1975 to discuss issues of importance, including economics and finance, transnational organized crime, terrorism, and the information society.

Since 1995, the G-8 has become increasing more involved in the issue of high-tech crime, and has created working groups and issued a series of communiqués from the leaders and actions plans from justice ministers. Much of this work has been coordinated by the Lyon Group, established formally in 1997.

At the Birmingham, England summit in May 1998, the G-8 adopted a recommendation on ten principles and a ten-point action plan on high-tech crime. The ministers announced:

> We call for close cooperation with industry to reach agreement on a legal framework for obtaining, presenting and preserving electronic data as evidence, while maintaining appropriate privacy protection, and agreements on sharing evidence of those crimes with international partners. This will help us combat a wide range of crime, including abuse of the Internet and other new technologies.

The G-8 has met several times with industry and is actively promoting requirements that Internet Service Providers maintain records of all of their users' activities in case there is a future need to investigate a crime that might have occurred. These requirements were strongly criticized at a meeting held by the G-8 in Japan in 2001 where industry and a civil liberties group were invited and a draft press release and guidelines that promoted data retention had to be withdrawn after they had already been made public.

The G-8 has continued its activity in the area of law enforcement and combating terrorism, however. Throughout 2002 a number of summits involving Finance Ministers, Justice and Interior Ministers, and heads of state have released a number of statements regarding increased surveillance, traceability of communications,[144] and data retention.[145] Increased cooperation across borders was discussed at length; and as with the Council of Europe convention, no requirements of dual-criminality or double-criminality are necessary.

The European Union

In July 2000, the Commission announced plans for a new directive for fighting cyber-crime.[146] A communication was released in January 2001.[147] While similar to the Council of Europe convention in many ways, the Commission's proposal also included proposals regarding data retention and the reduction of anonymity. These policies were sought within "public forums" (only with limited invited speaking slots) in the fall of 2001, with unclear and unpublished results.

The retention proposal was sought in the alternative forum of the electronic services data protection directive in the European Parliament. The substantive law measures of criminalizing data and systems interference and defining other such offences are being pursued as a Council Framework Decision, currently in draft mode.[148] This initiative is designed to be consistent with the Council of Europe and G-8 activities.

The Organisation for Economic Co-Operation and Development (OECD)

In contrast to many of these law enforcement-driven initiatives, the Organisation for Economic Co-Operation and Development (OECD) has tended to take a broader view of security issues. In 1992, the OECD issued Guidelines for the Security of Information Systems.[149] Containing nine principles, the Guidelines stress the importance of ensuring transparency, proportionality and other democratic values when establishing measures, practices and procedures for the security of information systems. In the fall of 2001, the OECD Working Party on

---

[144] Recommendations for Tracing Networked Communications Across National Borders in Terrorist and Criminal Investigations, published at the G8 Justice and Interior Ministers' Meeting in Mont-Tremblant, Quebec, May 2002.

[145] Principles on the Availability of Data Essential to Protecting Public Safety, published at the G8 Justice and Interior Ministers' Meeting in Mont-Tremblant, Quebec, May 2002.

[146] "European Union Ministers Vow Cyber Crime Crackdown," Reuters, July 29, 2000.

[147] Communication from the Commission to the Council, the European Parliament, the Economic and Social Committee and the Committee of the Regions, Creating a Safer Information Society by Improving the Security of Information Infrastructures and Combating Computer-related Crime, COM(2000) 890 final, January 26, 2001, available at <http://www.privacyinternational.org/issues/cybercrime/eu/>.

[148] Commission Proposal for a Council Framework Decision on Attacks against Information Systems (COM (2002) 173 final), April 19, 2002.

[148] OECD Guidelines for the Security of Information Systems, adopted November 1992, available at <http://www.oecd.org/EN/document/0,,EN-document-29-nodirectorate-no-24-10249-29,00.html>

Information Security and Privacy (WPISP) established a group of experts to conduct a review of these guidelines (such a review must take place every five years). The group of experts met four times between December 2001 and June 2002 and recommended a number of changes. The OECD is expected to formally release the revised guidelines in the fall of 2002. Although the guidelines have been substantially revised, the need to ensure key democratic values, such as openness, transparency and the protection of personal information, is nonetheless reiterated in the principles.

National Security, Intelligence Agencies and the "Echelon system"

In the past several years, there has been considerable attention given to mass surveillance by intelligence agencies of international and national communications. Investigations have been opened and hearings held in parliaments around the world about the "Echelon" system coordinated by the United States.

Immediately following the Second World War, in 1947, the governments of the United States, the United Kingdom, Canada, Australia and New Zealand signed a National Security pact known as the "Quadripartite," or "United Kingdom - United States" (UKUSA) agreement. Its intention was to seal an intelligence bond in which a common national security objective was created. Under the terms of the agreement, the five nations carved up the earth into five spheres of influence, and each country was assigned particular signals intelligence (SIGINT) targets.

The UKUSA Agreement standardized terminology, code words, intercept handling procedures, arrangements for cooperation, sharing of information, Sensitive Compartmented Information (SCI) clearances, and access to facilities. One important component of the agreement was the exchange of data and personnel.

The strongest alliance within the UKUSA relationship is the one between the United States National Security Agency (NSA), and Britain's Government Communications Headquarters (GCHQ). The NSA operates under a 1952 presidential mandate, National Security Council Intelligence Directive (NSCID) Number 6, to eavesdrop on the world's communications networks for intelligence and military purposes. In doing so, it has built a vast spying operation that can reach into the telecommunications systems of every country on earth. Its operations are so secret that this activity, outside the United States, occurs with little or no legislative or judicial oversight. The most important facility in the alliance is Menwith Hill, a Royal Air Force base in the north of England. With over two dozen domes and a vast computer operations facility, the base has the capacity to eavesdrop on vast chunks of the communications spectrum. With the creation of Intelsat and digital telecommunications, Menwith Hill and other stations developed the capability to eavesdrop on an extensive scale on satellite-borne fax, telex and voice messages.

The current debate over NSA activities has focused on the existence of a signals intelligence system known as "Echelon." United States officials have refused to confirm the existence of this or any other surveillance systems. In May 2001, the European Parliament's Temporary Committee on the Echelon Interception System (established in July 2000) issued a report concluding that "the existence of a global system for intercepting communications . . . is no longer in doubt."[150] According to the committee, the Echelon system (reportedly run by the United States in cooperation with Britain, Canada, Australia and New Zealand) was set up at the beginning of the Cold War for intelligence gathering and has developed into a network of intercept stations around the world. Its primary purpose, according to the report, is to intercept private and commercial communications, not military intelligence.

The report recommended "self-protection" by EU citizens and companies, and encouraged further development and use of encryption technology within Europe to protect communications against surveillance. The report also recommended actions to be taken by the European Parliament during its September 2001 session in Strasbourg. These included provisions for the United States to (1) Negotiate and sign an agreement with European Union (European Union) requiring both parties to "observe, vis-à-vis the other, the provisions governing the protection of the privacy of citizens and the confidentiality of business communications applicable to its own citizens and firms;" (2) Sign the international covenant on civil and political rights so complaints by individuals could be submitted to Human Rights Committee created by the covenant; (3) Negotiate with member states code of conduct akin to that of European Union; and (4) Begin a dialog with the European Union on economic intelligence gathering. (On this point the Committee did not find widespread evidence of Echelon being used primarily for economic intelligence gathering). The Committee also recommended that Germany and United Kingdom condition

---

150 European Parliament, Temporary Committee on the Echelon Interception System, Report on the Existence of a Global System for the Interception of Private and Commercial Communications (ECHELON interception system) (2001/2098(INI)), May 18, 2001 (adopted July 11, 2001), available at <http://www.europarl.eu.int/tempcom/echelon/pdf/prechelon_en.pdf>.

further authorization of United States communications interception operations within their territories on United States compliance with European Convention on Human Rights. No further action on these recommendations has been taken.

Prior to issuing its report, the Temporary Committee traveled to Washington DC to meet with senior Bush administration government and intelligence officials to discuss Echelon. When they arrived, however, their meetings with these officials at the Departments of State, Commerce and Defence, the CIA and the NSA were cancelled at the last minute. The European Parliament subsequently issued a Resolution protesting this move.[151]

The work of the recent Temporary Committee was based on two earlier reports of the European Parliament. The first, "An Appraisal of the Technologies of Political Control,"[152] was published in 1997 and stated that the NSA had established an integrated communications surveillance capability in Europe. It described Echelon as a communications intelligence sharing sub-system capable of scanning particular communications to detect information of interest. In 1999, the second European Parliament report, "Interception Capabilities 2000" set out the technical specifications of the interception system. [153] The report described the merger of Echelon and the International Law Enforcement Telecommunications Seminar (ILETS) stating that in time, the two vast systems - one designed for national security and one for law enforcement - would merge, and in the process will compromise national control over surveillance activities.

These recent events have left observers contemplating two profound conclusions. First, as long as the UK-USA SIGINT partners police and govern their own operations outside of actual effective parliamentary and judicial oversight, there is good reason to believe that SIGINT can be turned against individuals and groups exercising civil and political rights. There is ample evidence that the activities of Greenpeace, Christian Aid, Amnesty International, the International Committee to Ban Landmines, the Tibetan government-in-exile, various anti-globalization movements like the Independent Media Center, and the International Committee of the Red Cross have been targeted by UKUSA agencies. Second, there is an increasing blurring between the activities of

---

[151] Steve Kettmann, "U.S. Echelon Snub Angers Europe," Wired News, May 18, 2001, available at <http://www.wired.com/news/privacy/0,1848,43921,00.html

[152] Published by STOA (Science and Technology Options Assessment). Reference Project No. IV/STOA/RSCH/LP/politicon.1

[153] Report to the Director General for Research of the European Parliament (Scientific and Technical Options Assessment programme office) on the development of surveillance technology and risk of abuse of economic information, available at <http://jya.com/echelon-dc.htm>.

intelligence agencies and law enforcement. The creation of a seamless international intelligence and law enforcement surveillance system has resulted in the potential for a huge international network that may, in practice, negate current rules and regulations prohibiting domestic communications surveillance by national intelligence agencies.

Audio Bugging

Advances in technology are also making it easier and cheaper to conduct covert audio surveillance. Bugs come in many shapes and sizes. They range from micro engineered transmitters the size of an office staple, to devices no bigger than a cigarette packet that are capable of transmitting video and sound signals for miles. Many of the bugs are cleverly camouflaged. They are hidden in everything from umbrella stands to light shades. Sometimes, the infiltrator will hide them in a business or sports trophy where they will stay indefinitely. The latest bugs remain active with their own power supply for around ten years.

Laws restricting the use of covert audio devices vary widely across the world. Many countries have provisions in their general wiretap laws that also cover the use of bugs. The European Court of Human Rights has ruled several times that all signatories of the Convention must enact laws governing their use. While it is illegal in most circumstances in the United States to use or sell such devices, the British market had no restrictions whatever until recently. As one private investigator told the London Daily Telegraph, "It's a game anyone can play." Millions of bugs are sold every year in Asian countries such as Hong Kong and Japan.

The devices are used for a variety of reasons. In many Asian countries, use of the devices for industrial espionage is widespread. They are also frequently used in the workplace or in homes. Law enforcement and intelligence agencies also use the devices but according to government records in the United States, Canada and other countries, they are used much less frequently than traditional wiretaps for law enforcement purposes.

Video Surveillance

Surveillance cameras (also called Closed Circuit Television or CCTV) are increasingly being used to monitor public and private spaces throughout the world. The leader is the United Kingdom, where between 150 and 300 million

---

pounds per year is spent on expanding a surveillance industry that has an estimated 1.5 million cameras watching public spaces.[154] Many Central Business Districts in Britain are now covered by surveillance camera systems involving a linked system of cameras with full pan, tilt, zoom and night vision or infrared capability. CCTV systems are also in wide use in several other European countries where they are closely regulated. Surveillance of public spaces has grown markedly in the United States and Australia. In New York City, the NYCLU Surveillance Camera Project identified 2,397 cameras in Manhattan.[155] The Mayor of Washington, D.C. has proposed a "London style" blanket surveillance of public areas to cover the several public protests that takes place in the capital.[156] In Singapore, cameras are widely deployed for traffic enforcement and to prevent littering. Several governments are now considering using surveillance systems as an anti-terrorism tool. Some observers believe the surveillance camera phenomenon is dramatically changing the nature of cities. The technology has been described as the "fifth utility," where CCTV is being integrated into the urban environment in much the same way as the electricity supply and the telephone network in the first half of the century.[157]

The camera system is designed to serve as a deterrent to crime and for evidence gathering purposes. Generally these systems have been rolled out with little prior research into the effectiveness or appropriateness of the technology, as in most cases the deployment is driven by a public relations need to create the impression of heightened security.[158] The evidence supporting the effectiveness of the camera system has been inconclusive. A new study announced in June 2002 found that in many areas with CCTV that crime increased and that street lighting was a more effective deterrent.[159] In March 2002, a report issued by researchers at the University of Hull, United Kingdom found that cameras do not have a major impact on most criminal activity, and even where they appear to have an effect it is because that crime is often just displaced elsewhere.[160] Recent sudies

---

[154] Jeffery Rosen, "A Cautionary Tale for a New Age of Surveillance," New York Times Magazine, October 7, 2001.

[155] NYCLU Surveillance Camera Project <http://www.nyclu.org/surveillance.html>. See also, New York Surveillance Camera Players <http://www.notbored.org/the-scp.html>.

[156] " Eyes in the Sky: DC Police Are Building a Network of Cameras To Keep Tabs on the Public," Wall Street Journal Classroom Edition, April 2002

[157] Stephen Graham, The Fifty Utility, Index on Censorship, Issue 3, 2000, available at <http://www.indexoncensorship.org/300/gra.htm>.

[158] See Michael McCahill & Clive Norris, "Literature Review," Urbaneye Working Paper No. 2, March 2002, available at <http://www.urbaneye.net>.

[159] " CCTV not a crime prevention cure-all, says report," NACRO, June 28 2002, available at <http://www.nacro.org.uk/templates/news/newsItem.cfm/2002062800.htm>.

[160] Michael McCahill and Clive Norris "CCTV in Britain," Working Paper No. 3, Urbaneye Project, Centre for Criminology and Criminal Justice, University of Hull, March 2002, available at <http://www.urbaneye.net>.

conducted by the Scottish Center for Criminolgy have yielded similar results.[161] Questions are now surfacing about the use of cameras in Australia.[162]

As surveillance systems appear poised to become a part of the urban landscape, scholars, data protection commissioners, legislators, and the public are beginning to grapple with the implications of this new technology.[163] In July 2000, the United Kingdom Data Protection Commissioner issued a code of practice on the use of CCTV. The code sets out guidelines for the operators of CCTV systems and makes clear their obligations under the recently implemented Data Protection Act 1998.[164] Also in 2000 the Greek Data Protection Commissioner issued a directive prohibiting the use of CCTV except in certain circumstances.[165] In Sweden, the 1998 Law on Secret Camera Surveillance restricts the use of video surveillance. Norway's Personal Data Registers Act of 2000 also provides specific rules for video surveillance. Canada's privacy commissioner has been very active in limiting surveillance cameras and has recently launched a lawsuit against the Royal Canadian Mountain Police, calling their use of the system an unconstitutional breach of privacy.[166] Washington, D.C. is considering regulations that will subject video surveillance to the same restrictions that are imposed on electronic surveillance, including requiring judicial and public oversight over the system's operation. Campaigns have begun in several countries to stop the spread of surveillance camera systems.[167] For the past four years, an international coalition composed of artists, scientists, engineers, scholars, and others have declared December 24 to be "World Sousveillance" day, and have staged several public protests to draw attention to the use of surveillance cameras.[168]

---

[161] The Scottish Centre for Criminology, Crime Prevention Publications, available at <http://www.scotcrim.u-net.com/researchc.htm>; and, Al Webb, "'Spy' Cameras vs Villains in Britain," UPI. March 8, 2002

[162] Bruce Andrews. "Here's Looking at You", Australian Center for Independent Journalism, April 2002 <http://www.reportage.uts.edu.au/stories/2002/social/cctv_24042002.html>

[163] See "On the Threshold to Urban Panopticon? Analysing the Employment of CCTV in European Cities and Assessing its Social and Political Impacts," a four year European Comission funded project, available at <http://www.urbaneye.net>.

[164] United Kingdom Data Protection Commission, CCTV Code of Practice, July 2000, available at <http://www.dataprotection.gov.uk/dpr/dpdoc.nsf/ed1e7ff5aa6def30802566360045bf4d/db76232b37b5bb648025691900413c9d?OpenDocument>.

[165] Hellenic Republic Data Protection Authority, Directive On Closed Circuit Television Systems, September 29, 2000.

[166] Charles Mandel, "Security Cams not OK in Canada?" Wired News. April 16, 2002 <http://www.wired.com/news/politics/0,1283,51821,00.html>.

[167] See generally Privacy International, CCTV Pages, <http://www.privacyinternational.org/issues/cctv/index.html>; "Watching Them, Watching Us," United Kingdom CCTV Surveillance Regulation Campaign, <http://www.spy.org.uk/>; EPIC, Observing Surveillance Project, <http://www.epic.org/privacy/surveillance>.

[168] World Sousveillance Day <http://wearcam.org/wsd.htm>.

The debate over the appropriateness of surveillance technology is likely to become sharper as the technology becomes increasingly sophisticated. New systems can digitally record images, which facilitate easy archiving, recovery, and sharing of information. Features include night vision, computer-assisted operation, and motion detection facilities that help improve the operator's attentiveness by sounding an alert if suspicious activity is taking place. The clarity of the pictures is usually excellent, with many systems being able to read a newspaper at a hundred meters. Technology is also being developed to spot patterns in the surveillance data such as recognizing faces, analyzing crowd behavior, and scanning the intimate area between skin surface and clothes using "passive millimeter wave technology" to search for contraband or weapons.[169] Research into these technologies is receiving significant government funding for crime fighting and anti-terrorism purposes.[170]

Face Recognition

Face recognition technology utilizes computerized pattern matching technology to automatically identify peoples' faces. While it is still very much in its infancy, it raises significant public policy questions because it enables the covert identification and classification of people in public. The borough of Newham in the United Kingdom first deployed a face recognition system to scan faces against a database to identify people "of interest." The Reykjavik airport in Iceland was among the first airports to use the technology. In the United States, this same kind of face recognition technology was used at the 2001 Super Bowl in Tampa, Florida to compare the faces of attendees to faces in a database of mug shots. There was widespread public outcry, prompting some to call the event the "Snooper Bowl."[171]

Face recognition technology is still not reliable. For instance, it was not accurate enough for use in the Salt Lake Winter Olympic games where the security chief said that "it's just not proven technology yet."[172] Studies sponsored by the United States Defense Department have also shown the system is right only 54% of the time and can be significantly compromised by changes in lighting, weight, hair,

---

[169] Ivan Amato. "Beyond X-ray Vision: Can Big Brother see right through your clothes?" Discover Volume 23 No. 7 (July 2002) < http://www.discover.com/july_02/feattechapterhtml>

[170] See United States Defense Department's Human ID at a Distance Project <http://www.darpa.mil/iao/HID.htm>

[171] For more information, see EPIC's Face Recognition page <http://www.epic.org/privacy/facerecognition/>.

[172] "Games Notebook," The Ottawa Citizen, February 10, 2002.

sunglasses, subject cooperation, and other factors.[173]   Tests on the face recognition systems in operation at Palm Beach Airport in Florida,[174] and Boston Logan Airport have also shown the technology to be ineffective and error-ridden.[175]

As the power and capabilities of surveillance technology increases while the cost and size of systems decreases, there will be further incentives to use the technology. Critics see this trend as a reason to develop appropriate regulations to safeguard privacy and to prevent the misuse of the technology.[176]

Satellite Surveillance

Developments in satellite surveillance (also called "remote sensing") are also occurring at a fast pace, and embrace features similar to those of more conventional visual surveillance. Satellite resolution has constantly improved over the past decade. Since the end of the Cold War, companies such as EarthWatch, Motorola and Boeing have invested billions of dollars to create satellites capable of mapping the most minute detail on the face of the earth.

A commercial satellite capable of recognizing objects the size of a student's desk was launched from the United States in September 1999 and began releasing images in October 2000.[177] The Ikonos is most powerful commercial imaging satellite ever built. Its parabolic lens can recognize objects as small as one meter anywhere on earth and the according to the company, viewers can see individual trees, automobiles, road networks, and houses. The satellite, owned by Denver company Space Imaging, will be the first of a new generation of high resolution satellites using technology formerly restricted to government security agencies. Another ten companies have received licenses to launch equally powerful satellites and several are expected to launch shortly.

---

173 Declan McCullagh and Robert Zarate, "Scanning Tech a Blurry Picture", Wired News, February 16, 2002, available at <http://www.wired.com/news/print/0,1294,50470,00.html>.

174 American Civil Liberties Union Press Release, "Data on Face-Recognition Test at Palm Beach Airport Further Demonstrates Systems' Fatal Flaws," May 14, 2002, available at <http://www.aclu.org/news/2002/n051402b.html>.

175 Hiawatha Bray, "'Face Testing' at Logan is Found Lacking," Boston Globe, July 17, 2002, available at <http://www.boston.com/dailyglobe2/198/metro/_Face_testing_at_Logan_is_found_lacking+.shtml>.

176 See Testimony of Marc Rotenberg before D.C. City Council, June 2002 <http://www.epic.org/privacy/surveillance/testimony_061302.html>

177 See <http://www.spaceimaging.com/>.

The technology is already being used for a vast range of purposes from media reporting of war and natural disasters, to detecting unlicensed building work and even illegal swimming pools. Public interest groups are using the information to show images of nuclear testing by countries and even images of secret United States bases such as Area 51 in Nevada.[178]

While industry looks for the opportunity to exploit current spy satellite technology, a great deal of effort is being made to integrate the existing images with ground-based Geographic Information System (GIS) databases than can provide detailed data on human activity. Double clicking on a satellite image of an urban area can reveal precise details of the occupants of a target house. The "Open Skies" policy accepted worldwide means that there are few restrictions of the use of the technology.[179]

But the companies have a distance to go before they catch up with governments. It is estimated that the current generation of secret spy satellites such as the Ikon/Keyhole-12 can recognize objects as small as 10cm across and some analysts say that it can image a license plate.[180] Boeing recently landed a 10-year contract from the United States Government for a Future Imagery Architecture (FIA) to replace the KH satellites and the ground infrastructure.[181] The FIA is based on a constellation of new satellites that are smaller, less expensive, and placed in orbit to allow for real-time surveillance of battlefields and other targets.

Electronic Commerce

Surveillance by law enforcement is not the only concern users should have about their online privacy. The growth of the Internet and electronic commerce has dramatically increased the amount of personal information that is collected about individuals by corporations. As consumers engage in routine online transactions, they leave behind a trail of personal details, often without any idea that they are doing so. Much of this information is routinely captured in computer logs.

Most on-line companies keep track of users' purchases. This information ranges from the trivial to the most sensitive and, unless adequately protected, can be

---

[178] See e.g, Federation of American Scientists, Dimona Photographic Interpretation Report, available at <http://www.fas.org/nuke/guide/israel/facility/dimona_pir.html>.
[179] Id.
[180] "Spy Satellites: the Next Leap Forward," International Defense Review, January 1, 1997.
[181] "Boeing to build new United States satellites," Jane's Defense Weekly, September 15, 1999.

used for purposes that seriously harm the interests of the consumer. Other companies gather personal information from visitors by offering personalized services such as news searches, free email and stock portfolios. They then sell, trade or share that information among third party companies without the consumer's expressed knowledge or consent. The perceived value of this kind of information is behind the stock-market valuations of many dotcom companies.

Spam

Many on-line companies, for example, provide lists of their customers' e-mail addresses to companies that specialize in sending unsolicited commercial e-mail (spam). Other companies mine e-mail address from sources such as messages posted on mailing lists, from newsgroups, or from domain name registration data. This results in consumers being barraged by advertisements and "once-off" deals by companies or people they have never even heard of. Studies show that consumers resent spam both for the time it takes to process and for the loss of privacy resulting from their e-mail address circulating freely on countless directories.[182] Furthermore, spam can result in significant economic loss to the consumer. A 2001 report by the European Commission found that "Internet subscribers worldwide are unwittingly paying an estimated 10 billion euros ($9.36 billion USD) a year in connection costs just to receive 'junk' e-mails."[183] The Commission's recently passed Electronic Communications Privacy Directive prohibits unsolicited commercial marketing by e-mail without "opt-in" consent.[184] In Japan two new anti-spam laws were passed in 2002. The laws allow users of the Internet and text-enabled mobile phones to opt-out of spammers' contact lists, and require that all unsolicited commercial e-mail be clearly identified.[185]

Profiling

Probably even more worrying is the increasing practice of "online profiling" Internet users. Companies, including Internet Service Providers, web site hosts

---

[182] For more information on SPAM generally and how to reduce it see <http://www.junkbusters.com> and <http://www.cauce.org/>.

[183] European Commission, Unsolicited Commercial Communications and Data Protection, January 2001 available at <http://europa.eu.int/comm/internal_market/en/dataprot/studies/spam.htm>.

[184] 2439th Council meeting, Luxembourg, June 25, 2002. Transcripts of proceedings available at <http://europa.eu.int/rapid/start/cgi/guesten.ksh?p_action.gettxt=gt&doc=PRES/02/180|0|AGED&lg=EN>.

[185] Toru Takahashi, "2 new laws aimed at cutting spam," Daily Yomiuri (Japan), July 2, 2002 <http://www.yomiuri.co.jp/newse/20020702wo32.htm>.

---

and others, monitor users as they travel across the Internet, collecting information on what sites they visit, the time and length of these visits, search terms they enter, purchases they make or even "click-through" responses to banner ads. In the off-line world this would be comparable to, for example, having someone follow you through a shopping mall, scanning each page of every magazine you browse though, every pair of shoes that you looked at and every menu entry you read at the restaurant. When collected and combined with other data such as demographic or "psychographic" data, these diffuse pieces of information create highly detailed profiles of net users. These profiles have become a major currency in electronic commerce where they are used by advertisers and marketers to predict a user's preferences, interests, needs and possible future purchases. Most of these profiles are currently stored in anonymous form. However, there is a distinct likelihood that they will soon be linked with information, such as names and addresses, gathered from other sources, making them personally identifiable.

The most pervasive tracking technology is the cookie. The cookie is a small file containing an ID number that is placed on a user's hard drive by a website. Cookies were developed to improve websites' ability to track users over a session. The cookie can also notify the site that the user has returned and can allow the site to track the user's activities across many different visits. The use of cookies expanded greatly when it was realized that a single cookie could be used across many different sites. This led to the development of advertising network companies that can track users across thousands of sites. The largest ad service, DoubleClick, has agreements with over 11,000 websites and maintains cookies on 100 million users; each linking to hundreds of pieces of information about the user's browsing habits. It is possible to configure the common browsers to reject or send a warning notice before cookies are set. This does not provide much protection, however, as websites will often refuse access to users who do not accept cookies or send out so many repeated attempts that the user accepts the cookie in order to get uninterrupted access.

A more secretive manner of monitoring online users takes place through the use of web bugs. Web bugs are invisible graphics that are placed on Web sites or in emails in order track visitors to that Web site or the recipients of emails (often spam). A Web bug on a Web site collects information such as the IP address of the visiting computer, the browser being used, the time of the 'hit', and also a previously set cookie value. In an email a Web bug is used to discover if and when the email message was read, how many times it was forwarded, and the IP address of the recipient. A marketing email directing users to Web sites can also be used to link the email addresses of those that later visit the site to their cookie data. Web bugs can also be used in newsgroup messages to track readers.[186]

In the offline world, profiling has been thriving for decades.[187] Profiling companies build personally-identifiable databases based a plethora of sources including supermarket purchases, product warranty cards, public records, census records, magazine and catalog subscriptions, and surveys. This is done in the absense of legislation to prevent dossier building. Companies also "enhance" dossiers that they already own by combining or "overlaying" information from other databases. These dossiers may link individual's identities to any number of facts deemed private by advanced societies including medical conditions, physical characteristics, and lifestyle preferences.

The line between online and offline profiling has become more and more blurred. In 1999, DoubleClick announced that it was buying Abacus, owner of the largest direct marketing lists in the country, with information on the purchasing habits of 90 percent of all United States households, and that DoubleClick was going to merge information from the purchasing databases with information from online browsing. Following a public outcry, the company suspended its plan to merge personal data with profiles. However, in July 2000 the Federal Trade Commission reached an agreement with the Network Advertisers Initiative, a group consisting of the largest online advertisers including DoubleClick, which will allow for online profiling and any future merger of such databases to occur with only "opt-out" consent.[188]

Another important player in this move towards complete identification of Internet users is the Microsoft Corporation. In 2001 Microsoft began aggressively promoting the Passport and Hailstorm services in preparation for the launch of Microsoft XP, the newest version of the Windows operating system. Passport is an online identification and authentication system, which employs a single sign-on system to facilitate e-commerce and browsing among different web sites that require a user to identify oneself. Once a user signs on to Passport, other affiliated sites visited by the user receive information about the user. Passport stores user information in a central database. The Passport service is intended to give Microsoft and Passport affiliates the ability to send unsolicited commercial email to Internet users and to profile their activities. To register for Passport, a

---

[186] For more information on Web bugs visit the Privacy Foundation
<http://www.privacyfoundation.net/resources/webbug.asp>.

[187] See EPIC's Profiling page <http://www.epic.org/privacy/profiling/>.

[188] Electronic Privacy Information Center (EPIC) and Junkbusters. "Network Advertising Initiative: Principles not Privacy," July 28, 2000, available at <http://www.epic.org/privacy/internet/NAI_analysis.html>.

user must submit an e-mail address. Users can also submit their real name, city/locale, gender, age, occupation, marital status, personal statement, hobbies and interest, favorite quote, favorite things, a personal photo, and a home page. Hailstorm was a group of services (including MyAddress, MyProfile, MyContacts, MyNotifications, MyInbox, MyCalendar, MyDocuments, MyApplicationSettings, MyWallet, MyUsage, and MyLocation) that Microsoft intended to provide from central servers. In theory it would have collected an extraordinary range of consumer information. Privacy and consumer groups in the United States filed a series of complaints against Passport and Hailstorm with the Federal Trade Commission in 2001, detailing the risks to privacy and security in these systems. In July 2002, European Union (European Union) officials confirmed publicly that they were pursuing an investigation into Passport for breach of European privacy laws.[189]

A competitor to Microsoft's Passport, Project Liberty, is being developed by a coalition of companies.[190] This identification system is similar to Microsoft's single sign-on, however, it allows users to choose what companies will receive personal information. The goal of Project Liberty is to facilitate information sharing so that companies can create and exchange profiles of individuals personal information.

Attempts at developing more permanent methods of identifying users have been underway for years. In 1999, Intel announced that it was including a serial number in each new Pentium III chip that could be accessed by websites and internal corporate networks. Most of the manufacturers suppressed the number after a consumer boycott was announced, and Intel announced in 2000 that it is dropping the serial number in future chips. Microsoft and RealAudio were discovered using the internal networking number found in most computers as another identifier for online users. Microsoft's Windows Media Player contains a globally-unique identifier (GUID) that can be tracked by website operators. The Internet Engineering Task Force has developed specifications for the next version of the Internet's underlying protocols called IPv6 that will assign a unique permanent ID number to every device hooked into the net, which could one day include refrigerators and VCRs.

---

[189] European Union Article 29 Data Protection Working Group, "First orientations of the Article 29 Working Party Concerning Online Authentication Services," July 2, 2002, available at <http://www.epic.org/redirect/eu_redirect.html>.

[190] See Project Liberty Homepage <http://www.projectliberty.org/>.

Security Breaches

The privacy of online consumers can also be seriously compromised by security breaches. Many web sites are poorly secured against accidental releases or deliberate attacks.[191] In March 2000, De Beers lost 35,000 names, addresses, phone numbers and e-mail addresses of people inquiring about buying diamonds following a security breach. In April 2000, it was revealed that an unknown Microsoft engineer had included a backdoor into its web server software. If someone typed, "Netscape engineers are weenies!" backwards, they would have access to the websites and associated data. In August 2000, Kaiser Permanente, a top United States health insurer, admitted that it had compromised the confidentiality and privacy of its members when it sent over 800 e-mail messages, many containing sensitive information, to the wrong members.[192] Similarly in July 2001, makers of the anti-depressant drug "Prozac" revealed the names and email addresses of over 700 patients that subscribed to the company's email service for information on the drug and other issues.[193]

Information Brokers and Seal Programs

Many companies offer what are known as "information brokering" services, whereby users provide information to the company, which then provides it to a third-party website with the consent of the user. These sites raise a question of trust. Given that many of them are run by the same Internet companies that are also major privacy invaders, the user must wonder why they should volunteer providing information to these companies.

A common practice among online companies is to sign on to a "seal" program in order to provide consumers with a sense of security that their personal information is being protected. These programs follow the traditional seal programs in laying down certain eligibility standards which participant companies must respect in order to get a compliance seal. The better seal programs conduct monitoring and compliance checks, provide educational information, offer consumer dispute resolution, and enforce sanctions against errant companies. There are many disadvantages of seal programs operating within a self-regulatory system. All too often, seal program operators have been

---

191 See, e.g., Eric Murray, SSL Server Security Survey, July 31, 2000 showing that encryption on most e-commerce sites is inadequate, <http://www.meer.net/~ericm/papers/ssl_servers.html>.

192 "Sensitive Kaiser E-Mails Go Astray," Washington Post, August 10, 2000.

193 "Prozac Maker Reveals Patient E-Mail Addresses," Washington Post, July 4, 2001, at E01.

shown to be ineffective and reluctant to take enforcement measures against their members including companies such as Microsoft.[194] A 1999 Forrester research report found that, "because independent privacy groups like TRUSTe and BBBOnline earn their money from e-commerce organizations, they become more of a privacy advocate for the industry – rather than for consumers."[195]

Privacy Enhancing Techniques

There are tools available that can be used to protect the privacy of users in many cases. These technologies are known as "Privacy Enhancing Technologies" (PETs) and are aimed at eliminating or limiting the collection and processing of identifiable data. Encryption is an important tool for protection against certain forms of communications surveillance. When properly implemented, a message is scrambled (encrypted) so that only the intended recipient will be able to unscramble (decrypt), and subsequently read, the contents. Pretty Good Privacy (PGP) is the best known encryption program and has hundreds of thousands of users. An alternative is the open source program called GNU Privacy Guard (GPG) that allows anyone to view the full source of the system to ensure that it does not allow for secret surveillance.[196] Cryptographic modules are also implemented in applications; for example web browsers, in order to maintain some confidentiality in electronic commerce transactions, include Secure Sockets Layer (SSL) to encrypt sessions between users and servers.

Traditional cryptography implementations protect only the confidentiality and integrity of the communications content. They do little to prevent the disclosure of traffic data; that is, it is still clear that person A is emailing person B, or that person A is visiting web site W. More sophisticated applications are required to maintain the privacy of these transactions. "Anonymous remailers" strip identifying information from e-mails and can stop traffic analysis. Services such as Anonymizer, provide anonymous websurfing, email messaging, banner ad and pop-up blocking and deletes cookies and web bugs after Internet sessions.[197]

During the past year there were significant setbacks in the effort to develop commercially viable privacy enhancing techniques. In October 2001, Zero Knowledge Systems ceased to operate the Freedom Network, which used to

---

[194] "Just How Trusty is Truste," Wired, April 9, 2002
<http://www.wired.com/news/exec/0,1370,51624,00.html>.

[195] Forrester Research Inc, "Privacy Wake-Up Call," September 1, 1999.

[196] See <http://www.gnupg.org/>

[197] See <http://www.anonymizer.com>.

provide a fully encrypted and pseudonymous link between the user and secure servers, and replaced it with a simpler proxy-based service. In February 2002, a number of flaws were discovered in SafeWeb, an anonymous-surfing technology originally funded by the CIA.[198] In March 2002, Network Associates, the company that provided the commercial version of PGP, discontinued support for the application.[199] The international (free) version continues to be available from PGP International.[200]

At the same time, human rights groups and even large corporations explored new techniques to protect online privacy. The Canadian-based Privaterra worked with NGOs to encourage the use of strong encryption techniques and other methods for online privacy.[201] Hacktivism efforts continued with new efforts to empower dissident political organizations operating over the Internet. In July 2002, the international hacker group, Hactivismo, announced a new free service called "Camera Shy" to allow users to conceal messages in ordinary image files on the Internet. The browser-based steganography application automatically scans and decrypts content straight from the Internet and leaves no traces on the user's system.[202] The global giant American Express is offering a system known as "Private Payments" to enable more private online commerce.[203] Under this system a limited life transaction number, instead of the cardholder's credit card number, is used to make online purchases.[204]

It is important to distinguish between genuine privacy enhancing techniques and data security technologies that seek to render processing safe but not to reduce the disclosure and processing of identifiable data.[205] Moreover, there are many products offered by industry that are not privacy protective. Many of these systems, such as Microsoft's Passport and the World Wide Web Consortium's (W3C) Platform for Privacy Preferences (P3P), are designed to facilitate data sharing rather than to limit disclosure of personal information.[206]

---

[198] Declan McCullagh, "SafeWeb's Holes Contradict Claims," Wired News, February 12, 2002, available at <http://www.wired.com/news/politics/0,1283,50371,00.html>.

[199] Sam Costello, "Network Associates Abandons Search for PGP Buyer, Axes 18," IDG News Service, March 6, 2002, available at <http://www.nwfusion.com/news/2002/0306naipgp.html>.

[200] Homepage <http://www.pgpi.com/>.

[201] Homepage <http://www.privaterra.com>

[202] Eric Auchard, "Hacker Group Targets Countries that Censor Internet," Reuters, July 14, 2002.

[203] http://www26.americanexpress.com/privatepayments/info_page.jsp?pers_home=shoppvtpaymts

[204] See Private Payments FAQ <http://www26.americanexpress.com/privatepayments/faq.jsp>.

[205] Herbert Burkert, "Privacy-Enhancing Technologies: Typology, Critique, Vision" in Philip Agre and Marc Rotenberg, eds, Technology and Privacy: The New Landscape 125 (MIT Press 1997).

[206] EPIC and Junkbusters, "Pretty Poor Privacy: An Assessment of P3P and Internet Privacy," June 2000 <http://www.epic.org/reports/prettypoorprivacy.html>.

Electronic Numbering

Electronic Numbering (ENUM) is an Internet infrastructure that will allow a single number to reference contact or other information in a public database.[207] Individuals or businesses holding an ENUM account will be able to store information, including phone numbers, e-mail addresses, voicemail numbers, fax numbers, or any other type of data in the ENUM database. Persons wishing to contact the entity would use the ENUM to query a public database for the stored information.

ENUM raises a host of privacy issues that are yet to be resolved. Most importantly, because of the different ways in which ENUM can provide means to contact a person, ENUM has the potential to become a Globally Unique Identifier (GUID). At a more fundamental level, issues of notice and individual participation have yet to be resolved.

The ENUM owner could also include certain suggestions for the use of the contact information. For instance, when using an ENUM to query the database at 10 PM on a Friday night, the database could respond with instructions to call a cell phone rather than a land line at the office. However, the person querying the ENUM database would receive all of the owner's contact information, and could simply choose to violate the instructions.

Since the ENUM database is public, one can assume that it will be mined for commercial purposes. This may lead to an unprecedented amount of spam, as a single ENUM can reveal multiple methods of contacting a person.

Public Records and Privacy, Public-Private Ventures

Increasingly, information is being harvested from public records to create detailed profiles on individuals. Public records may contain many types of personal information that are commercially valuable. These include: Social Security numbers, birth records, arrest information, civil case history, criminal case history, addresses, drivers license information, land sales transactions,

---

[207] Current information on the development of ENUM is available at<http://www.enum-forum.org/>. See also EPIC's ENUM page <http://www.epic.org/privacy/enum/>.

---

records of asset holdings, ownership of corporations, marital status, presence of children, employment status, and health information.

Maintaining accessible public records is important for scholarship, research, journalism, and governmental accountability. However, allowing unrestricted use of public records enables private, commercial, and governmental interests to invade individuals' privacy.[208]

The advent of remote electronic access to public records systems has raised the specter of vastly increased data mining and profiling. Mining a public records database soon will no longer require the time and expense involved in traveling to the physical location of the records. Data miners will be able to remotely access public records systems and use widely available software to harvest personal information. This harvesting of personal information already has had a substantial impact on individuals. In 2002, the Wall Street Journal reported that drug maker Eli Lilly had terminated employees for decade-old convictions discovered in dossiers aggregated from public records.[209]

Unrestricted commercial harvesting of public records has enabled the American government to obtain detailed dossiers on citizens with ease. Through private-public partnerships, several profiling companies make consumer dossiers available to the government. One company in particular, ChoicePoint, has emerged as the leading provider for law enforcement and other government agencies.[210] ChoicePoint maintains web pages customized for individual federal agencies to facilitate the sale of public record information to police.[211] As a result of FOIA requests initiated by EPIC, it was discovered that ChoicePoint was selling the national ID databases of several Latin American countries to the American immigration law enforcement agency.[212]

---

[208] Daniel J. Solove, Access and Aggregation: Public Records, Privacy, and the Constitution, 86 Minnesota Law Review 6 (2002).

[209] "Firms Dig Deep Into Workers' Pasts Amid Post-Sept. 11 Security Anxiety," Wall Street Journal, March 12, 2002.

[210] "If the FBI Hopes to Get the Goods on You, It May Ask ChoicePoint," Wall Street Journal, April 13, 2001.

[211] See ChoicePoint FBI <http://www.cpfbi.com>; ChoicePoint DEA <http://www.cpdea.com>; ChoicePoint Government <http://www.cpgov.com>.

[212] Documents available at <http://www.epic.org/privacy/publicrecords/inschoicepoint.pdf>.

Digital Rights Management

In an effort to stem content and software piracy, a number of companies have developed Digital Rights Management (DRM) systems to prevent the unauthorized use of digital files.[213] DRM technologies can control file access (number of views, length of views), altering, sharing, copying, printing, and saving. These technologies may be contained within the operating system, program software, or in the actual hardware of a device. Some DRM technology can disable users' machines for unauthorized access to files. InTether Point-to-Point, for instance, imposes "penalties" for those who attempt an "illegal use" of a digital file.[214] Penalties include automatic rebooting of the users' machine, or destruction of the file the user is attempting to access.

These technologies have been developed with little regard for privacy protection. DRM technology usually requires the user to reveal his or her identity and rights to access the file. Upon authentication of identity and rights to the file, the user can access the content.

These systems can prevent anonymous consumption of content, and could be employed to profile users' preferences or to limit access to digital books, music, or programs. DRM technologies may "…enable an unprecedented degree of intrusion into and oversight of individual decisions about what to read, hear and view."[215] For instance, a DRM technology called Copyright Agent quietly scans peer to peer networks to discover whether users possess illegal content. If a copyright violation is found, the program automatically informs the users' Internet Service Provider that his or her service should be severed.[216]

In February 2002, the European Commision Information Society Directorate held a workshop on DRM technologies to examine, among other issues, their effects on privacy.[217]

In June 2002, Microsoft released information regarding its new "Palladium" initiative. Although, not much is known about the initiative, Palladium appears to

---

[213] See EPIC's DRM page <http://www.epic.org/privacy/drm/>.

[214] InTether Point to Point Product Page <http://www.infraworks.com/p2p.html>.

[215] Julie Cohen, A Right to Read Anonymously: A Closer Look at "Copyright Management" in Cyberspace, 28 Connecticut Law Review 981 (1996).

[216] Dawn C. Chmielewski, "Stealth Software Robot Puts Bootleggers on Notice," San Jose Mercury News <http://www.chicagotribune.com/business/printedition/article/0,2669,SAV-0103190188,FF.html>.

[217] More information and the final report of the workshop are available at <http://europa.eu.int/information_society/topics/multi/digital_rights/events/index_en.htm>.

be a more comprehensive version of its Hailstorm and Passport services. Through software and hardware controls, Palladium would place Microsoft as the gatekeeper of identification and authentication. Additionally, systems embedded in both software and hardware would control access to content, thereby creating ubiquitous DRM schemes that can track users and control use of media. Microsoft expects to have elements of the system in place by 2004.

Authentication and Identity Disclosure

As the architecture of authentication is developed and established through de jure, de facto, and technical standards, there are significant privacy implications. While authentication is considered essential for computer security, it may detract from individual privacy, depending on how authentication is implemented. In the best case scenario, individuals could choose to not authenticate in order to receive a given service, and authentication would involve the selective disclosure of some information that allows for the verification of the integrity of a transaction. In the worst case scenario, authentication can be implemented in such a way that every transaction an individual enters in, whether surfing the web, sending mail, accessing government services, and purchasing on-line, will be traced, tracked, audited, and compiled to an unprecedented degree. The resulting issue is what exactly is disclosed when authentication occurs, whether this involves the disclosure of personally identifiable information, and whether this is necessary and proportionate.

Defining Identity Disclosure

Policy processes often predetermine the form of authentication being considered in the very definition of the terms. Many of these processes, however, began in the midst of the cryptography policy debate in the 1990s, and carry much of the baggage from that era, such as the reliance on Trusted Third Parties[218] and X.509 identity certificates with limited signing capabilities.[219]

---

[218] Licensing Of Trusted Third Parties For The Provision Of Encryption Services Public Consultation Paper on Detailed Proposals for Legislation, Department of Trade and Industry (1997); archived at
<http://www.fipr.org/polarch/ttp.html>.

[219] Building Confidence in Electronic Commerce - A Consultation Document, Department of Trade and Industry (1999); archived at
<http://www.dti.gov.uk/cii/ecommerce/ukecommercestrategy/archiveconsultationdocs/introduction.shtml>.

The ISO[220] defines authentication as "the provision of assurance of the claimed identity of an entity." Industry Canada's definition, found in a 2000 consultation document on an authentication framework,[221] is "proof that users are who they claim to be (or that computer devices, software, etc. are what they purport to be)." Digital signature statutes around the world have been developed to allow for digital signatures to be used to sign legal documents (and extended logically to sales transactions, or signing documents and messages); embedded within these statutes again is identity-centrism, which is not a requirement necessarily of analogue-world signatures. UNCITRAL developed a model law on electronic signatures to meet this requirement, and define electronic signatures as "data in electronic form in, affixed to, or logically associated with, a data message, which may be used to identify the signatory in relation to the data message and indicate the signatory's approval of the information contained in the data message."[222]

As these articulations of digital signatures and certificates are used for purposes beyond signing legal documents, such as access control, the interpretive application of authentication becomes suspect. This poses a serious conflict with privacy principles, most notably informational self-determination as every time authentication occurs, assured-identity is disclosed, either through direct identification or through personally identifiable information. Likewise, at commercial level, identity disclosure is supported by the terminology. Consider the following statement from a senior vice president of the Information Technology Association of America:[223]

> When people are online, they want to know with whom they are dealing. They want to know that people are who they say they are, and are going to follow through with commitments made over the Internet and thus supporting identity-disclosure for electronic transactions. Public Key Infrastructure vendors are supporting this view with the use of the X.509 standard of certificates that are bound to an identity by a Certificate Authority.

Even the Internet Engineering Task Force defines authentication as being identity-centric that is, "[t]he process of verifying an identity claimed by or for a

---

[220] Glossary of IT Security Terminology, SC 27 Standing Document no 6, ISO/IEC JTC 1/SC 27, Doc. No.: SC 27 N 1954, Date: March 5, 1998.

[221] Building Trust and Confidence in Electronic Commerce: A Framework for Electronic Authentication, Industry Canada (2000) <http://e-com.ic.gc.ca/english/documents/framework.pdf>.

[222] United Nations Commission on International Trade Law (UNCITRAL) Model Law on Electronic Signatures (2001). Report of the Drafting Group, 34th session, Vienna, June 25 - July 13, 2001.

[223] "Are You Who You Say You Are?" Wired News, March 31, 1999.

system entity."[224] Additionally, the IETF has also been working on Public Key Infrastructure standards that bind identities to public keys.

Authentication services have another application beyond verifying signatures, however. While certificates and keys can be used for digitally signing documents, these certificates also act as an access control mechanism to provide a secure session. That is, traditionally if a user of a specific on-line service wishes to connect to that service, the user may present a username and password. Using authentication services instead, a user may present a certificate that contains a public key and identity signed by the service provider or another trusted third party, and this is in turn used to set up a secure session (Trusted Layer Session, or Secure Sockets Layer) with that service provider so that all communications between the user and the service provider are encrypted. The obligatory passage point is the disclosure of a greater level of personally identifiable information than previously, and in a more non-repudiable form (which thus introduces greater risks).[225]

Inscribing Identity into Policy

At the political level, authentication and identity are often synonymous. The Group of 8 industrialized countries (G8) has been working on the issue of authentication on two fronts. Under the auspices of the Lyon Subgroup on high-technology crime, the G8 has been proposing repeatedly[226] the use of user authentication when on-line, and the use of machine authentication to create traceability in electronic transactions for investigative purposes and to gather evidence. In a separate forum, the G8 developed the Okinawa Charter on Global Information Society where the requirement for authentication was bound with initiatives to resolve the digital divide.[227] As a result, the two foras and the two set of interests converge around authentication: the ability to support verification of the validity of transactions for the purpose of security, and the ability to identify individuals for surveillance.

---

[224] Internet Security Glossary, RFC 2828, IETF Network Working Group, May 2000 <http://www.ietf.org/rfc/rfc2828.txt>.

[225] Bohm, Nicholas, Ian Brown and Brian Gladman, "Electronic Commerce: Who Carries the Risk of Fraud?" The Journal of Information, Law and Technology (2000).

[226] Communiqué Annex: Principles and Action Plan To Combat High-Tech Crime, G7 meeting of Justice and Interior Ministers, Washington DC, December 10, 1997 <http://www.g8summit.gov.uk/prebham/washington.1297.shtml>.

[227] The charter is available at <http://www.dotforce.org/reports/it1.html>.

Inscribing Identity into Infrastructure

A public key infrastructure (PKI) has been heralded as the solution to many security problems. The infrastructure involves individuals with public and private keys which are semantically altered into certificates and signature keys respectively. Trust is developed through this transformation of the public key into a certificate: the owner of the public key registers the key with a CA who binds the identity of the individual with the key, creating the certificate. This certificate is then used to verify transactions signed with the private/signature key, and parties in a transaction can therefore ascertain the identity of the individual. The issue then becomes one of scale: if one certificate is issued by government for the use of gaining access to government services (as is often the proposed scheme under the auspice of Information Society projects, including the G8 Charter for example), then this very same certificate, or at least infrastructure of CAs may be used for purchases on-line with a number of service providers, or merely gaining access to information.[228]

Inscribing Identity into Technology

Authentication mechanisms are used within multiple applications varying from toll-machines through to copyright protection mechanisms. The inscription of identity within these technologies is occurring already. Mobile phones have authentication techniques that assure that a specific card is registered to a specific phone which is then registered to a specific individual; with next generation mobile phone applications, these devices will be used for electronic transactions, and geographic-based transactions -- which will all be based upon the identity of the individual. There have been proposals to also implement national ID cards into these mobile telephones.

Smartcards are the proffered technology for enabling digital signatures; these cards will be used for credit card transactions, and gaining access to other services such as prescription medicine, tolls for transportation, telephone calling cards, and even age-verification. Smartcards are thus built upon an identity-centric authentication infrastructure. In the future this trend of privacy-invasion may continue on to biometrics, and the prevention of piracy; but so long as

---

[228] The Privacy Risks of Public Key Infrastructures, by Austin Hill and Gus Hosein, presented at the 21st Data Protection Commissioners Conference, Hong Kong, September, 1999.

authentication details are kept on the card, the cards will remain not only a privacy threat, but a security risk as well.[229]

Authentication without Identification

As a result of the political, infrastructural, and technological initiatives on authentication that tend towards identity-centrism, we are not only left with a situation where privacy is vastly reduced in all levels of life, i.e. not just on-line, but we also face challenges of functionality.

From the privacy perspective, the worst case scenario is that every transaction from purchasing transport tickets through to accessing information on government web-sites will be identity-centric. The Microsoft Corporation is attempting to create such an identity-centric system through the promotion of the Microsoft Passport and Hailstorm services platform.[230] Passport is an online identification and authentication system that requires the submission of personal information. Increasingly, Passport membership is becoming a requirement for access to services on the Internet. Microsoft has stated that its "dream" is for every Internet user to have a Passport.[231]

Shifting to a world of perfect-identity may meet the interests of industry and government in ascertaining the identity of who they are transacting with; however there are rising functionality challenges. The source of these challenges range from data protection regimes, efficiency of data communications and storage, resources and costs, and issues surrounding revocation and non-repudiation. These challenges may provide sufficient incentives for government and industry to begin looking for alternative regimes of authentication that are not necessarily identity-centric.

Although the political and commercial emphasis has been placed often upon identity-centric infrastructure where identity disclosure is required, alternative solutions do exist that allow for informational self-determination. That is, a user may select which personal information is to be disclosed in the authentication process while still maintaining the security benefits of identity-centric authentication. Such solutions promote the notion of user control over personal

---

[229] Privacy Increases Smartcard Security, by Stefan Brands, Gus Hosein, and Stephanie Perrin, presented at the 22nd Data Protection Commissioners Conference, Venice, Italy, September 2000.

[230] See EPIC's Passport Page <http://www.epic.org/privacy/consumer/microsoft/>.

[231] See <http://www.microsoft.com/presspass/legal/apr02/04-22ntranscriptam.asp>.

data, and minimizing the risks of all of the interested actors due to the above-mentioned functional challenges.[232]

Without considering these alternatives and resisting full disclosure, we will be forced to endure the political, commercial, and technical settlement of identity-disclosure for all transactions, both on-line and off, resulting in an infrastructure of surveillance that will transform how we view traditional controls such as checkpoints, ID cards, and passport controls.

Spy TV: Interactive Television & "T-Commerce"

The convergence of communications networks, computers and mass media into an interactive network combining television and the Internet is the next progression of the technology currently being developed. Already, the new boxes are replacing the traditional cable TV set-top box with an interactive device that also includes the functions of a limited personal computer and video recorder. At the same time, personal computers are regularly equipped with TV tuner cards to handle advanced video operations.

The designers of these new appliances paint a pleasant picture of the conveniences that will be available with these new systems. They anticipate that viewers will be able to make spur of the moment purchases over their boxes, based on what their favorite star is wearing or on an individually tailored ad that appears between shows. Communities will be formed as people chat live about the plots of their favorite shows or sporting events. Vast libraries of movies and shows will be available for renting on demand by just pressing a button on the remote control. The industry calls this "T-Commerce" for Television Commerce. Millions of users are expected to be using these in just the next few years, and the ad revenue to justify the new expensive boxes is expected to hit $5 billion by 2004.

Interactivity has been the dream of the television industry since the invention of the TV. For several decades, there have been a series of expensive tests that have failed because the technology has been crude and expensive.[233] The change that now makes ITV possible is the evolution of the Internet and its underlying

---

[232] Stefan Brands, Rethinking Public Key Infrastructures and Digital Certificates -- Building in Privacy (MIT Press 2000)

[233] L. J. Davis, The Billionaire Shell Game: How Cable Baron John Malone and Assorted Corporate Titans Invented a Future Nobody Wanted (1998).

protocols and the advancement of digital television. These protocols are now being used to allow for interactive high-speed access to the Internet over existing cable lines. Slowly, intelligent cable TV boxes, which connect to broadband and interactive cable systems, are being deployed.

A number of companies have jumped into this new market in the last few years. The largest players are America Online and Microsoft. Microsoft purchased WebTV in 1998 and has also been including interactive television abilities in their operating systems for several years. Thus far, because of poor service, little interactive programming, and relatively high prices, the number of users has not significantly grown. They also are hampered by the need to use telephone lines to communicate with the service in most areas as cable lines are slowing becoming converted to interactive communications. America Online has announced that it will start deploying AOL TV in the United States in 2000. When its merger with media giant Time-Warner is complete, it will have control over a significant portion of the cable television lines and television shows in the United States It is expected that AOL will use that market power to force the development of more interactive television and the deployment of interactive boxes that will be capable of tracking users even if they do not wish to use the functions.

Meanwhile, there are other companies that have developed devices that will automatically record television shows for viewers and make recommendations for new shows based on viewers' previous behavior. The new systems are being designed, like their Internet predecessors, to track every activity of users as they surf the net through the boxes. They also are being designed to track the shows and commercials users watch and to use that information to tailor advertising for the greatest effect.[234] Rupert Murdoch said in the NewsCorp annual report, "It will tell us not only who our customers are, but what they buy, what they watch, what they read and what they want."[235] George Orwell's vision of the television that watches you will soon be a standard consumer appliance.

Even where systems are designed not to report back this kind of information, there is increasing pressure from the content industries to build systems this way so that they can monitor viewer's habits and protect against copyright infringement. This year, SONICBlue Inc., the maker of Replay TV, a personsal video recorder, was sued by the entertainment studios who argued that features allowing users to pause, fast forward, and skip commercials violated their

---

[234] See David Burke, Spy TV (Slab-O-Concrete Press 1999), available at
<http://www.spyinteractive.com/spyinteractive/>.
[235] Cited in Privacy Journal, October 1999.

copyrights. As part of the lawsuit, the studios requested all data that the company had on its customers viewing habits, including what shows were recorded, watched, and forwarded to friends. Because the ReplayTV 4000 product did not transmit this sort of data back to the company, SONICblue had no data to provide to the studios. It was, therefore, ordered by a court to re-engineer its product and install software to record TV usage data and transmit that data back to SONICblue so that it could then be turned over to the studios. This order was overturned in May 2002 but the issue is likely to resurface.[236]

Unlike personal computers that give users control over their actions and choices, the new ITV systems are generally based on a sealed "black box" controlled by the company that gives the user little or no control. In the WebTV box, users are not able to refuse cookies or delete them afterwards. The systems are closed and it is difficult, if not impossible, for even advanced users to identify what the system is doing. It will also prevent users from being able to use their own software.

There are other significant differences in that the media is more top-down, and corporatized than the Internet, which is decentralized and allows nearly any user to set up his own web site and become a content producer. Many of the ITV providers describe their systems as "closed gardens" that will only show content that the providers have a financial interest in. Other information will either be banned or be slower or more difficult to locate and view.

Genetic Privacy

Genetic data poses unique privacy issues since it can serve as an identifier and can also convey sensitive personal information. Not only does genetic information provide a fingerprint through variations in genetic sequences; it also provides a growing amount of information about genetic diseases and predispositions.

Errors in the genetic code are responsible for an estimated 3,000 to 4.000 hereditary diseases, including Huntington's disease, cystic fibrosis, neurofibromatosis, Duchenne muscular dystrophy, and many others. What's more, altered genes are now known to play a part in cancer, heart disease, diabetes, and many other common diseases. In these more common and complex

---

[236] Paramount Pictures Corp., et al. v. ReplayTV, Inc. and SONICblue, Inc., United States District Court, Central District of California, Case No. 01-09358 FMC (Ex). See EPIC's page on this case at <http://www.epic.org/litigation/replaytv/>.

disorders, genetic alterations increase a person's risk of developing that disorder. The disease itself results from the interaction of such genetic predispositions and environmental factors, including diet and lifestyle.[237]

Even more controversial than genetic predisposition to disease is the fact that "genes do appear to influence behavior."[238] Genes have been found to influence homosexuality, thrill seeking and tendencies towards violent criminal behavior.[239] Twin and adoption studies have shown that "nearly all behaviors that have been studied show moderate to high inheritability - usually to a somewhat greater degree than do many common physical diseases."[240]

The prevailing scientific opinion is that most behavior and human diseases are not the result of a single mutation or gene. Rather, most facets of human development "represent the culmination of lifelong interactions between our genome and the environment."[241] Currently available scientific knowledge thus does not seem to provide a strong link between an individual's genetic sequence and that person's eventual development of disease or personality traits; such conclusions are often speculative or, at best, matters of probability.

However, it is an area of scientific development that is undergoing rapid change and the body of knowledge about the human genome is increasing rapidly. The human genome sequence was published in February 2001, immediately kicking off a debate of the future of genetic technology and its impact on society - including privacy.[242] For example, United States Senators James M. Jeffords and Tom Daschle have commented, "[o]ne of the most difficult issues is determining the proper balance between privacy concerns and fair use of genetic information."[243]

---

[237] "From Maps to Medicine: About the Human Genome Research Project," National Human Genome Research Institute,
<http://www.nhgri.nih.gov:80/Policy_and_public_affairs/Communications/Publications/Maps_to_medicine/about.html>

[238] Leroy Hood and Lee Rowen, "Genes, Genomes, and Society," Genetic Secrets: Protecting Privacy and Confidentiality in the Genetic Era, Edited by Mark A. Rothstein 27 (Yale University Press 1997).

[239] Id.

[240] Peter McGuffin, Brien Riley, Robert Plomin, "Genomics and Behavior: Toward Behaviorial Genomics," Science 291 (5507): 1232, available at <http://www.sciencemag.org/cgi/content/full/291/5507/1232>.

[241] Leena Peltonen and Victor A. McKusick, "Genomics and Medicine: Dissecting Human Disease in the Postgenomic Era," Science 291 (5507): 1224, available at
<http://www.sciencemag.org/cgi/content/full/291/5507/1224>.

[242] Genome Landmark, Science <http://www.sciencemag.org/feature/data/genomes/landmark.shl>.

[243] James M. Jeffords and Tom Daschle, "Policy Issues: Political Issues in the Genome Era," Science 291 (5507): 1249, available at <http://www.sciencemag.org/cgi/content/full/291/5507/1249>.

Both the general public and scientific researchers have recognized that safeguards for genetic information are needed. For example, polls have found that 86% of adults believe that doctors should ask permission before conducting any genetic testing and 93% believe that researchers should do the same before any analysis.[244] Dr. Francis S. Collins, Director of the National Human Genome Research Institute, has observed that "in genetics research studies, we are seeing individuals who opt not to participate in research because of their fear that this information could fall into the wrong hands and be used to deny them a job or a promotion."[245]

Genetic Identification

Unlike fingerprints, DNA sequences are not unique (identical twins have different fingerprints but the same DNA profiles). DNA identification works by comparing particular regions of two samples and looking for differences rather than comparing entire DNA sequences. Identification is actually a process of combining several such comparisons and calculating the probability that the two samples are a false match. "Provided that tests are actually looking at different regions of the genome, and provided that the genetic patterns aren't 'structured' within a community by inbreeding, using multiple tests can reduce the chance of a false match from one in a hundred to one in a million or even one in 500 million. But they can't entirely eliminate the chance of a false match."[246] That has proven to be true in at least one instance. In Britain, a DNA match between evidence left at the scene of a robbery and an individual who had already been entered into that country's DNA database turned out to be false despite calculated odds of 37 million to one that a false match would occur. According to a FBI spokesman, "[t]here's a greater chance that you'll find a close match as the databases get bigger."[247] Besides false matches, some criminals have become reportedly more savvy at manipulating results of DNA identification.[248]

---

[244] Public Attitudes Toward Medical Privacy, conducted by the Gallup Poll for the Institute for Health Freedom, September 2000, available at <http://www.forhealthfreedom.org/Gallupsurvey/IHF-Gallup.html>.

[245] Testimony of Francis S. Collins, M.D., Ph.D., Director, National Human Genome Research Institute, National Institutes of Health, Testimony Before the Health, Education, Labor, and Pensions Committee, United States Senate, Hearing on Genetic Information in the Workplace, July 20, 2000, available at <http://labor.senate.gov/Hearings/july00hrg/072000wt/072000jmj/collins720/collins720.htm>.

[246] Simson Garfinkel, Database Nation: The Death of Privacy in the 21st Century 49 (O'Reilly 2000).

[247] Rebecca Pollard, "Crime Genes: A DNA Mismatch Raises Fears," ABCNews.com, June 19, 2000 <http://abcnews.go.com/sections/tech/MITTechReview/techreview000608.html>; Richard Willing, "Mismatch calls DNA tests into question," USA Today, February 8, 2000.

[248] Richard Willing, "Criminals try to outwit DNA," USA Today, August 28, 2000.

Law enforcement agencies are increasingly relying upon DNA evidence thus making it important that any genetic data collected is uncontaminated and accurately processed. Judges and courts have issued warrants[249], indictments[250] and even convictions[251] based solely on DNA identification.

DNA identification is also heavily relied upon in order to exonerate previously convicted criminals. One of the best-known efforts is the Innocence Project at the Cardozo School of Law, Yeshiva University. Founded in 1992 by Professor Barry Scheck, the clinical law program provides legal assistance to persons challenging their convictions based on DNA evidence. The clinic has participated in thirty-six of the sixty-three convictions that have been overturned on the basis of DNA evidence since the 1980s. On the basis of the proportion of cases that have been overturned and related FBI data, the Innocence Project estimates that thousands of individuals wrongly convicted could be freed if provided with easier access to DNA testing.[252] Similar Innocence Project programs have also started at the University of Wisconsin Law School, the University of Washington School of Law and the Santa Clara University of Law. [253]

Despite the recognition of such limitations, there is a push for more and larger DNA databases. DNA databases are often created from a strictly law enforcement purpose, usually related to violent offenders, but have expanded in purpose and scope. "In less than a decade, we have gone from collecting DNA from convicted sex offenders – on the theory that they are likely to be recidivists and that they frequently leave biological evidence – to data banks of all violent offenders; to juvenile offenders in 29 states; to testing of persons who have been arrested, but not convicted of a crime."[254] In the United States, local, state and federal law enforcement agencies contribute samples from crime scenes and those convicted of violent crimes into a national database to look for potential matches.[255] In the United States, some officials have urged that non-violent

---

[249] Richard Willing, "Police expand DNA use: Charge man with rape using only genetic profile," USA Today, October 25, 2000.

[250] Michael Luo, "Unnamed Man Indicted by DNA: Suffolk DA Charges Suspect in 6 South Shore Rapes," Newsday, August 9, 2000.

[251] Bruce Hight, "DNA Can Carry Conviction," Austin-American Statesman, April 14, 2000.

[252]Cardozo Law Innocence Project <http://www.cardozo.yu.edu/innocence_project/>.

[253] Frank J. Remington Center, Innocence Project <http://www.law.wisc.edu/FJR/innocence/>; Innocence Project Northwest <http://www.law.washington.edu/ipnw/>; Northern California Innocence Project <http://www.scu.edu/scu/law/clinic/Special_Projects/Innocence_Project/innocence_project.html>.

[254] Testimony of Barry Steinhardt, Associate Director of the American Civil Liberties Union, Before the House Judiciary Committee, Subcommittee on Crime, March 23, 2000, available at <http://www.aclu.org/congress/l032300a.html>.

[255] FBI Press Room, Press Release, October 13, 1998, DNA Index, available at <http://www.fbi.gov/pressrel/pressrel98/dna.htm>.

---

criminal offenders, such as burglars, to also be included in DNA databases.[256] Other countries such as Great Britain are similarly considering proposals to expand their own national DNA databases.[257] Several Australian states have been considering laws that would permit the creation of a national DNA database.[258] One Australian legislator has even called for collecting DNA samples from babies at birth.[259]

Other, non-law enforcement related DNA databases have also emerged. Since the early 1990s, all personnel serving in the United States Armed Forces have been required to submit DNA samples to ensure later identification. The United States military's DNA depository "contains 2.1 million index card-sized files with the name, Social Security number, fingerprint and blood sample of every active duty military person."[260] However, the program has faced resistance within the military's own ranks. In 1996, two United States Marines faced court-martials when they refused to provide DNA samples for the identification program.[261]

In addition to government-related DNA identification, a new industry - paternity testing - has emerged, placing large amounts of genetic data wholly under private sector control. Despite the controversy surrounding law enforcement collection of DNA, a larger proportion of genetic identification is done to establish paternity. In the United States, part of the reason for the rise in paternity DNA testing are federal requirements for identifying fathers in order to receive child support.[262] Paternity testing previously required blood samples and was more difficult to perform than currently used DNA tests - which may only require a few strands of hair.[263]

---

[256] "Slow Spiral: State DNA Lag Databases," Government Technology, April 2000, <http://www.govtechapternet/publications/crimetech/Apr00/CTEDNA.phtml>; "Maryland Seeks DNA of Criminals," Washington Post, March 24, 1999; Geraldine Sealey, "Debating DNA: The Ultimate Crimefighting Tool, or the Ultimate Invasion of Privacy," ABCNews.com, August 4, 1999.

[257] "New doubts over DNA register," The Guardian, September 2, 2000, available at <http://www.guardian.co.uk/Print/0,3858,4058441,00.html>; Melissa Kite and Richard Ford, "Blair orders DNA register of criminals," The Times, September 1, 2000.

[258] "Concern over proposed DNA databases," Australian Broadcasting Corporation (ABC) Online, January 24, 2000 <http://www.abc.net.au/worldtoday/s95485.htm>; Stewart Taggart, "DNA Testing Furor in Wee Waa," Wired News, April 18, 2000 <http://www.wired.com/news/print/0,1294,35727,00.html>.

[259] "Call to take DNA from newborn babies to fight crime," Independent News, April 25, 2001 <http://news.independent.co.uk/world/australasia/story.jsp?story=68669>.

[260] "Will DNA identification end Unknown Soldier tradition?" Associated Press, May 29, 1998 <http://www.onlineathens.com/1998/052998/0529.a3soldier.html>.

[261] Neil A. Lewis, "2 Marines who Refused to Comply with Genetic-testing Order Face a Court-Martial," The New York Times, April 13, 1996.

[262] Genelex: The Paternity DNA Testing Site, "Chapter 4: DNA in Parentage Testing, Updated for the Web Edition," April 2000 <http://www.genelex.com/paternitytesting/paternitybook4.html>.

[263] DNAnow.com, "Frequently Asked Questions," <http://www.dnanow.com/faq.html>.

Genetic Testing

Advances in technology have made genetic testing easier and faster. According to genetic testing companies, kits costing $100-$2,000 are available for over 400 diseases with hundreds more coming on the way.[264] The easy availability of tests vastly increases the amount of information at an individual's disposal. More problematic is the possibility that individuals will not able to control when such testing is conducted or how the results may be used. The two most controversial areas of genetic testing are in the workplace and the provision of medical and life insurance. Also, as in genetic identification, genetic testing is prone to quality control issues. A 1999 survey of genetic testing facilities found that of the 245 laboratories examined, 36 failed to meet high quality assurance standards.[265]

A number of countries, such as Iceland and Estonia are building nationwide DNA databases for medical research. Many of these undertaking are encouraged by pharmaceutical companies and other business enterprises looking to make profits from new medical procedures and services. Some efforts have be made to establish legal frameworks for these databanks.[266]

Right Not to Know

While genetic screening has become easier and cheaper, treatment of genetic disease lags behind. Thus, while someone may have the ability to determine if they are at high-risk of disease, many people may choose not to find out due to the inability to take any precautionary measures. The concept of a "right not to know" would apply in these situations, allowing a person to control whether she has a certain genetic make-up.

For example, Huntington's disease is an inherited neurological disease that results in death by a person's late 30s or early 40s after extended deterioration of both mental and physical control. There is no treatment for the condition yet a reliable test for Huntington's does exist. The inheritability of the disease is straightforward; the children of a person with Huntington's will have a fifty-percent chance of also being affected. The resistance to knowing one's propensity

---

[264] Lisa M. Krieger, "Genetic testing leaps ahead of social implications," San Jose Mercury News, July 3, 2001 <http://www.siliconvalley.com/docs/news/depth/gene070301.htm>.

[265] Margaret M. McGovern, MD, PhD; Marta O. Benach; Sylvan Wallenstein; Robert J. Desnick, PhD, MD; Richard Keenlyside, MD, MS, "Quality Assurance in Molecular Genetic Testing Laboratories," Journal of the American Medical Association, Volume 281 No. 9, March 3, 1999, at 835-40 <http://jama.ama-assn.org/issues/v281n9/abs/jto90000.html>.

[266] See, e.g., Iceland Act on Bio Banks.

for Huntington's is borne out in surveys finding that only 66 percent of those at risk of developing Huntington's would test themselves with 15 percent of that group indicating they would contemplate suicide if they tested positive. Of those indicating that they would not want to test themselves, 30 percent indicated they would consider suicide if they did find out that they would manifest the disease.[267] Due to the emotional and psychological impact that such information would have, many people in these situations exercise their "right not to know" by refusing to test themselves.

In practice, maintaining a "right not to know" can be difficult. Due to the simple inheritability of Huntington's, one family member's decision to test herself for Huntington's will reveal information about other family members. For example, if a daughter decides to test herself for Huntington's due to a history of the disease through her mother's side of the family, the test results would indicate whether or not her mother also has the disease - thus compromising the mother's desire not to know.[268]

In the Workplace

As DNA and genetic databases become more common world-wide, there has been a concurrent rise in the use of testing by employers. Although there are legitimate uses of genetic testing, such as the prevention of occupational diseases, there is also a serious danger that employers will use these tests to discriminate against current or potential employees. Without legal intervention, information indicating, for example, whether someone is prone to a debilitating illness or even an "undesirable" condition (such as laziness or depression) may be used by employers to discriminate against employees.

Genetic screening in the workplace has been conducted for decades but, based on limited polling of employers, still seems relatively rare when compared to general medical information accessed by employers. Some of the earliest genetic screening took place as early as the 1960s. Dow Chemical conducted genetic monitoring (genetic tests conducted over time to detect possible mutagenic

---

[267] Office of Technology Assessment (OTA): Genetic monitoring and screening in the workplace, OTA-BA-455 (Washington, United States Government Printing Office, October 1990), p. 13. (As cited in Conditions of Work Digest, "Workers' privacy III: Testing in the workplace," (International Labour Office 1993), at 66.)

[268] See Margaret R. McLean, " When What We Know Outstrips What We Can Do," Markkula Center for Applied Ethics, Issues in Ethics - V. 9, N. 2, available at
<http://www.scu.edu/SCU/Centers/Ethics/publications/iie/v9n2/outstrips.html>; Sally Lehrman, "Predictive Genetic Testing: Do You Really Want to Know Your Future?" The DNA Files, November 1998, available at <http://www.dnafiles.org/about/pgm4/topic.html>.

effects of the workplace environment) from 1964-1977.[269] In 1982, a United States federal government survey found that 1.6 percent of companies were using genetic testing for employment purposes.[270]

Despite the uncertainty about how commonly workplace genetic testing takes place, it has happened. In 1994, employees at the Lawrence Berkeley National Laboratory at the University of California - Berkeley discovered the laboratory's surreptitious practice of testing its employee blood and urine samples for syphilis, sickle cell anemia and pregnancy.[271] The laboratory, funded by the United States Department of Energy, conducts non-classified research and had been testing its employees for decades.[272] In subsequent litigation, the government argued that since its employees had agreed to a general medical examination, they had no reason to expect that genetic testing would not also be conducted. The government also argued notice was provided via a list of tests to be conducted posted on an examining room wall. The government won at in the federal district court but the United States Court of Appeals for the Ninth Circuit reversed and concluded the conditions being tested for raised "the highest expectations of privacy."[273] In 2000, the laboratory settled with employees for $2.2 million, ceased conducting the tests and allowed earlier test results to be reviewed and deleted.

More recently, in February 2001, an employee of the Burlington Northern Santa Fe Railroad in the United States sued the company for conducting tests for a genetic predisposition associated with carpal tunnel syndrome. The company had allegedly collected blood samples from 125 employees and tested 18 of those samples without employee consent. The employee filing the suit had refused to contribute a blood sample and was told he would be investigated. The lawsuit

---

[269] United States Congress, Office of Technology Assessment, Genetic Monitoring and Screening in the Workplace 44-45 (1990); Are Your Genes Right for Your Job? 3 Cal Law 25, 27 (May 1983). (As cited in Employee Privacy Law, ed. L. Camille Hébert, (West Group 2000) § 12:03.)

[270] United States Congress, Office of Technology Assessment, The Role of Genetic Testing in the Prevention of Occupational Diseases 33-35 (1983); United States Congress, Office of Technology Assessment, Genetic Monitoring and Screening in the Workplace 173-177 (1990).

[271] Dana Hawkins, "A bloody mess at one federal lab: Officials may have secretly checked staff for syphilis, pregnancy, and sickle cell," United States News and World Report, June 23, 1997.

[272] Even more shocking was the practice of the research facility to test certain minority employees for particular traits. For example, while all new hires were tested for syphilis, only African-American and Latino employees were re-tested during subsequent medical examinations. Only one Caucasian employee was repeatedly tested for syphilis; he was married to an African-American woman. African-American employees were also repeatedly tested for sickle cell anemia although one test is normally sufficient.

[273] Norman-Bloodsaw v. Lawrence Berkeley Laboratory, 135 F.3d 1260, 1269-70 (9th Cir. 1996). See also L. Camille Hébert, Employee Privacy Law § 12.07 (West Group 2000); "Court declares right to genetic privacy," United States News and World Report, February 16, 1998 <http://www.usnews.com/usnews/issue/980216/16upda.htm>.

---

alleges violation of disability law and existing legal prohibitions on genetic testing by employers.[274]

Insurance

While closely tied to workplace genetic testing (as employers may avoid hiring certain individuals to due to a perceived increase in the amount need for insurance coverage), genetic testing has also begun to be used in the provision of life and medical insurance directly. In February 2001, Norwich Union Life, one of Britain's largest insurers, admitted using genetic tests for breast and ovarian cancer and Alzheimer's disease to evaluate applicants. Moreover, Norwich Union Life was violating the industry's code of conduct since the genetic tests had not been approved by the government's Human Genetics Commission.[275] The controversial practice resulted in some individuals paying higher insurance premiums based on genetic predispositions, creating political pressure to outlaw the use of genetic data by insurers in the United Kingdom altogether.[276]

While representatives of Norwich Union Life claimed that the genetic tests were not compulsory, simply providing lower premiums for people that do not test positive for genetic tests can lead to rampant genetic testing. An "assessment spiral" will result when one company offers discounts for those with a particular genetic profile, creating pressure on competitors to offer similar discounts in order to keep "low-risk" policy holders and resulting in higher premiums for those that are not tested or do not possess the correct genetic make-up.[277] Thus, non-compulsory genetic testing can easily lead to genetic discrimination.

Legal Safeguards

Recognizing the issues implicated in widespread genetic testing, a number of international bodies have recommended that genetic testing should be carefully circumscribed by law. In 1989, the European Parliament issued a resolution recommending legislation to prohibit genetic testing for the purposes of selecting workers or examining employees without their consent. It advised that employees must be informed of any analysis and implications of genetic data before tests are

---

[274] Dana Hawkins, "The dark side of genetic testing: Railroad workers allege secret sampling," United States News, February 19, 2001.

[275] Melissa Kite, "Insurance firm admits using genetic screening," The Times, February 8, 2001.

[276] T. R. Reid, "Britain Moves to Ban Insurance Gene Tests," The Washington Post, April 30, 2001.

[277] See Mark A. Rothstein, "Genetic Secrets: A Policy Framework," Genetic Secrets: Protecting Privacy and Confidentiality in the Genetic Era, Edited by Mark A. Rothstein (Yale University Press 1997), at 469-70.

carried out and allowed withdraw from testing at any time.[278] The Council of Europe has also recommended that "the admission to, or the continued exercise of . . . employment, should not be made dependent on the undergoing of tests or screening."[279] Similarly, the World Medical Association (WMA) has issued statements to this effect. In 1992, issuing a Declaration on the Human Genome Project, it recommended the adoption of laws similar to those that prohibit "the use of race discrimination in employment or insurance."[280] In May 2000, it announced that it would draw up guidelines on the development of centralized health storage databases that will address "the issues of privacy, consent, individual access and accountability."[281] In 1997, the United Nations Educational, Scientific and Cultural Organization (UNESCO) adopted a Universal Declaration on the Human Genome and Human Rights, outlining the rights of individuals to control the collection and use of genetic information.[282]

In many cases, genetic testing may be indirectly prohibited by existing labor codes.[283] It is also possible that the use of genetic data by employers to discriminate against workers may violate equal opportunity or anti-discrimination laws. In the United States, for example, genetic testing may violate the 1964 Civil Rights Act that prohibits discrimination in employment on the basis of "race, sex, national origin, and religion," or the Americans with Disabilities Act of 1990, which prohibits discrimination in employment against a "qualified individual with a disability."[284]

Governments are also beginning to address the privacy issues directly. In the United States, most laws applying to genetic discrimination, testing or identification have been passed by states rather than the federal government. As of 1997, twelve states prohibit genetic discrimination in employment, 16 states prohibit genetic discrimination in insurance and more than 40 states have

---

[278] European Parliament, "Resolution on the Ethical and Legal Problems of Genetic Engineering," OJ, No. C.96, April 17, 1989.

[279] Council of Europe, Committee of Ministers: Recommendation No. R(92)3 on Genetic Testing and Screening for Heath Care Purposes, Principle 6 (a) <http://www.cm.coe.int/ta/rec/1992/92r3.htm>.

[280] See International Labour Office, Conditions of Work Digest: Worker's Privacy Part II: Monitoring and Surveillance in the Workplace (1993) 12(1).

[281] WMA To Draw Up Health Database Guidelines, WMA Press Release, 8 May 2000, <http://www.wma.net/e/press/00_11.html>.

[282] United Nations Educational, Scientific and Cultural Organization (UNESCO), "Universal Declaration on the Human Genome and Human Rights," November 11, 1997 <http://unesdoc.unesco.org/images/0010/001096/109687eb.pdf>. Also see "Implementation of the Universal Declaration on the Human Genome and Human Rights: Report by the Director-General," September 22, 1999 <http://unesdoc.unesco.org/images/0011/001173/117335e.pdf>.

[283] See generally, International Labour Office, Conditions of Work Digest: Worker's Privacy Part III: Testing in the Workplace, (1993) 12(2).

[284] Pub. L. No. 101-335 (1990), codified at 42 United StatesC. §§ 1201.

---

established DNA databases for law enforcement purposes.[285] In 2000, President Clinton issued an executive order prohibiting the use of genetic information in federal agency hiring and promotion decisions.[286]

Workplace Privacy

Workers around the world are frequently subject to some kind of monitoring by their employers.[287] Employers supervise work processes for quality control and performance purposes. They collect personal information from employees for a variety of reasons, such as health care, tax, and background checks.

Traditionally this monitoring and information gathering involved some form of human intervention and either the consent, or at least the knowledge, of employees. The changing structure and nature of the workplace, however, has led to more invasive and often, covert, monitoring practices which call into question employee's most basic right to privacy and dignity within the workplace. The progress in technology has facilitated an increasing level of automated surveillance. Now the supervision of employee's performance, behavior and communications can be carried out by technological means, with increased ease and efficiency. The technology currently being developed is extremely powerful and can extend to every aspect of a workers life. Software programs can record keystrokes on computers and monitor exact screen images, telephone management systems (TMS) can analyze the pattern of telephone use and the destination of calls, and miniature cameras and "Smart" ID badges can monitor an employee's behavior, movements, and even physical orientation

Advances in science have also pushed the boundaries of what personal details and information an employer can acquire from an employee. Psychological tests, general intelligence tests, performance tests, personality tests, honesty and background checks, drug tests, and medical tests are routinely used in workplace recruitment and evaluation methods. Since the discovery of DNA there has also been an increased use of genetic testing, allowing employers to access the most intimate details of a person's body in order to predict susceptibility to diseases, medical or even behavioral conditions. The success of the Human Genome Project will likely make this kind of testing more prevalent.

---

[285] Mark A. Rothstein, Genetic Secrets: A Policy Framework 456.

[286] Executive Order 13145 - To Prohibit Discrimination in Federal Employment Based on Genetic Information, February 10, 2000, available at <http://www.nara.gov/fedreg/eo2000.html#13145>.

[287] See EPIC's Workplace Privacy Page <http://www.epic.org/privacy/workplace/>.

Employers' collection of personal information and use of surveillance technology is often justified on the grounds of health and safety, customer relations or legal obligation. However, according to a recent study of the Privacy Foundation, it is actually the low cost of surveillance technologies, more than anything else that contributes to the increased monitoring.[288] In many cases workplace monitoring can seriously compromise the privacy and dignity of employees. Surveillance techniques can be used to harass, discriminate and to create unhealthy dynamics in the workplace.

Legal Background

Privacy advocates have long maintained that providing notice of a monitoring or surveillance policy should, as a bare minimum, be required before employers can engage in such invasive activities. They support strong privacy principles in the workplace such as the International Labor Office's "Code of Practice on the Protection of Workers' Personal Data," which protect employees' personal data and fundamental right to privacy in the technological era.[289] These guidelines were issued by the ILO in 1997, following three comprehensive studies on international workers' privacy laws.[290] The general principles of the code are:

- personal data should be used lawfully and fairly; only for reasons directly relevant to the employment of the worker and only for the purposes for which they were originally collected;
- employers should not collect sensitive personal data (e.g., concerning a worker's sex life, political, religious or other beliefs, trade union membership or criminal convictions) unless that information is directly relevant to an employment decision and in conformity with national legislation;
- polygraphs, truth-verification equipment or any other similar testing procedure should not be used;
- medical data should only be collected in conformity with national legislation and principles of medical confidentiality; genetic screening should be prohibited or limited to cases explicitly authorized by national

---

288 The Privacy Foundation, The Extent of Systematic Monitoring of Employee E-mail and Internet Use, July 9, 2001 <http://www.sonic.net/~undoc/extent.htm>

289 "Protection of workers' personal data," An ILO Code of Practice, Geneva, International Labour Office (1997).

290 International Labour Office, Conditions of Work Digest: Worker's Privacy Part I: Protection of Personal Data (1991) 10 (2); Worker's Privacy Part II: Monitoring and Surveillance in the Workplace (1993) 12(1); and Worker's Privacy Part III: Testing in the Workplace, (1993) 12(2).

legislation; and drug testing should only be undertaken in conformity with national law and practice or international standards;

- workers should be informed in advance of any advance monitoring and any data collected by such monitoring should not be the only factors in evaluating performance;
- employers should ensure the security of personal data against loss, unauthorized access, use, alteration or disclosure; and
- employees should be informed regularly of any data held about them and be given access to that data.

The code does not form international law and is not of binding effect. It was intended to be used "in the development of legislation, regulations, collective agreements, work rules, policies and practical measures." Unfortunately, however, the laws differ greatly from country to country and in some there are few legal constraints on workplace surveillance. In the United States, for example, the courts have typically been slow to recognize employees' rights to privacy. There has not yet been any satisfactory and uniform determination of what level of privacy employees are entitled to and how that privacy should be protected. Many believe that since employers have ownership or "control" over the working premises, its contents and facilities, and that employees give up all rights and expectations to privacy and freedom from invasion. Others simply avoid the question by making employees consent to surveillance, monitoring and testing as a condition of employment. Legislation has recently been introduced, however, which would prevent employers from secretly monitoring the communications and computer use of their employees.[291]

In European countries, the collection and processing of personal information is uniformly protected by the Data Protection Directive. The 1997 Telecommunication directive, however, provides for the confidentiality of communications for "public" systems and therefore would not cover privately owned systems in the workplace.[292] Nonetheless, many European countries, such as Austria, Germany, Norway and Sweden have strong labor codes and privacy laws that directly or indirectly prohibit or restrict this kind of surveillance. In Finland, a new law on Data Protection in Working Life entered into force in October 2001. In October 2000, the United Kingdom Privacy Commissioner

---

[291] The "Notice of Electronic Monitoring Act" (S.2898 and H.R.4908), introduced July 20, 2000.

[292] Directive Concerning the Processing of Personal Data and the Protection of Privacy in the Telecommunications Sector (Directive 97/66/EC of the European Parliament and of the Council of 15 December 1997) <http://www2.echo.lu/legal/en/dataprot/protection.html>.

issued a draft code of guidance for employer/employee relationships.[293] In March 2002 the first part of this code, on data protection in recruitment and selection of employees was issued.[294] Three further parts on employment records, monitoring at work and medical information and testing will be issued over the next few months. In 1999 the Swedish government established a Committee to study workplace privacy issues. In March 2002 the Committee issued a proposal recommending specific legislation to protect the personal information of current employees, former employees and employment applicants in both the private and public sectors.[295] In May 2002, the European Union Article 29 Data Protection Working Party issued a working paper on monitoring and surveillance of electronic communications in the workplace. The document set out a list of questions to be asked before any monitoring measure is put in place for example: Is the monitoring activity transparent to the workers? Is it necessary? Could not the employer obtain the same result with traditional methods of supervision? Is the processing of personal data proposed fair to the workers? Is it proportionate to the concerns that it tries to ally? It set out examples of what could be considered as legitimate monitoring activities and acceptance limits of surveillance of employees.[296]

There have also been developments outside of Europe on this issue. In June 2002, the Hong Kong Data Protection Commission issued a draft a code of practice on workplace for public consultation. The draft code covers telephone, CCTV, email and computer usage and possibly location monitoring.[297] In Australia the Privacy Amendment (Private Sector) Act 2000 put in place limited restrictions on employer's monitoring of communications by requiring the establishment of formal email use policies that must be made clear to all employees. It also requires employers to prove that the monitoring of e-mails is justifiable for instance on grounds of excessive use of email, distributing offensive material, suspected criminal activities or passing on sensitive

---

[293] Data Protection Commissioner, Employment: (Draft COP), October 2000, available at <http://www.dataprotection.gov.uk/dpr/dpdoc.nsf>.

[294] Data Protection Commissioner, Employment: Part 1: Recruitment & Selection, Employment Practices, Data Protection Code, March 2002, available at <http://wood.ccta.gov.uk/dpr/dpdoc.nsf - 25/02/99>.

[295] The proposal (in Swedish with a summary in English) is available at <http://naring.regeringen.se/propositioner_mm/sou/pdf/sou2002_18a.pdf>.

[296] Article 29 Data Protection Working Party, Working Document on The Surveillance Of Electronic Communications In The Workplace, 5401/01/EN/Final WP 55, May 29, 2002, available at <http://europa.eu.int/comm/internal_market/en/dataprot/wpdocs/wp55_en.pdf>.

[297] Privacy Commissioner for Personal Data, Draft Code of Practice on Monitoring and Personal Data Privacy at Work, (Hong Kong, PCO, 2002), available at <http://www.pco.org.hk/english/ordinance/codes.html>.

information.[298] However, the legislation grants exemptions to small businesses and the media and also exempts all employee records in any industry sector.

Performance Monitoring

Automated workplace monitoring has become increasingly common in recent years. Even in workplaces staffed by highly skilled information technology specialists, bosses demand the right to spy on every detail of a workers performance. Modern networked systems can interrogate computers to determine which software in being run, how often, and in what manner. A comprehensive audit trail gives managers a profile of each user, and a panorama of how the workers are interacting with their machines. Software programs can also give managers total central control individual PCs. A manager can now remotely modify or suspend programs on any machine, while at the same time reading and analyzing email traffic and Internet activity. A recent report by the American Management Association found that nearly 80 percent of major U.S companies monitor employees at work by checking communications such as telephone conversations, computer files, emails and Internet connections or by using video surveillance for performance evaluation and security purposes.[299]

An employer can monitor the level of use of a computer through monitoring the number of keystrokes a word processing employee enters in a specified period of time or the amount of time a computer is idle during the workday. Numerous technologies are available which monitor and analyze the performance of IT workers. Some allow network administrators to observe an employee's screen in real time, scan data files and e-mail, analyze keystroke performance, and even overwrite passwords. Once this information is collected, it can be analyzed by standard processing programs to determine a worker's performance profile. These monitoring products are sold at very low prices and have infiltrated the market. These snooping programs have also become popular not just among employers but also law enforcement agencies, private attorneys, investigators, and suspicious lovers.

The use of video cameras and closed circuit televisions (CCTV) is another common way of monitoring employees within the workplace. Even areas where employees would previously have enjoyed high expectations of privacy, such as

---

[298] Helene Zampetakis, "Email snooping almost banned," Information Technology News Service, June 26, 2001 <http://it.mycareer.com.au/news/2001/06/26/FFXDJRS4DOC.html>.

[299] American Management Association, Annual Survey on Workplace Monitoring and Surveillance 2001, April 18, 2001.

bathrooms or locker rooms, have come under increasing surveillance. The American Civil Liberties Union (ACLU) reports cases of postal workers in New York City finding hidden cameras in the restroom stalls and of waiters in the Boston Sheraton being secretly videotaped in the hotel locker room.[300] Where staff are more mobile, companies are now using a range of technologies to track geographic movements.[301] Some hospitals now require nurses to wear badges on their uniforms so they can be located constantly.[302] Advances in this area now allow carrier companies to place an electronic mechanism (described as a geostationary satellite-based. mobile communications system)[303] on trucks that then sends back to a main terminal the exact position of the vehicle at all times. In this way, carrier companies can ensure that no side trips nor other deviations are taken from the prescribed route.[304] Wide area systems such as Trackback are in use throughout the United Kingdom.

Telephone Monitoring

Telephone surveillance has become endemic throughout the private and public sector. In the United States, employers have broad discretion to monitor employees' calls for "business purposes." Companies are extensively using telephone analysis technology. Call center workers for British Telecom are regularly presented with a comprehensive analysis sheet, showing their performance relative to other workers. Airline reservations clerks in the United States and elsewhere wear telephonic headsets that monitor the length and content of all telephone calls, as well as the duration of their bathroom and lunch breaks.[305] In one instance, telephone calls received by airline reservation agents were electronically monitored on a second-by-second basis: agents were allowed only 11 seconds between each call and 12 minutes of break time each day.[306] Other airline agents have complained that they are evaluated based on how many times they use a customer's name during a call or how often they try to overcome a customer's initial objections to buying a ticket.

---

300 ACLU, Workplace Rights, Electronic Monitoring <http://www.aclu.org/library/pbr2.html>.
301 Laura Pincus Hartman, "The Economic and Ethical Implications of New Technology on Privacy in the Workplace," Business and Society Review, March 22, 1999.
302 "Monitoring Shrinks Worker Privacy Sphere," Eric Auchard, Reuters, May 29, 2001.
303 "Bulkmatic Equips Fleet with OmniTRACS System," Qualcomm Press release, December 19, 1996. <http://www.qualcomm.com/Press/pr961219c.html>.
304 Qualcomm Press release, December 19, 1996.
305 Laura Pincus Hartman, "The Economic and Ethical Implications of New Technology on Privacy in the Workplace," Business and Society Review, March 22, 1999.
306 Charles Pillar, "Bosses with X-Ray Eyes," MacWorld., July 1993.

The level of sophistication of telephone surveillance systems can be astonishing. Some systems can record all transactional activity on a phone, together with destination numbers and times. Other technology can then process and analyze this data. A British program called "Watcall," produced by the Harlequin company, can analyze telephone calls and group them into "friendship networks" to determine patterns of use.[307] Voice mail systems are also subject to systematic or random monitoring by managers. Most new systems have default pass codes for administrators, and these can open all message boxes.

E-mail and Internet Use Monitoring

Computers and networks are particularly conducive to surveillance. The Privacy Foundation study (above) found that 14 million employees in the United States are subject to this kind of surveillance on a continuous basis. This number obviously increases dramatically when random surveillance checks are included. Employers can monitor e-mail by randomly reviewing e-mail transmissions, by specifically reviewing transmissions of certain employees, or by selecting key terms to flag e-mail. In the latter case software analyses a company's entire e-mail traffic phrase by phrase, and draws conclusions about whether a message is legitimate company business. It can be instructed to search for specific keywords and "damaging" phrases. Some programs can even use algorithms to analyze communications patterns and turn them into images. Monitors can then look at these images to follow traffic patterns and detect whether sensitive data is at risk.

Many employers rely on software for remote monitoring of e-mail messages. With a few clicks they can see every e-mail message that employees send or receive and determine whether they are "legitimate" or not. Managers give a variety of reasons for installing such software. Some say it is to protect trade secrets or preventing sexual harassment incidents. Others want to prevent oversized-mails clogging networks and using too much bandwidth. Others simply don't want employees "wasting" company time by using the systems for personal activities. In an ideal world, this monitoring should follow the conventional format, i.e., identical to the quality check that has applied to correspondence sent out on company letterhead. However, the speed and efficiency of e-mail means that digital communication involves a vast intersection with personal correspondence. It also has features more in common with an internal memo, for which there has always been less monitoring and management.

---

307 Simon Davies, "Watch out for the Old Bill," Daily Telegraph, April 29, 1997.

According to the American Management Study (above) nearly two thirds of all companies discipline employees for abuse of email or Internet connections and 27% dismiss employees for those reasons. In 2000, Dow Chemical Company in the United States fired 50 employees and threatened 200 others with suspension after they found "offensive" material in their e-mail. The company opened the personal e-mail of more than 7,000 employees.[308] Similarly, the New York Times fired 23 employees in 1999 for sending "obscene" messages.

These cases raise complex legal and ethical questions concerning an employee's fundamental right to privacy and due process. What if employees are sent "offensive" e-mails by accident or maliciously? The e-mail cannot simply be deleted. It remains logged on the company server, threatening the relationship of trust between employee and management. Or what if an employee is dismissed on the grounds of sensitive personal information (for example relating to sexual preferences, a medial condition, etc.) gathered through a system? This problem also arises when companies monitor all Internet activity looking for visits to "inappropriate" sites. At first sight, such surveillance has elements in common with traditional surveillance for hard copy pornography, but there are significant dangers to workers in the realm of electronic surveillance. The use of spam e-mail to advertise X rated sites results in workers entering sites that appear to be quite benign. Or websites may be accidentally visited when displayed as a "hit" in response to a perfectly innocent search query. The surveillance technology does not, however, distinguish between an innocent mistake and an intentional visit.

The monitoring of chat room visits has also created some distress in the workplace. There is an increasing trend among companies to dismiss and/or sue employees for divulging company "trade secrets" or defaming the company in chat rooms. These have become known as "John Doe" cases. As most people log on to chat rooms anonymously or using an alias, once a company observes a certain party in a chat room engaging in "illegitimate" speech, they must subpoena the message-board services such as Yahoo or America Online, to obtain the identify the specific author. The service providers often turn over identifying information when presented with a subpoena without any notice to the individual. The number of these cases is rapidly increasing and threatens not only the privacy of employees but also their rights to anonymity and free speech.

---

308 'Dow Chemical Fires Employees Over Inappropriate E-mails', ABCNEWS.com, July 27, 2000

Drug Testing

There is also an increasing amount of drug testing in many countries. The number of companies using these tests has risen proportionately with the decreasing costs of the tests. For many employees, drug testing is now a standard part of working life. Companies routinely administer tests in the recruitment stage or at intermittent periods during employment even where there is no evidence of misconduct, poor performance or any other reason to suspect drug use. There are thousands of easy to use kits, which can detect traces of drugs within minutes and without the need for a laboratory, available on the market today. Most of these tests analyze hair or urine samples to detect traces of drugs such as amphetamines, marijuana, cocaine, opiates and methamphetamines.

The issue of wide scale "preventative" drug testing raises a whole host of questions concerning privacy, bodily integrity, freedom and the presumption of innocence. The process of testing itself can be hugely invasive. Observers are often present to prevent employees tampering with samples. In the case of urine testing this can be particularly offensive. Consider the case of one employee who wrote:

> I waited for the attendant to turn her back before pulling down my pants, but she told me she had to watch everything I did. I am a 40-year-old mother of three: nothing I have ever done in my life equals or deserves the humiliation, degradation and mortification I felt.[309]

This type of test can quickly turn from a necessary evil needed to protect lives and reputations to intimidation and harassment. It raises questions about whether the benefits to employers really outweigh the rights and dignity of workers. Manufacturing companies wishing to sell their products obviously claim they can. They extol the advantages of drug tests, claiming they can save employers thousands by reducing incidences of absenteeism, low productivity, accidents, injuries, compensation and health care claims. Governments generally have also encouraged testing as part of a larger war on drugs. What employers are not told, however, is that there are also numerous ethical and economic disadvantages to drug testing.

Drug testing fosters a climate of negativity based on suspicion and secrecy rather than trust, openness and respect. Low morale or resentment among workers may

---

309 From a letter to the American Civil Liberties Union describing a workplace drug test. See, ACLU, Drug Testing: A Bad Investment, September 1999 <http://www.aclu.org/issues/worker/drugtesting1999.pdf>.

consequently lead to low productivity or profits. In addition, even though individual tests may no longer be expensive, because they are so sweepingly administered among employees, they may be costing employers far more than they are saving them. Catching one or two light drug users for every few thousand people tested is hardly an economical justification for the initial outlay. Even if tests do reveal traces of drugs there is no clear evidence to suggest that mild drug use has a greater effect on productivity than, for example, alcohol. Dismissing workers on grounds of policy and suspicion rather than performance and proof, may result in the loss of valuable employees to the employer. Testing does not involve good management policy. Evidence has not shown that drug testing can deter future use, and it is in no way a substitute for proper guidance, support and counseling. In fact, in an ironic twist, routine testing may even encourage more serious drug usage among employees. As one commentator says:

> If one wants to get inebriated on a Friday night and still pass a urine test Monday, smoking a joint would be foolish. Cocaine and alcohol would represent the "safer" choices of intoxicants because alcohol is "legal" and cocaine cannot be detected in the body as long.[310]

Finally, drug testing is inaccurate and can often lead to false and misleading results. A report by the Ontario Information and Privacy Commissioners' Office says up to 40 per cent of tests are inaccurate.[311.] Highly sensitive tests can be positive even when the drug sought is not present. Some say positive reactions may result from a carry-over following a strongly positive earlier or from human error, such as contamination due to failure to cleanse equipment.[312] Others note that certain legal substances can also result in positive tests for illegal drugs. For example, there have been reports of Vicks inhalers resulting in positive tests for amphetamines and methamphetamines, standard anti-inflammatory drugs like Ibuprofen showing up positive on marijuana tests, and even traces of morphine being detected from poppy seeds. [313]

---

310 Ethan A. Nadelmann, "Drawing the Line on Drug Testing". IntellectualCapital.Com, October 14, 1999, available at <http://www.lindesmith.org/library/ethan_drugtesting2.html>.

311 Information and Privacy Commissioner/Ontario, Workplace Privacy: The Need for a Safety-Net, November 1993. <http://www.ipc.on.ca/english/pubpres/sum_pap/papers/safnet-e.htm>.

312 Morgan, John P. "Problems of Mass Urine Screening for Misused Drugs." Journal of Psychoactive Drugs. Volume 16(4) (1984): 305-317. available at The Lindesmith Center - Drug Policy Foundation <http://www.lindesmith.org/library/grmorg2.html>.

313 National Academy of Sciences, "Under the Influence? Drugs and the American Work Force," 1994. Also, ACLU, Drug Testing: A Bad Investment, September 1999.
<http://www.aclu.org/issues/worker/drugtesting1999.pdf>.

Country Reports

Argentine Republic

Articles 18 and 19 of the Argentine Constitution provide (in part), "The home is inviolable as is personal correspondence and private papers; the law will determine what cases and what justifications may be relevant to their search or confiscation. The private actions of men that in no way offend order nor public morals, nor prejudice a third party, are reserved only to God's judgment, and are free from judicial authority. No inhabitant of the Nation will be obligated to do that which is not required by law, nor be deprived of what is not prohibited." Article 43, enacted in 1994, provides a right of habeas data: "Every person may file an action to obtain knowledge of the data about them and its purpose, whether contained in public or private registries or databases intended to provide information; and in the case of false data or discrimination, to suppress, rectify, make confidential, or update the data. The privacy of news information sources may not be affected."[314] Habeas data is also included in the constitutions of many provinces of Argentina. Several cases of habeas data have dealt with correction of commercial information.

In 1999, the Supreme Court of Argentina ruled in two important cases on the scope of habeas data. The leading case is *Urteaga v. Estado Nacional*.[315] There, the Supreme Court allowed an individual access to personal information about his brother, who had disappeared during the military government, presumably in an armed conflict.[316] The lower courts dismissed the action of habeas data for lack of standing. The Court of Appeals reasoned that habeas data grants access only to personal information, and the claimant was trying to access data related to a third person. However, the Supreme Court reversed the ruling. The core of the judgment indicated an expanding approach to the interpretation of habeas data,

---

[314] Constitucion de la Nacion Argentina (1994), available at <http://www.constitution.org/cons/argentin.htm>.

[315] Supreme Court of Argentina, Urteaga c. Estado Nacional (October 15, 1998), in Derecho y Nuevas Tecnologias No. 1-2 (2000), at 193.

[316] This case was decided one month after a case where the Supreme Court denied a mother the right to access to information about her daughter, who had also disappeared during the military regime. In "Aguiar de Lapaco," the Court based its opinion in the principle of *non bis in idem* or guarantee against double prosecution (double jeopardy) because the right of access was used being claimed criminal proceedings and the defendants were benefited by a Presidential pardon. But the Court opinion was the object of strong political and scholarly criticism, and the high tribunal distinguished "Aguiar de Lapaco" from "Urteaga" since the last one was a civil case. Justice Boggiano's dissidence in "Aguiar de Lapaco" stated that habeas data could be used in the case to access to any kind of information held by government.

---

granting a wide right of access to personal information. The other case is *Ganora v. Estado Nacional*,[317] where the Supreme Court of Argentina established that habeas data can be used against any kind of public database. The claim was initiated by two lawyers who were defending Adolfo Scilingo, an ex-navy official who confessed his participation in crimes during the military regime. Arguing investigation and surveillance from the Government, the lawyers requested access to data in official databases about them. The district court judge and the Court of Appeals refused access, even without hearing the government's arguments based on a national security exception. The Supreme Court of Argentina restated its holding in *Urteaga* and the need to interpret habeas data in light of the international and foreign legislation. They cited the European Human Rights case *Leander*[318] and also made a reference to *Nixon v. United States,*[319] where the United States Supreme Court rejected the arguments of President Nixon, who alleged a confidential privilege over information. Finally they concluded that habeas data allowed access to government databases, and that an exception based on public interest should be subject to judicial review. This case shows the expanding interpretation of habeas data by the Supreme Court of Argentina.

In November 2000, Argentina passed the Law for the Protection of Personal Data.[320] It is in conformance with Article 43 of the Constitution and based on the European Union Data Protection Directive and the Spanish Data Protection Act of 1992. The law covers electronic and manual records. It requires express consent before information can be collected, stored, processed, or transferred. Collection of sensitive data is given additional protections and is prohibited unless authorized by law. International transfer of personal information is prohibited to countries without adequate protection. Individuals have an express right of habeas data to access information about themselves held by government or private entities. The law sets up an independent commission within the Ministry of Justice to enforce the law. The law has been considered adequate in terms of the standard set by the European Union Directive[321], although no formal declaration from the European Union Commission has yet been adopted.

---

[317] Ganora, Mario c/ Estado Nacional y otrs s/habeas corpus y habeas data (Supreme Court of Argentina, September 16 1999), 1-2 Derecho y Nuevas Tecnologías, at 229 (2000).

[318] Leander Case, 116 Eur. Ct. H.R. (ser. A) at 9 (1987).

[319] 418 United States 683 (1974).

[320] Law number 25.326, text available at < <http://www.ulpiano.com/Dataprotection_argentina.htm>.

[321] See Pablo Andrés Palazzi "Transmision internacional de datos personales y protección de la privacidad", Ed. Ad- Hoc, 2002.

The data protection agency is not functioning yet, due to the financial crisis of Argentina. On November 2001 the Government enacted the regulation of the Privacy Law. The first director was nominated in February 2002, but he resigned a month later.

Meanwhile, courts have started to interpret the new data protection statute. A civil court held in the year 2000 that information about marriage is not within the kind of personal data requiring consent from the data subject. The Commercial Court of Appeals ruled in March 2002 that the term "private databases whose purpose is to provide reports" encompasses all kind of databanks, including banks and financial companies, even if their database was not intended initially to provide reports,[322] and also that the data protection law applies to bank and finnacial entities in general.[323] Also, courts are applying the prohibition to provide information about credit card transactions and correcting information that is not kept up to date. In an interesting case that applied the data protection act, another trial Court ordered Equifax/Veraz to provide personal data without any kind of codification and in an intelligible way.

The data protection law was also applied to a case of surveillance by the Federal Police of a political party. The president of this political party, Gustavo Beliz, sued the police under the data protection law and habeas data clause of the Constitution requesting all the information that the police have obtained from his party. The Administrative Court of Appeals held that the plaintif had the right to acces the personal information that the police have collected about him without any suspicious of criminal activity. It also held unconstitutional the secret regulation opposed by the defendant for the collection of this data. Finally, in February 2002, a leading case was decided by the Civil Court of Appeals of Buenos Aires. The Court held that companies trading personal information are to be held strictly liable for damages produced by them.

The Civil Code prohibits "that which arbitrarily interferes in another person's life: publishing photos, divulging correspondence, mortifying another's customs or sentiments or disturbing his privacy by whatever means."[324] This article has been applied widely to protect the privacy of the home, private letters and a number of situations involving intrusive telephone calls, and neighbor's

---

[322] CNCom, Sala C, 26/3/2002, "Halabi, Ernesto c/ Citibank NA s/amparo."

[323] CNCom, Sala E, 15/5/2002, "Becker, José c/Banco de la Provincia de Buenos Aires s/amparo", with a sounded opinion of the Attorney General (Fiscal de Cámara).

[324] Código Civil, Article 1071bis, incorporated by Law No. 21.173.

intrusions into one's private life. This provision has been applied widely to private and public plaintifs.

In 1998, the Argentine Congress enacted the Credit Card Act.[325] The object of this bill is to regulate credit card contracts between consumers and financial institutions and specifically the interest rates that banks charge to consumer credit cards. Article 53 restricts the possibility of transferring information from banks or credit card companies to credit reporting agencies.[326] There is also a specific right of access to personal data of a financial character. The Central Bank of Argentina, whose jurisdiction includes the overview of the monetary policy in the Argentine financial market, has authority to regulate banks. Under that authority it created a public debtor's database,[327] requiring financial entities and banks to collect and classify debtors within a range of risk and to send the information to the database. Under Article 8.1 of the regulation[328] the data subject (a client of a bank) has a right of access to his information and to know the reason why she was included in the database.[329]

Under the Criminal Code the illegal sale of personal data and data trafficking over the Internet may be prosecuted. The Attorney General and the Ministry of Justice, are currently drafting a bill to specifically deal with computer crimes. The bill will prohibit violation of privacy by any means and illegal access to computer systems and networks. Government is pursuing the enactment of this bill due to a recent case of hacking to the web site of the Supreme Court. The Federal judge investigating the case concluded that the Criminal Code from the year 1921 had no crimes related to computer damage or illegal acces. After this decision the Supreme Court asked the Ministry of Justice to draft a bill to cover this new kind of crimes.

Under the Code of Penal Procedure, "A judge may arrange, for the purposes of building a case, the intervention of telephone communications or whatever other means of communication." The Penal Code provides penalties for publishing

---

[325] Law 25.065 of December 7, 1998 (Official Bulletin of January 14, 1999).

[326] Credit Card Act, Article 53 ("Bar to inform. Credit Card entities, companies and banks and other financial entities shall not transfer information about credit card debts to credit report agencies when the data subject has not paid its debts or is having financial problems, without prejudice of personal data that must be transferred to the Central Bank under current regulations. Those who transfer this information to third parties shall be liable for the damages produced by the release of the personal data.")

[327] See Financial System Debtors Database "Central de Deudores del Sistema Financiero," regulated by the Central Bank Circular A 2729 (consolidated version by Circular 2930).

[328] Article 8.1, Central Bank Circular A 2729 (consolidated version by Circular 2930).

[329] The information is published also on the Internet <http://www.bcra.gov.ar> and on CD-ROMs. The last CD-ROM contained a list with 1,950,000 individuals including data on their financial status.

private communications.[330] The National Defense Law prohibits domestic surveillance by military personnel.

In April 1999, the Criminal Court of Appeals in Buenos Aires recognized a right to privacy in electronic mail communications applying a section of the Penal Code related to the protection of secrets. Although the criminal provision was drafted in 1921, the Court had an open approach to the interpretation of the statute.[331] Under this case, data such as stored files and e-mail is not to be examined by anyone else without the user's permission.

The UN Human Rights Committee in 1995 expressed concern that the judicial authorization for wiretaps was too broad.[332] In December 2001, a new Intelligence law was enacted with implementing regulations to be issued 180 days later. The law provides for legislative oversight of government intelligence activities. It also prohibits the unauthorized interception of telephone, postal, facsimile, and other communications and private documents. Previously the Penal Code, dating from the year 1921, did not punish wiretapping. There have been numerous scandals relating to unauthorized wiretapping over the years and several cases of wiretapping were dismissed because of the lack of a criminal statute.

In 1996, the national government began a new crackdown on tax evaders. Measures included reviewing citizens' credit cards, insurance, and tax records. One bill allowed citizens whose credit card records had been obtained to sue for invasion of privacy.[333] The same year, the Argentina Passport and Federal Police Identification System, developed by Raytheon E-Systems, was inaugurated at the Buenos Aires airport. The system combines personal data, color photos and fingerprints.[334]

In November 1998, the City of Buenos Aires approved a law on access to information. The law gives all persons the right to ask for and to receive information held by the local authorities and creates a right of judicial review. Individuals have the right under habeas data to updating, rectification,

---

[330] Código Penal de la República Argentina, Art 153-157 <http://www.codigos.com.ar/penal/indice.htm>.

[331] Criminal Court of Appeals in Buenos Aires (Sixth chamber), 4.3.99 "Lanata c. Dufau," in El Derecho, (E.D.) 17.5.99.

[332] United Nations, 19th Annual Report of the Human Rights Committee, A/50/40, October 3, 1995.

[333] New York Times, June 10, 1996.

[334] Business Wire, September 12, 1996.

confidentiality or suppression of information.[335] But critics say that government agencies jealously keep public records and that it is very difficult to obtain information.[336]

In 1984, Argentina adopted the American Convention on Human Rights into domestic law. The Convention was incorporated into the Constitution in 1994 and since then has been by the Argentine Supreme Court to determine domestic cases.[337] In a recent case the Court decided that a famous sportsman had the right to forbid the media to broadcast the existence of a lawsuit related to his natural child base under the right to privacy provided in the American Convention on Human Rights and section 19 of the Federal Constitution.[338] In September 2001, the Court ruled that a weekly news magazine had violated the privacy of former president Carlos Menem when it reported, in 1994 and 1995, that he had used his office to advance the career of Congresswoman with whom he was having an affair.[339]

Commonwealth of Australia

While privacy issues are now featured prominently in the daily news in Australia, the legal safeguards for personal information remain limited. Neither the Australian Federal Constitution nor the Constitutions of the six States contain any express provisions relating to privacy. There is periodic debate about the value of a Bill of Rights, but no current proposals.[340] The Constitution limits the legislative power of the Commonwealth (federal) government, with areas not expressly authorized being reserved for the States. The constitutionality of federal laws imposing privacy rules on the private sector has been questioned, but not so far challenged. Most commentators believe that the Commonwealth could found any private sector privacy law on a 'cocktail' of constitutional

---

[335] See Pablo Andrés Palazzi, El derecho de acceso a la información pública en la ley N° 104 de la Ciudad Autónoma de Buenos Aires. REDI, Número 11 - Junio de 1999, available at
<http://publicaciones.derecho.org/redi/index.cgi?/N%FAmero_11_-_Junio_de_1999>.

[336] See La Nación, "Es de difícil cumplimiento la ley de acceso a la información," July 11, 2000.

[337] See Janet Koven Levit, "The Constitutionalization of Human Rights in Argentina: Problem or Promise?" 37 Columbia Journal of Transnational Law 281. See also Néstor Pedro Sagues, Judicial Censorship of the Press in Argentina, 4 Sw. J. Of L. & Trade Am 45 (1997) (explaining the importance of understanding the make-up of both the Inter-American Court and the Inter-American Commission on Human Rights because the Argentine Supreme Court relies on their opinions as a guide for interpreting personal rights issues).

[338] See Supreme Court, Fallos 324:975.

[339] See Supreme Court, Fallos 324:2895, Menem v. Noticias.

[340] The Commonwealth of Australia Constitution Act, available at
<http://www.republic.org.au/const/cconst.html>.

---

powers including those giving authority over telecommunications, corporations and foreign affairs (e.g. treaties).

Privacy Law in Australia comprises a number of Commonwealth (federal) statutes covering particular sectors and activities, some State or Territory laws with limited effect, and the residual common law protections, which have very occasionally been used in support of privacy rights through actions for breach of confidence, defamation, trespass or nuisance. The principal federal statute is the Privacy Act of 1988[341] which has four main areas of application, and which gives partial effect to Australia's commitment to the OECD Guidelines and to the International Covenant on Civil and Political Rights (ICCPR), Article 17. It creates a set of eleven Information Privacy Principles (IPPs), based on those in the OECD Guidelines that apply to the activities of most federal government agencies. A separate set of rules about the handling of consumer credit information, added to the law in 1989, applies to all private and public sector organizations. The third area of coverage is the use of the government issued Tax File Number (TFN), where the entire community is subject to Guidelines issued by the Privacy Commissioner, which take effect as subordinate legislation. The origins of the Privacy Act were the protests in the mid-1980s against the Australia Card scheme – a proposal for a universal national identity card and number. The controversial proposal was dropped, but use of the tax file number was enhanced to match income from different sources with the Privacy Act providing some safeguards. The use of the tax file number has been further extended by law to include benefits administration as well as taxation. Some controls over this matching activity were introduced in 1990.[342]

After several policy reversals, the re-elected conservative government introduced legislation to extend privacy protection to the private sector in April 2000. The Privacy Amendment (Private Sector) Act 2000 was passed in December 2000 and took effect in December 2001. The law puts in place National Privacy Principles (NPPs) based on the National Principles for Fair Handling of Personal Information originally developed by the Federal Privacy Commissioner in 1998 as a self-regulatory substitute for legislation. Private companies are now required to observe these principles although they can apply to the Privacy Commissioner for approval of a self-developed Code of Practice containing principles that are an "overall equivalent" to the NPPs. The Act has been widely criticized as failing to meet international standards of privacy protection. Privacy expert Roger

---

[341] Privacy Act 1988 (Cwth)
[342] The Data-matching program (Assistance and Tax) Act 1990.

Clarke describes the Act as "the world's worst privacy legislation" or "the Anti-Privacy Act."[343]

The NPPs impose a lower standard of protection in several areas than the European Union Directive. For example, organizations are required to obtain consent from customers for secondary use of their personal information for marketing purposes where it is "practicable"; otherwise, they can initiate direct marketing contact, providing they give the individual the choice to opt out of further communications. Controls on the transfer of personal information overseas are also limited, requiring only that organizations take "reasonable steps" to ensure personal information will be protected, or "reasonably believes" that the information will be subject to similar protection as applied in the Australian law. In addition, the Act provides for a number of broad exemptions for employee records (defined as a record of personal information relating to the employment of the employee including, for example, health information, contact details, salary or wages, performance and conduct, trade union membership, recreation and sick leaves, banking affairs etc); media organizations (defined to include organizations which provide information to the public and political parties); and small businesses (defined as receiving under $A3m annual turnover and not disclosing personal information for a benefit). According to the Federal Government the small business exemption exempts about 94 percent of all Australian businesses but only 30 percent of total business sales.[344] Small businesses that are otherwise exempt from the Act may choose to "Opt-in" if they so wish. In January 2002, the Commissioner issued a news release detailing the relevant procedures for doing so. However, these companies retain the right to opt-out at a later stage.[345] There are also weaknesses in the enforcement regime including, for example, allowing privacy complaints to be handled by an industry-appointed code authority with limited oversight by the Privacy Commissioner. The Act does, however, include an innovative principle of anonymity. Principle 8 states that: "Wherever it is lawful and practicable, individuals must have the option of not identifying themselves when entering into transactions with an organisation."

In March 2001 the Article 29 Data Protecting Working Party of the European Commission expressed many reservations about the Act, suggesting that it would not, as currently written, satisfy the adequacy test in Articles 25 and 26 of the

[343] See Roger Clarke's Homepage <http://www.anu.edu.au/people/Roger.Clarke/>.

[344] Partick Gunning, 'Central Features of Australia's Private Sector Privacy Law', Privacy Law and Reporter, Volume 7, Number 10, May 2001 at 1. Back issues available at <www.austlii.edu.au/au/other/plpr>.

[345] BNA World Data Protection Report, Volume 2, Issue 2, February 2002.

European Union directive for data to flow to third countries.[346] The group recommended the introduction of additional safeguards to address these concerns. In response, the Attorney General issued a press release stating that the Committee's comments "display an ignorance about Australia's law and practice and do not go to the substance of whether our law is fundamentally "adequate" from a trading point of view." He acknowledged that officials from Australia and Europe would "obviously" continue to talk but that "Australia will only look at options that do not impose unnecessary burdens on business." The AG's Department has, however, begun a joint review with the Department of Employment, Workplace Relations and Small Business to examine State, Territory and Commonwealth workplace relations legislation and the privacy protection of employee records. The timeline for this review is unclear, although it is expected to be completed within two years of the commencement of the legislation. The Department is also looking into the need for specific privacy protection for children's personal information.

The Office of Privacy Commissioner,[347] which enforces the Privacy Act, was initially established as a member of the Human Rights and Equal Opportunity Commission but has been operating as a separate statutory agency since 1st July 2000. The Office has wide range of functions, including handling complaints, auditing compliance, promoting community awareness, and advising the government and others on privacy matters. The Commissioner's office, which was cut back in the late 90's, recently received additional resources in anticipation of the new private sector jurisdiction.

In September 2001, the Privacy Commissioner issued the finalized Guidelines on the implementation of the NPPs and a revised draft of the Guidelines on the development of industry codes. In April 2002, the Privacy Commissioner approved the first private sector code, submitted by the Insurance Council of Australia (ICA).[348] Under the new General Insurance Information Privacy Code, complaints concerning the general insurance industry will be handled by complaints the Privacy Compliance Committee, a committee of the Insurance Enquiries and Complaints Ltd, rather than the Privacy Commissioner. The Internet Industry Association is also drafting a code that it hopes will meet the

---

[346] European Union Article 29 Data Protection Working Group, Opinion 3/2001 on the level of protection of the Australian Privacy Amendment (Private Sector) Act 2000, available at <http://europa.eu.int/comm/internal_market/en/media/dataprot/wpdocs/index.htm>.

[347] Homepage <http://www.privacy.gov.au/>.

[348] Office of the Federal Privacy Commissioner, Media Release, "Federal Privacy Commissioner Approves Australia's First Privacy Act Privacy Code," April 17, 2002, available at <http://www.privacy.gov.au/news/media/02_4.html>.

European Union requirements.[349] Other industries that have already adopted self-regulatory initiatives (e.g. the direct marketing and telecommunications industries) will have to decide whether to apply to register their Codes of Practice, and their alternative dispute resolution schemes, under the Privacy Act.

In March 2002 the Commissioner signed an agreement with the Australian Competition and Consumer Commission, which enforces existing fair trading rules, to facilitate cooperation and coordination between the offices where standards overlap.[350]

There are two other federal privacy related laws for which the federal Privacy Commissioner is also the supervisory and complaint handling agency:

- Part VIIC of the Crimes Act enacted in 1989, which provides some protection to individuals who have had criminal convictions in relation to so-called 'spent' convictions (i.e.: convictions for relatively minor offences which they are allowed to 'deny' or have discounted after a set period of time).
- The Data-matching Program (Assistance and Tax) Act 1990 that provides detailed procedural controls over the operation of a major program of information matching between federal tax and benefit agencies.

In the period of 2000-2001, the Commissioners Office received 8177 telephone and 884 email inquiries. Of the 8177 calls, 46 percent (3831) related to matters falling within the Commissioner's jurisdiction. Of these 3831 calls, 1353 (35 percent) related to credit reporting; 896 (23 percent) to information handling practices under the Information Privacy Principles (IPPs); 112 (2.9 percent) to Tax File Numbers 157; 96 (2.5 percent) to spent convictions, 19(0.5 percent) to data-matching. The remaining inquiries were requests for general information or publications. Some 464 written inquiries were received (under the Privacy Act a complaint alleging interference with privacy must be lodged in writing). Of these, 20 (15 percent) were declined and 270 (58.2 percent) fell outside the Commissioners jurisdiction. The remaining were formally investigated as complaints.[351]

---

[349] Karen Dearne, Privacy Safety Net for European Union, Australia IT News, December 11, 2001 available at <http://australianit.news.com.au/articles/0,7204,3408777%5E15319%5E%5Enbv%5E15306,00.html>.

[350] Office of the Federal Privacy Commission, "Regulators Co-Operate to Improve Privacy Compliance," Media Release, 12 March 2002, available at <http://www.privacy.gov.au/>.

[351] Federal Office of the Privacy Commissioner, The Operation of the Privacy Act, Annual Report 1 July 2000 – 30 June 2001, available at <http://www.privacy.gov.au/>.

On July 31, 2001 the Privacy Commissioner released the results of a comprehensive research project into public attitudes towards privacy issues that was commissioned earlier in the year.[352] The research findings were incorporated into three separate reports: Privacy and the Community; Privacy and Business; and Privacy and Government. The results indicate overwhelming support for privacy protection. For example, 91 percent of the public said that they would like businesses to seek permission before engaging in direct marketing; 89 percent would like organizations to advise them who would have access to their personal information and 92 percent would like to be told how it would be used; 42 percent have refused to deal with organizations they felt did not adequately protect their privacy. When asked what kind of data they considered most sensitive 40 percent identified financial details, 11 percent identified income, 7 percent identified medical or health information, 4 percent identified home address, 3 percent identified phone number and 3 percent identified genetic information.[353] The Privacy Commissioner says that the results of the survey will be used in setting out a future work plan for the office including informing the marketing and communications strategy, and providing information for other areas of responsibility such as the development of industry codes and guidelines.

A mix of privacy standards applies to the telecommunications sector. The Telecommunications Act 1997 contains a detailed list of 'exceptions' from a basic presumption of confidentiality of customer records. These exceptions are similar to those in the use and disclosure principles of the federal Privacy Act. These provisions are now supported by a Code of Practice on the Protection of Customer Personal Information that is binding on all telecommunications carriers and service providers,[354] with complaints handled by a Telecommunications Industry Ombudsman. The Code incorporates a draft version of all of the Privacy Act National Privacy Principles, and the telecommunications industry will be deciding whether to register a revised version of the Code under the Privacy Act, or submit themselves directly to the Privacy Commissioner's jurisdiction. There is also a Code of Practice on Calling Number Display, which requires carriers to offer free per call and per line blocking (but only on an opt-out basis) and attempts to impose guidelines on telephone users' use of CND information. Other

---

[352] Office of the Federal Privacy Commissioner, "The results of Research into Community, Business and Government attitudes towards Privacy in Australia." July 31, 2001
<http://www.privacy.gov.au/research/index.html#1.1>.

[353] Office of the Federal Privacy Commissioner, "Privacy and the Community: Main Findings," available at <http://www.privacy.gov.au/publications/rcommunity.html#4>.

[354] Australian Communications Industry Forum, Code C523, 2000, now registered by the Australian Communications Authority, available at <http://www.acif.org.au and http://www/aca.gov.au>.

Codes deal incidentally with privacy issues such as directories, numbering and emergency calls.

Public sector privacy issues continue to raise concerns. As part of reforms to the Australian tax system from July 2000, the Australian Taxation Office required all enterprises to obtain an Australian Business Number. The ATO collected registration details including address and email contact, and planned to make this available to the public through the Australian Business Register and through selling it to database companies. A storm of protest occurred in June 2000 when it was realized that the register would include the home address and other details of almost 2 million individuals, who were sole traders, contractors or even had just a minor income from a hobby or some other activity. The Government agreed to amend the legislation, limit the content of the Australian Business Register and allow individuals to suppress their details. At the same time, the Government was forced into another backdown after receiving legal advice that the Australian Electoral Commission had illegally disclosed information on around 10 million registered Australian voters, after the Prime Minister had asked for this information in order to conduct a targeted direct mailing campaign outlining the benefits of the tax reform package.

During 2000, Commonwealth and State governments announced plans to move towards unique patient identifiers in the health sector, likely to be centered around a health smart card. Health services are primarily delivered by the public sector in Australia, with only around a third of the population having private health insurance. The responsibility for delivery of health services is shared between the Commonwealth Government, which is responsible for much of the funding of the health system, and the States, which operate hospitals and community health services. The Commonwealth's proposal, HealthConnect, is intended as a voluntary national health information network under which health-related information about an individual would be collected in a standard, electronic format at the point of care.[355] As a first phase of this system the Department of Health and Aged Care drafted the Better Medication Management System Bill that would establish individual electronic medication records in order to improve access to information about drugs for doctors and patients. The system was widely criticized by consumers and doctors groups concerned about patient confidentiality and professional liability.[356] In July 2001, the Department of Health announced that all negotiations on the implementation of this system and the introduction of the enabling legislation had been postponed due to

---

[355] For details see <http://www.health.gov.au/healthonline/connect.htm>.

[356] "Medicos Oppose Data Bill," Karen Dearne, Australian IT July 24, 2001.

"technical difficulties." [357] In the interim the Department is consulting with the Privacy Commissioner in order to ensure standards for patient privacy.[358]

In December 2001, the National Health and Medical Research Council (NHMRC) issued guidelines (under section 95A of the Privacy Act 1988) on privacy in medical research. In June 2002, the Privacy Commissioner released guidelines on health data and fact sheet on use of commonwealth identifiers, including the medicare number.

Genetic privacy is currently under joint review by the Australian Law Reform Commission and the Australian Health Ethics Committee of the National Health and Medical Research Council. The group was scheduled to issue its final report by June 2002 but has recently extended the deadline by nine months until March 2003. On June 20, 2001 the Prime Minister, announced the establishment of a national digital database of DNA and fingerprint samples in order to facilitate law enforcement.[359] The database will hold DNA samples of convicted criminals and suspects. In deference to privacy concerns, the identities of those who supply the samples will be held by state and territory forensic laboratories rather than in the database itself. All states and territories, except Western Australia now have laws permitting DNA databasing.

The Telecommunications (Interception) Act of 1979 regulates the interception of telecommunications. A warrant is required under the Act and it also provides for detailed monitoring and reporting. However, the Interception Act safeguards need to be read alongside Parts 14 and 15 of the Telecommunications Act 1997 that place obligations on telecommunications providers to, at their own cost, positively assist and provide an interception capability for law enforcement interceptions. There have been a number of changes to the Interception regime in recent years, including broadening the range of offences for which warrants can be obtained; allowing more law enforcement agencies to apply for warrants and more of them to execute warrants themselves; and transferring the warrant issuing authority from federal court judges to designated members of the Administrative Appeals Tribunal (who are on term appointments rather than tenured and are arguably less independent). Significant loopholes exist within the legislation, such as section 6(2) which some experts argue allows the recording and monitoring of communications in specific circumstances such as when the equipment is provided by a telecommunications carrier. There remains

---

357 'Medical E-Files 'Delayed For Poll' by John Kerin, Australian IT, July 30 2001.

358 "Your Health On The Line," Australian Financial Review, May 25, 2002.

359 "Australia Launches DNA Database to Fight Crime," Reuters, June 20, 2001.

considerable uncertainty as to the position of e-mail and other stored communications, under the telecommunications laws – it is not clear which communications are subject to the strict Interception Act safeguards and which only to the lesser controls of the Telecommunications Act.

Interception warrants have steadily increased over the last few years. In 2000/2001 reporting year, there were 2157 new warrants issued compared to 1696 in 1999/2000, 1,284 in 1998/1999, and 675 in 1997/1998.[360] This excludes an undisclosed number of interception warrants issued to the Australian Security Intelligence Organisation by the Attorney General.

In December the Telecommunications (Interception) Act 1979 was amended by the Royal Commissions and Other Legislation Amendment Act 2001 to include Royal Commissions as "eligible Commonwealth authorities" for the purposes of receiving intercepted information and carrying out intercepts. In July 2002, there was considerable scandal when labor and union officials discovered that a Royal Commission into the Building and Construction Industry received intercepted communications transcripts in the course of its investigation. The Minster of Justice and Customs dismissed any criticisms saying that the Commission only had the power to receive intercepted information in certain circumstances and could not conduct interceptions itself.[361]

In March 2002, the government introduced the Telecommunications (Interception) Legislation Amendment Bill 2002. The bill was part of a larger package of anti-terrorism measures called the Security Legislation Amendment (Terrorism) Bill 2002 [No.2] and Related Bills. The proposal would have allowed law enforcement to intercept electronic communications (such as email, SMS and voice mail messages) without a warrant because these communications were considered access to "stored" data rather than "intercepted" in real-time. Commenting on the proposal before the Senate Legal and Constitutional Legislation Committee, the federal Privacy Commissioner argued that there was "little justification for reducing the privacy protection of a communication as intimate as a voice mail message or SMS, in comparison with alive communication simply because the transmission of the former is temporarily

---

[360] Attorney General's Department, Report on the Telecommunications (Interception) Act 1979 for the year ending 30 June 2001, available at
<http://www.ag.gov.au/publications/telecomar2000/Annual%20Report00-01.pdf>.
[361] Minister for Justice and Customs, Use of Telecommunications Interception Product by Royal Commissions, Press Release, July 9, 2002, available at
<http://www.law.gov.au/aghome/agnews/2002newsjus/e88_02.htm>.

delayed."[362] In June 2002 the government agreed to join opposition members in the Senate in voting against this proposal in order to ensure passage of the rest of the anti-terrorism legislation.[363] However similar proposals are likely to resurface at a later stage. According to the Minister for Justice and Customs, the government "remains of the view that the approach adopted in the bill with respect to stored information is appropriate. However, to avoid holding up this important package of legislation, the government has agreed to remove these provisions from the bill and to deal with the issue at a later date."[364]

In November 1999, the Australian Security Intelligence Organisation Legislation Amendment Act 1999 was passed by the Commonwealth Parliament. The Act came into effect on 10 December 1999. It gives ASIO new powers to access e-mails and data inside computers, use-tracking devices on vehicles, obtain tax and cash transaction information and intercept mail items carried by couriers. ASIO is authorized to modify private computer files as long as there is reasonable cause to believe that it is relevant to a security matter.[365] In addition, amendments to the Telecommunications (Interception) Act, passed in June 2000, granted further powers to granted the ASIO. The amendments allow the agency to obtain telecommunications interception warrants targeting "named persons". These warrants are based on a name of person only, not specifying the location of the tap to allow for the interception of multiple services without a new warrant. The amendments also expanded the use of wiretap information in other proceedings. Intelligence agencies can now get a "foreign communications warrant" to "enable ASIO, operating 'within Australia,' to intercept communications 'sent or received outside Australia' for the purposes of collecting foreign intelligence."

The Crimes Act contains a range of other privacy related measures, such as offenses relating to unauthorized access to computers, unauthorized interception of mail and telecommunications and the unauthorized disclosure of Commonwealth government information. It also contains provisions relating to "spent" convictions, allowing individuals convicted of minor offenses to lawfully "deny" them in most circumstances after a period of time.

---

362 Report of the Senate Legal and Constitutional Legislation Committee, Consideration of Legislation Referred to the Committee, Security Legislation Amendment (Terrorism) Bill 2002[No.2], Suppression of the Financing of Terrorism Bill 2002, Criminal Code Amendment (Suppression of Terrorist Bombings) Bill 2002, Border Security Legislation Amendment Bill 2002, Telecommunications Interception Legislation Amendment Bill 2002, May 2002, available at
<http://www.aph.gov.au/senate/committee/legcon_ctte/terrorism/report/Security.pdf>.

363 Electronic Frontiers Australia, Media Release: Senate Rejects Email Snooping Law - Victory For Online Privacy, June 28, 2002.

364 Statement of Senator Ellison, Minister of Justice and Customs, Senate Official Hansard No.6 2002, June 27, 2002, available at <http://www.aph.gov.au/hansard/senate/dailys/ds270602.pdf>.

365 "Orwellian Nightmare Down Under?" Wired News, December 4, 1999.

In late June 2001, the Government introduced legislation to target online crime. Despite widespread criticism from civil liberties and computer users groups such as the Australian Computer Society and Electronic Frontiers Australia,[366] on October 1, 2001 the Cybercrime Act 2001 passed into law.[367] The Act establishes seven new computer offenses: unauthorised access, modification or impairment with intent to commit a serious offence (defined as those punishable by 5 years imprisonment or more); unauthorised modification of data to cause impairment; unauthorised impairment of electronic communication; unauthorised access to, or modification of, restricted data; unauthorised impairment of data held on a computer disk etc.; Possession or control of data with intent to commit a computer Offence; and producing, supplying or obtaining data with intent to commit a computer offence. Sanctions include imprisonment of up to 10 years. The new Act also amends the Crimes Act to provide police with increased search and seizure powers including the authority to demand release of encryption keys or decrypted data.

The federal Freedom of Information Act of 1982[368] provides for access to government records. The Commonwealth Ombudsman promotes the Act and handles complaints about procedural failures. Merits review (appeal) of adverse FOI decisions is provided by the Administrative Appeals Tribunal, with the possibility of further appeals on points of law to the Federal Court. Budget cuts have severely restricted the capacity of the AGs Department and Ombudsman to support the Act and there is now little central direction, guidance or monitoring.

State and Territory Laws

The Australian States and Territories have varying privacy laws. *New South Wales*, the most populous State, passed the Privacy and Personal Information Protection Act 1998 which applies privacy principles (since July 2000) to most state government agencies – although there are numerous and generous exemptions, and agencies can apply for Codes of Practice that can weaken the principles. The former Privacy Committee (which acted as an Ombudsman since 1975 and also issued a number of reports and guidelines over, recent examples being reports on video surveillance and smart cards) has been replaced by a part time Privacy Commissioner with a very small staff. The Act is based on a set of

---

[366] 'Cyber-Crime Bill Excessive," Karen Dearne, Australia IT July 24, 2001.

[367] Cybercrime Act 2001, No.161, 2001.

[368] Freedom of Information Act 1982, Freedom of Information (Fees and Charges) Regulations 1982, Freedom of Information (Miscellaneous Provisions) Regulations 1982.

OECD-style Information Protection Principles and requires all government departments and agencies to develop a Privacy Management Plan demonstrating their compliance plans. It also allows government agencies to weaken the Information Protection Principles, which form the foundation of the legislation. In 1998 New South Wales enacted a Workplace Video Surveillance Act (partly in response to the Privacy Committee report). In December 2001, the NSW Law Reform Commission issued a report recommending that this Act and the Listening Devices Act 1984 be replaced by a new technology neutral law governing all types of surveillance. The Government has not yet acted on this recommendation.[369] In August 2001, NSW became the first state to enact Cybercrime legislation. Modeled on the federal proposal, the Crimes Amendment (Computer Offences) Act creates three new computer related offences; unauthorized access to data, modification of data and impairment of data with penalties ranging between two and ten years of imprisonment.[370] The law also criminalizes the authorized access, modifications or impairment of data in order to commit another unrelated offence. In July 2002 IBM secured a contract to conduct a pilot contract for a NSW electronic health data network. The network is based on the national HealthConnect project (above).[371]

The state of *Victoria* has enacted the Information Privacy Act 2000, which applies privacy principles (in fact an exact copy of the NPPs in the federal Act) to most state government agencies. There are relatively few exemptions and while there is provision for Codes of Practice, they cannot weaken the principles. The Act created an office of Privacy Commissioner with a monitoring, enforcement and education role and to conciliate complaints. The Civil and Administrative Tribunal can determine unresolved complaints. Victoria passed the Health Records Act in 2001 which came into effect in July 2002. The law complements the information privacy legislation by requiring Victorian health service providers to handle health information responsibly. The Health Records Act also gives patients a right of access to their records held by private practitioners. In July 2002, the State of Victoria announced plans to pass new legislation prohibiting person's images being posted on a website without permission. The Law Reform Commission is currently reviewing the issue. In May 2002, the Law Reform Commission issued a report on Powers of Entry, Search, Seizure and Questioning by Authorised Persons. The report found that that there were too few provisions in current acts to "safeguard citizens' rights

---

[369] Caitlin Fitzsimmons, "Email Snooping in Legal Limbo," Australian IT, July 16, 2002.

[370] "NSW Testbed for Federal Laws," Australian IT, August 7, 2001
<http://australianit.news.com.au/common/storyPage/0,3811,2524070%5E442,00.html>.

[371] "IBM Comes Up With Right IT Prescription," Australian Financial Review June 7, 2002.

and ensure transparency and accountability." It recommended additional safeguards to ensure that these powers would be used with restraint.[372]

The government of the *Australian Capital Territory*, which used to be a local authority under Commonwealth (federal) law, and was consequently covered by the federal Privacy Act, achieved self-government as a separate Territory in 1989. The Privacy Act was amended to continue coverage, intended as an interim measure, but this remains the position, with the Privacy Commissioner in effect serving also as the ACT's Commissioner, responsible to its own government. However, in 1997 the ACT government passed its own Health Records (Access and Privacy) *Act*, which applies to personal health information held by anyone - public or private sector. It provisions are similar to those of the IPPs in the Privacy Act, and supercedes them for ACT government agencies in this area of data handling.

Queensland had a purely advisory Privacy Committee from 1984 to 1991[373] and has a limited privacy statute[374] covering the use of listening devices, credit reporting (operating alongside the 1989 amendments to the federal Privacy Act) and physical intrusions into private property. In April 1998, after a yearlong review, a Parliamentary Committee recommended privacy legislation, at least for the public sector.[375] The government has indicated that it intends to legislate but no timetable has been set.

All of the States and the ACT (but not the Northern Territory) also have Freedom of Information laws that include rights for individuals to access and correct personal information about themselves.

Republic of Austria

The Austrian Constitution does not explicitly recognize the right of privacy.[376] Some sections of the data protection law (Datenschutzgesetz – DSG) have constitutional status and may only be restricted under the conditions of Article 8 of the European Convention of Human Rights (ECHR). The entire ECHR has

---

[372] Victorian Law Reform Committee, "The Powers of Entry, Search, Seizure and Questioning by Authorised Persons," May 30, 2002 available at <http://www.parliament.vic.gov.au/lawreform/>.

[373] Privacy Committee Act 1984 (Qld).

[374] Invasion of Privacy Act 1971 (Qld).

[375] Privacy in Queensland, Report No 9, Legal Constitutional and Administrative Review Committee, April 1998, available at <http://www.parliament.qld.gov.au/comdocs/legalrev/lcarc9.PDF>

[376] Constitution of Austria, <http://www.uni-wuerzburg.de/law/au00t___.html>.

---

constitutional status and Article 8 is often cited by the constitutional court in privacy matters.

A new data protection law (Datenschutzgesetz 2000) was approved in December 1999 and went into force in January 2000.[377] The Act replaces a 1978 law[378] of the same name and incorporates the European Union Directive. It protects the right of individuals in relation to the processing of their personal data irrespective of the mode of data processing. Individuals have the right to access, correct, delete, or keep confidential personal data.[379] Data controllers are required to notify the data subject who has right to access the data, its origin, and the identity of any recipients. Disclosure to third parties is only allowed when the data subject gives express written permission; it is in the legitimate objective of the data controller to disclose the information; if information is not anonymous, or if it is necessary for the protection and interests of a third party.[380] Claims against private sector data controllers can be brought under the law by an individual data subject or by the Data Protection Commission. Civil and criminal provisions apply.[381] Experts have criticized the new law as inadequate because it retains the cumbersome structure of the original 1978 Act rather than replacing it.[382]

Under the 2000 Act, a Data Protection Commission (DPC) and a Data Protection Council are established and have powers of investigation and enforcement to ensure compliance with the Act. The Commission is an advisory body responsible for resolving private sector complaints, investigating public sector data processing, and reporting bi-annually to the federal government on public sector data processing. It oversees all private sector activity including the authorization of international data transmissions and applications for data processing registration. The DPC will only deny the export of data if such transport conflicts with public interests, violates international legal obligations, disregards data disclosure requirements, damages the interests of the person warranting protection or has inadequate safeguards. The DPC is also responsible

---

[377] See <http://www.ad.or.at/office/recht/dsg2000.htm>.

[378] Datenschutzgesetz – DSG, BGBl 1978/565 changed by 1981/314, 1982/228, 1986/370, 1987/605, 1988/233, 1989/609, 1993/91, 1994/79, 1994/632, available at <http://www.ad.or.at/office/recht/dsg.htm>.

[379] Christopher Millard and Mark Ford,Data Protection Laws of the World, Austria Report (Clifford Chance 2001).

[380] id.

[381] id.

[382] See Viktor Mayer-Schoenberger and Ernst Brandl, Datenschutzgesetz 2000, (Line Publishing Vienna, 1999).

for submitting proposals to federal and state government on improvements to the Data Protection Act. [383]

As of May 2001, there were 100,000 registered Data Controllers who are defined as "the legal person ordering the collection, processing or disclosure of data or causing it to take place."[384] Data controllers are required to notify the data subject who has right to access the data, its origin, and the identity of any recipients. Disclosure to third parties is only allowed when the data subject gives express written permission; it is in the legitimate objective of the data controller to disclose the information; if information is not anonymous, or if it is necessary for the protection and interests of a third party. Claims against private sector data controllers can be brought under DSG by an individual data subject or by the DPC on behalf of data subjects and civil and criminal provisions both apply.

There are also a number of sectoral privacy laws. The telecommunication law contains special data protection provisions for telecommunication systems, particularly problems like phone directories, unsolicited calls or ISDN calling line identification.[385] The Genetic Engineering Act of 1994 requires prior written consent for information to be used for purposes other than the original purpose. While there are no specific provisions in the Act relating to medical data, there are provisions in other statutes dealing with the transmission of medical or health data. These include section 2 and 3 of the AIDS Act, which requires hospitals and physicians to report every case of Aids to the Federal Ministry of Health and Social Affairs.[386]

The Banking Act of 1993 deals with special requirements in relation to credit data. Section 18 of the DPA states that a data application containing information regarding a person's creditworthiness requires prior authorization. Moreover, financial institutions cannot use or share any information derived from secrets their customers revealed during business transactions. In their regular business relations, all financial institutions must comply with DPA provisions stating that they cannot use personal data obtained through client accounts for other purposes. Austrians can have an anonymous "Sparbuch" bank account. The Financial Action Task Force, an anti-money laundering group coordinated by the OECD, has been pressuring Austria to change its laws to require that each

---

[383] Privacy Exchange, Austria Country Report, May 30, 2001, available at
<http://www.privacyexchange.org/legal/nat/omni/austriaum.html>.
[384] Id.
[385] § 87 to § 101, Telekommunikationsgesetz – TKG, BGBl I 1997/100.
[386] Christopher Millard and Mark Ford, Data Protection Laws of the World, Austria Report (Clifford Chance 2001).

account be personally identified.[387] In June 2000, the First Chamber of the Parliament approved legislation to identify anyone who withdraws or deposits from an account by 2002.[388]

In 2000, the "Lander" adopted various laws relating to data protection. Some have passed legislation regarding notification about suspicions of neglect, mistreatment or sexual abuse, and the collection of personal data related thereto. There are also additional laws adopted regarding military authorities' standards regarding the use of personal data for military affairs.[389]

Over the past few years, Austria has been working on introducing a smart card for social security. This smart card, which would replace the present health insurance certificate, would be given to every person. It would be used as a "citizens card" and will possibly contain a digital signature. All personal, tax, but also social security and health data could be saved on this electronic identity card.[390] The government plans to introduce the smart cards for the social insurance system by 2005.[391] There are concerns about the card's functions and safety features as well as privacy protection issues.[392] Currently, while all Austrian citizens have identity cards, only aliens must be prepared to show their personal documents and give information for the purpose and duration of their stay in Austria. Citizens are not required to carry their identity cards.

Wiretapping, electronic eavesdropping and computer searches are regulated by the code of criminal procedure.[393] Telephone wiretapping is permitted if it is needed for investigating a crime punishable by more than one year in prison. Electronic eavesdropping and computer searches are allowed if they are needed to investigate criminal organizations or crimes punishable by more than ten years in prison. The provision concerning electronic eavesdropping and computer searches became effective between October 1, 1997, and July 1, 1998. Due to long and intensive discussion, the provisions are in effect only until December

---

[387] Financial Action Task Force on Money Laundering Issues: a Warning about Austrian Anonymous Savings Passbooks, February 11, 1999.

[388] Financial Action Task Force, FATF welcomes proposed Austrian legislation to eliminate anonymous passbooks, 15 June 2000.

[389] Article 29 Data Protection Working Group Party, Fifth Annual Report of the Situation Regarding the Protection of Individuals with Regard to the Processing of Personal Data and privacy in the European Union and in Third Countries Covering the Year 2000, March 6, 2002, available at <http://europa.eu.int/comm/internal_market/en/dataprot/wpdocs/wp62_en.pdf>.

[390] United States Department of Justice, International Trade Administration. Report on Austria E-Government, March 29, 2001, available at <http:// exportit.ita.doc.gov/Ocbe/ForeignM.nsf/>.

[391] Id.

[392] European Union Data Protection Working Party. Fifth Annual Report, supra, n.389.

[393] § 149a to § 149p Strafprozeßordnung – StPO.

31, 2001. Criticism of the drafts for this law has led to a number of restrictions, but whether or not these provisions can effectively prevent eavesdropping on innocent persons remains unresolved. In February 2001, the Federal Minister of Transport, Innovation and Technology issued a draft ordinance that would require all telecommunication operators to install technical equipment to facilitate the surveillance of telecommunication traffic in accordance with the code of criminal procedure.[394]

On October 15, 2001, in response to the terrorist attacks in the United States, the federal government announced a package of measures to fight money laundering and terrorism. Police forces increased surveillance on diplomatic missions, airports, and other sensitive sites.[395] A week later the government passed legislation increasing punishment for those found guilty of terrorist hoaxes, increased spending on additional security personnel and equipment including a helicopter and voted on an extension of police permission to carry out electronic surveillance.[396]

The Auskunftspflichtgesetz is a Freedom of Information law that obliges federal authorities to answer questions regarding their areas of responsibility.[397] However, it does not permit citizens to access documents, just to receive answers from the government on the content of information. The nine Austrian Provinces have laws that place similar obligations on their authorities.

In April 2001, the Ministry of Justice presented draft amendments of the Criminal Procedure code, which would bring about important changes to the Austrian judicial system. According to the draft law on the security of information, authorities, journalists and other persons who disclose classified information could face sanctions if the disclosure impairs Austria's public security, national defense, foreign relations or economic interests.[398] It would be possible, thus, to imprison journalists who publicly disclose secret documents from public officials even if its publication would be of public interest. Violations could lead to up to one year in prison. While the main aim of the law is to protect military secrets, critics claim that since the law is so poorly

---

[394] Draft Ordinance of the Federal Minister of Transport, Innovation and Technology over the Surveillance of Telecommunications , February 7, 2001, available at <http://www.vibe.at/misc/uevo.en.html>.

[395] "Austrian Federal Government supports United States Actions," Republic of Austria News Report, October 21, 2001.

[396] "Stronger Sentences for Terror-Hoaxes," Republic of Austria News Report, October 24, 2001.

[397] BGBl 1987/285 (15 May 1987). available at <http://www.rz.uni-frankfurt.de/~sobotta/Austria.htm>.

[398] International Helsinki Federation for Human Rights, 2002 Report on Austria (Events of 2001), May 28, 2002, available at <http://www.ihf-hr.org/reports/AR2002/country%20 links/austria.htm>.

formulated it could potentially adversely affect the free flow of information. Moreover it seems that since any official could declare their files classified, they could also restrict public scrutiny of their actions and limit freedom of information access.[399]

Austria is a member of the Council of Europe and has signed and ratified the Convention for the Protection of Individuals with Regard to Automatic Processing of Personal Data (ETS No. 108).[400] It has signed and ratified the European Convention for the Protection of Human Rights and Fundamental Freedoms.[401] In November 2001, it signed the Council of Europe Convention on Cybercrime.[402] It is a member of the Organization for Economic Cooperation and Development and has adopted the OECD Guidelines on the Protection of Privacy and Transborder Flows of Personal Data.

Kingdom of Belgium

The Belgian Constitution recognizes the right of privacy and private communications.[403] Article 22 states, "Everyone has the right to the respect of his private and family life, except in the cases and conditions determined by law. . . . The laws, decrees, and rulings alluded to in Article 134 guarantee the protection of this right." Article 29 states, "The confidentiality of letters is inviolable. . . . The law determines which nominated representatives can violate the confidentiality of letters entrusted to the postal service." Article 22 was added to the Belgian Constitution in 1994. Prior to the constitutional amendment, the Cour de cassation ruled that Article 8 of the European Convention applied directly to the law and prohibited government infringement on the private life of individuals.[404]

The Data Protection Act of 1992 governs the processing and use of personal information. Amending legislation to update this Act and make it consistent with the European Union Directive was approved by the Parliament in December 1998.[405] A Royal Decree ("Arrêté royal") to implement the Act was approved in

---

[399] Id.

[400] Signed January 28, 1981; Ratified March 30, 1988; Entered into force July 1, 1988

[401] Signed December 13, 1957; Ratified September 3, 1958; Entered into force Septmber 3,1958.

[402] Signed November 23, 2001.

[403] Constitution of Belgium, available at <http://www.fed-parl.be/constitution_uk.html>.

[404] Cour de Cassation, September 26, 1978.

[405] Act concerning the protection of privacy with regard to the treatment of personal data files, December 8, 1992, as amended by the Act of December 11, 1998 transposing European Union Directive 95/46/CE of

---

July 2000. The Decree, as a whole, broadens the scope of application of the law by extending the definition of "processing" and reinforces data subjects' rights. The Decree was finally adopted in February 2001, and the law came into effect in September 2001. Two months after the entry into force of the new data protection regime, the government announced that it had put in place an "*Observatoire des droits de l'Internet*" (the Internet Rights Observatory)[406] in order to better assess and analyze the impact of the Internet on the economy and consumer protection. The Observatory aims, through its composition, at being an open forum for all Internet stakeholders, and will issue advisory opinions and annual reports, organize a dialogue between economic actors, and inform the public.

The Commission de la Protection de la Vie Privée oversees the law.[407] The Commission investigates complaints, issues opinions and maintains the registry of personal files. [408]. In 1999 and 2000, the Commission answered approximately 800 complaints and requests for information per year. In 2001, this number increased to reach almost 1,100. The number of public requests also increased from about 6,200 in 1999 to about 7,400 in 2001. In the last three years, the commission has issued a number of recommendations relating, among others, to workplace privacy[409], video surveillance[410], the compatibility of the ten-yearly census survey with the Belgian privacy regulations[411], the protection of privacy in the context of electronic commerce.[412]. As of 2001, there are only 19 permanent staff members compared to 28 in 2000.

Surveillance of communications is regulated under a 1994 law.[413] Prior to its enactment, there was no specific law. The law requires permission of a *juge*

October 24, 1995. <http://www.law.kuleuven.ac.be/icri/papers/legislation/privacy/tabel/index.html>. An unofficial English translation is available at
<http://www.law.kuleuven.ac.be/icri/papers/legislation/privacy/engels/>.

[406] <http://www.internet-observatory.be/>.

[407] Commission de la protection de la vie privée homepage: http://www.privacy.fgov.be/

[408] As of July 2002, there were 22,896 records in the Commission's registry.

[409] Avis d'initiative n° 10/2000 du 3 avril 2000 relatif à la surveillance par l'employeur de l'utilisation du système informatique sur le lieu de travail, available at <http://www.privacy.fgov.be>.

[410] Avis d'initiative n° 34/99 relatif aux traitements d'images effectués en particulier par le biais de systèmes de vidéo-surveillance, available at <http://www.privacy.fgov.be/av034def.pdf>; Avis d'initiative n° 3/2000 relatif à l'utilisation de systèmes de vidéo-surveillance dans les halls d'immeubles à appartements, available at <http://www.privacy.fgov.be/av003def.pdf>.

[411] Avis d'initiative No. 37/2001 of October 8, 2001 concernant l'enquête socio-économique 2001, available at <http://www.privacy.fgov.be>.

[412] Avis d'initiative No. 34/2000 of November 22, 2000 relatif à la protection de la vie privèe dans le cadre du commerce électronique, available at <http://www.privacy.fgov.be>.

[413] Loi du 30 juin 1994 relative à la protection de la vie privée contre les écoutes, la prise de connaissance et l'enregistrement de communications et de télécommunications privées.

---

d'instruction before wiretapping can take place. Orders are limited to a period of one month. There were 114 orders issued in 1996.[414] The law was amended in 1997 to remove restrictions on encryption.[415] The Parliament also amended the law in 1998 to require greater assistance from telecommunications carriers.[416] In 1995, the Belgian Government admitted spying on the peace and environmental movements.[417]

In November 2000, the Belgian Parliament enacted a law on computer-related crime.[418] The law creates 4 new crimes (computer forgery ("*faux en informatique*"), computer fraud ("*fraude informatique*"), hacking, and sabotage of computer data ("*sabotage de données informatiques*"), and amends the Code of Criminal Procedure to give the *juge d'instruction and the Attorney General ("Procureur du Roi") more powers*. The *juge d'instruction* now has the authority to request the cooperation of experts or network managers to help decrypt telecommunications messages which have been intercepted. The experts, network managers, etc. cannot refuse providing cooperation; criminal sanctions are possible in cases of refusal. The law also provides that telecommunications network operators and telecommunications service providers have to record and store calling data ("*données d'appel*") and telecommunications services subscribers' identification data for future law enforcement authorities' needs during a minimum period of 12 months. The law is very vague as to the duration of data retention ("a certain time"). It does not prevent an upcoming implementing decree, which is still being drafted by the Ministry of Justice and Telecommunications, from increasing this period for much longer.[419]. The Belgian police are officially in favor of a 3-year general retention policy.[420]

---

[414] "Ecoutes: une pratique décevante et. flamande! Le résultat judiciaire des écoutes téléphoniques est médiocre. La Chambre va modifier la donne," Le Soir, December 12, 1997.

[415] Chapitre 17, Loi modifiant la loi du 21 mars 1991 portant réforme de certaines entreprises publiques économiques afin d'adapter le cadre réglementaire aux obligations en matière de libre concurrence et d'harmonisation sur le marché des télécommunications découlant des décisions de l'Union européenne, 19 Decembre 1997.

[416] Loi modifiant la loi du 30 juin 1994 relative à la protection de la vie privée contre les écoutes, la prise de connaissance et l'enregistrement de communications et de télécommunications privées, 10 Juin 1998. See "Le GSM en toute sécurité ? Pas sûr," Le Soir, 20 Feb. 1998.

[417] Statewatch Bulletin, Volume 5 No 6, November-December 1995.

[418] Loi du 28 novembre 2000 relative à la criminalité informatique.

[419] The implementing decree, in addition to fixing the maximum period of retention of data, will determine the conditions in which the telecommunications service providers and network operators have to cooperate with police on data retention.

[420] The European Commission ("EC") made strong critiques of the law before its enactment. However, most of its critiques were not addressed, and most of them rejected without adequate motivation. Some of the Commission's critiques mentioned that the law was too vague and could not be considered a "law" pursuant to current case law of the European Court of Human Rights ("ECHR"). The European institution also specified that the law, by not restricting the strictures within which the government has to implement data retention measures, is too vague and gives the government *carte blanche* to act in a discretionary fashion. According to

---

In December 1999 the Commission de la Protection de la Vie Privée had issued an opinion on the bill, in which it raised serious concerns about its potential negative impact on the protection of privacy. It recommended certain amendments to the Bill including the establishment of a "police monitoring system," which would report back to the Commission, and a three-year review provision.[421] These suggestions were not included in the law, and the data retention provision goes against the Commission's official opinion. However, the law provides that the Privacy Commission's opinion is mandatory before any royal decree is enacted on the issue of data retention.

Almost unnoticed, a law, enacted in December 2001, bans anonymity for subscribers and users of telecommunications network operators and services providers, while the application of the law is, however, subject to a proportionality requirement. A royal decree may prohibit the exploitation of telecommunications services if they render the identification of the caller impossible, or otherwise make it difficult to track, monitor, wiretap, or record communications. With this new rule, the government can now prohibit any telecommunications service that hinders the application of the wiretapping laws.[422]

After almost a year of negotiations, a national collective labor organization of employers and employees' representatives (the "Conseil national du travail") eventually agreed on common rules regulating the electronic surveillance of workers' computers in the workplace. The common agreement (called "convention collective de travail" or "CCT") entered into force on June 29, 2002 through a royal decree[423] and applies to all employers and employees in the

---

the EC, the data retention provision of the Belgian law is also disproportionate with respect to the Court of Justice of the European Community's case law. One has to note that, even though the new European Union Directive on privacy in electronic communications allows European Union Member States to allow data retention for a reasonable period, the Belgian law, as it is now written, could be considered in violation of current ECHR's case law. For more information, see European Commission, Opinion regarding Belgian bill on computer crime ("Notification 2000/151/B – Projet de loi relatif à la criminalité informatique – Emission d'un avis circonstancié au sens de l'article 9, paragraphe 2 de la directive 98/34/CE du 22 juin 1998 – Emission d'observations au sens de l'article 8, paragraphe 2 de la directive 98/34/CE"), ca June 2000, appended to the Parliamentary report of the Justice Commission, Chamber of Representatives of the Belgian Parliament, Oct. 19, 2000, DOC 50 0213/011.

[421] Opinion 33/99 de la Commission de la protection de la vie privée, available at <http://www.privacy.fgov.be/>.

[422] The wording of the law is so vague that a decree might prohibit any kind of anonymization software, the use of proxys by ISPs, since they all make the identification or tracking of communications "difficult". See Etienne Wéry, "Surfer anonymement devient illegal en Belgique", March 18, 2002, available at <www.droit-technologie.org/fr/1_2.asp?actu_id=553>.

[423] Arrêté royal rendant obligatoire la Convention Collective de Travail no. 81 du 26 avril 2002, conclue au sein du Conseil National du travail, relative à la protection de la vie privée des travailleurs à l'égard du contrôle des données de communication électroniques en réseau, Mon. b., pp. 29489-29501.

---

country.   It provides for rules implementing to the specific setting of the workplace the already existing and enforceable European and Belgian general data protection regulations, by ensuring the workers of fairness, information, and compliance with the basic data processing principles of proportionality, purpose specification, and transparency.[424] The data protection authority had previously released an opinion[425] on the same topic in which it refered to the general principles applicable: a general prohibition of the interception of telecommunications, proportionality and transparency, balance of the interests and limited storage of personal data.   Also in the field of workplace privacy, another CCT was released in 1998 to regulate the surveillance of workers by video surveillance cameras.[426]

There are also laws relating to consumer credit,[427] social security,[428] electoral rolls,[429] the national ID number,[430] professional secrets,[431] and employee rights.[432] The Constitution recognizes that "everyone has the right to consult any administrative document and to have a copy made, except in the cases and conditions stipulated by the laws, decrees, or [regional council decrees].[433] There are Freedom of Information laws, implementing this constitutional right, on the right of access to administrative documents on the national[434], regional[435], and

---

[424] Cfr Bertrand Géradin, "La convention collective de travail relative à la protection de la vie privée des travailleurs à l'égard du contrôle des données des communications électroniques en réseau du 26 avril 2002," June 14, 2002.

[425] Commission de la protection de la vie privée, Avis d'initiative relatif à la surveillance par l'employeur de l'utilisation du système informatique sur le lieu de travail, avis no. 10/2000, April 3, 2000, available at <http://www.privacy.fgov.be>.

[426] Convention Collective de Travail No. 68 relative à la protection de la vie privée des travailleurs à l'égard de la surveillance par cameras sur le lieu de travail, June 16, 1998, available at <http://www.privacy.fgov.be/textes_normatifs/cct-68_FR.pdf>.

[427] La loi du 12 juin 1991 relative au crédit à la consommation, http://www.privacy.fgov.be/textes_normatifs/loicrdit.PDF,l'arrêté royal du 11 janvier 1993 modifiant l'arrêté royal du 20 novembre 1992 relatif à l'enregistrement par la Banque Nationale de Belgique des défauts de paiement en matière de crédit à la consommation. <http://194.7.188.126/justice/index_fr.htm>.

[428] Loi du 15 janvier 1990 relative à l'institution et à l'organisation d'une banque-carrefour de la sécurité sociale. Modified by the loi du 29 avril 1996.

[429] Loi du 30 juillet 1991.

[430] Loi du 8 août 1993: le registre national.

[431] Article 458 of the Penal Code.

[432] See Roger Blanpain, Employee Privacy Issues: Belgian Report, 17 Comp. Lab. L. 38, Fall 1995. The employer generally has no right to obtain medical information from his employee, unless the information is absolutely necessary for the appropriate fulfillment of the employee's obligations under the employment contract.

[433] Constitution of Belgium, 1994, available at <http://www.uni-wuerzburg.de/law/be00000_.html>.

[434] Loi (Law) du 11 avril 1994 relative à la publicité de l'administration, loi du 12 novembre 1997 relative à la publicité de l'administration dans les provinces et les communes.

[435] Région flamande (Flemish Region), Décret relatif à la publicité de l'administration, May 18, 1999, Mon. b., June 15, 1999; Région wallonne (Walloon Region), Décret relatif à la publicité de l'administration dans les intercommunales wallonne March 7, 2001, Mon. b., March 20, 2001; Région wallonne (Walloon Region),

---

community levels.[436] The basic exemptions to the general rule of access are public security, the protection of fundamental rights, international interests, public order, security or defense, confidentiality, privacy etc. Each jurisdiction has a Commission d'accès aux documents administratifs which oversees the act.

From the end of 2000, IFPI Belgium, the recording industry trade association, started tracking people downloading and uploading music files from MP3 audio file-sharing web sites such as Napster, Gnutella or KaZaa. In a move that left many Belgian music fans outraged, IFPI collaborated by simple "gentlemen's agreements"[437], and outside any legal framework, with ISPs to get the names and addresses of high-speed Internet connection subscribers in order to send them personalized letters threatening them with legal action if they did not stop their file-sharing practices. In November 2001, the Privacy Commission released an initial opinion[438] severely condemning the way IFPI had behaved with respect to the protection of people's privacy, noticing that they were violating several Belgian and European telecommunications privacy and data protection laws.[439]

The Parliament is currently working on a bill that would implement European Union Directive on electronic commerce[440] into Belgian law.[441]

Belgium is a member of the Council of Europe and has signed and ratified the Convention for the Protection of Individuals with Regard to Automatic Processing of Personal Data (ETS No. 108).[442] It has signed and ratified the

---

Décret relatif à la publicité de l'Administration (March 30, 1995), Mon. b., June 28, 1995, available at <http://www.cass.be/cgi_loi/legislation.pl>.

[436] Commission Communautaire Commune de Bruxelles-Capitale, Ordonnance relative à la publicité de l'administration, June 26, 1997; Commission communautaire française, Décret relatif à la publicité de l'administration, July 11, 1996, Mon. b., August 27, 1996.

[437] Olivier Van Vaerenbergh, "L'IFPI poursuit, mais la justice renâcle – Napster: plaints en Belgique", Le Soir, February 16, 2000.

[438] Avis No. 44/2001 of November 12, 2001, "Avis d'initiative concernant la compatibilité de la recherché d'infractions au droit d'auteur commises sur Internet avec les dispositions juridiques protégeant les données à caractère personnel et les télécommunications", available at <http://www.privacy.fgov.be>.
For additional commentary, see Etienne Wery, "La Commision vie privée n'aime pas les manières de l'IFPI de traquer les pirates sur l'internet" (December 17, 2001), available at <http://www.droit-technologie.org/1_2_1.asp?actu_id=497>.

[439] The Commission found that IFPI had violated Belgian data protection law of December 8, 1992, Belgian telecommunications privacy laws, and European Union Directive 2000/31/EC on electronic commerce. Cfr Avis No. 44/2001, op. cit.

[440] Directive 2000/31/EC of the European Parliament and of the Council of 8 June 2000 on certain legal aspects of information society services, in particular electronic commerce, in the Internal Market, <http://europa.eu.int/cgi-bin/eur-lex/udl.pl?REQUEST=Seek-Deliver&COLLECTION=oj&SERVICE=eurlex&LANGUAGE=en&DOCID=2000l178p0001>.

[441] Avant-projet de loi sur certains aspects juridiques des services de la société de l'information (November 30, 2001), <http://www.droit-technologie.org/3_1.asp?legislation_id=92>.

[442] Signed May 7, 1982, Ratified May 28, 1993, Entered into Force September 1, 1993 .

European Convention for the Protection of Human Rights and Fundamental Freedoms. In November 2001, Belgium signed the Council of Europe Convention on Cybercrime.[443] It is a member of the Organization for Economic Cooperation and Development and has adopted the OECD Guidelines on the Protection of Privacy and Transborder Flows of Personal Data.

Federative Republic of Brazil

Article 5 of the 1988 Constitution of Brazil[444] provides, in part: "the privacy, private life, honor and image of persons are inviolable, and the right to compensation for property or moral damages resulting from their violation is ensured; the home is the inviolable refuge of the individual, and no one may enter therein without the consent of the dweller, except in the event of 'flagrante delicto' or disaster, or to give help, or, during the day, by court order; the secrecy of correspondence and of telegraphic, data and telephone communications is inviolable, except, in the latter case, by court order, in the cases and in the manner prescribed by the law for purposes of criminal investigation or criminal procedural finding of facts; access to information is ensured to everyone and the confidentiality of the source shall be safeguarded, whenever necessary to the professional activity; Finally, the Consitution provides for a unique right named Habeas Data, which guarantees the rights: a) to ensure the knowledge of information related to the person of the petitioner, contained in records or databanks of government agencies or of agencies of a public character; and, b) for the correction of data, when the petitioner does not prefer to do so through a confidential process, either judicial or administrative.

These constitutional guarantees to privacy and data protection have since been augmented with additional statutory protections.

In 1990, Brazilian law provided protection for the privacy of children, outlawing the total or partial unauthorized divulgence of a child or adolescent's name, or police, agency or judicial documents.[445] Soon after, broad consumer rights in data were created under the 1990 Consumer Protection Law[446], which provides that: The consumer will have access to personal data, consumer files and other information stored in files, archives, registries, and databases about themselves,

---

[443] Signed November 23, 2001.

[444] The Constitution of Brazil, 1988, available at <http://www.senado.gov.br/bdtextual/const88/const88i.pdf>.

[445] Law No. 8.069, July 13, 1990

[446] Law No. 8.078, Article 43, September 11, 1990.

as well as about their respective sources. Consumer files and data shall be objective, clear, true, in easily comprehensible language, and shall not contain derogatory information regarding periods prior to five years ago. In addition, the opening of a consumer file, archive, registry, or database should be communicated in writing to the consumer, if not opened at the behest of the consumer. Also, whenever consumers find incorrect data and files concerning their person, they can demand immediate correction, and the archivist shall communicate the due corrections within five days. Finally, once the consumer has settled his/her debts, Credit Protection Services shall not provide any information which may prevent or hinder further access to credit for that consumer.

The Telecommunications Act 1997 states as one of its operating principles that users of telecommunications services have the right to have their privacy respected in the usage of their personal data.[447]

The scope of the constitutional right to *habeas data* was clarified with the passage of additional procedures and definitions in 1997.[448] Under *habeas data*, the individual now has a right to petition for rectification of incorrect data. However, if the maintaining organization disputes or chooses not to make the correction, the petitioner only has the right to annotate the data with an explanation, rather than force a correction.

Finally, the forthcoming Brazilian Civil Code provides further rhetorical protection by declaring, "the private life of an individual is natural and inviolable" and evinces that the judiciary, at the request of an individual, must adopt measures to protect against actions to the contrary.[449]

In addition to the enacted legislation, there are a number of proposed laws under consideration that will affect individual privacy interests. A bill promoting the privacy of personal data in conformance with the OECD guidelines, to affect both public and private sector databases, was proposed in the Senate in 1996 and has yet to be voted on. The bill provides that, "No personal data nor information shall be disclosed, communicated, or transmitted for purposes different than those that led to structuring such data registry or database, without express authorization of the owner, except in case of a court order, and for purposes of a criminal investigation or legal proceedings . . . It is forbidden to gather, register,

---

[447] Law No. 9.472, July 16, 1997. Book 1, Art 3, IX. (Telecommunications Act)
[448] Law No. 9.507, November 12, 1997.
[449] Law No. 10.406, January 12, 1997.

archive, process, and transmit personal data referring to: ethnic origin, political or religious beliefs, physical or mental health, sexual life, police or penal records, family issues, except family relationship, civil status, and marriage system . . . Every citizen is entitled to, without any charge; access to his/her personal data, stored in data registries or databases, and correct, supplement, or eliminate such data, and be informed by data registry or database managers of the existence of data regarding his/her person."[450]

Since then, proposed laws have been introduced both protecting and infringing upon individual privacy. A trio of bills[451] were introduced in the Senate and House requiring ISP's to maintain personally identifiable information such as name, ID #, and address along with all of an individual's Internet connections, including IP address, login & logout time. Divulgence of the information could be made only in accordance with the law, with a penalty for unauthorized indulgence.

A general law was introduced in 1999[452] delineating information crimes, including restrictions on the collection, processing and distribution of information. In addition, it would outlaw computer crimes such as unauthorized access to or alteration of data or computer programs.

Finally, in 2000, evincing a concern with data profiling practices, a law[453] was proposed to restrict collection of personal data and data residing on an individuals computer. The proposal states that such data can only be collected with prior notice, under the express permission of the subject, and used for the sole purpose for which it was collected, under penalty of a statutory fine.

In addition to laws specifically addressing individual privacy rights and data protection, Brazil has apparently unrelated laws and treaties that have privacy implications. The Brazilian national policy on access to government information[454] grants individuals the right to receive information of general or individual concern. However, the right is self-limited by individual privacy: "the inviolable intimacy, private life, and honor and image of people."

---

[450] Proposed Law No. 61, 1996.

[451] Proposed Law No. 151, 2000; Proposed Law No. 3891, 2000; Proposed Law No. 4.972, 2001.

[452] Proposed Law No. 84, 1999.

[453] Proposed Law No. 3.360, 2000.

[454] Law No. 8.159, January 8, 1991. Chapter 1, Article 4.

Brazil signed the American Convention on Human Rights[455] on September 25, 1992. The Convention provides that every person has "the right to have his honor respected and his dignity recognized." Additionally, "no one may be the object of arbitrary or abusive interference with his private life, his family, his home, or his correspondence, or of unlawful attacks on his honor or reputation. And, everyone has the right to the protection of the law against such interference or attacks."

In 1996, a law regulating wiretapping was enacted.[456] Official wiretaps are permitted for 15 days, renewable on a judge's order for another 15 days, and can only be resorted to in cases where police suspect serious crimes punishable by imprisonment, such as drug smuggling, corruption, contraband smuggling, murder and kidnapping. The granting of judicial eavesdropping permits by judges was previously an ad hoc process without any legal basis.[457] Illegal wiretapping by police and intelligence agencies is still common. In 1992, amid a scandal that toppled President Fernando Collor de Mello, it was discovered that Vice President Itamar Franco's phones at his official residence in Brasilia and in a Rio de Janeiro hotel room had been tapped.[458] Several ministers resigned in 1998 after tapes of wiretapped conversation involving the Brazilian Development Bank were disclosed in what was called the "Telegate scandal." The Agencies Brasileira de Informacoes (Abin) was suspected of wiretapping President Cardoso after tapes of his conversations were leaked to the press in May 1999.[459] A newsmagazine released wiretaps in 2000 implicating a powerful former presidential aide, a member of the economic cabinet, a senator and several congressional deputies in an illegal patronage and influence-trafficking network.[460]

The Federal Penal Code was altered in 2000 to criminalize certain information crimes. The insertion of false data into an information system is punished by a prison sentence of 2 to 12 years. Unauthorized alteration of an information system is punishable by detention from 3 months to 2 years.

---

[455] American Convention on Human Rights, Article 11, July 18, 1978, available at <http://www1.umn.edu/humanrts/oasinstr/zoas3con.htm>.

[456] Law No. 9.296, July 24, 1996.

[457] "Brazil makes police phone-taps legal," Reuters World Service, July 24, 1996.

[458] "Brazil vice-president claims his phone was tapped," Reuters North American Wire, September 9, 1992.

[459] "Is Abin behind Telegate?," Latin America Weekly Report, June 8, 1999.

[460] "Wiretaps Lift Brazilian Scandal Into Top Ranks of Government," New York Times, July 15, 2000

Republic of Bulgaria

The Bulgarian Constitution of 1991 recognizes rights of privacy, secrecy of communications and access to information. Article 32 states, "(1) The privacy of citizens shall be inviolable. Everyone shall be entitled to protection against any illegal interference in his private or family affairs and against encroachments on his honor, dignity and reputation. (2) No one shall be followed, photographed, filmed, recorded or subjected to any other similar activity without his knowledge or despite his express disapproval, except when such actions are permitted by law." Article 33 states, "(1) The home shall be inviolable. No one shall enter or stay inside a home without its occupant's consent, except in the cases expressly stipulated by law. (2) Entry into, or staying inside, a home without the consent of its occupant or without the judicial authorities' permission shall be allowed only for the purposes of preventing an immediately impending crime or a crime in progress, for the capture of a criminal, or in extreme necessity." Article 34 states, "(1) The freedom and confidentiality of correspondence and all other communications shall be inviolable. (2) Exceptions to this provision shall be allowed only with the permission of the judicial authorities for the purpose of discovering or preventing a grave crime." Article 41 states, "(1) Everyone shall be entitled to seek, obtain and disseminate information. This right shall not be exercised to the detriment of the rights and reputation of others, or to the detriment of national security, public order, public health and morality. (2) Citizens shall be entitled to obtain information from state bodies and agencies on any matter of legitimate interest to them which is not a state or other secret prescribed by law and does not affect the rights of others."[461]

The Personal Data Protection Act was adopted by the National Assembly in December 2001 and came into effect in January 2002. Adoption of the law was a key part of the administrative reforms being undertaken in preparation for accession to the European Union. The law closely follows the European Union Data Protection Directive. It sets out rules for the fair and responsible handling of personal information by the public and private sector. Personal information is defined as "any information relating to a natural person, legal entity or group of individuals revealing physical, psychological, mental, economic, cultural or social identity, regardless of the form or method used for its recording."[462] Entities collecting personal information must inform people why their personal

---

[461] Constitution of the Republic of Bulgaria of 13 July 1991, available at <http://www.uni-wuerzburg.de/law/bu00t___.html>.

[462] "Bulgarian Assembly Passes Personal Data Protection Bill on First Reading," BBC Worldwide Monitoring, November 13, 2001.

information is being collected and what it is to be used for; allow people reasonable access to information about themselves and the right to correct it if it is wrong; ensure that the information is securely held and cannot be tampered with, stolen or improperly used; and limit the use of personal information, for purposes other than the original purpose, without the consent of the person affected, or in certain other circumstances. Sensitive information, including information concerning racial or ethic origin, political or religious affiliation, health, sexual life, and beliefs, is given special protection and can only be processed with the express written consent of an individual.[463] Some concerns have been raised that the law is over broad in scope. The Bulgarian Access to Information Programme note that the definition of "personal data" includes information relating to the performance of government officials and management or supervisory bodies of legal entities and as such may have a negative impact on access to information rights and government accountability.[464]

The law creates a Commission on Protection of Personal Data, to supervise compliance and implementation; maintain a national register of data controllers; examine complaints and take legal action for violations. The members of the Commission and the Chairperson serve a five-year term and may be re-elected once. They are nominated by the President and approved by the National Assembly. The first Commission was established in June 2002.

Separate laws are expected to be introduced in Bulgaria to regulate the processing of information for the purposes of law enforcement and national security; the judicial, health and insurance systems; the postal service and telecommunications; and research and statistics. [465]

Electronic surveillance used in criminal investigations is regulated by the criminal code and requires a court order.[466] The Telecommunications Law also requires that agencies must ensure the secrecy of communications.[467] The 1997 Special Surveillance Means Act regulates the use of surveillance techniques by the Interior Ministry for investigating crime but also for loosely defined national security reasons. A court order is generally required but the Ministry of the Interior has a discretionary power to authorize wiretaps without judicial review.

---

[463] "The Current Situation of the Access to Public Information in Bulgaria in 2001," Access to Information Project 2002, available at <http://www.aip-bg.org>.

[464] Id.

[465] "Draft Bulgarian Personal Data Protection Act Examined," by Vladimir M. Vassilev, World Data Protection Report, Volume 1, Issue 5, May 2001

[466] Article 170-171 (1) (As amended - SG, Nos. 28/1982, 10/1993).

[467] Telecommunications Law, Article 5.

The full extent of this power is not well known but there are regular complaints of abusive and illegal bugging of individuals.

In January 2001, it was announced that approximately 10,000 wiretaps were authorized during the year 2000. According to the Bulgarian Helsinki Federation only two to three percent of the intercepts were ever used in criminal proceedings.[468] No reasons for this surveillance were given.[469] A Parliamentary Commission held hearings in 2001 on the activities of "public order "agencies which includes the National Intelligence Service, the National Bodyguard Service and the National Security Service[470] In October 2001 the Interior Ministry reported that they had found illegal wiretapping devices, in recording mode, in the Central Telephone Exchange in Sofia and preparations for such devices in a number of the city's other exchanges. The bugging of telephone subscribers had been taking place since 1994 and was said to be economically motivated.[471] In November 2001, the director of the National Security Service (NSS) resigned his position. A number of allegations of wiretapping politicians had been made against him but these were never substantiated.[472] In August 2000, listening devices were found in the apartment of the Prosecutor General Nikola Filchev and several politicians. Filchev blamed the bugs on the Interior Ministry's Criminal Intelligence Service (CIS). A parliamentary session was held after 53 Democratic Left Parliamentarians demanded a hearing.[473] Following the debate members of the opposition Bulgarian Socialist Party [BSP] submitted draft amendments to put in place a system of judicial oversight for the use of surveillance.[474] In November 2000, the Movement for Rights and Freedoms (DPS), a party of Ethnic Turks, reported that its leaders were being monitored by the security services.[475]

In December 1998, the Bulgarian Committee for Post and Telecommunications issued an executive decree to license Internet Service Providers. The decree gave

---

468 Annual Report of the Bulgarian Helsinki Committee, "Human Rights in Bulgaria in 2000," March 2001 available at <http://www.bghelsinki.org/frames-reports.htm>.

469 Annual report of the Bulgarian Helsinki Committee, "Human Rights in Bulgaria in 2001," March 2002 available at <http://www.bghelsinki.org/frames-reports.htm>.

470 United States Department of State, Country Reports on Human Rights Practices 2001, March 4,2002 available at <http://www.state.gov/g/drl/rls/hrrpt/2001/eur/8238.htm>.

471 "Buggin Affair 'Economically Motivated', Interior Ministry Says," BBC Worldwide Monitoring, October 4, 2001.

472 "Security Chief Says 'Low Confidence' in Office Led to Resignation," BBC Worldwide Monitoring, November 28, 2001.

473 "Buggate Scandalizes Bulgaria." Transitions online, 31 July - 6 August 2000.

474 "Courts Should Be Involved In Controlling Bugging Devices," The British Broadcasting Corporation, August 09, 2000.

475 "Security Services Bugged Ethnic Turk's Leaders," BBC Worldwide Monitoring, November 26, 2000.

governmental employees the authorization to enter ISPs' offices at any time and obtain any documentation, including user names and passwords, as well as other private information.[476] The decision was extensively criticized by Internet users, service providers and others, including German Chancellor Shroeder who said that licensing was not appropriate. The Bulgarian Internet Society (ISOC) chapter filed a case at the Supreme Administrative Court to stop the decree in January 1999. The Court ordered a temporary restraint of the decree on June 17, 1999. In November 1999, the Bulgarian Prime Minister ordered the Minister of Telecommunications to negotiate an out of court agreement with ISOC. A few weeks later, the decree was changed, and the ISPs were removed from the licensing requirements and placed in the "free regime" category.

There are additional provisions relating to privacy in laws such as the Statistics Law, Tax Administration Law, Insurance Law,[477] and Social Assistance Law.[478] The Radio and Television Act sets limits[479] on broadcasting of personal information.

The Law for Access to Information to provide access to government records was enacted in June 2000 and went into force in July 2001.[480] The law allows for access to records except in cases of state security or personal privacy. Amendment of the Act is currently underway in order to implement Council of Europe Recommendation R(2000)2 on Access to Official Documents, adopted in Febraury 2001.[481] A new Archives Act is also pending. The 1997 Access to Documents of the Former State Security Service Act regulates the access, proceedings of disclosure and use of information kept in the documents of the former State Security Service. A draft Classified Information Protection Act has been introduced to further restrict access to classified information.[482]

Bulgaria is a member of the Council of Europe and has signed and ratified the European Convention for the Protection of Human Rights and Fundamental Freedoms.[483] It has signed but not ratified the Convention for the Protection of

---

[476] Committee for Post and Telecommunications, "List of telecommunication services, December 18, 1998. published in the State Gazette on December 29. 1998.

[477] Insurance Law, Article7 par. 1.

[478] Social Assistance Law, Article 32 par. 2.

[479] Radio and Television Act, Articles 10, 15.

[480] Access to Public Information Act (draft), available at <http://www.aip-bg.org/documents/access.htm>.

[481] The Current Situation of the Access to Public Information in Bulgaria in 2001," Access to Information Project 2002, available at <http://www.aip-bg.org>.

[482] Id.

[483] Signed May 10, 1992; Ratified September 7,1992; Entered into force September 7, 1992.

Individuals with Regard to Automatic Processing of Personal Data (ETS No. 108).[484] In November 2001, Bulgaria signed the Council of Europe Cybercrime Convention(ETS No. 185).[485]

Canada

There is no explicit right to privacy in Canada's Constitution and Charter of Rights and Freedoms.[486] However, in interpreting Section 8 of the Charter, which grants the right to be secure against unreasonable search or seizure, Canada's courts have recognized an individual's right to a reasonable expectation of privacy.[487]

Privacy is regulated at both the federal and provincial level. At the federal level, privacy is protected by two acts: the 1982 federal Privacy Act and the 2001 Personal Information and Electronic Documents Act (PIPEDA).

The federal Privacy Act of 1982 regulates the collection, use and disclosure of personal information held by federal public agencies and provides individuals a right of access to personal information held by those agencies, subject to some exceptions.[488] Individuals can appeal to a federal court for review if access to their records is denied by an agency, but are not authorized to challenge the collection, use, or disclosure of information. In 1999, in order to tighten exemptions and loopholes, the Privacy Commissioner finished an extensive review of the Act and recommended over 100 changes to the law to improve and update it. Some of the changes included giving the Commission primary authority over all information collected by the federal government, extending its coverage beyond "recorded" information, increasing notice of disclosures, expanding court reviews, creating rules on data matching, controlling "publicly available" information and expanding the mandate of the Privacy Commissioner.[489]

---

[484] Signed June 2, 1998.

[485] Signed November 23, 2001.

[486] *Canadian Charter of Rights and Freedoms*, Part I of the *Constitution Act, 1982*, being Schedule B to the *Canada Act 1982* (United Kingdom), 1982, c. 11, s. 8, online: Department of Justice <http://laws.justice.gc.ca/en/charter/> (date accessed: 25 May 2002).

[487] Hunter v. Southam, 2 S.C.R. 145, 159-60 (1984).

[488] Privacy Act, c. P-21, available at <http://canada.justice.gc.ca/stable/EN/Laws/Chap/P/P-21.html>.

[489] Privacy Commissioner, 1999-2000 Annual Report, May 2000, available at <http://www.privcom.gc.ca/english/02_04_08_e.htm>.

The Personal Information Protection and Electronic Documents Act (PIPEDA) was approved by Parliament in April 2000.[490] The Act adopts the CSA International Privacy Code (a national standard: CAN/CSA-Q830-96) into law for private sector organizations that process personal information "in the course of a commercial activity," and for federally regulated employers with respect to their employees. It does not apply to information collected for personal, journalistic, artistic, literary, or non-commercial purposes. Part 1 of the PIPEDA establishes the parameters for the collection, use, disclosure, retention, and disposal of personal information. It sets out 10 privacy principles as standards that organizations must comply with when dealing with personal information including: accountability, purpose, openness, consent, limiting use and collection, disclosure, retention, individual access, safeguards, accuracy, and challenging compliance. Part 2 deals with the use of electronic transactions and documents to facilitate electronic commerce and electronic communication within judicial proceedings.

PIPEDA has a tiered implementation schedule. In January 2001, it went into effect for personal information, excluding health information, held by federally regulated private sector entities, such as telecommunications and broadcasting businesses, banks and airlines, or businesses and organizations that disclose personal information across provincial or national borders. Health information was excluded for one year as a last minute concession to a powerful health sector lobby. As of January 1, 2002, personal health information processed by the organizations outlined above is covered by the Act. In January 2004, the Act will finally extend to every organization that collects, uses, or discloses personal information in the course of a commercial activity, whether or not the organization is federally regulated. It will cover all commercial activity in provincially regulated sectors unless the province enacts "substantially similar" laws, such as those of Québec.

In January 2001, the Data Protection Working Party of the European Commission issued a decision stating that PIPEDA provided an adequate level of protection for certain personal data transferred from the European Union to Canada.[491] This will allow certain personal data to flow freely from the European Union to recipients in Canada subject to PIPEDA without additional safeguards being needed to meet the requirements of the European Union Data Protection

---

[490] Bill C-6, Personal Information Protection and Electronic Documents Act, available at <http://www.parl.gc.ca/36/2/parlbus/chambus/house/bills/government/C-6/C-6_4/C-6_cover-E.html>.

[491] European Union Article 29 Data Protection Working Group, Opinion 2/2001 on the Adequacy of the Canadian Personal Information and Electronic Documents Act, January 26, 2001, available at <http://europa.eu.int/comm/internal_market/en/dataprot/wpdocs/wp39en.htm>.

Directive. However, the Commission's decision of adequacy does not cover any personal data held by federal sector or provincial bodies or information held by personal organizations and used for non-commercial purposes, such as data handled by charities or collected in the context of an employment relationship.[492] For this, transfers to recipients in Canada, operators in the European Union will have to put in place additional safeguards, such as the standard contractual clauses adopted by the Commission in June 2001 before exporting the data.

Both the Privacy Act and PIPEDA are overseen by the independent Privacy Commissioner of Canada.[493] Under the Privacy Act the Commissioner has the power to investigate, mediate, and make recommendations, but cannot issue orders or impose penalties. During the course of an investigation the Commissioner may subpoena witnesses and compel testimony, and enter premises in order to obtain documents and conduct interviews. The Commissioner is also charged with conducting periodic audits of federal institutions to determine compliance with the Privacy Act, and to recommend changes where necessary. The Commissioner can initiate a Federal Court review in limited circumstances relating to denial of access to records.

Between April 1, 2000, and March 31, 2001, the office received a total of 1,713 complaints under the Privacy Act, an almost ten percent increase from the previous year.[494] The office closed 1,542 investigations, again an increase of 10 percent from the previous year. 339 of these cases related to issues of collection, use, disclosure, or disposal, 630 related to access, and 573 to time limits.[495] Since November 2001, the office has received more than 8,047 requests for information concerning the Privacy Act.[496]

The Commissioner's powers under PIPEDA are very similar to those under the Privacy Act. Again, the Commissioner has powers of recommendation only with regard to complaints submitted under the Act. Once a complaint is received, the Commissioner assigns an investigator to look into the matter. The investigator then submits his findings to the Commissioner who then considers the case and issues a report with recommendations. He can also request the organization in

---

[492] Commission Decision of December 20, 2001, Official Journal of the European Communities L 2/13, available at <http://www.europa.eu.int/comm/internal_market/dataprot/adequacy/canada-faq_en.htm>

[493] Privacy Commissioner of Canada Homepage<http://www.privcom.gc.ca>.

[494] Privacy Commissioner of Canada Annual Report to Parliament 2000-2001, Part One–Report on the Privacy Act, December 2001, available at <http://www.privcom.gc.ca/information/ar/02_04_09_e.asp#000.htm>.
[495] Id.

[496] Email from Dona Vallieres, Senior Director General, Communications and Policy, Privacy Commission of Canada to Nicole Anastasopoulos, Research Assistant, Electronic Privacy Information Center, July 10, 2002 (on file with the Electronic Privacy Information Center).

question to submit, with a specified period of time, notice of any action taken or proposed to be taken to implement these recommendations.[497] However, if the Commissioner is satisfied that there are reasonable grounds to investigate a matter under the Act, he may initiate his own complaint.[498] Under PIPEDA the Commissioner is also authorized to conduct broad research into privacy issues and promote awareness and understanding of privacy issues among Canadians.

The Office of the Privacy Commissioner began receiving complaints under PIPEDA on January 1, 2001. By January 17, 2001, it was reported that the office had already received four formal requests for investigations and numerous telephone inquiries.[499] As of November 2001, the Office had received more than 8,859[500] requests for information concerning PIPEDA, 95 formal complaints (half of which involved banks) and initiated 198 investigations.[501] The Commissioner's office completed and issued findings and recommendations on 27 complaints.[502]

The Privacy Commissioner of Canada has been very active in a number of high profile cases. For example under the Privacy Act he has investigated:

- Canadian Customs and Revenue Agency (CCRA) following reports that customs officials were opening mail coming into Canada and passing information relating to immigration cases to Citizenship and Immigration Canada (CIC).[503]
- Human Resources Development Canada (HRDC) regarding the existence of a government database called the Longitudinal Labour Force File, which could contain up to 2,000 pieces of information on Canadian citizens.[504] Department of National Defense (DND) for workplace

---

[497] See generally , "Your Privacy Responsibilities: A Guide for Business and Organizations," Office of the Privacy Commissioner of Canada, December 2000.

[498] Stephanie Perrin, Heather Black, David Flaherty and T. Murray Rankin, The Personal Information Protection and Electronic Documents Act: An Annotated Guide (Toronto, 2001).

[499] Tyler Hamilton, "Confidentiality Fears Swamping Privacy Watchdog," The Toronto Star, January 17, 2001.

[500] Email from Dona Vallieres, Privacy Commission of Canada, to EPIC supra, n.496.

[501] Privacy Commissioner of Canada Annual Report to Parliament 2000-2001, Part Two– Report on the Personal Information Protection and Electronic Documents Act, December 2001, available at <http://www.privcom.gc.ca/information/ar/02_04_09_e.asp#000.htm>.

[502] Id.

[503] Office of the Privacy Commissioner, News Release, March 19, 2001, available at <http://www.privcom.gc.ca/media/nr-c/02_05_b_010319_e.asp>.

[504] Minister of Human Resources Development Canada, HRDC Dismantles Longitudinal Labour Force File Databank, News Release, May 29, 2000, available at <http://www.hrdc-drhc.gc.ca/common/news/dept/00-39.html>

privacy violations, which entailed accessible online employee information.[505]

Under PIPEDA the Commissioner has investigated:
- Air Canada for sharing its customers' personal and financial information with its partners.[506]
- U.S-based international marketing firm that was disclosing personal information by gathering and selling data on physicians' prescribing patterns.[507]
- A Canadian bank's refusal to grant a customer's request for access to their credit score.[508]

Since last year, the federal Privacy Commissioner initiated two important surveillance cases that have created much controversy in Canada and are considered to be of national importance as they may set the standards for the future use of private and public surveillance cameras in Canada. While both the Kelowna and Yellowknife cases refer to privacy violated through closed circuit television, the former was a public safety issue, while the latter a commercial case.

On February 22, 2001, the Royal Canadian Mountain Police (RCMP) began video surveillance of downtown Kelowna with the aim to prevent or deter crime. According to the Privacy Commissioner this kind of monitoring and recording was considered to be excessive of the legal requirement to collect only the minimal amount of personal information required for the intended purpose.[509] The RCMP Commissioner complied with the Privacy Commissioner's request to cease continuous recording except when a violation of the law is detected, in which case the area under surveillance will be videotaped. The Privacy Commissioner did not consider this an adequate response and on June 21, 2002, announced that he is launching a Charter challenge of the RCMP's video surveillance activities as a contravention of the Canadian Charter of Rights and Freedoms, arguing the surveillance was excessive and intrusive. The Privacy Commissioner is concerned that there is no guarantee that the cameras are not

---

[505]Privacy Commissioner of Canada Annual Report to Parliament 2000-2001, Part One, supra n.494.

[506] Letter from Privacy Commissioner George Radwanski to Air Canada, July 18, 2001, available at <http://www.privcom.gc.ca/media/nr-c/02_05_b_010718_e.asp>.

[507] Federal Privacy Commissioner George Radwanski Findings-September 21, 2001, available at <http://www.privcom.gc.ca/cf-dc/cf-dc_010921_e.asp>.

[508] Office of the Privacy Commissioner, News Release, February 27, 2002, available at <http://privcom.gc.ca/media.an/wn_020227_e.asp>.

[509] Office of the Privacy Commissioner, News Release, October 4, 2001 available at <http://privomc.goc.ca/media/nr-c/02_05_b_011004_e.asp>.

recording at all times and that this case will lead to the proliferation of video surveillance cameras in public spaces as well as citizen profiling.[510]

In June 2001, the Commissioner investigated a case concerning the installation of security cameras in the town of Yellowknife by a local security company, Centurion Security Services. The company installed surveillance cameras on the main street to monitor crimes as a marketing demonstration intended to generate business. The Commissioner issued a decision stating that both live video pictures and recorded video pictures of individuals would qualify as "personal information" under the Act and therefore could only be collected with consent of the individuals. The Commissioner also stated that since the company's video surveillance activity was a commercial activity, PIPEDA rules apply, and public places should only be monitored for public safety reasons where a demonstrated need had been shown, and not for commercial activities without individuals' consent.[511]

Part VI of Canada's Criminal Code makes the unlawful interception of private communications a criminal offense.[512] Police are required to obtain a court order and interception is only authorized in cases "where other investigative procedures are unlikely to succeed." In December 2000, the Supreme Court of Canada clarified this requirement, stating that in order to obtain a wiretapping warrant police must submit documents showing that "there is no other reasonable alternative method of investigation." The Court stressed that it is not enough to show that wiretaps are simply the most efficient way to investigate a crime because this standard could threaten civil liberties.[513] Amendments to the Radiocommunication Act[514] also forbid the divulgence of intercepted radio-based telephone communications. The Canadian Security Intelligence Service Act[515] authorizes the interception of communications for national security reasons. A federal court in Ottawa ruled in 1997 that the Canadian Security Intelligence Service was required to obtain a warrant in all cases.[516]

---

[510] Office of the Privacy Commissioner, News Release, 21, 2001, available at <http://www.privcom.gc.ca/media/nr_c/02_05_b_020621>.

[511] Office of the Privacy Commissioner, News Release, June 20, 2001, available at <http://www.privcom.gc.ca/media/nr-c/nt_010620_e.asp>.

[512] Criminal Code, c. C-46. ss. 184, 184.5, 193, 193.1.

[513] Janice Tibbetts, "Top Court Sets Ground Rules For Wiretaps," The Ottawa Citizen, December 15, 2000.

[514] Radiocommunication Act, R.S.C. 1985, c. R-2, s. 9.

[515] Chapter C-23, Canadian Security Intelligence Service Act, <http://canada.justice.gc.ca/STABLE/EN/Laws/Chap/C/C-23.html>.

[516] "CSIS has wiretap green light," The Hamilton Spectator, October 1, 1997.

In October 1998, Industry Minister John Manley announced a new Liberal government policy for encryption that allows for broad development, use, and dissemination of encryption products.[517] There are no restrictions on the private use of encryption in Canada.

The Telecommunications Act[518] has provisions to protect the privacy of individuals, including the regulation of unsolicited communications. Also, the Bank Act,[519] Insurance Companies Act,[520] and Trust and Loan Companies Act[521] permit regulations regarding the use of information provided by customers. A poll in April 1999 found that 88 percent of people said the government should "not allow banks to use information about their customers' bank accounts and other investments to try to sell customers' insurance."[522] There are sectoral laws for pensions,[523] video surveillance,[524] immigration,[525] and Social Security.[526] The Young Offenders Act[527] regulates the information that can be disclosed about offenders under the age of 18 while the Corrections and Conditional Release Act[528] speaks to the information that can be disclosed to victims and their families.

The events of September 11th caused much concern in Canada about the need for government policy to protect against future terrorist activity. In response to public safety concerns, the government hastily introduced legislation, Bill C-36, designed to institute the necessary procedures and mechanisms to define, deter, and punish terrorism at home and cooperate with other states abroad.[529]

As originally introduced the bill ambiguously defined terrorist groups and terrorist activity; made it an offense to knowingly participate or facilitate, harbor,

---

[517] Industry Canada, Building Trust in the Digital Economy, available at <http://e-com.ic.gc.ca/english/crypto/631d1.html>.

[518] Telecommunications Act, 1993, c. 38, s. 39, s. 41.

[519] Bank Act, c. 46, ss. 242, 244, 459.

[520] Insurance Companies Act, s. 489, s. 607.

[521] Trust and Loan Companies Act, s. 444.

[522] "88% of Canadians Oppose Banks Target-Marketing Insurance: Compass Poll," Canada Newswire, April 27, 1999.

[523] Canada Pension Plan, R.S.C. 1985, c. C-8, s. 104.07.

[524] Criminal Code, c. C-46, s. 487.01.

[525] Immigration Act, S.C. 1985, c. I-2, s. 110.

[526] Old Age Security Act, c. O-9, s. 33.01.

[527] Young Offenders Act, C. Y-1, s. 38.

[528] Corrections and Conditional Release Act, 1992, c. 20, s. 26, 142.

[529] Department of Justice Press Release, 'Government of Canada introduces Anti-Terrorist Act," October 15, 2001, available at <http://canada.justice.gc.ca/en/news/nr/2001/doc_27785.html>.

or fund terrorist activity; increased police electronic surveillance tools; limited disclosure of information and increased exemptions on access to subject data for national security reasons; required individuals with knowledge of a terrorist activity to be detained "preventively" and appear before a judge to offer information under the pretense of "investigative hearings," and substantially enhanced the interception capabilities and investigative powers of security services. The bill would have also given the Attorney General of Canada the power to issue blanket certificates that prohibit the disclosure of any information for the purpose of protecting international relations, national defense, or security. Critics were concerned with the bill's limited oversight applications and sunset clauses, and with the possibility that the government, by issuing certificates, could render federal privacy law powerless, especially against the power of Canadian Security Intelligence Services (CSIS) and other security departments or agencies.

Due to widespread protest,[530] the bill was amended with provisions that preventative arrest and investigative hearing powers would sunset after five years unless the government extended them[531] The bill also stated that ministers responsible for policing would now be required to report annually to Parliament on the use of preventative arrest and investigative hearing provisions Provisions dealing with Attorney General certificates would be amended so that the certificate could no longer be issued at any time, but only after an order or decision for disclosure has been made in a proceeding. The certificates would also be subject to review by a judge of the Federal Court of Appeal. A new interpretive clause was set which clarified that any political, religious, or ideological beliefs would not be considered a terrorist activity unless they specifically met the definition of "terrorist activity." Finally, some of the bill's measures would be subject to parliamentary review in three years. While the federal Privacy Commissioner George Radwanski was satisfied that these amendments would safeguard privacy rights, the Information Commissioner John

---

[530] This was the general consensus at the University of Toronto Law School's conference "The Security of Freedom," in November 2001, where law faculty and leading experts in criminology and political science analyzed Bill C-36 and questioned the government's efforts to expand its powers at the expense of civil rights and liberties. The presenters called for increased "democratic deliberation" and were skeptical not only of the transfer of emergency powers to the state, but were also concerned whether these new criminal laws and tougher penalties would prevent such crimes in the future. There were concerns regarding the bill's expansion of information gathering and information suppressing powers, which could threaten citizens' privacy and lead to information warehousing, profiling, or the monitoring of legitimate political protests and the stifling of legitimate speechapter Finally there were concerns with the bill's excessive preventative arrest provisions and limited safeguards, sunset clauses, and oversight measures. Ronald Daniels, Patrick Maclem, and Kent Roachapter (Eds). The Security of Freedom: Essays on Canada's Anti-Terrorism Bill. (Toronto, 2001).

[531] Department of Justice. Amendments to Bill C-36. News Release, available at <http://canada.justice.gc.ca/en/news/nr/2001/doc_27902.html>

Reid, among others, expressed concern that the amendments to the bill did not go far enough.[532] The Bill passed into law on December 2001.

Five weeks after tabling Bill C-36, the government introduced a complementary bill, the Public Safety Act (Bill C-42). The bill amended 19 existing acts and enacted new statutes to implement the Biological and Toxin Weapons Convention of 1975. Due to heavy criticism both within government and from the public, Bill C-42 was abandoned because it increased government surveillance power at the expense of civil liberties. The controversy centered around four provisions. The first allowed the Minister of National Defense to authorize the interception of private communication; the second gave the responsible minister the power to make interim orders in situations where immediate action is necessary; the third proposed information sharing among security agencies and federal departments to allow for screening of airline and travel agents' passenger information; and the fourth gave the Minister of National Defense the power to establish temporary military security zones for the protection of international relations, defense or security for up to a year, but which could be renewed.[533] Critics were concerned that this would allow the Minister to designate as a military security zone an area where an international summit meeting is taking place.[534]

In April 2002, Bill C-42 was abandoned and the government proposed Bill C-55, the Public Safety Act 2002, which included many of Bill C-42's provisions, but also incorporated many amendments to improve the legislation.[535] The Bill included most of Bill C-42's controversial proposals including ministers' interim powers, information-sharing power of passenger lists between security agencies and federal departments, and the establishment of temporary military zones. Important amendments were, however, included so that federal ministers' powers to suspend environmental, health, and other laws in emergencies and issue decrees in the name of national security must now be approved by the full cabinet within 45 days. The provision regarding the information-sharing of passenger lists restricted this information only to a small group of security agencies and only for restricted purposes such as transportation security, the Air Carrier Protective Program, warrants of arrest for serious offences, and counter-

---

[532] Federal Privacy Commission News Release. "Amendments to Bill C-36," November 21, 2001, available at <http://www.privcom.gc.ca/media/nr-c/02_05_b_011121_e.asp>.

[533] David Goetz et al., Library of Parliament, Parliamentary Research Branch, Bill C-42: The Public Safety Act LS-419E (2001).

[534] Id.

[535] Bruce, Cheadle, "Despite Liberal Unease over Revamped Anti-Terror Bill, PM Promises Fast Track," Canadian Press Newswire, May 6, 2002.

terrorism.[536] In June 2002, the Federal Privacy Commissioner publicly expressed his concern with this provision, stating that it went far beyond the purported anti-terrorism and security aims of the legislation and would "strike unjustifiably" at Canadians' right to privacy and anonymity.[537] Finally, "military security zones" were replaced by "controlled access military zones" with amendments restricting time and renewal of zones and requiring public notification.[538] The bill is still being debated in parliament.

The Federal Access to Information Act[539] provides individuals with a right of access to information held by the federal public sector. The Act gives Canadians and other individuals and corporations present in Canada the right to apply for and obtain copies of federal government records. "Records" include letters, memos, reports, photographs, films, microforms, plans, drawings, diagrams, maps, sound and video recordings, and machine-readable or computer files. About 12,000 requests are made annually for government records.[540] The Commissioner can initiate a Federal Court review in limited circumstances relating to denial of access to records.

The Office of the Information Commissioner of Canada oversees the Act.[541] The Commissioner can investigate and issue recommendations, but does not have power to issue binding orders. The Office handed 1,670 complaints in 1998-99. It also released report cards on several agencies and issued seven subpoenas to government officials. The Canadian Federal Court has ruled that government has an obligation to answer all access requests regardless of the perceived motives of the requesters. Similarly, the commissioner must investigate all complaints even if the government seeks to block him from so doing on the grounds that the complaints are made for an improper purpose. Each of the provinces also has a Freedom of Information Law.[542]

According to the Access to Information Review Task Force's June 2002 Report, 'Access to Information: Making it Work for Canadians,' "Canadians are making

---

[536] Solicitor General of Canada, RCMP and CSIS Access to Airline Passenger Information, available at <www.sgc.gc.ca/Epub/POL/eAirPassInfo.htm>.

[537] Federal Privacy Commission. News Release, "Amendments to Bill C-55," June 18, 2002.

[538] Department of National Defense Newsroom, "New Public Safety Act Proposes Amendments to the National Defense Act," April 2002, available at www.dnd.ca/eng/archive/2002/apr02/3ONDA_b_e.htm>.

[539] Access to Information Act, C. A-1.

[540] Office of the Information Commissioner of Canada, Annual Report 1998-9, July 21, 1999. <http://fox.nstn.ca/~smulloy/oic98_9e.pdf>.

[541] Information Commissioner of Canada <http://magi.com/~accessca/>.

[542] See Alasdair Roberts, Limited Access: Assessing the Health of Canada's Freedom of Information Laws, April 1998. <http://qsilver.queensu.ca/~foi/foi.pdf>.

---

relatively modest use of the Access to Information Act.... After 20 years, the Act is still not well-understood by the public."[543] The report, moreover, goes on to state that the events of September 11th require one to balance the government's need to protect sensitive information with the public's right to access information and suggests 139 recommendations for modernizing access to information.[544]

Canada is a member of the OECD and relied the OECD's 1980 Guidelines on the Protection of Privacy and Transborder Flows of Personal Data in the drafting of the federal Privacy Act of 1982.[545] Canada also has observer status at the Council of Europe and although it was not a member, it was a key player in the negotiations on the Cybercrime Convention. It has signed, but not yet ratified the Convention.[546]

Provinces

Privacy legislation on a provincial level is separated into three categories: (a) public sector (data protection) law, (b) private sector law and (c) sector-specific laws. Public sector legislation covering government bodies exists in almost all provinces and territories.[547] Nearly every province has some sort of oversight body, but they vary in their powers and scope of regulation. New Brunswick and Prince Edward Island were the last provincial governments to introduce provincial public sector legislation. With the passing of these two acts, every territory and province in Canada, except Newfoundland and Labrador, will have statutory protection for personal information held by government agencies.

In May 2002, the Federal Privacy Commissioner sent a report to Parliament concerning provincial legislation that is "substantially similar" to the federal PIPEDA. According to the report, every province has passed privacy legislation for the public sector, while Québec has comprehensive protection for both the private and public sectors. The commissioner only considers Quebec's Respecting the Protection of Personal Information in the Private Sector legislation to be substantially similar to PIPEDA in terms of protecting personal

---

[543] Report of the Access to Information Review Task Force. June 2002 Report Access to Information: Making it Work for Canadians. June 2002. <http: www.atirtf-geai-gc.ca/accessreport-e.pdf>.

[544] Access to Information: Making it Work for Canadians, June 12, 2002.

[545] Stephanie Perrin et al., The Personal Information Protection and Electronic Documents Act: An Annotated Guide (Toronto, 2001).

[546] Council of Europe. Cybercrime Convention available at <conventions.coe.int/Treaty/EN/CadreListeTraites.htm>.

[547] A list of state laws and commissions is <http://infoweb.magi.com/~privcan/other.html>.

information.[548] Some provinces are currently working on their own legislation in order to avoid having PIPEDA apply to intra-provincial transactions.

To date, only Québec has comprehensive legislation that applies to personal information held by the private sector. In Québec the fundamental character of the right to privacy is held in its Charter of Rights and Freedoms and its Civil Code.[549] More detailed requirements aimed at the public sector are found in legislation adopted in 1982, while Quebec enacted the first piece of legislation covering the entire private sector in North America in 1994. The latter regulates the collection, confidentiality, correction, disclosure, retention and use of personal information by these businesses. It also provides individuals with a right of access and correction. The Québec Commission D'accès à L'information has broad powers over the public and private sectors.

With respect to provincial sector-specific legislation, many provinces have specific laws to protect personal information, including health-specific privacy laws, consumer credit reporting laws, laws regulating information from credit unions, and legislation imposing restrictions on the disclosure of personal information held by private investigators and other professionals. Alberta, Manitoba, and Saskatchewan have all passed health-specific privacy legislation, which sets rules for the collection, use, and disclosure of personal health information. These laws apply to personal health information held by hospitals, government ministries, regulated health professionals, and other health care facilities. Ontario is currently working on including health privacy legislation in its general private sector legislation. Sectoral laws, however, only provide a partial and fragmentary approach to the problem of regulation.[550]

Republic of Chile

Article 19 of Chile's Constitution secures for all persons: "Respect and protection for public and private life, the honor of a person and his family. The inviolability of the home and of all forms of private communication. The home

---

[548] Privacy Commissioner, Report to Parliament on Substantially Similar Provincial Legislation. May 2002. <http://www.privcom.gc.ca/legislation/leg-rp_e.asp.htm>.

[549] <http://www.cai.gouv.qc.ca/commiss.htm>.

[550] Privacy Commissioner, Report to Parliament on Substantially Similar Provincial Legislation, May 2002, available at <http://www.privcom.gc.ca/legislation/leg-rp_e.asp.htm>.

---

may be invaded and private communications and documents intercepted, opened, or inspected only in cases and manners determined by law."[551]

Recently, Chile became the first Latin American country to enact a data protection law. The Act No. 19628, titled "Law for the protection of Private Life,"[552] came into force on October 28, 1999. The law has 24 articles, covering processing and use of personal data in the public and the private sector and the rights of individuals (to access, correction, and judicial control). The law contains a chapter dedicated to the use of financial, commercial and banking data, and specific rules addressing the use of information by government agencies. The law includes fines and damages for the unlawful denial of access and correction rights. Only databanks in the government must be registered.

There is no data protection authority, and each affected person enforces the law individually. There is no case law yet interpreting the law. Another deficiency is that the law does not contain restrictions on transfers to third countries.

Chile's transition to democratic rule in 1990 did not eliminate personal privacy violations by government agencies. The Investigations Police – a plainclothes civilian agency that functions in close collaboration with the International Criminal Police Organization (Interpol) and with the intelligence services of the army, navy, and air force – keeps records of all adult citizens and foreign residents and issues identification cards that must be carried at all times.[553] The personal data compiled during military rule was never destroyed. In January 1998, former dictator Gen. Augusto Pinochet threatened to use "compromising information" from secret military intelligence files against those who were trying to keep him from becoming a Senator for Life, a position which would provide immunity from civil suits and public accountability for crimes which took place during his dictatorship.[554] Under current law, the voter registration list is publicly disclosed and used for direct marketing purposes. In 1999, the UN Human Rights Committee criticized the requirement that hospitals report all women who receive abortions.[555]

---

[551] Constitution of Chile, 1980, available at
<http://www.georgetown.edu/LatAmerPolitical/Constitutions/Chile/chile97.html>.

[552] Law for the Protection of Private Life (Ley Sobre Proteccion de la Vida Privada), Law No.19628 of August 30, 1999, published in the Official Journal in August 28, 1999.

[553] Chile: A Country Report, 1994: United States Library of Congress.

[554] "Chile's Ex-Dictator Tries to Dictate His Future Role," The New York Times, February 1, 1998.

[555] Human Rights Committee Consideration of Chile's Fourth Periodic report, March 25, 1999.

Under a 1995 law the collection of information by recording, wiretapping or other secretive means, is prohibited. Such surveillance may be conducted in narcotics-related cases upon the issuance of a judicial order.[556] In August 1996, the head of the Direccion de Inteligencia Policial (Dipolcar), the police intelligence service, was charged with authorizing a surveillance operation against the defense ministry official responsible for Carabineros, the militarized national police force. His resignation in disgrace allowed a greater role for the civilian security police, Investigaciones, in anti-drug operations.[557] In 1992, a surveillance center with 24-hour scanning devices was uncovered in downtown Santiago. It was run by an active army intelligence unit (DINE, incorporating former members of the secret police, the CNI) and, among other incidents, was found to have tapped into presidential candidate Sebastian Pinera's cellular phone[558] and taped the calls of President Patricio Aylwin.[559] The Army admitted to tapping telephones in order to comply with its mission, but reaffirmed that it "does not tap phones in an attempt to interfere with peoples' privacy."[560] The scandal provoked the retirement of General Ricardo Contreras, head of the Army Telecommunications Command.[561]

Chile signed the American Convention on Human Rights on August 20, 1990.

People's Republic of China

Privacy remains a largely foreign concept for many Chinese, and the "right to privacy" is not seen as integral to the rights of the person. People often have had no clear idea how to distinguish between "shameful secret" or "yinsi," and "privacy," also connoted by the word "yinsi."[562] However, as China drifts from a socialist lifestyle to a more market-based one, privacy is becoming increasingly valued.

There are limited rights to privacy in the Chinese Constitution. Article 38, the source from which all legislation on the protection of personal rights

---

[556] Ley No.19.423.

[557] "Rows grow over security services," Southern Cone Report, September 12, 1996.

[558] "Television Nacional de Chile," BBC Summary of World Broadcasts, September 26, 1992.

[559] "Army's bugging centre uncovered," Latin America Weekly Report, October 8, 1992.

[560] "Navy, Air Force Deny Allegations of Telephone Tapping," BBC Summary of World Broadcasts, September 28, 1992.

[561] "Chile army to take action against servicemen involved in telephone-tapping case," BBC Summary of World Broadcasts, November 27, 1992.

[562] G. Zhu, "The Right to Privacy: An Emerging Right in Chinese Law" 18(3) Statute Law Review 208 (1997).

emanates,[563] provides that the personal dignity of citizens of the People's Republic of China is inviolable and further, that insult, libel, false accusation or false incrimination directed against citizens by any means is prohibited.[564] Articles 37 and 39 define, respectively, the protection of freedom of the person and the residence. However, certain law enforcement officials can issue search warrants on their own authority or else simply ignore legal requirements for independent oversight.[565] Article 40 of the Constitution provides for the freedom and privacy of correspondence of the citizen.[566]

Article 101 of the General Principles of Civil Law (1986) provides a 'right of reputation' to citizens and corporations. The personality of citizens shall be protected by law, and the use of insults, libel or other means to damage the reputation of citizens or legal persons shall be prohibited.[567] Two articles of the General Principles of Criminal Law (1979)[568] provide further bases for the protection of the right. Article 145 states "whoever by violence or other methods, including the use of 'big character posters' and 'small character posters',[569] publicly insults another person or fabricates facts to defame him, if the circumstances are serious, shall be sentenced to fixed-term imprisonment of not more than three years, criminal detention or deprivation of political rights." Article 149 states "whoever conceals, destroys or unlawfully opens another person's letters, infringing upon the citizens' right to freedom of correspondence, if the circumstances are serious, shall be sentenced to fixed-term imprisonment of not more than one year or criminal detention."[570]

---

[563] Id., at 211.

[564] People's Republic of China Constitution (Constitution Act, 1993) Chapter II (Fundamental Rights and Duties of Citizens), § 38, translation available at <http://www.qis.net/chinalaw/prccon5.htm.

[565] United States Department of State, Country Reports on Human Rights Practices 2001, March 2002, available at <http://www.state.gov/g/drl/hrrpt/2001/>.

[566] People's Republic of China Constitution, supra n.564 § 37, 39-40.

[567] General Principles of Civil Law, article 101, available at <http://www.qis.net/chinalaw/prclaw27.htm>. This right would seem to roughly correspond with the American tort of invasion of privacy, as defined by Prosser, that of placing a person in a false light in the public eye, see W. Prosser, The Law of Torts 863-866 (St. Paul: West Group, 5th ed. 1984).

[568] General Principles of Criminal Law, article 145, 149, available at <http://www.qis.net/chinalaw/prclaw60.htm>.

[569] H. Sheng, "Big Character Posters in China: A Historical Survey" 56(4) Journal of Chinese Law 234 (1990), "during the past fifty years, the writing of big- and small-character posters (dazibao) emerged as a principle form of political expression and have accompanied nearly every major political movement in the PRC. In a society that prizes reputations, outward appearances, and conformance with social norms, dazibao create a public spectacle, the very existence of which implies that the leadership has failed and that the community is disaffected. Moreover, dazibao reach a relatively wide audience at minimum cost and provide some anonymity for the writer. Because of these unique characteristics dazibao represent one of the few effective vestiges of free speech that may be used to voice political dissent in China.

[570] Zhu, supra n. 562, at 211.

The Law on the Protection of Minors (1991) provides that "no organization or individual may disclose the personal secrets of minors" and "with regard to cases involving crimes committed by minors, the names, home addresses and photos of such minors as well as other information which can be used to deduce who they are, may not be disclosed, before the judgment, in news reports, films, television programs and in any other openly circulated publications.[571] The Law on the Protection of Rights and Interests of Women (1992) provides that "women's right of reputation and personal dignity shall be protected by law. Damage to women's right of reputation and personal dignity by such means as insult, libel or giving publicity to private affairs shall be prohibited."[572] The Law on Lawyers (1996) requires lawyers to protect the personal secrets of their clients;[573] the Law on Statistics (1983) provides that data collected from investigations shall not be disclosed without the consent of data subjects;[574] and, the Provisional Regulations Relating to Bank Management (1986) provide that all information concerning the savings of clients shall not be disclosed.[575]

These provisions taken together provide a minimum legal protection of the privacy of the citizen. However, in practice, there has been a degree of confusion in applying them in cases concerning privacy. Consequently, the Supreme People's Court has issued two general judicial interpretations regarding the application of The General Principles of Civil Law to privacy. In Opinions on Several Questions concerning the implementation of the 'General Principles of Civil Law of the PRC' (1998) the Court held:

> The cases in which a person discloses personal secrets in written or oral way, or fabricates facts to publicly vilify the personal dignity, or damages the reputation by such means as insults and defamation of the others, and these acts have causes a certain negative impact on the persons concerned, shall be treated as an invasion of the right of reputation.[576]

More recently, in the case Yu Meifang v. Xinzhou Prefectural People's Hospital, the Xinzhou Intermediate People's Court of Shanxi Province ordered the defendant hospital to pay Yu 20,000 yuan (~$2400 USD) in compensation for the

---

[571] Law on the Protection of Minors, article 42, Zhu, id., at n.17.

[572] Law on the Protection of Rights and Interests of Women, article 39, Zhu id., at n.18.

[573] Law on Lawyers, article 23, Zhu, id., at n.19.

[574] Law on Statistics, article 14, Zhu, id., at n.20.

[575] Provisional Regulations Relating to Bank Management, article 47, Zhu, id., at n.21.

[576] Opinions on Several Questions concerning the implementation of the 'General Principles of Civil Law of the PRC' at paragraph 140, Zhu, id., at n. 22.

anguish and humiliation she experienced when the hospital released false information about her medical condition.[577] In February 2000, Yu had gone to the orthopedics section of the hospital for treatment. A doctor from the hospital tested her blood and suspected her of being HIV-positive. The hospital separated her from other patients immediately and informed both the Xinzhou Epidemic Prevention Station, and the shopping center where Yu worked, that she was infected with HIV. The shopping center subsequently refused to rent her retail space and her business partner severed their partnership.

The Practicing Physician Law requires that doctors not reveal health information obtained during treatment. Doctors who violate the law face criminal penalties. In May of 1999, the Ministry of Health, with the approval of the State Council, published an administrative order declaring that personal information about HIV/AIDS sufferers be kept secret, and that the legal rights and interests of those people and their relatives should not be infringed. The Ministry of Health order asked all units and individuals in charge of diagnosis, treatment, and management work not to publish any personal information about HIV/AIDS sufferers, such as the name and the family address. In 2001, Ministry of Health officials again called for more attention to the protection of the right to privacy of HIV/AIDS patients, following a court ruling that a hospital damaged a patient's reputation by releasing false HIV-related information about her.[578]

The Maternal and Child Health Care Law requires premarital and prenatal examinations to determine whether couples have acute infectious diseases or certain mental illnesses (not including mental retardation), or are at risk for passing on debilitating genetic diseases. Based on medical advice, the Ministry of Health can recommend sterilization or abortion. At least five provincial governments have implemented local regulations seeking to prevent persons with severe mental disabilities from having children.[579] In August 1998, the Government issued an "explanation" to provincial governments clarifying that no sterilization of persons with genetic conditions could be performed without their signed consent. In practice, most areas still do not have the capacity accurately to determine the likelihood of passing on hard to detect debilitating genetic diseases.

Last year, the China Psychiatric Association ceased listing homosexuality as a mental illness. Many gays and lesbians saw the move as a sign of increased

---

[577] "Patient's Privacy Rights Become an Issue in China" China Daily, July 17, 2001.

[578] "Patient's Privacy Rights Become an Issue in China" China Daily, July 17, 2001.

[579] 2001 United States State Dept. Report, supra n.565.

government tolerance. Nonetheless, most gatherings of gays and lesbians still take place clandestinely.[580]

There is no general data protection law in China and very few laws that limit government interference with collection, use and disclosure of personal information. Article 6 of the Postal Law prohibits postal enterprises and staff from providing information to any organization or individual about users' dealings with postal services except as otherwise provided for by law.[581] However, Article 21 permits postal staff to examine, on the spot, the contents of "non-letter postal materials." Mail handed in or posted by users must be in accordance with the stipulations concerning the content allowed to be posted; postal authorities have the right to examine mail, when necessary.[582] However, in an age when email is replacing letters as the preferred mode of written communication, China continues to ramp up massive and systematic surveillance of electronic communications.

The Chinese government announced[583] and then retracted a broad-sweeping rule that required all entities other than embassies to register any software using encryption technology. The original rule was announced on November 10, 1999 by the PRC State Encryption Management Commission and required registration by January 31, 2000.[584] However, few companies registered by the due date, and under increasing pressure from the international community officials reversed the hugely unpopular law, which likely would have delayed or prevented the launch of Microsoft's Office 2000 and Cisco's installation of new mobile phone networks.[585]

Business travelers in China carrying laptops with "ordinary business software" are no longer required to register with the government, even if there computers have software with encryption capabilities, as they would have been under the original interpretation of the law.[586] The law now only requires that certain special hardware and software products, primarily used for encryption, be

---

[580] Id.

[581] Postal Law of the People's Republic of China, (December 2, 1986) § 6.

[582] Id. § 21.

[583] "United States to push China on encryption," Reuters, January 27, 2000 <http://www.wired.com/news/politics/0,1283,33950,00.html>.

[584] State Council Order Number 273, October 22, 1999.

[585] M. Forney, "Ban Raised Fears Involving Privacy in Communications," Wall Street Journal, March 13, 2000. See also EPIC, Cryptography and Liberty 2000: An International Survey of Encryption Policy (EPIC 2000).

[586] M. Forney, "China Relaxes Strong Rules on Net Encryption Programs", Wall Street Journal, March 13, 2000.

registered with the government. Beijing has also decided not to require foreign businesses to hand over the keys to their encryption codes.

China has had a long-standing policy – dating back to the 4th Century BC – of keeping close track of its citizens. Even in those early times, many Chinese provinces were often remarkably successful in keeping records of their whole populations, so that they could be taxed and conscripted: "The state had the surname, personal name, age and home place of every subject and was also able to ensure that nobody could move far from home without proper authorization."[587]

Freedom of association remains tightly controlled. All social organizations – from book clubs to congregations and visiting relatives – must be reported to and registered with the Ministry of Civil Affairs. Any group that operates without registering risks prosecution.[588] Failure to notify local authorities concerning visiting guests is also punishable by fine.[589] Labor unions remain illegal.[590] Government authorities systematically monitor[591] some individuals and groups more closely than others, including: advocates of democratic reform,[592] human rights activists,[593] minorities,[594] and members of Falun Gong.[595]

---

[587] W.J.F Jenner "China and Freedom" in D. Kelly and A. Reid, Asian Freedoms: the idea of freedom in East and Southeast Asia (Cambridge University Press, 1998).

[588] M. Jendrzejczyk, "China: Human Rights and United States Policy," Statement to Congressional Human Rights Caucus, May 15, 2001, available at <http://www.hrw.org/press/2001/05/chinastatement.htm>, eight members of a book club were arrested in May 2001 for failing to register with local authorities.

[589] Regulations of the People's Republic of China on Administrative Penalties for Public Security, September 5, 1986.

[590] China ratified the International Convenant on Economic, Social and Cultural Rights in February, 2002, but reserved the right to freely organize and join trade unions.

[591] For a discussion of possible modalities of class-based surveillance see J. Young, "On the Fringe: State Surveillance and Differential Privacy Rights in Canada" Lex Informatica, (April, 2000), available at <http://www.lexinformatica.org/dox/panopticsort.pdf>.

[592] In June 2000, authorities arrested Huang Qi, operator of a web site on missing children at http://www.6-4tianwang.com for posting an article critical of the PRC leadership's handling of Tianamen Square. He was tried in secret and has not been heard from since, see e.g. V. Pik-Kwan Chan, "Amnesty says 200 in prison over June 4," South China Morning Post, May 31, 2002.

[593] No independent watchdog organizations were permitted in China, see Human Rights Watch, HRW World Report 2002 (New York: HRW, 2002), available at <http://www.hrw.org/wr2k2/asia4.html>.

[594] Authorities monitor and regular detain "splittist" activists in Tibet and Xianjiang, id.

[595] T. Ee Lyn, "HK Bars More Falun Gong members before anniversary" Reuters, June 29, 2002, quoting one Australian Falun Gong member "As soon as the authorities punched my name into the computer, [the Customs Officer] sent for guards right away and I was taken to a waiting room." R. Callick, "Out of China to Outer Melbourne" Australian Financial Review, June 21, 2002, documenting the story of Zeng Zheng, a Falun Gong supporter, who was arrested when she tried to explain the movement to her parents in an email, which authorities intercepted.

The Constitution provides for freedom of religious belief and the freedom not to believe; however, the government seeks to restrict religious practice to government-sanctioned organizations and registered places of worship and to control the growth and scope of the activity of religious groups.[596] There are five officially recognized religions: Buddhism, Taoism, Islam, Protestantism, and Catholicism. For each faith, there is a government-affiliated association to monitor and supervise its activities.[597]

In late 2000, six million census takers attempted an accurate count of the number of Chinese citizens in the fifth ever national census, but privacy and economic concerns made citizens less cooperative than in the past. Zhang Weimin, a statistician at China's National Statistics Bureau, noted that "under the planned economy, people had no privacy. Everybody's income was the same across the country. But now [China has] a market economy, and people want to protect their secrets... cooperation... will not be as good as before."[598]

An estimated 5 million children go unreported because of China's "one-child policy," under which authorities heavily fine parents who have more than one child, subject to some exceptions. In the recent census, enumerators were so concerned with accuracy that they promised not to divulge census results to the police, the family planning commission or any other state organization. They also promised to burn the paper results once computer data entry was complete, in order to ease the fears that these records would be used for other purposes.[599]

Since 1984, all Chinese citizens over the age of 16 have been required to carry identification cards issued by the Ministry for Public Security. Identification cards include name, sex, nationality, date of birth, address and expiry date, which varies depending on the age of the cardholder. Public security agencies and other government and quasi-government agencies have the right to demand the production of identification at any time.[600] Failure to register for an identification card, forging or otherwise altering a residence registration, or assuming another person's registration are all prohibited by law and punishable by fine.

---

[596] PRC Const., § 36, supra n.564.

[597] 2001 United States State Dept. Report, supra n.565.

[598] M. Cernetig, "Census takers in China can count on mistrust" *The Globe & Mail*, November 16, 2000,

[599] "Massive miscount looms as privacy issues, 'one child' policies hinder China census" *China Online*, October 31, 2000.

[600] "Regulations of the People's Republic of China Concerning Resident Identity Cards" *Xinhua News Agency*, May 7,1984, via BBC Summary of World Broadcasts.

Reportedly, the national identification system is being liberalized and the ability of most citizens to move around the country to live and work continues to improve.[601] Authorities have retained the ability to restrict freedom of movement through other mechanisms, and increased restrictions on movement during the year, particularly during politically sensitive anniversaries and to forestall Falun Gong demonstrations.[602]

Smart card development is well underway in China, with both domestic and international players competing to develop chips and modules to meet design and regulatory specifications.[603] In 2001, the city of Shanghai adopted a smart social security card designed to hold driving licenses, passports and even marriage registration. Currently, over 5 million Shanghai residents have applied for the card and the government hopes that by 2003 most Shanghai citizens will be using the card. The information on the card comes from, and can be verified by, social security, police, medical insurers, public housing and other local authorities.[604]

In 1988 and 1992, as the result of "invasion of privacy" litigation, many journalists were imprisoned. This stimulated much academic and public debate on such issues as the role of journalism in matters of public interest, the proper balance between the right to privacy and the right to know, the appropriate ethical norms which should govern the conduct of the journalist and the freedom of the press. Some judicial decisions during this period emphasized these debates; for example, Two Art Models v. The Organizers of the Exhibition, The Rock 'n' Roll Star Cui Jian v. The Writer Zhao Jianwei and his Publisher.[605]

It is well documented that the Chinese government is committed to monitoring media – online and in more traditional channels – for information that might harm unification of the country, endanger national security, or subvert government authority.[606] In February 1999, the government announced the creation of the State Information Security Appraisal and Identification Management Committee which "will be responsible for protecting government and commercial confidential files on the Internet, identifying any net user, and

---

[601] 2001 United States State Dept. Report, supra n.565

[602] Id.

[603] "With eye on Security, China nurtures domestic IC cards," Electronic Engineering Times, August 9, 1999.

[604] "Electronic Social Security Card in Shanghai" BNA World Data Protection Report, September 2001, at 6.

[605] Zhu, supra n.562, at n. 27.

[606] See, e.g., Human Rights Watch, Freedom of Expression and the Internet in China: A Human Rights Watch Backgrounder (2001), available at <http://www.hrw.org/backgrounder/asia/china-bck-0701.htm> see also Revised Provisional Regulations Governing the Management of Chinese Computer Information Networks Connected to International Networks § 6, May 20, 1997 which prohibits connection to international networks except through approved "access channels".

defining rights and responsibilities... [t]he move is intended to guard both individual and government users, protect information by monitoring and keep them from being used without proper authorization."[607] According to Human Rights Watch, by December 2000, China had over 300,000 Internet police.[608]

Frank Lu, the head of the Hong Kong-based Information Center of Human Rights and Democratic Movement in China, reported in November 1999 that 300 computer graduates had been recruited by Shanghai security officials to carry out cyber-surveillance in 1999.[609] Canadian, American, and British members of the Falun Gong movement claimed to be targets of such surveillance in Fall of 1999, reporting assaults on their web sites by various means commonly used to block or penetrate sites.[610]

In October 2000, the Ministry of Information Industry ("MII") promulgated the Internet Information Services Regulations aimed at controlling Internet usage. Promoting "evil cults" was prohibited, as was providing information that "disturbs social order or undermines social stability." One regulation, covering chat rooms, requires all service providers to monitor content and restrict controversial topics. Content providers must keep files of what they post and who reads it, for 60 days. Other regulations make it illegal to store, process, or retrieve information deemed to be "state secrets" from international computer networks. Authorities do not consider persons who receive dissident e-mail publications responsible, but forwarding those messages to others is illegal.[611]

Another provision of the regulations requires Internet café patrons to register with "software managers" and produce a valid ID card to log on.[612] The English chatroom of SOHU.com, partly owned by Dow Jones, posted a list of prohibited topics including criticism of the Constitution, topics which damage China's reputation, discussion that undermines China's religious policy, and "any discussion and promotion of content which PRC laws prohibit." The posting continues: "If you are a Chinese national and willingly choose to break these laws, SOHU.com is legally obligated to report you to the Public Security

---

[607] "China forms information security oversight committee," Xinhua News Agency, February 12, 1999.

[608] Human Rights Watch, HRW World Report 2002 (New York: HRW, 2002), available at <http://www.hrw.org/wr2k2/asia4.html>.

[609] K. Platt, "China's 'cybercops' clamp down," Christian Science Monitor, November 17, 1999.

[610] M. Laris, "China sniffing out dissent on the Internet; Government accused of web sabotage" Washington Post, August 5, 1999.

[611] "China Enacts Sweeping Rules On Internet Firms," Reuters, October 2, 2000.

[612] United States Embassy Beijing, Kids, Cadres And "Cultists" All Love It: Growing Influence Of The Internet In China (Beijing 2001) available at <http://www.usembassy-china.org.cn/english/sandt/netoverview.html>.

Bureau." An internal AOL memo recommended that if AOL were asked what it would do if the Chinese government demanded records relating to political dissidents, AOL staff should respond "It is our policy to abide by the laws of the country in which we offer services."

Article 7 of the Computer Information Network and Internet Security, Protection and Management Regulations states "the freedom and privacy of network users is protected by law. No unit or individual may, in violation of these regulations, use the Internet to violate the freedom and privacy of network users."[613] However, articles 8, 10 and 13 stipulate that individuals must be registered, that transferring accounts is prohibited and all those engaged in Internet business are subject security supervision, inspection, and guidance, including assisting in incidents involving law violations and criminal activities involving computer information networks."[614] Articles 285 to 287 of the criminal code make unauthorized intrusions into computer systems illegal.[615]

By law, all Internet cafés must be licensed. However, due to the labyrinthine licensing requirements and registration – for both the operator and the user – and pent up demand, it is estimated that more than 60 per cent of China's 200,000 plus Internet cafés remain unlicensed. Licensed cyber cafés require patrons to provide identification and register each time they visit. It is unsurprising that a significant percentage of China's estimated 55 million Internet users log on – using prepaid, anonymous phone cards – through unlicensed cyber cafés.[616] These cafés offer inexpensive access and a unregulated degree of freedom that might not otherwise be possible.[617]

In early 2001, more than 1,700 Internet cafes in Chongqing began operating "security management" software distributed by the local bureau of public security. The program filters materials deemed to be objectionable by the government and is capable of "capturing" computer screens and "casting" them onto screens at local public security bureaus.[618] The product was designed in part

---

[613] Computer Information Network and Internet Security, Protection and Management Regulations, article 7 (December 11, 1997), available at <http://www.qis.net/chinalaw/prclaw54.htm>.

[614] Id., articles. 8, 10, 13.

[615] General Principles of Criminal Law, articles. 285-287, available at <http://www.qis.net/chinalaw/prclaw60.htm>.

[616] "China launches crackdown on 'harmful' Internet content" Yahoo! News Singapore, May 1, 2002, <http://sg.news.yahoo.com/020501/1/2otr6.html>.

[617] The anonymity provided by Internet cafés hearkens to the use of "big-character posters" of an earlier era and provides a unique opportunity for Chinese citizens – particularly students – to express personal opinions.

[618] HRW Backgrounder 2001, called "Internet Police 100" the software comes in versions designed for home, cafés and schools.

to keep "unhealthy" information, such as cults, sex, and violence, off the Internet. Local police departments stated that strengthening the administration and control over the Internet cafes would benefit the healthy development of this fledgling industry.

On April 10, 2001, the State Council ordered a three-month investigation into all public Internet service providers and announced that no new Internet cafes could be opened during that time. By June 2001, the Shenzhen Legal Daily reported that Chinese police had inspected over 56,800 cafes. Over 6,000 of these were disconnected and 2,300 shut down completely.[619] The Shanghai Daily said the move was China's second major clampdown in a little more than a year. In May 2002, a devastating fire in an unlicensed café killed 25 people and prompted another nationwide crackdown.[620]

Throughout the inspections and closures, authorities have given various rationale for their methods, from protecting youth from corruption on the Internet, to public safety. Ultimately, the closure or increased regulation of cyber cafés – for any reason – impacts the ability of average Chinese, particularly students, from access to foreign news sources and denies them a degree of expression they do not otherwise enjoy.

The "Great Firewall"

China's Internet regulations and legislation are guided by the principle of "guarded openness" – seeking to preserve the economic benefits of new information and communication technologies, while guarding against foreign economic domination and the use of technology to coordinate anti-government activity.[621] According to Human Rights Watch, China has enacted at least 60 sets of regulations aimed at controlling Internet content – or access to content outside of China – since commercial Internet accounts were first authorized in 1994.[622]

Using technological assistance and equipment from Western companies such as Nortel Networks and IBM, China's Ministry for Public Security (MPS) passes all international connections through proxy servers at official gateways, where MPS

---

[619] "Chinese man sentenced for posting articles on net" Digital Freedom Network, June 19, 2000
<http://www.dfn.org/focus/china/liuweifang.htm>.

[620] "Mass Shutdown of Chinese Internet Cafes," The Guardian, July 10, 2002, available at
<http://www.guardian.co.uk/internetnews/story/0,7369,752802,00.html>.

[621] G. Walton, China's Golden Shield: Corporations and the Development of Surveillance Technology in the People's Republic of China, (Rights and Democracy, 2001) at 9
<http://serveur.ichrdd.ca/english/commdoc/publications/globalization/goldenShieldEng.html>.

[622] HRW Backgrounder 2001.

officials identify individual users and content, define rights, and carefully monitor network traffic into and out of the country.[623] Derisively termed the "Great Firewall" by hacktivists and journalists worldwide, the Ministry of Information Industry (MII) also uses the firewall to periodically filter access to Western web sites, particularly media organizations, such as the Washington Post and Voice of America,[624] human rights organizations, such as Amnesty International, or any other web site deemed subversive.[625] Recently, the government has taken public steps to relax filtering on a case-by-case basis.[626]

The pace and scale of the development of the Internet has reduced the significance of the Great Firewall. Economic modernization is leading to exponential growth in the demand for international bandwidth and the sheer volume of Internet traffic today poses a serious challenge to state control at the network level. China observers hold out the existence of many anti-government postings on the Internet as evidence that censorship regulations are inconsistently enforced. Further, data from a 2001 Chinese Academy of Social Sciences (CASS) survey on Internet use shows that 10 per cent of users admit to regularly using, and 25 per cent occasionally using, proxy servers to defeat censorship measures.[627] However, heavy restrictions on international connectivity remain a key principle in China's nascent Internet security strategy and penalties for Internet-related offences include life imprisonment or the death penalty.

Beyond the Great Firewall: Golden Shield

At a recent security industry conference, the PRC government announced an ambitious successor to its Great Firewall strategy. Rather than relying solely on a national intranet, separated from the global Internet by a massive firewall, China will now build surveillance intelligence into the network, allowing it to "see", "hear" and "think."[628] Content-filtration will shift from the national level to

---

[623] Golden Shield, supra n..621 at 9.

[624] See *e.g.* J. Lee, "United States Backs Plan to Help Chinese Evade Government Censorship of Web" *New York Times*, August 30, 2001, at A10. At other times, the Australian Broadcasting Corporation, the New York Times and the BBC have been blocked.

[625] M. Cohn, "China Seeks to Build the Great Firewall; Controlled modernization the mantra," Toronto Star, July 21, 2001, at A01.

[626] The Australian Broadcasting Corporation and the New York Times were separately removed from the "blacklist" after complaints to the PRC government. See, e.g., D. Miklovic et al., "Internet Shutdown: 200,000 China Cybercafes Shut in a Day" Gartner Group, June 25, 2002, available at <http://www3.gartner.com/resources/107700/107751/107751.pdf>.

[627] See China Academy of Social Sciences, Survey of Internet Use 2001, (May 2001); see also United States Embassy Beijing, China's Internet Information Skirmish, (Beijing 2000), available at <http://www.usembassy-china.org.cn/english/sandt/webwar.htm>.

[628] Golden Shield, supra n.621, at 15.

---

millions of digital information and communications devices in public places and people's homes.[629] This project is dubbed "Golden Shield."

The technology behind Golden Shield is incredibly complex and is based on research developed largely by Western technology firms, including Nortel Networks, Sun Microsystems and others. The Golden Shield efforts do not signal an abandonment of other avenues of access and content control. For example, details are only beginning to emerge about a new "black box" device, derived from technology previously used in airline cockpit data recorders, and broadly similar to the Carnivore system developed by the United States government.[630] Once attached to a server at the ISP, Carnivore works by intercepting all incoming transmissions and then parsing out pertinent material, based on keywords provide by the administrator. Chinese Internet police would use the black box technology to monitor dissidents and collect evidence on illegal activities.[631]

On February 28, 2002, China ratified the International Covenant on Economic, Social and Cultural Rights but took a reservation on the right to freely organize and join trade unions. China still has not ratified the International Covenant on Civil and Political Rights, which it signed in 1998. In February 2000, Chinese lawmakers attending the 20th session of the Standing Committee of the 9th National People's Congress (NPC) expressed support for its early ratification.[632]

Czech Republic

The 1993 Charter of Fundamental Rights and Freedoms provides for extensive privacy rights. Article 7(1) states, "Inviolability of the person and of privacy is guaranteed. It may be limited only in cases specified by law." Article 10 states, "(1) Everybody is entitled to protection of his or her human dignity, personal integrity, good reputation, and his or her name. (2) Everybody is entitled to protection against unauthorized interference in his or her personal and family life. (3) Everybody is entitled to protection against unauthorized gathering, publication or other misuse of his or her personal data." Article 13 states,

---

[629] B. Rappert, "Assessing the Technologies of Political Control" (1999) 36(6) J. of Peace Research 741. The Golden Shield Project contemplates automated voice recognition through digital signal processing; distributed; network video surveillance; and, content-filtration of the Internet.

[630] EPIC, Carnivore FOIA Litigation page, at <http://www.epic.org/privacy/carnivore/>.

[631] See e.g. L. Weijun, "China Plans to Build Internet Monitoring System," China News Daily, March 20, 2001 <http://www.cnd.org/Global/01/03/20/010320-3.html>.

[632] 'Chinese Lawmakers Urge Early Ratification of Human Rights Convention,' Xinhua News Service, February 27, 2001, at <http://202.84.17.11/english/htm/20010227/378782A.htm>.

"Nobody may violate secrecy of letters and other papers and records whether privately kept or sent by post or in another manner, except in cases and in a manner specified by law. Similar protection is extended to messages communicated by telephone, telegraph or other such facilities."[633]

On April 4, 2000 the new Act "On Personal Data Protection" was enacted and went into effect in on June 1, 2000.[634] The act replaces the 1992 Act on Protection of Personal Data in Information Systems.[635] The act implements the basic requirements of the European Union Data Protection Directive, however, it grants exceptions to the police and intelligence services from many of the key provisions. The European Union had been pressuring the Republic to move more quickly in adopting this legislation for several years.[636] Negotiations between the European Commission's Article 29 Committee and the Czech Office for Personal Data Protection have already taken place on the question of adequacy but no formal recommendation has yet been made. Under the act, data controllers were required to register their systems by December 1, 2000 and to fully comply with the other provisions of the law by June 1, 2001. In May 2001, the President signed an amendment to the act exempting political parties, churches, sports clubs and other civic organizations from certain of the act's requirements. These organizations will no longer need to register their data protection activities or obtain the consent of individuals before collecting personal information.[637]

The act established an Office for Personal Data Protection as an independent oversight body.[638] The office is responsible for supervising the implementation of the act; maintaining a register of databases; investigating complaints; imposing fines for violations; conducting audits and providing consultations on data protection; and commenting on legislative proposals. The Office also has authority over the certificate authorities for digital signatures under Act No. 227 of June 29, 2000 on Electronic Signatures.

In August 2000, Karel Neuwirt was appointed President of the Office and took office the following month. Three inspectors were also appointed to the Office, effective as of October 1, 2000. As of December 2001, a total of 17,082 notifications of personal data processing have been registered with the Office by

---

[633] Charter of Fundamental Rights and Freedoms, 1993.

[634] Act no. 101 of 2000 "On Personal Data Protection."

[635] Act of April 29, 1992 on Protection of Personal Data in Information Systems (No. 256/92).

[636] "European Union warns applicants on slow preparations," Financial Times, November 5, 1998.

[637] "Czech President Signs Amendment to Law on Personal Data Protection," BBC Worldwide Monitoring, May 25, 2001.

[638] Home Page<http://www.uoou.cz/>.

13,736 controllers. During the year 2001 the Office handled approximately 200 written complaints, ordered remedies for breaches of the Act in 25 cases, issued decisions on 322 applications for the transfer of personal data abroad. The Office also received an average of 500 telephone inquiries a month, and 195 requests for comment on legislative proposals.[639]

In his first annual report, the President noted that since its in the period between June 1, and December 31 2000, the office had received 40 written complaints, had registered data 108 controllers, and had issued decisions on in 29 cases.[640] In mid-March 2001 the Data Protection Office asked the Czech Statistical Office (CSO) to stop processing the results of the national census (carried out earlier that month) because of doubts as to the ability of the CSO to safeguard the data and because of the involvement of private company, DELTAX Systems, in the processing.

Electronic surveillance, wiretapping, and the interception of mail is regulated under the criminal process law and requires a court order.[641] A judge can approve an initial wiretap order for up to six months. There are special rules for intelligence services. Electronic surveillance, the tapping of telephones, and the interception of mail require a court order, and violations are subject to effective legal sanction. Over the years there have been many reports of illegal searches including wiretaps. In May 2001, the Foreign Ministry confirmed that bugging devices had been found in the Stirin conference center, which was used by the Ministry to host major negotiations during January 2000.[642] In December 1999, former Health Minister Ivan David alleged that a bugging device was installed in his office a few months prior to his resignation.[643] Also in 1999 there were complaints that the police conducted several searches without warrants of Romani homes, following a letter Romani activists sent to the mayor protesting racial discrimination.[644] In 1996, the Czech secret service (BIS) was accused of monitoring politicians, civic and environmental groups such as Greenpeace.[645] In

---

[639] E-mail from Karel Neuwirt, President, Office for Personal Data Protection, Czech Republic, to Sarah Andrews, Research Director, Electronic Privacy Information Center, May 15, 2002 (on file with the Electronic Privacy Information Center).

[640] Office for Personal Data Protection, Annual Report, June 1 –December 31 2000, available at <http://www.uoou.cz/eng/vyroc_zprava.php3>.

[641] Article 88 of Criminal Process Law.

[642] "Bugging Device found in Czech Foreign Ministry Conference Centre," BBC Worldwide Monitoring, May 22, 2001.

[643] United States State Department, Human Rights Report, 1999 <http://www.state.gov/g/drl/rls/hrrpt/1999/index.cfm?docid=325>.

[644] Id.

[645] CTK National News Wire, November 8, 1996.

1993, Justice Minister Jiri Novak's telephone was reportedly tapped. A secret service employee found a bugging device in the ministry's central telephone switchboard in the middle of September 1993.

The Penal Code covers the infringement of the right to privacy in the definitions of criminal acts of infringement of the home,[646] slander[647] and infringement of the confidentiality of mail.[648] There are also sectoral acts concerning statistics, medical personal data, banking law, taxation, social security and police data. Unauthorized use of personal data systems is considered a crime.[649] The law on the Police of the Czech Republic was recently amended in order to bring it into conformity with the Council of Europe Recommendation R (87) 15. Compliance with this recommendation is one of the requirements for accession to EURPOL and to the Schengen Agreements. During the drafting period the President of the Data Protection Office submitted comments on the proposed amendments. The Constitutional Court received several complaints about police misconduct, including violations of privacy, following the September 2000 meetings of the International Monetary Fund (IMF) in Prague.[650]

The Parliament approved the Freedom of Information Law in May 1999.[651] The law is based on the United States FOIA and provides for citizens' access to all government records held by State bodies, local self-governing authorities and certain other official institutions, such as the Chamber of Lawyers or the Chamber of Doctors, except for classified information, trade secrets or personal data.[652] A 1998 act governs access to environmental information.[653]

In April 1996, the Parliament approved a law that allows any Czech citizen to obtain his or her file created by the Communist-era secret police (StB). Non-Czech citizens are not allowed to access their records. The Interior Ministry holds 60,000 records but it is estimated that many more were destroyed in 1989. In October 1998, there was a controversy over the rumors that the records showed that former Vienna Mayor Helmut Zilk, who was about to receive an

---

[646] Penal Code, section 238.

[647] Penal Code, section 206.

[648] Penal Code, section 239.

[649] Centre de Recherches Informatique et Droit, Legal Aspects of Information Services and Intellectual Property Rights in Central and Eastern Europe, Feb 1995.

[650] "Constitutional Court to Deal with Complaints Against Police," CTK National News Wire, November 29, 2000.

[651] Act no. 106/1999 Coll., on free access to information

[652] "Freedom of info clears last hurdle," The Prague Post, May 19, 1999.

[653] Act no. 123/1998 Coll., on the right to information about the environment.

award from Czech President Vaclav Havel, was a collaborator with the StB. It was suspected that the Office for the Documentation and Investigation of the Crimes of Communism was the source of the documents.

The Czech Republic is a member of the Council of Europe and has signed and ratified the European Convention for the Protection of Human Rights and Fundamental Freedoms.[654] In September 2000, the Czech Republic signed the Council of Europe Convention 108 on the Protection of Individuals with Regard to Automatic Processing of Personal Data. This Convention was finally ratified on July 9, 2001. The Czech Republic is also a member of the Organization for Economic Cooperation and Development. It has adopted the OECD Guidelines on the Protection of Privacy and Transborder Flows of Personal Data.

Kingdom of Denmark

The Danish Constitution of 1953 contains two provisions relating to privacy and data protection. Section 71 provides for the inviolability of personal liberty. Section 72 states, "The dwelling shall be inviolable. House searching, seizure, and examination of letters and other papers as well as any breach of the secrecy to be observed in postal, telegraph, and telephone matters shall take place only under a judicial order unless particular exception is warranted by Statute."[655] Section 72 also applies to all kinds of telecommunication and electronic data. The European Convention on Human Rights was formally incorporated into Danish law in 1992.

The Act on Processing of Personal Data entered into force on July 1, 2000.[656] The act implements the European Union Data Protection into Danish law. It replaces the Private Registers Act of 1978, which governed the private sector,[657] and the Public Authorities' Registers Act of 1978, which governed the public sector.[658] The law divides personal information into three categories: ordinary, sensitive and semi-sensitive and provides different conditions for the processing

---

[654] Signed February 21, 1991; Ratified March 18, 1992, Entered into Force January 1, 1993.

[655] Constitution of Denmark 1953, available at <http://www.uni-wuerzburg.de/law/da00t___.html>.

[656] The Act on Processing of Personal Data, Act No. 429 of May 31, 2000 (Lov om behandling af personoplysninger), available at <http://147.29.40.90/_GETDOC_/ACCN/A20000042930-REGL>.

[657] Private Registers Act of 1978 (Lov nr 293 af 8 juni 1978 om private registre mv), in force January 1,1979.

[658] Public Authorities' Registers Act of 1978 (Lov nr 294 af 8 juni 1978 om offentlige myndigheders registre), also in force January 1, 1979.

of each.[659] A broad exemption from the Act is provided for law enforcement activities.[660]

An independent agency, the Data Protection Agency (Datatilsynet), enforces the act. The Agency supervises registries established by public authorities and private enterprises in Denmark. It ensures that the conditions for registration, disclosure and storage of data on individuals are complied with. It mainly deals with specific cases on the basis of inquiries from public authorities or private individuals, or cases taken up by the agency on its own initiative. Staff of the DPA are allowed to enter any premise where a file is operated without a court order. Decisions made by the DPA are final and may not be appealed any other administrative body. They may, however, be brought before the courts. Under the new Act, the DPA is required to give an opinion before any new laws or regulations that have an impact on privacy are issued.

In 2001 the DPA received 1029 inquires and complaints and initiated 112 investigations. As of June 2002, there were 8286 databases registered and a further 767 notifications for registration. In the past year there was a decrease in numbers, to 29, of staff employed by the agency.[661]

Other laws regulating the processing of personal information by the public sector include the Public Administration of 1985, the Publicity and Freedom of Information Act of 1985, the Public Records Act of 1992, and the National Registers Act of 2000. These laws set out basic data protection principles and determine what data should be available to the public and what should be kept confidential.[662] Sectoral laws also provide special protections for medical information[663] and credit card details[664] and lay down restrictions on direct marketing (including spam).[665] Provided that they are in accordance with Denmark's international and community obligations, these sectoral laws take priority over the general Data Protection Act.[666]

---

[659] Peter Blume et al, Nordic Data Protection 19-20 (DJOF Publishing Copenhagen 2001).

[660] Id. at 23.

[661] E-mail from Kira Kolby Christensen, Legal Adviser, Datatilsynet, to Sarah Andrews, Research Director, Electronic Privacy Information Center, June 14, 2002 (on file with the Electronic Privacy Information Center).

[662] Peter Blume et al., supra n.659, at 13.

[663] Patients' Rights Act of 1998.

[664] Credit Cards Act of 2000.

[665] Marketing Practices Act of 2000.

[666] Peter Blume et al., supra n.659, at 14.

Wiretapping is regulated by the Penal Code.[667] In March 2001, the Danish Minister of Justice proposed a new law (L194) that would dramatically increase police surveillance powers by allowing them to access a list of all mobile phones that were in operation near the scene of a crime at the time the crime was committed. This law was approved by the parliament in June 2001. Also in March 2001, Denmark amended its laws on search and seizure in accordance with its obligations under the Agreement on Trade-Related Aspects of Intellectual Property Rights (TRIPS) and under pressure from the United States software industry. The Administration of Justice Act now authorizes physical searches for copyright infringements without "prior notification of the defendant if it is assumed that the notification would cause a risk of removal, destruction or modifications of objects, documents, information in computer systems or anything else that are comprised by the petition for investigation." The law took effect on April 1, 2001.[668]

In October 2001, the Ministry of Justice and the Ministry of the Interior issued a package of "anti-terrorism" proposals in order to implement the UN Security Council's Resolution 1373 (2001) On Combating Terrorism and to prepare for the UN's International Convention for the Suppression of the Financing of Terrorism.[669] These proposals were postponed because of the general election but were re-introduced, with minor changes, by the new government in January 2002. In May 2002, the Parliament approved the Anti-Terrorism bill despite vocal opposition from NGOs and industry groups. The bill became law in June 2002.[670] Among other things, the legislation establishes mandatory registration and storage of traffic data for one year by telecommunications and Internet providers. It also gives law enforcement the power to secretly install snooping software on the computers of criminal suspects. The software will record keystroke data and transmit it electronically to the law enforcement agency. This power may only be used for serious crimes and will require an interception warrant. Serious crimes are defined as those punishable by jail for six years or more, including narcotics offences, homicide, assault and battery, causing danger to other peoples lives and health, theft, computer crimes, trafficking of refugees and child pornography, crimes against national security and the public order. During the passage of the law there was considerable debate on what kind of

---

[667] Penal Code Section 263.

[668] "Denmark Enacts Anti-Piracy Search and Seizure Law," Cluebot, July 20, 2001 <http://www.cluebot.com/article.pl?sid=01/06/26/042210>.

[669] "The Danish 'Anti-Terror Package," Danish Center for Human Rights, available at <http://www.humanrights.dk>.

[670] Law No. 378, June 6, 2002, Law Concerning the Change of Penal Code, Administration of Justice Act, Law of Competition and Consumer Regulation of theTelecommunications Market, Law of Small Arms, Law of Extradition and Law of Extradition of Criminals to Finland, Iceland, Norway And Sweden.

traffic data would have to be retained by service providers and, also, what constitutes a service provider for the purposes of the retention requirement. An administrative order will be issued by the Ministry of Justice later in the year to determine these issues.

All citizens in Denmark are provided with a Central Personal Registration (CPR) number that is used to identify them in public registers. The number can only be processed by private entities if they have specific legal authority to do so. Both the public and private sectors can only disclose this number with the consent of the individual.

Under the Aliens Act, immigration authorities may require DNA samples from applicants for residency or persons with whom the applicant claims family ties for the purposes of residency. In its report of October 2001, the United Nations Human Rights Committee expressed concern about the privacy implications of this practice and called on Denmark to ensure that such testing is used only when "necessary and appropriate to the determination of the family tie on which a residence permit is based."[671]

The Access to Information Act and the Access to Public Administration Files Act[672] govern access to government records.

Denmark is a member of the Council of Europe and has signed the Convention for the Protection of Individuals with Regard to Automatic Processing of Personal Data (ETS No. 108).[673] It has signed and ratified the European Convention for the Protection of Human Rights and Fundamental Freedoms.[674] Denmark has not yet signed the Council of Europe Convention on Cybercrime (ETS No. 185). It is a member of the Organization for Economic Cooperation and Development and has adopted the OECD Guidelines on the Protection of Privacy and Transborder Flows of Personal Data.

---

[671] Report of the Human Rights Committee, A/56/40,Volume 1, October 26, 2001

[672] lov nr 572 af 19 desember 1985 om offentlighed i forvaltningen).
<http://www.au.dk/da/regler/1985/lov572/index.html>.
< http://www.vissenbjergkommune.dk/postli/offlov.htm>.

[673] Signed January 28, 1981; Ratified October 23, 1989; Entered into Force February 1, 1990.

[674] Signed February 21, 1991; Ratified March 18, 1992; Entered into Force January 1, 1993.

Greenland

The original (unamended) Danish Public and Private Registers Acts of 1978 and Guidelines regarding Notification of Data Processing Bureaus 1979 continue to apply within Greenland, a self-governing territory. The Danish Data Surveillance Agency oversees compliance with the law. The 1988 amendments that brought Denmark into compliance with the Council of Europe's Convention 108 do not apply to Greenland. Greenland is not part of the European Union and therefore has not adopted the European Union Privacy Directive. Greenland's data protection requirements are much less stringent than those of Denmark and the other nations of the European Union.

Republic of Estonia

The 1992 Estonia Constitution recognizes the right of privacy, secrecy of communications, and data protection. Article 42 states, "No state or local government authority or their officials may collect or store information on the persuasions of any Estonian citizen against his or her free will." Article 43 states, "Everyone shall be entitled to secrecy of messages transmitted by him or to him by post, telegram, telephone or other generally used means. Exceptions may be made on authorization by a court, in cases and in accordance with procedures determined by law in order to prevent a criminal act or for the purpose of establishing facts in a criminal investigation." Article 44 (3) states, "Estonian citizens shall have the right to become acquainted with information about themselves held by state and local government authorities and in state and local government archives, in accordance with procedures determined by law. This right may be restricted by law in order to protect the rights and liberties of other persons, and the secrecy of children's ancestry, as well as to prevent a crime, or in the interests of apprehending a criminal or to clarify the truth for a court case."[675]

The Riigikogu – Estonia's Parliament – enacted the Personal Data Protection Act in June 1996.[676] The Act protects the fundamental rights and freedoms of persons with respect to the processing of personal data and in accordance with the right of individuals to obtain freely any information which is disseminated for public use. The Personal Data Protection Act divides personal data into two groups – non-

---

[675] Constitution of Estonia, available at <http://www.uni-wuerzburg.de/law/en00t___.html>.

[676] Law on the protection of personal data (RT I 1996, 48, 944), available at <http://www.dp.gov.ee/eng/Personal_Data_Protection_Act.html>.

---

sensitive and sensitive personal data. Sensitive personal data are data which reveal political opinions, religious or philosophical beliefs, ethnic or racial origin, health, sexual life, criminal convictions, legal punishments and involvement in criminal proceedings. Processing of non-sensitive personal data is permitted without the consent of the respective individual if it occurs under the terms that are set out in the Personal Data Protection Act. Processed personal data are protected by organizational and technical measures that must be documented. Chief processors must register the processing of sensitive personal data with the data protection supervision authority.

In April 1997, the Riigikogu passed the Databases Act.[677] The Databases Act is a procedural law for the establishment of national databases. The law sets out the general principles for the maintenance of databases, prescribes requirements and protection measures for data processing, and unifies the terminology to be used in the maintenance of databases. Pursuant to the Databases Act, the statutes of state registers or databases that were created before the law took effect must be brought into line with the Act within two years. The Databases Act also mandates the establishment of a state register of databases that registers state and local government databases, as well as databases containing sensitive personal data maintained by persons in private law. The chief processor of the register has the right to make proposals to the government, to the chief processors of various databases, and to the state information systems. He or she would also be responsible for coordinating authority with respect to the expansion, merger or liquidation of databases, database cross-usage, or the organization of data processing or data acquisition in a manner aimed at avoiding duplication of effort or substantially repetitive databases.

There have been several amendments to both of these acts over the last number of years but most have been of technical importance with no principal changes. The Government is currently working on an amendment bill to the Data Protection Act to bring it into full compliance with the 1995 European Union Data Protection Directive. This bill is expected to be introduced in the Parliament in August 2002. At the time of writing a bill to amend the Databases Act was also being debated in Parliament. The changes will mostly relate to support systems for state and local registers.[678] On January 1, 2001, a significant amendment was made to the list of sensitive data in Data Protection Act. According to the amendment, information relating to criminal charges is now

---

[677] Databases Act (RT* I 1997, 28, 423), available at <http://www.dp.gov.ee/eng/Databases_Act.html>.

[678] E-mail from Erki Podra, Head of Analysis and Development Department, Data Protection Inspectorate, Slovakia, to Sarah Andrews, Research Director, Electronic Privacy Information Center, June 4, 2002 (on file with Electronic Privacy Information Center).

treated as sensitive only if it is announced prior to the trial or before the judgment. Such data is deemed sensitive if it is necessary to protect morality or individual's private or family life, or necessary in the interests of a minor, a victim, a witness or a fair trial. The amendment also added information about heredity to the list of sensitive data.

The Data Protection Inspectorate is the supervisory authority for the Personal Data Protection Act and the Databases Act. The Inspectorate, a division of the Ministry of Internal Affairs, monitors compliance, issues licenses, takes complaints, and settles disputes. The agency can conduct investigations and demand documents, impose fines, and impose administrative sanctions.[679] In 2001, the Inspectorate received a total of 103 complaints under the Personal Data Protection and Public Information Act. It issued 57 orders and referred eight cases of criminal violations to relevant authorities. It received 88 registration applications for processing of sensitive data. As of July 2002, there were seventeen staff members, up from eight in 1999.[680]

The Inspectorate maintains close relations with the data protection authorities in other central and eastern European countries. In December 2001, the Data Protection Commissioners from the Czech Republic, Hungary, Lithuania, Slovakia, Estonia, Latvia and Poland signed a joint declaration agreeing to closer cooperation and assistance. The Commissioners agreed to meet twice a year in the future, to provide each other with regular updates and overviews of developments in their countries, and to establish a common website for more effective communication.[681]

In August 2000, the Cabinet approved a bill to create a national genetic database to be used for research into disease.[682] Under a pilot project, which began in January 2002, health data and tissue samples on 10,000 donors is being collected on a voluntary basis. The purpose of the pilot is to test the security and processes of the database. United States registered company, EGeen International Corporation, has agreed to provide financing for the project.[683] Estonia is

---

[679] Home Page <http://www.dp.gov.ee/>.

[680] E-mail from Erki Podra, supra n.678.

[681] E-mail from Karel Neuwirt, President, Office for Personal Data Protection, Czech Republic, to Sarah Andrews, Research Director, Electronic Privacy Information Center, May 15, 2002 (on file with the Electronic Privacy Information Center).

[682] "Estonia To Set Up One Of World's First Gene Banks," Associated Press, August 10, 2000. See also, Estonian Genome Foundation Web site <http://www.genomics.ee/genome/>.

[683] "Estonian Genome Foundation Signs Pilot Project Financing Accords," Baltic News Service, January 2, 2002.

cooperating closely with Iceland in setting up of this database and the two countries are expected to launch joint research projects on human genes.[684]

A new Law on Personal Identity Documents, requiring mandatory ID cards for all Estonian citizens and resident aliens, took effect in January 1, 2002. Although the cards are, at first, to be used for identification purposes only, the Government plans to widen their application in the future. On its face, the card contains standard personal information including name, sex, date of birth, citizenship, personal identification code, date of expiration and signature, and a photograph of the holder.[685] The card also incorporates a microchip storing an electronic identification certificate and an asymmetric key pair allowing for digital identification and digital signatures. Under the Digital Signatures Act of 2000,[686] electronic signatures are given the same legal status as hand written signatures. A PIN is currently used to activate the card but this may eventually be replaced by a biometric.[687] In May 2002, it was discovered that the sealed security envelopes containing the secret PIN and PUK codes issued with the cards were see through when placed under an ordinary light bulb. The Citizen and Migration Board stated that it would immediately change the printing practices.[688] In June 2001 members of the Reform Party introduced a bill seeking to reform the law and make the cards voluntary rather than compulsory. The bill was defeated in Parliament in December 2001.

In 2000, a government backed proposal to amend the tax laws and provide for publication of income tax paid by individuals sparked controversy among the public and opposition parties. Responding to this criticism in Government told the Parliament in October to discuss the bill but not to enact it as law. [689]

The 1994 Surveillance Act regulates the interception of communications, covert surveillance, undercover informants and police and intelligence databases.[690] Surveillance can be approved by a "reasoned decision made by the head of a

---

[684] "Iceland's Premier Confirms Support for Estonian NATO Membership," Newsline, Central and Eastern Europe, May 29, 2001.

[685] Regulation No. 370 of December 4, 2001 on the Establishment of Format and Technical Description of Identity Card and List of Data Entered on Identity Card and Determination of Period of Validity of Digital Data Entered on Identity Card.

[686] Digital Signatures Act, (RT I 2000, 26, 150), passed March 8, 2000, entered into force December 15, 2000. <http://www.riik.ee/riso/digiallkiri/digsignact.rtf>.

[687] "European States Roll out EID Cards," Cards International, February 22, 2002.

[688] "Estonian ID-Card Security Envelopes Shine Through," Baltic News Service, May 3, 2002.

[689] "Estonian Govt Advises Parlt Not To Pass Income Tax Publication Bill," Baltic News Service, October 3, 2000.

[690] Surveillance Act (RT* I 1994, 16, 290, February 22, 1994), available at <http://vlf.juridicum.su.se/master99/library2/teste/Surv.htm>.

---

surveillance agency." "Exceptional surveillance" requires the permission of a judge in the Tallinn Administrative Court for serious crimes. The punishment for illegal surveillance is a fine and three years imprisonment for general surveillance activity, and five years imprisonment for special measures like opening correspondence or telephone bugging.[691] Illegally obtained evidence is not admissible in court. Citizens have a right under the Surveillance Act to obtain access to information held about them by surveillance agencies. Agencies must respond within three months if the agency maintains information about them.[692] In October 1999, the Estonian Police Department refused to grant the Tallinn city police authority the right to plant eavesdropping devices in apartments, offices and telephones to combat organized crime.[693] The law was amended in May 2000 to allow the tax police to conduct surveillance.[694] Under the Telecommunications Act approved in February 2000, surveillance agencies can obtain information on the sender and receiver of messages by written or oral request.[695] Telecommunications providers are also required to delete data within one year and prevent unauthorized disclose of users' information.

In May 1996, the Estonian Intelligence Service started an inquiry on the involvement of former Vice Prime Minister Edgar Saavisar in a politically motivated wiretapping scandal. It eventually led to a change of government.[696] Swedish papers reported in January 2000 that the Estonian secret services had spied on Swedish diplomats.[697] In March 2002, the Estonian United People's Party issued a statement alleging that the national security police engaged in secret surveillance of politicians and members of parliament. The national security police denied these allegations.[698]

The Public Information Act was approved by the Parliament and entered into force in January 1, 2001. Supervision and enforcement of the Act will be conducted by the Data Protection Inspectorate. The law includes significant provisions on electronic access. Government departments and other holders of

---

[691] Criminal Code article 134.

[692] Surveillance Act (RT* I 1994, 16, 290, February 22, 1994)
<http://vlf.juridicum.su.se/master99/library2/teste/Surv.htm>.

[693] Baltic News Service, October 8, 1999.

[694] Estonian government approves plans for tax police, BBC Worldwide Monitoring, May 16, 2000.

[695] Telecommunications Act passed February 9, 2000 (RT I 2000, 18, 116), entered into force March 19, 2000.
<http://www.legaltext.ee/tekstid/X/en/X30063.HTM>.

[696] "Estonian intelligence begins probe into former premier Saavisar," Deutsche Presse-Agentur, May 16, 1996.

[697] "Estonian MP rejects reports that Estonian secret services spied on Swedes," BBC Worldwide Monitoring, January 13, 2000.

[698] "Estonian Security Police is not Involved in Politics," Baltic News Service, March 14, 2002.

public information will have a duty to post information on the web, and e-mail requests must be treated as official requests for information. Citizens have a right under the Surveillance Act to obtain access to information held about them by surveillance agencies. Agencies must respond within three months if the agency maintains information about them.[699]

Estonia is a member of the Council of Europe and has signed and ratified the European Convention for the Protection of Human Rights and Fundamental Freedoms.[700] In November 2001, Estonia ratified the Convention for the Protection of Individuals with Regard to Automatic Processing of Personal Data (ETS No. 108).[701] Also In November, Estonia signed the Council of Europe Convention on Cybercrime.[702]

Republic of Finland

Section 8 of The Constitution Act of Finland states, "The private life, honor and home of every person shall be secured. More detailed provisions on the protection of personal data shall be prescribed by Act of Parliament. The secrecy of correspondence and of telephone and other confidential communications shall be inviolable. Measures impinging on the sphere of the home which are necessary for the protection of fundamental rights or the detection of crime may be prescribed by Act of Parliament. Necessary restrictions on the secrecy of communications may also be provided by Act of Parliament in the investigation of offenses which endanger the security of society or of the individual or which disturb domestic peace, in legal proceedings and security checks as well as during deprivation of liberty."[703] Section 10 of the Constitution also provides for a fundamental right of access to "documents and other records in the possession of public authorities."

The Personal Data Protection Act 1999[704] went into effect on June 1, 1999. The law replaced the 1987 Personal Data File Act[705] to make Finnish law consistent with the European Union Data Protection Directive. The law does not apply to

---

[699] Surveillance Act (RT* I 1994, 16, 290, 22 February 1994)
<http://vlf.juridicum.su.se/master99/library2/teste/Surv.htm>.

[700] Signed May 14, 1993; Ratified April 16, 1996; Entered into Force April 16, 1996.

[701] Signed January 24, 2000; Ratified November 14, 2001; Entered into Force March 01, 2002.

[702] Signed November 23, 2001.

[703] Constitution of Finland, available at <http://www.eduskunta.fi/kirjasto/Lait/constitution.html>.

[704] Personal Data Act (523/99), available at <http://www.tietosuoja.fi/uploads/hopxtvf.HTM>.

[705] Personal Data Files Act (Law No. 471/87).

---

processing of personal data for a private or purely personal use. Activities of "the media, the arts and literary expression" are also excluded from its scope. Exemptions for defense and public security are included in separate legislation. The new act introduces the concept of informed consent and self-determination into Finnish law. The previous act regulated the use and disclosure of information in a personal data file but did not generally require the individual's consent or provide for the same level of notice and access.[706] Processing without consent may still occur, however, under the new system, for example, if there is "assumed consent" or the Data Protection Board has granted permission or if the matter concerns publicly available data on the "status, duties or performance" of a public figure.[707] The law lays down civil and criminal sanctions (including imprisonment of up to one year) for unlawful processing.

The Data Protection Ombudsman (DPO) enforces the Act and receives complaints. In 2000 the number of new cases brought before the DPO increased by nearly one third.[708] The DPO says that this increase is, in part, a result of switching from telephone to electronic customer service. The DPO usually receives 5,000 to 8,000 requests for advice each year.[709] A Data Protection Board resolves disputes and hears appeals of decisions rendered by the DPO. The DPO must be heard during the preparation of legislative or administrative reforms which may impact upon individual privacy rights. In 2000, the DPO issued 43 statements on legislative proposals.[710] The Data Protection Ombudsman issues guidance and consultation documents and assists in the compilation and review of Codes of Conduct by the private sector. In 2001 the DPO issued a guidance paper on the transfer of personal data to third countries.[711]

Telecommunications privacy is regulated by the Protection of Privacy and Data Security in Telecommunications Act, which came into force in July 2000. The law is broad in scope. It covers all telecommunications, including email and communications on the Internet.

---

[706] Peter Blume et al, Nordic Data Protection 49, (DJOF Publishing 2000).

[707] Id.

[708] The Data Protection Ombudsman's Year in Review 2000, available at <http://www.tietosuoja.fi/10993.htm>.

[709] Home Page <http://www.tietosuoja.fi/>.

[710] European Union Article 29 Data Protection Working Party, Fifth Annual Report on the Situation Regarding the Protection of Individuals with Regard to the Processing of Personal Data and Privacy in the European Union and in Third Countries Covering the Year 2000, Part II, March 6, 2002, available at <http://europa.eu.int/comm/internal_market/en/dataprot/wpdocs/wp54en_2.pdf>.

[711] Data Protection Ombudsman, Transfer of Personal Data to a Foreign Country According to the Personal Data Act, Issues About Data Protection 1/2001, January 2001.

In May 2001 a specific law on Data Protection in Working Life[712] was adopted and entered into force in October 2001. This law determines the legality of a number of issues in the workplace, such as psychological, genetic and drug tests, the processing of medical histories and the use of video and audio surveillance devices. In addition, the Telecommunications Privacy Act applies equally in the workplace. Therefore employers in Finland may not monitor the contents of employee's email messages.[713]

The Finnish government has enacted special ordinances that apply to particular personal data systems. These include those operated by the police such as criminal information systems,[714] the National Health Service, passport systems, population registers,[715] farm registers, and motor vehicle registers.[716] In January 2001, a new law on the status and rights of social welfare clients came into force and includes data protection provisions relating to the use of social services. The Public Access to Government Activities Act, which came into force in December 1999, also contains provisions on privacy.[717] In October 1999 the government amended the laws and granted the police a new high-tech means of enforcing traffic fines, which in Finland are based on the driver's income. Whereas before the police would simply ask violators for their income and calculate the fine manually based on that income, they now use cellular phones to access the official tax records. Within seconds the drivers reported income appears up on the screen along with the corresponding fine.[718]

Electronic surveillance and telephone tapping by the government are authorized by the Criminal Law. A judge can give permission to tap the telephone lines of a suspect if the suspect is liable for a jail sentence for crimes that are exhaustively listed in the Coercive Criminal Investigations Means Act. Transactional data of a suspect's telecommunications activity can be obtained if the suspect faces at least four months of jail. Electronic surveillance is possible, with the permission of the judge, if the suspect is accused of a drug related crime or a crime that can be punished with more than four years in jail. There were 12 orders for wiretapping in 1997. Although cases of political telecommunications eavesdropping are rare

---

[712] Law 477/2001.

[713] Peter Blume et al., supra n.706, at 71.

[714] Criminal Records Act (770/93).

[715] Act on Population Information (1993/507).

[716] Jorma Kuopus, "Data Protection Regulatory System," Data Transmission and Privacy, D. Campbell and J. Fisher, eds., (Netherlands: Martinus Nijhoff Publishers, 1994).

[717] Peter Blume et al., supra n.706, at 75-76.

[718] Steve Stecklow, "Finnish Driver's Don't Mind Sliding Scale, But Instant Calculation Gets Low Marks," Wall Street Journal, January 2, 2001.

in Finland, there have been published reports that the Finnish military has either supported Western signals intelligence operations (via its large base at Santahamina on the outskirts of Helsinki), or acquiesced to a Swedish/United States eavesdropping collaborative effort from the Swedish embassy in downtown Helsinki.[719] In 1996, the PENET anonymous remailer was forced to shut down after Scientologists demanded that the identity of users posting critical messages be revealed to the Church. The court order was later enjoined by the Court of Appeals.[720]

National identification numbers have long been in use in Finland. Since the 1970's all citizens have been issued a national identification number consisting of their date of birth and four other characters. The number is used extensively in the public and private sectors. It is included on passports, driving licenses and other personal data files held by the public administration.[721] The Finnish government in December 1999 began issuing new national ID cards (FINEID) based on smart card technology.[722] The cards include digital signatures to communicate online with government agencies and companies. The Finnish Population Register Centre operates as the digital signature certificate authority. The cards can be used in smart card readers in PCs and there are plans to put them in the SIM cards in mobile phones[723] and interactive television systems. The Electronic Services in Administration Act was passed in early 2000 to encourage the use of these digital identity cards but, so far, they have not proved very popular among the public.[724]

The Public Access to Government Activities Act went into effect in 1999 replacing the Publicity of Official Documents Act of 1951.[725] It provides for a general right to access any document created by a government agency, or sent or received by a government agency, including electronic records. Finland is a country that has traditionally adhered to the Nordic tradition of open access to government files. In fact, the world's first Freedom of Information act dates back as far as the Riksdag's (Swedish Parliament) 1766 "Access to Public Records Act." This Act also applied to Finland, then a Swedish-governed territory.[726]

---

[719] See <http://www.qainfo.se/~lb>.

[720] See <http://www.penet.fi/injuncl.html>.

[721] Peter Blume et al., supra n.706, at 41.

[722] See Finnish Population Register Centre <http://www.vaestorekisterikeskus.fi/>.

[723] "Your phone is you," New Scientist.Com, <http://www.newscientist.com/hottopics/tech/yourphoneisyou.jsp>.

[724] Peter Blume et al, supra n.706, at 42.

[725] Act 83/9/2/1951.

[726] Wayne Madsen, Handbook of Personal Data Protection (Stockton Press 1992).

Finland is a member of the Council of Europe and has signed and ratified the Convention for the Protection of Individuals with Regard to Automatic Processing of Personal Data (ETS No. 108).[727] Finland has signed and ratified the European Convention for the Protection of Human Rights and Fundamental Freedoms.[728] In November 2001, Finland signed the Council of Europe Convention on Cyber-Crime.[729] Finland is a member of the Organization for Economic Cooperation and Development and has adopted the OECD Guidelines on the Protection of Privacy and Transborder Flows of Personal Data.

Aland Islands

The Parliament of the self-governing Aland Islands (Landsting) passed its own Data Protection Act in 1991 and independently ratified the Council of Europe's Convention 108.[730] Although the Aland act makes reference to the Finnish Data Protection Act, there has always been some resistance by the Aland Swedish-speaking majority to following orders from Helsinki. Constitutionally, the Aland Parliament may nullify Finnish laws on its territory.[731]

French Republic

The right of privacy is not explicitly included in the French Constitution of 1958. The Constitutional Court ruled in 1994 that the right of privacy was implicit in the Constitution.[732]

The Data Protection Act was enacted in 1978 and covers personal information held by government agencies and private entities.[733] Anyone wishing to process personal data must register and obtain permission in many cases relating to processing by public bodies and for medical research. Individuals must be informed of the reasons for collection of information and may object to its

---

[727] Signed April 10, 1991; Ratified December 2, 1991; Entered into force April 1, 1992.

[728] Signed May 5, 1989; Ratified May 10, 1990; Entered into force May 10, 1990.

[729] Signed November 23, 2001

[730] Kuopus, supra n.716.

[731] Madsen, supra n.726.

[732] Dècision 94-352 du Conseil Constitutionnel du 18 Janvier 1995.

[733] Loi N° 78-17 du Janvier 1978 relative à l'informatique, aux fichiers et aux libertés. J.O., January 7, 1978 and arratum at J.O., January 25, 1978, modified by Law No. 88-227 of March 11, 1988, Law No. 92-1336 of December 16, 1992, Law No. 94-548 of July 1st, 1994, Law No. 99-641 of July 27, 1999, and Law No. 2000-321 of April 12, 2000., <http://www.cnil.fr/textes/text02.htm> and <http://www.cnil.fr/textes/index.htm>. Cfr English approved but not updated version at <http://ccweb.in2p3.fr/secur/legal/a78-17-text-local.html>.

processing either before or after it is collected. Individuals have rights to access information being kept about them and to demand the correction and, in some cases, the deletion of this data. Fines and imprisonment can be imposed for violations.

As a member of the European Union, France should have amended its data protection regime to make it consistent with the European Data Protection Directive (95/46/EC) by October 1, 1998.[734] In July 2000, pre-draft legislation to update the law was sent to the data protection authority for review and consultation.[735] The Council of Ministers then examined the text on July 18, 2001 which passed the first reading by the National Assembly on January 30, 2002.[736] The bill is now before the Senate since the end of January 2002. First reading by the Senate is expected in Autumn 2002.

The new data protection law would generally increase the powers of the data protection authority by allowing it to investigate, issue warnings, and impose sanctions (by fines of up to EUR 150,000). The data protection authority is the Commission nationale de l'informatique et des libertés (CNIL), an independent agency which enforces the Data Protection Act and other related laws.[737] The Commission takes complaints, issues rulings, sets rules, conducts audits, makes reports, and ensures the public access to information by being a registrar of all data controllers' processing activities. The new law would give the CNIL more authority over commercial data processing files. Further, the bill implements the legal framework for personal data transfers to third countries. It also strengthens individuals' rights of access and correction. However, it would weaken the commission's control over large government information systems by creating a new data system category, known as "sovereignty files" over which the CNIL would loose key powers.[738] Whereas before the approval of the commission was needed before any government processing system could be established, this would no longer be necessary for these sovereignty files. They are defined to include files relating to the safety of the State, defence, public security or penal

---

[734] Arrêt de la Cour (deuxième chambre) du 14 février 2001. Commission des Communautés européennes contre République française. Manquement d'Etat - Manquement non contesté - Directive 95/16/CE.Affaire C-219/99.

[735] Avis de la Commission nationale de l'informatique et des libertés sur le projet de loi modifiant la loi du 6 janvier 1978 relative à l'informatique, aux fichiers et aux libertés, available at <http://www.cnil.fr/actu/actualites/doc/aviscnildonneesperso.pdf>.

[736] The draft law and related documents are available at <http://www.legifrance.gouv.fr/html/actualite/actualite_legislative/prepa/cnil.htm>.

[737] Homepage <http://www.cnil.fr>.

[738] Philippe Astor and Jérôme Thorel, "L'ombre du fichier Stic plane sur La réforme de la CNIL," ZDNet France, July 18, 2001, available at <http://news.zdnet.fr/story/0,,s2091559,00.html>.

---

repression, or those that use the NIR (social security number). It is thought that this revision is a response to the difficulties experienced by the government in implementing the STIC. This system was first envisioned in 1995 but was not implemented until July 2000 following the reluctant approval of the CNIL. Since 1978 the CNIL has received over 11,500 requests for advice and 36,200 complaints. It reported in its 1999 annual report that the number of inquiries received annually had more than doubled since 1995.[739] It received a total of 5,617 inquiries[740] in 2000.[741] In 2001,[742] the total of inquiries was 5,729.[743]

The CNIL's 2000 report addresses in detail the establishment of the Système de Traitement des Infractions Constatées ("STIC"), an initiative by the Minister of Interior to merge police and other records; the use of biometrics as access control devices; spamming; the rise in workplace surveillance; online health services; children web sites; security in credit cards, and the globalization of privacy protections. After a study of 100 e-commerce web sites in 2000, the CNIL noticed a increasing level of awareness on their part, although negative findings included the lack of information on the data subject's right of access and on the purposes of 'cookies'.

In September 2001, the CNIL hosted the 23rd Annual Meeting of the World Data Protection Commissioners.[744]

Electronic surveillance is regulated by a 1991 law that requires permission of an investigating judge before a wiretap is installed. The duration of the tap is limited to four months and can be renewed.[745] The law created the Commission Nationale de Contrôle des Interceptions de Sécurité, which sets rules and reviews wiretaps each year. From 1995 – 1999 the number of wiretaps granted annually was between 4,500 and 4,700. This number decreased slightly in 2000. There

---

[739] CNIL, 20e rapport d'activite 1999, July 5, 2000.

[740] Of these 3,399 were complaints, 1049 were requests for advice, 817 were access requests, 208 were requests for the registration lists maintained by the CNIL and 144 were requests to be removed from commercial files. In particular, the number of requests by private individuals for checking files held on them by police forces rose by 21%, leading to 1,300 investigations. In response to complaints, the CNIL also carried out about 40 on-the-spot checks, especially at credit institutions and social housing bodies.

[741] CNIL, 21e rapport d'activité 2000, July 9, 2001.

[742] CNIL, 22e rapport d'activité 2001, July 10, 2002, available at <http://www.ladocumentationfrancaise.fr/brp/notices/024000377.shtml>.

[743] Of these 3,754 were complaints (+5.1%), 973 were requests for advice, (-7.2%), 836 were access requests (+2.3%), 252 were requests for the registration lists maintained by the CNIL (+21.1%) and 94 were requests to be removed from commercial files (-34.7%).

[744] 23rd International Conference of Data Protection Commissioners, Paris, September 2001.

[745] La loi n° 91-636 du 10 juillet 1991 relative au secret des correspondances émises par la voie des télécommunications.

were 4,289 requests for wiretaps in 2000. In total, 4175 wiretaps (2689 new and 1486 renewals) were authorized by the Commission.[746] The interception of cellular telephones rose from 12 percent of all wiretaps in January 1999 to 27.5 percent in December 1999.[747]

The European Court of Human Rights has ruled against France a number of times for violations of Article 8 of the Convention. The Court's 1990 decision in *Kruslin v. France* resulted in the enactment of the 1991 law.[748] Most recently, the court fined France FRF 25,000 for wiretap law violations.[749] There have been many cases of illegal wiretapping, including most notably a long running scandal over an anti-terrorist group in the office of President Mitterand monitoring the calls of journalists and opposition politicians.[750] The CNCIS estimated that there were over 100,000 illegal taps conducted by private companies and individuals in 1996, many on behalf of government agencies. A decree was issued in 1997 to limit the dissemination of tapping equipment.[751] In June 2001 the investigative weekly *Le Canard Enchaîné* reported that a prosecution judge was sued by a lawyer who was wiretapped at the judge's request. The Court found that the wiretap was an unfair act against the lawyer. In France only Government interceptions requests are under review by the CNCIS. There is a separate control scheme for wiretap requests by the judiciary.

The tort of privacy was first recognized in France as far back as 1858[752] and was added to the Civil Code in 1970.[753] There are additional specific laws on administrative documents,[754] archives,[755] video surveillance,[756]

---

[746] 9e rapport d' activité 2000, Commission nationale de contrôle des interceptions de sécurité, July 2001.

[747] 8e rapport d' activité 1999, Commission nationale de contrôle des interceptions de sécurité, May 2000.

[748] *Kruslin v. France*, 176-A, Eur. Ct. H.R. (ser. A) (1990).

[749] La France condamnée par la Cour européenne des droits de l'homme, Le Monde, August 27, 1998.

[750] See Capitaine Paul Barril, Guerres Secrètes à L'Élysée (Albin Michel, 1996) ; Francis Zamponi, Les RG à l'écoute de la France: Police et politique de 1981 à 1997 (La Découverte, 1998).

[751] 5e rapport d' activité 1997, Commission nationale de contrôle des interceptions de sécurité, May 1998.

[752] The *Rachel* affaire. Judgment of June 16, 1858, Trib. pr. inst. de la Seine, 1858 D.P. III 62. See Jeanne M. Hauch, Protecting Private Facts in France: The Warren & Brandeis Tort is Alive and Well and Flourishing in Paris, 68 Tul. L. Rev. 1219 (May 1994).

[753] Civil Code, Article 9, Statute No. 70-643 of July 17, 1970.

[754] Loi n° 78-753 du 17 juillet 1978 portant diverses mesures d'amélioration des relations entre l'administration et le public et diverses dispositions d'ordre administratif, social et fiscal. (Journal officiel du 18 juillet 1978, page 2851). <http://www.cnil.fr/textes/text05.htm>.

[755] Loi n° 79-18 du 3 janvier 1979 sur les archives (Journal officiel du 5 janvier 1979, page 43, rectificatif au journal officiel du 6 janvier 1979, page 55).

[756] Loi d'orientation et de programmation n° 95-73 du 21 janvier 1995 relative à la sécurité (Journal officiel du 24 janvier 1995, page 1249). <http://www.cnil.fr/textes/text054.htm>. Also see Décret n° 96-926 du 17 octobre 1996 relatif à la vidéo-surveillance pris pour l'application de l'article 10 de la loi n° 95-73 du 21 janvier 1995 d'orientation et de programmation relative à la sécurité (Journal officiel du 20 octobre 1996, page 15432). <http://www.cnil.fr/textes/text055.htm> and Circulaire du 22 octobre 1996 relative à l'application de l'article 10

correspondence,[757] and employment.[758] There are also protections incorporated in the Penal Code.[759]

The French Liberty of Communication Act was adopted on June 28th, 2000.[760] The Act requires all persons wishing to post content on the Internet to identify themselves, either to the public, by publishing their name and address on their website (in the case of a business) or to their host provider (in the case of a private individual). Earlier provisions, which would have imposed large penalties and jail sentences on anybody violating this requirement and required Internet Service Providers (ISPs) to check the accuracy of the personal details given to them, were dropped in the final version of the legislation.[761] The law requires ISPs to keep logs of all data which could be used to identify a content provider in the case of later legal proceedings. This provision will enter into force when its implementing decree (décret d'application) will be published. ISPs are subject to the "professional secret" rule regarding this data, meaning that they cannot disclose it to anyone except a judge. The law, as passed, also held ISPs liable for failing to delete content once ordered to do so by a judge or for failing to "take appropriate actions" once informed by a third party that they are hosting illegal or harmful content. In a review of this law, however, brought before it on June 29, 2000 by 60 opposition members of Parliament,[762] the French Constitutional Council struck down this provision as contrary to Art 34 of the Constitution.[763] This article states that any measures that could impact upon civil liberties must be detailed in the law. In this case, the Council ruled that the "appropriate actions" to be taken by ISPs should have been specified in the law. As a result, the law was subsequently amended to remove the impugned provision and ISPs may now only be made liable if they fail to delete content having been told to do so by a judge. The passage of this law provoked widespread criticism from civil liberties groups and privacy advocates who argued that it would restrict rights to

de la loi n° 95-73 du 21 janvier 1995 d'orientation et de programmation relative à la sécurité (décret sur la vidéosurveillance) (Journal officiel du 7 décembre 1996, page 17835). <http://www.cnil.fr/textes/text056.htm>.

[757] Code of Post and Telecommunications, L. 41.

[758] Loi n° 92-1446 du 31 décembre 1992 relative à l'emploi, au développement du travail à temps partiel et à l'assurance chômage. (Journal officiel du 1er janvier 1993, page 19).

[759] Penal Code, Article 368.

[760] Loi n° 553 du 28 juin 2000, modifiant la loi n° 86-1067 du 30 septembre 1986 relative à la liberté de communication.

[761] A full history of the developments since the law was first introduced in May, 1999 is available (in French) at <http://www.iris.sgdg.org/actions/loi-comm/index.html>.

[762] Saisine du Conseil constitutionnel par plus de 60 députés, June 29, 2000.

[763] Conseil Constitutionnel, Décision n° 2000-433 DC, July 27, 2000.

anonymity and free speech. In June 2000, IRIS, a French civil liberties group, drew up a petition in opposition to the law.[764]

On June 13, 2001, the Government introduced the draft "Law on the Information Society" (or LSI).[765] This law, which purports to implement the European Union E-Commerce Directive and includes many provisions affecting data protection rules, seeks to expand liability for illegal content on the Internet. ISPs would now be made civilly liable for failing to delete or deny access to content once they have been informed that it is illegal. This liability would extend not only to host providers but also to access providers and telecoms operators. The proposed law would also have a negative impact on privacy and anonymity. ISPs would be required to store log files on all their customers' activities for up to one year. In submitting comments to the Government on this proposal earlier this year, the CNIL recommended that a distinction should be drawn between information necessary for invoicing purposes and information kept solely for law enforcement purposes and that there should be a three month limitation for retention of the latter. The draft law also proposes government access to private encryption keys, import and export restrictions on encryption software, and strict sanctions for using cryptographic technique to commit a crime. Another section of the bill compels government ministries to give access to their digital data to all citizens free of charge. It also sets forth short mandatory delays for the publication of classified information in public archives. The French civil liberties group IRIS launched a campaign against this law, arguing among other things that the data retention provisions of the law violate the European Union Telecommunications Privacy Directive 97/66/EC. IRIS made a comprehensive dossier of all relevant documents publicly available.[766]

On November 15, 2001, the Parliament enacted the *Loi sur la Sécurité Quotidienne* (or LSQ)[767], a legislation in which new anti-terrorism provisions were added, in direct response to the September 11, 2001 terrorist attacks. The enacted law includes provisions on data retention[768] and compelled access for the government to cryptography keys. These provisions have been extracted from the draft "Law on the Information Society" (or LSI). They still need, however, the

---

[764] Loi sur la liberté de communication, Déclaration des acteurs d'Internet, available at <http://www.iris.sgdg.org/actions/loi-comm/declaration.html>.

[765] Text (in French) available at <http://www.legifrance.gouv.fr/html/actualite/actualite_legislative/prepa/pl_pli.htm>.

[766] Due to French Presidential and Legislative elections in May and June 2002, this draft law would need a resubmission by the new French government to be examined by the French Parliament.

[767] Law No. 2001-1062 of November 15, 2001, J.O. November 16, 2001.

[768] Internet Service Providers and telecommunications companies now are compelled to record and store traffic and location data of their subscribers for a period of maximum one year.

publication of an implementing decree (*décret d'application*) to enter into force. The LSQ was contested by many civil liberties groups because it heavily curtails human rights, was adopted hurriedly in defiance of regular legislative procedure, and under the pretext of the fight against terrorism.[769]

Two orders ("*ordonnances*") have implemented parts of the European Union Directive for the protection of privacy in the telecommunications sector (97/66/EC) and the Distance Sales Directive (97/7/EC).[770]

Two laws in France provide for a right to access administrative documents held by public bodies.[771] The *Commission d'accès aux documents administratifs ("CADA")* is charged with enforcing the acts.[772] It can mediate and issue recommendations but its decisions are not binding. According to the CADA, it handled 4,000 inquiries per year between 1996 and 1999, and 4,900 in 2000.[773] The law was amended in April 2000 to clarify access to legal documents and also identify the civil servant processing the request.[774]

Case law in the field of surveillance at the workplace significantly progressed in clarity with a landmark decision by the Cour de cassation last year. The French Supreme Court established that an employee has the right to privacy even at the workplace and during working hours, and that, as a result, deserves respect of the secrecy of his correspondence by his employer. The employer is now prohibited from getting access to his employee's e-mails if they are labeled private, even if the employer were to provide that the e-mail is limited to professional matters.[775]

---

[769] See <http://www.iris.sgdg.org/actions/loi-sec/>.

[770] Orders of July 25, 2001 (J.O., July 28, 2001, p. 12132, <http://www.legifrance.gouv.fr>) and of August 23, 2001 (J.O., August 25, 2001, p. 13645, <http://www.legifrance.gouv.fr>) provide that direct marketing by automated calling systems or facsimile machines towards a subscriber or a user of telecommunications network is forbidden where such subscriber or user has not given his prior consent. Other means of communication may be used only where there is no objection from the consumer.

[771] Loi no. 78-753 du 17 juillet 1978 de la liberté d'accès au documents administratifs; Loi no. 79-587 du juillet 1979 relative à la motivation des actes administratifs et à l'amélioration des relations entre l'administration et le public. Amended by Loi no. 2000-321 du 12 avril 2000 relative aux droits des citoyens dans leurs relations avec les administrations (J.O., April 13, 2000).

[772] Rapport d'activité - 9ème rapport Commission d'accès aux documents administratifs (CADA) Edition 1999, available at <http://www.ladocfrancaise.gouv.fr/fic_pdf/cada.pdf>.

[773] For more details, see David Banisar, Freedom of Information and Access to Government Records Around the World, available at <http://www.freedominfo.org/survey/>.

[774] Loi n°2000-321 du 12 avril 2000 relative aux droits des citoyens dans leurs relations avec les administrations (J.O. du 13 avril 2000).

[775] Cass. fr. October 2, 2001 S.A. Nikon France v. Frédérick Onof. See also Christophe Guillemin, "L'entreprise n'a aucun droit de regard sur les couriers personnels", ZDNet France, <http://news.zdnet.fr/cgi-bin/fr/printer_friendly.cgi?id=2096632>.

France is a member of the Council of Europe and has signed and ratified the Convention for the Protection of Individuals with Regard to Automatic Processing of Personal Data (ETS No. 108).[776] and earlier, the European Convention for the Protection of Human Rights and Fundamental Freedoms.[777] In November 2001, the French government signed the Council of Europe Cyber-crime Convention.[778] France is a member of the Organization for Economic Cooperation and Development and has adopted the OECD Guidelines on the Protection of Privacy and Transborder Flows of Personal Data.

Federal Republic of Germany

Article 10 of the Basic Law states: "(1) Privacy of letters, posts, and telecommunications shall be inviolable. (2) Restrictions may only be ordered pursuant to a statute. Where a restriction serves to protect the free democratic basic order or the existence or security of the Federation, the statute may stipulate that the person affected shall not be informed of such restriction and that recourse to the courts shall be replaced by a review of the case by bodies and auxiliary bodies appointed by Parliament." Attempts to amend the Basic Law to include a right to data protection were discussed after reunification, when the Constitution was revised, and were successfully opposed by the then-conservative political majority.

In a 1983 case against a government census law, the Federal Constitutional Court formally acknowledged an individual's "right of informational self-determination" which is limited by the "predominant public interest." The central part of the verdict stated, "Who can not certainly overlook which information related to him or her is known to certain segments of his social environment, and who is not able to assess to a certain degree the knowledge of his potential communication partners, can be essentially hindered in his capability to plan and to decide. The right of informational self-determination stands against a societal order and its underlying legal order in which citizens could not know any longer who what and when in what situations knows about them."[779] This landmark court decision derived the "right of informational self-determination" directly from Articles 1(1) and 2(1) of the Basic Law, which declare the personal right (Persönlichkeitsrecht) to freedom to be inviolable.

---

[776] Signed January 28; 1981; Ratified March 24, 1983; Entered into Force October 1, 1985.

[777] Signed November 11, 1950; Ratified May 3, 1974; Entered into Force May 3, 1974.

[778] Signed November 23, 2001.

[779] BverfGE 65,1.

Prior to the terrorist attacks in the United States in September 2001, Germany had the strictest data protection laws of any European Union state.[780] The world's first data protection law was passed in the German Land of Hessen in 1970. In 1977, a Federal Data Protection Law (BDSG) followed, which was reviewed in 1990, amended in 1994 and 1997. The general purpose of this law is "to protect the individual against violations of his personal right (Persönlichkeitsrecht) by handling person-related data." The law covers collection, processing and use of personal data collected by public federal and state authorities (as long as there is no state regulation), and by non-public offices, if they process and use data for commercial or professional aims.

Germany was slow to update its law to make it consistent with the European Union Data Protection Directive. Under the terms of the directive Germany should have harmonized its law by October 1998. The European Commission announced in January 2000 that it was going to take Germany to court for failure to implement the directive. An amending bill was approved by the Government on June 14, 2000 and finally passed into law in May 2001. The 2001 revisions to the BDSG include regulations on transmitting personal data abroad, video surveillance, anonymization and pseudonymization, smart cards, and sensitive data collection (relating to race/ethnic origin, political opinions, religious or philosophical convictions, union membership, health, and sexual orientation). It grants data subjects greater rights of objection. It also states that companies must now appoint a data protection officer if they collect, process, or use personal information; that databases collecting such information must be registered with Germany; and that consent from the individual whose data is collected is required after full disclosure of data collection and its consequences. According to the Data Protection Commission, secondary legislation will need to be introduced on the auditing requirements and a more general revision of German data protection law may be outlined by the end of 2002.[781] In an effort to improve investigative measures to target sexual abuse of children, the German Budesrat approved a proposal in May 2002 to make the current maximum allowed time for data retention the new minimum required time, effectively permitting limitless data retention. The Bundestag was expected to vote on this proposed law by late 2002.

---

[780] "Terrorism Reaches Germany Amid Warnings on Extremists," Deutsche Presse-Agentur, April 17, 2002.

[781] E-mail from Helmut Heil, Federal Data Protection Commission, to Sarah Andrews, Research Director, the Electronic Privacy Information Center, June 26 2001 (on file with the Electronic Privacy Information Center).

The Federal Data Protection Commission (Bundesbeauftragte für den Datenschutz) is responsible for supervision of the Data Protection Act.[782] Its chief duties include receiving and investigating complaints, as well as submitting recommendations to parliament and other governmental bodies. In 2001 there were between 10,000 and 20,000 data controllers registered by the agency.[783] However, the number of controllers is steadily decreasing as federal agencies, in compliance with the 2001 changes to the Act, appoint in-house data protection officers office,(as an alternative to registration under the Act).[784] The Commission, which has 70 persons on staff, handles about 4,500 written and oral complaints and carries out around 45 investigations each year.[785]

All of the 16 Länder have their own specific data protection regulations that cover the public sector of the Länder administrations. Thirteen of the Länder (Brandenburg, Baden-Württemberg, Bayern, Hessen, Nordrhein-Westfalen, Schleswig-Holstein)Schleswig-Holstein, Berlin, Hamburg, Niederschsen, Saarland, Sachsen-Anhalt, Thüringen, and Mecklenburg-Vorpommern[786]) have adopted new data protection laws pursuant to the European Union Directive. Each Land also has a commission to enforce the Länder data protection acts.[787] Supervision, however, is carried out for the private sector by the Land authority designated by the Land data protection law (usually the Land Data Protection Commissioner).

Another important Federal law in Germany is the G-10 law, which imposes limitations on the secrecy of certain communications. The G-10 law was amended in 2001 to require that service providers give law enforcement the means to monitor data as well as voice lines.[788] Officials are trying to convince Internet Service Providers to self-regulate content,[789] and European ISPs and data protection commissioners continue to resist demands from police agencies that they allow expanded surveillance of e-mail and store related data. These demands

---

[782] Home Page <http://www.bfd.bund.de/>.

[783] Fax from Ulrich Dammann, Bundesbeauftragte für den Datenschutz, to Sarah Andrews, Research Director, the Electronic Privacy Information Center, July 27, 2000 (on file with the Electronic Privacy Information Center).

[784] E-mail from Helmut Heil, Federal Data Protection Commission, to Marcia Hoffman, IPIOP Clerk, the Electronic Privacy Information Center, June 7, 2002 (on file with the Electronic Privacy Information Center).

[785] Id.

[786] Id.

[787] Links to the Ländesbeauftragten für den Datenschutz are available at <http://www.datenschutz-berlin.de/sonstige/behoerde/ldbauf.htm>.

[788] "Germany: New Law Allows More Extensive Government Monitoring of Phone Calls and Email," World Socialist Web Site, February 20, 2001.

[789] "ISPs Must Help Stop Hate Web Content," Newsbytes, July 27, 2001.

stem from the telecommunications surveillance directive (TKUV) proposed by the ministry in February 2001 and are similar to the Enfopol 38 proposals at the European Union level.

In May 2002 the European Parliament voted to adopt a series of amendments that will modify current telecommunications privacy law and will take effect near the end of 2003. (See section on Electronic Communications Privacy Directive). In October 2001, the German government passed a law to take effect in 2005 requiring fixed and wireless telecommunication companies to install technology that gives police and security agencies access to most German communications. ISPs are not affected by this law.[790] In an effort to improve investigative measures to target sexual abuse of children, the German Budesrat approved a proposal in May 2002 to make the current maximum allowed time for data retention the new minimum required time, effectively permitting limitless data retention. The Bundestag was expected to vote on this proposed law by late 2002.

Wiretapping is also regulated by the G-10 law and requires a court order for criminal cases.[791] In July 1999, the Constitutional Court issued a decision on a 1994 law which authorizes warrantless automated wiretaps (screening method) of international communications by the intelligence service (BND) for purposes of preventing terrorism and illegal trade in drugs and weapons. It was reported in 1999 that the BND had 1,400 operatives listening in on satellite communications.[792] The Constitutional Court ruled in December 1999 that the government could conduct surveillance of political parties if it is believed that they are hostile to the constitution and information can not be obtained by public means.[793] Also, telephone monitoring has been on the increase since 1997, when there were 7,776 instances of monitoring, up to 9,802 in 1998 and 12,651 in 1999. This renewed rise of interventions in secret communications gives the Federal Commissioners great concern for data security. For years, the Commissioners have appealed to prosecution authorities to use this means sparingly.

---

[790] Steve Gold, "German Carriers Told To Install Cyber-Snooping Tech," Newsbytes, October 25, 2001.

[791] "Gesetz zur Beschraenkung des Brief-, Post- und Fernmeldegeheimnisses - Gesetz zu Artikel 10 des Grundgesetzes (GG10)" (Law on Restriction of the Right of Secrecy of Letters, Mail and Telecommunication - Law Applying to Article 10 of the Constitution). 13. August 1968 (G10 BGBl. I, p. 949) and was changed the last time by the bill of 28.10. 1994 (BGBl. I, p.3186ff) "Verbrechensbekaempfungsgesetz" ("Crime-Fighting Law").

[792] "German Phone Taps are Routine," The Independent, July 10, 1999.

[793] "Constitutional Court Upholds Covert Investigation of Political Parties," The Week in Germany, December 10, 1999.

After a fiercely fought six-year political debate, a two-thirds majority of the German parliament eventually approved a change to Section 13 of the Constitution in April 1998, making it legal for police authorities to place bugging devices even in private homes (provided there is a court order). The change was the provision for the "law for the enhancement of the fight against organized crime," which became effective in 1999. In April 1998, a law was passed that allows the Bundeskrimalamt to run a nationwide database of genetic profiles related to criminal investigations and convicted offenders. One month later, the Bundesgrenzschutz, originally a para-military border police force, now responsible for guarding railways and stations, received permission to check persons' identities and baggage without any concrete suspicion.[794]

Wherever they deal with the handling of personal information on natural persons, either directly or by amendments, nearly all German laws contain references to the respective data protection law or carry special sections on the handling of personal data that reflect the right to privacy. Most recently there have been a number of laws relating to communications privacy. The Telecommunications Carriers Data Protection Ordinance of 1996, revised in 2000, protects privacy of telecommunications information.[795]

The Information and Communication Services (Multimedia) Act of 1997 sets protections for information used in computer networks.[796] Despite these statutory protections, a September 2001 poll revealed that two of every five German PC owners over the age of 14 voluntarily go without the Internet because of data security concerns.[797] The Act also sets out the legal requirements for digital signatures, which were made legally binding by legislation passed in 2001 to conform to the European Union directive.[798] In January 2002 the German government announced plans to provide within three years more than 200,000

---

[794] "New Powers For The Border Police: Checks Anywhere At Any Time," Fortress Europe, FECL 56 (December 1998).

[795] Telecommunications Carriers Data Protection Ordinance (TDSV) of July 12, 1996 (Federal Law Gazette I at 982), Federal Ministry of Posts and Telecommunications, available at <http://www.datenschutz-berlin.de/gesetze/medien/tdsve.htm>.

[796] Federal Act Establishing the General Conditions for Information and Communication Services - Information and Communication Services Act - (Informations- und Kommunikationsdienste-Gesetz - IuKDG) June 13, 1997, available at <http://www.datenschutz-berlin.de/gesetze/medien/iukdge.htm>. Also see Resolution of the Conference of Data Protection Commissioners of the Federation and the Länder of April 29, 1996 on key points for the regulation in matters of data protection of online services, available at <http://datenschutz-berlin.de/sonstige/konferen/sonstige/old-res2.htm>.

[797] "Data Theft Terror: German PC Owners Refuse to Surf," Deutsche Presse-Agentur, September 23, 2001.

[798] European Union Article 29 Data Protection Working Party, Fifth Annual Report on the Situation Regarding the Protection of Individuals With Regard to the Processing of Personal Data and Privacy In the European Union and In Third Countries, Part II, March 6, 2002, available at <http://europa.eu.int/comm/internal_market/en/dataprot/wpdocs/wp54en_2.pdf>.

---

federal employees with the ability to sign electronic documents with chip cards containing encrypted keys. Such signatures would hold the same legal weight as handwritten signatures on paper documents.[799]

Additionally, there are some privacy issues addressed by laws covering other areas. For example, it is an offense under Section 1 of the German Unfair Competition Act to send unsolicited commercial communications in Germany. This effectively means that sending direct marketing e-mail without the consumer's consent is illegal under German law, as the e-mail would be regarded as unsolicited.[800] Despite these legal protections, a June 2002 study conducted by the German Electronic Commerce Forum revealed that spam e-mail is a considered a significant problem by German consumers.[801]

In 1996, the Berlin Data Protection Commissioner reached an agreement with German Railway and a United States bank (Citibank), who were planning to issue combined Railway and Visa cards. As all processing of information would have taken place in the United States, the Berlin Data Protection Commissioner invoked the European Union Directive's prohibition on transborder flows of data to stop the deal. The transaction was allowed to go through once German Railway and Citibank signed a contract guaranteeing German citizens the same protection for their personal information in the United States as they enjoyed in Germany.[802] The agreement was an important precursor for transborder dataflows to the United States and other countries without privacy laws.[803]

In June 2001, the German Ministry of the Economy and Technology presented a software prototype that would let consumers make anonymous Internet purchases and payments. The software was scheduled for general availability in 2002. This is part of a project called Data Protection in Teleservices (DASIT), the goal of which is to develop software that can accommodate data privacy law requirements. State Secretary for the Ministry of the Economy and Technology Margareta Wolf said that 79 percent of online shops fail to adequately inform customers about their data privacy rights, and that 84 percent of Germans have

---

[799] Rick Perera, "German Federal Employees Get Digital Signatures," CNN.com, January 21, 2002 <http://www.cnn.com/2002/TECH/ptech/01/21/german.government.idg/index.html>.

[800] "Personal Protection," The Lawyer, May 14, 2001.

[801] "Spam Fuelling Consumer Backlash: Study," The Sydney Morning Herald, June 6, 2002, available at <http://www.smh.com.au/articles/2002/06/06/1022982732852.html>.

[802] Christopher Millard and Mark Ford, Data Protection Laws of the World, (Sweet and Maxwell 2000), Volume 1, at 9.

[803] Dr.iur. Alexander Dix, "Case Study: North America and the European Directive - The German RailwayCard: A model contractual solution of the "adequate level of protection" issue?" September 1996, available at <http://www.datenschutz-berlin.de/sonstige/konferen/ottawa/alex3.htm>.

---

privacy concerns about surfing the web. The program meets the quality criteria for Internet data privacy protection and the teleservices data privacy law.

In early 2001, German government agents entered the homes of 103 people who they claimed were trading music files of "skinhead bands" online. Police seized computers and pressed charges that could lead to 3-year prison sentences. Even though it is legal under German law to listen to such MP3 files, law enforcement officials argued that transferring those files over the Internet is illegal. The government stresses that it is looking for any possible "lawful ways" to fight against far-right websites, which may involve such tactics as allowing government agents to send large amounts of e-mail to those websites in an attempt to disrupt their servers.[804]

In May 2002, Germany's Minister of Health, Data Protection Commissioner, and healthcare organizations announced plans for the development of an electronic universal healthcare card. The proposed card will contain, among other data, a patient's identification and emergency healthcare information. Patients will be able to use the card to fill prescriptions and disclose healthcare information to physicians on a voluntary basis. The card will likely be implemented in 2003.[805] There is currently no general Freedom of Information act in Germany. On June 22, 2001, the Federal Government presented the design for a Freedom of Information law (*Informationsfreiheitsgesetz*, or IFG). The law, which was supposed to be modeled after the United States Freedom of Information Act, would have allowed citizens to request access to basically all information on federal authorities. In 2002, however, the Bundestag elected not to enact the proposed law.[806] Some Länderalready have their own FOI laws in effect. The Land of Brandenberg adopted an FOI law in 1998 to allow citizen access to government records.[807] The Information and Data Protection Commissioner enforces the act. More recently, Berlin,[808] Schleswig-Holstein,[809] and Nordrhein-Westfalen[810] have also adopted FOI laws.

---

[804] "German Government Searches Net Music Lovers' Homes," BNA World Data Protection Report, Volume 1, Issue 5, May 2001.

[805] "Heathcare Groups Agree Parameters For Health Card," World Data Protection Report, Volume 2, Issue 6 (June 2002).

[806] E-mail from Alexander Dix, Commissioner for Data Protection and Access to Information, Brandenburg,to Marcia Hoffman, IPIOP Clerk, Electronic Privacy Information Center, June 5, 2002 (on file with the Electronic Privacy Information Center).

[807] Akteneinsichts- und Informationszugangsgesetz (AIG), 1998.

[808] See generally, <http://www.datenschutz-berlin.de/recht/bln/ifg/ifg.htm>.

[809] See generally, <http:// www.datenschutzzentrum.de/material/recht/infofrei/infofrei.htm>.

[810] E-mail from Alexander Dix, supra n.806.

Since 1990, a law has allowed for access to the files of the Stasi, the security service of former East Germany, by individuals and researchers.[811] The law created a Federal Commission for the Records of the State Security Services of the Former GDR (the Gauck Authority), which has a staff of 3,000 piecing together shredded documents and making files available.[812] There have been 1.6 million requests from individuals for access to the files and 2.7 million requests for background checks since the archives became available.[813] Many of the files were destroyed in 1989, but sometime in 1990, the United States Central Intelligence Agency was able to obtain the names, aliases and payment histories of 4,000 spies who worked in various countries for Stasi or informers from the Soviet Union. The United States Government refused to give the files to the German government until December 1999, claiming that it would harm the people in the files.[814] In May 2000, files about former Chancellor Helmut Kohl's telephone calls were found to be missing from the archives when they were going to be used to investigate corruption. The Stasi had conducted extensive wiretapping of Kohl for years.[815] In late 2000, Kohl's lawyers launched legal action to prevent the publication of transcripts of his telephone conversations recorded by the Stasi. The government wanted to release those it believes are of historical interest, but Kohl's lawyers argued say that the information was gathered illegally.[816] In July 2001, the Federal Administrative Court ruled that no information collected by the Stasi about public figures should be disclosed to researchers or the media without express consent of that person.[817] In July 2002, Parliament passed a law to reverse the effects of the ruling and allow journalists and historians to access these files but only for the purposes of examining the operations of the Stasi.[818]

Germany enacted a number of provisions intended to deter terrorist activity after the September 2001 attacks in the United States. The Counterterrorism Act, which took effect in January 2002, comprehensively changed a number of existing laws. Among the most prominent revisions are those that create legal bases for biometric identification in passports and identity cards; make it easier for authorities to share information; allow the Secret Service to request user information from ISPs, airlines, and travel agencies; and create a speech

---

[811] For an English translation of the Stasi Records Act, see <http://www.bstu.de/englisch/index.htm>.

[812] Homepage <http://www.bstu.de/home.htm>.

[813] "Gauck Reports Steady Flow of Inquiries About Stasi Records," The Week in Germany, July 16, 1999.

[814] "United States-Held Files Seen Uncovering E. German Spies." Reuters, February 4, 1999.

[815] "Stasi Files on Kohl's Tapped Calls Vanish," The Times, May 17, 2000.

[816] "Kohl Sues to Gag Stasi Files," BBC News, December 8, 2000.

[817] "Kohl's Stasi Files Stay Closed," BBC News, July 4, 2001.

[818] Geir Moulson, "German Archive Welcomes File Opening," Associated Press, July 5, 2002.

framework database to make possible speech recognition of asylum seekers.[819] In February 2002, the Interior Ministry announced that its counterterrorist efforts would include encrypted biometric identification cards for all citizens, as well as fingerprinting and face recognition technologies.[820] Citizens have challenged a number of the tactics used by German law enforcement to uncover terrorist suspects. By February 2002, courts in Berlin and Frankfurt had upheld objections to the use of computerized searches of government records (*Rasterfahndung*) to profile terrorist suspects based partly on religious identification.[821] In April 2002, Germany submitted to the European Union a proposal to make it possible to conduct investigations *Rasterfahndung* throughout the Union to help combat terrorism.[822]

Germany is a member of the Council of Europe and has signed and ratified the Convention for the Protection of Individuals with Regard to Automatic Processing of Personal Data (ETS No. 108),[823] and later signed an Additional Protocol to this convention.[824] It has also signed and ratified the European Convention for the Protection of Human Rights and Fundamental Freedoms. In November 2002 Germany signed the Convention on Cybercrime.[825] It is a member of the Organization for Economic Cooperation and Development and has adopted the OECD Guidelines on the Protection of Privacy and Transborder Flows of Personal Data.

Hellenic Republic (Greece)

The Constitution of Greece recognizes the rights of privacy and secrecy of communications. Article 9 states: "(1) Each man's home is inviolable. A person's personal and family life is inviolable. No house searches shall be made except when and as the law directs, and always in the presence of representatives of the judicial authorities. (2) Offenders against the foregoing provision shall be

---

[819] Text of the Terrorismusbekämfungsgesetz is available at
<http://www.bmi.bund.de/Annex/de_15999/Terrorismusbekaempfungsegsetz_PDF-Datei.pdf>.

[820] Teresa Anderson, American Security Management, February 1, 2002.

[821] John Hooper, German Courts Put Terror Hunt In Doubt," The Gaurdian, February 2, 2002, available at <http://www.guardian.co.uk/international/story/0,3604,643720,00.html>.

[822] Jelle van Buuren, "Rasterfahndung at European Level?" Telepolis, April 4, 2002
<http://www.heise.de/tp/english/inhalt/te/12274/1.html>.

[823] Council of Europe, Legal Affairs, Treaty Office <http://conventions.coe.int/>.

[824] Council of Europe, Additional Protocol to the Convention For the Protection of Individuals With Regard to the Automatic Processing of Personal Data, Regarding Supervisory Authorities and Transborder Data Flows, available at <http://conventions.coe.int/Treaty/EN/searchsig.asp?NT=181&CM=8&DF=>.

[825] Signed November 23, 2001.

punished for forced entry into a private house and abuse of power, and shall be obliged to indemnify in full the injured party as the law provides."[826] A Constitutional amendment in 2001 added a new provision to this article granting individuals a direct right to protection of their personal information. The new provision, Article 9A, states: "All persons have the right to be protected from the collection, processing and use, especially by electronic means, of their personal data, as specified by law. The protection of personal data is ensured by an independent authority, which is established and operates as specified by law." Article 19 of the Constitution protects the privacy of communications. It states: "Secrecy of letters and all other forms of free correspondence or communication shall be absolutely inviolable. The guaranties under which the judicial authority shall not be bound by this secrecy for reasons of national security or for the purpose of investigating especially serious crimes, shall be specified under law." The 2001 amendment also added two new provisions to this article. Article 19(2) now states: "The matters relating to the establishment, operation and powers of the independent authority ensuring the secrecy of paragraph 1 shall be specified by law." Article 19 (3) states: "The use of evidence acquired in violation of the present article and of articles 9 and 9A is prohibited."

The Law on the Protection of Individuals with regard to the Processing of Personal Data (Data Protection Act) was approved in 1997.[827] Greece was the last member of the European Union to adopt a data protection law and its law was written to directly adopt the European Union Directive. The Act was also necessary for Greece to join the Schenghen Agreement. There were major protests during the ratification of the Schengen Agreement for border controls and information sharing. According to news reports, police used tear gas to disperse a group of about 1,000 protesters, including Orthodox priests, when they tried to push their way into Parliament as the pact was being debated.[828]

The Hellenic Data Protection Authority (DPA) was established in November 1997 as an independent authority set to monitor privacy violations in Greece. It was created to supervise the implementation of the Data Protection Act and all regulations referring to the protection of personal data.[829] It also exercises other powers delegated to it from time to time.

---

[826] Constitution of Greece, 1975 (as amended), available at <http://confinder.richmond.edu/greek_2001.html>.

[827] Law no. 2472 on the Protection of Individuals with regard to the Processing of Personal Data.

[828] The Reuters European Community Report, June 10, 1997.

[829] Home Page<http://www.dpa.gr/>.

The Authority is responsible for archival audits, issuing regulatory acts arising from legislation on data protection, and providing information and recommendations to interested parties to ensure compliance with data protection regulations. Its mandate includes issuing directives to enhance uniformity in implementation and to protect personal data vis-à-vis technological developments; assisting controllers in drafting codes of conduct; examining complaints; reporting violations; and issuing decisions related to the right to access information. The authority grants permits for the collection and processing of sensitive personal data and is accountable for the interconnection of files, including sensitive data and the trans-boundary flow of personal data. The Authority's communications office is in charge of all public relations and communication with private and public services and institutions, the media, foreign data protection authorities, European Union authorities, and international organizations and institutions.

In 2001, the Hellenic DPA received 944 complaints and inquires.[830] From September 2001 to June 2002, there have been approximately 500 requests referring mainly to unlawful collection and processing of personal data by companies involved in direct marketing, banks and financial institutions, debt recording and telecommunications companies, maternity hospitals, closed-circuit television systems/communication of data to third parties and entries in the Schenghen information system.[831] Since the entry into force of Greek law on the protection of personal data, the DPA has performed 51 audits on privacy policies and standards. During 2001, the DPA conducted 15 audits of files held by general hospitals and clinics, data banks, and debt-recording companies.

In the past few years, the DPA has issued directives relating to state identity cards, direct marketing, closed-circuit television (CCTV), DNA testing, and workplace surveillance. The Authority has also issued guidelines covering data protection in the workplace in particular surveillance of phone calls and emails.[832] On May 4, 2000 in a controversial ruling, the Agency ruled that religious affiliations must be removed from state identity cards. The decision was opposed by the Greek Orthodox Church and led to massive protests and

---

[830] Email from Ms. Amalia Logiaki, Communications Director, Hellenic Data Protection Authority, Greece, to Nicole Anastasopoulos, IPIOP Clerk, Electronic Privacy Information Center, June 15, 2002 (on file with the Electronic Privacy Information Center).

[831] Id.

[832] Article 29 Data Protection Working Group Party, Fifth Annual Report on the Situation regarding the Processing of Individuals with Regard to the Processing of Personal Data and Privacy in the European Union and in Third Countries, Part II, March 6, 2002, available at <http://europa.eu.int/comm/internal_market/en/dataprot/wpdocs/wp54en_2.pdf>.

challenges to the ruling.[833] In March 2001 Greece's highest administrative court upheld the ruling finding that stating citizens' religious affiliation on the compulsory identity cards was unconstitutional.[834] Prior to the ruling, Greece was the only member of the European Union that required citizens to list their religious beliefs on citizen identity cards. The new Greek identity cards do not include religion, even on a voluntary basis. In addition to the removal of religious affiliation, new identity cards also no longer include fingerprints, names and surnames of the cardholder's spouse, maiden names, profession, home addresses, or citizenship.

The DPA considers the trading of personal data for direct marketing or sales to be lawful under specific conditions and only with the consent of the individual or when the data is collected from public sources. It has specific guidelines for the ascertainment of credibility of information and only for specific purposes.[835] In May 2000, the DPA issued a directive regarding direct marketing companies that were collecting personal data directly from mothers in maternity hospitals. The directive required that hospitals act as controllers by drafting a consent form for mothers who wanted to receive advertising literature to fill out. The hospital would then forward the consent form to marketing firms.[836]

In September 2000, the Authority set out guidelines prohibiting the recording, use, monitoring, and retention of personal information through the use of closed circuit television (CCTV) on a regular, continuous, or permanent basis.[837] Recording is only lawful when it is done for the protection of individuals or goods or for traffic violations and only under the principles of necessity and proportionality. In these exceptional cases, the DPA must grant permission, and the rules on accuracy and notification must be followed. With respect to crime prevention or repression, the DPA must grant special permission to judicial and legal authorities to use cameras, with strict guidelines for use and retention. In the course of the past year, the authority received five complaints concerning CCTV systems in the private sector, two of which were infractions. The authority upon examining these infractions ordered the relocation of the cameras and the prior notification of individuals entering the area monitored by CCTV.

[833] "Greek Church at War over Plans to Change ID Cards," The Guardian, May 24, 2000.

[834] "Greek Church Causes Fresh Identity Crisis," The Guardian, August 29, 2001.

[835] Hellenic Data Protection Authority, Decision No. 050/20.01.2000.

[836] Hellenic Data Protection Authority, Decision No. 523/18, May 25, 2000.

[837] Hellenic Data Protection Authority, Decision No. 1122, September 07, 2000.

With respect to DNA analysis for the purpose of criminal investigation and prosecution, the Authority issued an opinion in 2001 expressing concern with the method and effects of collection of citizens' sensitive data. According to the opinion, the genetic analysis of DNA must be limited to the "non-codified section of DNA" and identity verification.[838] The DPA advised that any methods that allow any conclusions about the personality traits of individuals from their DNA should be forbidden, including personality profiling.[839] This method of investigation should only be used for verification of offenders' and victims' identity and for criminal investigations and should be destroyed once the fulfillment of the intended aim is achieved. Finally, the Authority does not support any effort to collect and analyze genetic material for preventative purposes.[840]

According to the Human Rights Watch 2002 World Report, in August 2001, the DPA asked the government to discard a provision of the law compelling hospital staff and hotel employees to notify the police if undocumented migrants sought their services because it violated Greece's privacy protection laws.[841]

In May 2001, there was a public outcry when it was revealed that Megalos Adelfos, the local version of the television show, Big Brother, was soon to be aired in Greece. The National Council for Radio and Television requested details of the show to determine whether it would breach the country's privacy regulations.[842] In July, the DPA issued an order for the termination of the processing of personal data for the show.[843] The show aired nonetheless. Citing privacy concerns, journalists and media students staged a protest outside the private Antenna network headquarters.

According to the Hellenic Bank Association, a nonprofit legal entity, that represents banks and other financial institutions operating in Greece and sets codes of banking ethics for its members, there are voluntary standards of confidentiality and banking secrecy that protect customers' financial records. These records can only be disclosed with the consent of the customers. However, the code also states that the exchange of consolidated information between banks relating to "groups of customers, as part of the electronic transfer of quantitative

---

[838] Hellenic Republic Data Protection Authority. Opinion No.15/2001, February 15, 2001, <http://www.dpa.gr>.

[839] Id.

[840] Id.

[841] Human Rights Watch, World Report 2002 (New York 2001).

[842] "Greek Protests over Big Brother," The Herald (Glasgow), May 28, 2001.

[843] Hellenic Data Protection Authority. Decision. No. 1346, July 3, 2001.

data on transactions and/or for statistical purposes, does not constitute a breach of confidentiality."[844]

While Law no. 2225/94 requires police who wish to conduct telephone taps to obtain court permission,[845] in the past there were continuing reports of government surveillance, including illegal wiretapping and interception of mail of human rights groups, Orthodox religious groups, and activist members of minority groups.[846] Although monitored in the past, this year the Greek Helsinki Monitor reported that it was not monitored by security services.[847]

In April 2001 the European Court of Human Rights, in the case of *Donald Peers v. Greece*, found that Mr. Peers was entitled to compensation for breach of privacy, under Article 8 of the European Convention, when prison administrators opened his mail while he was incarcerated for drug offences in Greece in 1994.[848]

Tough security measures, including military patrols, special commando units and more than 1,000 surveillance cameras are being put in place for the 2004 Olympic Games in Athens.[849] Greek law enforcement authorities are being provided training and intelligence assistance from seven countries: Australia, Britain, France, Germany, Israel and Spain, and the United States.[850] There appears to be little concern over the violation of citizen privacy through the use of these cameras.

In 1999, Greece created Article 5 of the Greek Code of Administrative Procedure (Law No. 2690/1999)[851] which is a new Freedom of Information Act that provides citizens the right to access administrative documents created by government agencies. It replaces Law 1599/1986, which regulated the use of the Single Register Code Number (EKAM).[852]

---

[844] Hellenic Banking Association, Code of Banking Ethics, available at
<www.Hba.gr/English/iabout/profile.htm#h1>.

[845] Law no 2225/94.

[846] United States Department of State, Greece Country Report on Human Rights Practices 2000, February 2001, available at <http://www.state.gov/g/drl/rls/hrrpt/2000/>. See also, Human Rights Watch World Report, 2002, available at <http://www.hrw.org/wr2k2/>.

[847] United States Department of State, Greece Country Report on Human Rights Practices for 2001, March 2002, available at <http://www.state.gov/g/drl/rls/hrrpt/2001/eur/8261.htm>.

[848] Id.

[849] "Athens to be on full alert for Games," The Ottawa Citizen, November 24, 2000.

[850] "OLYMPICS; More to It Than Games," The New York Times, July 24, 2001.

[851] See <http://www.rz.uni-frankfurt.de/~sobotta/greecenew.htm>.

[852] Law no 1599/1986 on the Relationship of a New Type of Identification Card and Other Provisions.

Greece is a member of the Council of Europe and has signed and ratified the Convention for the Protection of Individuals with Regard to Automatic Processing of Personal Data (ETS No. 108)[853] and the European Union Convention for the Protection of Human Rights and Fundamental Freedoms.[854] In November 2001, Greece signed the Council of Europe Convention on Cybercrime.[855] Greece is also a member of the Organization for Economic Cooperation and Development (OECD) and has adopted the OECD's Guidelines on the Protection of Privacy and Transborder Flows of Personal Data.

Special Administrative Region of Hong Kong

On July 1, 1997, the People's Republic of China (PRC) resumed exercise of its sovereignty over Hong Kong and established it as a "Special Administrative Region" (SAR). The laws of the Hong Kong SAR were incorporated into the Chinese legal system by the enactment of the Basic Law, often described as Hong Kong's mini-constitution.[856]

The Basic Law of the Hong Kong SAR contains several privacy protections. Article 29 provides that the "homes and other premises of Hong Kong residents shall be inviolable. Arbitrary or unlawful search of, or intrusion into, a resident's home or other premises shall be prohibited." Article 30 provides that the "freedom and privacy of communications of Hong Kong residents shall be protected by law. No department or individual may, on any grounds, infringe upon the freedom and privacy of communications of residents except that the relevant authorities may inspect communications in accordance with legal procedures to meet the needs of public security or of investigation into criminal offenses."

---

[853] Signed February 17, 1983; Enacted August 11, 1995; Entered into Force December 1995.

[854] Signed November 28, 1950; Enacted November 28, 1974; Entered into Force November 28, 1974.

[855] Signed November 23, 2001

[856] Adopted on April 4, 1990 by the Seventh National People's Congress of the People's Republic of China at its Third Session. The authority of the Congress to establish a special administrative region and decide on the systems to be implemented there is given by arts. 31 and 62(13) of the *Constitution* of the PRC. See Y. Ghai, *Hong Kong's New Constitutional Order: The Resumption of Chinese Sovereignty and the Basic Law* 56 (Hong Kong University Press 1997). Legally, the *Basic Law* should not be considered as the constitution of Hong Kong, although it may have certain constitutional functions. The relationship between the Chinese central government and the Hong Kong SAR government is not the one between the federal government and a state. Although the Hong Kong SAR is a highly autonomous administrative region of China, it has no independent sovereignty. The power over Hong Kong absolutely belongs to China and the central government delegates certain powers to the Hong Kong SAR through the *Basic Law*. The powers not delegated to the Hong Kong SAR remain vested with the central government.

In 1996, after six years of study by the Law Reform Commission,[857] Hong Kong enacted a Personal Data (Privacy) Ordinance (the Ordinance),[858] The Ordinance came into effect in December of that year, with the exception of the provisions concerning the transfer of data outside Hong Kong[859] and data-matching.[860] No substantial amendments to the Ordinance have been made to date, other than the provision which provided that the Ordinance prevails over any other ordinance in case of inconsistencies,[861] which the Standing Committee of the National People's Congress of the PRC found contravened the Basic Law and declared invalid.[862]

Following the standard set by the OECD Guidelines for Protection of Privacy and Transborder Flows of Personal Data, the Ordinance adopts six 'fair information principles' to regulate notice, collection, accuracy, use, security and access to 'personal data', broadly defined as "any representation of information (including an expression of opinion) in any document, and includes a personal identifier."[863] It also imposes additional restrictions on certain processing, namely data matching and direct marketing. The former requires the prior approval of the Privacy Commissioner while the latter requires that a "data user" inform the 'data subject' of the opportunity to opt-out from further approaches.[864]

The Ordinance applies to public and private 'data users' and to manual and electronic records. However, under the Interpretation and General Clauses Ordinance,[865] it is not applicable to PRC government agencies in the Hong Kong SAR.[866] In June 1999, the High Court dismissed a legislator's civil suit over the failure of the then New China News Agency (NCNA) to respond within the Ordinance-specified time frame to the legislator's request for information about herself in the agency's files, because the NCNA Director named in the suit was not in Hong Kong at the time the incident occurred. In October 2000, the Director of the NCNA, now known as the Liaison Office, served the legislator a

---

[857] Hong Kong Law Reform Commission, 1994 Report on the Law Relating To The Protection Of Personal Data (1994).

[858] Personal Data (Privacy) Ordinance, chapter 486, (June 30, 1997). See generally, M. Berthold & R. Wacks, Data Privacy Law in Hong Kong (FT Law & Tax, 1997).

[859] Personal Data (Privacy) Ordinance, chapter 486, § 33 (June 30, 1997).

[860] Id., §§ 30-32. The provisions relating to datamatching subsequently came into force on August 1, 1997.

[861] Id., § 3.2.

[862] R. Denny and P. Yung, "Hong Kong" 3, in C. Millard and M. Ford, Data Protection Laws of the World, (London: Sweet & Maxwell, 2002), no statutory amendment has been made to this effect.

[863] Personal Data (Privacy) Ordinance, (Hong Kong), 1996, chapter 486, § 2, "data".

[864] Id., § 35.

[865] Interpretation and General Clauses Ordinance, chapter 1.

[866] See J. Holvast et al., The Global Encyclopedia of Data Protection Regulation, (Kluwer, 2000).

---

writ requiring the legislator to pay his court costs, as is allowed under Hong Kong law. The pro-democracy legislator eventually paid her opponent's court costs with a combination of public donations and personal funds.[867]

The Ordinance establishes an oversight body, the Office of the Privacy Commissioner ("PCO"), to promote and enforce compliance with statutory requirements.[868] The Commissioner is given strong enforcement powers modeled on those contained in the United Kingdom Data Protection Act.[869] In addition to investigating complaints, the commissioner may initiate independent investigations and conduct audits of selected data users. Some violations of the Ordinance constitute criminal offenses. In other cases, an injured party may seek compensation through civil proceedings. If the Commissioner believes that violations may continue or be repeated, it may issue enforcement notices to direct remedial measures.

The Commissioner may issue codes of conduct to provide guidance on compliance with the Ordinance's provisions. Codes are legally subordinate, but have evidentiary relevance in determining whether a contravention of the Ordinance has occurred. To date the Commissioner has issued five codes; the Code of Practice on the Identity Card Number and other Personal Identifiers;[870] the Code of Practice on Consumer Credit Data;[871] the Code of Practice on Human Resource Management;[872] the Code of Practice on Protection of Customer Information for Fixed and Mobile Service Operators[873] and, most recently a draft Code of Practice on Monitoring and Personal Data Privacy at Work.[874] In 2000, the Privacy Commissioner jointly issued a voluntary code of practice and a consumer guide on how to deal with 'spam' with the Telecommunications Authority and the Hong Kong Internet Service Providers

---

[867] United States Department of State, Greece Country Report on Human Rights Practices for 2001, March 2002, available at <http://www.state.gov/g/drl/rls/hrrpt/2001/eur/8261.htm>.

[868] Personal Data (Privacy) Ordinance, (Hong Kong), 1996, c. 486, § 5.

[869] Data Protection Act 1998 (United Kingdom), 1998, c. 29.

[870] Privacy Commissioner for Personal Data, Code of Practice on the Identity Card Number and other Personal Identifiers, (Hong Kong, PCO, 1997).

[871] Privacy Commissioner for Personal Data, Code of Practice on Consumer Credit Data, (Hong Kong, PCO, 2002). Issued on 27 February 1998, effective November 27, 1998; see also Privacy Commissioner for Personal Data, Consultation Paper on Amendments

[872] Privacy Commissioner for Personal Data, Code of Practice on Human Resource Management, (Hong Kong, PCO, 2000).

[873] Office of the Privacy Commissioner for Personal Data, Press Release, "New Code Launched for Fixed and Mobile Service Operators to Protection Customer Information," June 17, 2002. See also Privacy Commissioner for Personal Data, Code of Practice on Protection of Customer Information for Fixed and Mobile Service Operators, (Hong Kong, PCO, 2002).

[874] Privacy Commissioner for Personal Data, Code of Practice on Monitoring and Personal Data Privacy at Work, (Hong Kong, PCO, 2002).

Association. In May 2001, the Privacy Commissioner held a public consultation on the Code of Practice for Consumer Credit Data.[875] In February 2002,[876] the Privacy Commissioner approved amendments which would make it easier for banks and other credit grantors to gain access to consumer credit reference files[877] and retain credit data for a much longer period of time than previously allowed.[878]

The recent economic downturn[879] has led to some companies outsourcing data processing functions to jurisdictions which have weaker privacy protections for personal data, particularly mainland China and India.[880] To date this development has largely gone unchecked by the Privacy Commissioner[881] because § 33 of the Ordinance, governing transborder data flows, has yet to be enacted.[882]

The Hong Kong SAR is the European Union's tenth largest trading partner, while the European Union is Hong Kong's third largest supplier, after China and Japan. Total bilateral trade in 1999 amounted to a significant €42 billion.[883] The Commissioner has had informal discussions with the European Union over the question of adequacy of data protection under the relevant European Union, but

---

[875] Privacy Commissioner for Personal Data, Consultation Paper on Amendments to the Consumer Credit Data Code (May 25, 2001).

[876] Privacy Commissioner for Personal Data, Press Release, "Privacy Commissioner Approves Amendments to the Consumer Credit Data Code," 8 February 2002, available at
<http://www.pco.org.hk/english/infocentre/press.html>.

[877] Privacy Commissioner for Personal Data, Code of Practice on Consumer Credit Data, (Hong Kong, PCO, 1998), § 3.1.

[878] Id., §§ 2.2, 2.4-2.5.

[879] See, e.g. E. Yiu, "Bankruptcies triple in first five months" *South China Morning Post,* (June 12, 2002), 1; E. Yiu, "WebTrust Seal of approval still awaits first client" *South China Morning Post* (January 30, 2002), 2.

[880] See, e.g. L. Leung, "HKMA pushes banks to share loan histories", *South China Morning Post* (September 21, 2001) 4, Hong Kong's Monetary Authority urged banks to share data on consumer credit to reduce default loans; L. Beckerling, "Sharing credit data offers benefits all round, says HSBC", *South China Morning Post* (May 21, 2002) 3, Hong Kong's biggest lender supports sacrificing privacy for the good of Hong Kong; "MAS bars Visa's new outsourced service for banks" *The Straits Times,* (June 17, 2002), naming Hong Kong as an adoptee of a new "Verified by VISA" which Singapore's Monetary Authority rejected for privacy reasons.

[881] Privacy Commissioner for Personal Data, Privacy, Security and Transborder Data Flows – Observations from Hong Kong, (May 20, 2002).

[882] Section 33 would prescribe several conditions for transborder transfer of personal data: 1) reasonable grounds for believing the country has in place a law which is "substantially similar" to Hong Kong's; 2) where 1 is not true, the data subject must give explicit consent to the transfer; 3) alternatively, the data user must have reasonable grounds to believe that the transfer is "for the avoidance or mitigation of adverse action against the data subject", it is not practicable to obtain consent and if it were, the data subject would give it; 4) the data transferred is exempt under the PD(P)O; or 5) the data user has taken *all* reasonable precautions to ensure the data will not be used in contravention to Hong Kong law.

[883] Third Annual Report by the European Commission on the Hong Kong SAR: Report from the Commission to the Council and the European Parliament, COM (2001)431 Final at 11.

---

has not received a formal reply.[884] Hong Kong will likely not be deemed adequate before the enactment of s. 33 of the Ordinance.[885]

In 1999, the Hong Kong Law Reform Commission issued a consultation paper calling for "a code of practice on all forms of surveillance in the workplace for the practical guidance of employers, employees and the general public."[886] In March 2002, the Commissioner responded with a more modest Draft Code of Practice on Monitoring and Personal Data Privacy At Work,[887] which covers the monitoring of telephone calls, email and computer usage and video surveillance.[888] He specifically recognized, but excluded from treatment, other privacy-invasive practices such as drug testing, psychological profiling and productivity monitoring by automated equipment. These may yet be covered by future codes of practice.

Opinion surveys conducted in 2000 and 2001 indicated that approximately 64 percent of Hong Kong businesses use at least one of the following five surveillance methods: closed circuit television, computer use (auditing), web-browsing, e-mail, phone.[889] While only around 22 percent of businesses engaged in surveillance had relevant written policies.

Employers, trade association and trade unions have criticized the draft – particularly the definition of "e-mail" – as problematically vague and have

---

[884] European Union Article 29 Data Protection Working Party Fourth Annual Report on the Situation Regarding the Protection of Individuals With Regard to the Processing of Personal Data and Privacy in the Community and in Third Countries Covering the Year 1999: Part II, May 17, 2001, 5019/EN/WP 46, 20. The Working Party entered into preliminary discussions on the level of protection in Hong Kong, but has not yet reported back.

[885] Data Protection Working Party Opinion 7/2001 on the Draft Commission Decision (version 31 August 2001) on Standard Contractual Clauses for the transfer of Personal Data to data processors established in third countries under Article 26(4) of Directive, September 13, 2001, 95/465061/01/EN/Final WP 47, 3, describing the general principle that the data importer is bound by the data exporter's legislation. See also C. Raab et al. Application of a Methodology Designed to Assess the Adequacy of the Level of Protection of Individuals with regard to Processing Personal Data: Test of the Method on Several Categories of Transfer: Final Report, European Commission Tender No. XV/97/18/D, 17-22, 57-65, 103-107,142-148,178-181.

[886] Law Reform Commission, "Consultation Paper on Civil Liability for Invasion of Privacy," August 1999, available at <http://www.info.gov.hk/hkreform/reports/index.htm>.

[887] Privacy Commissioner for Personal Data, Draft Code of Practice on Monitoring and Personal Data Privacy at Work, (Hong Kong, PCO, 2002).

[888] E-mail from Stephen Lau, Privacy Commissioner for Personal Data, Hong-Kong to Sarah Andrews, Research Director, Electronic Privacy Information Center, June 11, 2001 (on file with the Electronic Privacy Information Center).

[889] University of Hong Kong, Social Sciences Research Centre, 2001 Opinion Survey: Personal Data (Privacy) Ordinance: Attitudes and Implementation – Key Findings, April 2002, the percentage reporting use of the enumerated surveillance types did not appreciate in 2001.

---

suggested that the nature of the workplace will be affected by companies reacting with more restrictive policies on the use of e-mail and the Internet at work.[890]

Since 1949, Hong Kong residents have carried laminated photo identity cards imprinted with biographical data and the cardholder's residency status. In 2002, the government introduced a smart identity card with a chip that will contain a digital replica of the cardholder's thumbprint, immigration data, a digital certificate and have room for other information, including medical and financial data and driving records.[891] The government plans to replace all 6.8 million of the old cards by 2007.[892]

In response to widespread sensitivity about privacy, Hong Kong's Secretary of Information Technology and Broadcasting stated in January of 2002 that there "will be no more data on the surface of the card, than the data that already appears" and that "…only minimal data will be stored in the card's chip. Except for essential immigration-related data and digital certificates, personal data in respect of non-immigration related applications will be kept at back-end computer systems of the concerned government departments. None of the proposed non-immigration applications (that is, using the card as a driving license and library card, storage of a digital certificate and change of address) will be mandatory. Cardholders will have a choice on whether to include the applications on the card."[893] Further, any data stored in the chip will be encrypted, data for separate applications will be segregated and only authorized persons will have access to the data on the card.[894]

In a classic example of "function creep," in April 2002, a senior Immigration Department official said that more services and functions are being considered, including storing a person's blood type on the card for emergencies.[895]

In commenting on the initial proposal, the Privacy Commissioner expressed concerns over the danger of identity theft and the secondary use of the personal

---

[890] C. Buddle, "Keeping Orwell out of the office" South China Morning Post, March 15, 2002, 18; A. Li and P. Moy, "Unclear code for workplace rejected" South China Morning Post, April 13, 2002, 6. See also Privacy Commissioner for Personal Data, Draft Code of Practice on Monitoring and Personal Data Privacy at Work, (Hong Kong, PCO, 2002), 22-23: e.g. the draft code differentiates between inbound and outbound e-mail, stating that "monitoring of inbound e-mails can rarely be justified."

[891] M. Landler, "Fine-tuning for privacy, Hong Kong plans digital ID" New York Times (February 18, 2002).

[892] M. Benitez, "ID card contract awarded," South China Morning Post, February 27, 2002.

[893] C. Yau, Letter to the Editor, South China Morning Post, January 25, 2002.

[894] Id.

[895] A. Lo, "New ID cards may get extra functions" South China Morning Post, April 24, 2002, quoting Raymond Wong Wai-main, assistant immigration director.

information that will be stored on the card.[896] Sin Chung-kai, a Democratic Party legislator, who led the debate on the ID card issue, stated "We're not opposed to people having to carry ID cards. The crux of the controversy is how much other information about a person should be stored on the card."[897]

In December 2000, an interdepartmental working group on computer crime issued a report for public consultation.[898] The report proposed a series of measures, both legislative and administrative, to address computer related crimes. Recommendations included strengthening the penalties for hacking and unauthorized access offenses,[899] compelling the disclosure of encryption keys or decrypted text,[900] and requiring Internet Service Providers to retain subscriber logs.[901] The government is still considering means to implement these proposals.[902]

Hong Kong banks already share a "blacklist" of loan defaulters and borrowers who have court judgments issued against them,[903] but faced with an unprecedented five-fold increase in bankruptcies in the past year, banks recently proposed an amendment to the Ordinance allowing them to share even more personal data through a newly created third-party agency. The so-called "positive data sharing agency" would be run by a private company and modeled after British and American institutions.[904] The agency would allow banks to share information between each other on the amount of a credit seeker's outstanding credit card debt, cards held, credit limit, past due accounts, residential mortgages and other types of consumer credit.[905] The Hong Kong Monetary Authority and the Privacy Commissioner supported the proposal, but SAR legislators, consumer advocates and the public did not, citing privacy concerns.[906] A representative of

---

[896] PCO Press Release, "Privacy Commissioner for Personal Data expresses views on ID Card Scheme," October 20, 2000.

[897] Landler, supra n. 891.

[898] S. Chung Kai, Cyber Office Legislative Councillor (Information Technology), Cyber 2005 (Issue No. 7), December 14, 2000.

[899] Security Bureau, Inter-departmental Working Group on Computer Related Crime Report, (Hong Kong, 2000).

[900] Id., paragraph 5.14.

[901] Id., paragraph 8.22.

[902] A. Creed, "Hong Kong Mulls Measures To Fight Computer Crime," Newsbytes, July 18, 2001.

[903] L. Beckerling, "Public gets say on credit bureau," South China Morning Post, May 4, 2002.

[904] J. Moir and L. Beckerling, "Privacy goes plastic," South China Morning Post, June 13, 2002.

[905] L. Beckerling, "First look at sample credit risks report," South China Morning Post, March 29, 2002.

[906] See L. Leung, "HKMA pushes banks to share loan histories", South China Morning Post, September 21, 2001) 4; L. Beckerling, "Public gets say on credit bureau" South China Morning Post, May 4, 2002, 1; E. Yiu, "Democrats to consider proposal for credit information sharing", South China Morning Post, June 24, 2002, 3,

---

one of Hong Kong's largest banks responded to these concerns by saying that "privacy [was] no longer relevant."[907]

As required by the Ordinance, the Privacy Commissioner opened a public consultation on the credit issue last year and proposed relaxing restrictions on data sharing between banks.[908] Specifically, amendments to the Consumer Credit Data Code would extend the period of retention of credit application data by a credit reference agency from 90 days to 5 years and extend the period for retention of file activity data from 12 months to 5 years. Further proposals would allow the release of file activity data by a credit reference agency to credit providers, and to prevent credit providers from accessing an individual's data held by a credit reference agency except where there was a relevant need to do so.

In early 2002, Hong Kong police proposed a pilot program to install a number of cameras in Lan Kwai Fong, a district of Hong Kong, aimed at preventing crime and controlling crowds.[909] The cameras would be linked to a police station and footage would be held for three months. The plan was supported by the local business association, but not by many local businesses who felt the surveillance might affect people's willingness to come to the area. Lawmakers and human rights groups also opposed the plan, saying it was an invasion of privacy.[910]

In May, Hong Kong police bowed to public and legislative opposition and suspended the proposal. In a paper submitted to legislators, Deputy Secretary for Security, Timothy Tong Hin-ming, said police would study the privacy concerns of the scheme before consulting the public and the Privacy Commissioner again.[911]

---

quoting Democratic Party financial affairs spokesman, Sin Chung-kai arguing that banks would only use credit sharing to boost profitability.

[907] L. Beckerling, "Public gets say on credit bureau," South China Morning Post, May 4, 2002, quoting Anna Borzi of HSBC Securities stating "Privacy is over. There are already more things being recorded, coded and monitored than we can poke a stick at. If anybody seriously believes privacy can still be protected they are seriously deluded. That battle has been fought and lost."

[908] See Privacy Commissioner for Personal Data, Code of Practice on Consumer Credit Data (Hong Kong, PCO, 2002); see also Privacy Commissioner for Personal Data, Consultation Paper on Amendments to the Consumer Credit Data Code, May 25, 2001.

[909] When asked for a specific example of the need for video surveillance in Lan Kwai Fong, Deputy Police Commissioner Dick Lee Ming-kwai cited a stampede in 1993 when 21 people were crushed to death on New Year's Eve.

[910] S. Lau, "Business backs push for video surveillance" South China Morning Post, February 19, 2002.

[911] C. Yeung and R. Ma, "Police drop spy camera scheme" South China Morning Post, May 14, 2002.

Also in May, the SAR Department of Corrections announced that it was installing thousands of surveillance cameras in all of Hong Kong's prisons – including dormitories, but not toilets – in an effort to prevent inmate gambling.[912]

Hong Kong's Independent Commission Against Corruption (ICAC) prosecuted two people, in 1998 and 1999, for unauthorized disclosure of telecom subscriber data to debt collectors.[913] In response to these incidents, ICAC issued a study that called for closer cooperation among the government agencies responsible for telecommunications in Hong Kong.[914]

In June 2002, the Privacy Commissioner jointly launched a voluntary Code of Practice on Protection of Customer Information for Fixed and Mobile Service Operators with Hong Kong's Consumer Council, ICAC, and the Office of the Telecommunications Authority.[915] The guidelines are the result of the year long effort to gather the privacy rules for telecommunication companies into one document.

The Code covers the following five areas: policy on protection of customer personal data; technical measures for protection of customer personal data; location security; staff security; and, transfer of customer personal data.[916] Specifically, the Code calls on companies to establish a data classification policy based on degrees of sensitivity for personal data and risk of exposure. It also recommends controlling access on a "need-to-know" basis, the introduction of an ethics policy and the prevention of bribery.

While the compliance with the guidelines in the Code are voluntary, the requirements listed in the code are not. For example, the Telecommunication Authority requires service providers to protect customers' data,[917] the Personal Data (Privacy) Ordinance sets out strict rules for the use and distribution of

---

[912] S. Lee, "Closed-circuit television cameras to monitor inmates' evening activities" South China Morning Post, May 17, 2002.

[913] S. Schwartz, "Phone firms urged to adopt pioneering data privacy code" South China Morning Post, June 18, 2002, 4. The type of data contemplated by the *Code* includes a customer's name, identity document number, residential address, etc. as well as service plan details, usage details, billing details, payment details.

[914] "Four Hong Kong Government Agencies Issue New Privacy Guidelines for Telecom Industry," BNA Privacy Law Watch, June 21, 2002.

[915] Privacy Commissioner for Personal Data, Press Release, "New Code Launched for Fixed and Mobile Service Operators to Protection Customer Information," June 17, 2002.

[916] Privacy Commissioner for Personal Data, Code of Practice on Protection of Customer Information for Fixed and Mobile Service Operators, (Hong Kong, PCO, 2002), 3-4.

[917] Telecommunications licensees have a license condition which provides that the licensee shall not disclose information of a customer except with the consent of the customer and that the licensee shall not use information provided by its customers or obtained in the course of provision of service to its customers for purposes other than those related to the provision of service by the licensees.

personal data; and, the ICAC has responsibility for all cases involving bribery in Hong Kong.

The interception of communications is regulated by the Telecommunications Ordinance[918] and the Post Office Ordinance.[919] Wiretaps require authorization for interception operations at the highest levels of government, but a court-issued warrant is not required. The Hong Kong government has refused to reveal how often the Chief Executive uses his powers to authorize telephone wiretaps and interception of private mail.[920] In 1999, an unofficial report estimated that the SAR government intercepted more than 100 conversations of private individuals a day.[921] The vagueness of the intercept powers and the lack of procedural safeguards are inconsistent with the Article 17 of the International Covenant on Civil and Political Rights, which is incorporated into Hong Kong's domestic law by article 14 of the Bill of Rights Ordinance.[922]

Republic of Hungary

Article 59 of the Constitution of the Republic of Hungary provides that "everyone has the right to the good standing of his reputation, the privacy of his home and the protection of secrecy in private affairs and personal data." "Everyone in the Republic of Hungary shall have the right to good reputation, the inviolability of the privacy of his home and correspondence, and the protection of his personal data."[923] In 1991, the Supreme Court ruled that a law creating a multi-use personal identification number violated the constitutional right of privacy.[924]

Act No. LXIII of 1992 on the Protection of Personal Data and Disclosure of Data of Public Interest covers the collection and use of personal information in both the public sector and private sector. It is a combined Data Protection and Freedom of Information Act. Its basic principle is informational self-

---

[918] Telecommunications Ordinance, chapter 106, § 33.

[919] Post Office Ordinance, chapter 98, § 13.

[920] United States Department of State, Country Report on Human Rights Practices 2001, March 2002, available at <http://www.state.gov/g/drl/hrrpt/2001/>.

[921] "Phone tap figures to remain secret," South China Morning Post, October 1, 1998.

[922] Bill of Rights Ordinance chapter 383, § 8, art 14 (June 30, 1997)

923 Constitution of the Republic of Hungary, Chapter XII, Article 59, unofficial translation available at:

<http://centraleurope.com/ceo/country/hungary/constit/hucons01.html>.

[924] Constitutional Court Decision No. 15-AB of 13 April 1991.

---

determination.[925] As regards data protection, the Act sets out general provisions on the request, collection, handling and transfer of personal information and provides legal remedies to individuals whose rights are violated. Under the Act personal data may only be collected and processed with the consent of the individual or if it is required by law. The individual must be fully informed of the purpose of the data processing. Only the data necessary to accomplish this purpose may be collected and it may only be stored until that purpose is fulfilled. The data must be accurate, complete and up to date. Individuals are granted the right to access their personal information and where necessary to request its correction or even deletion. Special protections are set out for "sensitive data," which is defined as data relating to "racial origin, nationality, and ethnic status, political opinion or party affiliation, religious or other conviction" or "medical condition, abnormal addiction, sexual life and criminal record." This kind of data may only be processed where the subject has consented in writing or if it is based on an international agreement or required by law for the purpose of enforcing a constitutional right, national security purposes, crime prevention or a criminal investigation.[926] The Act also expressly prohibits the use of all purpose identification numbers or codes.

Hungary is an applicant for European Union membership. In June 1999, the Parliament amended the Act to create a distinction between 'data handling' and 'data processing' in accordance with the European Union Directive.[927] The Article 29 Working Group of the European Commission recommended in September 1999 that "the Commission and the Committee established by Article 31 of Directive 95/46/EC note that Hungary ensures an adequate level of protection within the meaning of Article 25(6) of this directive."[928] In July 2000, the European Commission formally adopted this position, thereby approving all future transfers of personal data to Hungary.[929] Some further revisions of the act are anticipated, for example, regarding the regulation of transfers abroad and automated decision making, in order to ensure full compliance with the European

---

[925] ACT LXIII OF 1992 on the Protection of Personal Data and the Publicity of Data of Public Interest, available at <http://www.osa.ceu.hu/yeast/AccessAndProtection/04.htm>.

[926] See Zita Orb, "Amended Rules on Data Protection," World Data Protection Report, Volume 1, Issue 1, January 2001 at 22.

[927] Act No. LXXII of 1999.

[928] European Union Article 29 Data Protection Working Group, Opinion 6/99 Concerning the level of personal data in Hungary, Adopted on 7 September 1999, available at
<http://europa.eu.int/comm/internal_market/en/media/dataprot/wpdocs/wp24en.htm>.

[929] European Commission, Press Release, "Commission adopts decisions recognising adequacy of regimes in United States, Switzerland and Hungary," July 27, 2000, available at
<http://europa.eu.int/comm/internal_market/en/media/dataprot/news/safeharbor.htm>.

Union Directive. Public drafts of these amendments have been released publicly but they have not yet been introduced in Parliament.

The Parliamentary Commissioner for Data Protection and Freedom of Information oversees the 1992 Act.[930] Besides supervising the implementation of the Act and acting as an ombudsman for both data protection and freedom of information, the Commissioner's tasks include investigating complaints, maintaining the Data Protection Register, and providing opinions on draft legislation. Under the Secrecy Act of 1995, the Commissioner is also entitled to review and propose changes to the classification of state and official secrets. The Commissioner (along with the two other Parliamentary Commissioners – one for human rights in general, the other for the ethnic minorities) was elected for the first time on June 30, 1995, for a six year term.

The Commission has been very active reviewing cases involving personal information.[931] The Commissioner conducts about 900 examinations each year.[932] In his annual report for the year 2000, the Commissioner noted that the single most important development of the year was the unprecedented rise in the number of complaints against private organizations.[933] He stated that whereas in 1997 there were three and a half more investigations of public data controllers than private ones, by 2000 the ratio was less than double (614 public versus 364 private). He also noted that in 2000 the majority of investigations into the private sector concerned collection agencies processing "intersectoral" information whereas previously the investigations seemed to concern the collection practices of banks, telecommunications and insurance companies. In June 2000, the Commission issued a Recommendation on the disclosure of personal information by private companies to debt collection and repayment organizations.[934] The number of complaints about workplace privacy also continued to increase. In September 2000, the Commissioner ruled against a state owned company that required employees to complete a personality test, containing 480 questions, and submit to a lie detector test in order to determine whether the employees had ever stolen company property or were likely to do so in the future.[935] In March 2000, the Commissioner expressed concern about United States FBI agents based in

---

[930] Homepage <http://www.obh.hu/>.

[931] See Hungarian Civil Liberties Union, Data Protection and Freedom of Information, 1997.

[932] Letters from László Majtényi, Parliamentary Commissioner for Data Protection and Freedom of Information, August 4, 1999, July 11, 2000.

[933] Annual Report of the Parliamentary Commissioner for Data Protection and Freedom of Information 2000, available at <http://www.obh.hu/adatved/indexek/besz/index.htm>.

[934] Recommendation of the Data Protection Commissioner, June19, 2000.

[935] Statement of the Data Protection Commissioner, September 4, 2000.

Hungary having access to personal information while being given diplomatic immunity.[936] Throughout the year the Commissioner also issued recommendations on the collection of records concerning the political views of military officers,[937] on the processing of data by car repair shops,[938] and on the use of image, recording devices in surveillance and information collection.[939] In February 2001, in response to a recommendation issued by the Commissioner, the Central Statistics Office (KSH) amended the national census questionnaire to omit the name and address of respondents.[940] There was a long delay in filling the post of Commissioner, following the departure of Dr. Laszlo Majtenjyi in 2001.

The Commission maintains close relations with the data protection authorities in other central and eastern European countries. In December 2001, the Data Protection Commissioners from the Czech Republic, Hungary, Lithuania, Slovakia, Estonia, Latvia and Poland signed a joint declaration agreeing to closer cooperation and assistance. The Commissioners agreed to meet twice a year in the future, to provide each other with regular updates and overviews of developments in their countries, and to establish a common website for more effective communication.[941]

Many laws contain rules for handling personal data including addresses,[942] universal identifiers,[943] medical information,[944] police information,[945] public records,[946] employment,[947] telecommunications,[948] and national security services.[949] In November 2001 passed an anti money laundering package

---

[936] "Ombudsman worry about use of personal data by Hungary-based FBI staff," BBC Monitoring Europe, March 23, 2000.

[937] Recommendation of the Data Protection Commissioner, September 14, 2000.

[938] Recommendation of the Data Protection Commissioner, December 14, 2000.

[939] Recommendation of the Data Protection Commissioner, December 20, 2000.

[940] "Census Questionnaire Amended at Ombudsman's Request," BBC Summary of World Broadcasts, February 1, 2001.

[941] E-mail from Karel Neuwirt, President, Office for Personal Data Protection, Czech Republic, to Sarah Andrews, Research Director, Electronic Privacy Information Center, May 15, 2002 (on file with the Electronic Privacy Information Center).

[942] Act No. LXVI of 1992 on the register of personal data and addresses of citizens.

[943] Act No. XX of 1996 on the identification methods replacing the universal personal identification number, and on the use of identification codes.

[944] Act XLVII of 1997 on the use and protection of medical and related data.

[945] Act No. XXXIV of 1994 on the Police (Chapter VIII: "Data handling by the Police").

[946] Act No. LXVI of 1995 on public records, public archives, and the protection of private archives (restricting rules on the publicity of documents containing personal data).

[947] Act No. IV of 1991 on furthering employment and provisions for the unemployed.

[948] Act No. LXXII of 1992 on telecommunications.

[949] Act No. CXXV of 1995 on the National Security Services etc.

outlawing anonymous bank accounts.[950] The Direct Marketing Act authorizes companies to process individuals' names and addresses for marketing purposes but requires consent for the processing of other information such as telephone numbers or email addresses.[951] There is no sectoral legislation covering the Internet, however, the Commissioner issued a recommendation on data protection in Cyber-Space in February 2001 calling for amendments or supplements to existing law to address this issue. The Criminal Code also has provisions on privacy.[952]

Surveillance by police requires a court order and is limited to investigations of crimes punishable by more than five years imprisonment.[953] Surveillance by national security services requires the permission of a specially appointed judge or the Minister of Justice, who can authorize surveillance for up to 90 days.[954] In April 1998, the government issued a decree ordering phone companies that offer cellular service to modify their systems to ensure that they could be intercepted. The cost was estimated to be HUF10 billion.[955] It has been reported that the NSS regularly install black boxes on ISP networks and intercept communications without warrants. Furthermore, it is reported that signing a contract to allow full access to data by the NSS is a precondition for obtaining an ISP operating license.[956]

There have been a number of scandals involving spying on politicians, environmental activists and ethnic minorities. In March 2001, the Chairman of the Hungarian Coalition Party (SMK) reported that its members were being monitored and their communications bugged.[957] In 1998 Prime Minister Viktor Orbán stated that members of the then-opposition political party FIDESZ were the targets of illegal secret surveillance by the secret services.[958] A parliamentary committee was established to investigate the matter but its final report released in the spring of 2000 did not find evidence to support the allegations.[959] In

---

[950] "OECD Removes Hungary From Money Laundering List," Hungarian News Agency, June 22, 2002.

[951] Act No. CXIX of 1995 on the use of name and address information serving the purposes of research and direct marketing.

[952] Criminal Code, Sections 177-178, available at
<http://www.privacy.org/pi/countries/hungary/hungary_criminal_code.html>.

[953] Act XXXIV of 1994 on Police.

[954] Act LXXV of 1995 on the National Security Services.

[955] "Technical costs of phone tapping estimated at HUF 10bn," MTI Econews, April 17, 1998.

[956] John Horvath, "Internet Backdoors in Hungary," Heise Online, April 5, 2002.

[957] "Hungarian Party's Phones Bugged," BBC Summary of World Broadcasts, March 8, 2001.

[958] "Fidesz 'bugging' probe underway," The Budapest Sun, September 3, 1998.

[959] United States Department of State, Country Reports on Human Rights Practices 2000, February 2001, available at <http://www.state.gov/g/drl/rls/hrrpt/2000/eur/index.cfm?docid=774>.

November 2001, the Justice Minister denied reports that there had been an increase in secret surveillance saying that the number of authorizations for this surveillance were 25 per cent less than under previous governments.[960]

In terms of access to information the1992 on the Protection of Personal Data and Disclosure of Data of Public guarantees access to information of public interest which is defined as any information being processed by government authorities except for personal information. Exemptions can be made for state secrets or official secrets and information related to national defense, national security, criminal investigations, monetary and currency policy, international relations and judicial procedure. In June 2002, the Government announced that it would ask the Parliament to pass legislation authorizing the further opening of the secret police files from the Communist era.[961] The announcement came following an admission by the Prime Minister that he had been a counter-intelligence officer in the secret police during that time.[962]

Hungary is a member of the Council of Europe and has signed and ratified the Convention for the Protection of Individuals with Regard to Automatic Processing of Personal Data (ETS No. 108).[963] It has signed and ratified the European Convention for the Protection of Human Rights and Fundamental Freedoms.[964] In November 2001, Hungary signed the Council of Europe Convention on Cybercrime.[965] It is a member of the Organization for Economic Cooperation and Development and has adopted the OECD Guidelines on the Protection of Privacy and Transborder Flows of Personal Data.

Republic of Iceland

Article 66 of the 1944 Constitution (as amended in 1991) provided: "The home shall be inviolate. Houses may not be searched, nor may any letters or other documents be detained and examined, except by judicial ruling or by a special provision of law." [966] In 1995 further amendments were made to the Constitution

---

[960] "Justice Minister Denies Increase in Secret Surveillance," BBC Worldwide Monitoring, November 20, 2001.

[961] Radio Free Europe, June 28, 2002.

[962] Radio Free Europe, June 20, 2002.

[963] Signed May 13, 1993; Enacted October 8, 1997; Entered into Force February 1, 1998.

[964] Signed November 6, 1990; Enacted November 5, 1992; Entered into Force November 5, 1992.

[965] Signed November 23, 2001.

[966] Constitution of the Republic of Iceland, 1944 (as amended), available at <http://oncampus.richmond.edu/~jjones//confinder/Iceland2.htm>.

and the personal privacy provision is now contained in Article 72. A translation of the 1995 amendments is not yet available.

As a member of the European Free Trade Association (EFTA), Iceland is obliged to ensure that its laws, in certain fields, are compatible with those of the European Union. On January 1, 2000 the Act on the Protection of Individuals with regard to the Processing of Personal Data came into force. The Act replaces the Registration and Processing of Personal Data of 1989 (as amended) and was adopted to bring Iceland's data protection regime into compliance with the European Union Data Protection Directive.[967] It covers both automated and manual processing of personal information. It distinguishes between sensitive and non-sensitive data and includes specific restrictions on the use of video surveillance and national identification numbers. It instructs the Statistical Bureau of Iceland to maintain a registry of individuals not willing to allow the use of their names in product marketing.

The Act established a new independent Data Protection Authority (Persónuvernd) to replace the former Data Protection Commission.[968] Persónuvernd supervises implementation and compliance with the Act and any pursuant regulations or orders. It maintains the registry of activities and can investigate and issue rulings. It can impose fines for non-compliance and can seek criminal sanctions. Persónuvernd is also responsible for supervising the handling of personal in the Schengen Information System[969] Persónuvernd has the authority to issue public guidelines and regulations. Over the last two years it has issued rules on consent; notification; security assessments and systematic safety measures. Since it's establishment Persónuvernd has received 847 notifications of personal data processing from 435 separate controllers. In 2001 it received 117 formal complaints and 220 requests for information. A total of 920 cases were investigated during the year. Persónuvernd hopes to reduce this figure significantly in the coming year through public awareness initiatives, controller education and more streamlined case processing. As of June 2002, there were seven full time staff employed by Persónuvernd.[970] In March 2001, the Ministry

---

[967] Act on Protection of Individuals with regard to the Processing of Personal Data No. 77/2000, available at <http://brunnur.stjr.is/interpro/tolvunefnd/tolvunefnd.nsf/pages/1E685B166D04084D002569050056BF6F>.

[968] Homepage at <http://www.personuvernd.is/tolvunefnd.nsf/pages/english>.

[969] Act on the Participation of Iceland in the Schengen Co-operation, No. 15/2000 and Act on the Schengen Information System, No. 16/2000.

[970] E-mail from Hordur Helgi Helgason, Deputy Commissioner, Icelandic Data Protection Authority (Persónuvernd), to Sarah Andrews, Research Director, Electronic Privacy Information Center, July 7, 2002 (on file with the Electronic Privacy Information Center).

of Justice issued a new regulation governing the practices of credit reporting agencies.[971]

In December 1998, the Parliament approved the Health Sector Database Act to create a nationwide centralized database of medical records to be used for genetic research.[972] In January 2000, the Minister of Health granted an exclusive 12-year license to operate that database to Íslensk Erf)agreining ehf, the Icelandic subsidiary of American bio-tech company deCode Genetics.[973] The database will incorporate non-personally identifiable data derived from the medical records held by Iceland's health services. Patients are to be granted a right to opt-out of the database by notifying the Director General of Public Health. The database is to be used to "develop new or improved methods of achieving better health, predication, diagnosis and treatment of disease, to seek the most economic ways of operating health services, and for making reports in the health sector." Measures to ensure security and privacy in the operation of the database must meet standards and conditions set out by the Data Protection Authority. In 2000, the Data Protection Authority issued regulations on the general security terms.[974] It is currently evaluating the design of the database system.[975]

The operating company is specifically authorized to use the data in the database for financial profit and, as long as confidentiality is ensured, to link it with other databases containing genealogical or genetic data. The company is reportedly spending $200 million over the next five years to research the country's gene-pool in order to find the genes related to common illnesses such as cancer, asthma, schizophrenia, Alzheimer's and Parkinson's diseases. According to one estimate presented at the 10th International Congress of Human Genetics in May 2001, the database will be worth approximately $14 billion.[976]

This proposal has been very controversial and is hotly debated both in Iceland and with medical and privacy experts around the world. In Iceland, the

---

[971] Regulation on Credit Reporting, No. 246/2001.

[972] Act on a Health Sector Database no. 139/1998, 17 December 1998.
<http://brunnur.stjr.is/interpro/htr/htr.nsf/pages/gagngr-log-ensk>.

[973] Operating Licence issued to Íslensk erf>agreining ehf, State Reg. No. 691295-3549, for the Creation and Operation of a Health Sector Database, Ministry of Health and Social Security, January 2000, available at <http://ministryofhealth.is/interpro/htr/htr.nsf/Files/oplic/$file/oplic.pdf>.

[974] General Security Terms of the Icelandic Data Protection Commission Document No. 1, January 19, 2000, available at <http://www.personuvernd.is/tolvunefnd.nsf/pages/C9519A42E967537E002569180036F54C>.

[975] E-mail from Hordur Helgi Helgason, supra n.970.

[976] What Is A Person's Dna Worth? Fair Compensation For Dna Access, J C Bear, Faculty of Medicine Memorial University of Newfoundland presented at the 10th International Congress of Human Genetics, Vienna, May 2001 available at <http://www.mannvernd.is/english/articles/jb_fair_compensation.html>.

Association of Icelanders for Ethics in Science and Medicine (Mannvernd) is leading the opposition to the project. Mannvernd reports that as of January 2002, 20,200 people had opted out of the database.[977] The Icelandic Medical Association is also opposing the effort and many doctors are refusing to hand over their patients' records without consent. The World Medical Association in April 1999 supported the Icelandic Medical Association's opposition to the database.[978] At their annual meeting in Santiago de Compostela, Spain in September 1998, the other European Data Protection Commissioners recommended that the Icelandic authorities reconsider the project in light of the fundamental principles laid down in the European Convention on Human Rights, the Council of Europe Convention and Recommendation (97)5 on medical data, and the EC Directive. In 1998, at the request of the Icelandic Medical Association, security expert Dr. Ross Anderson evaluated the proposed system. He concluded that the privacy and ethical implications of the proposed database were "outside the boundaries of what would be acceptable elsewhere in Europe" and advised the association to oppose its establishment.[979]

In May 2000, the Government enacted the Act on Biobanks.[980] This Act sets rules for the "collection, keeping, handling and utilization of biological samples from human beings" to ensure confidentiality and prohibit discrimination. The Act requires informed consent from the person for the collection of samples. However, this requirement does not apply to samples in biobanks that are already exist, such as the health sector database. The Act came into force in January 2001. In October 2000, the Commission ruled that four researchers in pharmacology and geriatrics, who had been granted a permit for a research project into Alzheimer's Disease, had breached the terms of the permit by collecting the medical records of people who were not participants in the Alzheimer project. The research project was financed by and conducted in association with Islenska Erfðagreining ehf.[981]

Under the Law on Criminal Procedure, wiretapping, tape recording or photographing without consent requires a court order and must be limited to a short period of time. After the recording is complete, the target must be informed

---

Opt-Out Graph, Association of Icelanders for Ethics in Science and Medicine (Mannvernd), available at <http://www.mannvernd.is/english/index.html>.

[978] "World Medical Association Opposes Icelandic Gene Database," EBMJ, 24 April 1999.

[979] Ross Anderson, "The DeCODE Proposal for an Icelandic Health Database," March 1998, available at <http://www.cl.cam.ac.uk/~rja14/iceland/iceland.html>.

[980] Act on Biobanks no. 110/2000, May 2000, available at <http://brunnur.stjr.is/interpro/tolvunefnd/tolvunefnd.nsf/pages/95EAE39BAC9DFA25002569050057034C>.

[981] "Illegal research on Alzheimer," Icelandic State Radio News Service, 28th October 2000, translation by Mannvernd at <http://www.mannvernd.is/english/news/alzheimer.illegal.html>.

and the recordings must be destroyed after they are no longer needed.[982] There were 42 wiretaps authorized between 1992 and February 1996.[983] Complaints against the orders can be submitted to the Supreme Court. Chapter XXV of the Penal Code also penalizes violations of privacy such as violating the secrecy of letters and revealing secrets to the public.

In June 2001, Keflavik International Airport began incorporating the facial recognition software, FaceIT, into its video surveillance. A police spokesperson said that the surveillance was being used to "identify known criminals and false asylum seekers" without disturbing European's citizens' rights to travel freely under the Schengen Agreement.[984]

The Freedom of Information Act of 1996 (Upplysingalög) governs the release of records.[985] Under the Act, individuals (including non-residents) and legal entities have a legal right to documents without having to show a reason for the document. There are exceptions for national security, commercial and personal information. Copyrighted material can be provided to requestors but it is then their responsibility if they republish the materials in a manner inconsistent with the copyright. Denials can be appealed to the Information Committee.

Iceland is a member of the Council of Europe and has signed and ratified the Convention for the Protection of Individuals with Regard to Automatic Processing of Personal Data (ETS No. 108).[986] It has signed and ratified the European Convention for the Protection of Human Rights and Fundamental Freedoms.[987] In November 2001, it signed the Council of Europe Convention on Cybercrime (ETS No.185).[988] It is a member of the Organization for Economic Cooperation and Development and has adopted the OECD Guidelines on the Protection of Privacy and Transborder Flows of Personal Data.

---

[982] Articles 86-87, Law on Criminal Procedure.

[983] See <http://www.icenews.is/daily/1996/09feb96.html>.

[984] "Icelandic Airport Installs New Surveillance Software," Airline Industry Information, June 20, 2001.

[985] Act no. 50/1996, <http://www.rz.uni-frankfurt.de/~sobotta/Enskthyd.doc>.

[986] Signed September 27, 1982; March 25, 1991; Entered into Force July 1, 1991.

[987] Signed November 11, 1950; Enacted June 29, 1953; Entered into Force September 3, 1953.

[988] Signed November 30, 2001.

Republic of India

The Constitution of 1950 does not expressly recognize the right to privacy.[989] However, the Supreme Court first recognized in 1964 that there is a right of privacy implicit in the Constitution under Article 21 of the Constitution, which states, "No person shall be deprived of his life or personal liberty except according to procedure established by law."[990]

There is no general data protection law in India. In June 2000 the National Association of Software and Service Companies (NASSCOM) urged the government to pass a data protection law to ensure the privacy of information supplied over computer networks and to meet European data protection standards.[991] The National Task Force on IT and Software Development had submitted an "IT Action Plan" to Prime Minister Vajpayee in July 1998 calling for the creation of a "National Policy on Information Security, Privacy and Data Protection Act for handling of computerized data." It examined the United Kingdom Data Protection Act as a model and recommended a number of cyber laws including ones on privacy and encryption.[992] No legislative measures, however, has been considered to date.

In May of 2000, the government passed the Information Technology Act, a set of laws intended to provide a comprehensive regulatory environment for electronic commerce.[993] The Act also addresses computer crime, hacking, damage to computer source code, breach of confidentiality and viewing of pornography. Chapter X of the Act creates a Cyber Appellate Tribunal to oversee adjudication of cybercrimes such as damage to computer systems (Section 43) and breach of confidentiality (Section 72). After widespread public outcry, sections requiring cybercafes to create detailed records about their customers' browsing habits were dropped. The legislation gives broad discretion to law enforcement authorities through a number of provisions – Section 69 allows for interception of any information transmitted through a computer resource and requires that users disclose encryption keys or face a jail sentence up to seven years. Section 80 allows deputy superintendents of police to conduct searches and seize suspects in

---

[989] Constitution of India, November 1949, available at <http://www.alfa.nic.in/const/a1.html>.

[990] Kharak Singh vs State of UP, 1 SCR 332 (1964); See Mr. R.C. Jain, National Human Rights Commission, India, Indian Supreme Court on Right to Privacy, July 1997.

[991] "Nasscom Urges Laws for Data Protection," Business Line -Internet Edition
<http://www.indiaserver.com/businessline/2000/06/29/stories/152939t5.htm>

[992] National Task Force on IT & SD, Basic Background Report, June 9, 1998, available at
<http://it-taskforce.nic.in/it-taskforce/bg.htm>.

[993] Information Technology Act 2000, No. 21 of 2000, available at <http://www.mit.gov.in/it-bill.htm>.

---

public spaces without a warrant. This section in particular appears to be targeted at cybercafe users where an estimated 75% of Indian Internet users access the web.[994] Section 44 imposes stiff penalties on anyone who fails to provide requested information to authorities, and Section 67 imposes strict penalties for involvement in the electronic publishing of materials deemed obscene by the government. Chapter III of the Act gives electronic records and digital signatures legal recognition, and Chapter VI authorizes the Government to appoint a Controller of Certifying Authorities, who will license certifying authorities before they can operate in India and will act as the repository of all Digital Signature Certificates issued under the Act. Following the enactment of the IT Act the Ministry of Information Technology adopted the Information Technology (Certifying Authorities) Rules in October 2000 to regulate the application of digital signatures and to provide guidelines for Certifying Authorities.[995] In April 2001 the Controller of Certifying Authorities announced that digital signatures would be available to Internet users by June 2002.[996]

There is also some right of personal privacy in Indian law. Unlawful attacks on the honor and reputation of a person can invite an action in tort and/or criminal law.[997] The Public Financial Institutions Act of 1993 codifies India's tradition of maintaining confidentiality in bank transactions.

In March 2000 the Central Bureau of Investigation set up the Cyber Crime Investigation Cell (CCIC) to investigate offences under the IT Act 2000 and other high tech crimes.[998] The CCIC has jurisdiction over all of India and is a member of the Interpol Working Party on Information Technology Crime for South East Asia and Australia. Similar cells have been set up at the state and city level, for example in the state of Karnataka and the city of Mumbai. In June 2002 the central government authorized the National Police Academy in Hyderabad to prepare a handbook on procedures to handle digital evidence in the case of

---

[994] Siddharth Varadarjan, "The Public Domain, "Policing the Net; The Dangers of India's New IT Act," Sarai Reader 2001, available at <http://www.sarai.net/journal/pdf/133-135%20(bill).pdf>.

[995] Information Technology (Certifying Authorities) Rules 2000, available at <http://www.mit.gov.in/rules/rulesfinal.htm>

[996] Baker & McKenzie, Global E-Commerce Law, available at <http://www.bmck.com/ecommerce/india.htm>.

[997] As the civil law pertaining to defamation is uncodified, the courts have to apply the corresponding rules of the English Common Law. In 1994 the Supreme Court decided in the *Auto Shankar* case that every citizen has the right to safeguard his or her privacy and that nothing could be published on areas such as the family, marriage and education, "whether truthful or otherwise", without the citizen's consent, but carved an exception to this rule for material based on public records and information about public officials' conduct that is "relevant to the discharge of their duties". See "Failure to Define Law on Privacy Could Cost Society Dear," Times of India, August 26, 2001, available at <http://timesofindia.indiatimes.com/articleshow.asp?artid=1912122924>.

[998] See <http://cbi.nic.in/cyber1.htm>.

computer and Internet-related crimes.[999] The government is also considering establishing an Electronic Research and Development Centre of India to be responsible for developing new cyber forensic tools. India's Intelligence Bureau is reported to have developed an e-mail interception tool similar to the Carnivore system, which it claims to use in anti-terrorist investigations.[1000] In April 2002, India and the United States launched a cyber security forum to collaborate on responding to cyber security threats.[1001]

Wiretapping is regulated under the Indian Telegraph Act of 1885. There have been numerous phone tap scandals in India, resulting in a 1996 decision by the Supreme Court which ruled that wiretaps are a "serious invasion of an individual's privacy." And laid out guidelines for wiretapping by the government.[1002] The guidelines define who can tap phones and under what circumstances. Only the Union home secretary or his counterpart in the states can issue an order for a tap. The government is also required to show that the information sought cannot to be obtained through any other means. The Court mandated the development of a high-level review committee to review the legality of each wiretap. Tapped phone calls are not accepted as primary evidence in India's courts. However, as is the case with most law in India, there continues to be a gap between the law and its enforcement. According to prominent Non-Government Organizations, the mail of many NGOs in Delhi and in strife-torn areas continues to be subjected to interception and censorship.[1003]

In March 2002 the Indian Parliament in a rare joint session passed the Prevention Of Terrorism Act or POTA over the objections of several Opposition parties and in the face of considerable public criticism. The National Human Rights Commission, an independent government entity, criticized the measure finding that the existing laws were sufficient to combat terrorism.[1004] The law codifies the Prevention of Terrorism Ordinance that in turn builds on the repealed

---

[999] Ashu Kumar. "Police Academy, ER&DCI Team Up to Take on Cybercrooks," Financial Express, June 11, 2002, available at <http://www.financialexpress.com/print.php?content_id=8322>.

[1000] Siddharth Srivastava, "Email Users Beware, Big Brother is Watching," Times of India, December 24, 2001, available at <http://timesofindia.indiatimes.com/articleshow.asp?art_id=37906058>. See also "India: Interception of E-Mails, Electronic Data," BNA World Data Protection Report, Volume 2, Issue 3, March 2002.

[1001] See United States State Department Press Release and Transcript of News Conference, available at <http://usinfo.state.gov/regional/nea/sasia/text/0502cyber.htm>.

[1002] Peoples Union for Civil Liberties (PUCL) vs. The Union of India & Another, December 18, 1996, on Writ Petition (C) No. 256 of 1991.

[1003] South Asia Human Rights Documentation Centre, Alternate Report and Commentary to the United Nations Human Rights Committee on India's Third Periodic Report under Article 40 of the International Covenant on Civil and Political Rights, July 1997, available at <http://www.hri.ca/partners/sahrdc/alternate/fulltext.shtml>.

[1004] See National Human Rights Commission Report, available at <http://nhrc.nic.in/whatsnew1.htm#1.OPINION>

Terrorists and Disruptive Activities (Prevention) Act or TADA. It gives law enforcement sweeping powers to arrest suspected terrorists, intercept communications, and curtail free expression. Critics argue that the experience of TADA and POTO shows that the power was often misused for political ends by authorities and that POTA does little to curb those excesses.[1005] Chapter V of the Act deals with the interception of electronic communication, which also creates an audit mechanism that includes some provision for judicial review and parliamentary oversight; however, it remains to be seen how effective such mechanisms will be in practice. In certain high-risk states such as Jammu and Kashmir, search warrants are not required and the government from time to time bans the use of cellular telephones, long distance phones, and cyber cafes.[1006] India's Enforcement Directorate, which investigates foreign exchange and currency violations, searches, interrogates and arrests business professionals, often without a warrant.[1007]

A prominent expose of government corruption by the web portal Tehelka has sparked a growing debate on the appropriate balance between the press and personal privacy. Telehka's investigative journalists covertly filmed high level officials accepting bribes and army officers groping call girls as part of their expose on how official corruption operates in India.[1008] While some critics admit that the journalists did shed much needed light on a murky subject, they argue that there should be some restrictions on the press' behavior.[1009] Indian allows the use of illegally obtained evidence and therefore the evidence collected by the journalists can be used in court. Similar questions arose in relation to the transcripts of tapped phone calls released to the press in a match fixing scandal surrounding the national sport of cricket in April 2000.[1010]

The Indian parliament is examining a draft Communications Convergence Bill, which was supposed to pass in May 2002, but has been delayed until the monsoon session that begins in July.[1011]   The bill aims to create a "super

---

[1005] Human Rights Watch, "India: Proposed Anti-Terror Law Should Be Rejected," October 18, 2001, available at <http://www.hrw.org/press/2001/10/india1018.htm>.

[1006] Tariq Ahmad Bhat, "Kashmir: Booth capture Ban on long distance calls affects business," The Week, March 17, 2002, available at < http://www.the-week.com/22mar17/events9.htm>.

[1007] United States Department of State, Country Report on Human Rights Practices 2001, March 4, 2002, available at <http://www.state.gov/g/drl/rls/hrrpt/2001/sa/8230pf.htm>.

[1008] Mukund Padmanabhan, "Sex, bribes, and videotape," The Hindu, September 8, 2001, available at <http://www.hinduonnet.com/thehindu/2001/09/08/stories/05082523.htm>.

[1009] Rajeev Dhavan, "Tehelka: what next?" The Hindu September 7, 2001, available at <http://www.hinduonnet.com/thehindu/2001/09/07/stories/05072523.htm>.

[1010] Manoj Joshi. "Phone-tap laws may trip Cronje case," April 15, 2000 <

[1011] Vandana Gombar. "Panel at IT, But Convergence Law Still Not In Sight," <http://www.financialexpress.com/print.php?content_id=8552>.

regulator", the Communications Commission for India, to oversee voice and data (including telecom, broadcasting, and Internet) communications.[1012] Chapter XIV of the bill deals with the interception of communication and punishment for unlawful interception. Section 63 has been criticized by business groups for placing a significant burden on service providers to provide information on their customers to the government, and allowing the government to intercept any communication under a very low standard.[1013]

The Supreme Court ruled in 1982 that access to government information was an essential part of the fundamental right to freedom of speech and expression[1014] A draft Freedom of Information Act was introduced into the Parliament in July 2000.[1015] The bill would provide a general right to access information and create a National Council for Freedom of Information and State Councils. It contains seven broad categories of exemptions. Campaigners who said that the bill provided only limited access to government records heavily criticized the draft.[1016] The National Centre for Advocacy Studies said, "Many of the aspects towards information availability have been left completely in the hands of bureaucrats, which defeats the very purpose of the bill." In 1997, the state of Tamil Nadu adopted the Act for Right to Information and the states of Gujarat and Rajasthan have administratively provided access to records. The state of Madhya Pradesh enacted a Right to Information Bill in March 1998.

Republic of Ireland

Although there is not an express reference to a right to privacy in the Irish Constitution, the Supreme Court has ruled an individual may invoke the personal rights provision in Article 40.3.1 to establish an implied right to privacy. This article provides that "The State guarantees in its laws to respect, and, as far as practicable, by its laws to defend and vindicate the personal rights of the citRizens." It was first used to establish an implied constitutional right in the case of *McGee v. Attorney General*,[1017] which recognized the right to marital privacy.

[1012] See draft bill, available at <http://www.tiaonline.org/policy/regional/asia/conbill.pdf>

[1013] See United States India Business Council, "Comment to GOI on Draft Communications Convergence Bill," available at <http://www.tiaonline.org/policy/submissions/USIBCConvergenceSubmission.pdf>.

[1014] S.P. Gupta vs. Union of India (AIR 1982 SC 149); See Government of India, Report of the Working Group on Right to Information and Promotion of Open and Transparent Government, May 1997.

[1015] Freedom on Information Bill, 2000. <http://www.humanrightsinitiative.org/RTI/foibill1.htm>.

[1016] "Open-government bill flawed, say activists," South China Morning Post, January 11, 2000. "NGOs oppose information bill," The Times of India, March 7, 2000.

[1017] 1974 IR 284.

This case has been followed by others such as *Norris v. Attorney General*[1018] and *Kennedy and Arnold v. Ireland*.[1019] In the latter case the Supreme Court ruled that the illegal wiretapping of two journalists was a violation of the constitution, stating:

> The right to privacy is one of the fundamental personal rights of the citizen which flow from the Christian and democratic nature of the State... The nature of the right to privacy is such that it must ensure the dignity and freedom of the individual in a democratic society. This can not be insured if his private communications, whether written or telephonic, are deliberately and unjustifiably interfered with.[1020]

In 1988, the Data Protection Act was passed in order to implement the 1981 Council of Europe Convention for the Protection of Individuals with Regard to Automatic Processing of Personal Data. The Act regulates the collection, processing, keeping, use and disclosure of personal information processed by both the private and public sectors, but it only covers information that is automatically processed. Individuals have a right to access and correct inaccurate information. Information can only be used for specified and lawful purposes and cannot be improperly used or disclosed. Additional protections can be ordered for sensitive data. Criminal penalties can be imposed for violations. There are broad exemptions for national security, tax, and criminal purposes. Misuse of data is also criminalized by the Criminal Damage Act 1991.

As a member of the European Union, Ireland should have amended this Act and extended its scope in order to implement the European Data Protection Directive by October 1, 1998. In January 2000, the European Commission initiated a case before the European Court of Justice against Ireland and four other countries for failure to implement the Directive on time.[1021] In December 2001, certain provisions of the Directive were implemented with the introduction of the European Communities (Data Protection) Regulations, 2001. The regulations took effect in April 2002 and govern the transfer of personal information to third countries (i.e. non European Economic Area countries). The Data Protection (Amendment) Bill was finally published in February 2002 to will implement the remaining provisions of the Directive. It was approved by the Seanad (the

---

[1018] 1984 I.R. 36.

[1019] 1987 I.R. 587.

[1020] Constitution of Ireland, available at <http://www.maths.tcd.ie/pub/Constitution/index.html>.

[1021] European Commission, Press Release, "Data protection: Commission takes five Member States to court," January 11, 2000, available at <http://europa.eu.int/comm/internal_market/en/media/dataprot/news/2k-10.htm>.

Senate) in May 2002 and is now being considered by the Dáil (the House of Representatives). It is expected to be enacted before the end of the year.

The bill amends the existing law in a number of ways. It extends protection to manual as well as automated files. It broadens the definition of "processing." It improves the rights of individuals in the areas of notice, access and consent. It clarifies, and in some cases increases, the responsibilities of data controllers. It provides additional protection for "sensitive" data, defined as information relating to: racial or ethic origin; political opinions; religious or philosophical belief; trade union membership; physical or mental health; sexual life; the commission or alleged commission of an offence and any proceedings arising there-from. It requires the registration of every data controller, unless specifically exempted under regulations issued by the Data Protection Commissioner. It increases the powers of the Data Protection Commissioner to ensure compliance with the Act and to issue Codes of Practice. Finally, it creates specific exemptions for "journalistic, artistic, or literary" processing.[1022]

The 1988 Act established the office of the Data Protection Commissioner to oversee enforcement of its principles. The Commissioner has powers to cinvestigate complaints, prosecute offenders, sponsor codes of practice, and supervise the registration process. The number of complaints received by the Commission increased significantly to 233 in 2001 from 131 in 2000. Of these 35 percent were upheld, 33 percent were rejected and 32 percent were resolved informally. [1023] Among others, during the year the Commissioner initiated investigations into MBNA Bank and Eircom (Ireland's leading communications company) for directing marketing practices; Ryanair (an airline company) for abusive credit card practices and disclosure on national radio of a named passenger; and Concern (a major charitable organization) for disclosure, without consent, of donors' details to a financial institution. The number of data controllers registered rose to 3100 during 2001. In January 2001, the Data Protection Commissioner issued regulations[1024] requiring all telecommunications companies and Internet service providers to register with his office.[1025] This was the first time the Commissioner had exercised his power to create additional categories of operators required to register. In his 2001 annual report the

---

[1022] Data Protection Commissioner, "What's New in the Bill: A Summary Guide," available at <http://www.dataprivacy.ie/3n.htm>.

[1023] Irish Data Protection Commissioner, Annual Report 2001, available at <http://www.dataprivacy.ie/images/annual_report_2001.pdf>.

[1024] The Data Protection (Registration) Regulations 2001.

[1025] "Data Protection Commissioner Requires Telecommunications Industry and Internet Service Providers to Register," January 9, 2001, available at <http://www.dataprivacy.ie/7nr0101.htm>

Commissioner specifically criticized members of the legal profession its for low level of compliance with the registration requirement. In July 2002, the Commissioner issued a public warning concerning a United Kingdom based company masquerading as an official registration service for Irish data controllers.[1026]

No codes of practice have been issued under the Data Protection Act. Whereas under the 1988 Act the Commissioner only had the power to approves codes drawn up by trade associations, the Data Protection (Amendment) Bill 2002 gives the him the power to propose and prepare his own codes. In his 2001 report, the Commissioner noted the need for a code of practice for the health sector. He noted that his Office has advised the Health Information Working Party, which was established by the Department of Health and Children to study the handling of medical data, to prepare such a code.

In May 2002, the European Communities (Data Protection and Privacy in Telecommunications) Regulations 2002 (S.I. No. 192 of 2002) were signed into law. These regulations give effect to European Directive 97/66/EC concerning data protection in the telecommunications sector. In November 2001 it was revealed that Irish mobile phone operators, Eircell and Digfone, were holding customer "locator records" for more than six years, stating that they believed they were required to do so under the law.

In 1998 the Government passed the Social Welfare Act of 1998 to create a unique personal identification number for use in dealing with public agencies. The Personal Public Service Number (PPSN) replaced the "Revenue and Social Insurance" (RSI) number, which for years, was used for social welfare and tax purposes only. The PPSN will eventually be used as a unique personal identifier in all communications between an individual and specified State Agencies. The Act allows for the exchange of personal data between these bodies in certain circumstances, and its provisions are expressly exempt from the Data Protection Act. The only privacy safeguard laid down by the Act is a provision making it an offence for anyone other than a State agency to attempt to obtain an individual's PPSN. The Data Protection Commissioner criticized this scheme while it was being debated, stating that "the proposed sharing of personal data, obtained and kept by legally separate entities, for such diverse purposes is fundamentally incompatible with ... the basic tenets of data protection law."[1027]

[1026] Data Protection Commissioner, News Release, "Warning: Unofficial Registration Services,"July 5, 2002.

[1027] Irish Data Protection Commissioner, Annual Report, 1996, at 35. See also "Remarks by the Data Protection Commissioner on the bill to the Dail Select Committee on Social, Community and Family Affairs," March 4, 1998.

The development of the PPSN is part of a much larger project to modernize public services and develop a fully functioning e-Government. In 1999, an independent government agency, known as Reach, was established by Government order to oversee this project. Reach is charged with building a central Public Service Broker, which is intended to facilitate transactions between individuals and Public Service Agencies. Personal data about citizens will be held in secure vaults and be released to public agencies in the course of particular transactions. Apart from the normal categories of information required for most services, individuals may chose to store additional data in these vaults for example, birth and marriage certificates, details of income or other means, digital photographs, credit card details, passport details, car registration and insurance details. Data in the system will be updated directly by individuals or by an agent acting on their behalf. Access will be limited to the individual customer or to authorized public servants in the course of a specific transaction. A Public Services Card is being developed as an individual's key to access his/her personal data and the connected public services. The card will display the cardholder's name, signature and PPSN. For basic transactions, the card and a PIN number will be enough to guarantee access. Technology to protect higher sensitivity transactions has not yet been chosen but may be based on a Public Key Infrastructure (PKI). [1028] The Data Protection Commissioner is in close consultation with Reach concerning the privacy and security implications of this system.

Ireland is recognized as having the most modern copyright and electronic signature laws in Europe.[1029] In July 2000 the E-Commerce Act was implemented, granting legal recognition to e-signatures, e-writings and e-contracts. The Copyright and Related Rights Act, which permits surprise searches and enacts stiff penalties against software theft, came into force in November 2000. Ireland's implementation of the European Union's E-Commerce Directive makes it one of the only European countries to place the burden of opting out of 'spam' on the consumer.[1030] This legislation has enabled Ireland to promote itself as an attractive e-commerce location, however, it may now need to be amended to comply with the new Telecommunications Privacy Directive (COM(2000)385).

[1028] For more details about the Reach Project visit <http://www.reachapterie/index.htm>.

[1029] "Cyber Champion Award presented to Taoiseach," The Irish Times, October 10, 2000.

[1030] "Republic Puts 'Spam' Burden on the Consumer," The Irish Times, June 29, 2001.

Wiretapping and electronic surveillance is regulated under the Interception of Postal Packets and Telecommunications Messages (Regulation) Act. The Act followed a 1987 decision of the Supreme Court ruling that wiretaps of journalists violated the constitution (see above). In October 2001, the Taoiseach (Prime Minister) publicly apologized on behalf of the State to three journalists whose phones were tapped during the 1980s as part of an effort to control leaks from the Government. The Taoiseach apologized for "the inappropriate invasion of their privacy and interference by the State with their role as journalists."[1031] In its June 1998 Report on "Privacy, Surveillance and the Interception of Communications," the Law Reform Commission recommended legislation to make illegal the invasion of a person's privacy through secret filming, taping and eavesdropping and the publication of information received from such surveillance.

The issue of employee monitoring is also causing growing concern in Ireland. In March 2002, Amarach Consulting released a survey finding that one in four employees say that their use of the Internet in the workplace is monitored or restricted.[1032] In 2000, the Manufacturing, Science and Finance Union (MSF) recently called for national and European Union legislation to limit the use of electronic surveillance in the workplace.[1033]

In September 2002, the 24th International Conference of Data Protection and Privacy Commissioners will be hosted by the British, Irish, Guernsey, Jersey and Isle of Man data protection authorities in Cardiff, Wales.[1034]

The Freedom of Information Act was approved in 1997 and went into effect in April 1998.[1035] The act creates a presumption that the public can access documents created by government agencies and requires that government agencies make internal information on their rules and activities available. The Office of the Information Commissioner enforces the act.

Ireland is a member of the Council of Europe and has signed and ratified the Convention for the Protection of Individuals with Regard to Automatic Processing of Personal Data (ETS No. 108).[1036] It has also signed and ratified the European Convention for the Protection of Human Rights and Fundamental

---

[1031] "Apology for Phone Tapping," The Irish Times, October 26, 2001.

[1032] Amarach Consulting, "Big Brother Watching Irish Internet Users," Press Release, March 14, 2002, available at <http://www.amarachaptercom/news/amarachpressrelease_14_03_02.doc>.

[1033] "Law to Limit Monitoring of Workers Urged," The Irish Times, March 7, 2000.

[1034] For more information visit <http://www.informationrights2002.org/>.

[1035] Freedom of Information Act, 1997, available at <http://www.irlgov.ie/finance/free1.htm>.

[1036] Signed December 18, 1986; Enacted May 25, 1990; Entered into Force August 1, 1990.

Freedoms.[1037] However, unlike every other European signatory country, Ireland has not incorporated this Convention into national law. In February 2002, Ireland signed the Council of Europe Convention on Cybercrime.[1038] Ireland is also a member of the Organization for Economic Cooperation and Development and has adopted the OECD Guidelines on the Protection of Privacy and Transborder Flows of Personal Data.

State of Israel

Section 7 of The Basic Law: Human Dignity and Freedom (1992) states: "(a) All persons have the right to privacy and to intimacy. (b) There shall be no entry into the private premises of a person who has not consented thereto. (c) No search shall be conducted on the private premises or body of a person, nor in the body or belongings of a person. (d) There shall be no violation of the secrecy of the spoken utterances, writings or records of a person."[1039] According to Supreme Court Justice Mishael Cheshin, this law elevated the right of privacy to the level of a basic right.[1040]

The Protection of Privacy Law regulates the processing of personal information in computer data banks.[1041] The law sets out 11 categories of prohibited activities and provides for civil and criminal penalties. Holders of data banks of more than 10,000 names must register with the Registrar of Databases. The law limits the use of information in these databases to the purposes for which they were intended, and database holders must provide access to database subjects. There are broad exceptions to the law for police and security services. The law also sets up basic privacy regulations relating to surveillance, publication of photographs and other traditional privacy features. The law was amended in 1996 to broaden the databases covered and increase penalties.[1042]

The Registrar of Databases within the Ministry of Justice enforces the law. The Registrar maintains the register of databases and can deny registration if he or she believes that a database is used for illegal activities. The Registrar also

---

[1037] Signed November 11, 1950; Enacted February 25, 1953; Entered into Force September 3, 1953.

[1038] Signed February 28, 2002.

[1039] The Basic Law: Human Dignity and Freedom (5752 - 1992). Passed by the Knesset on the 21st Adar, 5754 (9th March, 1994), available at <http://www.mfa.gov.il/mfa/go.asp?MFAH00hi0>.

[1040] Israeli Business Law: An Essential Guide.

[1041] The Protection of Privacy Law 5741-1981, 1011 Laws of the State of Israel 128, amended by the Protection of Privacy Law (Amendment) 5745-1985.

[1042] Law of April 11, 1996.

investigates violations of the law. As of mid-1998, 5,200 databases were registered.[1043] A public council for the protection of privacy has also been set up to advise the Justice Minister on legislative matters related to the Protection of Privacy Law and its subsidiary regulations and orders. The council sets guidelines for the protection of computerized databases and guides the work of the Registrar of Databases. The European Commission considers Israel's data protection laws to likely offer an adequate level of protection for personal data transferred to Israel from countries in the European Union.[1044]

The Credit Data Service Law was enacted in 2002 to create a shared center for storing consumers' credit information among different competing creditors and break up the dominance of the two banks that controlled most credit information.[1045] Although the law gives consumers access to their information and the opportunity to correct information collected, includes "positive" records, such as evidence of good credit, and features a procedure for opting out of collection, some politicians have argued that it unduly invades privacy by automatically sharing credit information and penalizing those who opt out of the database.[1046]

The Jerusalem Attorney's office indicted 46 public-sector workers in December 2001 for selling information from the classified database on the country's inhabitants. The information—some of which was sold to private detectives—included criminal records, lists of outgoing telephone calls, salaries and property ownership. The defendants, employed by the police, tax, insurance, telecommunications and other government departments, were charged with accepting bribes, violation of privacy, illegal use of the database and conspiracy.[1047]

Interception of communications is governed by the Secret Monitoring Law of 1979, which was amended in 1995 following a finding by the State Comptroller that police were abusing wiretap procedures. The amendments were designed to tighten procedures and cover new technologies, such as cellular phones and e-mail. In addition, the amendments increased penalties for illegal taps and allowed interception of privileged communications, such as those with a lawyer or

---

[1043] United Nations Human Rights Committee, Initial Report of States Parties Due in 1993, Israel. 09/04/98. CCPR/C/81/Add.13. (State Party Report), April 9, 1998.

[1044] "Global data protection and security issues in the cards arena," Cards International, September 26, 2001.

[1045] Credit Data Service Law, 5762-2002.

[1046] "MKs to duke it out in credit data service law battle," Israel Business Arena, July 5, 2001.

[1047] "46 indicted for selling confidential data," The Jerusalem Post, December 5, 2001.

doctor.[1048] The police must receive permission from the President of the District Court to intercept any form of wire or electronic communication or plant a microphone for a period up to three months, which can be renewed. According to the Israeli government, the number of wiretap orders "has averaged roughly 1,000 to 1,100 annually over the last several years. Roughly half of these wiretap permits are given in connection with drug-related offences."[1049] Intelligence agencies may wiretap people suspected of endangering national security after receiving written permission from the Prime Minister or Defense Minister. The agencies must present an annual report to the Knesset. The Chief Military Censor may also intercept international conversations to or from Israel for purposes of censorship.[1050] Although courts are supposed to weigh privacy concerns against law enforcement needs before authorizing wiretaps, in practice authorization is almost automatic upon request; out of more than 1,700 wiretap requests made in 1999, only six were refused.[1051]

According to an Internal Security Ministry report released in May 2002, Israeli police carried out 1,685 wiretaps in 2000. The report, an internal review of police wiretapping procedures, cited "lack of oversight and supervision" regarding police wiretapping and said police consistently fail to destroy non-essential evidence uncovered by wiretapping.[1052] The Knesset Interior Committee held a session in February to discuss the wiretapping of prominent Israeli politicians, including former Prime Minister Benjamin Netanyahu, and decided at the close of the session to establish a subcommittee to monitor classified work by the police. However, the approval of the Knesset speaker and legal advisers must be obtained before the subcommittee can be established.[1053]

In June 2000, the Tel Aviv District Court held that the State could not order an Internet Service Provider to collect subscriber e-mails to provide to the police, finding that such a practice constituted the equivalent of an illegal wiretap. However, the Court determined that police could request e-mails already collected by the ISP from subscribers against whom an indictment is pending and could then use the e-mails upon indictment if a court found the collection to be

---

1048 The Secret Monitoring Law, 5739-1979, Laws of the State of Israel, Volume 33, at 141-146.

1049 United Nations Human Rights Committee, Initial Report of States Parties Due in 1993, supra n.1043.

1050 Herb Keinon, "Shas disputes linking wiretap to Yishai-Deri rivalry," The Jerusalem Post, November 27, 1998.

1051 "Courts quick to authorize wiretaps," Ha'aretz, August 10, 2000.

1052 "Problems revealed with police wiretaps," The Jerusalem Post, May 20, 2002.

1053 Nina Gilbert, "Knesset to scrutinize widespread use of wiretaps," The Jerusalem Post, February 12, 2002.

justifiable—even if illegal at the time of seizure—when balanced against individual privacy rights.[1054]

In 1996 a Defense Forces employee was tried for misusing the phone records of a journalist.[1055] Several people, including Ma'ariv publisher Opher Nimrodi, were convicted in 1998 of ordering wiretaps on business people and media personalities, including Science Minister Silvan Shalom in 1994.[1056] In November 1998, wiretaps were discovered on the phone of Labor and Social Affairs Minister Eli Yishai. It was suspected that he was wiretapped by a rival political faction inside the Shas party.

Unauthorized access to computers is punished by The Computer Law of 1995.[1057] In June 2002, an Israeli teen-ager was sentenced under this law to 18 months in jail for masterminding a series of high-profile hacks into the computer systems at the Massachusetts Institute of Technology, NASA, the FBI, the United States Air Force and the United States Department of Defense.[1058] An appeals court overruled the teen-ager's original sentence of six months community service after the Israeli government, under pressure from the United States, pushed for a stricter sentence.[1059]

The Postal and Telegraph Censor, which operates as a civil department within the Ministry of Defense, has the power to open any postal letter or package to prevent harm to state security or public order.[1060]

The 1996 Patient Rights Law imposes a duty of confidentiality on all medical personnel.[1061] A Genetic Privacy Bill passed its second and third readings by the Knesset's Science and Technology Committee in November 2000. The bill is designed to limit disclosure of private DNA information.[1062] In August 1999, the Cabinet called on the Ministry of Justice to develop legislation creating a national

---

[1054] "Courts quick to authorize wiretaps," Ha'aretz, August 10, 2000.

[1055] Evelyn Gordon, "IDF officer involved in phone record scandal accuses others of involvement," The Jerusalem Post, July 11, 1996.

[1056] "Media wiretapper found guilty," The Jerusalem Post, September 4, 1998.

[1057] The Computer Law (5755-1995), 1534 Laws of the State of Israel 366, See Miguel Deutch, Computer Legislation: Israel's New Codified Approach, 14 J. Marshall J. Computer & Info. L. 461 (Spring 1996).

[1058] Boaz Guttman, "The Analyzer: Following the State's Appeal," May 6, 2002, available at <http://www.bgrg.co.il/206.pdf>.

[1059] Bob Sullivan, "Analyzer gets 18-month jail term, " MSNBC, June 6, 2002, available at <http://www.msnbc.com/news/762951.asp>.

[1060] Regulation 89 of the Mandatory Defence (Emergency) Regulations, 1945.

[1061] Patient Rights Law, 5756-1996.

[1062] Nina Gilbert, "Genetic privacy bill passed," The Jerusalem Post, November 16, 2000.

DNA database for police investigations.[1063] The Health Ministry issued regulations on the use of video surveillance in hospitals in September 1998 after it was disclosed that cameras had been moved to watch patients undressing.[1064]

Criminal records are governed by the Criminal Register and Rehabilitation Law, which allows 30 government agencies to access the records.[1065]

Finance Minister Yaakov Ne'eman issued an authorization in March 1998 giving the director of the Bureau for Counterterrorism full access to the databases of all Israeli taxation authorities, including the Income Tax Authorities and Customs. It gives the Bureau access to the financial records of any citizen in Israel, including the status of their bank account "for urgent cases of preventing terrorist acts."[1066]

Israel contracted with Electronic Data Systems in 1999 to install a biometrics-based border control system to monitor the entrance and exit of about 50,000 Palestinians workers through the Gaza Strip using hand geometry and facial recognition technology.[1067] Israel has also installed a biometrics identification system in Tel Aviv's Ben Gurion Airport. Frequent travelers who submit biographic information and biometric hand-geometry data may use automatic inspection kiosks to go through airport security. Travelers use a credit card for initial identification and then scan their palms into the kiosk to verify their identity. The machine prints a receipt that allows the traveler to proceed through security. Nearly 80,000 Israeli citizens have enrolled in the biometric identification system.[1068]

The Supreme Court ruled in *Shalit v. Peres* that there was a fundamental right for citizens to obtain information from the government.[1069] The Freedom of Information Law was approved unanimously by the Knesset in May 1998. It provides for broad access to records held by government offices, local councils and government-owned corporations. Requests for information must be

---

[1063] Herb Keinon, "Filing our most secret codes," The Jerusalem Post, September 8, 1999.

[1064] Judy Siegel, "Embarrassed by Ichilov disclosure: Ministry issues regulations for hospital cameras," The Jerusalem Post, September 10, 1998.

[1065] Criminal Register and Rehabilitation Law, 5741-1981.

[1066] "Anti-terror chief to see all tax files," Ha'aretz, May 29, 1998.

[1067] "Consortium led by EDS wins award to develop leading-edge biometric border crossing system for the Israeli borders," EDS News Releases, September 6, 1999, available at <http://www.eds.com/news/news_release_template.shtml?rowid=2051>.

[1068] John Mesenbrink, "Biometrics plays big role in airport safety," Security, December 1, 2001.

[1069] H.C. 1601-4/90 Shalit et al. v. Peres et al., 44(3) P.D. 353. See Debbie L. Rabina, Access to government information in Israel: stages in the continuing development of a national information policy, available at <http://www.ifla.org/IV/ifla66/papers/018-160e.htm>.

processed within 30 days. A court can review decisions to withhold information. A Jerusalem Post survey in June 1999 found that many agencies had not begun to prepare for the law.[1070]

Italian Republic

The 1948 Constitution has several limited provisions relating to privacy. Article 14 states, "(1) Personal domicile is inviolable. (2) Inspection and search may not be carried out save in cases and in the manner laid down by law in conformity with guarantees prescribed for safeguarding personal freedom. (3) Special laws regulate verifications and inspections for reasons of public health and safety, or for economic and fiscal purposes." Article 15 states, "(1) The liberty and secrecy of correspondence and of every form of communication are inviolable. (2) Limitations upon them may only be enforced by decision, for which motives must be given, of the judicial authorities with the guarantees laid down by law."[1071]

The Italian Data Protection Act was enacted in 1996 after twenty years of debate.[1072] The Act is intended to fully implement the European Union Data Protection Directive. It covers both electronic and manual files, for both government agencies and the private sector. There have also been decrees approved relating to security requirements[1073], to the processing of medical information,[1074] processing of information for journalistic purposes,[1075] for scientific or research purposes,[1076] and by public bodies.[1077]

[1070] Judy Siegel, "Ministries not ready for info law," The Jerusalem Post, June 25, 1999.

[1071] Constitution of the Republic of Italy, adopted December 22, 1947, available at <http://www.uni-wuerzburg.de/law/it00t___.html>.

[1072] Legge `31 dicembre 1996 n. 675, Tutela delle persone e di altri soggetti rispetto al trattamento dei dati personali. Amended by Legislative Decree No. 123 of 09.05.97 and 255 of 28.07.97.
<http://elj.strath.ac.uk/jilt/dp/material/l675-eng.htm (Unofficial translation). Legge 31 Dicembre 1996, N. 676, Delega al Governo in materia di tutela delle persone e di altri soggetti rispetto al trattamento dei dati personali. <http://www.privacy.it/legge96676.html>. For list of decrees see <http://www.privacy.it/normativ.html>.

[1073] Presidential Decree No. 318, July 28, 1999.

[1074] Decreto legislativo del 30/7/1999 n. 282 "Disposizioni per garantire la riservatezza dei dati personali in ambito sanitario," available at <http://www.privacy.it/dl1999282.html>.

[1075] Decreto legislativo 13 maggio 1998, n. 171. Disposizioni in materia di tutela della vita privata nel settore delle telecomunicazioni, in attuazione della direttiva 97/66/CE del Parlamento europeo e del Consiglio, ed in tema di attività giornalistica, available at <http://www.privacy.it/dl1998171.html>.

[1076] Decreto legislativo del 30/7/1999 n. 281 "Disposizioni in materia di trattamento dei dati personali per finalità storiche, statistiche e di ricerca scientifica," available at <http://www.privacy.it/dl1999281.html>.

[1077] Decreto legislativo 11/5/1999, n.135 Disposizioni integrative della legge 31/12/1996, n. 675, sul trattamento di dati sensibili da parte dei soggetti pubblici available at <http://www.privacy.it/dl1999135.html>.

The Act is enforced by the Supervisory Authority (Garante) for Personal Data Protection.[1078] The Garante maintains a register of databases, conducts audits and enforces the laws. It can also audit databanks not under its jurisdiction, such as those relating to intelligence activities. The Decree on the internal organization of the Authority was published in the Official Journal on February 1, 1999. The decree establishes the procedures for keeping the Register of Data Processes, access to the register by citizens, investigations, registrations and inspections.[1079] As of June 2002, the Garante had 69 staff persons.[1080]

In February 2001, the Garante issued a Code Of Conduct And Ethics Regarding The Processing Of Personal Data For Historical Purposes. The Code came into effect on March 14, 2001. In March 2001, the Garante also issued guidelines on the protection of personal data in electoral activities such as campaign literature and elections.[1081] During the period of December 2000 and February 2001 the Garante ruled the following: that employees are entitled to access information about them included in evaluation reports drafted by their employers;[1082] that political associations can not collect email addresses from the Internet to send unsolicited out unsolicited political messages;[1083] that the processing operations of the Italian armed forces corps the Carabinieri failed to comply with the Data Protection Law;[1084] that the personal information on identification badges worn by employees who are in regular contact with the public should be relevant and not excessive to the purpose;[1085] that banks can not take fingerprint scans of those entering the premises as this is out of all proportion to their security needs;[1086] and that the personal data in medical expert opinions in insurance liability cases must be accessible to the data subject but may be temporarily deferred in order not to affect the outcome of the investigation.[1087] In October 1998 it ruled that phone companies need not mask the phone numbers on bills

---

[1078] Home Page <http://www.dataprotection.org/>.

[1079] Decreto del presidente della repubblica, 31 marzo 1998, n.501 Regolamento recante norme per l'organizzazione ed il funzionamento dell'Ufficio del Garante per la protezione dei dati personali, a norma dell'articolo 33, comma 3, della legge 31 dicembre 1996, n. 675. (GU n. 25 del 1-2-1999), available at <http://193.207.119.193/MV/gazzette_ufficiali/25/2.htm>.

[1080] E-Mail from Antonio Caselli (on behalf of Mr. Giovanni Buttarelli, Secretary General to the Italian Data Protection Authority) to Dwayne Nelson, IPIOP Clerk, Electronic Privacy Information Center, June 17, 2002. (on file with the Electronic Privacy Information Center).

[1081] Personal Data and Elections- Instructions for Use, March 7, 2001

[1082] Employee Evaluation Data Are Personal Data, February 6, 2001

[1083] The Garante Says No to Political Spamming, January 11, 2001.

[1084] Flawed Data Protection Approach by a Police Corps, January 11, 2001.

[1085] Employee's Badges: Less Personal Data for More Privacy, December 11, 2000.

[1086] No Taking of Fingerprints to Enter a Bank, December 11, 2000.

[1087] Right of Access- Personal Data Included in Medical Expert Opinions for Insurance Purposes: Access May be Deferred, December 28, 2000.

and that phone companies should allow for anonymous phone cards to protect privacy. The Garante has also held investigations into the Echelon surveillance system. In March 2002, it hosted a conference on "Juridical and Psychosocial Implications of Human Genetics."

A Milan court ruled in September 1999 that the Data Protection Act only is concerned with the controls on the processing of personal information and is not a general privacy act. The court reversed the Garante ruling against a newpaper for publishing incorrect details about a countess.[1088]

Wiretapping is regulated by articles 266-271 of the penal procedure code and may only be authorized in the case of legal proceedings.[1089] Government interceptions of telephone and all other forms of communications must be approved by a court order. They are granted for crimes punishable by life imprisonment or imprisonment for more than five years; for crimes against the administration punishable by no less than five year imprisonment; for crimes involving the trafficking of drugs, arms, explosives, and contraband; and for insults, threats, abusive activity and harassment carried out over the telephone. The law on computer crime includes penalties on interception of electronic communications.[1090] Interception orders are granted for 15 days at a time and can be extended for the same length of time by a judge. The judge also monitors procedures for storing recordings and transcripts. Any recordings or transcripts that are not used must be destroyed. The conversations of religious ministers, lawyers, doctors or others subject to professional confidentiality rules can not be intercepted. There are more lenient procedures for anti-Mafia cases. Some 44,000 orders were approved in 1996, up from 15,000 in 1992.[1091] A June report indicated that Rome, by itself, had nearly 13,000 wiretaps over the period of a year.[1092] In March 1998, the Parliament issued a legislative decree adopting the provisions of the European Union Telecommunications Privacy Directive.[1093]

In October 2001, the Italian Parliament passed a decree (no. 374/2001, converted into Act no. 438/2001) in which the offense of criminal association for purposes

---

[1088] See http://www.andreamonti.net/jus/demi990927.htm

[1089] Intercettazioni di conversoni o comunicazioni, Art 266-271 du code di procedura penale issus de la loi du Septembre 22, 1988.

[1090] Legge 23 dicembre 1993 n 547.

[1091] French Commission National de Control des Interceptions de securite, Annual Report 1996.

[1092] British Broadcasting Corporation Worldwide Monitoring, June 7, 2002

[1093] Decreto legislativo 13 maggio 1998, n. 171. Disposizioni in materia di tutela della vita privata nel settore delle telecomunicazioni, in attuazione della direttiva 97/66/CE del Parlamento europeo e del Consiglio, ed in tema di attività giornalistica, available at <http://www.privacy.it/dl98171.html>.

---

of terrorism was re-defined; however, the blanket surveillance of communications by law enforcement bodies was expressly ruled out. Telephone tapping and electronic surveillance were facilitated, only with the authorization and under the supervision of judicial authorities and only with regard to very serious offences. Additional safeguards apply to the use of investigational findings and the prohibition to disclose such findings.

There are also sectoral laws relating to workplace surveillance,[1094] statistical information, and electronic files and digital signatures.[1095] The Workers Charter prohibits employers from investigating the political, religious or trade union opinions of their workers, and in general on any matter which is irrelevant for the purposes of assessing their professional skills and aptitudes.[1096] The 1993 computer crime law prohibits unlawfully using a computer system and intercepting computer communications.[1097]

In October 2000, medical researchers from the International Institute of Genetics and Biophysics opened a "genetic park" in Southern Italy. The inhabitants of ten remote villages will be part of an elaborate experiment to identify the causes of diseases such as Alzheimer's, asthma, cancer and hypertension. Over the next two years the researchers plan to build a database combining the church records, medical histories, blood and DNA samples of the inhabitants.[1098]

Italy is a member of the Council of Europe and has signed and ratified the Convention for the Protection of Individuals with Regard to Automatic Processing of Personal Data (ETS No. 108)[1099] and has signed its additional protocol (ETS No. 181). It has signed and ratified the European Convention for the Protection of Human Rights and Fundamental Freedoms.[1100] In November 2001, Italy signed the Council of Europe's Convention for Cybercrime (ETS No. 185).[1101] Italy is a member of the Organization for Economic Cooperation and Development and has adopted the OECD Guidelines on the Protection of Privacy and Transborder Flows of Personal Data.

[1094] Legge 29 marzo 1983, n. 93 - Legge quadro sul pubblico, ITNTDI, p. 296, § 1114.

[1095] Presidential Decree No. 513 of 10 November 1997, "Regulations establishing criteria and means for implementing Section 15(2) of Law No. 59 of 15 March 1997 concerning the creation, storage and transmission of documents by means of computer-based or telematic systems," available at <http://www.aipa.it/english/law2/pdecree51397.asp>.

[1096] Section 8 of Law No. 300 of 20 May 1970.

[1097] Law No. 547 of 23 December 1993

[1098] Rory Caroll, "Meet the People of Genetic Park," The Guardian (London), October 30, 2000.

[1099] Signed February 2, 1983; Ratified March 29, 1997; Entered into Force July 1, 1997.

[1100] Signed November 11, 1950; Ratified October 26, 1955; Entered into force October 26, 1955.

[1101] Signed November 23, 2001.

Japan

Article 21 of the 1946 Constitution states, "Freedom of assembly and association as well as speech, press and all other forms of expression are guaranteed. 2) No censorship shall be maintained, nor shall the secrecy of any means of communication be violated." Article 35 states, "The right of all persons to be secure in their homes, papers and effects against entries, searches and seizures shall not be impaired except upon warrant issued for adequate cause and particularly describing the place to be searched and things to be seized .2) Each search or seizure shall be made upon separate warrant issued by a competent judicial officer."[1102]

The 1988 Act for the Protection of Computer Processed Personal Data Held by Administrative Organs governs the use of personal information in computerized files held by government agencies.[1103] Additionally, some local governments have similar laws: the Prefecture of Kanagawa has legislation that protects privacy in both the public and private sectors.[1104] The federal law is based on the OECD guidelines and imposes duties of security, access, and correction. Agencies must limit their collection to relevant information and publish a public notice listing their file systems. Information collected for one purpose cannot be used for a purpose "other than the file holding purpose." The Act is overseen by the Government Information Systems Planning Division of the Management and Coordination Agency. The agency reports that there have been 1,700 notices filed. The agency does not have any powers to investigate complaints.

Some privacy advocates point out that the law specifically does not include the paper-based "koseki" family recond-keeping system, which tracks birth, death, marriage, divorce, amongst other family events. This information was traditionally available to any public requestor, and was frequently used by prospective employers or in-laws to check for illegitimacy, impure ethnic background, or other scandals. Since the 1980s, the information has not been publicly available, but the records still exist and are relatively unprotected.[1105]

[1102] Constitution of Japan, 1946, available at <http://www.ntt.co.jp/japan/constitution/english-Constitution.html>.

[1103] The Act for the Protection of Computer Processed Personal Data held by Administrative Organs, Act No. 95, 16 December 1988 (Kampoo, 16 December 1988).

[1104] Kanagawa Prefecture Ordinance on the Protection of Personal Data, Ordinance No. 6, dated 30 March 1990.

[1105] Philip Brasor, "Japanese tradition that violates privacy rights," Japan Times, June 9, 2002.

Until recently, the Japanese government has promoted a policy of self-regulation for the private sector, especially relating to electronic commerce. However, since the summer of 1999, lawmakers have been working on the Personal Data Protection Bill, which would provide a framework for both governmental and commercial usage of personal information. The proposed legislation requires that such private and public entities abide by five principles:[1106] 1) to explicitly specify the purpose for data collection and hold to the scope of that purpose 2) to gather personal information "by lawful and appropriate means" 3) to maintain accuracy and currency of data 4) to protect the security of personal information 5) to infuse transparency into the collection and use of data. Further, the bill specifically requires private business to disclose to individuals any personal information collected from them and the purposes of such collection; it also prohibits companies from sharing personal information with third parties.[1107]

Journalists and opposition party members have opposed certain aspects of the bill. Although the bill does exempt the press—and academic institutions—from the restrictions placed on private companies, opponents assert that the law would violate free speech protections under Article 21 of the Constitution by restricting the media from collecting and reporting certain information.[1108] Journalists fear that, because government officials will be the ultimate arbiters as to what constitutes exempted "reporting" that they will exclude pieces that pry too deeply into their own misdeeds.[1109]

In March 2000[1110] and again in 2001, the Prime Minister's Cabinet approved the bill and submitted it to the Diet.[1111] However, deliberations over the bill have once again been delayed due to continued criticism by media groups and opposition parties.[1112]

The Ministry of Finance and Ministry of International Trade and Industry announced plans to introduce legislation to protect individual credit data in 2000 after a task force issues proposals.[1113] Japan's Ministry of Posts and

---

[1106] Japan Proposed Law Concerning Protection of Personal Information (Unofficial Transcript); "Cabinet approves bill to protect personal info," Yomiuri Shinbun, March 28, 2001.

[1107] "Bill must serve freedom of the press," Yomuiri Shinbun, March 28, 2001.

[1108] "Freedom of Expression," Mainichi Daily News, March 30, 2001.

[1109] "New Tokyo Law may out end to 'exposes,'" Straits Times (Singapore), June 1, 2001.

[1110] "Current Diet unlikely to OK info bill," Yomiuri Shinbun, June 3, 2001.

[1111] "Bill on data Protection approved by Cabinet," Japan Times, March 28, 2001.

[1112] "Advisory Panel to Japanese Government Drafts Law to Protect Personal Information," BNA Daily Report for Executives, June 8, 2000.

[1113] "Japan Ministries To Compile Credit Data Protection Bill," Nikkei, July 4, 1999.

Telecommunications (MPT) announced plans in June 1998 to study privacy in telecommunications services, establishing a study group to look into the matter.[1114] An October 1999 survey by the MPT found that 92 percent of respondents believed that their personal information had been disclosed without their consent. Eighty-three percent believed that organizations and individuals who hold personal information should be regulated.[1115]

Japanese ISPs issued draft guidelines for protecting users' online privacy in 2002 in response to the Internet Provider Responsibility Law of 2001. The guidelines limit dissemination of private information without specific consent, allow the ISPs to delete user information, and require ISPs to maintain information posted by users about public figures.[1116]

In February 1998, MITI established a Supervisory Authority for the Protection of Personal Data to monitor a new system for the granting of "privacy marks" to businesses committing to the handling of the personal data in accordance with the MITI guidelines, and to promote awareness of privacy protection for consumers. The "privacy mark" system is administered by the Japan Information Processing Development Center (JIPDEC) – a joint public/private agency.[1117] Companies that do not comply with the industry guidelines will be excluded from relevant industry bodies and not granted the privacy protection mark. It is assumed that market forces will then penalize them. However, in addition, the new Supervisory Authority will investigate violations and make suggestions as necessary to the relevant administrative authorities.[1118] An analysis of the marks done for the European Union by four academic privacy experts found that there were serious shortcomings in the system.[1119] In the first two years of the JIDPEC program, companies seeking certification were dominated by businesses that handle personal information like marriage bureaus; in total, the JIPDEC awarded about 140 licenses.[1120] In May 2000, the JIPDEC agreed with BBBOnline, a

---

[1114] Newsbytes, June 1, 1998.

[1115] Ministry of Post and Telecommunications Press Release, "More than 90% of Telecommunications Service Users Are Interested in Privacy Protection," October 14, 1999.

[1116] "Japanese ISPs, Carriers, Users Release Guideline for ISP Privacy Protection Duties," Bureau of National Affairs Privacy Law Watch, April 17, 2002.

[1117] Home Page <http://www.jipdec.or.jp/security/privacy/index-e.html>.

[1118] Nigel Waters, 'Reviewing the Adequacy of Privacy Protection in the Asia Pacific Region, IIR Conference Information Privacy - Data Protection, June 15, 1998, Sydney; see also Ministry of International Trade and Industry (MITI), Japan's views on the Protection of Personal Data, April 1998.

[1119] Raab, Bennett, Gellman & Waters, European Commission Tender No XV/97/18/D, Application of a Methodology Designed to Assess the Adequacy of the Level of Protection of Individuals with Regard to Processing Personal Data: Test of the Method on Several Categories of Transfer, September 1998.

[1120] "Japan, United States bodies ink deal on data-privacy certification," The Yomiui Shimbun, May 19, 2000.

---

division of the United States-based Better Business Bureau, to mutually recognize each other's privacy protection marks.

Wiretapping traditionally has been considered a violation of the Constitution's right of privacy and has been authorized only a few times. However, in August 1999, the Diet passed the controversial Communications Interception Law authorizing wiretapping phone or faxes, and monitoring email, when investigating cases involving narcotics, gun offenses, gang-related murders and large-scale smuggling of foreigners.[1121] Under the new law, which went into effect in August 2000, the use of wiretaps is restricted to prosecutors and police officers at the rank of superintendent and above, and requires police officers to obtain warrants from district court judges in order to use wiretaps. The warrants are good for 10 days and can only be extended for a total of 30 days. Further, the presence of a third, independent party, for instance an employee of Nippon Telegraph and Telephone Company, is required during monitoring. Finally, police and prosecutors must in principle notify individuals who have been monitored within 30 days after the investigation. Strict penalties are possible for those who abuse the wiretap policy.[1122] The National Police Agency (NPA) and Ministry of Justice (MOJ) recently requested about 170 million yen (USD 1.4 million) in 2001 for the development of a "temporary mailbox" technology for intercepting email.[1123]

The Federation of Bar Associations, journalists and trade unions opposed the wiretap law.[1124] Opponents argue that Diet proponents of wiretapping forced a vote on the bill before the legislatures could host a full airing of the potential privacy problems it would create.[1125] Professor Toshimaru Ogura, of the Japanese Net Workers against Surveillence Taskforce (NaST) and Toyama University, asserts the law does not restrict the storage and use of information gathered, possibly providing the government with a mandate to maintain databases on citizens that can be shared by other domestic—and possibly foreign—agencies.[1126] Further, Professor Ogura argues that the MOJ officials have a free hand to broadly intercept communications from innocent people in the process of targeting criminals; for example, the MOJ proposed in a Diet

---

[1121] Reuters, June 1, 1999.

[1122] "Diet passes wiretap, ID bills," Asia Intelligence Wire, August 13, 1999.

[1123] Toshimaru Ogura, "Toward Global Communication Rights: Movements against Wiretapping and Monitoring in Japan," October 30, 2000.

[1124] "Diet eyes allowing police to bug phones," Mainichi Daily News June 16, 1998.

[1125] Toshimaru Ogura,"Police Gain Right to Tap Phone Email," The Standard, August 15, 2000.

[1126] Id.

session that it could tap all of the in/outcoming phone calls of a shipping company in an effort to capture drug smugglers.[1127]

The new law was applied for the first time in May 2002 to break up a Tokyo drug ring. Police monitored cell phones and email based on a warrant, and arrested nine suspects.[1128]

Many have protested the wiretapping law as too large of a grant of power, including one lawmaker who sued alleging the police had illegally tapped his phone.[1129] Over 180,000 people have signed a petition for the repeal of the wiretapping law. The signature-collecting Committee for the Repeal of the Wiretapping Law submitted the petition to the Diet on May 24, 2000.[1130] In August, NTT asked that its employees not be required to be present when taps are installed, saying it would likely have a detrimental effect on company performance.[1131] Wiretapping is also prohibited under article 104 of the Telecommunications Business Law and article 14 of the Wire Telecommunications Law.[1132]

In June 1997, the Tokyo High Court upheld a lower court's finding that the Kanagawa Prefectural Police had illegally wiretapped the telephone at the home of a senior member of the Japanese Communist Party. The court awarded damages of four million yen.[1133] A number of NTT employees have also been caught recently selling information about customers.[1134] A number of companies that provide for pre-paid cellular phone service announced in May 2000 that, in order to prevent crime, they would start requiring users to provide identification before using the service. [1135]

In the same anti-crime package of bills under which the wiretapping law was passed, the Diet also provisionally approved the Basic Resident Registers Law, granting Tokyo the authority to issue a 11-digit number to every Japanese citizen and resident alien, and requiring all citizens and resident aliens to provide basic

---

[1127] Id.

[1128] BNA World Data Protection Report, Volume 2, Issue 6, June 2002.

[1129] "Prosecutors drop bug case by lawmaker, TV Asahi," Yomiuri Shinbun, December 29, 2000.

[1130] See NaST Homepage <http://www.jca.apc.org/privacy/>.

[1131] "DoCoMo urges NPA not to seek tapping aid," Yomiuri Shimbun, August 16, 2000.

[1132] Telecommunications Business Law, LAW No. 86 of 25 December 1984) as amended last by Law No. 97 of June 20, 1997 <http://www.mpt.go.jp/policyreports/english/laws/Tb_index.html>.

[1133] "Police wiretapping," Mainichi Daily News, June 29, 1997.

[1134] NTT Staffers Leaking Customer Information, Newsbytes, July 2, 1999.

[1135] Prepaid cell phone companies to require, Kyodo News Service, May 12, 2000

information – name, date of birth, sex, and address – to the local police. Due to privacy concerns, the bill was supposed to go into effect within three years of its passage on the condition that new privacy-protection legislation is enacted.[1136]It is unsure, in light of the recent postponement of that privacy legislation, whether the registration bill will still be implemented.

The Ministry of Transportation announced in June 1999 a plan to issue "Smart Plates" license plates with embedded IC chips. These new licenses could be issued as early as 2004,[1137] and will contain driver and vehicle information and be used for road tolls and traffic control.[1138] Since 1986, the National Police Agency has also operated a comprehensive video surveillance system called the "N-system" at least 540 locations on expressways and major highways throughout the country, which automatically records the license plate number of every passing car.[1139] Whenever a "wanted" car is detected, the system immediately issues a notice to police.[1140] Eleven motorists filed a lawsuit challenging the system in 1997. The latest model of N-system can also photograph the faces of drivers.[1141]

Two new anti-spam laws were also implemented in 2002. The laws allow users of the internet and text-enabled mobile phones to opt-out of spammers' contact lists, and require that all unsolicited commercial e-mail be clearly identified. The Public Management Ministry will enforce the law, imposing fines of up to 500,000 yen (USD 4,170) for failure to comply. Repeat or egregious offenders can be fined up to 3 million yen (USD 25,000) or 2 years in prison. [1142] Corporate violators can face up to 300 million yen (USD 2.5 million) fines.

In response to rising crime rates, Tokyo police have begun operating surveillance cameras on utility poles and buildings to monitor pedestrians in the densely populated Kabukicho district of the city.[1143] Lawyers opposing the move assert that this surveillance is unconstitutional, pointing to a 1969 Supreme Court decision against a police officer who secretly photographed a student activist in

---

[1136] "Diet passes wiretap, ID bills," Asia Intelligence Wire, August 13, 1999.

[1137] "NPA reports on IC chip data to be implanted in licenses," Kyodo News Services, June 21, 2001.

[1138] "License Plates to Bear IC Chips with Driver, Auto Info," Comline, June 9, 1999.

[1139] "Cameras to give police in Kabukicho 'peep' show," Japan Times, June 5, 2001.

[1140] Christian Science Monitor, April 8, 1997.

[1141] Ogura, supra n.1123.

[1142] Toru Takahashi, "2 new laws aimed at cutting spam," Daily Yomiuri (Japan), July 2, 2002 <http://www.yomiuri.co.jp/newse/20020702wo32.htm>.

[1143] Japan Times, June 5, 2001.

Kyoto.[1144] In response to the criticism, Tokyo police will place signs near cameras to give pedestrians notice they are being filmed.[1145] Other areas of the country are following Tokyo's lead, but many privacy groups, such as NaST and the Japan Consumers' Union, are reporting on video surveillance and publicizing all new camera installations.

Private surveillance is also on the rise. The Japan Institute of Labor reported that 35% of Japanese companies are monitoring their employees' email and Web use.[1146] Companies cited fear of viruses, sexual harassment, and other concerns as the reasons for surveillance.

In March 2000, it was discovered that a research company had secretly conducted genetic tests on 1,000 blood samples obtained from people who had donated blood to the Japanese Red Cross Society. The Health and Welfare Ministry launched an investigation in November 1999 into reports that a dealer was selling private information on people receiving medical treatment, including their clinical histories. Several months later, Tohoku University in Sendai and the National Cardiovascular Center in the Osaka Prefecture city of Suita also disclosed that they had studied the genes of blood donors without obtaining their consent. A poll conducted by the Mainichi newspaper suggests that this is standard practice, finding that 70 percent of medicine faculties in 64 universities around Japan are conducting gene tests.[1147] Health and Welfare Minister Yuya Niwa said that the ministry is investigating the case and will consider setting up laws regulating such leakage of patients' medical data.

The Law Concerning Access to Information Held by Administrative Organs was approved by the Diet in May 1999 after 20 years of debate.[1148] The law allows any individual or company to request government information in electronic or printed form. A nine-person committee in the Office of the Prime Minster will receive complaints about information that the government refuses to make public and will examine whether the decisions made by the ministries and agencies were appropriate. Government officials will still have broad discretion to refuse requests but requestors will be able to appeal decisions to withhold documents to one of eight different district courts. The law went into effect in April 2001. A

[1144] Id.

[1145] Id.

[1146] "35% of companies monitor online browsing, email by employees," Japan Today, May 14, 2002.
[1147] Manabu Yoshikawa and Yasuyoshi Tanaka Mainichi Shimbun, "Ethicists OK gene-sample research," Mainichi Daily News, May 8, 2000.

[1148] The Law Concerning Access to Information Held by Administrative Organs, available at. <http://www.somucho.go.jp/gyoukan/kanri/translation.htm>.

survey by Kyodo News in May 1999 found that 31 city and prefectural governments are in the process of adopting legislation consistent with the new law. Sixteen of them are including a principle of "right to know."[1149]

In June 2002, the Defense Agency revealed that it had been collecting names of people requesting information via the new law and cross-referencing the list with private information, such as the political affiliations of the requestor.[1150] While it is as yet unclear whether the list constitutes a clear violation of the law, it has sparked a huge outcry by the public, including calls for the resignation of defense officials.[1151]

In a controversial international development during the summer of 2001, a New Zealand researcher testified before the European Union that New Zealand was intercepting electronic transmission from Japanese embassies as part of the Echelon spy network.[1152] He claimed that the United States was primarily interested in information on Japan's economic influence in the South Pacific.[1153] A group of Japanese civic groups have requested that their government lodge a complaint against the United States and the four other suspected member nations of Echelon: New Zealand, Australia, the United Kingdom, and Canada.[1154]

Japan is a member of the Organization for Economic Cooperation and Development and a signatory to the OECD Guidelines on Privacy and Transborder Data Flows. Japan participated as a non-member observer country in the negotiations on the Council of Europe Convention on Cybercrime and signed the Convention in November 2001.[1155]

Jordan

Jordan's Constitution does not expressly address the individual's right to privacy. However, the right to privacy is included through Islamic beliefs and traditions, which maintains high respect for individual privacy and the right of every

---

[1149] Kyodo News, May 22, 1999.

[1150] "MSDF officer compiled personal data on people seeking Defense Agency info," Japan Times, May 29, 2002 <http://www.japantimes.com/cgi-bin/getarticle.p15?np20020529a2.htm>.

[1151] "Private data kept by all SDF arms," Japan Times, June 4, 2002, available at <http://www.japantimes.com/cgi-bin/getarticle.p15?nn20020604a2.htm>.

[1152] "Japanese diplomatic dispatches infiltrated by English-speaking spies," Mainichi Shinbun, June 27, 2001.

[1153] Id.

[1154] "Japanese Call To Shut Out Satellite Spy Group," The Age, June 28, 2001.

[1155] Convention on Cybercrime, Chart of signatures and ratifications, available at <http://conventions.coe.int/>.

member of society to protect his personal life against interference.[1156] Jordan is a signatory to the United Nations' Declaration of Human Rights.

While still relatively low, Internet penetration and e-commerce is expanding in Jordan. Coupled with this growth, concerns over privacy and data collection are also developing. The majority of potential e-commerce users feel that their rights of privacy and transparency are not protected under current laws.[1157] In order to address e-commerce growth and privacy issues, in July 2000 the private sector established the 'Reach 2.0 Initiative'. This was a ten week event for Jordan's IT industry. At its closing, the participants made a number of recommendations aimed at developing and improving the IT sector in Jordan, one of which include enacting a law that would ratify digital signatures on the Internet in order to ensure legitimacy and authentication.[1158]

Jordan and the US have issued a joint statement on electronic commerce in which both States endorse principles and policies pertaining to the recognition and enforcement of electronic authentication methods and protection of internet privacy with regard to the processing and collection of personal data.[1159]

There is no data protection law in Jordan. In 1999 it was reported that the government had initiated a system of national numbers in order to create a data bank for all citizens. This system is still in the process of development.[1160]

Jordan has not enacted wiretapping or electronic surveillance legislation. Article 18 of the Constitution provides that all postal, telegraphic and telephonic communications shall be treated as secret and as such shall not be subject to censorship or suspension except in circumstances prescribed by law. The Constitution also requires that security force obtain a warrant from the Prosecutor General or a judge before conducting searches and seizures. In practice, however, authorities do not always respect these constitutional restrictions. According to the United States, Department of State, notes in its Human Rights report,

---

[1156] Akhal Al Ahmad, The Virtual Law Firm: Privacy Issue World Wide Activities Middle East - Jordan <http://vlf.juridicum.su.se/master99/staff/akhal/privacy.html>

[1157] Obeidat, Mohammad, "Consumer Protection and Electronic Commerce in Jordan – An Exploratory Study,"
<http://www.thepublicvoice/org/events/dubai01/Presentations/HTML%20/M..Opeidat/m.opeidatpaper.htm>

[1158] Mashagbeh and Gannon, "Expanding the usage of the Internet and bridging the digital divide," <http://63.104.165.4/fri/features/features3.htm>

[1159] US-Jordanian Joint Statement on Electronic Commerce <http:www.ecommerce.gov/joint_statements/jordan/html>.

[1160] Akhal Al Ahmad, The Virtual Law Firm: Privacy Issue World Wide Activities Middle East - Jordan <http://vlf.juridicum.su.se/master99/staff/akhal/privacy.html>

"[s]ecurity forces monitor telephone conversations and Internet communication, read private correspondence, and engage in surveillance of persons who are considered to pose a threat to the Government or national security….Judges complain of unlawful telephone surveillance."[1161]

Republic of (South) Korea

The Constitution of the Republic of Korea provides for the protection of secrecy and liberty of private life. Article 16 states, "All citizens are free from intrusion into their place of residence. In case of search or seizure in a residence, a warrant issued by a judge upon request of a prosecutor has to be presented."[1162] Article 17 states that "the privacy of no citizen shall be infringed."[1163] Article 18 states, "The privacy of correspondence of no citizen shall be infringed."[1164] In general, the government respects the integrity of the home and family.[1165]

South Korea has adopted a data protection regime similar to the United States and Japan, with one act covering the public sector and sectoral legislation for the private sector.[1166] The statute in the former category is the Act on the Protection of Personal Information Maintained by Public Agencies (1994),[1167] which is generally applicable to the automated processing of personal data in the public sector, but not to manual records.[1168] It has a provision recommending private entities respect the data protection principles in the statute, but has no appropriate administrative or enforcement mechanism to that effect.[1169]

The Act on the Protection of Personal Information Maintained by Public Agencies imposes an obligation on public agencies to maintain records of personal information databases and to report these databases to the Ministry of

---

1161 United States, Department of State, Country Report on Human Rights Practices 2001, March 2002, available at <http://www.state.gov/g/drl/rls/hrrpt/2001>.

1162 Constitution of The Republic of Korea, chapter II (Rights and Duties of Citizens), § 16; Section 9 further stating that "it shall be the duty of the State to confirm and guarantee the fundamental and inviolable human rights of individuals."

1163 Id., § 17.

1164 Id., § 18.

1165 United States Department of State, Country Report on Human Rights Practices 2001, March 2002, available at <http://www.state.gov/g/drl/hrrpt/2001/>.

1166 C. Chung and I. Shin, "On-Line Data Protection and Cyberlaws in Korea" 27 Korean J. of Int'l and Comp. L. 21, 24 (1999).

1167 Act No. 4734.

1168 Id. §§ 1, 2(3).

1169 C. Chung and I. Shin, "On-Line Data Protection and Cyberlaws in Korea," 27 Korean J. of Int'l and Comp. L. 21, 31 (1999).

Government Administration and Home Affairs ("MOGAHA"), the ministry responsible for the Act.[1170] The MOGAHA publishes lists of these databases in an official journal, which is publicly-available.[1171] In addition, the MOGAHA can request relevant information from the data holding entities and issue opinions on their data processing practices.[1172] A "data subject" has a right of access to and correction of personal information held by public agencies.[1173]

The Act establishes a Data Protection Review Commission, under the Premier's Office, headed by the Vice-Minister of the MOGAHA, to recommend and review proposals on improving data protection policy.[1174]

The Act has been criticized for its ineffectiveness.[1175] The MOGAHA has not placed much emphasis on rigorous application of the legislation and reportedly has little will to uphold privacy versus administrative efficiency. In January 1999, the Act was amended to give even more power to the MOGAHA, streamline the procedure for access to personal information by data subjects, and limit exemptions to disclosure. However, there remains no independent oversight of government application of the Act.

Acts governing the collection, use and disclosure of personal information in the private sector include the Protection of Communications Secrets Act (1993);[1176] the Telecommunications Business Act (1991);[1177] the Medical Service Act (1973);[1178] the Real Name Financial Trade and Secrecy Act;[1179] the Use and Protection of Credit Information Act (1995);[1180] the Framework Act on Electronic Commerce (1999);[1181] and the Digital Signatures Act (1999).[1182]

[1170] Act No. 4734 § 6.

[1171] Id. §§ 7-8.

[1172] Id. §§ 18-19.

[1173] Id. §§ 12, 16.

[1174] Act No. 4734 § 20.

[1175] C. Chung and I. Shin, "On-Line Data Protection and Cyberlaws in Korea" 27 Korean J. of Int'l and Comp. L. 21, 33 (1999).

[1176] Act No. 4650. Article 54 of this act provides that: No personal shall encroach upon or divulge communications secrecy held by a telecommunications business operator. The one engaged or has been engaged in telecommunications service shall not divulge others' communication secrets obtained while in office. When related authorities ask for perusal or submission of documents regarding telecommunications service in writing for investigatory purposes, the telecommunications business operator or the one entrusted with partial treatment of telecommunications service under Article 12 of this act may accede.

[1177] Act No. 4394.

[1178] Act No. 2533.

[1179] Act No. 5493.

[1180] Act No. 4866.

[1181] Act No. 5834.

As early as 1997, legislators and academics proposed a general privacy law for the private sector.[1183] However, the government proposed and later adopted a narrower alternative, targeting the information and telecommunications industries. The Act on Promotion of Information and Communications Network Utilization and Data Protection[1184] modeled after the German Online Service Data Protection Act of 1997,[1185] came into effect in 2000. It adopts common 'fair information principles'[1186] and rules for the collection, use and disclosure of personal data by "providers of information and communications services", such as common carriers, Internet service provider and other intermediaries, particularly content providers. The Korean Act also covers specific off-line service providers such as travel agencies, airlines, hotels, and educational institutes.

The Act requires that "data users" seek consent from "data subjects" for collection, use, and disclosure to a third party "beyond the notification as prescribed in the Act or the limit specified in a standardized contract for the utilization of the information and communication services".[1187] Data users should collect only as little personal data as is necessary[1188] and are prohibited from collecting sensitive personal information, including ideology, faith and medical data without explicit consent of the data subject.[1189] However, consent is not required where it is necessary to give effect to a contract, adjust fees, or where the personal information is provided after having been rendered unidentifiable to the individual, such as for the compilation of statistics, academic research or market surveys.[1190]

The Act allows the data subject to withdraw consent for collection, use and disclosure at any time and requires the data user to comply unless the preservation of such personal information is required by another Act. Further,

---

[1182] Act No. 5792.

[1183] See C. Chung, "International Developments in the Data Protection and Some Proposals for Korean Legislation", The Korean J. of Info. Soc. (1997).

[1184] Act No. 5835.

[1185] Gesetz zur Regelung der Rahmenbedingungen für Information sund Kommunikationsdienste: IuKDG, chapter 2.

[1186] The fair information principles of the Act are derived from the eight principles found in the OECD Guidelines on the Protection of Privacy and Transborder Flows of Personal Data, September 23, 1980.

[1187] Act No. 5835, § 16(2). See also Personal Information Dispute Mediation Committee, Korea Information Security Agency, Personal Data Protection in Korea, March 2002, at 3.

[1188] Id., § 16(1).

[1189] Id., at 4.

[1190] Id., at 3.

every data subject has a right of access and correction to his or her personal information.[1191]

A data user must obtain consent from an appropriate legal guardian when collecting, using or disclosing personal information from children under 14, and may request appropriate minimum information of the guardian in order to effect that consent. A legal guardian has a right of access and correction to the child's personal information and upon receiving a guardian's request for correction, the data user must cease to use or disclose erroneous information until they have made the correction.[1192]

The Act prohibits sending unsolicited commercial e-mail (spam) contrary to an addressee's explicit refusal of such mails.[1193] All UCE must contain the word "Advertisement" in the subject line of each and every message and must contain opt-out instructions and contact information for the sender.[1194] Additionally, a number of direct marketers established the Association for the Improvement of the E-Mail Environment in early 2002 to help cope with the increasing UCE problem in Korea.[1195]

Criminal and administrative penalties are imposed for breaches of data protection principles; processing of personal information without consent or beyond the scope of the purpose for which the collection was made attracts penalties of up to one year in prison or a fine of 10 million Won.[1196] Data subjects may file damage claims for breaches of the Act with the Personal Information Mediation Committee or with a court. The onus is on the data user to prove good faith intentions to comply or non-negligence.[1197]

There is significant overlap between the aforementioned act and the Framework Act on Electronic Commerce and the Digital Signatures Act. For this reason and

---

[1191] Act No. 5835, § 18(2).

[1192] Id., § 18(4).

[1193] Act No. 5835, § 19(3).

[1194] Id 5. Due to the volume of UCE, the government is contemplating an amendment which would curtail distribution and punish senders. Further, the amendment proposes the addition of "Adult" or "Consent" in the subject line of each and every UCE and punitive measures for UCE senders who use false contact information or hinder technologically the tracing or deletion of UCE.

[1195] Personal Information Dispute Mediation Committee, Korea Information Security Agency, Personal Data Protection in Korea, March 2002, at 18.

[1196] Act No. 5835, § 30. Additionally, § 32 imposes lesser administrative penalties of 5 million Won for violations of other data protection principles.

[1197] Personal Information Dispute Mediation Committee, Korea Information Security Agency, Personal Data Protection in Korea, March 2002, 6.

others, some legal commentators have called for comprehensive reform.[1198] The Framework Act on Electronic Commerce requires data users to give data subjects sufficient information regarding purpose of collection to give informed consent.[1199] The data user must obtain explicit consent from the data subject prior to collecting personal information and is prohibited from using the personal information collected for inconsistent purposes.[1200] Additional requirements include appropriate security,[1201] and a right of access, correction or deletion.[1202] The Digital Signatures Act prohibits the fraudulent use of another person's private key or issuance of a key in the name other than your own.[1203] It also has data protection provisions[1204] similar to the Electronic Commerce Act and penalties equal to the Act on Promotion of Information and Communications Network Utilization and Data Protection.

In October 2000, the MIC proposed a cyber-crime prevention system to combat an increase in fraud, gambling and privacy intrusion on the Internet. The system would establish a monitoring network, a cyber conflict coordination committee and damage control centers.[1205] In March 2001, the MIC announced that it would invest 277.7 billion Won (~$237 million USD) over the next five years to develop the country's information security industry, including public-key infrastructure, biometrics, and high-density/high speed ciphers.[1206]

In December 2001, the MIC established the Personal Information Dispute Mediation Committee, as an alternative to civil litigation, to facilitate a prompt, convenient and appropriate settlement of data protection disputes.[1207] Members – including lawyers, IT engineers, professors, consumer advocates and representatives from industry – are appointed for three year terms.

[1198] See C. Chung, supra n.1183, at 42-43 citing the lack of an appropriate oversight authority as the major weakness of the Korean data protection regime; I. Kim, "A Study on the Data Protection Act" 26 Public Law 2 (June 1998) (in Korean); I. Lee, "Trends in the Korean Data Protection Legislation" Road to the Information Society (November 1999) (in Korean).

[1199] Act No. 5834, §§ 30-31.

[1200] Id.,§ 13(2).

[1201] Id., § 13(3).

[1202] Id., § 13(4).

[1203] Act No. 5792, §§ 19-23.

[1204] Id., § 24.

[1205] Ministry Of Information To Set Up Cyber Crime Prevention System, Korea Herald, October 16, 2000.

[1206] "Gov't Unveils 5-Year Plan For Security Technology," Korea Herald, March 14, 2001.

[1207] Personal Information Dispute Mediation Committee, Korea Information Security Agency, Personal Data Protection in Korea, March 2002, at 13-14.

Either data subjects or data users can initiate mediation, free of charge. The Committee first engages in informal fact-finding and makes non-binding recommendations for settlement. If parties cannot reach a settlement, they can begin formal mediation. If parties fail to reach a mediated settlement, they can pursue matters in a competent civil court. They can also bypass the Committee process altogether and go directly to court.[1208]

The Korea Association of Information and Telecommunication (KAIT) has instituted a privacy "trust mark" for web sites and other online businesses which satisfy appropriate data processing standards. Qualified trust mark applicants provide notice and purpose of collection, use and disclosure of personal information; provide appropriate safeguards for personal data; special treatment for children under 14; and remedies for data subjects.

Extending the doctrine of privacy law, Korean courts have tacitly recognized a "right of publicity," as an every individual's right to control the commercial use of his or her identity.[1209] Plaintiffs in tort invasion of privacy and defamation cases have the burden of proving both the facts and that the standard for the action is met.[1210] If successful, plaintiffs are entitled to compensatory, but not punitive damages for as little as "hurt feelings".[1211] Actions related to the right of privacy or defamation are rarely brought before Korean courts because of the cultural dislike of bringing private matters into such a public forum.[1212]

In an attempt to resolve the tension between the right of privacy and the constitutionally protected "freedom of speech and press"[1213] or "freedom of the arts",[1214] Korean courts have held that "a decedent's right of privacy should be recognized only if his personal honor would be severely injured..."[1215] In another case, a Seoul court found that five female university students were entitled to damages when a Newsweek photographer published a photo of them

---

[1208] Id.

[1209] H. Nam, "The Applicability of the Right of Publicity in Korea," 27 Korean J. of Int'l and Comp. L. 45, 49 (1999). See also W. Han, "Infringement of the Right of Publicity and Civil Liability," 12 Human Rights and Justice 109, 116 (1996) (in Korean).

[1210] H. Nam, id., at 88 (1999).

[1211] Id.

[1212] Id. But see "Grassroots Pro-privacy Movements on the Rise" BNA World Data Protection Report, Volume 1, Issue 11, November 2001, at 8, as evidence that Koreans are generally concerned about privacy issues.

[1213] Constitution of Korea, article 21

[1214] Id., article 22, clause 1.

[1215] Marianne Sim Lim v. Jin-Myung Kim, Seoul Dist. Ct., 94 Kahab 9230 (June 23, 1995), involving a "model novel" which depicted the life of the deceased subject in a fictional manner.

at school without their permission and in conjunction with an unfavorable accompanying article.[1216]

State security services have a history of conducting surveillance of political dissidents. The Protection of Communications Secrets Act of 1993 and the reform of the National Intelligence Service ("NIS", formerly known as the National Security Planning Agency) were designed to curb government surveillance of civilians and, according the United States Department of State largely "appear to have succeeded".[1217]

The Protection of Communications Secrets Act lays out broad conditions under which the monitoring of telephone calls, mail, and other forms of communication are legal.[1218] It requires government officials to secure a judge's permission before placing wiretaps, or, in the event of an emergency, soon after placing them, and it provides for jail terms for persons who violate this law. Revisions, intended to protect privacy more stringently, have been submitted to the National Assembly and are under discussion.[1219] As yet, there is no consensus on whether those monitored should be subsequently informed after the wiretap is discontinued, on the scope and type of crimes which require wiretapping as part of an investigation, and on the legal procedure required by investigating authorities to gain access to telephone records. Some human rights groups argue that a considerable amount of illegal wiretapping, shadowing, and surveillance photography still occurs, and they assert that the lack of an independent body to investigate whether police have employed illegal wiretaps hinders the effectiveness of the anti-wiretap law.

Under previous administrations, there were widespread surveillance and wiretapping abuses by intelligence and police officials. In October 1998, President Kim Dae-jung ordered a full-scale probe into illegal wiretapping. Rep. Kim Hyong-o of the opposition Grand National Party (GNP) stated that he believed that over 10,000 taps were actually placed in 1998.[1220] The government proposed amendments to the Telecommunications Law in November 1999 which would allow victims of illegal wiretapping to sue in court, limit the number of

---

[1216] Sun-Jeong Kwon, Hyun-Ju Kim and Yun-Hwa Kim v. Newsweek Inc., Seoul Civil Dist. Ct., 92 Gadan 57989 (July 8, 1993).

[1217] United States State Department Report 2001, supra n.1165.

[1218] Act No. 4650.

[1219] "Ruling party to seek early revision of human rights-related laws" Yonhap News Agency, October 18, 2000.

[1220] "Kim Hyong-o Says More Than 10,000 May Be Exposed to Gov't Taps," Korea Times, February 13, 1999.

crimes for which wiretapping is allowed, and provide for notice to targets of wiretapping. The government set up a wiretapping complaint center under the MIC in October 1999.[1221] The United Nations Human Rights Commission heard testimony on Korean wiretapping at its meeting in October 1999.[1222]

In 1998, several opposition legislators broke into the NIS liaison office in the National Assembly and removed documents that they claim substantiated allegations that the NIS was conducting surveillance of Assembly members.[1223] The members further alleged that their homes, offices, and cellular telephones were tapped. They have called for either tightening or abolishing a provision in the existing law that allows government officials to obtain retroactive judicial permission to monitor a conversation (especially a cellular telephone call) in the event of an emergency.[1224]

According 2001 statistics released by the MIC, the number of wiretapping cases by prosecutors and police in the computer communications field stood at 224 last year, up 23.8 percent from a year earlier. In particular, the number of cases in which communications service providers rendered assistance to investigators' wiretapping, increased 222.3 percent from 1,075 to 3,465. Eavesdropping on wired and wireless telecommunications decreased 26.4 percent from 3,234 in 1999 to 2,380 in 2000, but cases of telecom operators providing data on communications to authorities such as subscriber names, addresses and communications records increased 3.9 percent from 154,390 to 160,485 during the period.[1225]

Fresh on the heels of similar developments in Hong Kong, the MIC stated in December 2001, that mobile service providers have been neglecting rules regarding user privacy and that companies need to clarify their legal obligations with respect to subscriber privacy. The MIC is proposing measures to this effect.[1226]

[1221] "Gov't to operate eavesdropping complaint center," Korea Herald, October 30, 1999.

[1222] United Nations Human Rights Committee, Summary record of the 1792nd meeting: Republic of Korea. 22/11/99. CCPR/C/SR.1792, 22 November 1999.

[1223] United States Department of State, Country Report on Human Rights Practices 2000, February 2001, available at <http://www.state.gov/g/drl/hrrpt/2000/>.

[1224] United States State Department Report 2001, supra n.1165.

[1225] "Carnivore goes global: Korean police Net-taps jump 24 percent," Korea Herald, March 27, 2001.

[1226] "MIC to Compel Protection of Mobile Phone Privacy" BNA World Data Protection Report, Volume 2, Issue 1, January 2002, at 12.

Amnesty International reports that the Korean government continued to require released political prisoners to report regularly to the police under the Social Surveillance Law.[1227]

According to the United States State Department, under the National Security Law, it is forbidden for South Koreans to listen to North Korean radio in their homes or read books published in North Korea if the government determines that they are doing so to help North Korea. However, in 1999 the government legalized the viewing of North Korean satellite telecasts in private homes. The government also allows the personal perusal of North Korean books, music, television programs, and movies as a means to promote understanding and reconciliation with North Korea.

Student groups make credible claims that government informants are posted on university campuses.[1228]

In 1997, the government proposed an "Electronic National Identification Card Project." The plan was based on a smart card system and according to a local human rights group would "include universal ID card, driver's license, medical insurance card, national pension card, proof of residence, and a scanned fingerprint, among other things." The government was scheduled to issue cards to all citizens by 1999.[1229] In November 1997, a law on the ID card project passed the National Assembly. In December 1997, Kim Dae Jung, a former dissident, won the Presidential election. He had publicly opposed the ID card project in his campaign and the project was publicly withdrawn. However, activists believe that government agencies are continuing to quietly develop the proposals. In 1999, the government began replacing existing cards with a plastic card.

The Act Relating to Use and Protection of Credit Information of 1995 protects credit reports.[1230] In July 2001, three large credit card companies were fined under this law. The companies were found to have disclosed personal information on their customers (including bank account numbers, pay levels and credit card transaction records, and customer identifiers such as names,

---

[1227] See Amnesty International, Republic of Korea (South Korea): On trial for defending his rights: the case of human rights activist Suh Jun-sik, (under the law, some released prisoners are required to report to the police when moving or traveling).

[1228] United States Department of State, Report 2001, supra n.1165.

[1229] Joohoan Kim, Ph.D., Digitized Personal Information and the Crisis of Privacy: The Problems of Electronic National Identification Card Project and Land Registry Project in South Korea, available at <http://kpd.sing-kr.org/idcard/joohoan2.html>.

[1230] No. 4866, Enforcement Decree for the Act Relating to Use and Protection of Credit Information.

addresses, phone numbers and resident-registration numbers) to insurance companies without giving notice to their customers or obtaining their consent in advance.[1231] Postal privacy is protected by the Postal Services Act.[1232]

In January 2001, the Ministry of Health and Welfare announced plans to establish a DNA database of missing children. Green Korea United and the People's Solidarity for Participatory Democracy criticized the proposal saying that may infringe on people's privacy. They also called on the government to prevent gene discrimination and impose sanctions on those who release personal genetic information.[1233]

The Act on Disclosure of Information by Public Agencies is a freedom of information act that allows Koreans to demand access to government records. It was enacted in 1996 and went into effect in 1998. The Supreme Court ruled in 1989 that there is a constitutional right to information "as an aspect of the right of freedom of expression, and specific implementing legislation to define the contours of the right was not a prerequisite to its enforcement."[1234]

South Korea is a member of the Organization for Economic Cooperation and Development and has adopted the OECD Guidelines on the Protection of Privacy and Transborder Flows of Personal Data.

Republic of Latvia

Article 96 of the Latvian Constitution established a fundamental human right to privacy: "Everyone has the right to inviolability of their private life, home and correspondence."[1235] Article 17 of the Constitutional Law on Rights and Obligations of a Citizen and a Person states: "(1) The State guarantees the confidentiality of correspondence, telephone conversations, telegraph and other communications. (2) These rights may be restricted by a judge's order for the investigation of serious crimes."[1236]

[1231] "Stricter Privacy Protection," Korea Herald, July 19, 2001.

[1232] Amended by Law No. 2372, Dec.16, 1972; Law No.3602, December. 31,1982.

[1233] "Civic Groups Oppose DNA Database Plan," Korea Times, February 8, 2001.

[1234] Right to Information 1 KCCR 176, 88 HunMa 22, Sep. 4, 1989.

[1235] Constitution of the Republic of Latvia, available at <http://www.saeima.lv/LapasEnglish/Constitution_Saturs.htm>.

[1236] Constitutional Law, The Rights and Obligations of a Citizen and a Person, 1991.

The Law on Personal Data Protection was adopted by the Parliament on March 23, 2000, and came into force in January 2001. The law is based on standard fair information practices and is fully compliant with the European Union Data Protection Directive. Data processing systems in the areas of "public safety, combating of crime or national security and defence" or those maintained "by institutions specially authorized by law" are exempt from this registration procedure. A further exemption from the Act is provided for "official secret matters" regulated by the Law on Official Secrets. Under the Act all pre-existing databases (whether controlled by state and local government or private sector institutions) had to be registered with the Inspectorate by January 2002. After this deadline, unregistered systems were to cease operations. As of July 2002, 7,613 personal data processing systems were registered under the Act.

The Act established a State Data Inspectorate within the Ministry of Justice. The Inspectorate, which has a staff of 17, is charged with making decisions and reviewing complaints, making formal recommendations, issuing permission for the transfer of information abroad, and maintaining and inspecting the national register of data processing systems. Since its creation, the Inspectorate has received, registered and adjudicated 35 complaints related to data protection. Training on personal data protection is provided for lawyers, information technology specialists and inspectors.[1237]

Amendments to the Personal Data Protection Law to ensure full implementation of European Union Directive 95/46/EC and its requirements regarding the degree of independence of the State Data Inspectorate were adopted by the parliament in May 2002. The amendments stipulate that personal data protection should also apply to the police sector and authorize the Inspectorate to impose administrative penalties for violations of personal data processing.[1238] The European Commission approved Latvia's proposal for financing under the 2002 Phare program to strengthen data protection. Phare is a program financed by the European Communities that is designed to assist the applicant countries of central Europe in their preparations for joining the European Union.

The Inspectorate maintains close relations with the data protection authorities in other central and eastern European countries. In December 2001, the Data

---

[1237] E-mail from Ms. Signe Plumina, Director of State Data Inspection, Latvia, to Sarah Andrews, Research Director, Electronic Privacy Information Center, June 07, 2002 (on file with the Electronic Privacy Information Center).

[1238] "Latvia's Contribution to the Regular Report from the Commission on Latvia's Progress Towards Accession (National Progress Report)," June 2002, available at <http://www.am.gov.lv/files/e/national_progress_report_2002.pdf>.

Protection Commissioners from the Czech Republic, Hungary, Lithuania, Slovakia, Estonia, Latvia and Poland signed a joint declaration agreeing to closer cooperation and assistance. The Commissioners agreed to meet twice a year in the future, to provide each other with regular updates and overviews of developments in their countries, and to establish a common Web site for more effective communication.[1239]

The Latvian parliament passed the final reading of a draft law on the introduction of compulsory ID cards for all residents on May 22, 2002. The law would require all citizens and non-citizens of Latvia over the age of 14 to be issued machine-readable ID cards bearing the owner's place of residence. The law was expected to take effect in July 2002, but the ID cards will not be compulsory for citizens until 2005 or for foreigners until 2004.[1240]

The Latvian Constitutional Court ruled in December 2001 that although government language regulations requiring surnames to be "Latvianized" in official documents, such as passports, implicated the constitutional right to privacy, the restriction on privacy was constitutional because it protected "the rights of other inhabitants of Latvia to use the Latvian language on all of Latvia's territory and to protect the democratic order." The plaintiff, a woman who filed the suit after the surname she acquired through marriage to a German citizen was "Latvianized" on her passport from Mentzen to Mencena, lodged an application before the European Court of Human Rights shortly after the Latvian court's decision.[1241] The woman's complaint was the first case to be brought before the constitutional court by a private individual since the law was amended on July 1, 2001, to broaden the class of those entitled to file a claim.[1242]

The Grand Chamber of the European Court of Human Rights has also accepted a case against Latvia for breach of privacy.[1243] The complaint was filed with the court in May 1999 by a Latvian woman married to a Russian ex-military man after she and her family were exiled from Latvia under terms of the 1994

[1239] E-mail from Karel Neuwirt, President, Office for Personal Data Protection, Czech Republic, to Sarah Andrews, Research Director, Electronic Privacy Information Center, May 15, 2002 (on file with the Electronic Privacy Information Center).

[1240] "Latvia's Parliament passes law on ID cards and new passports," Baltic News Service, May 23, 2002.

[1241] International Helsinki Federation for Human Rights,"Human Rights in the OSCE Region: The Balkans, the Caucasus, Europe, Central Asia and North America," Report 2002 (events 2001), available at <http://www.ihf-hr.org/reports/AR2002/country%20links/Latvia.htm>.

[1242] "Latvian Constitutional Court opens first case at claim by private individual," Baltic News Service, July 18, 2001.

[1243] "European human rights court to consider ex-military family's case as first from Latvia," Baltic News Service, April 30, 2001.

Latvian-Russian treaty on the withdrawal of Russian troops from the newly independent country.[1244] The complaint alleges that Latvian authorities violated the family's right to privacy by confiscating their documents and searching their apartment and discriminated against them by forcing them to leave the country.[1245] In January 2002 the court agreed to hear three of the 11 complaints filed by the family under the 1950 European Convention on Human Rights. The court will decide whether Latvia's actions constitute violations of the family's right to liberty and security, to respect for private and family life, and freedom from discrimination.[1246]

The Electronic Document Law, adopted in the first reading by the parliament in October 2001 to implement European Union Directive 1999/93/EC, was expected to come into force in July 2002. The law defines the legal status of an electronic document and a digital signature. The regulation implementing the European Union Directive on e-commerce (2000/31/EC) is being elaborated and will be adopted by October 2002. Latvia also adopted a regulation in April 2002 on the archiving of documented data and electronic documents stored in information systems in accordance with European Union Recommendation 2000/13. In addition, the State Information Systems Law was adopted in May 2002 to provide a legal framework for the operation of the state information systems and cooperation of involved units.[1247]

In January 2002 Sweden and Latvia signed a joint agreement on cooperation in areas relating to justice and interior affairs. The agreement will stay in place until December 2003 and will involve cooperation on a number of issues including judicial training, information sharing and data protection, crime prevention and probation services.[1248]

Under the Penal Code, it is unlawful to interfere with correspondence.[1249] Wiretapping or interception of postal communications requires the permission of a court.[1250] In April 2001 the parliament passed legislative amendments requiring mobile telephone operators to install wiretapping facilities, at their own cost, for

---

[1244] Leah Bower, "Expulsion tug of war in international court," The Baltic Times, February 1, 2002.

[1245] "Latvia rejects Russia's accusations over counterfeit documents in human rights court," Baltic News Service, July 6, 2002.

[1246] Bower, supra n.1244.

[1247] "Latvia's Contribution to the Regular Report from the Commission on Latvia's Progress Towards Accession (National Progress Report)," supra n.1238.

[1248] "Swedish--Latvian justice, interior affairs agreements signed," Baltic News Service, January 31, 2002.

[1249] Criminal Code of Latvia, article 132.

[1250] Criminal Procedure Code of Latvia, articles 168, 176, 176.1.

operations of the top national security agency, the Bureau for the Protection of the Constitution.[1251] On November 16, 1995, it was reported that telephones in the Latvian Defense Ministry were tapped. The Latvian Defense Ministry responded by stating Latvia's "military counterintelligence service reserves the right to ensure the security of communications at the Ministry of Defense and structures of the national armed forces."[1252] In April 1994, a bugging device was found on the switchboard of the "Dienas Bizness" newspaper.[1253] The United States State Department report on Human Rights Practices, released by the Bureau of Democracy, Human Rights, and Labor for the year 2001, found no credible reports of illegal surveillance by the Latvian government.[1254]

Latvia joined the Council of Europe in 1995 and held the six-month rotating presidency from November 2000 to May 2001. It has signed and ratified both the European Convention for the Protection of Human Rights and Fundamental Freedoms[1255] and the Convention for the Protection of Individuals with Regard to Automatic Processing of Personal Data (ETS No. 108).[1256]

Republic of Lithuania

Article 22 of the Constitution states, "The private life of an individual shall be inviolable. Personal correspondence, telephone conversations, telegraph messages, and other intercommunications shall be inviolable. Information concerning the private life of an individual may be collected only upon a justified court order and in accordance with the law. The law and the court shall protect individuals from arbitrary or unlawful interference in their private or family life, and from encroachment upon their honor and dignity."[1257]

Lithuania's predominant data protection regulation, the Law on Legal Protection of Personal Data[1258], was first passed in 1996 and has since been amended

---

[1251] "Latvian mobile telephone operators to pay for tapping facilities," BBC Worldwide Monitoring, April 5, 2001.

[1252] "Defense Ministry issues a statement in response to reports of bugging," Latvian Radio, Riga, November 16, 1995, BBC Summary of World Broadcasts, November 20, 1995.

[1253] BBC Summary of World Broadcasts, April 16, 1994.

[1254] United States Department of State, Country Reports on Human Rights Practices 2001, March 2002, available at <http://www.state.gov/g/drl/rls/hrrpt/2001/eur/8279.htm>.

[1255] Signed February 10, 1995; Ratified July 26, 1996; Entered into Force July 26, 1996.

[1256] Signed October 31, 2000; Ratified May 30, 2001; Entered into Force September 1, 2001.

[1257] Constitution of the Republic of Lithuania, available at <http://www.litlex.lt/Litlex/Eng/Frames/Laws/Documents/CONSTITU.HTM>.

[1258] The Law on Legal Protection of Personal Data (No. I-1374, 1996) (State News, 1996, No. 63-1479).

multiple times to account for both domestic and European concerns. In 1998 the law was extended to regulate privately, in addition to publicly, held computerized information.[1259] It was further amended in 2000[1260] to ensure compliance with the European Union Directives on Data Protection and Telecommunications, and most recently in 2002[1261] to further bring Lithuania in line with European data protection standards.

The stated purpose of the Law on Legal Protection of Personal Data is to protect the private lives of people by establishing the rights of individuals and regulations for data processors. Individuals are entitled to know about the processing of their personal data; have access to that data; familiarise themselves with the processing method; demand rectification or destruction of their personal data; and, object to the processing of their personal data. These rights are, however, contingent upon several enumerated exceptions, such as national security, law enforcement and important economic or financial interests of the state.

Once consent from the data subject is obtained, data processors are subject to both regulations on both their means and ends. Personal data can only lawfully be processed if used for predefined purposes such as compliance with a legal obligation or as a necessary adjunct to a commercial transaction. The use must be accurate, fair and lawful and not excessive in relation to the predefined purpose. Finally, personal data can only be further disclosed under a personal data disclosure contract, specifying the purposes for which the data will be used and the conditions and procedures of its use.

As a complement to the protections described above, in 1998 the Code of Administrative Offenses[1262] was supplemented with monetary penalties for unlawful personal data processing, unlawful state information systems processing.[1263] In addition, the Law on State Registers[1264] provides further controls on the use and legitimacy of state data registers that contain personal information, and mandates that data registers may only be erased or destroyed in cooperation with the State Data Protection Inspectorate.

[1259] Law No.VII-662, March 12, 1998.

[1260] Law No. VIII-1852, July 17, 2000 (State News, 2000, No.64-1924).

[1261] Law No. IX-719, February 6, 2002.

[1262] (State News, 1998, No.40-1065). See Data Protection Development Programme for the Year 2002-2004, II, Current Statement, available at <http://www.ada.lt/en/legal.html>.

[1263] See Ona Jakstaite, "Regulating Data Security in Lithuania," Baltic IT Review.

[1264] The Law on the Public Registers (13 August 1996, No. I-1490), (State News, 1996, No.86-2043), available at <http://www.ada.lt/en/docs/Ist_reg.htm >.

In order to enforce the provisions of the Law on Legal Protection of Personal Data and the Law on State Registers, the State Data Protection Inspectorate was established in 1996.[1265] It registers data controllers, supervises processing, handles appeals for denial of access to records, and approves Transborder data flows. The office previously operated within the Ministry of Public Administration Reforms and Local Authorities but was granted full independence under the 2000 Act. The Inspectorate has eight staff members. As of December 2000 it had registered 695 data controllers, conducted 25 direct inspections, drafted 21 legal acts, granted ten permissions for transfers of data abroad and issued two protocols for violation of the law.[1266] The office has prepared a strategic plan for the development of data protection and measures of implementation for the years 2002-2004[1267]. The plan has three main objectives: to create a reliable and efficient data protection system in harmonization with European Union regulations; to foster an environment that respects constitutional rights to privacy; and to encourage the development of privacy enhancing technologies.

The Inspectorate maintains close relations with the data protection authorities in other central and eastern European countries. In December 2001, the Data Protection Commissioners from the Czech Republic, Hungary, Lithuania, Slovakia, Estonia, Latvia and Poland signed a joint declaration agreeing to closer cooperation and assistance. The Commissioners agreed to meet twice a year in the future, to provide each other with regular updates and overviews of developments in their countries, and to establish a common website for more effective communication.[1268]

Although it appears that Lithuania has implemented a comprehensive legal and governmental regime for the protection of personal data, the concepts, duties and rights conferred are still unfamiliar. Compliance with the laws, while growing, still has much room to improve. According to one report "[t]wo percent of

---

[1265] Resolution No. 1185, "Concerning the Setting up of the State Data Protection Inspectorate," October 10, 1996.

[1266] The State Data Protection Inspectorate, Overview of The First Four Years (1997-2000), available at <http://www.ada.lt/en/activity-s.html>.

[1267] The State Data Protection Inspectorate, Data Protection Development Programme for the Year 2002-2004, available at <http://www.ada.lt/en/legal.html>

[1268] E-mail from Karel Neuwirt, President, Office for Personal Data Protection, Czech Republic, to Sarah Andrews, Research Director, Electronic Privacy Information Center, May 15, 2002 (on file with the Electronic Privacy Information Center).

Lithuanian hotels, seven percent of electronic shops and seventy percent of banks observe the requirements of the law."[1269]

Government observation of and intrusion into individuals is limited by the Constitution and the law.[1270] Wiretapping requires a warrant issued by the Prosecutor General or a judge. In practice, the boundaries of lawful surveillance are still being contended. According to the United States Department of State Human Rights Report for the year 2001:

> [I]t is assumed widely that law enforcement agencies have increased the use of a range of surveillance methods to cope with the expansion of organized crime. In July in the case of Juozas Valasinas v. Lithuania [...], the ECHR found that officials in his correctional institution were reading his correspondence without the approval of the court. During the first half of the year, the Parliament controller confirmed a violation of prisoner's correspondence rights. Pursuant to a change in the law, since April prisoners' complaints to courts, the Parliament controller, and human rights groups have not been censored, and censorship of their private correspondence has been subject to stricter control by prison authorities.
>
> Local media reported that the security services monitored the activities of the nongovernmental organization (NGO), Collegiate Association for the Research of the Principle, Jehovah's Witnesses, and a visiting member of the Russian Vissarion Church.
>
> In May a member of the Parliament complained that a government agency had monitored his cell phone calls in 2000, when he was not yet a member of the Parliament; a printout of his calls were published in a national daily newspaper during a political dispute.[1271]

There are specific privacy protections in laws relating to telecommunications,[1272] radio communications,[1273] statistics,[1274] the population register,[1275] and health

---

[1269] "Protection of Personal Data on the Internet Poor in Lithuania – Research," Baltic News Service, May 16, 2002.

[1270] Law on Operative Activities, 1991.

[1271] United States Department of State, Country Reports on Human Rights Practices 2001, March 2002, available at <http://www.state.gov/g/drl/rls/hrrpt/2001/eur/8287.htm>.

[1272] The Law on Telecommunications, November30, 1995, No. I-1109.

[1273] Law on Radio Communication, November 7, 1995, No.I-1086.

[1274] The Law on Statistics, 12 October 1993, No.I-270.

information.[1276] The Penal Code of the Republic of Lithuania provides for criminal responsibility for violations of the inviolability of a residence, infringement on secrecy of correspondence and telegram contents, on privacy of telephone conversations, persecution for criticism, secrecy of adoption, slander, desecration of graves and impact on computer information. Civil laws provide for compensation for moral damage because of dissemination of unlawful or false information demeaning the honor and dignity of a person in the mass media.[1277] In February 2001, the European Court of Human Rights accepted two cases against Lithuania filed by a former prosecutor and a former tax inspector who allege that their privacy was violated when they were fired from their positions and prohibited from taking certain posts in the private sector because of their previous collaboration with the KGB.[1278]

The 1996 Law on the Provision of Information to the Public provides for a limited right of access to official documents and to documents held by political parties, political and public organizations, trade union and other entities.[1279] A more comprehensive Law on the Right to Receive Information from the State and Municipal Institutions, drafted by the Lithuanian Centre for Human Rights, is currently being reviewed by the Parliament.[1280]

Lithuania is in the process of preparing for membership in the European Union and has a National Program for the Adoption of European Union Regulations. It is a member of the Council of Europe and in June 2001 ratified the Convention for the Protection of Individuals with Regard to Automatic Processing of Personal Data (ETS No. 108).[1281] It has signed and ratified the European Convention for the Protection of Human Rights and Fundamental Freedoms.[1282]

[1275] Law on the Population Register, January 23, 1992, No. I-2237.

[1276] Law on the Health System, 19 July 1994, No.I-552.

[1277] United Nations Human Rights Committee, Consideration of Reports Submitted by States Parties Under Article 40 of the Covenant, Initial reports of States parties due in 1993, Addendum, Lithuania, 1996, available at <http://www.hri.ca/fortherecord1997/documentation/tbodies/ccpr-c-81-add10.htm>.

[1278] "Strasbourg Probing 2 Cases Of Ex-KGB Agents Vs. Lithuania," Baltic News Service, February 8, 2001.

[1279] The Law on the Provision of Information to the Public, July 2, 1996 No.I-1418 (as amended on January 23, 1997).

[1280] Memorandum on the Submission of ARTICLE 19 Critique - Lithuanian Draft Law on "The Right to Receive Information," available at <http://www.article19.org/docimages/404.doc>.

[1281] Convention for the Protection of Individuals with regard to Automatic Processing of Personal Data (ETS no: 108). Signed February 11, 2000; Ratified June 1, 2001; Entered into force October 1, 2001.

[1282] Signed May 14, 1993; Ratified June 20, 1995; Entered into force June 20, 1995.

Grand Duchy of Luxembourg

Article 28 of the Constitution states, "(1) The secrecy of correspondence is inviolable. The law determines the agents responsible for the violation of the secrecy of correspondence entrusted to the postal services. (2) The law determines the guarantee to be afforded to the secrecy of telegrams." [1283]

Luxembourg's Act Concerning the Use of Nominal Data in Computer Processing was adopted in 1979.[1284] The law pertains to regulate individually identifiable automated personal records in both public and private computer files. All databanks including personal data have to be authorized, and data subjects have the right to correct their personal and correct them if inaccurate. The law also requires licensing of systems used for the processing of personal data.[1285]

As a member of the European Union, Luxembourg should have amended this law by October 1, 1998, in order to implement the European Data Protection Directive (95/46/EC). An amending bill was introduced in the Parliament in 1997, but was withdrawn in 1998 and not reintroduced due to Parliamentary elections.[1286] In January 2000, the European Commission initiated a case before the European Court of Justice against Luxembourg and four other countries for failure to implement the Directive on time.[1287] A new bill was finally drafted and submitted to Parliament in October 2000.[1288] As yet, no measure has been introduced to implement the 1997 Telecommunications Privacy Directive.

A Grand-Ducal decree of August 1979 created the Commission à la protection des données nominatives (the Commission). The Commission is charged with overseeing the law and assisting the Minister of Justice with the management of the National Register of Databanks. If an application for personal data processing is granted, and there is an objection raised, or if the application is refused, or the

---

[1283] Constitution of the Grand Duchy of Luxembourg, available at
<http://www.uni-wuerzburg.de/law/lu00t___.html>.

[1284] Act on the Use of Nominal Data in Computer Processing, March 31,1979. See Charles E.H. Franklin, Business Guide to Privacy and Data Protection Legislation 306 (1996).

[1285] A good outline of the law is available at
<http://www.privacyexchange.org/legal/nat/omni/luxemsum.html>.

[1286] Act on the protection of individuals with regard to the processing of their personal data, no. 4357. Document is available at <http://www.chd.lu> under Portail Documentaire, recherche d'archives, recherche avancée, Dossier parlementaire No. 4357.

[1287] European Commission, "Data protection: Commission Takes Five Member States to court," January 11, 2000, available at <http://europa.eu.int/comm/internal_market/en/media/dataprot/news/2k-10.htm>.

[1288] European Commission, Status of implementation of Directive 95/46, available at
<http://europa.eu.int/comm/internal_market/en/dataprot/law/impl.htm>.

original authorization is withdrawn for some reason, an appeal can be made to the Disputes Committee of the Council of State. The Minister for Justice maintains a national register of all systems containing personal information. Public sector personal data systems can only be established upon the issuance of a special law or regulation. The Advisory Board reviews such proposed laws or regulations. In 1992, the law was amended to include special protection requirements for police and medical data. In 1993, the law was modified to establish an independent control authority pursuant to the Schengen Agreement.

Articles 88-1 and 88-2 of the Criminal Code regulate telephone tapping.[1289] Judicial wiretaps are authorized if it can be shown: that a serious crime or infringement, punishable by two or more years imprisonment, is involved; that there is sufficient evidence to suspect that the subject of the interception order committed or participated in the crime; or received or transmitted information to, from, or concerning the accused; and that ordinary investigative techniques would be inadequate under the circumstances. Orders are granted for 1-month periods and may be extended repeatedly as long as the cumulative period does not exceed one year. Administrative wiretaps may also be authorized for national security reasons by a special tribunal appointed by the head of government. These interceptions are granted for three months at a time and must stop once the requested information is received. The communications of persons bound by professional secrecy rules cannot be intercepted and any recordings of such must be destroyed immediately. Information, gathered during judicial and administrative interceptions, but not subsequently used, must be destroyed. In the case of judicial warrants, persons who formed the subject of the warrant will sometimes be informed of the action taken. This law was highly criticized by human rights activists and the socialist workers party when it was first introduced. In fact the law was challenged on numerous occasions before the European Court of Human Rights. That Court, however, ruled that the law violated neither article 8 (concerning the right to private and family life) nor article 13 (concerning the right to due process) of the European Convention on Human Rights.[1290]

A law on electronic commerce that implements three European Union Directives (Dir. 99/93 on electronic signatures, Dir. 2000/31/EC on Electronic Commerce, and Dir. 97/7 on Distance-Selling) was adopted on August 2000.[1291] This law

---

[1289] Art 88-1 - 88-4 of the Criminal Code, Law of 26 November 1982, modified by the law of July 7, 1989.

[1290] Commission nationale de contrôle des interceptions de sécurité, (France) 8e Rapport d'Activité 1999, at 66-67.

[1291] Loi du 14 août 2000 relative au commerce électronique modifiant le code civil, le nouveau code de procédure civile, le code de commerce, le code penal et transposant la directive 99/93 relative à un cadre

contains provisions on the privacy rules certification authorities have to comply with, spamming, and the liability of online service providers. A Grand-Ducal regulation on electronic signatures, electronic payments and the setting up of the Electronic Commerce Committee was adopted on June 1, 2001.

The Numerical Identification of Natural and Legal Persons Act of 1979[1292] provides for the introduction of an identity number, consisting of 11 digits (including digits to represent date of birth and sex, nationality, marital status and spouse's name) for every person resident in the country, and a numbering system for companies. The law contains specifications for use of this number: the identification number and other related information can only be used by the public services that are authorized to have access to the index, and is restricted to an internal use. These specifications are loosely drafted, however, and leave it open for the number to be widely circulated. The data protection authority is said to be monitoring the adoption of this number closely.[1293]

There are also sectoral laws on privacy relating to telecommunications,[1294] and banking secrecy. Luxembourg's status as a financial haven ensures that unwarranted surveillance of individuals is forbidden. This may change as Luxembourg comes under increasing pressure to amend its financial confidentiality laws to permit greater access to personal financial records by European and American investigators.

There is no general freedom of information law in Luxembourg. Under the 1960 decree on state archives, the archives are to be open to the public, but citizens must make a written request explaining why they want access and ministers have broad discretion to deny requests.[1295] The government announced in August

---

communautaire pour les signatures électroniques, la directive relative à certains aspects juridiques des services de la société de l'information, certaines dispositions de la directive 97/7 concernant la vente à distance des biens et des services autres que les services financiers, *Mémorial*, September 8, 2000, at 2176., available at <http://www.chd.lu> under Portail Documentaire, recherche d'archives, recherche avancée, Dossier parlementaire No. 4641.

1292 Loi du 30 mars 1979 organisant l'identification numérique des personnes physiques et morales <http://www.etat.lu/ECP/30-3-79.doc>. Règlement grand-ducal du 7 juin 1979 déterminant les actes, documents et fichiers autorisés à utiliser le numéro d'identité des personnes physiques et morales, available at <http://www.etat.lu/ECP/7-6-79.doc>. Règlement grand-ducal modifié du 21 décembre 1987 fixant les modalités d'application de la loi du 30 mars 1979, available at <http://www.etat.lu/ECP/21-12-87.doc>.

1293 The Council of Europe, The introduction and use of personal identification numbers: the data protection issues, 1991, available at <http://www.coe.fr/DataProtection/Etudes_Rapports/epins.htm>.

1294 Loi du 21 mars 1997 sur les telecommunications,<http://www.etat.lu/ILT/co/legal/loi-t.htm>, Règlement grand-ducal du 22 décembre 1997 fixant les conditions du cahier des charges pour l'établissement et l'exploitation de réseaux fixes de telecommunications, <http://www.etat.lu/ILT/co/legal/lic-b.htm>.

1295 Arrêté grand-ducal fixant l'organisation et les conditions de fonctionnement des Archives de l'Etat.

1999 that it was planning to develop a new press bill including a right to access records.[1296]

Luxembourg is a member of the Council of Europe and has signed and ratified the Convention for the Protection of Individuals with Regard to Automatic Processing of Personal Data (ETS No. 108).[1297] It has signed and ratified the European Convention for the Protection of Human Rights and Fundamental Freedoms.[1298] It is a member of the Organization for Economic Cooperation and Development and has adopted the OECD Guidelines on the Protection of Privacy and Transborder Flows of Personal Data.

Malaysia

The Constitution of Malaysia does not specifically recognize the right to privacy.[1299]

The Ministry of Energy, Communications and Multimedia (MECM) is currently drafting a Personal Data Protection Act as part of the "National Electronic Commerce Master Plan." Work began on the bill in 1998 but has been delayed for several years. The bill was expected to be enacted in March 2002,[1300] but MECM Minister Datuk Amar Leo Moggie said increasing requests for exemptions to the act complicated the drafting process.[1301] According to the MECM, the proposed legislation is "envisaged to be a world-class, leading-edge cyberlaw that provides for a secure electronic environment."[1302] The law sets out nine data protection principles governing the collection, use, disclosure, accuracy, retention, access to and security of personal data. If enacted, it will establish a data protection Commissioner (to be appointed by the Minister) with the power to: monitor and supervise compliance; promote awareness and understanding; encourage trade bodies to prepare and comply with the codes of practice; cooperate with counterparts in foreign countries; carry out inspections

---

[1296] Le programme gouvernemental: Accord de coalition PCS/PDL, August 1999.
<http://www.gouvernement.lu/gouv/fr/gouv/progg/coalfr.html#1>.

[1297] Signed January 28, 1981; Ratified February 10, 1988; Entered into Force June 1, 1988.

[1298] Signed November 11, 1950; Ratified September 3, 1953; Entered into Force September 3, 1953.

[1299] Constitution of Malaysia, available at
<http://www.eur.nl/frg/iacl/armenia/constitu/constit/malaysia/malays-e.htm >.

[1300] "Data protection law to safeguard Internet users," BNA World Data Protection Report, Volume 2, Issue 1, January 2002.

[1301] "ICT a must for companies, says Moggie," Malaysia Economic News, October 11, 2001.

[1302] Datuk Amar Leo Moggie, "Official opening of Jagat's cyber law seminar series: Data protection and its far-reaching implications," November 29, 2001.

of data systems; and conduct prosecutions for non-compliance.[1303] Penalties for violating the law will include criminal fines of up to 250,000 ringgit ($65,790) and imprisonment of up to four years. Civil damages for data subjects (including compensation for injury to feelings) are also provided.[1304]

Malaysia announced plans in November 2001 to provide data protection and Internet law training for its judges, public prosecutors and police officers in anticipation of the enactment of the Personal Data Protection Act.[1305] The Prime Minister's Department said training for the judiciary and law enforcement would "better equip them to deal with computer-related crimes."[1306]

In 1998, the Parliament approved the Communications and Multimedia Act, which includes several sections on telecommunications privacy. Section 234 prohibits unlawful interception of communications. Section 249 sets rules for searches of computers and allows for access to encryption keys. Section 252 authorizes police to intercept communications without a warrant if a public prosecutor believes a communication is likely to contain information relevant to an investigation.[1307] There are regular reports of illegal wiretapping, including on former Deputy Premier Anwar Ibrahim in 1998. Police detained four people under the Internal Security Act on suspicion of spreading rumors of disturbances in Kuala Lumpur in August 1998. Inspector General of Police Tan Sri Abdul Rahim Noorsaid told the media then that the suspects were detained after police tracked their activities on the Internet with the assistance of Internet service provider Mimos Berhad.[1308] The provider said later that it did not screen private e-mail.[1309]

Several other laws relating to technology were approved in 1997, including the Digital Signature Act, the Telemedicine Act, the Copyright (Amendment) Act and the Computer Crimes Act.[1310] The Computer Crimes Act is based on the United Kingdom Computer Misuse Act of 1990. It outlaws unauthorized access to computer material; the use of a computer to commit an offense involving

---

[1303] Loh Chyi Jen, "Framing the country's privacy laws," New Straits Times (Malaysia), July 18, 2001.

[1304] Sarban Singh, "Hackers risk tough penalty," New Straits Times (Malaysia), April 16, 2001.

[1305] "Training for judges, prosecutors to keep in touch with cyber world," New Straits Times-Management Times," November 30, 2001.

[1306] "Judiciary to have data protection training," BNA World Data Protection Report, Volume 2, Issue 2, February 2002.

[1307] Communications and Multimedia Act 1998.

[1308] Tony Emmanuel, "Rumours over Internet: Four to be charged soon," New Straits Times (Malaysia), September 24, 1998.

[1309] "E-mail not screened, says service provider," New Straits Times (Malaysia), August 17, 1998.

[1310] MECM Cyberlaws, available at <http://www.ktkm.gov.my/comm/cyberlaws.html>.

fraud, dishonesty or which causes injury; the unauthorized modification (permanent or temporary) of the contents of any computer; and the wrongful communication of codes, passwords, etc. The law applies to these acts even when they are committed outside of the country. The law allows police to inspect and seize computer equipment of suspects without a warrant or notice. Suspects are also required to turn over all encryption keys for any encrypted data on their equipment.[1311] In July 2001, the Chief Inspector of the technology crime investigation team (a unit under the Royal Malaysian Police) called for updates to the Computer Crimes Act, arguing that "it focuses much on the ICT scenario of the early 90s and thus is rendered inadequate for addressing computer crimes of 2000 and beyond."[1312] Prime Minister Datuk Seri Dr Mahathir Mohamad has also stressed the need for greater security measures to tackle "the rising number of cybercrime incidents and the increased use of the Internet for misinformation."[1313] In January 2001, following a high profile hack into the Parliament's Web site, it was reported that the government may apply the Internal Security Act, which allows for indefinite detention without trial, to hackers of government Web sites. Malaysia's Banking and Financial Institutions Act 1989, Pt XIII, also has provisions on privacy.

In April 2001, the National Registration Department (NRD) launched the Government Multi-Purpose Card, also called MyKad, making Malaysia the first nation to introduce a multi-application national identity card.[1314] MyKad is embedded with a microchip and is used as a national identity card, driver's license, passport and electronic purse. Officials plan additional card applications that will allow users to withdraw cash from automated teller machines and digitally sign documents on the Internet.[1315] The cards will also be used to store users' health and immigration information.[1316] Users can see information stored on their cards by inserting them into readers at government kiosks or offices and verifying their identity by scanning a thumbprint that is compared with a digitized version stored on the card. In addition to the thumbprint biometric, the cards also feature photos of their owners. The Malaysian government originally proposed putting the religious affiliation of all citizens on the front of the cards, but complaints from the country's non-Muslim ethnic groups prompted the government to only include the religious affiliation of Muslims in order to

---

[1311] Computer Crimes Act 1997.

[1312] Shyla Sangaran, "Keeping pace with computer crime cases," New Straits Times-Computimes, July 9, 2001.

[1313] "PM calls for increased net security to curb cybercrimes," FT Asia Intelligence Wire, July 13, 2001.

[1314] Sarban Singh, "MyKad for multipurpose use," New Straits Times (Malaysia), September 6, 2001.

[1315] Dan Balaban, "Getting serious about citizen ID," Card Technology, December 2001.

[1316] "MyKad can be used for all transactions, says NRD," Malaysia General News, November 2, 2001.

enforce Islamic law. [1317] By May 2002, 1.7 million MyKad had been issued, mostly to people in the Klang Valley.[1318] MyKad is currently optional to the public, except for people who need to reapply for national identity cards due to loss, damage, change of address or those who are getting their identification cards for the first time. A nationwide rollout of the cards is expected to take place in 2003, but full implementation of the project will take five to eight years.[1319]

The Consumers Association of Penang has criticized the cards, arguing that they make individuals' personal and confidential information too vulnerable. The association has recommended that the proposed Personal Data Protection Act address these risks specifically and provide a proper definition for the term "sensitive data."[1320] The Federation of Malaysian Consumers Association also questioned the security of the information contained on MyKad, contending that the storage of private information on a centralized system makes it vulnerable to tampering and sabotage. The federation also criticized the Malaysian government for not implementing clear guidelines on how MyKad is to be used and for not consulting the public about the project during development.[1321]

All Malaysians over the age of 12 are issued national ID cards. The government announced in 1998 that if citizens do not carry their cards, they risk being detained by immigration police.[1322] The National Registration Department said in January 2002 that it will suspend the issuing of new identity cards to citizens who have lost their cards three times. Instead, the Department will issue them a temporary receipt, which cannot be used for official transactions without an endorsement from the Department. Applications for replacement identity cards submitted by people who have lost their cards more than five times will be thoroughly investigated by the Department before it makes a decision to issue a new card, according to the Department's director.[1323] In January 1999, it was announced that Muslim couples married in the Malaysian capital will be issued cards with computer chips so that Islamic police equipped with portable card readers can instantly verify their vows.

[1317] Dan Balaban, supra n.1315.

[1318] "New I/C applicants issued with GMPC from May 1," Malaysia General News, May 8, 2002.

[1319] Rina Omar, "MyKad has it all," New Straits Times (Malaysia), March 29, 2002.

[1320] "Smart IC open to abuse," The Star, April 18, 2001.

[1321] Sarban Singh, supra n.1314.

[1322] Annie Freeda Cruez, "Malaysians told: Carry ICs or risk detention," New Straits Times (Malaysia), May 14, 1998.

[1323] Annie Freeda Cruez, "NRD plans higher fines and six months' suspension," New Straits Times (Malaysia), Janary 4, 2002.

In December 1998, the government began requiring cyber cafes to obtain name, address, and identity card information from patrons but lifted the requirement in March 1999.[1324] The National Registration Department recently proposed the introduction of smart identity cards for all newborns. The card will store information previously written in the birth certificate such as a number, name, parent's names, address and citizenship status. It will include health information such as immunization history, allergies and blood type. Unlike the adult smart card, however, it will not include photographs or thumbprints. The card will be optional, but all parents will be encouraged to apply. The card is expected to be implemented in 2002.

In August 2001, the Malaysian Bar Council ruled that body searches by school authorities to look for tattoos on students were a gross violation of privacy and should only be conducted if a student is suspected of having committed an offense. The searches were mostly carried out on students in religious and residential schools who were believed to have been targeted by occult groups.[1325]

United Mexican States

Article 16 of the 1917 Mexican Constitution provides in part: "One's person, family, home, papers or possessions may not be molested, except by virtue of a written order by a proper authority, based on and motivated by legal proceedings. The administrative authority may make home visits only to certify compliance with sanitary and police rules; the presentation of books and papers indispensable to verify compliance with the fiscal laws may be required in compliance with the respective laws and the formalities proscribed for their inspection. Correspondence, under the protective circle of the mail, will be free from all inspection, and its violation will be punishable by law."[1326]

There is no comprehensive data protection law in Mexico. Provisions in the Federal Consumer Protection Code, however, place restrictions on restrict direct marketing and credit reporting agencies. On June 7, 2001 the Mexican E-Commerce Act took effect. The law amends the Civil Code, the Commercial Code, the Rules of Civil Procedure and the Consumer Protection Act. It covers consumer protection, privacy and digital signatures and electronic documents. It

---

[1324] "Cabinet: Cybercafes not subjected to restrictions," New Straits Times (Malaysia), March 18, 1999.

[1325] "Body searches 'violate students' privacy,'" New Straits Times (Malaysia), August 4, 2001.

[1326] Constitucion Politica de los Estados Unidos Mexicanos, available at <http://info.juridicas.unam.mx/cnsinfo/fed00.htm>.

includes a new article in the Federal Consumer Protection Act giving authority to the government "to provide for the effective protection of consumer in electronic transactions or concluded by any other means, and the adequate use of the data provided by the consumer" (Art. 1.VIII); and also to coordinate the use of Code of Ethics by providers including the principles of this law. The law also creates a new chapter in the Consumer Law titled: "Rights of Consumers in electronic transactions and transactions by any other means." The new article 76 now provides, "This article will be applied to the relation between providers and consumers in transactions effectuated by electronics means. The following principles must be observed: I. Providers shall use information provided by consumers in a confidential manner, and shall not be able to transfer it to third parties, unless there is express consent from the consumer or a requirement from a public authority. II. Providers must use technical measures to provide security and confidentiality to the information submitted by the consumer, and notify the consumer, before the transaction, of the characteristics of the system. VI. Providers must respect consumer decisions not to receive commercial solicitations."

Article 214 of the Penal Code protects against the disclosure of personal information held by government agencies.[1327] The General Population Act regulates the National Registry of Population and Personal Identification. The Registry's purpose is to register all persons making up the country's population using data enabling their identity to be certified reliably. The aim is ultimately to issue the citizen's identity card, which will be the official document of identification, fully endorsing the data contained in it concerning the holder.[1328]

Chapter 6 of Mexico's Postal Code, in effect since 1888, recognizes the inviolability of correspondence and guarantees the privacy of correspondence.[1329] The 1939 General Communication Law provides penalties for interrupting communications and divulging secrets.[1330] The Federal Penal Code establishes penalties for the crime of revealing personal secrets by any means, including personal mail.[1331] In 1981, the Penal Code was amended to

---

[1327] Código Penal Federal, Article 214.

[1328] See United Nations Commission on Human Rights, Question of the follow-up to the guidelines for the regulation of computerized personal data files: report of the Secretary-General prepared pursuant to Commission decision 1995/114, available at
<http://www.hri.ca/fortherecord1997/documentation/commission/e-cn4-1997-67.htm>.

[1329] El Código Postal de los Estados Unidos Mexicanos (1884).

[1330] Ley de Vías Generales de Comunicación de 30 de diciembre de 1939, Arts 571. 576, 578.

[1331] Código Penal Federal, Art 210.

include the interception of telephone calls by a third person.[1332] The Law Against Organized Crime, passed in November 1996, allows for electronic surveillance with a judicial order.[1333] The law prohibits electronic surveillance in cases of electoral, civil, commercial, labor, or administrative matters and expands protection against unauthorized surveillance to cover all private means of communications, not merely telephone calls.[1334]

The Law has been widely criticized by Mexican human rights organizations as violating Article 16 of the Constitution.[1335] They noted that the ruling PRI party "to keep the opposition in check" had historically used telephone espionage.[1336] There are numerous reports of illegal wiretapping. In September 2001, thirteen people were arrested on suspicion of involvement in the illegal wiretapping of state government employees and former employees. The wiretapping was allegedly run out of the state governor's office who has denied any involvement.[1337] In December 2000 President Fox formed a committee to review the practices of CISEN, the Government civilian intelligence agency, following allegations of illegal phone tapping.[1338] In 1997, the telephones of the Jalisco State Supreme Court were found to have been wiretapped.[1339] In March 1998, a large cache of government electronic eavesdropping equipment which had been used since 1991 to spy on members of opposition political parties, human rights groups and journalists was discovered in Campeche.[1340] Thousands of pages of transcripts of telephone conversations were uncovered along with receipts for $1.2 million in Israeli surveillance equipment. More than a dozen other cases of government espionage in four other states were exposed, ranging from hidden microphones and cameras found in government offices in Mexico City, to tapes of a state governor's telephone calls. Every government agency identified with the electronic surveillance operations – the federal attorney general and interior ministry, the military, the national security agency and a plethora of state institutions – denied knowing anything about them.[1341] The new President-elect,

---

[1332] Id., Article. 167, part 9.

[1333] Ley Federal Contra la Delincuencia Organizada, November 7, 1996.

[1334] "Zedillo to sign sweeping organized crime package," The Los Angeles Times, October 30, 1996.

[1335] "Exigen siete ONG la renuncia del titular de Seguridad Publica," La Jornada, October 7, 1997.

[1336] "Con la reforma anticrimen, el espionaje entraría a la Constitución," La Jornada, April 28, 1996.

[1337] United States Department of State, Country Report on Human Rights Practices 2001, March 2002, available at <http://www.state.gov/g/drl/rls/hrrpt/2001/>.

[1338] Id.

[1339] Associated Press, January 18, 1997.

[1340] "Spy Network Stuns Mexicans, Raid Opens Door to Exposure of Government Snooping," The Washington Post, April 13, 1998.

[1341] "Anger as Big Brother spy tactics exposed," The Guardian (London), April 14, 1998.

Vicente Fox, has promised to eliminate the security police division that is responsible for much of the illegal government wiretapping in Mexico.

The United States-Mexican border has been an area of increased surveillance. Mexican authorities now routinely perform "security sweeps" of homes in areas bordering the United States.[1342] On the United States side, biometric facial feature recognition systems have been implemented by the Immigration and Naturalization Service at the Otay Mesa border crossing (San Diego-Tijuana) for frequent United States commuters to Mexican maquiladora factories. The biometric data is stored with driver's license numbers, vehicle registration numbers and passport status information in an INS database. When a commuter in the program approaches the United States border, a transponder under his vehicle sends a signal to the checkpoint booth, activating the database and displaying the driver's image. Other commuters use a voice-activated device in addition to the facial scan.[1343]

In June 2002, President Fox signed into law the Federal Transparency and Access to Public Government Information Law, which was approved by Parliament in April 2002. The law will go into effect in May 2003 and allow access to information held by all government bodies. The law creates a National Commission on Access to Public Information to supervise the implementation of the law. Exemptions are made for a number of categories of information.

Mexico is a member of the Organization for Economic Cooperation and Development, but has not adopted the OECD Guidelines on the Protection of Privacy and Transborder Flows of Personal Data. Mexico has also signed the American Convention on Human Rights.

Kingdom of the Netherlands

The Constitution grants citizens an explicit right to privacy.[1344] Article 10 states: "(1) Everyone shall have the right to respect for his privacy, without prejudice to restrictions laid down by or pursuant to Act of Parliament. (2) Rules to protect privacy shall be laid down by Act of Parliament in connection with the recording and dissemination of personal data. (3) Rules concerning the rights of persons to

---

1342 "En marcha, amplia operacion anticrimen en la frontera con European Union," La Jornada, November 5, 1996.

1343 "Human bar codes," The San Diego Union-Tribune, May 13, 1998.

1344. Constitution of the Kingdom of the Netherlands 1989, available at <http://www.uni-wuerzburg.de/law/nl00000_.html>.

---

be informed of data recorded concerning them and of the use that is made thereof, and to have such data corrected shall be laid down by Act of Parliament." Article 12 states: "(1) Entry into a home against the will of the occupant shall be permitted only in the cases laid down by or pursuant to Act of Parliament, by those designated for the purpose by or pursuant to Act of Parliament. (2) Prior identification and notice of purpose shall be required in order to enter a home under the preceding paragraph, subject to the exceptions prescribed by Act of Parliament. A written report of the entry shall be issued to the occupant." Article 13 states, "(1) The privacy of correspondence shall not be violated except, in the cases laid down by Act of Parliament, by order of the courts. (2) The privacy of the telephone and telegraph shall not be violated except, in the cases laid down by Act of Parliament, by or with the authorization of those designated for the purpose by Act of Parliament."

In May 2000, the government-appointed commission for "Constitutional rights in the digital age" presented proposals for changes to the Dutch constitution. The commission was set up after confusion about the legal status of e-mail under the constitutionally protected privacy of letters. The commission's task was to investigate if existing constitutional rights should be made more technology-independent and if new rights should be introduced. According to this proposal, Article 10 will be expanded to the right of persons to be informed about the origin of data recorded about them and the right to correct that data. Article 13 would be made technology-independent and would give the right to confidential communications. Breaches of this right could only be authorized by a judge or a minister. The discussion about possible changes is still ongoing.

The Personal Data Protection Act of 2000 was approved by the Parliament in June 2000.[1345] This bill is a revised and expanded version of the 1988 Data Registration Act that will bring Dutch law in line with the European Data Protection Directive and will regulate the disclosure of personal data to countries outside of the European Union. The Act replaces the Data Registration Act of 1988. The new law went into effect in September 2001.

The College Bescherming Persoonsgegevens (CBP) serves as the Data Protection Authority and exercises supervision of the operation of personal data files in accordance with the Act.[1346] Previously known as the Registratiekamer, the CBP's functions have remained largely the same with the implementation of the

---

[1345] Personal Data Protection Act, Staatsblad 2000 302, July 6, 2000, unofficial translation, available at <http://www2.unimaas.nl/~privacy/wbp_en_rev.htm>.
[1346] Homepage <www.cbpweb.nl>.

new Act, although it has been given new powers of enforcement. It can now apply administrative measures and impose fines for non compliance with a decision. It can also levy fines, of up to 4540 euro for breach of the notification requirements. Otherwise, the CBP continues to advise the government, deal with complaints submitted by data subjects, institute investigations and make recommendations to controllers of personal data files. In 2001 the CBP received approximately 9,000 requests, a large increase over previous years. This increase is attributed to the increased public attention surrounding the passage of the new law. The CBP received approximately 300 complaints and requests for mediation, of which many related to requests for access to police records. The CBP issued a number of public education reports during 2001 and a policy framework for the transfer of data to third countries. A focus of the CBP recently has been on establishing privacy protections within information communication technology. It is a major participant in the European Privacy Incorporated Software Agents (PISA) project which was established to develop privacy enhancing techniques to protect user information in electronic transactions.[1347] In January 2001, it issued a report on email and Internet privacy in the workplace setting out 17 guidelines for employers. According to the Chamber the report "argues in favor of a balanced and common sense approach to e-mail and Internet checks at the workplace." It concludes that although employees retain a reasonable expectation of privacy in the workplace, employers should be entitled to monitor email and Internet usage under certain conditions.[1348] In its annual report for the year 2000, issued in May 2001, the Chamber drew attention to the increasing use of video surveillance cameras in public spaces, threats to privacy in the health sector, and the need for further privacy protection on the Internet.

Two decrees have been issued under the Data Registration Act. The Decree on Sensitive Data[1349] sets out the limited circumstances when personal data on an individual's religious beliefs, race, political persuasion, sexuality, medical, psychological and criminal history may be included in a personal data file. The Decree on Regulated Exemption[1350] exempts certain organizations from the registration requirements of the Data Registration Act.

The Telecommunications Act 1998 implements the European Union Telecommunications Privacy Directive. In March 2002, Internet Service Provider

---

[1347] College Bescherming Persoonsgegevens, Annual Report for the Year 2001, July 2002, available at <http://www.cbpweb.nl/structuur/blok_publ_jv.htm>.

[1348] Dutch Data Protection Authority, Working Well in Networks, January 2001, English summary available at <http://home.planet.nl/~privacy1/>.

[1349] Decree on Sensitive Data, March 5, 1993.

[1350] Decree on Regulated Exemption, July 6, 1993.

XS4ALL won a court order preventing well known spam company Abfab from sending unsolicited commercial email to its subscribers. Afbab has appealed the decision.[1351] There are sectoral laws dealing with the Dutch police,[1352] medical exams,[1353] medical treatment,[1354] social security,[1355] entering private homes,[1356] and the employment of minorities.[1357]

Interception of communications is regulated by the criminal code and requires a court order.[1358] The Intelligence services do not need a court order for interception, but obtain their authorization from the responsible minister. The Special Investigation Powers Act which came into effect in February 2000 streamlines criminal investigatory methods.[1359] A new Telecommunications Act was approved in December 1998, requiring all Internet Service Providers have the capability by August 2000 to intercept all traffic with a court order and maintain users logs for three months.[1360] The deadline for compliance was later extended to April 2001. The bill was enacted after ISP XS4ALL, refused to conduct a broad wiretap of electronic communications of one of its subscribers. The Dutch Forensics Institute has developed a so-called "black-box" that is used to intercept Internet traffic at an ISP. The black box is under control of the ISP and is turned on after receiving a court order. The box is believed to look at authentication traffic of the person to wiretap and divert the person's traffic to law enforcement if that person is online.[1361] The costs of installing this technology are estimated to be between 500,00 guilders ($201,400) and 1.5 million guilders ($604,100) and are reportedly forcing many of the smaller ISPs out of businesses.[1362] In May 2000, Dutch Internet providers canceled a deal with the Justice Department to provide names and addresses of Internet users under criminal investigation without a court order if the case involves a serious crime. Dutch privacy law gives the holder of a data registry the right to give out

---

[1351] See XS4ALL Spam page at <http://www.xs4all.nl/uk/news/overview/spam_e.html>.

[1352] Dutch Police Registers Act 1990.

[1353] Dutch Medical Examinations Act 1997.

[1354] Dutch Medical Treatment Act 1997.

[1355] Dutch Social Security System Act 1997, Compulsory Identification Act.

[1356] Dutch Act on the Entering of Buildings and Houses 1994.

[1357] Dutch Act on the Stimulation of Labor by Minorities 1994.

[1358] Article 125g of the Code of Criminal Procedure.

[1359] See Ministry of Justice, Fact Sheet on the Special Investigation Powers Act, available at <http://www.minjust.nl:8080/a_beleid/fact/specialpow.htm>.

[1360] Telecommunications Act 1998. Rules pertaining to Telecommunications (Telecommunications Act), December 1998.

[1361] Homepage <http://www.holmes.nl/>.

[1362] "Dutch Cyber-Police Could Boost ISP Consolidation," by Caroline Jacobs, December 2000, available at <http://www.infowar.com/law/00/law_120700e_j.shtml>.

personal data to third parties in "pressing cases." The agreement between the providers and the Justice Department had to be halted nevertheless after a court ruled that the Justice Department was requesting information without a clear urgency.[1363]

A survey by the Dutch Ministry of Justice in 1996 found that police in the Netherlands intercept more telephone calls than their counterparts in the United States, Germany or Britain.[1364] The Parliamentary Investigations Commission into police methods released a 4,700-page report in 1996. The report was critical of legal controls on police surveillance[1365] and found that there was a failure among judges, prosecutors and other officials to limit police abuses. Some analysts say that the reason for the high number of taps is that the Netherlands prohibits other forms of investigations such as informers.

There have been a number of proposals over the last year to grant law enforcement increased authority. In 2001 the Committee on the Gathering of Information in Criminal Investigations (the Mevis Committee) issued a report proposing a wide range of increased powers for police to allow them carry out "pro-active investigations". The proposals would grant the police access, without judicial warrant, to the personal information of whole groups of citizens stored by a wide variety of private entities, such as banks, telephone companies, credit card companies, hospitals travel agents, in order to determine crime patterns.[1366] The Mevis Committee specifically recommended that telecommunications data be excluded from the constitutional guarantee for confidential communications stating that it should not be necessary for police to always obtain a warrant to intercept communications.[1367]

In October 2001, the Government released an Action Plan containing 43 specific measures to be taken to combat terrorism and promote security.[1368] Among these were proposals to: expand information and security agencies; promote better cooperation among information and security services and the police; develop biometric identifiers; expand investigative and prosecuting capacity; regulate the

---

[1363] "Dutch Internet Providers Cancel Deal with Law Enforcement on Voluntary Assistance in Criminal Investigations," Telepolis, July 12, 2000 <http://www.heise.de/tp/english/inhalt/te/8367/1.html>.
[1364] Id.
[1365] Tappen in Nederland, WODC, 1996
[1366] "Dutch Law Enforcement Should Get Easier Access to Personal Data Stored by Companies," Jelle van Buuren, Telepolis, May 21, 2001.
[1367] Report of the Mevis Commission, May 2001, available (in Dutch) at <http://www.minjust.nl/c_actual/rapport/gegevens.pdf>.
[1368] Ministry of Justice, Plan of Action for Combating Terrorism and Promoting Security, October 5, 2001, available at <http://www.minjust.nl:8080/c_actual/persber/pb0775.htm>.

use of strong encryption and force Trusted Third Parties (TTPs) to use key escrow or key recovery techniques to enable access to encrypted communications; ensure the quick implementation of the 1998 interception requirements for ISPs (above); expand satellite interception capacity to combat terrorism and "investigate further" the issue of data retention by telecommunications operators.

Data retention requirements and changes to article 13 of the Constitution, as recommended by the Mevis Committee, have recently been officially proposed by the Government in the Telecommunications Data Requisition Bill. In its annual report for 2001, the data protection authority criticized this proposal saying that "constitutional protection should not be restricted to the content of communications, but should extend to 'traffic data', i.e. information about the communications."[1369]

A new law was also adopted this year giving a broad range of new powers to Dutch intelligence services. The Governmental Intelligence and Security Forces Act authorizes the interception, search and key word scanning of satellite communications. It also allows the intelligence services to store intercepted communications for up to one year. Previously, irrelevant communications had to be deleted immediately. Encrypted data can be stored for an unlimited time to facilitate possible decryption in the future.[1370]

In February 2002 privacy and civil liberties organization, Bits of Freedom, organized the first Dutch Big Brother Awards (awards for most egregious privacy violations given each year by Privacy International and affiliate NGOs around the world). The awards were granted to: the Health Institute RIVM for archiving over one million blood samples of children, without any legal basis or permission from the children's; the Mevis Committee for its 2001 report (above); the Organisation for Applied Scientific Research (TNO) for the development of the Automatic Aggression Detection video processing software; and to the State Secretary of Transport, Public Works and Water Management Monique de Vries for re-introducing proposals for data retention.[1371]

[1369] College Bescherming Persoonsgegevens, Annual Report for the year 2001, supra n.1347.

[1370] Jelle van Buuren, "Dutch Government Wants to Regulate Strong Cryptography," Heise Online, October 9, 2001 available at <http://www.telepolis.de/english/inhalt/te/9763/1.html>.

[1371] Dutch Big Brother Awards 2002 <http://www.bigbrotherawards.nl/index.en.html>.

The Government Information (Public Access) Act of 1991[1372] is based on the constitutional right of access to information. It creates a presumption that documents created by a public agency should be available to everyone. Information can be withheld if it relates to international relations of the state, the "economic or financial interest of the state," investigation of criminal offenses, inspections by public authorities or personal privacy. However, these exemptions must be balanced against the importance of the disclosure. Requestors can appeal denials to an administrative court that renders the final decision.

The Netherlands is a member of the Council of Europe and has signed and ratified the Convention for the Protection of Individuals with Regard to Automatic Processing of Personal Data (ETS No. 108).[1373] It has signed and ratified the European Convention for the Protection of Human Rights and Fundamental Freedoms. In November 2001, the Netherlands signed the Council of Europe Convention on Cybercrime.[1374] It is a member of the Organization for Economic Cooperation and Development and has adopted the OECD Guidelines on the Protection of Privacy and Transborder Flows of Personal Data.

New Zealand

Article 21 of the New Zealand Bill of Rights Act 1990, states that "Everyone has the right to be secure against unreasonable search or seizure, whether of the person, property, or correspondence or otherwise."[1375] This has been interpreted by the New Zealand Court of Appeal in a number of cases as protecting the important values and interests which make up the right to privacy.[1376]

New Zealand's Privacy Act was enacted in 1993 and has been amended several times.[1377] It regulates the collection, use and dissemination of personal information in both the public and private sectors. It also grants to individuals the right to have access to personal information held about them by any agency. The Privacy Act applies to "personal information," which is any information about an identifiable individual, whether automatically or manually processed. Recent

---

[1372] Act of 31 October 1991, containing regulations governing public access to government information. This replaced the Act on Public Access to Information of November 9, 1978.

[1373] Signed May 7, 1982; Ratified May 28, 1993; Entered into Force September 1, 1993.

[1374] Signed November 23, 2001.

[1375] Bill of Rights Act, 1990, available at <http://www.uni-wuerzburg.de/law/nz01t___.html>.

[1376] Tim McBride, "Recent New Zealand Case Law on Privacy: Part I: Privacy Act and the Bill of Rights Act," Privacy Law & Reporter January 2000, 107.

[1377] The Privacy Act 1993, The Privacy Amendment Act 1993, The Privacy Amendment Act 1994, Privacy Amendment Act 1996, Privacy Amendment Act 1997, Privacy Amendment Act 1998.

---

case law has held that the definition also applies to mentally processed information.[1378] The news media are exempt from the Privacy Act in relation to their news activities.

The Act creates twelve Information Privacy Principles generally based on the 1980 OECD guidelines and the information privacy principles in Australia's Privacy Act 1988. In addition, the legislation includes a new principle that deals with the assignment and use of unique identifiers. The Information Privacy Principles can be individually or collectively replaced by enforceable codes of practice for particular sectors or classes of information. At present, there is only one complete sectoral code of practice in force, the Health Information Privacy Code 1994. There are several codes of practice that alter the application of single information privacy principles: the Superannuation Schemes Unique Identifier Code 1995, the EDS Information Privacy Code 1997, and the Justice Sector Unique Identifier Code 1998. In May 2001 the Commissioner released a Proposed Code on Post-Compulsory Education Unique Identifier for public comment. This code was finalized and issued in August 2001. The Commissioner has also released the drafts of two new privacy codes, Draft Credit Information Privacy Code and the Draft Telecommunications Code. The public consultation period on the telecommunications code closed in March 2002. In addition to the information privacy principles, the legislation contains principles relating to information held on public registers; it sets out guidelines and procedures in respect to information matching programs run by government agencies, and it makes special provision for the sharing of law enforcement information among specialized agencies.

The Office of the Privacy Commissioner is an independent oversight authority that was created prior to the Privacy Act by the 1991 Privacy Commissioner Act.[1379] The Privacy Commissioner oversees compliance with the Act, but does not function as a central data registration or notification authority. The Privacy Commissioner's principal powers and functions include promoting the objects of the Act, monitoring proposed legislation and government policies, dealing with complaints at first instance, approving and issuing codes of practice and authorizing special exemptions from the information privacy principles, and reviewing public sector information matching programs. As of June 30 2001, the Commissioner had 24 full time and 6 part-time staff.

[1378] See Re Application by L information stored in person's memory (1997) 3 HRNZ 716 (Complaints Review Tribunal).

[1379] Home Page <http://www.privacy.org.nz/>.

Complaints by individuals are initially filed with the Privacy Commissioner who attempts to conciliate the matter. In the year ending June 2001 the office received 881 new complaints and 6,563 enquiries. 806 complaints (new and from last year) were closed during the year. Eighty percent were resolved without issuing a final opinion.[1380] The Commissioner regards the power to investigate and to require answers during investigations as "a vital element" in securing such a high conciliation rate. When conciliation fails, the Proceedings Commissioner[1381] or the complainant (if the Proceedings Commissioner is unwilling) can bring the matter before the Complaints Review Tribunal, which can issue decisions and award declaratory relief, issue restraining or remedial orders, and award special and general damages up to NZ $200,000.

In March 2002, the Commission hosted a meeting of the International Working Group on Data Protection in Telecommunications, a group created by the International Conference of Data Protection and Privacy Commissioners. In conjunction with that meeting the Commissioner also organized a one-day symposium on freedom of information and privacy.[1382]

The Law Commission is currently undertaking a review of the legal protection of privacy rights and the working of the 1993 Privacy Act. In February 2002, the Commission issued a discussion paper "Protecting Personal Information from Disclosure" for public comment.[1383]   In the summer of 2001, the Mental Health Commission began a study of privacy procedures in mental health services. The Privacy Commissioner participated in the work of the review board. In February 2002, the board issued its report: "A Review of the Implementation of the Privacy Act and Health Information Privacy Code by Mental Health Units of District Health Boards."[1384]

New Zealand is one of a number of countries involved in negotiations with the European Commission concerning the "adequacy" of its privacy regime in relation to the 1995 European Union Data Protection Directive. Since 1998 the Commission has been urging the Government to introduce two minor amendments to the Privacy Act in order to secure a finding of adequacy. The first

---

[1380] New Zealand Privacy Commission, Annual Report for the year ended June 30, 2001, November 2001 available at <http://www.privacy.org.nz/recept/annrep01.pdf>.

[1381] The Proceedings Commissioner is a member of the Human Rights Commission, to which the Privacy Commissioner also belongs. The Proceedings Commissioner is empowered to take civil proceedings before the Complaints Review Tribunal on behalf of a complainant if conciliation fails.

[1382] International Symposium On Freedom Of Information And Privacy, Auckland, 28 March 2002, <http://www.privacy.org.nz/media/isfoip.html>.

[1383] Available at <http://www.lawcom.govt.nz/>.

[1384] Available at <http://www.mhc.govt.nz/publications/Publications/Privacy%20Review.pdf>.

amendment would remove the existing requirement that in order to make an access or correction request, an individual must be a New Zealand citizen, permanent resident or present in New Zealand at the time the request is made. The second would introduce a limited data export control to regulate the transfer of personal information outside New Zealand. In December 12, 2000 these changes were finally included in the Statutes Amendment Bill and submitted to Parliament. A statutes amendment bill is a procedure designed for the introduction of non-controversial legislation. Accordingly, it was expected that these amendments would be approved and enacted without delay.[1385] In the fall of 2001, however, one party withdrew its support of one of the amendments. In his annual report, the Privacy encouraged "those responsible for the business of the House of Representative [to] ensure that whatever vehicle these amendments proceed in is given priority."

The High Court ruled in July 2000 that the implementation of a nationwide drivers license system with a digitized photograph that was required by the 1998 Land Transport Act was legal. The law creates a national database of digitized photographs. The individual challenging the law appealed the ruling. The Court of Appeals rejected her appeal in April 2001 saying much of the case was based on misconceptions of the law.[1386]

The New Zealand Crimes Act and Misuse of Drugs Act govern the use of police interception powers.[1387] Interception warrants authorize not just the interception of communications but also the placing of listening devices. A judge authorizes warrants where there is reasonable grounds to believe that certain offences that been committed or are being contemplated. Emergency permits may be granted for the bugging of premises and, following the 1997 repeal of a prohibition, for telephonic interceptions. Those who illegally disclose the contents of private communications illegally intercepted face two years in prison. However, those who illegally disclose the contents of private communications lawfully intercepted are merely liable for a NZ$500 fine. In 2000/2001 the New Zealand Police sought and obtained 19 (new and renewed) interception warrants under the Misuse of Drugs Act and 20 (new and renewed) interception warrants under the Crimes Act. No applications were made for emergency permits under either

[1385] Office of the Privacy Commissioner, Press Release, "Proposed Amendments to the Privacy Act-addressing the questions of adequacy under the European Union Data Protection Directive, December 15, 2000 <http://www.privacy.org.nz/media/prppaam.html>.

[1386] "Photo licence appeal rejected," The Dominion (Wellington) April 12, 2001

[1387] Part XIA, Crimes Act 1961; Misuse of Drugs Act 1978.

statute.[1388] A total of 84 warrants (new and renewed) were obtained under the Telecommunications Amendment Act 1997 for obtaining call data analyzers (pen registers and trap and trace devices that obtain call information but not the contents of communications).

The New Zealand Security Intelligence Service (NZSIS), established under the New Zealand Security Intelligence Service Act of 1969, is also permitted to carry out electronic interceptions. The NZSIS has a staff of 115 and an annual budget of $11 million. The majority of it work is devoted to threats to national security.[1389] The Act was amended in 1999 to allow for the service to enter premises to install taps following a Court of Appeal case that prohibited entering of premises without a warrant. The amendment also created a "foreign interception warrant."[1390] Another amendment created a Commissioner of Security Warrants to jointly issue warrants with the Prime Minister.[1391] The Minister in Charge of the NZSIS is required to submit an annual report to the House of Representatives. During the year ending June 2001, the Minister reported that seventeen domestic interception warrants were in force. Of these, nine were new interception warrants and eight were carried over from the previous year. The average length of time for which these warrants were in force was 208 days.[1392] According to the Minister's report "the methods for interception and seizure used were listening devices and the copying of documents." The report also states that foreign interception warrants were in force during the year but does not give any statistics for these warrants.

One agency not governed by the restrictions imposed on law enforcement and the NZSIS is the Government Communications Security Bureau (GCSB), the signals intelligence (SIGINT) agency for New Zealand. The GSCB was established by Executive Authority in 1977 and focuses on foreign intelligence. Operating as a virtual branch of the United States National Security Agency, this agency maintains two intercept stations at Waihopai and Tangimoana. The Waihopai station routinely intercepts trans-Pacific and intra-Pacific communications and passes the collected intelligence to NSA headquarters. David Lange, a former Prime Minister of New Zealand, said he and other ministers were told very little

---

[1388] New Zealand Police Annual Report 2001, Information Required by Statute, October 24, 2001, available at <http://www.police.govt.nz/resources/2001/annualreport/>.

[1389] "SIS gives MPs new details of NZ terrorist links," by John Armstrong, New Zealand Herald, December 9, 2000, available at
<http://www.nzherald.co.nz/storydisplay.cfm?thesection=news&thesubsection=&storyID=163879>.

[1390] New Zealand Security Intelligence Service Amendment Act 1999.

[1391] New Zealand Security Intelligence Service Amendment (No 2) Act 1999.

[1392] Report of the New Zealand Security Intelligence Service to the House of Representatives for the year ended June 30, 2001, available at <http://www.nzsis.govt.nz/ar01/part2.html>.

about the operations of GCSB while they were in power. Of particular interest to GCSB and NSA are the communications of the governments of neighboring Pacific island states.[1393] GCSB was specifically exempted from the provisions of the Crimes Act in 1997.[1394] A Bill to place the GCSB on a statutory was introduced in early 2001 and is still pending. In August 2001, the Government announced that it is setting up a new unit within the Government Communications Security Bureau dedicated to the protection of nation's critical infrastructure from cyber threats by Internet hackers or computer viruses. The Centre for Critical Infrastructure Protection (CCIP) was scheduled to begin operations in April 2002.[1395]

The Government has proposed major new surveillance powers for these state agencies. The Crimes Amendment Bill (No. 6), introduced in November 2000, would prohibit the unauthorized interception of electronic communications and would make hacking and denial of service attacks illegal but would grant broad exemption to the police, the NZSIS and the GCSB, allowing them to secretly hack into individual's computers and intercept virtually all e-mail communications passing through New Zealand. The bill would require individuals to hand over computer passwords and encryption keys. The bill was approved by the Select Committee on Law and Order in July 2001 despite criticism from the Green party, the New Zealand Council for Civil Liberties and the Privacy Commissioner.[1396] The Privacy Commissioner appeared twice before the Committee and issued two reports on the bill.[1397] In his comments the Commissioner welcomed the broadening of laws against interception of private communications and the introduction of the new computer related offences but expressed 'serious misgivings' about the exemptions provided for state surveillance allowing them to hack into systems without interception warrants. As of July 2002 the Bill was still pending.

Even more controversial is the Telecommunications (Interception Capabilities) Bill currently being drafted by the Government. Similar to the United States

---

[1393] Nicky Hager, Secret Power: New Zealand's Role in the International Spy Network (Nelson, MZ: Craig Potton, 1996).

[1394] Crimes (Exemption of Listening Device) Order 1997 (SR 1997/145).

[1395] "New Zealand Center To Combat Cyber Threats," Newsbytes, August 8, 2001, available at <http://www.newsbytes.com/news/01/168792.html>.

[1396] New Zealand Crimes Bill Raises Cybersnooping Concerns, by Adam Creed, Newsbytes, July 23, 2001 <http://www.newsbytes.com/news/01/168208.html>.

[1397] Report by the Privacy Commissioner to the Minister of Justice on Supplementary Order Paper Non 85 to the Crimes Amendment Bill (No 6), December 12, 2000; Supplementary Report by the Privacy Commissioner to the Law and Order Committee in relation to Supplementary Order Paper Non 85 to the Crimes Amendment Bill (No 6), May 10, 2001. Both are available at <http://www.privacy.org.nz>.

Communications Assistance for Law Enforcement Act (CALEA) of 1994, this legislation would require all Internet Service Providers and telephone companies to upgrade their systems so that they are able to assist the police and intelligence agencies (GCSB and SIS) intercept communications. The legislation would also require a telecommunications operator to decrypt the communications of a customer if that operator had provided the encryption facility.[1398] It would not require individuals to hand over encryption keys.

Prior to introducing the proposals the Government sought the advice of the Law Reform Commission on whether such a requirement would violate section 21 of the New Zealand Bill of Rights on unreasonable searches and seizures. In its responsive report, issued in February 2002, the Law Reform Commission concluded that "the existence of comparable obligations in other democracies establishes reasonably conclusively either that the search is not thereby rendered unreasonable or that if there is a limitation of the rights described in section 21 it can be demonstrably justified in a free and democratic society." The Commission recommended that the law be amended to impose an obligation on third parties to provide all reasonable and necessary information and assistance (including passwords and decryption keys) to enable law enforcement officer(s) to access, copy or convert the data into intelligible form.[1399]

The Broadcasting Act of 1989 requires broadcasters to maintain standards that are consistent with 'the observance of good taste and decency...the maintenance of law and order and the privacy of the individual'.[1400] It establishes a Broadcasting Standards Authority (BSA) to oversee enforcement and to rule on complaints. The BSA has ruled on a number of privacy cases.[1401] Recently, particular controversy surrounded several television broadcasts unreasonably intruding on the privacy of children. In March 1999 one program, widely publicized in advance, revealed the results of a DNA paternity test live on TV with mother, father and young child present.[1402] The Broadcasting Amendment Act of 2000, which came into effect on July 1, 2000, empowers the BSA to encourage the development and observance by broadcasters of codes of broadcasting practice in relation to the privacy of the individual.

[1398] New Zealand Government Executive Press Release, "Interception Capability – Government Decisions," March 21, 2002, available at <http://www.executive.govt.nz/speechaptercfm?speechralph=37658&SR=0>.

[1399] New Zealand Law Reform Commission, Study Paper 12, "Electronic Technology And Police Investigations: Some Issues," February 2002, available at <http://www.lawcom.govt.nz/Documents/Publications/SP%2012%2028-2-02.pdf>.

[1400] Available online at <http://www.spectrum.net.nz/archive/acts.shtml>.

[1401] See for example "Recent New Zealand Case Law on Privacy: Part II: the Broadcasting Standards Authority, the Media and Employment," by Tim McBride, Privacy Law & Reporter, February 2000, at 133.

[1402] "Dna Test Matches Father and Son on TV," The Dominion (Wellington) March 30, 1999.

The Criminal Investigations (Blood Samples) Act of 1995 authorized the establishment of a national DNA databank. Police have to get an order from a High Court judge before a compulsory test can be conducted and they can only take samples from suspects of violent crimes and convicted burglars. Voluntary samples from anybody can be included in the databank. In October 2000, police were ordered to reduce the number of voluntary DNA due to budgetary concerns. By 2002, however, it was reported that police were being advised to increase this number again and to try and obtain voluntary samples from anyone arrested with a prior criminal record.[1403] In February 2001 the Justice Minister announced that he plans to introduce legislation to allow DNA samples to be taken from burglary suspects. [1404] As of June 2001, the total number of DNA profiles stored in the national database was 17,188. Of these, 13,629 were obtained by consent and 3,559 were obtained by compulsory order.[1405] In May 2002, a new $3 million purpose-built laboratory was opened in Auckland for forensic DNA testing.[1406] Testing is carried out by the Institute of Environmental Science and Research (ESR).

The Official Information Act of 1982[1407] and the Local Government Official Information and Meetings Act of 1987[1408] are freedom of information laws governing the public sector. There are significant interconnections between this freedom of information legislation and the Privacy Act in subject matter, administration, and jurisprudence, so much so that the three enactments may be viewed, in relation to access to information, as complementary components of one overall statutory scheme. The Office of the Ombudsman supervises enforcement.[1409] The Ombudsman hears around 1,100 complaints each year under the Official Information Act and 170 each year under the Local Government Official Information and Meetings Act. The Privacy Commissioner and the Ombudsmen work closely together Official Information Act requests involve privacy issues.

New Zealand is a member of the Organization for Economic Cooperation and Development and has adopted the OECD Guidelines on the Protection of Privacy and Transborder Flows of Personal Data.

[1403] "Police DNA Drive," The Evening Post (Wellington) March 21, 2002.

[1404] "Police Say They Can Afford Bigger DNA Database," The Dominion (Wellington) February 13, 2001.

[1405] New Zealand Police Annual Report 2001, supra n.1388.

[1406] "DNA Laboratory to be Ready in May," The Dominion (Wellington), February 23, 2002.

[1407] Official Information Act 1982.

[1408] Local Government Official Information and Meetings Act 1987.

[1409] Homepage <http://www.ombudsmen.govt.nz/>.

Self-governing territories

The Privacy Act does not apply to self-governing territories associated with New Zealand, the Cook Islands and Niue. Nor does it apply to the soon-to-be self-governing territory of Tokelau.

Kingdom of Norway

The Norwegian Constitution of 1814 does not have a specific provision dealing with the protection of privacy.[1410] The closest provision is section 102, which prohibits searches of private homes except in "criminal cases." More generally, section 110c of the Constitution places state authorities under an express duty to "respect and secure human rights." In 1952, the Norwegian Supreme Court held that there exists in Norwegian law a general legal protection of "personality" which embraces a right to privacy. This protection of personality exists independently of statutory authority but helps form the basis of the latter (including data protection legislation), and can be applied by the courts on a case-by-case basis.[1411]

The Data Inspectorate (Datatilsynet), created by the Personal Data Registers Act of 1978, is an independent administration body set up under the Ministry of Justice in 1980.[1412] The Inspectorate employed twenty-two staff members as of 1999. The responsibilities of the Inspectorate are as follows: accept applications for licenses for data registers , evaluate the licenses, enforce the privacy laws and regulations, and provide information about the protection of privacy and the rules of data registers. The Inspectorate can conduct inspections and impose sanctions. Decisions of the Inspectorate can be appealed to the Ministry of Justice. As of 1999, the Inspectorate has issued 65,000 licenses.

The Personal Data Registers Act of 2000 went into effect on January 1, 2001, and it replaced the Personal Data Registers Act of 1978.[1413] Although Norway is not a member of the European Union, the Act was designed to update Norwegian law to comply with the European Union Directive since Norway was a party to the 1992 Agreement on the European Economic Area (EEA), which required

---

[1410] The Constitution of the Kingdom of Norway, available at <http://odin.dep.no/ud/nornytt/uda-121.html>.

[1411] Supreme Court decision of 13 December 1952, reported in Rt. 1952, at 1217.

[1412] Homepage <http://www.datatilsynet.no/>.

[1413] LOV 2000-04-14 nr 31: Lov om behandling av personopplysninger (personopplysningsloven), available at <http://www.lovdata.no/all/hl-20000414-031.html>.

compliance with the Directive.[1414] It covers all data linked directly to individuals. The Act applies to both the public and private sectors, and it covers both manual and computerized registers. The Act requires that licenses must be acquired from the Data Inspectorate to create data registers for credit reporters, data processing of personal information for third party ads, addressing and distribution services that consist of the sale or supply of addresses or advertising materials, and opinion polls and market surveys. Sensitive information, such as racial origin, religion, or criminal record, cannot be used in a data register unless the information is necessitated by the purpose of the data register as determined by the Data Inspectorate. The Inspectorate also has the power to make on-site visits to data register licensees to determine compliance with the Act.

The Personal Data Registers Act of 2000 provides strong protections for data subjects about whom data has been collected. The Act provides that all persons have a right to demand information concerning themselves. Also, according to the Act, all incorrect data must be corrected and all persons shall have the right to block their name from use. Finally, data cannot be transferred to another country without the permission of the Data Inspectorate, and the data cannot be transferred to a country with less protection than that provided for in the European Union Directive.[1415] Also similar to the European Union Directive, data subjects must be informed that their personal data is being collected and the name of the controller collecting the personal data.[1416] Violations of the Personal Data Registers Act of 2000 are punishable by fines or imprisonment of up to one year.

The new law also provides specific rules for video surveillance. Video Surveillance that does not create actual files falls under weaker protection than regular personal data registers. However, if the surveillance results in the actual recording of pictures, then the surveillance falls in the Act and the Data Inspectorate must be informed.[1417] The Inspectorate has the power to intervene and prohibit the surveillance. Finally, if the video surveillance is performed in a public place, there must be clear notice such as a sign.[1418] However, the Criminal Procedure Act allows police to perform covert video surveillance of public areas

---

[1414] Lee A. Bygrave & Ann Helen Aaro, International Privacy, Publicity, and Personality Law, (London: Butterworths, 2001), at 333-346.

[1415] Dag Wiese Schartum, Nordic Data Protection, (Copenhagen: DJOF Publishing, 2001).

[1416] Christopher Millard & Mark Ford, Data Protection Laws of the World, (London: Sweet & Maxwell, 2000).

[1417] Dag Wiese Schartum, supra n.1415.

[1418] Christopher Millard, supra n.1416.

if the surveillance is of "essential significance" for investigating suspected criminal conduct that can result in more than six years in prison.[1419]

The Personal Data Registers Act of 2000 provides an exception for the processing of personal data for historical, statistical, or scientific purposes that are not incompatible with the original purposes of the data collection if "the public interest in the process clearly outweighs any inconvenience to the data subject."[1420] It also provides that the Data Inspectorate cannot license data registers related to national security or preparedness.

Wiretapping requires the permission of a tribunal and is initially limited to four weeks.[1421] The total number of telephones monitored was 360 in 1990, 467 in 1991, 426 in 1992, 402 in 1993, 541 in 1994 and 534 in 1995.[1422] A Supervisory Board reviews the warrants to ensure the adequacy of the protections. A Parliamentary Commission of Inquiry (The Lund Commission) was created in 1994 to investigate the post-World War II surveillance practices of Norwegian police and security services. The Commission delivered a 600 page report in 1996, causing a great deal of public and political debate on account of its finding that much of the undercover surveillance practices, including wiretapping of left wing political groups until 1989, had been instituted and/or conducted illegally and that the courts had not generally been strong enough in their oversight.[1423] This included keeping files on children as young as eleven years old.

Provisions of the Criminal Procedure Act allow for wiretapping without the permission of the tribunal in two circumstances. First, section 16a allows wiretapping for narcotics investigations with the permission of a magistrate court. Second, section 216b allows wiretapping for "grounded suspicion" of a national security threat with the permission of a magistrate court.[1424]

A new act to monitor the secret services was approved in 1995 following the Commission's recommendations.[1425] It created a new Control Committee to monitor the activities of the Police Security Services, the Defense Security Services and the Defense Intelligence Services. The former Minister of Justice

---

[1419] Lee A. Bygrave & Ann Helen Aaro, supra n.1414.

[1420] Christopher Millard, supra n.1416.

[1421] Law of 17 December 1976, Law of 24 Juin 1915. Criminal Procedure Act, chapter 16 a, by Act No. 52 of 5 June 1992. See also Regulation No. 281 of 31 March 1995 on Telephone Monitoring in Narcotics Cases.

[1422] Government of Norway report to the UN Human Rights Commission, CCPR/C/115/Add.2, May 26, 1997.

[1423] "Judicial Inquiry into Norwegian Secret Surveillance," Fortress Europe, FECL 43, April/May 1996.

[1424] Lee A. Bygrave & Ann Helen Aaro, supra n.1414.

[1425] Act No. 7 of 3 February 1995 on the Control of the Secret Services.

and the head of the Norwegian security police (POT) were forced to resign from the government in 1996 after it was revealed that the POT had placed a member of the Lund Commission under surveillance and requested a copy of her Stasi file from the German authorities four times.[1426] Later it was discovered that the POT had also investigated several key members of the Storting who have oversight over the agency.[1427] In 1997, the Parliament agreed to allow people who were under surveillance by the POT to review their records and to obtain compensation if the surveillance was unlawful. The POT has records on over 50,000 people.[1428]

The Telecommunications Act imposes a duty of confidentiality on telecommunications providers.[1429] However, the Telecommunications Authority can demand information for investigations. The Norwegian police in January 2000 called for new laws requiring telecommunications providers and Internet Service Providers to keep extensive logs of usage for six months to one year.[1430]

A large number of other pieces of legislation contain provisions relevant to privacy and data protection. These include the Administrative Procedures Act of 1967,[1431] and the Criminal Code of 1902.[1432] The criminal code first prohibited the publication of information relating to the "personal or domestic affairs" in 1889.[1433] The Criminal code also prohibits the unauthorized opening of sealed correspondence, including cracking security mechanisms.[1434] The Criminal Code also prohibits covert monitoring or recording of telephone conversations or other conversations in closed settings.[1435] In December of 2000, a Norwegian news service reported that Norwegian military and police intelligence units entered into an agreement with the country's fifteen largest companies to perform Internet surveillance. The system was reported to be similar to the United States FBI's carnivore system, which intercepts and monitors any information sent across the Internet. The Norwegian Justice Department confirmed the existence of the system, but sources claimed that it has not been implemented on a large

---

[1426] "Minister resigns," Statewatch bulletin, November-December 1996, Volume 6, Number 1.

[1427] FECL 49 (December 1996/January 1997).

[1428] "Parliament says people can see files," Statewatch bulletin, May-June 1997, Volume 7, Number 3.

[1429] The Telecommunications Act of 23 June 1995.

[1430] "Norwegian police has called for law on logging," M2 Communications, January 19, 2000.

[1431] Administrative Procedures Act of 1967.

[1432] Almindelig borgerlig Straffelov 22 mai 1902 nr 10.

[1433] See Prof. Dr. Juris Jon Bing, Data Protection in Norway, 1996, available at <http://www.jus.uio.no/iri/rettsinfo/lib/papers/dp_norway/dp_norway.html>.

[1434] Lee A. Bygrave & Ann Helen Aaro, supra n.1414.

[1435] Id.

scale. The Norwegian Parliament has demanded a review of the project, which was created to defend the national IT infrastructure.

The Public Access to Documents in the (Public) Administration provides for public access to government records.[1436] Under the Act, there is a broad right of access to records. The Act has been in effect since 1971. The Act does not apply to records held by the Storting (Parliament), the Office of the Auditor General, the Storting's Ombudsman for Public Administration or other institutions of the Storting. There are exemptions for internal documents; information that "could be detrimental to the security of the realm, national defence or relations with foreign states or international organizations"; subject to a duty of secrecy; "in the interests of proper execution of the financial, pay or personnel management"; the minutes of the Council of State, photographs of persons entered in a personal data register; complaints, reports and other documents concerning breaches of the law; answers to examinations or similar tests; and documents prepared by a ministry in connection with annual fiscal budgets. The King can make a determination that historical documents in the archive that are otherwise exempted can be publicly released. If access is denied, individuals can appeal to a higher authority under the act and then to a court.

A news report early in the year 2000 indicated that Norway's Data Protection Registrar intended to investigate the fused banking giant Postbanken/DnB, which had been criticized for using postmen to collect information and make lists of potential clients. The investigations were to determine whether the postmen and women were breaching regulations governing the privacy of postal service clients. An article published in February, 2002, indicates the state welfare agency, Trygdeetaten, would like to order banks to advise of any "unusual" transactions involving accounts held by welfare recipients. The proposal, which would require the relaxation of existing privacy laws, has prompted opposition from the banking industry and some politicians. The banking industry has warned against law changes which would threaten client confidentiality. The agency, however, feels that it is the only way they will be able to "crack down" on welfare cheating.

Norway is a member of the Council of Europe and has signed and ratified the Convention for the Protection of Individuals with Regard to Automatic Processing of Personal Data (ETS No. 108) and has signed ETS No. 181.[1437] It

---

[1436] The Freedom of Information Act of 1970, amended by Act No. 47 of 11 June 1982 and Act no. 86 of 17 December 1982 and Act of 10 January 1997 No. 7.

[1437] Signed March 13, 1981; Ratified February 20, 1984; Entered into Force October 1, 1985.

has signed and ratified the European Convention for the Protection of Human Rights and Fundamental Freedoms.[1438] In Novmber 2001, Norway signed the Council of Europe's Convention for Cybercrime.[1439] It is a member of the Organization for Economic Cooperation and Development and has adopted the OECD Guidelines on the Protection of Privacy and Transborder Flows of Personal Data.

Republic of Peru

The 1993 Constitution sets out extensive privacy, data protection and freedom of information rights.[1440] Article 2 states, "Every person has the right: To solicit information that one needs without disclosing the reason, and to receive that information from any public entity within the period specified by law, at a reasonable cost. Information that affects personal intimacy and that is expressly excluded by law or for reasons of national security is not subject to disclosure. Secret bank information or tax information can be accessed by judicial order, the National Prosecutor, or a Congressional investigative commission, in accordance with law and only insofar as it relates to a case under investigation. V. To be assured that information services, whether computerized or not, public or private, do not provide information that affects personal and family intimacy. VI. To honor and good reputation, to personal and family intimacy, both as to voice and image. Every person affected by untrue or inexact statements or aggrieved by any medium of social communication has the right to free, immediate and proportional rectification, without prejudice to responsibilities imposed by law…IX. To secrecy and the inviolability of communications and private documents. Communications, telecommunications or instruments of communication, may be opened, seized, intercepted or inspected only under judicial authorization and with the protections specified by law. All matters unconnected with the fact that motivates the examination are to be guarded from disclosure. Private documents obtained in violation of this precept have no legal effect. Books, ledgers, and accounting and administrative documents are subject to inspection or investigation by the competent authority in conformity with law. Actions taken in this respect may not include withdrawal or seizure, except by judicial order."

[1438] Signed November 11, 1950; Ratified January 15, 1952; Entered into Force September 3, 1953.

[1439] Signed November 23, 2001.

[1440] Constitution of Peru, available at <http://www.asesor.com.pe/teleley/5000%2Din.htm>.

A Data Protection Bill was introduced in Parliament by the Union del Peru political party in September 1999.[1441] The bill is based on the new Spanish Data Protection Act, the Italian Data Privacy Act, the Australian Privacy Act, the United States Restatement of Torts and the European Union Data Protection Directive. The bill proposes the creation of a Data Protection Commissioner. If approved, the bill will make Peru fully compatible with the European Union Directive legal system. In March 2002, the Ministry of Justice published a Resolution in the Official Gazette establishing a special commission to draft a new Data Protection Bill.[1442]

In August 2001, Peru enacted a data protection law covering private credit reporting agencies.[1443] The law puts in place a set of principles to protect both individuals and companies whose information is recorded in databases. It regulates the incorporation of credit bureaus, qualifications for shareholders of these companies, and the sources of information they can use. Similar to Article 11 of European Union Directive, it sets out the information that must be provided to the data subject where the data has not been obtained from him or her. In addition, the law prohibits credit bureaus from collecting (1) sensitive information, (2) data violating the confidentiality of bank or tax records; (3) inaccurate or outdated information; (4) bankruptcy records older than 5 years; (4) other debtor records 5 years after the debt was paid. It provides that credit agencies must adopt security measures and grants individuals have the following rights: (1) the right to access to information; (2) the right to modify or cancel their personal data; (3) judicial relief for non-consumers or consumer protection law. The law also creates strict liability for damages. The Government Agency for Consumer Protection is in charge of applying fines for violation of the law and issuing injunctions to correct errors.

Article 154 of the Penal Code[1444] states that "a person who violates personal or family privacy, whether by watching, listening to or recording an act, a word, a piece of writing or an image using technical instruments or processes and other means, shall be punished with imprisonment for not more than two years."[1445]

[1441] Proyecto No. 5233, Ley Sobre La Privacidad de los Datos Informaticos y la Creacion del Comisionado paragraph la Proteccion de la Privacidad, presentado por miembros del grupo parlamentario del Partido Popular Cristiano, 1999.

[1442] Minsterial Resolution No. 094-2002-JUS.

[1443] Law No. 27489. Ley que Regula las Centrales Privadas de Información de Riesgos y de Protección al Titular de la información, available at
<http://www.leyes.congreso.gob.pe/DetalleLey.asp?wC_NORMA=6&wN_LEY=27489>.
1444 Código Penal, available at
<http://www.congreso.gob.pe/out_of_domain.asp?URL=http%3A//www.leyes.congreso.gob.pe/>.

[1445] The United Nations High Commissioner For Human Rights, Third periodic report of Peru: CCPR/C/83/Add.1, March 21, 1995.

Article 157 criminalizes the disclosure of sensitive data including "political and religious convictions" and other aspects of intimate life.

Article 161 of the Penal Code states "that a person who unlawfully opens a letter, document, telegram, radio telegram, telephone message or other document of a similar nature that is not addressed to him, or unlawfully takes possession of any such document even if it is open, shall be liable to imprisonment of not more than 2 years and to 60 to 90 days' fine."[1446] A sentence of not less than one year nor more than three years is to be given to any "person who unlawfully interferes with or listens to a telephone or similar conversation." Public servants guilty of the same crime must serve not less than three or more than five years and must be dismissed from their post. A person who unlawfully tampers with, deletes, or misdirects "the address on a letter or telegram," but does not open it, "is liable to 20 to 52 days' community service."

In April 2002, Peru passed a new law to govern the interception of communications and private documents. [1447] Under the new law, a judicial warrant is needed to seize documents or intercept communications. The law requires telecommunications operators to provide all necessary technical assistance and facilities to carry out interceptions. The powers may be used in the investigation of crimes including kidnapping, trafficking of minors, drug trafficking, customs violations, terrorism, crimes against the humanity, and treason.

In its most recent report on Human Rights Practices, the United States Department of State noted that "unlike in previous years, there were few complaints that the Government violated " rights to privacy of communications. In the past there were numerous reports of abuse of surveillance authority by Peru's National Intelligence Service (Servicio Nacional de Inteligencia or SIN). The SIN conducted widespread surveillance and illegal phone tapping of government ministers and judges assigned to constitutional cases, beginning in the early 1990s. Army agents used sophisticated Israeli phone-tapping equipment to monitor telephone conversations, and copies of the conversations were delivered to Montesinos.[1448] The SIN maintains close ties with the United States Central Intelligence Agency, including a covert assistance program to combat

---

[1446] The United Nations High Commissioner For Human Rights. Third periodic report of Peru: 21/03/95. CCPR/C/83/Add.1.

1447 Law 27697. Ley que otorga facultad al fiscal paragraph la intervención y control de comunicaciones y documentos privados en caso excepcional . Publicada en el Diario Oficial El Peruano el 12 de Abril del 2002. http://www.leyes.congreso.gob.pe/LeyNume.asp

[1448] "Former Agent Accuses Peru Spy Chief," AP, March 17, 1998.

drug trafficking.[1449] The SIN has allegedly conducted a nationwide surveillance campaign with the sole purpose of intimidating political opposition figures. In 1990, an opposition congressman's house was blown up after he delivered a congressional report on domestic surveillance of opposition politicians, journalists, human rights workers and companies suspected of tax evasion.[1450] In August, 1997 former UN Secretary General Javier Perez de Cuellar filed charges against the SIN with the Peruvian Attorney General and the Inter-American Human Rights Commission for taping 1,000 conversations he made from his home telephone between October 1994 and August 1995 while he ran for President against Alberto Fujimori.[1451] President Fujimori absolved the SIN of the accusations against it, asserting that private individuals with commercial scanners had carried out the wiretapping.[1452] The allegations prompted the resignation of the Defense Minister and a special prosecutor was appointed to investigate the incident.[1453] The Defense Commission's three-month inquiry confirmed accusations of the widespread wiretapping but concluded that there was no evidence the intelligence services carried out the spying.[1454] A member of Congress and several journalists filed a suit on grounds that their constitutional rights had been violated (an *acción de amparo*), and to put an end to the tapping of their telephone calls.[1455]

In July 2000 a Computer Crimes Act was adopted and is codified in Article 207(A)(B)(C) of the Penal Code.[1456] The Act prohibits unlawful access, use, interference or damage to a system, database, or network of computers. Sanctions include up to five years imprisonment.

The Organic Law of the National Identification Registry and Civil Society (1995) created an autonomous agency which may "collaborate with the exercise of the functions of pertinent political and judicial authorities in order to identify persons" but is "vigilant regarding restrictions with respect to the privacy and identity of the person" and "guarantees the privacy of data relative to the persons

---

[1449] Human Rights Watch, World Report 1998, available at
<http://www.hrw.org/hrw/worldreport/Americas.htm>.

[1450] "As Lima Talks Hit Snag, Some Ex-Hostages Are Complaining," The New York Times, January 13, 1997.

[1451] "Former U.N. chief charges Peru tapped his phone," Reuters, August 4, 1997.

[1452] "President Fujimori denies intelligence services behind phone-tapping," America Television, Lima, BBC Summary of World Broadcasts, July 19, 1997.

[1453] "Peru defense head resigns in crisis," Reuters, July 17, 1997.

[1454] "Peru Congress probe fails to catch phonetappers," Reuters World Report, May 29, 1998.

[1455] International Freedom of Expression eXchange (IFEX) Clearing House (Toronto), July 21, 1997
<http://www.ifex.org/alert/00002190.html>.

1456 Ley Nª 27309 publicada en el Diario Oficial el Peruano el 17 julio 2000 incorpora el artículo 207 A, B y C del Código Penal.

who are registered." The Law also requires all persons to carry a National Identity Document featuring a corresponding number, photograph and fingerprint.[1457] The court must provide all personal data kept on file at the Public Registry upon request within 15 days.[1458] In January 2002, a new law creating a National Registry of Persons with Disabilities was adopted.[1459] The registry will be administered by the National Council of Integration of Persons with Disabalities (CONADIS).

Freedom of information is constitutionally protected under the right of habeas data. The first case to test the habeas data clause, which reviewed clause 7 of Article 2, was brought in the criminal court system in January 1994. The Supreme Court ruled in March 1994 that the case should not have been brought in the criminal courts, nullified all previous decisions on the case, and ordered it resubmitted to the civil court system.[1460] Several cases have allowed the courts to establish their jurisdiction over, and support for, habeas data. In 1996 the Supreme Court, citing clause 5 of Article 2 of the Constitution, ordered the Ministry of Energy and Mines to release environmental surveys of a private mining operation to the Peruvian Society of Environmental Rights.[1461] Also in 1996, the Supreme Court sided with the Civil Labor Association against the General Director of Mining and ordered the release of an environmental impact study submitted by the Southern Perú Cooper Corporation.[1462]

In May 1994, Law N° 26301 was passed in order to set temporary legal standards for the legal application of habeas data.[1463] The Law requires that all habeas data actions be notarized, although reasons for the requested action need not be given, and filed with the legal authority from which information or an action is desired. The Law sets out the time periods and procedures for taking actions under clauses 5, 6 and/or 7 of Article 2 of the Constitution. The Law was updated in

---

[1457] Ley Organica Del Registro Nacional De Identificacion Y Estado Civil, Ley No. 26497, July 11, 1995. <http://www.congreso.gob.pe/ccd/leyes/cronos/1995/ley26497.htm>.

[1458] Ley de aplicación de la acción constitucional del habeas data, Ley No. 26301, Nov. 13, 1995, available at <http://www.asesor.com.pe/teleley/bull505.htm>.

1459 Ley General de la Persona con Discapacidad Nª 27050, available at <http://www.leyes.congreso.gob.pe/Imagenes/Leyes/27050.pdf>.

[1460] "AUTOS & VISTOS, "Comentarios jurisprudenciales," Colegio de Abogados de Lima y Gaceta Juridica, January, 1996, 41-53.

[1461] VerExp. N° 1658-95, published in the Diario Oficial El Peruano, "Jurisprudencia" September 4, 1996, 2297.

[1462] VerExp. N° 263-96. published in the Diario Oficial El Peruano, December 28, 1996, 2698.

[1463] Ley N° 26301, Aprueban Ley Referida a la Aplicacio de la Accion Constitucional de Habeas Data, May 2, 1994, available at <http://www.asesor.com.pe/teleley/bull505.htm>.

June 1995 to give a right of action, provide greater access to records, and to limit its use as a means of censorship.[1464]

In June 2002, the Parliament approved a long awaited Transparency and Access to Information of the Public Administration Law.[1465] The law establishes a general principle that State information belongs to the public. The Peruvian Press Council, which led the call for access to information has called the law "a step in the right direction" but says that it needs to be made stronger "to bring an end to the culture of secrecy and enable the State to work toward greater transparency."[1466]

Peru signed the American Convention on Human Rights on July 28, 1978, but withdrew from the jurisdiction of the American Court of Human Rights in July 1999.

Republic of the Philippines

Article III of the Constitution of the Philippines contains the Bill of Rights. Section 1 of the Bill of Rights states that the "Congress shall give highest priority to the enactment of measures that protect and enhance the right of all the people to human dignity."[1467] Section 2 states that "the right of the people to be secure in their persons, houses, papers, and effects against unreasonable searches and seizures of whatever nature and for any purpose shall be inviolable, and no search warrant or warrant of arrest shall issue except upon probable cause to be determined personally by the judge after examination under oath or affirmation of the complainant and the witnesses he may produce, and particularly describing the place to be searched and the persons or things to be seized."[1468] Section 3(1) states that the "privacy of communication and correspondence shall be inviolable except upon lawful order of the court, or when public safety or order requires otherwise, as prescribed by law."[1469] It further states that "any evidence obtained in violation of this or the preceding section shall be inadmissible for any purpose

---

[1464] IFEX, "Habeas Data law modified and approved," 1995/04/25; IFEX, "President's Office promulgates reforms to Habeas Data laws," 1995/06/12.

[1465] Ley de Transparencia y Acceso a la Información. Proyecto aprobado el 27 de Junio del 2002 pero aun no publicado en el diario Oficial El Peruano.

[1466] Elizabeth Cavero, Interview with Jorge Santiestevan de Noriega Legal Counsel, Peruvian Press Council, La Republica, June 29, 2002. Translation by Freedominfo.org, available at <http://www.freedominfo.org/news/peru1/>.

[1467] Constitution of the Philippines, article. VIII, § 1.

[1468] Id., § 2.

[1469] Id., § 3(1).

---

in any proceeding." Section 7 states that "the right of the people to information on matters of public concern shall be recognized. Access to official records, and to documents and papers pertaining to official acts, transactions, or decisions, as well as to government research data used as basis for policy development, shall be afforded the citizen, subject to such limitations as may be provided by law."[1470]

The Supreme Court ruled in July 1998 that Administrative Order No. 308, the Adoption of a National Computerized Identification Reference System, introduced by former President Ramos in 1996, was unconstitutional. The Court found the order, would "put our people's right to privacy in clear and present danger... No one will refuse to get this ID for no one can avoid dealing with government. It is thus clear as daylight that without the ID, a citizen will have difficulty exercising his rights and enjoying his privileges." While stating that all laws invasive of privacy would be subject to "strict scrutiny," the Court also was careful to note that "the right to privacy does not bar all incursions to privacy."[1471] President Joseph Estrada reiterated his support for the use of a national identification system in August 1998 stating that only criminals are against a national ID.[1472] Justice Secretary Serafin Cuevas authorized the National Statistics Office (NSO) to proceed to use the population reference number (PRN) for the Civil Registry System-Information Technology Project (CRS-ITP) on August 14, claiming that it is not covered by the decision.[1473]

There is no general data protection law but there is a recognized right of privacy in civil law.[1474] The Civil Code of the Philippines states that "[e]very person shall respect the dignity, personality, privacy, and peace of mind of his neighbors and other persons," and punishes acts that violate privacy by private citizens, public officers, or employees of private companies.[1475]

Article 26 of the Civil Code states that "every person shall respect the dignity, personality, privacy and peace of mind of his neighbors and other persons. The

---

[1470] Id., § 7.

[1471] Philippine Supreme Court Decision of the National ID System, July 23, 1998, G.R. 127685, available at <http://bknet.org/laws/nationalid.html>.

[1472] "Erap wants nat'l ID system (Only criminals disagree with it, says the President)," Business World (Manila), August 12, 1998.

[1473] Opinion Number 91; See "Foundation laid for proposed Nat'l ID," Business World (Manila), August 14, 1998.

[1474] Cordero v. Buigasco, 34130-R, April 17, 1972, 17 CAR (2s) 539; Jaworski v. Jadwani, CV-66405, December 15, 1983.

[1475] Civil Code, article 26; See n. 35 of the Philippine Supreme Court Decision of the National ID System, supra n.1471.

---

following and similar acts, though they may not constitute a criminal offense, shall produce a cause of action for damages, prevention and other relief:

(1) Prying into the privacy of another's residence:
(2) Meddling with or disturbing the private life or family relations of another;
(3) Intriguing to cause another to be alienated from his friends;
(4) Vexing or humiliating another on account of his religious beliefs, lowly station in life, place of birth, physical defect, or other personal condition.[1476]

Article 32(11) of the Civil Code states that "any public officer or employee, or any private individual, who directly or indirectly obstructs, defeats, violates or in any manner impedes or impairs the privacy of communication and correspondence shall be liable to the latter for damages."[1477]

The Philippines has only one law on data transfer, Presidential Decree No. 1718 ("P.D. 1718") entitled "Providing For Incentives In The Pursuit of Economic Development Programs By Restricting The Use of Documents and Information Vital To The National Interest in Certain Proceedings and Processes." While the law was passed in 1980, it lacks force because rules and regulations have not been issued to allow enforcement. Broadly, P.D. 1718 prohibits the export of all documents and information from the Philippines to other countries that may adversely affect the interests of Philippine corporations, individuals, or government agencies. P.D. 1718 contains exceptions for exportation of information that are a matter of form, in connection with business transactions or negotiations that require them, in compliance with international agreements, or made pursuant to authority granted by the designated representative of the President.[1478]

Bank records are protected by the Bank Secrecy Act[1479] and the Secrecy of Bank Deposits Act,[1480] the latter provides that all deposits of whatever nature with banks or banking institutions are absolutely confidential and may not be examined, inquired, or looked into by any person, government official, bureau or office, absent exceptional circumstances. Those circumstances include: the

---

[1476] Civil Code, article 26.
[1477] Id., article 32(11).
[1478] E-com Legal Guide, The Philippines, Christopher Lim, Baker & McKenzie, Manila, January 2001.
[1479] Bank Secrecy Act, No. 7653.
[1480] Secrecy of Bank Deposits Act, No. 1405.

written permission of the depositor, cases of impeachment, court orders in cases of bribery or dereliction of duty of public officials, cases where the money deposited or invested is the subject matter of litigation, and cases covered by the Anti-Graft and Corrupt Practices Act.[1481] Ernest Leung, the president of the Philippine Deposit Insurance Corporation, has made several attempts to eliminate the deposit secrecy act because he believes that no less than total access can ensure the stability of the Philippines banking system.[1482] In March 2001, the Senate debated a proposal in to force three million citizens to file an annual "Statement of Assets and Liabilities."[1483]

In May 2000, the ILOVEYOU email virus was traced to a hacker in the Philippines, focusing international attention on the country's cyberlaw regime. The lack of any internet-specific laws frustrated investigation efforts, and prosecutors finally were able to gain a warrant under the Access Devices Regulation Act of 1998,[1484] a law intended to punish credit card fraud that outlaws the use of unauthorized access devices to obtain goods or services broadly.[1485]

On the heels of the virus attack, in May, President Joseph Estrada signed into law the Electronic Commerce Act of 2000.[1486] Section 3(e) of the Electronic Commerce Act of 2000[1487] stipulates the "protection of users, in particular with regard to privacy, confidentiality, anonymity and content control" through policies "driven by choice, individual empowerment, and industry-led solutions." Further, wherever possible, "business should make available to consumers and, where appropriate, business users the means to exercise choice with respect to privacy, confidentiality, content control and, under appropriate circumstances, anonymity."[1488] Section 23 mandates a minimum fine of PP100,000 (~$2000 USD) and a prison term of 6 months to 3 years for unlawful and unauthorized access to computer systems. Section 31 provides that only individuals with legal right of possession shall be granted access to electronic files or electronic keys. Section 32 imposes an obligation of confidentiality on persons receiving

---

[1481] Internet Banking – Key Legal Considerations, Natividad Kwan and Cornelio B. Abuda, Baker & McKenzie, Manila, November 2000.

[1482] "Bangko Sentral favor deposit secrecy lifting," Business World (Manila), (January 17, 2000).

[1483] House Bill 5345.

[1484] Access Devices Regulation Act of 1998, No. 8484.

[1485] Id.

[1486] Electronic Commerce Act of 2000, No 8972.

[1487] Electronic Commerce Act of 2000, No. 8792.

[1488] Id., § 3(e).

electronic data, keys, messages, or other information not to convey it to any other person.[1489]

In June of 2001 the Philippine National Bureau of Investigation announced their intention to bring the first formal hacking and piracy charges under the Electronic Commerce Act. The charges involve two former employees of a business school who allegedly broke into the school's computer system and stole an undisclosed amount of proprietary digital material.[1490]

While restrictions on search and seizure within private homes are generally respected, searches without warrants do occur. In August of 2000, the Philippine National Police (PNP) conducted random searches of person for illegal firearms at checkpoints in Manila that their own government characterized as in violation of citizen's privacy rights.[1491]

The Act to Prohibit and Penalize Wire Tapping and Other Related Violations of the Privacy of Communication and for Other Purposes[1492] contains a notwithstanding clause that supersedes all inconsistent statutes.[1493] Section 1 states that all parties to a communication must give permission for a recorded wiretap or intercept and makes it illegal to knowingly possess any recording made in prohibition of this law, unless it is evidence for a trial, civil or criminal.[1494] Section 2 assesses liability for any person who contributes to the actions described in § 1.[1495] Section 3 provides certain exceptions to the conditions found in §§ 1-2 but adopts stringent criteria for wiretap warrants, including the identity of the wiretap target; who may execute the warrant; reasonable grounds that a crime has been, is or will be committed; and, a reasonable belief that the evidence obtained via the wiretap will aid in a conviction or prevention of a crime.[1496] Further, predicate offences – or offences for which a court may authorize a wiretap – are limited to a number of

---

[1489] Internet Banking – Key Legal Considerations, Natividad Kwan and Cornelio B. Abuda, Baker & McKenzie, Manila, November 2000.

[1490] "Philippines' NBI Clamps Down on 'Cyberthieves,'" Metropolitan Computer Times, June 13, 2001.

[1491] United States Department of State, Country Report on Human Rights Practices for 2001, March 2002, available at <http://www.state.gov/g/drl/hrrpt/2001/>.

[1492] Act to Prohibit and Penalize Wire Tapping and Other Related Violations of the Privacy of Communication and for Other Purposes, No. 4200, June 19, 1965.

[1493] Id., § 5.

[1494] Id., § 1.

[1495] Penalties include imprisonment, disqualification from public office or deportation, in the case of a foreign alien.

[1496] No. 4200, § 3.

particularly onerous severity.[1497] Section 4 states that any communication obtained in violation of this Act shall not be admissible as evidence in any court.

In April 1999, the National Bureau of Investigation and the Ombudsman started investigations after reports that police had tapped up to 3,000 telephone lines including top government officials, politicians, religious leaders, businessmen and print and television journalists. In May 1998, Director Gen. Santiago Alino, chief of the Philippine National Police, ordered an investigation of the alleged electioneering and illegal wiretapping activities by members of the National Police's Special Project Alpha (SPA). The House and the Senate held investigations in August 1997 after officials of the telephone company admitted that their employees were being paid to conduct illegal wiretaps.[1498]

Section 5 of the Rape Victim Assistance and Protection Act of 1998, stipulates that "any stage of the investigation, prosecution and trial of a complaint for rape, the police officer, the prosecutor, the court and its officers, as well as the parties to the complaint shall recognize the right to privacy of the offended party and the accused." It further states that a police officer, prosecutor or court may order a closed-door investigation, prosecution or trial and that the name and personal circumstances of the offended party and/or the accused, or any other information tending to establish their identities, and such circumstances or information on the complaint shall not be disclosed to the public.[1499] Section 3 provides for the establishment of a rape crisis center in every province and city "for the purpose of: ensuring the privacy and safety of rape victims."[1500]

Section 8 of the Proposed Rule on Juveniles in Conflict with the Law stipulates that "the right of the juvenile to privacy shall be protected at all times. All measures necessary to promote this right shall be taken, including the exclusion of the media."[1501] Section 9 of the Rule, dealing with the fingerprinting and photographing of a juvenile, states "while under investigation, no juvenile in conflict with law shall be fingerprinted or photographed in a humiliating and degrading manner." and stipulates procedural guidelines such as separate storage

---

[1497] Offences falling into this category include: crimes of treason, espionage, provoking war and disloyalty in case of war, piracy, mutiny in the high seas, rebellion, conspiracy and proposal to commit rebellion, inciting to rebellion, sedition, conspiracy to commit sedition, inciting to sedition, kidnapping as defined by the *Revised Penal Code*, and violations of Commonwealth Act No. 616, punishing espionage and other offenses against national security.

[1498] "Wiretapping probe," Business World (Manila), August 26, 1997.

[1499] Rape Victim Assistance and Protection Act of 1998, No. 8505, § 5.

[1500] Id., § 3(d).

[1501] Proposed Rule on Juveniles in Conflict With the Law A. M. NO. 02-1-18-SC, April 15, 2002, available at <http://www.chanrobles.com/amno02118sc.htm>, § 8.

of fingerprint files from adult files; restricted access by prior authority of the Family Court; and automatic destruction if no charges are laid or when the juvenile reaches the age of majority (21). Section 26(k) of the Rule confers a duty on the Family Court to respect the privacy of minors during all stages of the proceedings.[1502]

The Local Government Code of the Philippines[1503] provides all barangay[1504] "proceedings for settlement shall be public and informal provided that the... chairman... may upon request of a party, exclude the public from the proceedings in the interest of privacy, decency, or public morals."[1505]

Section 14 of Alien Social Integration Act of 1995[1506] provides that "information submitted by an alien applicant pursuant to this Act, shall be used only for the purpose of determining the veracity of the factual statements by the applicant or for enforcing the penalties prescribed by this Act."[1507]

The use of biometric technologies has been rising in the Philippines. Since March of 1996, dozens of companies and government agencies have been adopted fingerscan technologies in applications ranging from time management and payroll systems to security access control. Many companies use the technology primarily to reduce fraudulent time card punching.[1508] Banks use the technology to reduce fraudulent transactions and to promote security. Additionally, GTE and IriScan Inc. introduced iris-scan technology in 1998 to ensure the security of online transactions. Other uses of biometric technology in the Philippines include the dispensation of health care and social services; privacy systems for database and records protection; travel security systems with passport, ticket, and baggage verification; business, residence, and vehicle security with access and operator authentication; processing and circulation control in the corrections or prison

---

[1502] Id., § 26.

[1503] Local Government Code of the Philippines.

[1504] As the basic political unit, the barangay serves as the primary planning and implementing unit of government policies, plans, programs, projects, and activities in the community, and as a forum wherein the collective views of the people may be expressed, crystallized and considered, and where disputes may be amicably settled.

[1505] Local Government Code of the Philippines, § 414.

[1506] Alien Social Integration Act of 1995, No. 7919.

[1507] Id., § 14.

[1508] The Government Service Insurance System, National Computer Center, Philippine Tourism Authority, Department of Social Welfare and Development, and the Light Railway Transit Authority use the figerscan as a means to ensure that employees are actually at the worksite.

environment; and portable systems for on-scene recognition of individuals for use in law enforcement.[1509]

In July of 2001 the Philippines' Civil Service Commission released a resolution requiring all government officials an employee to refrain from sending indecent messages. The resolution takes effect on August 5, 2001 and bans public officials from sending sexist jokes, pornographic pictures and lewd letters or mails through electronic means including mobile phones, fax machines and e-mails. Individuals who feel sexually harassed may report cases directly to the Civil Service Commission. The resolution is a follow-up to a proposal by the Commission on Elections and the National Telecommunications Commission to monitor, track and prosecute senders of "politically motivated text messages."[1510]

The Code of Conduct and Ethical Standards for Public Officials and Employees[1511] mandates the disclosure of public transactions and guarantees access to official information, records or documents. Agencies must act on a request within 15 working days from receipt of the request. Complaints against public officials and employees who fail to act on request can be filed with the Civil Service Commission or the Office of the Ombudsman.

A recent study by MasterCard Inc. entitled "Asian Ideals," indicates that individuals in the Philippines have a moderate level of confidence in the confidentiality of their personal information. The survey included 400 respondents each from 13 different Pacific Rim countries. The privacy portion of the survey used a privacy scale with a score of 1 indicating "absolutely no privacy" and 10 indicating "total privacy." 41% of Filipinos gave scores of 8 to 10 regarding the confidentiality of their medical records. Another 24% gave a middle score of 5.[1512] With regard to privacy in office e-mail, telephone, and employee records, 23% believe they have "enough privacy" (5 on the privacy scale) and 9% believe they have "total privacy" (10 on the scale). On the specific issue of e-mail privacy, 22% Filipinos believe they have "enough privacy." Filipinos have a little less confidence in the privacy of their office telephone conversations with 23% believing they have a high level of privacy (8-10 on the scale), 22% believing they have enough privacy, and 17% believing they have "absolutely no privacy."[1513] Bank privacy got significantly better scores. 60% of

---

[1509] "Biometrics system usage rises," Business World (Manila), February 17, 1998.

[1510] "Philippine Agency Acts on 'E-Harrassment' In Gov't Workplaces," Metropolitan Computer Times, July 23, 2001.

[1511] Republic Act 6713 of 1987.

[1512] "Spouses are Asians' most trusted family members," Business World (Manila), May 17, 2001.

[1513] "Asia-Pacific consumers note work privacy," Business World (Manila), March 23, 2001.

---

the respondents gave a score of 6 or higher when asked to rate the privacy of personal information kept at the bank. 22% gave a middle score of 5, and 19% had some apprehension concerning the privacy of their bank accounts. Filipinos consumers also had mixed feelings about privacy and security on the Internet. 27% gave a middle score of 5 and almost an equal number of respondents believe the Internet is safe and unsafe – 37% give a score of 4 or lower while 36% give a score of 6 or higher. 15% said that the Internet was "absolutely unsafe" and only 1% said that it is "totally safe."[1514]

Republic of Poland

The Polish Constitution recognizes the rights of privacy and data protection. Article 47 states, "Everyone shall have the right to legal protection of his private and family life, of his honor and good reputation and to make decisions about his personal life." Article 49 States, "The freedom and privacy of communication shall be ensured. Any limitations thereon may be imposed only in cases and in a manner specified by statute." Article 51 states, "(1) No one may be obliged, except on the basis of statute, to disclose information concerning his person. (2) Public authorities shall not acquire, collect nor make accessible information on citizens other than that which is necessary in a democratic state ruled by law. (3) Everyone shall have a right of access to official documents and data collections concerning himself. Limitations upon such rights may be established by statute. (4) Everyone shall have the right to demand the correction or deletion of untrue or incomplete information, or information acquired by means contrary to statute. (5) Principles and procedures for collection of and access to information shall be specified by statute."[1515]

The Law on the Protection of Personal Data Protection was approved in October 1997 and took effect in April 1998.[1516] The law is based on the European Union Data Protection Directive. Under the Law, personal information relating to identity may only be processed with the consent of the individual. Special rules are provided for the processing of sensitive data, which is defined as data relating to race, ethnic origin, religion, political opinions, union membership, genetic code, sexual preferences, and medical history including addictions. Everyone has the right to verify his or her personal records held by government agencies or private companies. Every citizen has the right to be informed whether such

---

[1514] "Filipinos fairly confident of bank account privacy Mastercard Asain Ideals TM survey shows," Business World (Manila), May 31, 2001.

[1515] The Constitutional Act of 1997.

[1516] Law on Protection of Personal Data, Dz.U. nr 133, poz. 833, October 29, 1997.

databases exist and who administers them; queries should be answered within 30 days. Upon finding out that data is incorrect, inaccurate, outdated or collected in a way that constitutes a violation of the Act, citizens have the right to request that the data be corrected, filled in or withheld from processing.[1517] Personal information cannot generally be transferred outside of Poland unless the country has "comparable" protections. The law sets out civil and criminal sanctions for violations. A 1998 regulation from the Minister of Internal Affairs and Administration sets out standards for the security of information systems that contain personal information.[1518] In August 2001, the Act was amended in order to bring it into full compliance with the European Union Data Protection Directive.[1519] Among other changes, the amendment redefined the term "personal data"; introduced a new provision relating to final decisions issued solely on the basis of automated processing of personal data; introduced a new provision on data processing in relation to performance of a contract; adjusted the lawful processing provision; and inserted a scientific research clause.

The Bureau of Inspector General enforces the Act for the Protection of Personal Data.[1520] Mrs. Ewa Kulesza, Ph.D. was appointed as the first Inspector General for the Protection of Personal Data by the Polish Parliament in April 1998. The Bureau has four central duties: to supervise compliance with the Act; to investigate complaints and issue administrative decisions; to comment on proposed new laws and regulations that impact upon data protection; and to maintain a central registry of databases. Registration details must include the name and address of the data controller, the scope and purpose of the data processing, methods of collection and disclosure, and the security measures.[1521] An inspector has the right to access data, check data transfer and security systems, and determine whether the information gathered is appropriate for the purpose that it is supposed to serve.[1522] The office monitors the activities of all central government, local government and private institutions, individuals and corporations. As of June 2002, the Bureau had 102 staff members, up from 51 in April 1999.

[1517] "The Info Boom's Murky Side," Warsaw Voice, November 9, 1997.

[1518] The Regulation of June 3, 1998 By the Minister of Internal Affairs and Administration As regards establishing basic, technical and organisational conditions which should be fulfilled by devices and information systems used for the personal data processing (Journal of Laws of June 30, 1998, No. 80, item 521).

[1519] Act of August 25, 2001 amending the Act on Personal Data Protection (Journal of Laws No. 100 item 1087).

[1520] Homepage <http://www.giodo.gov.pl>.

[1521] See Christopher Millard and Mark Ford, Data Protection Laws of the World, Volume 2 (Sweet and Maxwell 2000).

[1522] "A One-Woman Orchestra," Warsaw Voice, June 21, 1998.

In 2001, the Bureau received 1555 inquires about the Act, 795 complaints and 534 legislative proposals for comment. The Bureau conducted 198 inspections, and issued 676 decisions and 52 notifications of breaches. There are 54 886 registered with the Bureau.[1523] Some of the more significant decisions issued by the Inspector General in 2001 were to prohibit: telecom and insurance companies from making photocopies of identity cards at the time of entering into a contract to provide their services; banks from using their former clients' personal data for marketing purposes; and employers from processing data on employees' sexual life by the during recruitment. The Inspector has also opened an investigation into a brokerage house that accidentally disclosed clients' personal data on the Internet.[1524] In November 2001 the Bureau, in conjunction with the Council of Europe, hosted a major conference on data protection.[1525]

The Bureau also maintains close relations with the data protection authorities in other central and eastern European countries. In December 2001, the Data Protection Commissioners from the Czech Republic, Hungary, Lithuania, Slovakia, Estonia, Latvia and Poland signed a joint declaration agreeing to closer cooperation and assistance. The Commissioners agreed to meet twice a year in the future, to provide each other with regular updates and overviews of developments in their countries, and to establish a common website for more effective communication.[1526]

There are sectoral laws in place to deal with the processing of medical and financial data. The 1996 Act on the Profession of a Doctor, imposes a duty of confidentiality, subject to certain exceptions, in relation to patient information on medical professionals. The Constitutional Tribunal ruled in March 1998 that requiring doctors to identify, on sick leave certificates, the disease of the patient violated the patients' right to privacy. The Banking Act 1997 imposes a requirement of secrecy on banks in relation to an individual's banking activities and identity, and limits the exchange and disclosure of personal data among banks and third parties except for the purpose of assessing credit risks or investigation fraud. Broad exemptions are granted to state entities however. In

---

[1523] Statistics Concerning the Activity of the Bureau of the Inspector General for the Protection of Personal Data, available at <http://www.giodo.gov.pl/English/english.htm>.

[1524] E-mail from Igor Kowalewski, International Relations Officer, Bureau of the Inspector General for Personal Data Protection, to Sarah Andrews, Research Director, Electronic Privacy Information Center, June 20, 2002 (on file with the Electronic Privacy Information Center).

[1525] European Conference on Data Protection, "Council of Europe Convention 108 for the Protection of Individuals with regard to Automatic Processing of Personal Data: Present and Future," November 19-20, 2001, Warsaw (Poland)

[1526] E-mail from Karel Neuwirt, President, Office for Personal Data Protection, Czech Republic, to Sarah Andrews, Research Director, Electronic Privacy Information Center, May 15, 2002 (on file with the Electronic Privacy Information Center).

April 2000, the Constitutional Tribunal dismissed a challenge to the rights of Polish tax authorities to request confidential information about any individual's bank accounts, bonds and securities. The court held that these powers were important in the fight against bribery and money laundering.[1527]

Chapter 33 of the 1997 Penal Code, "Offences against the Protection of Information," deals with computer related offences. Unauthorized access to computer systems, computer eavesdropping, interference with data, and computer sabotage are crimes by up to eight years imprisonment. The code also prohibits telecommunications fraud, the handling of stolen software, computer espionage, causing harm from interference with automatic data processing.[1528]

The government of Poland carries out a large number of wiretaps with limited oversight. Under the Criminal Code, the Minister of Justice and the Minister of the Interior, must authorize the use of wiretaps by the police and intelligence services. The law specifies for which cases the interception of communications may be authorized. In exceptional cases, the police may initiate a wiretap at the same times as they apply for authorization. Furthermore, under the Police Code electronic surveillance may be used for the prevention of crime as well as for investigative purposes. The government does not openly release statistics on the number of wiretaps applied for and authorized, tending to view this as a state secret. In 1997 there were reports of numbers of wiretaps varied from 2000 to 4000.[1529] There are unsubstantiated reports that these numbers increased further in 1999 and 2000. [1530] The United States Department of State, in its annual Country Reports on Human Rights Practices, has been consistently critical of high number of wiretaps authorized in Poland. In it's most recent report it noted that "[t]here is no independent judicial review of surveillance activities, nor is there any control over how the information derived from investigations is use. A growing number of agencies have access to wiretap information."[1531] In its 1999 report, the United Nations Human Rights Committee said it was "concerned that the Prosecutor (without judicial consent) may permit telephone tapping and that

---

[1527] "Constitutional Tribunal Allows Treasury to Screen Bank Accounts," Polish News Bulletin, April 12, 2000.

[1528] Andrzej Adamski, "Computer Crime in Poland: Three Year's Experience in Enforcing the Law," presented to the Council of Europe Conference on Cybercrime, Budapest, November 2001, available at <http://www.coe.int/T/E/Legal%5FAffairs/Legal%5Fco%2Doperation/Combating%5Feconomic%5Fcrime/Cybercrime/International_conference/3National_reports.asp#TopOfPage>.

[1529] Some Remarks on Human Rights Protection in Poland (in connection with the fourth periodic report of Republic of Poland on implementation of the International Covenant on Civil and Political Rights), Helsinki Foundation for Human Rights, available at <http://www.hfhrpol.waw.pl/en/index.html>.

[1530] United States Department of State, Country Reports on Human Rights Practices 2001, March 4, 2002, available at <http://www.state.gov/g/drl/rls/hrrpt/2001/eur/8321.htm>.

[1531] Id.

---

there is no independent monitoring of the use of the entire system of tapping telephones." The Committee recommended that Poland "review these matters so as to ensure compatibility with article 17 [of the International Covenant on Civil and Political Rights], introduce a system of independent monitoring, and include in its next report a full description of the system by then in operation."[1532] Poland's fifth periodic report is due in July 2003.

A number of different proposals to expand law enforcement surveillance capabilities over the last few years have been put forward. In July 2001, amendments to the Police Act gave the police increased powers to monitor individuals in public places including through the use of visual surveillance. The International Helsinki Committee noted in its 2002 report that the amendments "were dubious in terms of the right to privacy."[1533] The Ministry of Internal Affairs and Administration announced in January 2000 that it was setting up a new unit of 1,500 officers based on the United States FBI to combat organized crime. The new unit will have the power to conduct electronic surveillance and create extensive databases.[1534] Efforts to require all service operators (including mobile phone and Internet access providers) to install equipment, to facilitate this increased monitoring, are also going forward.

Controversy still surrounds the expanded national id system. The Electronic Census System (PESEL) number, which has been issued since the mid-1970s, is the biggest collection of personal data in Poland. Every identity card contains a PESEL number, which is a confirmation of the owner's date of birth and sex. The system is fully computerized. The Government began issuing the new ID cards in January 2001.

The Parliament approved the Act on Access to Public Information in September 2001. It went into effect in January 2002. The Act creates a presumption of access to information held by all public bodies, private bodies that exercise public tasks, trade unions and political parties. The bodies are also required to publish material online. There are exemptions for official or state secrets, confidential information, personal privacy and business secrets. Appeals are

---

[1532] United Nations, Report of the Human Rights Committee, A/54/40, October 21, 1999.

[1533] International Helsinki Federation for Human Rights, "Human Rights in the OSCE Region: The Balkans, the Caucasus, Europe, Central Asia and North America," Report 2002 (events 2001) available at <http://www.ihf-hr.org/reports/AR2002/country%20links/Poland.htm>.

[1534] "New Police Unit to Combat Organised Crime," Polish News Bulletin, January 4, 2000.

made to a court. Parliament is currently discussing amendments that would create an independent commission to enforce the Act.[1535]

Poland enacted the Classified Information Protection Act in January 1999 as a condition to entering NATO.[1536] The act covers classified information or information collected by government agencies that disclosure "might damage interests of the state, public interests, or lawfully protected interests of citizens or of an organization." There have also been efforts to deal with the files of former employees of the communist era secret police. A law creating a National Remembrance Institute (IPN) to allow victims of this secret police agency access to records was approved by the Parliament in October 1998. The files were opened to the public in February 2001.[1537] The Screening Act of 1997 created a special commission to examine the records of government officials who might have collaborated with the secret police. The Commission began work in November 1998. Under the Data Protection Act, individuals have the right to access and correct records that contain personal information about them from both public and private bodies.

Poland is a member of the Council of Europe and has signed and ratified the European Convention for the Protection of Human Rights and Fundamental Freedoms. In May 2002 it ratified the Convention for the Protection of Individuals with Regard to Automatic Processing of Personal Data (ETS No. 108).[1538] In November 2001, it signed the Council of Europe Cybercrime Convention (ETS No. 185).[1539] Poland is a member of the Organization for Economic Cooperation and Development and has adopted the OECD Guidelines on the Protection of Privacy and Transborder Flows of Personal Data.

Republic of Portugal

The Portuguese Constitution has extensive provisions on protecting privacy, secrecy of communications and data protection.[1540] Article 26 states, "(1) Everyone's right to his or her personal identity, civil capacity, citizenship, good

---

[1535] See "Freedom of Information and Access to Government Records Around the World," David Banisar, Privacy International, June 2002, available at <http://www.freedominfo.org/survey/>.

[1536] The Classified Information Protection Act of 22 January 1999.

[1537] See "Freedom of Information and Access to Government Records Around the World," supra n.1535.

[1538] Signed April 21, 1999; Ratified May 23, 2002; Entry into Force September 1, 2002.

[1539] Signed November 23, 2001.

[1540] Constitution of the Portuguese Republic, available at <http://www.parlamento.pt/leis/constituicao_ingles/IND_CRP_ING.htm>.

name and reputation, image, the right to speak out, and the right to the protection of the intimacy of his or her private and family life is recognized. (2) The law establishes effective safeguards against the abusive use, or any use that is contrary to human dignity, of information concerning persons and families. (3) A person may be deprived of citizenship or subjected to restrictions on his or her civil capacity only in cases and under conditions laid down by law, and never on political grounds." Article 34 states, "(1) The individual's home and the privacy of his correspondence and other means of private communication are inviolable. (2) A citizen's home may not be entered against his will, except by order of the competent judicial authority and in the cases and according to the forms laid down by law. (3) No one may enter the home of any person at night without his consent. (4) Any interference by public authority with correspondence or telecommunications, apart from the cases laid down by law in connection with criminal procedure, are prohibited."

In 1997, Article 35 of the Constitution was amended to give citizens a right to data protection. The new Article 35 states, "1. All citizens have the right of access to any computerised data relating to them and the right to be informed of the use for which the data is intended, under the law; they are entitled to require that the contents of the files and records be corrected and brought up to date. 2. The law shall determine what is personal data as well as the conditions applicable to automatic processing, connection, transmission and use thereof, and shall guarantee its protection by means of an independent administrative body. 3. Computerised storage shall not be used for information concerning a person's ideological or political convictions, party or trade union affiliations, religious beliefs, private life or ethnic origin, except where there is express consent from the data subject, authorisation provided for under the law with guarantees of non-discrimination or, in the case of data, for statistical purposes, that does not identify individuals. 4. Access to personal data of third parties is prohibited, except in exceptional cases as prescribed by law. 5. Citizens shall not be given an all-purpose national identity number. 6. Everyone shall be guaranteed free access to public information networks and the law shall define the regulations applicable to the transnational data flows and the adequate norms of protection for personal data and for data that should be safeguarded in the national interest. 7. Personal data kept on manual files shall benefit from protection identical to that provided for in the above articles, in accordance with the law."

The 1998 Act on the Protection of Personal Data adopts the European Union Data Protection requirements into Portuguese law.[1541] It limits the collection, use and dissemination of personal information in manual or electronic form. It also applies to video surveillance or "other forms of capture, processing and dissemination of sound and images." It replaces the 1991 Act on the Protection of Personal Data with Regard to Automatic Processing.[1542]

The Act is enforced by the National Data Protection Commission (Comissão Nacional de Protecção de Dados - CNPD).[1543] The Commission is an independent Parliament-based agency that registers databases, authorizes and controls databases, issues directives, and oversees the Schengen information system. The number of investigations conducted has risen steadily from 5 in 1994 to 42 in 1997, 78 in 1998 and 151 in 2000. The number of referrals for criminal prosecution to the Public Prosecution Service, has remained rougly static at around 20 per year in recent years. The Commission authorized 483 databases in 2000, for a total of 3161 approvals between 1994 and 2000. The Commission also handled 133 inspections in 2000, mostly relating to financial services.[1544] It issued opinions on obtaining subscriber information from telecommunications providers, access to marketing databases by the Criminal Investigation Police, denied access by the Information and Security Service to the information system of the Aliens and Frontiers Department and approved transborder dataflows to the United States when the parent company promised to protect the information under European law. In June 1997, the Supreme Administrative Tribunal upheld the Commission in a case against a shoe company that used smart cards to control employees' bathroom visits.

The penal code has provisions against unlawful surveillance and interference with privacy.[1545] Evidence obtained by any violation of privacy, the home, correspondence or telecommunications without the consent of the interested party is null and void.[1546] An inquiry was opened in October 1994 on illegal

---

[1541] Act n° 67/98 of 26 October. Act on the Protection of Personal Data (transposing into the Portuguese legal system Directive 95/46/EC of the European Parliament and of the Council of 24 October 1995 on the protection of individuals with regard to the processing of personal data and on the free movement of such data). <http://www.cnpd.pt/Leis/lei_6798en.htm>.

[1542] Law No. 10/91 - Lei da Protecção de Dados Pessoais face à Informática, amended by Lei n.º 28/94, de 29 de Agosto. Aprova medidas de reforço da protecção de dados pessoais.

[1543] Homepage <http://www.cnpd.pt/>.

[1544] National Commission for the Protection of Computerised Personal Data (NCPCPD), 2000 Report, available at <http://www.cnpd.pt/relat/relatorio.htm >.

[1545] Chapter VI, Penal Code, Section 179-183.

[1546] Article 126 of the Code of Penal Procedure paragraph 3. See United Nations, "Committee Against Torture Consideration of Reports Submitted by States Parties Under Article 19 of the Convention," Addendum, Portugal, 10 June 1997.

surveillance of politicians after microphones were discovered in the offices of a state prosecutor and several ministers.[1547] The Portuguese government ordered cellular telephone companies to assist with surveillance in October 1996.[1548] Law 69/98 implements the European Union Telecommunications Directive 97/66/EC.[1549]

There are also specific laws on the Schengen Information System,[1550] computer crime,[1551] and counseling centers.[1552]

Law n° 65/93, of 26 August 1993 provides for access to government records in any form by any person.[1553] Documents can be withheld for "internal or external security," secrecy of justice, and personal privacy. It is overseen by the Commission for Access to Administrative Documents (CADA), an independent Parliamentary agency. The CADA can examine complaints, provide opinions on access, and decide on classification of systems. CADA issued 177 opinions in 1998.

Portugal is a member of the Council of Europe and has signed and ratified the Convention for the Protection of Individuals with Regard to Automatic Processing of Personal Data (ETS No. 108).[1554] In November 2001, it signed the Council of Europe Convention on Cybercrime (ETS No. 185).[1555] It has signed and ratified the European Convention for the Protection of Human Rights and Fundamental Freedoms.[1556] It is a member of the Organization for Economic Cooperation and Development and has adopted the OECD Guidelines on the Protection of Privacy and Transborder Flows of Personal Data.

[1547] "Bug Found in Portuguese State Prosecutor's Office," The Reuters European Business Report, April 27, 1994.

[1548] "Portugal to tap mobile phones in drugs war," Reuters World Service, October 9, 1996.

[1549] Law 69/98.

[1550] Law No. 2/94 .

[1551] Law No. 109/91.

[1552] Act No. 3/84.

[1553] Law No. 65/93, including the alterations made by Laws No. 8/95 and 94/99.

[1554] Signed May 14, 1981; Ratified September 2, 1993; Entered into force January 1, 1994.

[1555] Signed Novemner 23, 2001.

[1556] Signed September 22, 1976; Ratified November 9, 1978; Entered into Force November 9, 1978.

Russian Federation

The Constitution of the Russian Federation recognizes rights of privacy, data protection and secrecy of communications. Article 23 states, "1. Everyone shall have the right to privacy, to personal and family secrets, and to protection of one's honor and good name. 2. Everyone shall have the right to privacy of correspondence, telephone communications, mail, cables and other communications. Any restriction of this right shall be allowed only under an order of a court of law." Article 24 states, "1. It shall be forbidden to gather, store, use and disseminate information on the private life of any person without his/her consent. 2. The bodies of state authority and the bodies of local self-government and the officials thereof shall provide to each citizen access to any documents and materials directly affecting his/her rights and liberties unless otherwise stipulated under the law." Article 25 states, "The home shall be inviolable. No one shall have the right to enter the home against the will of persons residing in it except in cases stipulated by the federal law or under an order of a court of law."[1557]

The Russian Supreme Court ruled in 1998 that regulations requiring individuals to register and obtain permission from local officials before they could live in Moscow violated the Constitution.[1558] However, there have been no significant changes; registration (propiska) is still needed for those who wish to stay in Moscow for longer than three days. For those attempting to move to Moscow, officials can make such registration a painful and complicated process.

The Duma approved the Law of the Russian Federation on Information, Informatization, and Information Protection in January 1995.[1559] The law covers both the government and private sectors and licenses the processing of personal information by the private sector. It imposes a code of fair information practices on the processing of personal information. It prohibits the use of personal information to "inflict economic or moral damage on citizens." The use of sensitive information (social origin, race, nationality, language, religion or party membership) is also prohibited. Citizens and organizations have the right of access to the documented information about them, to correct it and supplement it.

[1557] Constitution of the Russian Federation 1993, available at
<http://www.friends-partners.org/oldfriends/constitution/russian-const-ch2.html>.
[1558] RFE/RL, March 11, 1998.
[1559] Russian Federation Federal Act No. 24-FZ, Law of the Russian Federation on Information, Informatization and Information Protection, January 25, 1995.

The Russian law does not establish a central regulatory body for data protection and efforts at data protection have not been effective. Application to the Internet has also been limited. The law specifies that responsibility for data protection rests with the data controllers. The law is overseen by the Committee of the State Duma on Information and Informatization and the State Committee on Information and Informatization under the Russian President Authority.

The Duma has not yet approved the proposed 'Law on Information of Personal Character". This would update the 1995 act to make it more compliant with the Council of Europe's Convention 108 and the European Union Directive. The bill has been pending for several years, and in November 2000 members of the Committee on Information and Informatization claimed the Bill was ready to be approved.

However, regulations for the protection of data have been enacted in conjunction with laws in other areas. In an effort to stabilize its troubled economy, the Russian Federation is passing many laws enabling it to do business with foreign corporations. Some of the many concerns Russia is addressing are the protection of e-commerce transactions and financial data protection.

On December 30, 2001, the President of the Russian Federation, Vladimir V. Putin, signed into law the new Labor Code which includes protection of personal data.[1560] The Code became effective on February 1, 2002.

On February 6, 2002, a roundtable discussion on Russian information security was held in Moscow.[1561] Experts and political figures recommended the adoption of laws on commercial trade secrets, the protection of personal data, and access to classified information. Regulations of Communications Ministry's State Radio Frequencies Commission in force from June 1,2002 made local wireless communication system licenses less expensive by an order of magnitude and easier to obtain.[1562] Officials recognize that as a result of these changes, a wide range of related problems will need to be solved including securing protection of data against unauthorized access.

Secrecy of communications is protected by the 1995 Communications Act. The tapping of telephone conversations, scrutiny of electronic communications,

---

[1560] "Improved Russian Labor Code Entered Into Force," International Law Update, Volume 8, No. 2, February 2002.

[1561] "Experts Suggest Modifying Russian Informational Security Doctrine," News Bulletin, February 6, 2002.

[1562] "Communications Ministry Opens Up a Multibillion Market," RusData Dialine - BizEkon News, June 4, 2002.

delay, inspection and seizure of postal mailings and documentary correspondence, receipt of information therein, and other restriction of communications secrets are allowed only on the basis of a court order.[1563] The Law on Operational Investigation Activity regulates surveillance methods of the secret services and requires a warrant issued by a judge.[1564] This law was amended in December 1998 by the State Duma. Guarantees for the protection of privacy were stressed and additional controls imposed on prosecutors. In December 1999, the law was expanded to allow surveillance by the tax police, Interior Ministry, Border Guards, the Kremlin security service, the presidential security service, the parliamentary security services and the Foreign Intelligence Service.[1565] It is widely rumored that the Federal Security Service (FSB) still conducts widespread illegal wiretapping. In July 2000, a tabloid newspaper posted files on hundreds of prominent Russians including politicians, bankers, and journalists showing that they were under surveillance.[1566] These rumors, however, have not been substantiated. A criminal investigation against Lt-Gen Voldkodav, the former head of the Internal Affairs Ministry's directorate in Stravropol Territory, is currently underway. Among other things, Voldkodav is charged with violating the right to privacy and illegal surveillance of a policeman, employees of the Federal Security Service, court and prosecutor's office.[1567]

In 1998, several agencies, including the FSB, disclosed the System for Operational Research Actions on the Documentary Telecommunication Networks (SORM-2). SORM-2 required Internet Service Providers (ISPs) to install surveillance devices and high speed links to the FSB which would allow the FSB direct access to the communications of Internet users, although with a warrant.[1568] These rather expensive devices and links are to be paid for by the ISP's themselves. Most ISPs have not publicly resisted the FSB demands to install the devices but one ISP in Volgograd, Bayard-Slavia Communications, challenged the FSB demands to install the system. The local FSB and Ministry of Communication attempted to have their license revoked but backed off after the ISP challenged their decision in court. The document was confirmed by the State Committee of the Russian Federation on Communication and Informization

---

[1563] Russian Federation Federal Act No. 15-FZ. Adopted by the State Duma on January 20, 1995.

[1564] "Yeltsin Signs Law Regulating Criminal Investigations, " OMRI, August 16, 1995.

[1565] "Police Get Window Of Access To E-mail," The Moscow Times, January 13, 2000.

[1566] "Alleged Russian Spy Files Posted," Associated Press, July 7, 2000.

[1567] "Former Regional Police Chief Charged with Abuse of Office," BBC Worldwide Monitoring, July 24, 2001.

[1568] "Russia Prepares To Police Internet," The Moscow Times, July 29, 1998. More information in English and Russian is available from the Moscow Libertarium Forum <http://www.libertarium.ru/libertarium/sorm/>.

(Goskomsvyaz, now Ministry of Communications) as Order No. 47 in March 23, 1999, and Order No. 130, July 25, 2000 which was registered in the Ministry of Justice on August 9, 2000.

Order No. 130 was challenged immediately in the Russian Supreme Court by Pavel Netupsky, a St. Petersburg journalist. Although the Court upheld SORM-2, it ruled part 2.6 illegal, and therefore made sure that ISP would know whom the FSB is monitoring.[1569] Netupsky lost on all other counts. SORM-2 has now been implemented, although there have been no announced arrests as of yet. In fact, SORM-2 appears to have dropped below the radar of public awareness and it has not been in the news for quite some time.

There are also privacy protections in the Civil Code[1570] and the Criminal Code, articles 137-139; the provided penalties are mostly fines.[1571] The United Nations Human Rights Committee expressed concerns over the state of privacy in Russia in 1995 and recommended the enactment of additional privacy laws. It noted: "The Committee is concerned that actions may continue which violate the right to protection from unlawful or arbitrary interference with privacy, family, home or correspondence. It is concerned that the mechanisms to intrude into private telephone communication continue to exist, without a clear legislation setting out the conditions of legitimate interference with privacy and providing for safeguards against unlawful interference. The Committee urges that legislation be passed on the protection of privacy, as well as strict and positive action be taken to prevent violations of the right to protection from unlawful or arbitrary interference with privacy, family, home or correspondence."[1572]

The Russian Orthodox Church issued an official protest about a brand new national Tax ID card in March 2000. The card, issued for tax collection, contained the series of numbers 666, and a similar type of card or ID number has never been issued. The tax ID is voluntary, although government officials have also proposed that the ID card be used as a social security card and eventually replace passports.[1573]

[1569] "Supreme Court Rules Phone-Tapping Clause in Decree to be Illegal," BBC World Monitoring, September 28, 2000.

[1570] Civil Code, Article 19. RF Act No. 51-FZ. Adopted By The State Duma on October 21, 1994.

[1571] The Criminal Code of the Russian Federation No. 63-FZ of June 13, 1996.

[1572] United Nations Human Rights Committee, Comments on Russian Federation, U.N. Doc. CCPR/C/79/Add.54 (1995), <http://www.law.wits.ac.za//humanrts/hrcommittee/RUSSIA.htm>.

[1573] "Devil in the Numbers for Russian Tax ID Card Plan," Reuters, March 23, 2000.

On November 20, 2001, as part of a Smart Cards of Russia 2001 exhibition, the Federal Agency for Government Communications and Information demonstrated electronic documents designed to identify Russian citizens and ensure cryptographic protection of identification data.[1574]

Law of the Russian Federation on Information, Informatization, and Information Protection of 1999 also serves as a Freedom of Information law. The scope of the law is generally limited. A more broad FOIA bill entitled "Federal Law on the Right to Access Information" was stalled in the Duma. The bill creates a presumption that information is "available and open," "reliable and complete" and "must be timely disclosed." Agencies must respond within 30 days. Information can be withheld if it is a "national, commercial, official, professional or banking secret" or related to a "valid investigation and fact-finding proceedings." If information is withheld, the person can appeal to the agency, then to a court and the Human Rights Ombudsman.

According to a United States Department of State Report for Travelers to Russia, the importation and use of Global Positioning Systems (GPS) and other radio electronic devices, such as cellular phones, are subject to special rules and regulations.[1575] Unauthorized use of such devices may result in seizure of the equipment and possible arrest of the user. The penalty for using a GPS device in a manner which is determined to have compromised Russian national security can be a prison term of ten to twenty years. There are no restrictions on bringing laptop computers into Russia. However, software can be confiscated if software encryption is used.

Russia is a member of the Council of Europe and has signed and ratified the European Convention for the Protection of Human Rights and Fundamental Freedoms.[1576] It has not signed the Convention for the Protection of Individuals with Regard to Automatic Processing of Personal Data (ETS No. 108). Russia participated in the negotiations on the Council of Europe (CoE) Convention on Cybercrime which was opened for signature in Nov. 23, 2001. The Convention requires party states to establish criminal offences under their domestic laws regarding various computer or computer-related crimes, including unauthorized access to a computer system and unauthorized interception of a data transmission. As of July 2002, Russia had not yet signed the treaty.

[1574] "Russia Exhibits its Latest Data Protection Systems," BBC Worldwide Monitoring, November 21, 2001.

[1575] "Information on using GPS Devices, Radio-Electronic Equipment, and Computers in Russia," United States Department of State, Bureau of Consular Affairs, March 1998, <http://travel.state.gov/gps.html >.

[1576] Signed February 28, 1996; Ratified May 5, 1998; Entered into Force May 5, 1998.

Autonomous Russian Republics

Some of the twenty-two autonomous republics of the Russian Federation have constitutional provisions on privacy. In some cases, these republics claim that their constitutions take precedence within their territories over that of the Russian Federation.

Republic of San Marino

The Act on Collection, Elaboration and Use of computerized personal data was enacted in 1983 and amended in 1995.[1577] The Act applies to any computerized filing system or data bank, both private and public. It prohibits the collection of personal and confidential data through fraudulent, illegal or unfair means. It requires that information is accurate, relevant and complete. Any individual is entitled both to inquire whether his or her personal data have been collected or processed, to obtain a copy, and to require that inaccurate, outdated, incomplete or ambiguous data, or data whose collection, processing, transmission or preservation is forbidden, be rectified, integrated, clarified, updated or canceled. The creation of a data bank requires the prior authorization of both the State Congress (the Government) and the Guarantor for the Safeguard of Confidential and Personal Data. There are additional rules for sensitive information. Infringements can be punished by means of administrative sanctions or penalties. There were a number of Regency's Decrees issued under the 1983 Act that remained in force after the 1995 revisions.[1578] The Regulation on Statistical Data Collection and Public Competence in Data Processing[1579] regulates data processing within the Public Administration.

The Act is enforced by the Guarantor for the Safeguard of Confidential and Personal Data, a judge of the Administrative Court. The Guarantor can examine any claim or petition relating to the application of the above-mentioned law and

---

[1577] Regulating the Computerized Collection of Personal Data, Law N. 70 of 23 May 1995 revising Law N. 27 of 1 March 1983, amended by law 70/95.

[1578] Decree N. 7 of 13 March 1984, "Establishment of a State Data Bank as provided for by Article 5 of Law N. 27 of 1 March 1983"; Decree N. 7 of 3 June 1986, "Integration to Decree N. 7 of 13 March 1984, Establishing a State Data Bank"; Decree N. 140 of 26 November 1987, "Procedures for the Establishment of Private Data Banks."

[1579] Regulation on Statistical Data Collection and Public Competence in Data Processing, Law N. 71 of 23 May 1995.

pass judgment whenever the confidentiality of personal data is violated. His judgment can be appealed to a higher court. The release of information to other countries is conditioned on the prior authorization of the Guarantor, who must verify that the country to which confidential information is being transmitted ensures the same level of protection of personal data as that established in Sammarinese legislation.

Under pressure from the Organization for Economic Co-operation and Development (OECD), San Marino has recently agreed to amend its tax laws and if necessary weaken financial privacy standards, in order to facilitate better "exchange of information in tax matters."[1580]

San Marino is a member of the Council of Europe but has not signed or ratified the Convention for the Protection of Individuals with Regard to Automatic Processing of Personal Data (ETS No. 108). It has signed and ratified the European Convention for the Protection of Human Rights and Fundamental Freedoms.[1581]

Republic of Singapore

The Singapore Constitution is based on the British system and does not contain any explicit right to privacy.[1582] The High Court has ruled that personal information may be protected from disclosure under a duty of confidences.[1583]

There is no general data protection or privacy law in Singapore. The government has been aggressive in using surveillance to promote social control and limit domestic opposition.[1584] In 1986, then-Prime Minister and founder of modern Singapore Lee Kwan Yew proudly described his stance on privacy:

> I am often accused of interfering in the private lives of citizens. Yet, if I did not, had I not done that, we wouldn't be here today. And I say without the slightest remorse, that we wouldn't be here, we would not have made economic progress, if we had not intervened on very personal

---

[1580] "The War on Tax Havens," The National Post, September 2001.

[1581] Signed November 16, 1988; Ratified March 22, 1989; Entered into Force March 22, 1989.

[1582] Constitution of the Republic of Singapore, September 1963, available at <www.uni-wuerzburg.de/law/sn00t___.html>.

[1583] X v CDE1992 2 SLR 996.

[1584] See Christophen Tremewan, The Political Economy of Social Control in Singapore (St. Martin's Press, 1994).

matters – who your neighbor is, how you live, the noise you make, how you spit, or what language you use. We decide what is right, never mind what the people think. That's another problem.[1585]

Singapore has no governmental authority affiliated with privacy or data protection, except for a small privacy division within the Ministry of Finance.[1586] The idea of data protection legislation had been officially "under review" by the government for twelve years. A recent Straits Times survey revealed that 80 percent of readers feel that personal information contained in databases is too freely accessible.[1587] For purposes of e-commerce, the National Internet Advisory Committee proposed the Model Data Protection Code for the Private Sector in February 2002[1588] and the National Trust Council will decide whether to implement it later in the year, though businesses will not be required to adopt its provisions.[1589]

In September 1998, the National Internet Advisory Board released an industry-based self-regulatory "E-Commerce Code for the Protection of Personal Information and Communications of Consumers of Internet Commerce."[1590] The ode encourages providers to ensure the confidentiality of business records and personal information of users, including details of usage or transactions. It prohibits the disclosure of personal information, and requires providers not to intercept communications unless required by law. The Code also limits collection and prohibits disclosure of personal information without informing the consumer and giving them an option to stop the transfer, ensures accuracy of records and provides a right to correct or delete data. In 1999 the Code was adopted by CaseTrust and incorporated into its Code of Practice as part of an accreditation scheme promoting good business practices among store-based and web-based retailers. CaseTrust is a joint project operated by the Consumers Association of Singapore, CommerceNet Singapore Limited and the Retail Promotion Centre in Singapore. The Info-Communications Development Authority (IDA), the lead

---

1585 "Lee Kwan Yew's Speech at National Day Rally," The Straits Times, April 20, 1987, cited in Christophen Tremewan, id.

1586 Report of the National Internet Advisory Board 1997/1998, September 1998. See also, Susan Long, "Guess Who's Reading Your Personal Data Today?" Singapore Press Holdings, May 18, 2002.

1587 Long, id.

1588 "Consultation on Protection Regime," BNA World Data Protection Report, Volume 2, Issue 4, April 2002.

1589 "Voluntary Singapore Web Codes to Protect Privacy," Reuters, February 5, 2002.

1590 "E-com Legal Guide, Singapore," Kien Keong Wong and Ken Chia, Baker & McKenzie, Singapore, available at January 2001, available at <http://www.bakerinfo.com/apec/singapec_main.htm#Privacy>.

agency in charge of e-commerce regulation, announced in March 2000 that it would endorse the TRUSTe system as "an industry 'trustmark' seal."[1591]

In June of 1998, the Singapore Declaration was released at the 3rd APEC Ministerial Meeting on the Telecommunications and Information Industry. The declaration recognizes that APEC's Electronic Commerce Task Force is developing a work plan to be considered at the APEC Economic Leaders meeting in Malaysia in November 1998, and directs the Telecommunications Working Group (TEL) to assist the development of that plan. The Declaration also instructs TEL to consider in its work "the identification of key issues that will affect consumer confidence and ability to use electronic commerce within the APEC region, in particular, issues of access, affordability, privacy and security."[1592]

The Singapore Broadcasting Authority is the regulatory authority for the electronic medium in Singapore. It is a statutory board under the Ministry of Information and the Arts (MITA).

In July 1998, the Singapore government enacted three major bills concerning computer networks. They are the Computer Misuse (Amendment) Act, the Electronic Transactions Act and the National Computer Board (Amendment) Act. The CMA prohibits the unauthorized interception of computer communications.[1593] The CMA also provides the police with additional powers of investigations. Under the amended Act, it is now an offense to refuse to assist the police in an investigation. Amendments also widened the provisions allowing the police lawful access to data and encrypted material in their investigations of offenses under the CMA as well as other offenses disclosed in the course of their investigations. Such power of access requires the consent of the Public Prosecutor. The Electronic Transactions Act imposes a duty of confidentiality on records obtained under the act and imposes a maximum SG$10,000 fine and twelve-month jail sentence for disclosing those records without authorization. Police have broad powers to search any computer and to require disclosure of documents for an offence related to the act without a warrant.[1594] More broadly, the government has wide discretionary powers under the Internal Security Act, the Criminal Law Act, the Misuse of Drugs Act, and the Undesirable

---

[1591] "Infocomm Development Authority Helping Singaporeans Go Online," March 2000, available at <http://www.ida.gov.sg>.

[1592] The Singapore Declaration, available at <http://www.apecsec.org.sg>.

[1593] Computer Misuse Act (Chapter 50A), available at <http://www.lawnet.com.sg/freeaccess/CMA.htm>.

[1594] Electronic Transactions Act (Act 25 of 1998), available at <http://www.lawnet.com.sg/freeaccess/ETA.htm>.

Publications Act to conduct searches without warrant, as is normally required, if it determines that national security, public safety or order, or the public interest are at issue.[1595] Defendants have the right to request judicial review of such searches.

Electronic surveillance of communications is governed by the Telecommunications Authority of Singapore (TAS). The government has extensive powers under the Internal Security Act and other acts to monitor anything that is considered a threat to "national security." The United States State Department in 1998 stated, "Divisions of the Government's law enforcement agencies, including the Internal Security Department and the Corrupt Practices Investigation Board, have wide networks for gathering information. It is believed that the authorities routinely monitor citizens' telephone conversations and use of the Internet. While there were no proven allegations that they did so in 1997, it is widely believed that the authorities routinely conduct surveillance on some opposition politicians and other critics of the Government."[1596] All of the Internet Services Providers are operated by government-owned or government-controlled companies.[1597] Each person in Singapore wishing to obtain an Internet account must show their national ID card to the provider to obtain an account.[1598] ISPs reportedly provide information on users to government officials without legal requirements on a regular basis. In 1994, Technet – then the only Internet provider in the country serving the academic and technical community – scanned through the e-mail of its members looking for pornographic files. According to Technet, they scanned the files without opening the mails, looking for clues like large file sizes. In September 1996, a man was fined United States$43,000 for downloading sex films from the Internet. It was the first enforcement of Singapore's Internet regulation. The raid followed a tip-off from Interpol, which was investigating people exchanging pornography online. Afterwards, the SBA assured citizens that it does not monitor e-mail messages, chat groups, what sites people access, or what they download.[1599]

In 1999, the Home Affairs Ministry scanned 200,000 users of SingNet ISP at the request of the company looking for the "Back Orifice" program without telling

---

[1595] United States Department of State, Country Report on Human Rights Practices 2000, February 2001, available at <http://www.state.gov/g/drl/rls/hrrpt/2000/>.

[1596] United States Department of State Singapore Country Report on Human Rights Practices for 1997, January 30, 1998.

[1597] Garry Roday, "The Internet and Social Control in Singapore," Pol. Sci. Q. Volume 113, No. 1, Spring 1998.

[1598] Id.

[1599] The Straits Times, September 27, 1996.

the subscribers. The Telecommunications Authority of Singapore said that the ISP had violated no law but SingNet apologized for the scans and the National Information Technology Committee announced that it would create new guidelines.[1600] The Infocomm Development Authority released guidelines in January 2000.[1601] Under the guidelines, a subscriber's explicit consent must be obtained before scanning can occur. The scanning must be minimally intrusive and must not intercept web browsing or electronic communications. A November 1999 study by the Singapore Polytechnic's business administration revealed 60 percent of consumers who stated they were unready for virtual shopping cited privacy concerns.[1602]

Employer monitoring of employee phone calls, emails, and Internet usage is also permissible under Singapore law. Under Singapore property law, workplace email, telephone and computer contents are the property of the employer. Thus, if an employee loses his job because of the contents of his communications technology, he has no grounds for defense based on an invasion of privacy.[1603]

The Minister for Home Affairs announced in March 2000 that it was creating a "Speakers Corner" based on the one in London. However, speakers are required to register with the local police station and show their national ID cards or passports. The personal information is held for five years.[1604] Home Affairs Minister Wong Kan Seng said that the records are kept for investigative purposes to ensure that the speaker has registered.[1605] It has been reported that the police investigated a number of human rights activists, who staged a peaceful rally in Speakers Corner in December 2000, for the offense of "assembly without a permit."[1606]

The Government is active in some areas normally considered private, in pursuit of what it considers the public interest. For example the Government continues to enforce ethnic ratios for publicly subsidized housing, where the majority of

---

[1600] "ISPs To Get Guidelines On Scanning," The Straits Times, May 12, 1999.

[1601] "Guidelines for IASPs on Scanning of Subscribers' Computers," Infocomm Development Authority of Singapore, for IASPs on Scanning of Subscribers' January 6, 2000, available at <http://www.ida.gov.sg>.

[1602] "Not Many Ready To Cyber-Shop, Says Poll," The Straits Times, November 18, 1999.

[1603] "Boss is Spying On You – And He Has the Right," The Straits Times, October 10, 2000.

[1604] "Singapore To Get `Speakers' Corner,'" Asian Wall Street Journal, April 25, 2000.

[1605] "Keeping Records of Speakers," The Straits Times, May 9, 2000.

[1606] Associated Press, February 9, 2000.

citizens live and own their own units, designed to achieve an ethnic mix more or less in proportion to that in the society at large.[1607]

In early 2001 the Ministry of Health launched MeetDoc.com, an Internet-accessible medical database.[1608] MeetDoc.com holds all patients' records from all hospitals and clinics in Singapore and is available to government and private doctors in Singapore and abroad. Because records are accessible only with a patient's username and password, physicians must obtain a patient's permission before obtaining medical information.

An extensive Electronic Road Pricing system for monitoring road usage went into effect in 1998. The system collects information on an automobile's travel from smart cards plugged into transmitters in every car and in video surveillance cameras.[1609] The service claims that the data will only be kept for 24 hours and does not maintain a central accounting system. Video surveillance cameras are also commonly used for monitoring roads and preventing littering in many areas.[1610] It was proposed in Tampines in 1995 that cameras be placed in all public spaces including corridors, lifts, and open areas such as public parks, car parks and neighborhood centers and broadcast on the public cable television channel.[1611] A man was prosecuted under the Films Act in May 1999 for filming women in bathrooms.[1612]

The Banking Act prohibits disclosure of financial information without the permission of the customer.[1613] Numbered accounts can also be opened with the permission of the authority. The High Court can require disclosure of records to investigate drug trafficking and other serious crimes. The Monetary Authority of Singapore issued new "Know Your Customer" guidelines to banks in May 1998 on money laundering. Banks are required to "clarify the economic background and purpose of any transactions of which the form or amount appear unusual in relation to the customer, finance company or branch office concerned, or whenever the economic purpose and the legality of the transaction are not

---

[1607] United States Department of State Singapore Country Report on Human Rights Practices for 2000, February 2001.

[1608] Edmund Tee, "Get All Your Medical Data Online," The Straits Times, February 17, 2001.

[1609] "You're on Candid Camera," The Straits Times, September 2, 1998.

[1610] "Video Cameras To Monitor Traffic at 15 Junctions," The Straits Times, March 12, 1995; "Surveillance System Set Up in Jurong East," The Straits Times, July 16, 1996.

[1611] "Do We Really Want an All-Seeing Camera?" The Straits Times, July 13, 1995.

[1612] "Peeping Tom Used Hidden Camera To Spy," The Straits Times, May 29, 1999.

[1613] Banking Act, Chapter 19, available at <http://www.mas.gov.sg>.

immediately evident.[1614] Banks must report suspicious transactions to the MAS. In 2002, the soon-to-be-instituted Credit Bureau asked CaseTrust to accredit its procedures and systems to allay consumer financial privacy concerns.[1615]

Despite the extensive and arguably invasive monitoring, most Singaporeans support placing surveillance cameras in public places according to a 2000 survey conducted by The Straits Times. According to one respondent, "Its like your big brother is watching you all the time. But if having a big brother means that I am safe from robbers and thieves, then I don't mind." The privacy concerns were generally dismissed because, as one member of Parliament explained, "you shouldn't be doing anything embarrassing in public."[1616]

In response to the terrorist attacks in the United States on September 11, 2001, Singapore strengthened its anti-terrorist efforts by passing laws that codified United Nations resolutions to punish criminally the funding of terrorist activities and the making of false terrorist threats.[1617] In June 2002, Singapore proposed that Asian and European law enforcement agencies organize a system to share intelligence information to combat terrorism and organized crime.[1618]

Slovak Republic

The 1992 Constitution provides for protections for privacy, data protection and secrecy of communications. Article 16 states, "(1) The inviolability of the person and its privacy is guaranteed. It can be limited only in cases defined by law." Article 19 states, "(1) Everyone has the right to the preservation of his human dignity and personal honor, and the protection of his good name. (2) Everyone has the right to protection against unwarranted interference in his private and family life. (3) Everyone has the right to protection against the unwarranted collection, publication, or other illicit use of his personal data." Article 22 states "(1) The privacy of correspondence and secrecy of mailed messages and other written documents and the protection of personal data are guaranteed. (2) No one must violate the privacy of correspondence and the secrecy of other written documents and records, whether they are kept in private or sent by mail or in

---

[1614] "Guidelines On Prevention Of Money Laundering," Monetary Authority of Singapore, May 26, 1999, available at <http://www.mas.gov.sg>.

[1615] Leong Chan Teik, "New Bank Credit Bureau Will Get Accredited," The Straits Times, June 4, 2002.

[1616] "Eyes Wide Open," The Strait Times, April 12, 2000.

[1617] "Singapore Tightens Anti-Terrorist Laws," BBC News, November 13, 2001, available at <http://news.bbc.co.uk/hi/english/world/asia-pacific/newsid_1653000/1653797.stm>.

[1618] "European Union/ASEM – Calls For Restraint in Middle East and Kashmir," European Report, June 12, 2002.

another way, with the exception of cases to be set out in a law. Equally guaranteed is the secrecy of messages conveyed by telephone, telegraph, or other similar means."[1619]

The Act on Protection of Personal Data in Information Systems was approved in February 1998 and went into effect in March 1998.[1620] The Act replaces the previous 1992 Czechoslovakian legislation.[1621] It limits the collection, disclosure and use of personal information by government agencies and private enterprises either in electronic or manual form. It creates duties of access, accuracy and correction, security, and confidentiality on the data processor. Processing of information on racial, ethnic, political opinions, religion, philosophical beliefs, trade union membership, health, and sexuality is forbidden. Special protections are provided for sensitive data, defined as data revealing "racial or ethnic origin, political opinions, religious or philosophical beliefs, trade-union membership and data concerning health or sex life and conviction." Transfers to other countries are limited unless the country has "adequate" protection. All systems are required to be registered with the Statistical Office of the Slovak Republic.[1622]

The Act created a new office, the Inspection Unit for the Protection of Personal Data, headed by the Commissioner for Personal Data Protection, to supervise and enforce the Act.[1623] The Commissioner is appointed by the Government on the basis of a recommendation by the President of the Statistical Office. Mr. Pavol Husar took office as the first Commissioner in February 1999. The Commissioner monitors the implementation of the law, reviews registered systems, inspects the processing of personal data in information systems, receives and handles complaints concerning the violation of personal data protection in information systems, initiates corrective actions whenever a breach of legal obligations is ascertained, and participates in the preparation of generally binding regulations in the field of personal data. The Commissioner is required to file an annual report on the status of data protection with the Government and the National Council. As of September 2001 the office had nine staff members.[1624] In January 2001, the Commissioner said publicly that the act was going to be much more vigorously enforced and large fines imposed for violations, including

---

[1619] Constitution of the Slovak Republic, September 1992, available at
<http://www.sanet.sk/Slovakia/Court/const.html>.

[1620] Act No. 52 of February 3, 1998 on Protection of Personal Data in Information Systems.

[1621] Act of April 29, 1992 on Protection of Personal Data in Information Systems (No. 256/92).

[1622] Registration is governed by the Decree of the Statistical Office of the Slovak Republic of 11 May .

[1623] Web site at <http://www.dataprotection.gov.sk/>.

[1624] E-mail from Natalia Krajcovicova, Inspection Unit for the Protection of Personal Data, Slovakia, to Sarah Andrews, Electronic Privacy Information Center, September 4, 2001 (on file with Electronic Privacy Information Center).

non-registration. He noted that there were only 400 information systems registered when the number should really be around 20,000.[1625] Since 2001 the Unit has received eighty two serious complaints under the Act and prepared over 300 informational documents for citizens and public administration bodies on data protection issues.[1626]

One of the top priorities for the Inspection Unit over the last year has been to secure amendments to the Act on Protection of Personal Data in Information Systems in order to bring it into full compliance with the European Union Directive.[1627] In September 2001 a draft amendment to the Act was submitted to the Legislative Council of the government for approval. In November 2001, the Legislative Council reviewed the draft and made a number of recommendations and suggestions, including the establishment of a new independent supervisory authority, to be called the Office for Personal Data Protection. At the Council's request the Commissioner drafted a completely new Act to incorporate these changes and resubmitted it in December 2001. The new bill was approved by the Government and submitted to Parliament in February 2002. Most of the bill's provisions deal with restructuring the supervisory authority. It also creates new protections for the processing of sensitive information, defined as information relating to racial or ethnic origin, political views, religion or ideology, membership of trade unions and health and places restrictions on the processing of the national identity number. The bill failed to pass into law, when in late June the President refused to sign it on the grounds that it did not clearly define the establishment of the new office. He also objected to the proposed implementation date of July 1, 2002 stating that it would interfere with the general election planned for September 2002. Under the current election laws, political parties must submit petition sheets containing over 10,000 signatures and including signatory's identity numbers, a requirement that would contradict the new law. On July 2, the Parliament passed an amended bill taking into account these objections and the new law is expected to take effect in September 2002.[1628]

The Inspection Unit maintains close relations with the data protection authorities in other central and eastern European countries. In December 2001, the Data Protection Commissioners from the Czech Republic, Hungary, Lithuania,

---

[1625] "Large Fines to be Imposed for Abuse of Personal Data in Slovakia," BBC Worldwide Monitoring, January 25, 2001.

[1626] E-mail from Natalia Krajcovicova, Inspection Unit for the Protection of Personal Data, Slovakia, to Sarah Andrews, Electronic Privacy Information Center, July 1, 2002 (on file with Electronic Privacy Information Center).

[1627] Id.

[1628] "Slovak MPs Approve Personal Data Protection Law," BBC Worldwide Monitoring, July 3, 2002.

Slovakia, Estonia, Latvia and Poland signed a joint declaration agreeing to closer cooperation and assistance. The Commissioners agreed to meet twice a year in the future, to provide each other with regular updates and overviews of developments in their countries, and to establish a common website for more effective communication.[1629]

Under the 1993 Police Law, the police are required to obtain permission from a court or prosecutor before undertaking any telephone tapping or mail surveillance.[1630] This type of activity is supposed to be used only in cases of extraordinarily serious premeditated crimes or crimes involving international-treaty obligations. However, the communist-era secret police still remain in positions of power and over the years there have been many public revelations of illegal wiretapping of opposition politicians, reporters and dissidents.[1631] In 2001 there were allegations that members of the SMK and SMER parties were being monitored and their telephones tapped.[1632] Active monitoring of The Church of Scientology by the Ministry of the Interior was also reported.[1633] Under the Criminal Code police require a judicial search warrant to enter a private home and the court may only issue this warrant with good cause. Police are required to present the warrant before conducting the search or within twenty-four hours. There are continuing reports of Roma homes being entered without warrants.[1634]

There are legal protections for privacy in the Civil Code. Article 11 states "everyone shall have the right to be free from unjustified interference in his or her privacy and family life." There are also computer-related offenses linked with the protection of a person (unjustified treatment of a personal data).[1635] The Slovak Constitutional Court ruled in March 1998 that the law allowing public prosecutors to demand to see the files or private correspondence of political parties, private citizens, trade union organizations and churches, even when not necessary for prosecution, was unconstitutional. Court chairman Milan Cic said this was "not only not usual, but opens the door to widespread violation of

---

[1629] E-mail from Karel Neuwirt, President, Office for Personal Data Protection, Czech Republic, to Sarah Andrews, Research Director, Electronic Privacy Information Center, May 15, 2002 (on file with the Electronic Privacy Information Center).

[1630] Code of Criminal Procedure, sections 86 to 88.

[1631] "Hungarian Politicians in Slovakia are Being Bugged," CTK National News Wire, February 21, 1995, "Deputy Brings Charges Against Slovak Secret Services Spokesman," CTK National News Wire, August 21, 1997.

[1632] United States Department of State, Country Reports on Human Rights Practices 2001, March 2002, available at <http://www.state.gov/g/drl/rls/hrrpt/2001/eur/8338.htm>.

[1633] Id.

[1634] Id.

[1635] European Commission, Agenda 2000 - Commission Opinion on Slovakia's Application for Membership of the European Union, Doc 97/20, July 15, 1997.

---

peoples' basic rights and their right to privacy."[1636] There are sector specific privacy provisions to protect an individual's medical, financial and tax records.[1637] A draft new media law, containing provisions on the protection of privacy and rights of correction, is also moving forward.[1638]

The Act on Free Access to Information was approved by the Parliament in May 2000. It sets broad rules on disclosure of information held by the government. There are limitations on information that is classified, constitutes a trade secret, would violate privacy, was obtained "from a person not required by law to provide information, who upon notification of the Obligee instructed the Obligee in writing not to disclose information," or "concerns the decision-making power of the courts and law enforcement bodies." Appeals are made to higher agencies and can be reviewed by a court. There are separate requirements for disclosure of environmental information that covers private organizations. It became effective January 1, 2001[1639] and revoked Act 171/1998 of the National Council on Free Access to Environmental Information. In February 2001, the government approved a draft law on confidential information to harmonize the handling of classified documents with NATO standards, despite the Data Protection Commissioner's objections that it violated human rights.[1640]

Slovakia is a member of the Council of Europe and has signed and ratified the Convention for the Protection of Individuals with Regard to Automatic Processing of Personal Data (ETS No. 108.[1641] In August 2001, it signed the Additional Protocol to Convention 108 regarding supervisory authorities and transborder data flows. It has signed and ratified the European Convention for the Protection of Human Rights and Fundamental Freedoms.[1642] Slovakia joined the OECD in September 2000.

[1636] "Court Rules Law on Public Prosecutors Unconstitutional," CTK National News Wire, March 4, 1998.

[1637] Act No. 277/1994 on Health Care; Act No. 21/1992 on Banks; and Act No. 511/1992 on Tax Administration. See, "Data Protection Laws of the World," Christopher Millard and Mark Ford, Clifford Chance, Sweet & Maxwell 2000.

[1638] "Culture Ministry to Draft Own Media Law," BBC Worldwide Monitoring, February 9, 2001.

[1639] Act on Free Access to Information, available (in Slovakian) at <http://www.infozakon.sk/zakon-schvalenyvnrsr.htm>.

[1640] "Government Approves New Version of Law on Confidential Information," BBC Summary of World Broadcasts, March 2, 2001.

[1641] Signed April 14, 2000; Ratified September 13, 2000; Entered into Force January 1, 2001.

[1642] Signed February 21, 1991; Ratified March 18, 1992; Entered into Force January 1, 1993. <http://conventions.coe.int/>.

Republic of Slovenia

The 1991 Constitution recognizes many privacy rights. Article 35 on the Protection of the Right to Privacy and of Personal Rights states, "The physical and mental integrity of each person shall be guaranteed, as shall be his right to privacy and his other personal rights." Article 37 on the Protection of Privacy of Post and other Means of Communication states, "The privacy of the post and of other means of communication shall be guaranteed. In accordance with statute, a court may authorize action infringing on the privacy of the post or of other means of communication, or on the inviolability of individual privacy, where such actions are deemed necessary for the institution or continuance of criminal proceedings or for reasons of national security." Article 38 on the Protection of Personal Data states, "The protection of personal data relating to an individual shall be guaranteed. Any use of personal data shall be forbidden where that use conflicts with the original purpose for which it was collected. The collection, processing and the end-use of such data, as well as the supervision and protection of the confidentiality of such data, shall be regulated by statute. Each person has the right to be informed of the personal data relating to him which has been collected and has the right to legal remedy in the event of any misuse of same."[1643]

A new Law on Personal Data Protection went into effect in August 1999.[1644] The law is based on the European Union Data Protection Directive and the COE Convention No 108 and replaces the earlier law of 1990.[1645] It provides that private entities may process personal data if they have acquired the written consent of individuals or if the data processing is determined by law. Public entities may only process personal data for which they have been granted legal authorization. Special protections are set out for "sensitive data" which is defined as data on racial or other origins, political, religious or other beliefs, trade union membership, sexual behavior, criminal convictions and medical data. This data must be specially labeled and may only be transferred across telecommunications networks if it is protected by "encryption methods" and an "electronic signature" that can guarantee illegibility. The law requires a catalogue to be created for each database containing personal information. It also imposes cross border

---

[1643] Constitution of the Republic of Slovenia 1991, available at <http://www.sigov.si/us/eus-usta.html>.

[1644] ESIS, Regulatory Developments: Slovenia, April 2000, available at <http://www.eu-esis.org/esis2reg/SIreg4.htm>.

[1645] Law on Personal Data Protection, March 7, 1990 (The Official Journal of the Republic of Slovenia, No. 8/90, 38/90 and 19/91).

restrictions stating that data may only be transferred to countries that have a system of data protection that applies to foreign citizens.

In July 2001 a new Act[1646] amending the 1999 law came into force. The primary purpose of the amendment was to establish an independent oversight mechanism in accordance with the requirements of the 1995 European Union Data Protection Directive. Previously supervision of the Act was conducted by a single Inspector within the Ministry of Justice. The new Act created an independent agency, the Inspectorate for Personal Data Protection within the Ministry of Justice. Supervision of the Act is divided between the Inspectorate and the Human Rights Ombudsman. The Inspectorate began work in September 2001 and, as of July 2002, employed three people. The Human Rights Ombudsman employs two people responsible for data protection. The Ministry of Justice remains responsible for maintaining the database registry. The Home Policy Committee within the National Assembly also performs oversight of the Act. [1647]

In July 2000, the Health Insurance Data Collections Act, came into force. The Act sets out restrictions on the collection, use and exchange of health data.[1648]

A judge's warrant must be issued prior to a house search or telephone tapping. A new Law on the Police was adopted in 1998 allows for surveillance to be authorized under special circumstances by a General Police Director.[1649] It was reported in October 2001 that, in response to the September 11th attacks on the United States, the Slovene Information Security Agency (SOVA) began monitoring the e-mail and telephone communications of prominent academics and NGO activists.[1650] In June 2002, the Parliamentary Commission for the Supervision of Work of Security and Intelligence Services began an inquiry into allegations that the Slovene police and SOVA were secretly wiretapping Peter Ceferin, lawyer for a man accused of human trafficking.[1651]

[1646] Act Amending the Personal Data Protection Act (Uradni list RS, 57/01).

[1647] E-mail from Joze Bagataj, Data Protection Inspector, to Sarah Andrews, Research Director, Electronic Privacy Information Center, July 12, 2002 (on file with the Electronic Privacy Information Center).

[1648] Id.

[1649] Law on the Police, 18 July 1998.

[1650] International Helsinki Federation for Human Rights, "Human Rights in the OSCE Region: The Balkans, the Caucasus, Europe, Central Asia and North America" Report 2002 (events 2001), available at <http://www.ihf-hr.org/reports/AR2002/country%20links/Slovenia.htm>.

[1651] "Slovene Inquiry Commission Investigates Wiretapping Allegations," BBC Worldwide Monitoring, June 28, 2002.

The Law on National Statistics regulates the privacy of information collected for statistical purposes.[1652] The Law on Telecommunications requires telecommunications service providers to "guarantee the confidentiality of transmitted messages and of personal and non-personal data known only to them." The Electronic Commerce and Electronic Signature Act was approved in June 2000.

Slovenia is a member of the Council of Europe and has signed and ratified the Convention for the Protection of Individuals with Regard to Automatic Processing of Personal Data (ETS No. 108).[1653] It has also signed and ratified the European Convention for the Protection of Human Rights and Fundamental Freedoms.[1654]

Republic of South Africa

Section 14 of the South African Constitution of 1996 states, "Everyone has the right to privacy, which includes the right not to have – (a) their person or home searched; (b) their property searched; (c) their possessions seized; or (d) the privacy of their communications infringed." Section 32 states, "(1) Everyone has the right of access to – (a) any information held by the state, and; (b) any information that is held by another person and that is required for the exercise or protection of any rights; (2) National legislation must be enacted to give effect to this right, and may provide for reasonable measures to alleviate the administrative and financial burden on the state."[1655] The interim Constitution contained an essentially similar provision to Section 14, in Section 13.[1656] It is clear that both sections are written in a way that directly responds to the experiences during the apartheid era of gross interferences with peoples' right to privacy.

The South African Constitutional Court has delivered a number of judgments on the right to privacy relating to the possession of indecent or obscene photographs,[1657] the scope of privacy in society,[1658] and searches.[1659] All the

---

[1652] Law on National Statistics, 25 July 1995.

[1653] Signed November 23; 1993; Ratified May 27, 1994; Entered into force September 1, 1994.

[1654] Signed May 14, 1993; Ratified June 28, 1994; Entered into Force June 28, 1994.

[1655] The Constitution of the Republic of South Africa, Act 108 of 1996, available at <http://www.parliament.gov.za/legislation/1996/saconst.html>.

[1656] The Interim Constitution (Act 200 of 1993).

[1657] Case and Another v Minister of Safety and Security and Curtis and Another v Minister of Safety and Security 1996 (3) SA 617 (CC).

---

judgments were delivered under the provisions of the Interim Constitution as the causes of action arose prior to the enactment of the Final Constitution. However, as there is no substantive difference between the privacy provisions in the Interim and Final Constitutions, the principles remain authoritative for future application.

In early 2002, the Law Commission gave notification of a project to begin work on drafting a comprehensive national Privacy Act. This could take 18 months to 2 years. Many important privacy provisions, specifically regarding data retention and personal privacy, originally intended for this Act have largely been left out of the new laws on Electronic Commerce, Surveillance and Access to Information, to be included in this general law when drafted. Although these laws do make efforts to cater for personal privacy protection, the result is that certain important gaps remain until the privacy law is promulgated.

On July 18, 2001, the Interception and Monitoring Bill of 2001 was introduced into South African Parliament, proposing amendments to the 1992 Act which had previously been amended to *strengthen* privacy concerns. According to Adv. Johnny de Lange, Chairperson of the South African Parliament's Portfolio Committee on Justice & Constitutional Development, the Bill "aims to regulate the interception and monitoring of certain communications ... to regulate authorized telecommunications monitoring," and "to prohibit the provision of certain telecommunication services which do not have the capacity to be monitored."[1660] Despite the constitutional implications of such a law, the Bill has received backing from the African National Congress (ANC). The ANC currently holds 266 of the 400 seats in the South African Parliament.[1661] A new Bill was introduced into Parliament in the May 2002 which authorizes Members of Parliament to 'cross the floor' to other parties, but still retain their seats. As such, it is likely that the ANC seat numbers in the National Assembly will increase when the law is finalized.[1662] The Interception and Monitoring Bill was fast tracked for a vote in mid-August 2001, giving interested members of the public only three weeks to make submissions. On August 13, 2001 Privacy International submitted a statement on the bill criticizing the proposal as

---

[1658] Bernstein and others v Von Weilligh Bester NO and others, 1996 (2) SA 751 (CC); 1996 (4) BCLR 449 (CC) - delivered March 27, 1996.

[1659] Mistry v The Interim National Medical and Dental Council of South Africa and others as yet unreported, CCT 13/97, May 29, 1998.

[1660] Press statement issued by Adv. Johnny de Lange, MP and Chairperson of the Portfolio Committee on Justice & Constitutional Development, available at <http://www.polity.org.za/govdocs/pr/2001/pr0718c.html>.

[1661] United States Dept. of State, Country Reports on Human Rights Practices 2000, February 2001, available at <http://www.state.gov/g/drl/rls/hrrpt/2000 >.

[1662] Loss or Retention of membership of National and Provincial Legislatures Bill, as certified, March 2002, available at <http://www.pmg.org.za/bills/020304floorcross.htm>.

"inconsistent with international standards on human rights and the legal requirements of the South African Constitution" and calling for its delay until a number of changes could be made.[1663] This Bill is intended to replace a 1992 law of the same name. It is based on the proposals of the South African Law Reform Commission, which in November 1998 recommended amendments to facilitate the monitoring of cellular phones and ISPs.[1664] These proposals were part of a wider project to rationalize the many former apartheid government security laws.[1665]

The passage of the Interception and Monitoring Bill was then disrupted, and the Bill effectively shelved in late 2001, pending finalization of the Council of Europe Convention on Cybercrime, which requires member states and non-member signatories to enact measures consistent with the Convention.[1666] South Africa is one of four non-member signatories to the Convention, along with the USA, Canada and Japan.

A new version of the surveillance law was circulated in the first quarter of 2002 and was revised a number of times following further consultation with law enforcement agencies and telecommunications service providers.[1667] The most recent draft was deliberated on June 18, 2002, but at the time of going to press, was not yet finalized.

The most recent version, newly titled, *the Regulation of Interception of Communications Act,* is in purpose and essence similar to previous versions. The Bill, when passed will continue to prohibit wiretaps and surveillance, except for law enforcement purposes. The Bill will require that all telecommunications services including ISPs make their services capable of being intercepted before they could offer the service to the public. There is a provision for the Minister to exempt Internet Service Providers from these provisions in certain circumstances. Providers will be required to pay for the costs of making their systems wiretap-enabled and those that are not capable of conforming to surveillance requirements may be shut down. No model of cost sharing is proposed at this stage and the state will be responsible for the costs of connecting central

---

[1663] Letter to Ms Collette Herzenberg and Ms. Zodwa Zenzile of the Committee on Justice & Constitutional Development, from David Banisar, Deputy Director, Privacy International, August 13, 2001, available at <http://www.privacyinternational.org/countries/south_africa/pi-sa-intercept-letter.html >.

[1664] Discussion Paper 78 (Project 105), Review of Security Legislation, The Interception and Monitoring Prohibition Act 127 of 1992 (November 1998) , available at <http://www.law.wits.ac.za/salc/discussn/monitoring.pdf>.

[1665] Id.

[1666] Specifically, Chapter II; Article 3. Council of Europe: Convention on Cybercrime. ETS No.: 185.

[1667] Working Draft 4 (IMB 78) and Working Draft 4A (IMB 79), [Bill 50-2001].

interception centres to telecommunications providers. Criminal penalties are also included should a service provider refuse to comply with the provisions of the Act or assist law enforcement. Repeat offenders may in addition face the revocation of their service license granted under the Telecommunications Act.[1668] The National Intelligence Agency (NIA) announced in February 2000 that it was creating a signals intelligence service based on the model of the United Kingdom's GCHQ.[1669] Under the authority of new Regulation of Interception of Communications Act, the NIA will have the authority to intercept all postal, telephone and Internet communications under the auspices of crime control and national security, actual or potential threats to public health and safety, and to assist foreign law enforcement agencies with interception regarding organized crime or terrorism, under a mutual assistance agreement. [1670]

Additional amendments contain new definitions which widen the scope of the Bill;[1671] an expanded list of grounds for obtaining a wiretap order; including a wiretap to ascertain the location of a person in the case of an emergency;[1672] an expanded range of interception directions that can be granted,[1673] such as decryption orders;[1674] and an augmented list of offences under the Act,[1675] which includes being in possession of a stolen cellphone and failure to report a SIM card stolen, lost or damaged.

New provisions on data retention require all telecommunication service providers (TSPs) to gather detailed personal data on individuals and companies (including photocopies of identity documents) before signing contracts or selling SIM[1676] cards for pre-paid mobile services. Provisions require that such data is made available to law enforcement agencies when requested to. There is no limit specified for the length of time TSPs are required to retain personal data, but a

---

[1668] Act No. 103 of 1996, as amended.

[1669] "South Africa to set up signals intelligence centre," Reuters, February 7, 2000.

[1670] Section 13(5).

[1671] The definition of "communication" has been augmented to include all 'direct' and 'indirect' communications, which together cover all traffic, signaling and other call related information, as well as the content of such communications.

[1672] Section 9

[1673] These include: broad interception direction; an archived communications direction (any communication related information in the possession of a telecommunications service provider and which is being stored by that TSP for up to one year, regarding the transmission of the indirect communication) and real time (real time information on an ongoing basis without interception) or supplementary direction or a combination thereof. Also on application are entry warrants (to rig premises and intercept postal articles) and decryption directions. All can be obtained as *oral directions* when urgent circumstances prevail.

[1674] Section 18.

[1675] Chapter 8.

[1676] Subscriber Identity module.

requirement to store communication related information is limited in duration to 12 months.

The Minister has a number of broad powers in the Act, including the discretion to stipulate all technical and security requirements for networks to be capable of surveillance, including capacity, the systems to be used, the facilities and devices to be acquired, and the type of communication related information to be stored. At this stage, consultation in developing these standards appears to be limited to the Minister, other relevant ministers and TSPs. There is no provision for public interest or technical bodies to be consulted.

In 1996, it was revealed that the South African Police Service was monitoring thousands of international and domestic phone calls without a warrant.[1677] In February 2000, the government apologized to the German government after it was found that an intelligence operative had placed spy cameras outside the Germany Embassy.[1678] The opposition Democratic Party announced in November 1999 that it found surveillance devices at its parliamentary offices and national headquarters.[1679]

The Department of Communications (DOC) released its long awaited Electronic Communications and Transactions Bill in early 2002, which at the time of printing, was still being deliberated by Parliament.

The E-commerce Bill followed a 2-year period of extensive public consultation. Its main aim is to facilitate e-commerce by creating legal certainty and promoting trust and confidence in electronic transactions. As such, it provides for functional equivalence of electronic documents, recognition of contracts, digital signatures, electronic filing and evidence etc.[1680] The Bill also contains statutory provisions on cyber crime and creates several computer crime offences, including unauthorized access to data; interception of or interference with data; computer related extortion; fraud, and forgery[1681] aimed at interference with commercial activities and hacking. Positive provisions are included on the restriction of ISP liability;[1682] promoting consumer rights; criminalizing spam and requiring all

---

[1677] "Newspaper Uncovers `Unlawful' Tapping by Intelligence Units," The Star, 21 February 1996.

[1678] "S.Africa admits to spying on German embassy," Reuters, February 6, 2000.

[1679] "Democratic Party Outraged By Bugging Of Its Offices," Africa News, November 23, 1999.

[1680] Chapter III

[1681] Chapter XIII.

[1682] Incorporating notice and take down procedures; mere conduit recognition and safe harbor provisions. Liability will only attach where and ISP has direct knowledge of illegal or objectionable material and fails to take effective action as required by law.

retail websites to have an accessible privacy policy. The Bill also provides for a national e-strategy to bridge the digital divide.

While awaiting a specific privacy and data protection law to be drafted, personal privacy protections are weak, and based on the voluntary adoption of a set of privacy principles by data collectors. While the principles cover explicit, written consent for collection and use of personal data, the purpose for which it is gathered, non-disclosure, etc. this is regulated as a matter of contract and agreement, with the sanction for breach to be determined between the parties. In addition, the provisions on personal privacy only apply to electronically collected personal data, ignoring information gathered in non-electronic ways but subsequently captured electronically.

The Bill proposes the registration of all cryptography providers and services and government accreditation of authentication providers. A new law enforcement 'cyber inspectorate' is proposed who will monitor websites and public information systems and investigate compliance by crypto and authentication providers.[1683]

Included in the Bill is a provision authorizing the Minister to declare both public and private databases critical in the "national interest" or the "economic and social well-being of SA." Once declared, the Minister can require the database to be registered, including all information about its location and the types of data stored. The law also proposes to authorize the minister to determine technical standards and set procedures for the general management of critical data bases, their security and disaster recovery procedures.[1684]

South Africa does not have a privacy commission but has a Human Rights Commission (HRC) which was established under Chapter 9 of the Constitution. The HRC's mandate is to investigate infringements of and protect the fundamental rights guaranteed in the Bill of Rights, and to take steps to secure appropriate redress where human rights have been violated. Additionally, the Commission has limited powers to enforce the PAIA.

There are no other specific pieces of legislation on general data protection law. Other than the Constitutional right to privacy, the South African common law

---

[1683] Inspectors are given investigative, search and seizure powers, subject to obtaining a warrant (which may be issued by any Court). They may also exercise these powers without a warrant if they have reason to believe that a warrant would be issued to them on application, and if delaying the search to obtain a warrant would defeat its purpose.
[1684] Chapter XI.

protects rights of personality under the broad umbrella of the *actio injuriarum.* The elements of liability for an action based on invasion of privacy are the same as any other injury to the personality, namely an unlawful and intentional interference with another's right to seclusion and to private life. The Law Commission is currently drafting a new computer crimes law.

Financial privacy is covered by a weak code of conduct for banks issued by the Banking Council in March 2000. Credit bureau Experian accidentally made available on its web site the records on 1.5 million clients in July 1999.[1685] The information was from cell phone company Vodac and banks Nedcor, Standard Bank, Mercantile, Teljoy and Homechoice and included names, addresses and identity, telephone and cellphone numbers, and bank account details. In February 2000, it was discovered that First National Bank's (FNB) telephone banking service allowed callers to obtain a balance statement and available credit level for the accounts of any client. The service was reported to get 170,000 calls a month.[1686]

The Cabinet approved a plan in March 1998 to issue a multi-purpose smart card that combines access to all government departments and services with banking facilities. This is part of the information technology strategy formulated by the Department of Communications to provide kiosks for access to government services.[1687] In the long term, the smart card is intended to function as passport, driver's license, identity document and bankcard. The driver's license will include fingerprints. The new smart cards have not yet been issued to date.[1688]

The Promotion of Access to Information Act (AIA) was brought into operation on March 9 of 2001.[1689] The Act goes beyond defining a right of access to information held by the state, and includes a constitutional right of access to information held by private organizations as well.[1690] While the PAIA contains legislative mandates for information retention in the public sector, it contains no such framework concerning information held in the private sector. As a result, information retention is primarily left to the whim of individual system managers. The PAIA's enforcement mechanism is primarily left in the hands of the South African Judiciary, whose role in balancing a serious of competing

---

[1685] "Fears That Website Listed Confidential Bank Data," Africa News, July 12, 1999.

[1686] "FNB allows access to account balance data," Business Day, February 21, 2000.

[1687] David Shapshak, "SA services get `smart'," Mail & Guardian, April 24, 1998.

[1688] "Smart Cards To Replace ID Books In SA In 2001," Africa News, February 1, 2000.

[1689] Act No. 2 of 2000.

[1690] "Concerns Raised over Access to Information Act," Mail Guardian, May 10, 2001.

values outlined in the PAIA has been called into question due to the judges lack of formal training for interpretation of the PAIA.[1691]

Originally introduced as the Open Democracy Bill, the proposed legislation also included comprehensive data protection provisions.[1692] However, the Parliamentary committee removed those provisions in November 1999, to form part of the specific privacy law to be drafted. The Committee wrote that, "it would be dealing with the right to privacy in section 14 of the Constitution in an ad hoc and undesirable manner…it is intended that South-Africa, in following the international trend, should enact separate privacy legislation. The Committee, therefore, requests the Minister for Justice and Constitutional Development to introduce Privacy and Data Protection legislation, after thorough research on the matter, as soon as reasonably possible."[1693] As noted above, the drafting of this law is pending.

Use of the PAIA has been extremely limited since its promulgation and official statistics are not yet available. The South African History Archives (SAHA) have been the major user of this Act in a number of projects seeking access to military records and documents collected by the Truth and Reconciliation Commission. SAHA suggest that use of the Act has been limited for a number of reasons: that the culture of freedom of information has not yet taken root and the Act has been poorly publicized. The fact that requirement for manuals and guides, to be produced by government departments were suspended for a year until February 2002, means that the public has little information about the available resources.[1694]

In November 2001 South Africa signed the Council of Europe Convention on Cybercrime as a non-member signatory.[1695]

Kingdom of Spain

The Constitution recognizes the right to privacy, secrecy of communications and data protection. Article 18 states, "(1). The right of honor, personal, and family

---

[1691] Id.

[1692] Open Democracy Bill No. 67, 1998. <http://www.parliament.gov.za/bills/1998/b67-98.pdf>.

[1693] Report of the Ad hoc Committee on Open Democracy Bill [B 67-98], Parliament of the Republic of South Africa, January 24, 2000.

[1694] Michele Pickover and Verne Harris, Freedom of Information in South Africa: A Far-off Reality?, May 2001, available at <http://www.wits.ac.za/saha/foi_reports.htm>

[1695] Signed November 23, 2001.

privacy and identity is guaranteed. (2) The home is inviolable. No entry or search may be made without legal authority except with the express consent of the owners or in the case of a flagrante delicto. (3) Secrecy of communications, particularly regarding postal, telegraphic, and telephone communication, is guaranteed, except for infractions by judicial order. (4) The law shall limit the use of information, to guarantee personal and family honor, the privacy of citizens, and the full exercise of their rights."[1696]

The first Spanish Data Protection Act (LORTAD) was enacted in 1992. The LORTAD was succeeded in 1999 by an amended Data Protection Act, the LOPD, which brought Spanish law into line with the European Union Data Protection Directive.[1697] It covers files held by the public and private sector. The law establishes the right of citizens to know what personal data is contained in computer files and the right to correct or delete incorrect or false data. Personal information may only be used or disclosed to a third party with the consent of the individual and only for the purpose for which it was collected. Additional protections are provided for sensitive data. Questions still remain about citizens who do not wish to be included in the "promotional census." Consumer groups are also concerned about the law's provisions allowing use of information without consent unless the consumer has opted out of the use. In 1999 regulations on the secondary measures to be taken to protect filing systems were issued.[1698]

The Agencia de Protección de Datos is charged with enforcing the LOPD.[1699] The Agency maintains the registry and can investigate violations of the law. The agency has issued a number of decrees setting out in more detail the legal requirements for different types of information. In December 2000 it issued guidance on international transfers of data.[1700] As of December 2001, the number of registered databases was 271,875. [1701] In 2001, the agency conducted 405 investigations most of which were carried out on the basis of individual complaints. 363 complaints were received regarding the refusal of data controllers to grant subjects access to their files.[1702] In September of 2000, the

---

[1696] Constitution of Spain, as amended August 1992, available at
<http://www.uni-wuerzburg.de/law/sp00t___.html>.

[1697] Ley Organica 5/1992 de 29 de Octubre de Regulación del Tratamiento Automatizado de los Datos de Caracter Personal (LORTAD). Ley Orgánica 15/99 de 13 de Diciembre de Protección de Datos de Carácter Personal.

[1698] Royal Decre No. 994/1999

[1699] Homepage <https://www.agenciaproteccciondatos.org>.

[1700] Data Protection Authority Instruction No. 1/2000.

[1701] E-mail from Emilio Aced Felez, Agencia de Proteccion de Datos, to Sarah Andrews, Research Director, Electronic Privacy Information Center, June 27, 2002 (on file with the Electronic Privacy Information Center).
[1702] Id.

---

agency fined Telefonica, the Spanish telephone company, 60,000 euros for a glitch in its computer systems that allowed improper access to customer files.[1703] A 180 million peseta fine was issued in January of 2001 to Zeppelin, the television company producing the Spanish version of the show "Big Brother," for releasing personal information on those who tried out for the show.[1704] A 100,000 peseta fine was issued to Caja Insular de Ahorros de Canarios in February 2001, and Microsoft Iberica was fined 10 million pesetas in April for improper use of client information.[1705] The agency has recently opened an investigation against the University of Zaragoza on allegations that the university sold alumni information without permission.[1706] Appeals against decisions of the Data Protection Authority may be brought before an administrative court. In 2000, 54 such appeals were brought. The court upheld the decisions of the Authority in the majority of these cases.[1707]

In 2000 the Constitutional Tribunal of Spain issued three judgments relating to data protection.[1708] The first was a constitutional challenge against the 1992 law for breach of the provisions relating to distribution of powers between the State and other agencies (in this case the Data Protection Agency). The court rejected this challenge. The second concerned another constitutional challenge which was originally filed against the 1992 law but which carried over to the 1999 law. Upholding the constitutionality of the law generally, the court struck down certain provisions allowing government agencies to transfer personal information on Spanish citizens inter se without citizen permission. The court ruled that these provisions infringed the privacy rights guaranteed to citizens by Title 18 of the Spanish Constitution.[1709] The third case concerned an employer's processing of an employee's health data. The court ruled that the applicant's constitutional privacy rights were breached when the employer noted the employee's medical diagnosis on the sick leave records.

[1703] "Proteccion de Datos Multa con 10 millones a Telefonica por el acceso en internet a la facturacion de sus clientes,"El Pais, September 29, 2000.

[1704] "Por la fuga de datos en "Gran Hermano" la APD multa con un millon de euros a la productora Zeppelin," Expansion, January 6, 2001.

[1705] "Multada una caja de ahorros por mantener en la lista de morosos a quien ya no lo era proteccion de datos requerda que no se pueden conignar antiguas deudas como 'Saldo O'," El Pais, February 17, 2001. "Microsoft Iberica, sancionada por utilizar datos de sus clientes," Cinco Dias, April 18, 2001.

[1706] "El defensor del pueblo requiere a la Universidad de Zaragoza sobre la venta de datos," El Pais, June 4, 2001.

[1707] European Union Article 29 Data Protection Working Party, Fifth Annual Report on the Situation Regarding the Protection of Individuals with Regard to the Processing of Personal Data and Privacy in the European Union and in Third Countries Covering the Year 2000, Part II, March 6, 2002, available at <http://europa.eu.int/comm/internal_market/en/dataprot/wpdocs/wp54en_2.pdf>.

[1708] Judgement Nos. 290/2000, 292/2000, and 202/1999 respectively. Summaries available in European Union Article 29 Data Protection Working Party, Fifth Annual Report, id.

[1709] Judgement No. 292/2000.

Under the criminal code interception of communications requires a court order.[1710] There have been a number of scandals in Spain over illegal wiretapping by the intelligence services. In 1995, Deputy Prime Minister Narcis Serra, Defense Minister Julian Garcia Vargas and military intelligence chief Gen. Emilio Alonso Manglano were forced to quit following revelations that they had monitored the conversations of hundreds of people, including King Juan Carlos.[1711] An exclusionary rule applies to evidence collected by means of illegal wiretaps or bugs, and in November of 2000, the Audiencia of Barcelona through out a case because the evidence was so tainted.[1712] In May of 2001, prosecutors asked for 12 year sentences for each of two detectives accused of placing illegal wiretaps.[1713]

The 1998 Telecommunications Act guarantees the rights of individuals to use strong cryptography but also contains a provision allowing for a mandatory key recovery system. This provision was strongly opposed by civil liberties advocates. [1714] It has, so far, not been enforced. There are also additional laws in the penal code, and relating to credit information[1715] video surveillance,[1716] and automatic tellers.[1717] The government issued a decree on digital signatures in September 1999.

In June 2002, the Parliament approved the controversial Law of Information Society Services and Electronic Commerce (LSSI). The law prohibits the distribution of 'spam'; requires web hosting companies to police content and shut down websites involved in illegal activities; and mandates retention for one year of Internet users traffic data. This latter requirement was a late addition to the proposal, which had been under consideration for nearly two years. It was introduced following the approval, in May 2002, by the European Parliament of the Directive on telecommunications privacy, which contained a provision

---

[1710] Ley Organica 11/1980 de 1 de Dec 1980. Penal Code, Sections 196-199.

[1711] "Spain Socialists seek opposition apology on bugging," Reuters, February 6, 1996.

[1712] "Secreto Communicaciones Audienceia invalida pruebas obtenidas por "pinchazo" telefono, Spanish Newswire Services, November 23, 2000.

[1713] "Pinchazos telefonicos: Fiscalia pide 24 anos paragraph detectives por pinchar telefonos," Spanish Newswire Service, May 7, 2001.

[1714] See Global Internet Liberty Campaign, New Spanish Telecommunications Law Opens a Door to Mandatory Key Recovery Systems, July 1998. <http://www.gilc.org/crypto/spain/gilc-crypto-spain-798.html>.

[1715] INSTRUCCION 1/1995, de 1 de marzo, de la Agencia de Protección de Datos, relativa a prestación de servicios de información sobre solvencia patrimonial y crédito. <http://www.onnet.es/ley0029.htm>.

[1716] Ley Organica 4/1997, de 4 de agosto por la que se regula la utilización de videocámaras por las Fuerzas y Cuerpos de Seguridad en lugares públicos.

[1717] Seguridad en cajeros automáticos y otros servicios. ORDEN de 23 de abril de 1997.

allowing for preventive data retention. Following Royal assent, the law has to be published in the Official Gazette. It will take effect three months after this publication. Prior to passage, the Data Protection Authority, in a formal submission to the Government, expressed its opposition to the routine storage of traffic data.[1718] Opponents have vowed to challenge the law before the Constitutional Court arguing that it breaches constitutional rights to privacy, freedom of expression and the presumption of innocence.[1719]

The law of 30/26/11/1992 provides for access to government information.[1720] The law was amended in 1998 by Ley 29/1998, de 13 de julio. Under Article 37.2, the right of access and correction can be denied if reasons of public interest prevail.

Spain is a member of the Council of Europe and has signed and ratified the Convention for the Protection of Individuals with Regard to Automatic Processing of Personal Data (ETS No. 108).[1721] It has signed and ratified the European Convention for the Protection of Human Rights and Fundamental Freedoms.[1722] In November 2001, Spain signed the Council of Europe Convention on Cybercrime.[1723] It is a member of the Organization for Economic Cooperation and Development and has adopted the OECD Guidelines on the Protection of Privacy and Transborder Flows of Personal Data.

Kingdom of Sweden

Sweden's Constitution, which consists of several different legal documents, contains several provisions that are relevant to data protection. Section 2 of the Instrument of Government Act of 1974[1724] provides for the protection of individual privacy. Section 13 of Chapter 2 of the same instrument states also that freedom of expression and information – which are constitutionally protected pursuant to the Freedom of the Press Act of 1949[1725] – can be limited with respect to the "sanctity of private life." Moreover, Section 3 of the same chapter

---

[1718] Letter from Emilio Aced Felez, June 27, 2002, supra n.1701.

[1719] "Foes Vow to Challenge Spanish Internet Law," Associated Press, July 1, 2002.

[1720] Ley 30/1992, de 26 de Noviembre, de Régimen Jurídico de las Administraciones Públicas y del Procedimiento Administrativo Común, available at. <http://www.um.es/siu/marco/30-92.htm>.

[1721] Signed January 28, 1982; Ratified April 31, 1984; Entered into Force October 1, 1985.

[1722] Signed November 24, 1977; Ratified October 4, 1979; Entered into Force October 4, 1979.

[1723] Signed November 23, 2001.

[1724] Regeringsformen, SFS 1974:152.

[1725] Tryckfrihetsförordningen, SFS 1949:105.

provides for a right to protection of personal integrity in relation to automatic data processing. The same article also prohibits non-consensual registration of persons purely on the basis of their political opinion. The European Convention on Human Rights was been incorporated into Swedish law in 1994. The ECHR is not formally part of the Swedish Constitution but has, in effect, similar status.

Sweden enacted the Personal Data Act (PDA) of 1998 to bring Swedish law into conformity with the requirements of the EC Directive on data protection.[1726] The PDA essentially adopts the European Union Data Protection Directive into Swedish law. It regulates the establishment and use, in both public and private sectors, of automated data files on physical/natural persons. The Act replaced the Data Act of 1973, which was the first comprehensive national act on privacy in the world.[1727] The 1973 Act continued to apply until October 2001 with respect to processing of personal data initiated prior to October 24, 1998. An extended transition period, up to 2007, is allowed for pre-existing manual files. Section 33 of the Act was amended in 1999 to adopt the European Union Directive standards on the transfer of personal data to a third country. According to the Data Inspection Board, the amendment will facilitate transfer of data through international communication networks, such as the Internet. Depending on the other circumstances, there may be situations where a third country - despite not having any data protection rules at all - still can be considered having an adequate level of protection. It is also possible that the level of protection in a third country may be assessed as adequate in some areas but not in others. The amendment entered into force in January 2000.

The Data Inspection Board (Datainspektionen) is an independent board that oversees the enforcement of the Data Act.[1728] In 2001, the board received 341 complaints. 69 of these were related to the previous Act, which was still in force transitionally until October 1, 2001. The remaining 272 complaints were processed under the new Act. The Board received 475 inquiries relating to the PDA which required in depth examination. The Board also answered 15, 000 telephone inquiries and 2,500 emails. There are 2016 notified processing operations registered with the Board. 4726 controllers have personal data representatives and as such are exempted from the notification requirements. [1729] As of August 2000, the Board had 39 employees. One of their most publicized cases was against SABRE, the airline reservation system, for transferring medical

---

[1726] Personuppgiftslagen, SFS 1998:204

[1727] Datalagen, SFS 1973:289.

[1728] Homepage <http://www.datainspektionen.se>.

[1729] Email from Elisabeth Walinn, Data Inspection Board, to Sarah Andrews, Electronic Privacy Information Center, June 20, 2002 (on file with the Electronic Privacy Information Center).

information of passengers without adequate controls. The Supreme Administrative Court recently declined to hear the case following decisions by lower courts upholding the Board's ruling.

The Act provides liberal exemptions for freedom of expression. It specifically states that in the case of a conflict the existing protections for freedom of the press (Freedom of the Press Act 1949) and freedom of speech (Freedom of Speech Act) will prevail. In July 2001, the Swedish Supreme Court ruled that the operator of a web site dedicated to the criticism of a number of Swedish banks and bank officials did not violate data protection act as he was protected by the free expression exemptions. The Supreme Court thereby reversed the decision of the court of appeals that had imposed criminal fines on the web site operator for permitting the transfer of personal information outside the country without the approval of the Data Inspection Board (DIB).[1730] A number of other cases on the freedom of expression exemptions have been decided by the DIB itself, often in favor of the speaker.[1731] The DIB has also proposed an amendment to the Act to cover "harmless data."[1732]

There are a number of so called 'register laws' in Sweden which supplement the PDA rules on files containing personal data. Some examples include the Health Care Register Act of 1998[1733], the Police Data Act of 1998[1734], the Land Register Act of 2000,[1735] and the Schengen Information System Act of 2000.[1736] Other statutes with provisions relating to data protection include the Secrecy Act of 1980,[1737] the Credit Information Act of 1973,[1738] the Debt Recovery Act of 1974,[1739] and the Administrative Procedure Act of 1986.[1740] In 2001 additional laws were adopted to cover the processing of personal data for taxation purposes

---

[1730] "Web Publication of Defamatory Text Shielded by Swedish Privacy Law's News Media Clause," by Stephen Joyce, BNA Daily Report for Executives, July 24, 2001.

[1731] For a review of these cases see, Peter Blume et al, Nordic Data Protection 132-137 (DJOF Publishing 2001).

[1732] Jacqueline Klosek, Data Privacy in the Information Age 106 (Quorum Books 2000).

[1733] SFS 1998:544

[1734] SFS 1998:622

[1735] SFS2000:224

[1736] SFS 2000:344

[1737] Sekretesslagen, SFS 1980:100. For information on the background to the new Act, see the report,Integritet-Offentlighet-InformationsteknikIntegrity-Publicity–Information Technology, SOU 1997:39.

[1738] Kreditupplysningslag, SFS 1973:1173, available at <http://www.datainspektionen.se/in_english/legislation/credit.shtml>.

[1739] Inkassolag, SFS 1974:182, available at <http://www.datainspektionen.se/in_english/legislation/debt.shtml>.

[1740] Förvaltningslagen, SFS 1986:223.

and social services.[1741] A bill to amend the Credit Reporting Act and bring it into line with the European Union Data Directive and the Swedish PDA was approved by the Finance Committee in April, 2001.[1742]

National identification numbers have been in use in Sweden for years. During the 1990s the 1973 Data Act was amended to introduce restrictions on their use. These restrictions were reproduced in the new PDA. Under section 22 of this Act information about personal identity numbers or classification numbers may only be processed without consent, if the processing is clearly justified having regard to the purpose of the processing, the importance of secure identification, or some other substantial reason.[1743]

In 1999 the Swedish government established a Committee to study workplace privacy issues. The Committee is chaired by former Justice Minister Reidunn Lauren and includes a member of the Data Inspection Board. In March 2002 the Committee issued a proposal recommending specific legislation to protect the personal information of current employees, former employees and employment applicants in both the private and public sectors.[1744] According to the Committee Chair a bill will likely not be introduced on this issue until Spring 2003.[1745]

In November 2000 the Parliament passed the Act on Electronic Signatures.[1746] This came into effect on January 1, 2001.

The 1998 Law on Secret Camera Surveillance restricts the use of video surveillance. Permits must be obtained, and clearly visible notices posted, for video surveillance of public places. Post offices, banks and stores, however, need only register by mail in order to set up cameras to film entrances, exits and cash points if the intention is crime prevention.[1747] Penalties for breach of the law include fines and one-year imprisonment. In April 2002 charges were brought

---

[1741] Email from Elisabeth Walinn, supra n.1729.

[1742] Baker & McKenzie, Global E-Commerce, What's New, April 9, 2001, available at <http://www.bmck.com/ecommerce/whatsnew-global-jan-july-2001.htm>.

[1743] Information on the Personal Data Act," Ministry of Justice, Sweden, available at <http://justitie.regeringen.se/inenglish/pressinfo/pdf/puleng.pdf>.

[1744] The proposal (in Swedish with a summary in English) is available at <http://naring.regeringen.se/propositioner_mm/sou/pdf/sou2002_18a.pdf>.

[1745] "Sweden Concerns Over Employer Monitoring," BNA World Data Protection Report, Volume 2, Issue 4, April 2002.

[1746] SFS 2000:832

[1747] International Helsinki Federation for Human Rights, "Human Rights in the OSCE Region: The Balkans, the Caucasus, Europe, Central Asia and North America," Report 2002 (events 2001), available at <http://www.ihf-hr.org/reports/AR2002/country%20links/Sweden.htm>.

---

against a man for installing a video camera, without a permit, on his balcony to watch the street below.[1748]

A court order is required to obtain a wiretap.[1749] The law was amended in 1996 to facilitate surveillance of new technologies.[1750] The Prosecutor General's Office submits a report to Parliament every year with details of all of electronic surveillance conducted. The Swedish Helsinki Committee has concluded that the state interference in the private lives of its citizens lacked in legal rights and transparency. They have recommended better oversight by parliament of these surveillance techniques as well as an independent assessment of their necessity and effectiveness "[1751] In 2000 the Minister of Justice proposed an amendment to expand the use of police wiretapping and other surveillance techniques.[1752] This proposal has not gone through and is still being reworked due to strong resistance from NGOs.

Internal security is the responsibility of the security police, an independent agency under the overall control of the National Police Board. Oversight is conducted by the Register Board which was established in 1996.[1753] The consolidated Act on Special Monitoring of Foreigners (1991) grants the security police the authority to conduct "exploratory" phone tapping.[1754] The Register Board released a report in December 1998 revealing that Sweden's police/security services carried out, over a long period, covert surveillance of thousands of Swedish citizens, mostly politically leftists, often on highly tenuous or trivial grounds from 1969 until 1996. The intelligence agency also used their files to attempt to prevent journalists critical of them from being hired by the national television and radio networks. The surveillance had been repeatedly denied to exist by high government officials such as the Justice Chancellor, who at the same time wrote secret reports about the investigations.[1755] The Lund/McDonald commission was set up in early 1999 in order to investigate these surveillance practices, which were demanded by the United States as a condition to receiving military technology. In April 1999 a new law on Police

---

[1748] "Man Could Go to Prison for Mounting Camera on his Balcony," National Post, April 3, 2002.

[1749] Law 1974/203 amended by Law 1989/529/.

[1750] Law of 8 May 1996.

[1751] See International Helsinki Federation for Human Rights, Report 2002, supra n. 1747.

[1752] United States State Department, Country Report on Human Rights Practices- 2001, March 2002, available at <http://www.state.gov/g/drl/rls/hrrpt/2001/eur/8338.htm>.

[1753] Report on Swedish Security Police, by Dennis Töllborg and Iain Cameron, available at <http://q-reportage.com/dennis/a8.htm>.

[1754] Id.

[1755] "Sweden: The personnel control system 1969-1996," Statewatch Bulletin, Volume 9, Number 1 (January-February 1999).

Data was introduced and specifically prohibits security police filing of individuals solely on the grounds of "ethnical background, political opinion, religious or philosophical conviction, trade union membership, health details, or sexual preferences."[1756]

Previously, it was also discovered that the Swedish statistical agency, Statistika, was monitoring 15,000 Stockholm residents born in 1953 in intimate detail. The information included statistics on drinking habits, religious beliefs, and sexual orientation. The DIB subsequently ordered the destruction of the master tape containing the data.[1757]

In May 2002 the Swedish Parliament approved two anti-terrorism laws. One implements the UN Convention on the Suppression of the Financing of Terrorism and entered in force on July 1, 2002. The second adopts the Framework Decision of the European Union Council on Combatting Terrorism which was issued in late 2001. In January 2002 Sweden and Latvia signed a joint agreement on cooperation in areas relating to justice and interior affairs. The agreement will stay in place until December 2003 and will involve cooperation on a number of issues including judicial training, information sharing and data protection, crime prevention and probation services.[1758]

Sweden is a country that has traditionally adhered to the Nordic tradition of open access to government files. The world's first freedom of information act was the Riksdag's (Swedish Parliament) "Freedom of the Press Act of 1766." The Act required that official documents should "upon request immediately be made available to anyone making a request" at no charge. The Freedom of the Press Act is now part of the Constitution and decrees that "every Swedish citizen shall have free access to official documents." Decisions by public authorities to deny access to official documents may be appealed to general administrative courts and ultimately, to the Supreme Administrative Court. The Parliamentary Ombudsman has some oversight functions for freedom of information.

Sweden is a member of the Council of Europe and has signed and ratified the Convention for the Protection of Individuals with Regard to Automatic Processing of Personal Data (ETS No. 108).[1759] It has signed and ratified the European Convention for the Protection of Human Rights and Fundamental

---

[1756] Act on Police Data (Polisdatalag 1998: 622) section 5.

[1757] Wayne Madsen, Handbook of Personal Data Protection, (New York: Stockton Press, 1992).

[1758] "Swedish- Latvian Justice, Interior Affairs Agreements Signed," Baltic News Service, January 31, 2002.

[1759] Signed January 28, 1981; Ratified September 29, 1982; Entered into Force October 1, 1985.

Freedoms.[1760] In November 2001 it signed the Council of Europe Convention on Cybercrime (ETS No. 185).[1761] It is a member of the Organization for Economic Cooperation and Development and has adopted the OECD Guidelines on the Protection of Privacy and Transborder Flows of Personal Data.

Swiss Confederation (Switzerland)

Article 36(4) of the 1874 Constitution guaranteed, "[t]he inviolability of the secrecy of letters and telegrams." This Constitution was repealed and replaced by public referendum in April 1999. The new constitution, which entered into force on January 1, 2000, greatly expanded the older privacy protection provision. Article 13 of the Constitution now states: "All persons have the right to receive respect for their private and family life, home, mail and telecommunications. All persons have the right to be protected against abuse of their personal data." [1762]

The Federal Act of Data Protection of 1992 regulates personal information held by federal government and private bodies.[1763] The Act requires that information must be legally and fairly collected and places limits on its use and disclosure to third parties. Private companies must register if they regularly process sensitive data or transfer the data to third parties. Transfers to other nations must be registered and the recipient nation must have equivalent laws. Individuals have a right of access to correct inaccurate information. Federal agencies must register their databases. There are criminal penalties for violations. To date, the Parliament is discussing a revision of the act, which in its main parts provides better regulations for the protection against the transfer of data especially by private bodies. It also tries to adapt Swiss data protection law to the standards of the European Union Data Protection Directive. However, the government also proposes a major change in a new art. 17a, which allows federal authorities to create new data banks and to process personal data without previous regulation by the law, "if major public interest does not allow a postponement of data processing or if a testing phase, before the law enters into force, is required." In this case, the government only has to produce a decree.[1764] There are also separate data protection acts for the "Cantons" (states). However there are still

---

[1760] Signed November 28, 1950; Ratified February 4, 1952; Entered into Force September 3, 1953.

[1761] Signed November 23, 2001.

[1762] Constitution of Switzerland, 1999, available at <http://www.uni-wuerzburg.de/law/sz00000_.html>.

[1763] Loi fédérale sur la protection des données (LPD) du 19 juin 1992.

[1764] Eidgenössisches Justiz- und Polizeidepartement: Entwurf zur Teilrevision dess Bundesdatenschutzgesetzes, Bern im August 2001 (Federal department of justice and police: Pre-draft for a partial revision of the federal data protection act, Berne August 2001

---

some cantons that do not have data protection laws and thus do not have data protection commissioners.

In June 1999, the European Union Data Protection Working Party determined that Swiss law was adequate under the European Union Directive.[1765] In July 2000, the European Commission formally adopted this position, thereby approving all future transfers of all personal data transfers to Switzerland.[1766]

The 1992 Act created the office of a Federal Data Protection Commissioner.[1767] The commissioner maintains and publishes the Register for Data Files, supervises federal government and private bodies, provides advice, issues recommendations and reports, and conducts investigations. The commissioner also consults with the private sector. In its most recent report covering the period from April 2000 to March 2001, the Commissioner addressed in detail, the use of video surveillance in the public and private sectors, monitoring of employee emails and Internet use, employee drug testing, DNA profiling by law enforcement, privacy in e-commerce, seal programs and the adequacy of Safe Harbor. The report also criticized certain practices of the postal service, and called for increased compliance of the medical sector with the legal requirements on the processing of personal information. Finally it addressed the need for strong technologies and amendments to the law to combat the increasing threat to privacy posed by the Internet.[1768] In previous reports, the Commissioner has recommended the introduction of legislation, similar to that in Germany, providing an explicit right to anonymity.[1769] In 2001, the commission also issued guidance on surveillance of Internet and email use in the workplace and the use of video surveillance technologies. There are currently 20 people employed by the Commissioner, most of them, however, working part-time.

Until the beginning of 2002, telephone tapping was governed by Art 179 *octies* of the Penal Code and corresponding regulations in the federal, the military and

---

[1765] Working Party on the Protection of Individuals with Regard to the Processing of Personal Data, Opinion 5/99 on the level of protection of personal data in Switzerland, 7 June 1999, available at <http://europa.eu.int/comm/dg15/en/media/dataprot/wpdocs/wp22fr.pdf>

[1766] European Union, Press Release, "Commission adopts decisions recognising adequacy of regimes in United States, Switzerland and Hungary," July 27, 2000, available at <http://europa.eu.int/comm/internal_market/en/media/dataprot/news/safeharbor.htm>.

[1767] Home Page <http://www.edsb.ch/>.

[1768] Préposé Fédéral De La Protection Des Données, 8eme Rapport d'Activités 2000/2001, available at <http://www.edsb.ch/framesf.html>.

[1769] Préposé Fédéral De La Protection Des Données, 7e Rapport D'Activités 1999/2000, available at <http://www.edsb.ch/framesf.html>.

---

the cantonal Penal Procedure Codes.[1770] Due to liberalization of the Telecom sector by the 1997 Telecommunication Act, the government issued a decree which established a specialized agency, Le Service des Tâches Spéciales (STS), within the Department of the Environment, Transport, Energy and Communications, to administer wiretaps.[1771] Until then, the technical procedures for wiretapping were carried out by a special service within the PTT-telecom, the state monopoly company. The STS now has the function of a connecting link between the special services of the different private and state owned telecom companies and the public prosecutors, who issue an interception order. Already under the old legal regulation, every interception order had to be confirmed by the allowance of a prosecution chamber of the federal court or the cantonal high court respectively.

On January 1, 2002, a new Federal Law on the surveillance of mail and telecommunications entered into force.[1772] It is the product of parliamentary debates that started in 1999, when the federal Department on Justice and Police (Justice Ministry) presented a first draft for that law, which replaces federal and cantonal regulations. The Law Commission of the National Council (Great Chamber of the federal Parliament) rejected this draft and prepared its own, which constitutes the basis of the new law. Whereas, until then, interception was possible in all investigations relating to crimes and offences (crimes for which a prison sanction can be issued), the new law prohibits any preventive interception and provides, for the first time, for a catalogue of offences. The requirements for an order by a prosecutor and the respective allowance of a prosecution chamber are more precise. The catalogue thus impedes interceptions like in the Canton of Berne where, in 1995, the phone of a family was tapped to investigate against the 18-year old son, who was suspected to be the author a series of graffitti. Nevertheless, the list of offences does not stop the avalanche of tapping actions since the beginning of the nineties. While at the beginning of that decade about 500 interception orders were issued annually, the number has continuously increased to about 2,000 orders since 1996 (2,138 cases).[1773] To these orders, another 2,000 cases of disclosure of traffic data has to be added. Traffic data have to be retained by the providers for six months backward. In the case of mobile

---

[1770] Art 66-73, Procédure pénale fédérale, Loi du 23 Mars 1979 sur la protection de la vie priveé.

[1771] Telecommunications Law (LTC) of 30 April 1997. Ordonnance du 1er décembre 1997 sur le service de surveillance de la correspondance postale et des télécommunications, available at <http://www.admin.ch/ch/f/rs/c780_11.html>.

[1772] Loi fédérale sur la surveillance de la correspondance postale et des télécommunications, (www.admin.ch/ch/f/rs/c780_1.html) and the respective new decree (www.admin.ch/ch/f/rs/c780_11.html)

[1773] Conseil National, Heures de Questions: Session d'hiver 1999. Réponse du Conseil fédéral concernant les écoutes téléphoniques, 20 Décembre 1999, available at <http://www.parlament.ch/afs/data/f/gesch/1999/f_gesch_19993427.htm>.

phones, this also includes information on the location of speakers. This, however, requires that the respective telephone companies constantly track phones, and that they store the data hereby collected. In the course of the parliamentary debate, the Conseil des Etats (Small Chamber of the Parliament) voted in the spring of 2000 in favor of the registration of all users of prepaid calling cards.[1774] This proposal was eventually dropped but is likely to resurface at a later date.

The new law also provides for the surveillance of e-mails, which are treated as every other telecommunication. Providers will thus have to create the respective interfaces to make surveillance possible. In these cases, traffic data will also have to be retained for 6 months. In December 1997, the newspaper *Sonntags Zeitung* had reported that Swisscom, (formerly PTT), was tracking the location of cellular phone users and maintaining those records for an extended period.[1775] The Data Protection Commissioner issued a report on this subject in July 1998.[1776] Swisscom at that occasion denied the tracking practice. Company speakers argued that the company was acting completely legal. Indeed, the article of the Sonntags Zeitung was wrong, in the sense, that location data only are transmitted to the police in case of a judicial order. However, the tracking of cellular phones itself is inevitable for the technical functioning of the net and the retainment of data was already at that time was proscribed by the Telecommunications law - for billing purposes on the one hand and for the purposes of a judicially ordered surveillance on the other.

There have been numerous public revelations of illegal wiretapping. A 1993 inquiry found that phones used by journalists and ministers in the Swiss Parliament were tapped.[1777] The Data Protection Commissioner also accused the Telecom PTT, the state telephone company, of illegally wiretapping telephones. There were considerable protests in 1996 when it was revealed that the federal prosecutor was wiretapping journalists to discover their sources after which Swiss President Arnold Koller described the taps as "excessive."[1778] In February 1998, an agent for Israel's Mossad Secret Service was arrested by the Swiss authorities for attempting to tap the phone of a Lebanese immigrant whom he believed had links to the Hizbollah. On July 7, 2000 the Swiss court handed down a one year sentence to be suspended for two-years.[1779]

[1774] "Les utilisateurs de portables devront être identifiables," Service de base française, June 20, 2000.

[1775] Digital Cellular Report, January 15, 1998.

[1776] See <http://cryptome.com/swisscom-nix.htm>.

[1777] Statewatch bulletin, Volume 3, Number 1, January-February 1993.

[1778] "Phone Taps Raise Ire Of Swiss Public, Media," Christian Science Monitor, March 14, 1997.

[1779] "Swiss court hands Mossad spy a suspended one-year sentence," Associated Press, July 10, 2000.

In 1989, a Parliamentary inquiry revealed that the Federal Police (the political police) had collected files on about 900,000 people, most of whom were not suspected of having committed any offence. In 1991 a citizens committee launched a popular initiative to abolish the political police. Surveillance should only be possible on the grounds of a criminal investigation. The vote on the initiative was postponed by the Government for years. In June 1998, nine years after the scandal 75 percent of the voters said no to the initiative. The Federal government had saved its political police, which since the beginning of the nineties had been completely modernized and, in July 1998, received for the first time in history a legal basis with the Law on Measures for Maintaining Internal Security.[1780] The former "federal police" now named "Service for Analysis and Prevention" is part of the "Federal Office for Police Matters", which also includes the Federal Criminal Police. It hosts two data banks: ISIS, which is the information system for internal security, which replaced the old paper files of the federal police. ISIS contains files on about 50,000 persons who are considered as "terrorists", "violent extremists" or possible spies. Files are opened on "preventive" grounds, which means that no criminal investigation is required. However, data resulting from criminal investigations and thus also from telephone surveillance can be maintained for preventive purposes, even if the person is acquitted before a court. The other data bank, JANUS, is the fusion of three information systems which have been built up during the nineties, and had been maintained separately until 1998: DOSIS, which held data on investigations in drug trafficking; ISOK, the information system on "organized crime"; and FAMP which includes information about false money, trafficking human beings (prostitution) and illicit pornography. Files in JANUS can be created on the grounds of simple suspicion. Most of the 62,500 persons filed in JANUS in July 2001 were registered for alleged drug trafficking, since registration of consumers is not allowed. The records on the 62,500 suspected persons *(Stammpersonen =* main Persons) also contain 116,500 references on third persons, which are not suspected. Among them, 13,500 are so-called "contact persons"; 13,000 are telephone subscribers (with their names and addresses); and about 90,000 are telephone numbers with only fragmentary information to the respective persons.[1781]

In May 2000 a decree was passed to establish a DNA database within the Federal Office for Police. The data protection commissioner strongly criticized the

---

[1780] Loi Fédérale BWIS verordnung VWIS. ISIS .

[1781] Conseil national 01-1068 - Question ordinaire de Dardel - Personnes enregistrées dans les systèmes de données JANUS et ISIS - Réponse du Conseil fédéral du 5 septembre 2001.

measure and insisted that a law should be quickly enacted to govern its use. The Conseil Fédéral presented a draft law on November 8, 2000, which is still subject to parliamentary debate. The draft does not provide a catalogue of offences, on the grounds of which DNA profiles could be taken. DNA profiling would be able for convicted persons and for those who are only suspected to have committed a crime or an offense. Profiling could be ordered by the police, without a judge's warrant.[1782]

Besides the Data Protection Act, there are also legal protections for privacy in the Civil Code[1783] and Penal Code,[1784] and special rules relating to workers' privacy from surveillance,[1785] telecommunications information,[1786] health care statistics,[1787] professional confidentiality including medical and legal information,[1788] medical research,[1789] and identity cards.[1790] The identity card is machine-readable as will be the new passport. During the discussion on the Law on Identity Papers (passports and ID cards), it was debated to include biometric data into the those papers. Although Parliament rejected the idea, the form of the new passport can be upgraded with such information. The draft for a new Foreigners Law, however, provides for biometric data to be included into the ID cards for foreigners. The law will also provide a definite legal basis for the Central Register of Foreigners, which at the moment holds data on about 4,5 million persons.

Banking records are protected by the Swiss Federal Banking Act 1934. This Act was passed to guarantee strong protections for the privacy and confidentiality of bank customers, allegedly for those subject to persecution for racial, political or religious reasons.[1791] Switzerland has come under increasing pressure from the

---

[1782] Verordnung über das DNA-Profil-Informationssystem vom 31.5.2000; Botschaft über das Bundesgesetz über die Verwendung von DNA-Profilen im Strafverfahren vom 8. November 2000 - 00.088

[1783] Section 28 of the Civil Code, 10 December 1907.

[1784] Code pénal, Titre troisiçme: Infractions contre l'honneur et contre le domaine secret ou le domaine privé, Art 173-179.

[1785] Section 328 of the Code of Obligations. See International Labour Organization, Conditions of Work Digest, Volume 12, 1/1993.

[1786] Telecommunications Law (LTC) of 30 April 1997.

[1787] Office fédéral de la statistique, La protection des données dans la statistique médicale, 1997. <http://www.admin.ch/bfs/stat_ch/ber14/statsant/ff1403c.htm>.

[1788] Code pénal, Art 320-322.

[1789] Ordonnance du 14 juin 1993 concernant les autorisations de lever le secret professionnel en matière de recherche médicale (OALSP), available at <http://www.admin.ch/ch/f/rs/c235_154.html>.

[1790] Ordinance du 18 mai 1994 relative à la carte d'identité Suisse, available at <http://www.admin.ch/ch/f/rs/c143_3.html>.

[1791] "Swiss News," Information Access Company, November 1, 1999. See also, Paolo S. Grassi and Daniele Calvarese, The Duty of Confidentiality of Banks in Switzerland, 7 Pace Int'l L. Rev. 329, on effects of money laundering legislation on limiting banking privacy.

European Union and OECD to weaken these laws and provide greater access to bank records for the purposes of tax collection. Swiss Finance Minister, Kaspar Villiger, initially rejected these calls, maintaining that the banking secrecy laws are essential for Switzerland's role as an important financial center.[1792] However, in October 2000, following the scandal involving the funds of Sani Abacha, former dictator of Nigeria, it was announced that the Swiss banking laws would be amended.[1793] In January 2001, Lukas Muhlemann, chairman of Credit Suisse, urged the government not to submit to European Union pressure, proposing alternative less privacy invasive means to fight tax evasion.[1794]

The Government has proposed new amendments in the criminal law to deal with "terrorist organizations" and "financing of terrorism" as well as for the ratification of the UN convention against terrorist financing.[1795] When presenting his annual report on July 1, 2002, the Data Protection Commissioner warned, that Switzerland is under foreign pressure to cut fundamental rights of privacy, saying "Perfect security is not possible. Those who go in this direction, are taking the risk of a totalitarian state"[1796]

Switzerland is a member of the Council of Europe and signed and ratified the Convention for the Protection of Individuals with Regard to Automatic Processing of Personal Data (ETS No. 108) in 1997.[1797] Switzerland has signed and ratified the European Convention for the Protection of Human Rights and Fundamental Freedoms. In November 2001, Switzerland signed the Council of Europe Convention on Cybercrime.[1798] It is a member of the Organization for Economic Cooperation and Development and has adopted the OECD Guidelines on the Protection of Privacy and Transborder Flows of Personal Data.

Republic of China (Taiwan)

Article 12 of the 1946 Republic of China Constitution states, "The people shall have freedom of privacy of correspondence." Additionally, the Constitution

---

[1792] "Switzerland's Villiger says bank secrecy still needed," AFX News Limited, June 7, 2000.

[1793] "Swiss Tighten Money Laundering Laws," Private Banker International, October 13, 2000.

[1794] "Fight European Union Stand on Secrecy, Swiss Banker Urges," Financial Times (London), January 23, 2001.

[1795] "lutte contre le terrorisme", www.ofj.admin.ch/themen/terror/intro-f.htm with further leading links

[1796] "Bilanz des Datenschutzbeauftragten", Wochenzeitung WoZ july 4, 2002

[1797] Signed October 2, 1997; Ratified October 2, 1997; Entered into force February 1, 1998.

[1798] Signed November 23, 2001.

protects many rights that have an impact on privacy, such as free exercise of religion (Article 13) and freedom of association (Article 14).[1799]

The most important statutory privacy provision in Taiwan is the Computer-Processed Personal Data Protection Law, enacted in August 1995.[1800] The Act governs the collection and use of personally identifiable information by government agencies and many areas of the private sector. It requires that "[t]he collection or utilization of personal data shall respect the rights and interests of the principal and such personal data shall be handled in accordance with the principles of honesty and credibility so as not to exceed the scope of the specific purpose." Individuals have a right of access and correction of their data, the ability to request cessation of computerized processing and use, and the ability to request deletion of their data. Data flows to countries without privacy laws can be prohibited, and damages can be assessed for violations. The Act also establishes separate principles for eight categories of private institutions: credit information organizations, hospitals, schools, telecommunication businesses, financial businesses, securities businesses, insurance businesses, and mass media, as well as "other enterprises, organizations, or individuals designated by the Ministry of Justice and the central government authorities in charge of concerned end enterprises."

There is no single privacy oversight body to enforce the Act. The Ministry of Justice enforces the Act for government agencies. For the private sector, the relevant government agency for that sector enforces compliance. For example, the Criminal Investigation Bureau (CIB) arrested several people in November 1998 for selling lists of more than 15 million voters and personal data of up to 40 million individuals in violation of the Act.[1801]

Several laws control spying or surveillance by private parties. Article 315 of Taiwan's Criminal Code states that a person who, without reason, opens or conceals a sealed letter or other sealed document belonging to another may be punished under the law. The 1996 Telecommunications Law states "Unauthorized third parties shall not receive, record or use other illegal means to infringe upon the secrets of telecommunications enterprises and telecommunications messages. A telecommunications enterprise should take

---

[1799] Constitution of the Republic of China, Adopted by the National Assembly on December 25, 1946, promulgated by the National Government on January 1, 1947, and effective from December 25, 1947. <http://www.president.gov.tw/1_roc_intro/index_e.html>.

[1800] Computer-Processed Personal Data Protection Law of August 11, 1995, available at <http://www.virtual-asia.com/taiwan/bizpack/legalcodes/cpdpl.htm>.

[1801] "Police arrest data thieves," China News, November 10, 1998.

proper and necessary measures to protect its telecommunications security."[1802] The Act was amended in October 1999 to increase penalties for illegal telephone taps to NT 1.5 million (USD 44,182) and up to five years in prison.

Illegal wiretapping by the government has been a widespread problem in Taiwan for years. Previously, under the martial law-era Telecommunications Surveillance Act and Code of Criminal Procedure, judicial and security authorities simply had to file a written request with a prosecutor's office to wiretap a suspect's telephone calls. In June 1999, the Parliament approved the Telecommunication Protection and Control Act in to impose stricter guidelines on when and how wiretaps can be used, although they can still be approved for broad reasons such as "national security" and "social order." The act also requires telecommunications providers to assist law enforcement and sets technical requirements for interception, which is opposed by mobile phone providers.[1803] In 1998, the Supreme Court ruled that evidence obtained through illegal wiretaps was not admissible in a criminal trial.

The Prosecutor General's Office revealed in 1999 that over 15,000 people were subject to wiretapping, including for "political intelligence" in the first half of 1999.[1804] According to the United States State Department, the number of wiretaps was reduced to 3377 in 2000 and 6505 in the year 2001 following the enactment of the new law.[1805] In January 2000, a wiretap was found at the campaign office of presidential candidate (now President) Chen Shui-bian.[1806] Independent presidential candidate James Soong alleged in November 1999 that the government was tapping his campaign and home phones.[1807]

The new law also regulates wiretapping by the intelligence services, which previously operated without any supervision. In October 2000, Chin Huei-chu, a People First Party legislator accused the Military Intelligence Bureau (MIB) of conducting political surveillance domestically. The MIB denied the allegations saying that all intelligence work was directed solely at mainland China.[1808] Many legislators also claim that the National Security Bureau, which oversees

---

[1802] Telecommunications Law 1996, February 5, 1996.

[1803] "Private cellular firms feel threatened by wiretap law," Taipei Times, November 13, 1999.

[1804] "Surveillance must not be abused," China News, November 7, 1999.

[1805] United States Department of State, Country Reports on Human Rights Practices 2001, March 4, 2002, available at <http://www.state.gov/g/drl/rls/hrrpt/2001/eap/8294.htm>.

[1806] "'Taiwan's Watergate,' says Chen after wiretap found," Taipei Times, January 26, 2000.

[1807] "Soong aides make wiretapping claim," China News, November 4, 1999.

[1808] "Military Intelligence Bureau Denies Political Surveillance At Home," British Broadcasting Corporation, October 11, 2000.

national law enforcement, routinely monitors the phone conversations of politicians. This charge is also denied by the NSB.[1809]

Under the HIV Prevention Law, the government can demand that foreigners who have been in Taiwan for over three months provide an HIV test, and may deport them if they test positive.[1810] This is a liberalization of the earlier rule, which called for mandatory deportation of HIV-positive foreigners.[1811]

Plans for a national ID system are still developing. In 1997, the Taiwanese government proposed a new national ID card called the "National Integrated Circuit Card." The plan called for a smart card based system with over 100 uses for the card including ID, health insurance, driver's license, taxation and possibly small-value payments. Following public outcry based on the privacy implications of the plan, the government held hearings to evaluate it again. Eventually, the government abandoned the plan[1812] in favor of a traditional paper ID which will not contain fingerprints or other biometric information.[1813] However, a based-based system just for health information, using the national ID number, has been developed and will be implemented next year.[1814]

Voyeurism and scandalous revelations in the media have prompted new demands for enhanced privacy protection. A video allegedly of a Taipei city council member engaged in sexual relations with her married lover – shot with a hidden pinhole camera – was released by a gossip magazine last year.[1815] Pornographic videos of female subjects taken without their knowledge have turned up on the internet.[1816] In March of 2002, President Chen's daughter was forced to publicly deny that a hidden "pinhole" video of an intimate couple was of her and her future husband.[1817] In response, lawmakers are looking to strengthen the 1999

[1809] Jimmy Chuang, "NSB denies bugging lawmakers," Taipei Times, April 5, 2002, available at <http://www.taipeitimes.com/news/2002/04/05/print/0000130595>.

[1810] "Legislature revises HIV Prevention Law regarding foreigners found to be positive," Taipei Times, July 1, 2000.

[1811] An Enforcement Ordinance of the HIV Prevention Law .

[1812] "When Smart Cards Get Too Smart," The Industry Standard, September 7, 1998.

[1813] Tsai Ting-I, "Fingerprint law likely to be axed," Taipei Times, January 1, 2002, available at <http://www.taipeitimes.com/news/2002/01/01/print/0000118132>.

[1814] Chuang Chi-ting, "Paperless health-cards unveiled," Taipei Times, November 12, 2001, available at <http://www.taipeitimes.com/news/2001/11/12/print/0000111165>..

[1815] Tsai Ting-I, "Legislators target hidden cameras," Taipei Times, March 12, 2002, available at <http://www.taipeitimes.com/news/2002/03/12/print/0000127325>.

[1816] Tsai Ting-I, "Legislators demand tougher legislation for candid cameras," Taipei Times, March 6, 2002, available at <http://www.taipeitimes.com/news/2002/03/12/print/0000126529>.

[1817] Lawrence Chung, "Stop fanning such voyeurism, Taipei govt tells media," Straights Times (Singapore), March 2, 2002.

criminal law (Article 315) punishing circulation of illegally recorded activities. Currently, the law mandates prison terms of 5 years or fines of NT 50,000 (USD 1,473).

Taiwan is one of only a few non-Muslim states to criminalize adultery.[1818] This law corresponds to a strong social condemnation of sexual adventurism, which encourages the media to look for indiscretions among the famous. In July 2001, Taiwan industries announced the production of a special mobile 'spy phones.' The phones have a special chip that is supposed to be able to pick up sounds and voices in the near vicinity of the phone. Dialing a special code can remotely activate the chip. They are being marketed towards housewives as a means to spy on their husbands to see if they are having an extra-marital affair.[1819]

An increasing number of Taiwanese access the Internet in cyber-cafes,[1820] and Taiwan has new regulations for browsing in such establishments. The city of Taipei implemented a law last year banning cyber-cafes within 200 meters of a school and limiting the hours children could enter the cafes. In response to protestations by owners of cyber-cafes, the national government superceded the Taipei law with new regulations. Now, the popular shops now must be no closer than 50 meters from schools, and need not restrict hours for children 15-18.[1821] Also, the management of the cafes agreed to keep customers from accessing "questionable" material, but will not required to directly monitor Internet use.[1822]

Kingdom of Thailand

Section 34 of the 1997 Constitution states, "A persons family rights, dignity, reputation or the right of privacy shall be protected. The assertion or circulation of a statement or picture in any manner whatsoever to the public, which violates or affects a person's family rights, dignity, reputation or the right of privacy, shall not be made except for the case which is beneficial to the public." Section 37 states, "Persons have the freedom to communication with one another by lawful means. Search, detention or exposure of lawful communication materials between and among persons, as well as actions by other means so as to snoop

---

[1818] "Adultery: the pursuit of happiness – or a crime against the state?" Asiaweek, November 16, 2001.

[1819] "Taiwan Wives Can Spy On Spouses With Special Phone," Straits Times (Singapore), July 22, 2001.

[1820] "Taiwan Internet Usage at Cybercafes Up 9.2% in Two Years," Chinese Information and Cultural Center, July 8, 2001, available at <http://www.taipei.org/teco/cicc/news/english/e-07-08-01/e-07-08-01-13.htm>.

[1821] "Government unveils Net café provisions," Taiwan Headlines, December 5, 2001, available at <http://www.taiwanheadlines.gov.tw/20011205/20011205s1.html>.

[1822] Adam Creed, "Taiwan drafts new rules for internet cafes," Washington Post, December 6, 2001.

---

into the contents of the communications materials between and among persons, is prohibited unless it is done by virtue of the power vested in a provision of the law specifically for the purpose of maintaining national security or for the purpose of maintaining peace and order or good public morality." Section 58 states, "A person shall have the right to get access to public information in possession of a State agency, State enterprise or local government organization, unless the disclosure of such information shall affect the security of the State, public safety or interests of other persons which shall be protected as provided by law." [1823]

The National Information Technology Committee (NITC) approved plans in February 1998 for a series of information technology (IT) laws. Six sub-committees under the National Electronics and Computer Technology Centre (Nectec) were set up to draft the following bills: E-Commerce Law, EDI Law, Privacy Data Protection Law, Computer Crime Law, Electronics Digital Signature Law, Electronics Fund Transfer Law and Universal Access Law. All six bills were reportedly submitted to the Cabinet in January 2000.[1824] In July 2000, the Cabinet approved, the Electronic Transactions Bill, a combined electronic commerce and digital signature measure.[1825] The bill was finally passed by Parliament in October 2001[1826] and became effective in April 2002.[1827] The law allows electronic documents to be used as evidence in Court and make digital signatures legally binding.

Work has been under way for a number of years on a draft data protection law but so far it has not been introduced in Parliament. The draft is based on eight principles of data protection, including consent, notice, purpose specification and use limitation, accuracy, access, security and enforcement.[1828] The law would also establish a data protection committee. The Association of Thai Computer Industry (ATCI) has said that it would welcome the introduction of a data protection law.[1829] A survey of ISP subscribers, conducted by the Bangkok Post in November 2001, found that 39 percent of all respondents were concerned about their privacy and possible abuse of personal data provided to their ISP.[1830]

1823 Constitution of the Kingdom of Thailand, 1997, available at
<http://www.krisdika.go.th/law/text/lawpub/e11102540/text.htm>.
1824 "IT laws will be reviewed today- Ready for Cabinet early next month," Bangkok Post, January 20, 2000.
1825 "Cabinet Okays E-commerce Law Draft," The Nation (Thailand) July 27, 2000
1826 "Thailand's Parliament Passes Electronic Transactions Law, Bangkok Post, October 30, 2001
1827 "E-Law Becomes Effective Today But Uncertainties Still Remain," Bangkok Post, April 3, 2002 available at <http://www.bangkokpost.com/030402_Database/03Apr2002_data82.html>.
1828 "Data Protection Laws under Discussion," Bangkok Post, July 4, 2001.
1829 "Industry body prods Govt on privacy issues - Laws needed to gain trust," Bangkok Post, May 10, 2000.
1830 "Slow Links The Biggest Issue That Dial-Up Users Face, But Over Two-Thirds Are Satisfied," Bangkok Post, December 12, 2001.

A draft of the Computer Crime law was approved, with reservations, by the Prime Minister in May 2002. Under the draft law the publication of child pornography would be punishable by five years imprisonment and a large fine and hacking into computer networks with malicious intent would be punishable by two years imprisonment. The law would also criminalize the use of computers for fraudulent purposes. It would grant "State Officers" defined as police and officials of any other organization established by the legislation, widespread powers of search and seizure. The Prime Minister expressed concern about these powers saying that the Council of State would have to review the proposal for infringement of human rights before submitting it to his Cabinet and the Parliament for approval.[1831] Nonetheless, it is expected that the legislation will be enacted within a year. According to the drafting committee, the law is based on computer crime laws in the United States and Europe including the recent Council of Europe Convention on Cybercrime.

In July 2001, the NITC announced its intention to crack down on "inappropriate" content on Web sites. It stated that it was going to introduce new measures requiring ISPs to keep subscriber's log files and caller ID for at least three months, to include a customer responsibility clause in their update their terms of use policy, and to react immediately and block access when informed of inappropriate content on web sites. The Royal Police Department was tasked with cooperating with the NITC in enforcing the new measures. It was instructed to work with technical and legal experts in analyzing Web sites, to establish an email hotline, and to monitor all Internet cafes.[1832]

The Official Information Act was approved in 1997.[1833] The Act guarantees access to public information for all citizens and sets a code of information practices for the processing of personal information by state agencies. Section 4 of the Act defines personal information as information relating to "the particular private matters" of a person that can identify that person.[1834] The agency must ensure that the system is relevant to and necessary for the achievement of the objectives of the operation of the State agency; make efforts to collect information directly from the subject; publish material about its use in the Government Gazette; provide for an appropriate security system; notify such

[1831] "New Legislation: Cyber –criminals Targeted," The Nation (Thailand) May 3, 2002.

[1832] "Thailand Moves to Crack Down on Web Content," Newsbytes, July 26, 2001.

[1833] Official Information Act, B.E. 2540 (1997), available at
<http://www.krisdika.go.th/law/text/lawpub/e02092540/text.htm>

[1834] "Information Access and Privacy Protection in Thailand," Kittisak Prokati, Commissioner, Official Information Commission, Thailand.

person if information is collected about them from a third party; not disclose personal information in its control to other State agencies or other persons without prior or immediate consent given in writing by the person except in limited circumstances; and provide rights of access, correction and deletion.

The Official Information Commission (OIC) oversees the Act.[1835] The Commission is under the Office of the Prime Minister. In November 2000, Mr. Chungtong Opassiriwit was appointed as the new director of the Commission, following the dismissal of the former director in August 1999. In April 2001, an Information Act Amendment Committee, comprising 18 members was established. The Committee is looking at ways to enforce the Act more efficiently and effectively.

The Central Juvenile and Family Court Act and the Children and Youth Conduct Promotion Act provide protection for the basic rights, including privacy, of children in crime and sexual harassment cases. In September 2001, the Office of the Attorney General issued a statement accusing the media of not respecting these rights.[1836]

Under the 1997 Constitution the police are required to obtain a warrant before conducting a search. In practice however, the procedures for obtaining warrants under the Criminal Procedure Code are said to be outdated and warrantless or overly intrusive searches are not uncommon.[1837] In 2002 the Ministry of Justice introduced a bill to establish a Special Investigation Department (SID). Under the bill, the SID would be authorized to investigate any criminal case and to search people's homes without a warrant. They would also be authorized and to conduct body searches if suspects refused to co-operate. In June 2002, a police committee issued a report opposing the proposal saying that it could infringe on individual human rights and could lead to inter agency conflict.[1838]

Phone tapping is a criminal offense under the 1934 Telegraph and Telephone Act.[1839] Violators can face up to five years in jail. Wiretaps can be conducted for certain law enforcement purposes upon the issuance of a warrant. Under the Ant-Money Laundering Law of 1999 police are empowered to wiretap the conversations between drug dealers, clients and producers. Illegal wiretapping is

---

[1835] Homepage<http://www.oic.thaigov.go.th/>.

1836 "Media Mistreats Juveniles," Bangkok Post, September 14, 2001

[1837] United States Department of State, Country Reports on Human Rights Practices 2001, March 4, 2002 available at <http://www.state.gov/g/drl/rls/hrrpt/2001/eap/8378.htm>

1838 "Panel Affirms Opposition to SID Plan," Bangkok Post, June 30, 2002.

1839 Telegraph and Telephone Act, B.E. 2476.

common in Thailand. Communications Minister Suthep Thuagsuban told reporters in June 2000, "Tapping telephones is not new in Thailand, everybody knows there is telephone tapping...When you return home you should check your line."[1840] In April 1997, tapes and transcripts from wiretaps of Sanan Kachornprasart, the opposition party Democrat secretary-general, were found in the compound of Government House.[1841] The Armed Forces Security Center was accused of being behind the tapping.[1842] Wiretaps were found on the telephone of, Mr Veera Somkwamkid the chairperson of the Civil Rights and Freedom Protection Group, an anti corruption group in June 2000. Following the arrest of two technicians from the Telephone Organisation of Thailand (TOT) for the tap, the president of the TOT resigned. The National Counter Corruption Commission took over the investigation and closed their inquiry in June 2001.[1843] Mr Veera, announced he would appeal the decision of the Commission not to arrest "the suspected masterminds", a police general and a police colonel to the Prime Minister.[1844] In March 2002, the editor in chief of the leading daily claimed his mobile phone was being bugged by Advanced Info Services Plc, a company owned by the Prime Minister.[1845]

This alleged illegal wiretapping by the Prime Minister is said to be part of a much larger campaign to silence the media and other critics of his government. In March 2002 there was widespread controversy when it was revealed that the government's Anti-Money Laundering Office (AMLO) had ordered a secret probe into the assets of prominent media figures and NGO officials. In June 2002, the Thai Administrative Court ruled that these investigations by AMLO were unlawful and a violation of privacy.[1846]

In 1997, Thailand began issuing a new national ID card with a magnetic strip. At present, these cards are in use nine provinces. The computer system links government departments including the Revenue Department, the Ministry of Foreign Affairs, the Ministry of Defense and the Office of the Narcotics Control Board. The new ID card can also be used as an ATM card, student card and social welfare card. The government also has plans to link the system with other governments to allow holders to travel in Asian countries without the need for a

---

[1840] "Thai telecoms chief resigns amid phone tapping scandal," Agence France Presse, June 6, 2000.

[1841] "Thailand: Politics - PM Denies Chuan's Wire-tapping Claim," Bangkok Post, April 8, 1997.

[1842] "Inside Politics Infuriated by tap rap," FT Asia Intelligence Wire, July 3, 1997.

[1843] "Anti-graft agency to probe bugging case," Bankok Post, June 16, 2000.

[1844] "Probe result upsets Veera: Activist wants to examine report," Bangkok Post, June 13, 2001

[1845] "Thai Editor Claims his Cell Phone is Bugged," The Straits Times (Singapore), March 15, 2002.

[1846] "AMLO: Sinister Criminal Plot and Cover-Up," The Nation (Thailand), June 27, 2002.

passport, using only the new card.[1847] Prime Minister Thaksin Shinawatra recently criticized plans by the Social Security Office to issue single purpose smart cards for social security fund members. Instead he encouraged integration of the service into the new ID card.[1848] In August 2000, in a move towards greater e-government, the Interior Ministry's Local Administration Department (LAD) developed its own web portal, which will be used to provide a wide range of services to citizens. Citizens register for an email account with khonthai.com by entering their ID card number. Once they have an account and password they can verify data included in their civil registration accounts including their ID card details, name, address and marital status changes, and voting eligibility. The portal site currently hosts government agencies, state enterprises and private sector firms. Political parties providing election information are also listed and the system will eventually be used for e-voting. LAD also intends to introduce the system in over 300 municipal schools in the next few years. [1849]

The Official Information Act allows for citizens to obtain government information such as the result of a consideration or a decision which has a direct effect on a private individual, work-plan, project and annual expenditure estimates, and manuals or order relating to work procedure of State officials which affects the rights and duties of private individuals. Individuals can appeal denials to the Official Information Commission. In 2001 the Commission received 150 complaints and 88 requests for appeals.[1850] In June 2000, following an investigation by the OIC, the Defence Ministry released he official report on the 1992 bloody Black May military crackdown on political protests.[1851]

The 1997 Constitution provided for the establishment of a National Human Rights Commission (NHRC) to supervise, monitor and promote human rights in Thailand. In June 2001, the Senate selected the final two of the eleven member Commission. The members will serve for a period of six years.[1852]

1847 "Thailand: Issuing Computerized National Identity Cards," Newsbytes, September 8, 1997.

1848 "Thaksin not in favour of 'unnecessary' smart cards," Bangkok Post, May 27, 2001

1849 "E-Government: Email Accounts Linked to ID card," Bangkok Post, August 2, 2000.

1850 "Your Right to Know," Bangkok Post, April 1, 2002.

1851 E-mail from Nit Wirudchawong, OIC Commissioner, to EPIC, May 18, 2001.

1852 "Human Rights Commission: Senate chooses last two panel members," Bangkok Post, June 2, 2001.

Republic of Turkey

Section Five of the 1982 Turkish Constitution is entitled, "Privacy and Protection of Private Life."[1853] Article 20 of the Turkish constitution deals with "Privacy of the Individual's Life," and it states, "Everyone has the right to demand respect for his private and family life. Privacy of individual and family life cannot be violated. Exceptions necessitated by judiciary investigation and prosecution are reserved. Unless there exists a decision duly passed by a judge in cases explicitly defined by law, and unless there exists an order of an agency authorized by law in cases where delay is deemed prejudicial, neither the person nor the private papers, nor belongings of an individual shall be searched nor shall they be seized." Article 22 states, "Secrecy of communication is fundamental. Communication shall not be impeded nor its secrecy be violated, unless there exists a decision duly passed by a judge in cases explicitly defined by law, and unless there exists an order of an agency authorized by law in cases where delay is deemed prejudicial. Public establishments or institutions where exceptions to the above may be applied will be defined by law." In October 2001, in a move aimed at improving its chances of accession to the European Union, Turkey passed the Constitutional Amendment Bill, containing thirty-four proposals for amendment to the Constitution.[1854] A number of the proposals strengthen the basic rights and freedoms of individuals, including increased protection for privacy of the person and the home.[1855]

The Turkish Ministry of Justice has been working on data protection legislation for several years without success. In the summer of 2000 a working party was established to facilitate this effort but so far there are no reports of any progress and a public draft has not been issued. A May 1998 report by the E-Commerce Laws Working Party[1856] emphasized both the importance of facilitating the collection and processing of personal data and the protection of personal data of individuals in the information age.

Within the Turkish national legislation, the protection of personal rights is regulated in the Civil Code. Pursuant to Article 24 of the Civil Code, an individual whose personal rights are violated unjustly may request protection

---

[1853] Constitution Republic of Turkey, available at <http://www.mfa.gov.tr/GRUPI/Anayasa/i142.htm>.

[1854] Nick Thorpe, "Mixed Reactions to Turkey's Reforms," BBC News, October 5, 2001, available at <http://news.bbc.co.uk/hi/english/world/europe/newsid_1580000/1580238.stm>

[1855] United States Department of State, Country Reports on Human Rights Practices - 2001, March 2002, available at <http://www.state.gov/g/drl/rls/hrrpt/2001>.

[1856] Turkish Republic Foreign Trade Office, E-Commerce Laws Working Party Report, 8 May 1998. A summary of the report in Turkish is available at <http://kurul.ubak.gov.tr/e-ticaret.html>.

---

against the violation from the judge. Individuals can bring action for violation of their private rights. However, there is no criminal liability for such violations of personal rights and currently there is no protection for personal data (through data protection laws or any other laws) under the current Turkish Criminal Code.

Articles 195-200 of the Turkish Criminal Code on the freedom of communications govern communication through letters, parcels, telegram and telephone. Government officials are required, subject to some exceptions, to obtain a judicial warrant before monitoring private correspondence. Despite the existing laws and regulations, rights to privacy and to private communications are not well respected in Turkey and there is widespread illegal wiretapping by the government.

In 1997 the Turkish parliament set up a telephone bugging committee to investigate allegations that the Security Directorate listens in on all telephone communications, including cellular calls. Responding to a request for information from this committee, then acting Security Director Kemal Celik, confirmed these allegations in a secret 50-page report documenting government bugging of telephones.[1857] In December 1999, a Turkish court convicted the deputy head of Ankara's police intelligence division Zafer Aktas of abuse of office for his part in a telephone tapping scandal, in which Ankara police were accused of bugging the prime minister's telephones.[1858] In March 2000, Chairman of the Supreme Court's 8th Department, Naci Unver, sued the Interior Ministry after finding out that his official phone is being bugged. The Interior Ministry defended the tapping saying that the claims of the suitor that the incident was a violation of personal freedom and of the independence of the juridical system were "obscure and pointless." The Ministry demanded the withdrawal of the lawsuit for compensation, saying, "Or else there would be no end to lawsuits filed." The Ministry also claimed that the police department had "just listened but not carried out a criminal recording and thus the events did not damage suitors in any concrete way. In the second report, it is also stated that if compensation were to be paid, it would result in an unnecessary wealth gain for the victim.[1859] The Interior Minister said that new guidelines would be issued soon and punishment for illegal wiretaps would be forthcoming.[1860] No such guidelines have been issued, however, and allegations of illegal wiretapping continue. In April 2001 Istanbul Security Director was accused of wiretapping

---

[1857] "Acting Security Director Confirms All Telephones Bugged," BBC Worldwide Monitoring, April 14, 1997 and "No Privacy on the Phone Lines," Asia Times, April 16, 1997.

[1858] "Turk policeman convicted in phone tapping scandal," Reuters, December 6, 1999.

[1859] "Comedy of phone bugging," Milliyet, March 16, 2000.

[1860] Hurriyet, March 13, 2000.

the Istanbul Governor's telephone calls. The Security Director denied the allegations as slanderous.[1861] In May 2001, the Foreign Ministry launched an investigation following reports that its phones were being tapped.[1862] The Parliament Speaker also expressed concern about the alleged surveillance of a deputy from the Motherland Party and referred the matter to the State Security Court (DGM).[1863] The Interior Ministry issued a statement calling allegations of continuing illegal wiretapping of people and institutions "baseless and unfair"[1864] but on June 15, 2001 released a decree establishing an inspection delegation of three chief inspectors from the Directorate General of Security, to determine whether officials have been abusing their authority.[1865] In May 2002 the Wiretapping and Investigation Committee (a sub-committee of the Human Rights Investigation Committee) issued its final report finding that cellular phones are easily monitored by operating companies that the Mafia engages in illegal wiretapping.[1866] In February 2002, a scandal broke out following the publication, in a weekly magazine, of the private emails of the European Union's ambassador to Turkey.[1867]

In April 2000, the government introduced a new bill proposing the establishment of a "Council for the Security of National Information and its Duties" within with the Prime Minister's office. The Council was to address issues including data protection, encryption, and security of information systems[1868] and would have been authorized to collect all types of Internet transmissions in secrecy. The draft Bill was heavily criticized and was eventually dropped.

In 1990, a parliamentary commission on human rights was established with the power to monitor the human rights situation in Turkey and abroad. Currently, the commission consists of 25 parliamentarians, three consultants and four secretaries. Since its inception, the commission has taken up some 20 cases on its own initiative. Most of these cases relate to alleged violations of physical

---

[1861] "Istanbul Police Chief Denies Ordering Governor's Phone Tapped," BBC Worldwide Monitoring, April 22, 2001.

[1862] "Turkish Foreign Ministry Investigates Wiretapping Allegations,'" BBC Worldwide Monitoring, May 3, 2001.

[1863] "Turkish Speaker Concerned Over Tapping Of Phones Without Court Order," BBC Worldwide Monitoring, May 10, 2001.

[1864] "Interior Ministry Denies Illegal Wiretapping," BBC Worldwide Monitoring, May 4, 2001.

[1865] "Body Probing Phone Tapping To Be Set Up," BBC Worldwide Monitoring, June 15, 2001.

[1866] "Parliamentary Report Reveals Illegal Wiretapping by Mafia, GSM Operators," Istanbul Hurriyet, May 24, 2002 (FBIS Translated Text).

[1867] "Fogg Email Scandal Said Attempt to Discredit Pro-European Union Circles at Home," Istanbul Milliyet, February 12, 2002 (FBIS Translated Text).

[1868] Elif Unal,"Turkey Debates Cyberspace Controls," Reuters, April 16, 2000.

integrity[1869] and it is unknown whether the Commission has dealt with any cases of individual privacy. A large number of cases against Turkey for violations of human rights have been brought before the European Court of Human Rights. In 1996 the Court ruled in *Akdivar and others v Turkey*,[1870] a case concerning attacks on a village in south-east Turkey, that the deliberate burning of villagers homes and their contents was an unjustified and serious interference with the right to respect for their family lives in violation of article 8 of the European Convention. In June 2002, the Court again ruled that relatives of Kurdish villagers who disappeared following a raid by the Turkish army in 1994 were entitled to compensation for violations of the right to privacy.[1871] In July 2001, the Interior Minister released a circular, "Violation Decisions of European Court of Human Rights", advising officials to respect individual's rights, so as to improve the country's record before the Court and other democratic nations.[1872] Among other issues, the Minister specified that, in order to comply with Article 8 of the Convention, judicial authorization is necessary before houses can be searched.

Turkey is a member of the Council of Europe and has accepted the Council's monitoring mechanism.[1873] It signed the Convention for the Protection of Individuals with Regard to Automatic Processing of Personal Data (ETS No. 108) in 1981 but has not ratified it. It has signed and ratified the European Convention for the Protection of Human Rights and Fundamental Freedoms.[1874] Turkey has also been a member of the Organization for Economic Co-operation and Development since 1961.

[1869] See Commission On Human Rights, Question of the Human Rights of All Persons Subjected to any Form of Detention or Imprisonment: Promotion and protection of the right to freedom of opinion and expression, report of the Special Rapporteur, Mr. Abid Hussain, submitted pursuant to Commission on Human Rights resolution 1996/53 Addendum Mission to Turkey, available at <http://www.unhchr.ch/html/menu4/chrrep/3197a1.htm>, Distr. General E/CN.4/1997/31/Add.1 February 11, 1997.

[1870] Case 99/1995/605/693, 1 BHRC 137

[1871] Case of Orhan v. Turkey (Application no. 25656/94), decided June 18, 2002

[1872] 'Interior Minister Issues Circular Warning of Human Rights Violations,' BBC Worldwide Monitoring, July 25, 2001.

[1873] See Republic of Turkey, Ministry of Foreign Affairs paper, "Human Rights in Turkey: V. Turkey's Place and Role in the International Context," available at <http://www.mfa.gov.tr/GRUPF/hrtur.htm>.

[1874] Signed November 11, 1950; Ratified May 18, 1954; Entered into force May 18, 1954.

Republic of Ukraine

The Constitution of Ukraine guarantees the right of privacy and data protection.[1875] Article 31 states, "Everyone is guaranteed privacy of mail, telephone conversations, telegraph and other correspondence. Exceptions shall be established only by a court in cases envisaged by law, with the purpose of preventing crime or ascertaining the truth in the course of the investigation of a criminal case, if it is not possible to obtain information by other means." Article 32 states "No one shall be subject to interference in his or her personal and family life, except in cases envisaged by the Constitution of Ukraine. The collection, storage, use and dissemination of confidential information about a person without his or her consent shall not be permitted, except in cases determined by law, and only in the interests of national security, economic welfare and human rights. Every citizen has the right to examine information about himself or herself, that is not a state secret or other secret protected by law, at the bodies of state power, bodies of local self-government, institutions and organizations. Everyone is guaranteed judicial protection of the right to rectify incorrect information about himself or herself and members of his or her family, and of the right to demand that any type of information be expunged, and also the right to compensation for material and moral damages inflicted by the collection, storage, use and dissemination of such incorrect information." There is also a limited right of freedom of information. Article 50 states, "Everyone is guaranteed the right of free access to information about the environmental situation, the quality of food and consumer goods, and also the right to disseminate such information. No one shall make such information secret."

There have been efforts to enact a data protection act for a number of years. A draft bill on Data Protection prepared by State Committee of Communications and Computerization was introduced to the Cabinet of Ministers for consideration in December 1999. The draft was loosely based on the Council of Europe Convention No. 108 and the State of Hesse's (Germany) 1970 data protection act and focused on property rights for privacy control. The Chief of the Parliament Committee on Legal Policy Mr. O. Zadorozhniy introduced an alternative draft bill on Personal Information to the Parliament on June 25, 2001. The bill was prepared with the assistance of Mr. A. Pazyuk director of NGO Privacy Ukraine. The draft covers public and private sectors, provides natural persons with the right to informational self-determination. It includes special provisions concerning sensitive data (racial origin, nationality, trade union

---

[1875] Constitution of Ukraine, Adopted at the Fifth Session of the Verkhovna Rada of Ukraine, June 28, 1996, available at <http://alpha.rada.kiev.ua/const/conengl.htm>.

membership, political, philosophical and religious beliefs, medical and health data, and data on criminal offenses) and imposes limitation of data transfer to third countries with inadequate level of data protection. The draft proposes the establishment of independent authority for supervision. The National Agency on Personal Data Processing Supervision would be empowered to conduct investigations, impose sanctions, maintain a national register of databases, and to adopt or approve codes of fair information practice proposed by private sector. The draft would require amendments to the Constitution to provide for the appointment of the National Agency chief nominated by the President of Ukraine and subject to the authority of the Parliament. The Agency would be required to submit annual reports to Parliament. As of June 2002, no data protection act has been enacted.

The 1992 Act on Information defines only general principles of citizens' access to information personally related to them. Article 9 provides individuals with access to information concerning them. Exceptions are to be defined by Law. Article 23 of the Statute prohibits collection of personal data without consent of the data subject, and provides the right to know about data collection.[1876] The Constitutional Court of Ukraine ruled in October 1997 that Article 23 prohibited not only the collection of information, but also the storage, use and dissemination of confidential personal information without the consent of the individual.[1877] There are exceptions for national security, economic well-being, and information that would affect another's rights and freedoms. Confidential information includes, in particular, information about a person such as education, marital status, state of health, date and place of birth, property status and other personal details.

The Act on the Operational Investigative Activity (OIA) of February 18, 1992 empowers law enforcement agencies to conduct surveillance. The agencies are obliged to obtain a warrant under the court procedure as implemented by the Act of the Supreme Court Plenary Session of November 1, 1996.[1878] The Statute does not provide wiretapping procedure rules. Those are regulated by secret rules, adopted by the joint Ministry of Internal Affairs and State Committee as Communications Order No 745/90 of September 30, 1999. The applications are registered and include the names of officials, and the date and type of

---

[1876] Act On information, October 1992 (# 2657-XII).

[1877] Verdict of the Constitutional Court of Ukraine Concerning the case of the official treatment of Articles 3, 23, 31, 47, 48 of the Law of Ukraine "On information" and Article 12 of the Law of Ukraine "On the Prosecutor's Office" (case of K. G. Ustimenko), October 30, 1997.

[1878] Directive of the Supreme Court of Ukraine, No.9 of November 1, 1996, "On referring to the Constitution in administering justice."

communications. Statistical data on wiretapping activity is not publicly available. Under article 11 of the Act, priests, doctors, and lawyers can not be asked about information concerning their clients, and any such information cannot be used as evidence in court. However, in practice, the courts regularly use such information. The special services investigated the Kazakhstan Energy Grid Operating Company in June 2000 for the illegal tapping of employee conversations and charged one employee with a violation of the criminal code.[1879]

On January 18, 2001 a new law was passed amending the OIA Act of 1992. The new Act clarifies the offences for which surveillance may be used and significantly improved procedures for judicial supervision and oversight. Individuals are not granted full access to the personal data collected by police during the investigation and are allowed only to receive an explanation of the human rights implications of the surveillance. The Act prohibits the dissemination of information about undisclosed crimes, information that might damage an open investigation, the interest of man or the security of the State. The disclosure of State secrets is also prohibited. An Order of the Chief of the Security Service dated March 1, 2001 defines a State secret as an data relating to "the preparation, performance and results of secret OIA measures used against persons who are preparing or have committed especially dangerous or heinous crimes against the State."

The ongoing political scandal concerning the case of murdered journalist and founder of the Ukrainska Pravda newspaper, Heorhiy Honhadze, centers on allegations of illegal wiretapping by the Secret Service Unit (SSU). On November 28, 2000 Oleksandr Moroz, the leader of the opposition Socialist Party faction in Parliament publicly released cassettes linking President, Leonid Kuchma, chief of the President's Office Volodymyr Lytvyn and Interior Minister Yury Kravchenko to the disappearance of the journalist in September 2000. Not long before his disappearance Honhadze had complained to the Attorney General that he was under continuous surveillance. The cassettes contained alleged recordings of conversations between the three officials during which the President gave the order for action to be taken against Honhadze. Moroz claimed that he received the cassettes from a telecommunications officer at the SSU, which maintained secret bugging devices in the President's office.[1880] Presidential office head, Lytvyn, and the president's representative in parliament,

---

[1879] "Power Company Denies Involvement in Telephone Tapping," BBC Summary of World Broadcasts June 2, 2000.

[1880] "Moroz Says Leaked Audio Tapes Link Kucmha to Gongadze Disappearance," by KPnews staff, KYIV Post, November 28, 2000.

Roman Besmertny, immediately denied the allegations claiming that the cassettes were clearly fakes. One week later the SSU released an official statement dismissing the Moroz report as slander and stating that it was impossible "from the technical or organizational or physical points of view' to wiretap the communications of state officials.[1881] On December 8, however, members of a committee of inquiry that had been set up to investigate the journalist's murder were detained and searched by custom and security officers while returning from a visit to the SSU telecommunications officer involved. The recordings of their interview with the SSU officer were taken from them and damaged. In May 2001, the Socialist and Peasant Parties issued an official statement demanding answers to some of the legal questions that arose during the scandal including the allegations of widespread wiretapping by the SSU.[1882]

As of June 13, 2002, the Ukrainian Prosecutor-General's Office has suspended the investigation into the case against former security officer Mykola Melnychenko who was granted United States political asylum after he publicized wiretapped conversations of Ukrainian President Leonid Kuchma suggesting the president's involvement in illegal activities.[1883] The tapes made in the president's office are said to implicate President Leonid Kuchma in the journalist's murder and a number of other crimes. Ukraine wants Melnychenko extradited for divulging state secrets.

Another high-profile incident of illegal wiretapping occurred in 2002. Investigators launched a criminal investigation into the bugging of telephone conversations between the Kiev mayor Oleksandr Omelchenko and the leader of the popular centre-right "Our Ukraine bloc," Viktor Yushchenko, during a 2001 election campaign.[1884] In Ukraine, it is a criminal offence to publicize private conversations, as well as to secretly record them. The leaders of the all-Ukrainian public movement "For Honesty in Politics" first published the recordings at a news conference on January 9, 2002. The wiretapping is believed to have been done in Kiev and investigators do not rule out the possibility that it was done

---

[1881] "Secret Police Say Wiretapping Government Phones Impossible," BBC Worldwide Monitoring, December 1, 2000.

[1882] "Party Demands Answers on Journalist Murder Tape Scandal," British Broadcasting Corporation, May 17, 2001.

[1883] "Ukraine suspends tape scandal inquiry, wants whistle-blower extradited," BBC Worldwide Monitoring, June 13, 2002.

[1884] "Latest Tape Scandal Triggers Probe into Phone Tapping," BBC Worldwide Monitoring, January 11, 2002.

legally by law enforcement agencies as part of a criminal investigation directed at non-public or -state figures.[1885]

The Ukrainian Supreme Council has supported a resolution to create a parliamentary ad hoc commission to investigate violations of constitutional human rights to the confidentiality of telephone conversations.[1886] Last year the Supreme Council parliament renewed prosecutor supervision over people's and politicians' constitutional right to privacy of telephone conversations and correspondence.

The Department of Special Telecommunication Systems and Information Safeguarding of the Security Service of Ukraine is authorized under an April 2000 Presidential Order to adopt regulations on the protection of information in data transmitting networks, as well as to establish the "application of the tools for the protection of state information resources."[1887] In July 2000, President Kuchma signed a decree on "development of national content of the global informational network (Internet) and wide access to this network in Ukraine." It sets rules on digital signatures, information security and protection of information "which can not be published according to the law."[1888]

In September 1999, President Leonid Kuchma proposed regulations requiring that Internet Service Providers install surveillance devices on their systems based on the Russian SORM system. The regulations had to be withdrawn because of a Constitutional issue and he proposed a bill to implement them. The bill was attacked by the Parliament and withdrawn. In June 2000, several high government officials (including the deputy chair of the security service, the chair of the headquarters of the Ministry of Defense, and the chair of the Presidential Committee on informational security) held closed meetings with representatives of the major Ukrainian ISPs to discuss new SORM regulations. A working group released a document announcing that the group had agreed to implement surveillance capabilities based on the European ENFOPOL 98 initiative and create a working group on filtering and monitoring of unlawful information.[1889]

[1885] "Prosecutor Warns Organizers of Recent Tape Scandal Of Imprisonment," BBC Worldwide Monitoring, February 6, 2002.

[1886] "Ukrainian parliament sets up ad hoc body to investigate wiretap," BBC Worldwide Monitoring, March 7, 2002.

[1887] Presidential Order No. 582/2000 of April 10, 2000.

[1888] Decree of 31.07.2000, No. 928/2000.

[1889] See Andriy Pazyuk, "Ukrainian ISPs demonstrate their willingness to be subservient to Big Brother," Privacy Ukraine, July 7, 2000.

The large ISPs are expected to support the regulations to eliminate competition from smaller ISPs who will not be able to afford the new systems.

There are a number of other laws that control personal information.[1890] The cabinet approved the creation of a Single State Automated Passport System in January 1997 as a component of the State Register of Population.[1891] The system will be used as an internal ID system and hold both textual and graphical data about every Ukrainian. The text data will include: first, patronymic and last name, date of birth, sex, identification number, date of registration and residence, data of another state citizenship, data of passport and its duplicates, data of job/study, matrimonial status, data of husband/wife and children, education, military draft status, date of documents for travelling abroad, and memorandums (disability care, restriction for travelling abroad). The graphical information will include: identifier, biometrics data and signature. Religious conservatives demonstrated in opposition to the application of personal identification numbers approved by the Act On State Register of Natural Persons – Taxpayers.[1892] The Parliament approved an amendment to the statute in July 1999 allowing for an alternative system of registration to be used for persons with religious grounds for opposing identity numbers.[1893] There are also laws relating to tax information,[1894] social insurance,[1895] domicile registration,[1896] retirement insurance,[1897] unemployment insurance,[1898] criminal investigations,[1899] juvenile records,[1900] former prisoners,[1901] military service records,[1902] medical records,[1903] and HIV and AIDS records.[1904]

[1890] See Andriy Pazyuk, Privacy Ukraine Privacy of Data Subject in Ukraine, 1999 for more details on the laws, available at <http://www2.datatestlab.com/privacy/>.

[1891] The Statutory Order of the Cabinet of Ministers (CM) of January 20, 1997 (No 40).

[1892] "On State Register of Natural Persons – Taxpayers" of December 22, 1994 (No.320/94).

[1893] Statute of July 16, 1999 (No.1003-XIV) on the alterations to the Statute "On State Register of Natural Persons – Taxpayers."

[1894] Law "On State Register of natural persons – taxpayers" of December 22, 1994 (No320/94).

[1895] The Basic legislation of Ukraine on Obligatory State Social Insurance, January 14, 1998 (No.16/98).

[1896] The MIA Order, February 3, 1992 (No.66).

[1897] Statutory Order of the CM, June 4, 1998 (No.794).

[1898] The Statutory Order of CM, May 27, 1998 (No.578).

[1899] The Order of Office of Public Prosecutor, December 21, 1995 (No.22/835); The MIA Order, January 14, 1994 (No.190).

[1900] The Law "On organs and services on juveniles and dedicated educational institution for juveniles"January 1995 (No.20/95); Ministry of Education Order, December 27, 1994 (No.362).

[1901] The Law "On Administrative Control the Former Prisoners," December 1, 1994 (No.264/94).

[1902] Department of Defense Orders of June 27, 1995 No 165, 166 approved the Regulation "On military record maintained at the place of employment or study (public or private)" and the Regulation "On military domiciliary registration."

[1903] Law of September 19, 1992.

The Parliament of Ukraine adopted a new edition of the Criminal Code in on April 5, 2001. The new code includes several articles relating to privacy violation and will go into effect in September 2001. Article 132 prohibits dissemination of information about AIDS or other incurable diseases data by medical personnel. Dissemination of other confidential medical data by a doctor is punishable under Article 145. Article 162 provides for criminal liability for unlawful entrance, search and seizure. Article 163 criminalizes the unlawful wiretapping or interception of electronic communications. Article 168 provides liability for disclosing confidential information regarding child adoption. Finally, Article 182 on 'Breaching the Inviolability of Private Life' provides that the

> [u]nlawful collection, storage, usage or dissemination of confidential information related to a person without consent or the dissemination of such information in a public speech, or production or in the mass-media , is punishable by a fine of up to 50 multiple tax free incomes or correctional labor of up to 2 years or imprisonment of up to 6 months or limitation of liberty of up to 3 years.

Considering that the Constitutional Court of Ukraine has interpreted "confidential information" to include all personal data related to individual, the broad scope of Article 182 poses a real threat to freedom of speech. In order to address this issue, the draft bill on Personal Information (introduced in June 2001) proposes that this article be amended to criminalize only the use of personal data for unlawful actions that endanger the life or health of the person concerned.

The 1992 Act on Information provides a right of access to government records.[1905] Article 21 sets out methods for making official information public, including disclosing it to interested persons orally, in writing or in other ways. Article 29 of the Statute prohibits the limitation of the right to obtain non-covert information. Article 37 sets out a long list of exceptions. The author of a rejected or postponed request has a right to appeal the decision to a higher echelon or court (Article 34). There is limited access to the files of the former secret police under the Act "on rehabilitation of victims of political repressions," which gives the rehabilitated citizen or his heirs the right to read his personal file kept in the KGB archives.

[1904] Law On prevention of AIDS contamination and social aid on civilians (in redaction of the 3rd of March 1998) as well as Article 13 of the Discipline of medical inspection on HIV results, registration of HIV and AIDS persons and medical care (approved by the Statutory Order of the CM, December 18, 1998).

[1905] Statute On Information adopted by Parliament on October 2, 1992 (No.2657-XII).

Ukraine is a member of the Council of Europe but has not signed or ratified the Convention for the Protection of Individuals with Regard to Automatic Processing of Personal Data (ETS No. 108). It has signed and ratified the European Convention for the Protection of Human Rights and Fundamental Freedoms.[1906] The European Parliament supported the European Union Common Strategy towards Ukraine in a vote on March 15, 2001, but at the same time it urged rapid changes to many current Ukraine policies. [1907] Ukraine was urged to adopt the necessary measures to guarantee an adequate level of data protection comparable to that required in the European Union.

United Kingdom of Great Britain and Northern Ireland

The United Kingdom does not have a written constitution. In 1998, the Parliament approved the Human Rights Act to incorporate the European Convention on Human Rights into domestic law, a process that establishes an enforceable right of privacy.[1908] The Act came into force on October 2, 2000. A number of cases, many related to celebrity privacy, have been decided or are pending in the courts.[1909]

The Parliament approved the Data Protection Act in July 1998.[1910] The legislation, which came into force on March 1, 2000, updates the 1984 Data Protection Act in accordance with the requirements of the European Union's Data Protection Directive.[1911] The Act covers records held by government agencies and private entities. It provides for limitations on the use of personal information, access to and correction of records and requires that entities that maintain records register with the Information Commissioner.

The Office of the Information Commissioner is an independent agency that maintains the register and enforces the Act.[1912] As of March 31, 2002, there were

---

[1906] Signed November 9, 1995; Ratified September 11, 1997; Entered into force September 11, 1997.

[1907] "European Union/Ukraine: Parliament Debates Strategy and Tactics," Europe Information Service, Euro-East, March 27, 2001

[1908] Human Rights Bill, CM 3782, October 1997, available at <http://www.official-documents.co.uk/document/hoffice/rights/rights.htm>.

[1909] See "Developments in Jurisprudence", Appendix, Information Commissioner – Annual report and accounts for the year ending March 31 2002, June 2002 available at <http://www.dataprotection.gov.uk/.

[1910] Data Protection Act 1998c. 29.

[1911] Data Protection Act 1984 (c. 35).

[1912] Home page of the Information Commissioner, formerly known as the Data Protection Commissioner and the Data Protection Registrar, <http://www.dataprotection.gov.uk/>

198,519 databases registered with the Commission.[1913] The agency received 12, 479 requests for assessment and inquiries in 2001-2002. There were 106 cases forwarded for prosecution resulting in 66 prosecutions and 33 convictions. The Commissioner has also issued a number of comprehensive reports for the public. She has published a Code of Practice for the use of Closed Circuit Television (CCTV)[1914] and a study of the availability and use of personal information in public registers.[1915] In October 2000, the Commissioner issued a draft code of guidance for employer/employee relationships.[1916] In March 2002, the first part of this code, on data protection in recruitment and selection of employees was issued.[1917] A second, on employee monitoring was released for public comment in April 2002.[1918] Two further parts on employment records, and medical information and testing will be issued over the next few months. The Commissioner is also responsible for enforcing the Telecommunications (Data Protection and Privacy) Regulations. These regulations came into force on March 1, 2000, and implement the 1997 European Union Telecommunications Directive.[1919] They replaced the Telecommunications (Data Protection and Privacy) (Direct Marketing) Regulations 1998 which came into effect on May 1, 1999. The current Commissioner, Elizabeth France announced in 2002 that she was not asking to be reappointed. In July 2002, Mr Richard Thomas was appointed as her successor. In September 2002, the 24th International Conference of Data Protection and Privacy Commissioners will be hosted by the British, Irish, Guernsey, Jersey and Isle of Man data protection authorities in Cardiff, Wales.[1920]

[1913] See Information Commissioner – Annual report and accounts for the year ending March 31, 2002, June 2002, available at <http://www.dataprotection.gov.uk/

[1914] CCTV Code of Practice, July 2000.

[1915] Study of the Availability and Use of Personal Information in Public Registers. Final Report to the Office of the Data Protection Registrar J.E. Davies and C. Oppenheim, Loughborough University, September 1999, available at <http://wood.ccta.gov.uk/dpr/dpdoc.nsf>.

[1916] Data Protection Commissioner, Employment: (Draft COP), October 2000, available at <http://www.dataprotection.gov.uk/dpr/dpdoc.nsf>.

[1917] Data Protection Commissioner, Employment Practices Data Protection Code: Part 1: Recruitment & Selection, Employment Practices, Data Protection Code, March 2002, available at <http://wood.ccta.gov.uk/dpr/dpdoc.nsf - 25/02/99>.

[1918] Data Protection Commissioner, Employment Practices Data Protection Code: Part 3: Monitoring at Work: an Employer's Guide, available at <http://www.dataprotection.gov.uk/dpr/dpdoc.nsf>.

[1919] Directive 97/66/EC concerning the processing of personal data and the protection of privacy in the telecommunications sector.

[1920] For more information visit <http://www.informationrights2002.org/>.

The Regulation of Investigatory Powers Act became law in July 2000,[1921] superceding the Interception of Communications Act of 1985.[1922] It authorizes the Home Secretary to issue warrants for the interception of communications and requires Communications Service Providers to provide a "reasonable interception capability" in their networks. Telephone taps for national security purposes are authorized by the Foreign Minister. It further allows any public authority designated by the Home Secretary to access "communications data" without a warrant. This data includes the source, destination and type of any communication, such as mobile phone location information and web browsing logs. Finally, it allows senior members of the civilian and military police, Customs, and members of the judiciary to demand that users hand over the plaintext of encrypted material, or in certain circumstances decryption keys themselves. It also sets rules on other types of investigatory powers that had not been previously regulated under United Kingdom law. Many legal experts, including the Data Protection Commissioner, believe that many of the provisions violate the European Convention on Human Rights and a legal challenge to the lawfulness of the Act is likely.

A number of draft codes and regulations have been issued by the Home Office.[1923] In June 2002, the Home Office announced that the list of government agencies allowed under the act to intercept web traffic and mobile location information without a warrant was being extended to over 1,000 different government departments including local authorities, health, environmental, trade and many other agencies. This resulted in a substantial controversy over the dramatic expansion of power, especially after the Surveillance Commissioner admitted in his annual report that "I clearly cannot carry out meaningful oversight of so many bodies without assistance" even before the proposed expansion.[1924] Home Secretary David Blunkett announced a few weeks later that he had "blundered" and withdrew the order.[1925]

In 2000, there were 1,711 interceptions allowed under the IOCA 1985 and 661 approved under the RIPA.[1926] The Interception of Communications Minister

---

[1921] Regulation of Investigatory Powers Act 2000, available at
<http://www.homeoffice.gov.uk/ripa/ripact.htm>. See the FIPR Regulation of Investigatory Powers Information Centre <http://www.fipr.org/rip/>.

[1922] Interception of Communications Act 1985, 1985 CHAPTER 56, available at
<http://www.butterworths.co.uk/academic/lloyd/Statutes/communications.htm>.

[1923] See Home Office RIPA Pages <http://www.homeoffice.gov.uk/ripa/ripact.htm>.

[1924] Report of the Chief Surveillance Commissioner for 2000-2001, Cm 5360, January 2002.

[1925] "Blunkett shelves access to data plans," The Guardian, June 19, 2002.

[1926] Report of the Interception of Communications Commissioner for 2000, Cm 5296, October 2001.

---

found that there were "a significant number of errors and breaches reported –26" in 2000. These including tapping the wrong numbers and technical errors such as a telecommunications companies who "inadvertently routed product [intercepted communications]" to the intelligence service. There were 2,565 authorizations including 371 for "intrusive" authorizations for breakins into homes under the Police Act 1997 and 310 under Part II of the RIPA between April 2000 and March 2001. There were 18 reported errors including wrong addresses and failures to obtain authorization or overly broad requests.[1927]

In December 2001, the Parliament approved the Anti-terrorism, Crime and Security Act 2001.[1928] The law allows the Secretary of State to issue a code of practice for "the retention of communications data by communications providers" for the purpose of protecting national security or preventing or detecting crime that relates to national security. A leaked submission by the police and intelligence services to the Home Office in 2000 proposed a 7 year data retention scheme. In September 1998, it was revealed that there were secret talks between the Association of Chief Police Officers (ACPO) and representatives for Internet Service Providers (ISPs) with the aim of reaching a "memorandum of understanding" to give the police access to private data held by ISPs.[1929] The High Court issued an injunction against the *Mail on Sunday* preventing the publication of further revelations.

There is a long history of illegal wiretapping of political opponents, labor unions and others in the United Kingdom.[1930] In 1985, the European Court of Human Rights ruled that police interception of individuals' communications was a violation of Article 8 of the European Convention on Human Rights.[1931] The decision resulted in the adoption of the Interception of Communications Act 1985. Most recently, the European Court of Human Rights ruled in 1997 that police eavesdropping of a policewoman violated Article 8.[1932] In the late 1970s and 80s, MI5, Britain's security service, tapped the phones of many left-leaning activists including the future Secretary of State for Trade and Industry Peter Mandelson, and kept files on Jack Straw, now Foreign Secretary, and Harriet

---

[1927] Report of the Chief Surveillance Commissioner for 2000-2001, Cm 5360, January 2002.

[1928] Anti-terrorism, Crime and Security Act 2001, available at <http://www.hmso.gov.uk/acts/acts2001/20010024.htm>.

[1929] "Police tighten the Net," The Guardian Online, September 17, 1998.

[1930] See, e.g., Patrick Fitzgerald & Mark Leopold, Stranger on the Line (Bodley Head 1987).

[1931] Malone v United Kingdom (A/95): (1991) 13 EHRR 448.

[1932] Halford v United Kingdom (Application No 20605/92), 24 EHRR 523, 25 June 1997.

Harman, former Social Security Secretary, as well as Guardian journalist Victoria Britain.

In late 1997, a report commissioned by the European Parliament and prepared by the United Kingdom-based research group Omega Foundation, confirmed that Britain was a key player in a vast global signals intelligence operation controlled by the United States National Security Agency (NSA).[1933] According to the report, the United States and its United Kingdom partner, GCHQ, "routinely and indiscriminately" intercepted large amounts of sensitive data that had been identified through keyword searching. The eavesdropping was carried out from a number of spy bases in the United Kingdom, most notably the Menwith Hill base in the north of England. The European Parliament created a one-year temporary committee to investigate allegations that the Echelon surveillance system violates individual privacy rights and is used to conduct industrial espionage.[1934]

There are also a number of other laws containing privacy components, most notably those governing medical records[1935] and consumer credit information.[1936] Other laws with privacy components include, the Rehabilitation of Offenders Act of 1974, the Telecommunications Act of 1984 (as amended by the Telecommunications Regulations of 1999), the Police Act of 1997, the Broadcasting Act of 1996, Part VI and the Protection from Harassment Act of 1997. Some of these acts are amended and may be repealed in part by the 1998 Data Protection Act. The Police and Criminal Evidence Act (1984) allows police to enter and search homes without a warrant following an arrest for any offense. And while police may demand identification before arrest only in limited circumstances, they have the right to stop and search any person on the street on grounds of suspicion. Following arrest, a body sample will be taken for inclusion in the national DNA database.[1937]The Crime and Disorder Act of 1998 provides for information sharing and data matching among public bodies in order to reduce crime and disorder. The Data Protection Commissioner issued a report on the privacy implications of the Act.[1938]

[1933] European Commission, Science and Technology Options Assessment Office (STOA), "Assessing the technologies of political control," Brussels, 1997.

[1934] "European Union to Search for Echelon," Reuters, July 5, 2000.

[1935] Access to Medical Reports Act 1988, Access to Health Records Act 1990, The Health and Social Care Act 2001.

[1936] Consumer Credit Act, 1974.

[1937] Criminal Justice and Public Order Act 1994, available at
<http://www.hmso.gov.uk/acts/summary/01994033.htm>.

[1938] "Crime & Disorder Act 1998: Data protection implications for information-sharing," available at
<http://wood.ccta.gov.uk/dpr/dpdoc.nsf>.

The privacy picture in the United Kingdom is mixed.[1939] There is, at some levels, a strong public recognition and defense of privacy. Proposals to establish a national identity card, for example, have routinely failed to achieve broad political support. On the other hand, crime and public order laws passed in recent years have placed substantial limitations on numerous rights, including freedom of assembly, privacy, freedom of movement, the right of silence, and freedom of speech.[1940]

There has been a proliferation of CCTV cameras in hundreds of towns and cities in Britain. The camera networks can be operated by police, local authorities or private companies, and are partly funded by a Home Office grant. Their original purpose was crime prevention and detection, though in recent years the cameras have become important tools for city center management and the control of "anti-social behavior." Between 250 million and 400 million pounds a year is spent expanding the web of 1,500,000 cameras covering public spaces in Britain,[1941] but despite the ubiquity of the technology, successive governments have been reluctant to pass specific laws to govern their use. Their use has come under greater criticism recently and recent research by the Scottish Centre for Criminology found that the cameras did not reduce crime, nor improved public perception of crime problems.[1942] As mentioned above, the Information Commission has also issued a code of practice for the use of these cameras. A new study announced in June 2002 found that in many areas with CCTV that crime increased and that street lighting was a more effective deterrent.[1943]

Home Secretary David Blunkett announced on July 3 a six month consultation period on "entitlement cards," a new name for a national ID card proposal.[1944] The cards would be mandatory for all persons over 16 and would be required to obtain heath care, jobs and other services. The proposal has already been widely criticized by politicians and major media across the political spectrum and is not expected to be approved. Blunkett first proposed the card shortly after September 11 but was forced to back away after it was also severely criticized.

[1939] See Simon Davies, Big Brother (Pan Books 1996).

[1940] See Criminal Justice and Public Order Act 1994

[1941] House of Lords, Science and Technology Committee, Inquiry: "Use of digital images as evidence," February 3, 1998, section 4.3.

[1942] Home Page <http://www.scotcrim.u-net.com/researchc.htm>.

[1943] "CCTV not a crime prevention cure-all, says report," NACRO, June 28 2002, available at <http://www.nacro.org.uk/templates/news/newsItem.cfm/2002062800.htm

[1944] See Privacy International ID Cards Page for more details <http://www.privacyinternational.org/issues/idcard/>.

In July 2002, Privacy International announced a campaign against the use of new finger print scanners in school libraries across the country.[1945] The electronic finger printing is being conducted in an effort to cut costs and increase the efficiency of libraries. Privacy International specifically criticized the role of the Office of the Information Commisioner in reviewing and endorsing the system.

The Freedom of Information Act was enacted in November 2000.[1946] The government announced in 2001 that implementation on the right to access provisions was being delayed until 2005. The Act has received considerable criticism from by many politicians across the political spectrum and NGOs as being insufficient and weaker than the existing code of practice. In June 2002, the Scottish Parliament approved a Freedom of Information bill[1947] that is regarded as stronger than the English FOIA Act. It also will not go into effect until 2005.

The United Kingdom is a member of the Council of Europe and has signed and ratified the Convention for the Protection of Individuals with Regard to Automatic Processing of Personal Data (ETS No. 108)[1948] and the European Convention for the Protection of Human Rights and Fundamental Freedoms.[1949] In November 2001, the United Kingdom signed the Council of Europe Convention on Cybercrime.[1950] The United Kingdom is a member of the Organization for Economic Cooperation and Development and has adopted the OECD Guidelines on the Protection of Privacy and Transborder Flows of Personal Data.

Territories

The Isle of Man Data Protection Act of 1986 is based on the 1984 United Kingdom Data Protection Act. The Office of the Data Protection Registrar

---

[1945] Privacy International Media Release, "Privacy Watchdaog Condemns Mass Finger Printing of UK Primary School Children," July 22, 2002, available at
<http://www.privacyinternational.org/countries/uk/kidsprint/>.

[1946] Freedom of Information Act 2000, available at <http://www.cfoi.org.uk/foiact2000.html>. For detailed information on the act, see the Campaign for Freedom of Information at <http://www.cfoi.org.uk>.

[1947] Available at <http://www.scotland.gov.uk/consultations/government/dfib-00.asp>.

[1948] Signed May 14, 1981; Ratified August 26, 1987; Entered into Force December 1, 1987.

[1949] Signed November 11, 1950; Ratified March 8, 1951; Entered into Force September 3, 1953.

[1950] Signed November 23, 2001.

enforces the Act.[1951] A new data protection bill was introduced in the House of Keys in March 2002.[1952]

The Data Protection (Bailiwick of Guernsey) Law 2001 was approved in March 2002.[1953] It is expected to go into force in late 2002, replacing the 1986 law. The Isle of Guernsey Data Protection Commissioner enforces the Act.[1954]

The Data Protection (Jersey) Law came into force in 1987. The law is equivalent to the 1984 United Kingdom Data Protection Act. The Data Protection Registry who registers databases and conducts investigations oversees the Act.[1955] The Registry is currently drafting a new law.

United States of America

There is no explicit right to privacy in the United States Constitution. The Supreme Court has ruled that there is a limited constitutional right of privacy based on a number of provisions in the Bill of Rights. This includes a right to privacy from government surveillance into an area where a person has a "reasonable expectation of privacy"[1956] and also in matters relating to marriage, procreation, contraception, family relationships, child rearing and education.[1957] However, the United States has taken a sectoral approach to privacy regulation so that records held by third parties, such as consumer marketing profiles or telephone calling records, are generally not protected unless a legislature has enacted a specific law. The Court has also recognized a right of anonymity[1958] and the right of political groups to prevent disclosure of their members' names to government agencies.[1959]

In January 2000, the Supreme Court heard *Reno v. Condon*, a case addressing the constitutionality of the Drivers Privacy Protection Act (DPPA), a 1994 law that protects drivers' records held by state motor vehicle agencies. In a unanimous

---

[1951] Home Page<http://www.gov.im/odpr/>.

[1952] Available at <http://www.gov.im/odpr/DataProtectionBill/dpbill.pdf>.

[1953] The Data Protection (Bailiwick of Guernsey) Law, 2001, available at <http://www.dpcommission.gov.gg/2001%20Law/2001%20Law.htm>.

[1954] Home Page <http://www.dpcommission.gov.gg/>.

[1955] Home Page <http://www.dataprotection.gov.je/>.

[1956] Katz v. United States, 386 U.S. 954 (1967).

[1957] See e.g., Griswold v. Connecticut, 381 U.S. 479 (1965); Whalen v. Roe, 429 United States 589 (1977); Paul v. Davis, 424 U.S. 714 (1976).

[1958] McIntyre v. Ohio Elections Commission, 514 U.S. 334 (1995).

[1959] NAACP v. Alabama, 357 U.S. 449 (1958).

decision, the Court found that the information was "an article of commerce" and can be regulated by the federal government.[1960] In June 2001, the Supreme Court ruled in the case of *Kyllo v. United States* that the use of a thermal imaging device, without a warrant, to detect heat emanating from a person's residence constituted an illegal search under the Fourth Amendment.[1961] In November 2000, the Supreme Court ruled held that suspicionless vehicle checkpoints, used to discover and interdict illegal narcotics, violate the Fourth Amendment.[1962] Also, in March 2001, the Supreme Court held that a state hospital cannot perform diagnostic tests to obtain evidence of criminal conduct without the patient's consent as such as test is unreasonable and violates the Fourth Amendment.[1963]

In the 2001 term, the Supreme Court addressed anonymity, searches on buses, and student privacy. In *Watchtower Bible*, the Court invalidated a law that required registration with the government before individuals could engage in door-to-door solicitation. The Court held that a pre-registration requirement violated the First Amendment and individuals' right to anonymity.[1964] In *United States v. Drayton*, the Court held that the Fourth Amendment does not require police officers to advise bus passengers of their right not to cooperate and to refuse consent to searches.[1965] Student privacy was diminished in a series of cases involving drug testing, "peer grading," the practice of allowing a fellow student to score a test, and the right to sue under a federal student privacy law. In *Earls*, the Court held that random, suspicionless drug testing of students involved in non-athletic extracurricular activities was justified under the "special needs" exception to the Fourth Amendment.[1966] In *Falvo*, the Court held that both peer grading and the reporting aloud of peer grades did not violate the Family Educational Rights and Privacy Act of 1974 (FERPA).[1967] In *Gonzaga*, the Court held that the FERPA does not give individuals a right to sue for violations of privacy.[1968]

[1960] Reno v. Condon, 528 U.S. 141 (2000).

[1961] Kyllo v. United States, 533 U.S. 27 (2001).

[1962] City of Indianapolis v. Edmond, 531 U.S. 32 (2000).

[1963] Ferguson v. City of Charlestown, 532 U.S. 67 (2000).

[1964] Watchtower Bible & Tract Soc'y of N.Y. v. Village of Stratton, 122 S. Ct. 2080 (2002).

[1965] United States v. Drayton, 122 S. Ct. 2105 (2002).

[1966] Bd. of Educ. v. Earls, 122 S. Ct. 2559 (2002).

[1967] Owasso Indep. Sch. Dist. No. I-011 v. Falvo, 534 U.S. 426 (2001).

[1968] Gonzaga Univ. v. Doe, 122 S. Ct. 2268 (2002).

The Privacy Act of 1974 protects records held by United States Government agencies and requires agencies to apply basic fair information practices.[1969] Its effectiveness is significantly weakened by administrative interpretations of a provision allowing for disclosure of personal information for a "routine use" compatible with the purpose for which the information was originally collected. Limits on the use of the Social Security Number have also been undercut in recent years because Congress has approved new purposes for the identifier[1970] and because the private sector employs the identifier for many purposes with virtually no safeguards for the individual.[1971]

There is no independent privacy oversight agency in the United States The Office of Management and Budget plays a limited role in setting policy for federal agencies under the Privacy Act, but it has not been particularly active or effective. In 1999 a Chief Counselor for Privacy was appointed within the Office of Management and Budget to coordinate federal stances towards privacy. The Counselor had only a limited advisory capacity. The new Bush Administration has eliminated this position.

The Federal Trade Commission has oversight and enforcement powers for the laws protecting children's online privacy, consumer credit information and fair trading practices but has no general authority to enforce privacy rights.[1972] The FTC has received thousands of complaints but has issued opinions in only a few cases. It has also organized a series of workshops and surveys, which have found that industry protection of privacy on the Internet is poor, but the FTC had long said that the industry should have more time to make self-regulation work. In a shift from this position, in June 2000, the FTC recommended in a report to the United States Congress that legislation is necessary to protect consumer privacy on the Internet due to the dismal findings in a survey of online privacy policies.[1973] Since issuing that report, the new Chairman of the Commission appointed by President Bush has recommended that more study is necessary

---

[1969] Privacy Act, Pub. L. No. 93-579 (1974), codified at 5 USC § 552a, available at <http://www.epic.org/privacy/laws/privacy_act.html>.

[1970] Social Security Numbers: Government Benefits from SSN Use but Could Provide Better Safeguards, General Accounting Office Report No. GAO-02-352 (May 2002), available at <http://www.gao.gov/new.items/d02352.pdf>.

[1971] Statewide Grand Jury Report: Identity Theft in Florida, SC: 01-1095 (January 2002), available at <http://www.idtheftcenter.org/attach/FL_idtheft_gj.pdf>; Social Security: Government and Private Sector Use of the Social Security Number is Widespread, General Accounting Office Report No. GAO/HEHS 99-28 (February 1999), available at <http://www.epic.org/privacy/ssn/gao_ssn_2_99.html>.

[1972] See FTC Privacy Pages <http://www.ftc.gov/privacy/index.html>.

[1973] Privacy Online: Fair Information Practices in the Electronic Marketplace: A Federal Trade Commission Report to Congress (May 2000), available at <http://www.ftc.gov/os/2000/05/index.htm#22>.

before legislation is passed to protect Internet Privacy.[1974] Instead, FTC has focused on enforcing existing law in the areas of telemarketing, spam, pretexting, and children's privacy.[1975] In January 2002, the FTC proposed changed to the Telemarketing Sales Rule to tighten use of individuals' account numbers, and to create a national do-not-call list for individuals who wish to opt-out of telemarketing.[1976]

The United States has no comprehensive privacy protection law for the private sector. A patchwork of federal laws covers some specific categories of personal information.[1977] These include financial records,[1978] credit reports,[1979] video rentals,[1980] cable television,[1981] children's (under age 13) online activities,[1982] educational records,[1983] motor vehicle registrations,[1984] and telemarketing.[1985] The end of 1999 brought increased scrutiny on financial privacy. In 1999, the Michigan Attorney General sued several banks for revealing that they were selling information about their customers to marketers. Other banks across the country subsequently admitted that they were also selling customer records. The Gramm-Leach-Bliley Act, which eliminated traditional ownership barriers between different financial institutions such as banks, securities firms and insurance companies, set weak protections on financial information that is likely to be shared among merged institutions. In spite of the low level of protections conferred, the effective date of the privacy provisions were pushed back from November 2000 until July 2001. The year 2000 also saw the sole federal law governing information use online go into effect. The Children's Online Privacy Protection Act (COPPA), passed by Congress in 1998 and requiring parental

---

[1974] Protecting Consumers' Privacy: 2002 and Beyond, Remarks of FTC Chairman Timothy J. Muris, October 2001, available at <http://www.ftc.gov/speeches/muris/privisp1002.htm>.

[1975] See FTC Privacy Initiatives <http://www.ftc.gov/privacy/index.html>.

[1976] The Proposed National "DO NOT CALL" Registry, Amendment to the Telemarketing Sales Rule, January 2002, available at <http://www.ftc.gov/bcp/conline/edcams/donotcall/index.html>.

[1977] See Marc Rotenberg, The Privacy Law Sourcebook: United States Law, International Law, and Recent Developments (EPIC 2001) <http://www.epic.org/bookstore/pls/>.

[1978] Right to Financial Privacy Act, Pub. L. No. 95-630 (1978).

[1979] Fair Credit Reporting Act, Pub. L. No. 91-508 (1970), amended by PL 104-208 (1996), available at <http://www.ftc.gov/os/statutes/fcra.htm>.

[1980] Video Privacy Protection Act, Pub. L. No. 100-618 (1988).

[1981] Cable Privacy Protection Act, Pub. L. No. 98-549 (1984), available at <http://www.epic.org/privacy/cable_tv/ctpa.html>.

[1982] See Center for Media Education, A Parent's Guide to Online Privacy, available at <http://www.kidsprivacy.org/>.

[1983] Family Educational Rights and Privacy Act, Public Law 93-380, 1974, available at <http://www.epic.org/privacy/education/ferpa.html>.

[1984] Drivers Privacy Protection Act, PL 103-322, 1994, available at <http://www.epic.org/privacy/laws/drivers_privacy_bill.html>.

[1985] Telephone Consumer Protection Act, PL 102-243, 1991.

consent before information is collected from children under the age of 13, went into effect in April 2000.[1986] Protections for medical records were finally introduced in the United States in 2001. In October 1999, the Department of Health and Human Services issued draft regulations protecting medical privacy. The final rules were issued on December 20, 2000 and went into effect in April 2001. The large number of exemptions provided limits the protection offered by the new rules. For example, patients' information can be used for marketing and fundraising purposes. Doctors, hospitals, and health services companies will be able to send targeted health information and product promotions to individual patients and there is no opt-out right to limit this marketing use of medical data.[1987] There is also a variety of sectoral legislation on the state level that may give additional protections to citizens of individual states.[1988] The tort of privacy was first adopted in 1905 and all but two of the 50 states recognize a civil right of action for invasion of privacy in their laws.[1989]

There has been significant debate in the United States in recent years about the development of privacy laws covering the private sector. The White House and the private sector maintain that self-regulation is sufficient and that no new laws should be enacted except for a limited measure on medical and genetic information. There have been many efforts in Congress to improve privacy. Since January 2001, there have been well over 100 bills introduced in the House and Senate.[1990]

There is also substantial activity in the states. In recent years, Massachusetts and Hawaii have considered comprehensive privacy bills for the private sector. California passed a Social Security Number bill that will prevent the printing of the identifier on forms, invoices, and identification badges. The bill also gives individuals greater power to control their credit report once fraud is suspected.[1991] Minnesota enacted a bill that requires ISPs to give notice and obtain user authorization before using personal information for secondary purposes.[1992] In a statewide referendum, North Dakota residents established opt-

---

[1986] FTC Privacy Pages <http://www.ftc.gov/privacy/index.html>.

[1987] Office of the Secretary; Standards for Privacy of Individually Identifiable Health Information; Proposed Rule 45 CFR Parts 160 and 164, §164.501 (March 27, 2002), available at <http://www.hhs.gov/ocr/hipaa/propmods.txt>.

[1988] Compilation of State and Federal Privacy Laws (2002 ed.), by Robert Ellis Smith and Privacy Journal <http://www.epic.org/privacy/consumer/states.html>.

[1989] See Lake v. WalMart Stores, Inc., 582 N.W.2d 231 (Minn. 1998), for a review of state adoption of common law privacy torts.

[1990] See EPIC Bill Track <http://www.epic.org/privacy/bill_track.html>.

[1991] California Senate Bill 168.

[1992] Minnesota S.F. 2908.

in protections for financial information.[1993] Additionally, Georgia enacted a privacy law that prohibits private businesses from discarding documents or computer components that contain personal information.[1994]

Internet privacy has remained the hottest issue of the past few years. A number of profitable companies, including eBay.com, Amazon.com, drkoop.com, and yahoo.com have either changed users' privacy settings or have changed privacy policies to the detriment of users.[1995] A series of companies, including Intel and Microsoft, were discovered to have released products that secretly track the activities of Internet users.[1996] Users have filed several lawsuits under the wiretap and computer crime laws. In several cases, TRUSTe, an industry-sponsored self-regulation watchdog group ruled that the practices did not violate its privacy seal program. Significant controversy arose around online profiling, the practice of advertising companies to track Internet users and compile dossiers on them in order to target banner advertisements. The largest of these advertisers, DoubleClick, set off widespread public outrage when it began attaching personal information from a marketing firm it purchased to the estimated 100 million previously anonymous profiles it had collected.[1997] The company backed down due to public opposition, a dramatic fall in its stock price and investigations from the FTC and several state attorneys general. In July 2000 the Federal Trade Commission reached an agreement with the Network Advertisers Initiative, a group consisting of the largest online advertisers including DoubleClick, which will allow for online profiling and any future merger of such databases to occur with only the opt-out consent.[1998] In January 2001, the FTC dropped its investigation of DoubleClick. However, a number of private lawsuits were filed against DoubleClick. In January 2001, DoubleClick closed its online profiling division, and in May 2002, privacy class actions suits against the company were settled that resulted in little or no benefit to Internet users.[1999] Intel announced in

---

[1993] Tena Friery, "Privacy Alert: North Dakota Votes for 'Opt-In' Financial Privacy," Privacy Rights Clearinghouse, June 21, 2002, available at <http://www.privacyrights.org/ar/nd_optin.htm>.

[1994] Georgia Senate Bill 475.

[1995] Chris Jay Hoofnagle, Consumer Privacy In the E-Commerce Marketplace 2002, Third Annual Institute on Privacy Law 1339, Practicing Law Institute G0-00W2 (June 2002), available at <http://www.epic.org/epic/staff/hoofnagle/plidraft2002.pdf>.

[1996] See Big Brother Inside Campaign <http://www.bigbrotherinside.org>.

[1997] See EPIC DoubleClick Pages <http://www.epic.org/privacy/doubletrouble/>.

[1998] For a detailed history and critical analysis of this agreement, see Electronic Privacy Information Center (EPIC) and Junkbusters, "Network Advertising Initiative: Principles not Privacy," July 2000 <http://www.epic.org/privacy/internet/NAI_analysis.html>.

[1999] Privacy advocates debate merits of DoubleClick settlement, Computerworld, May 22, 2002, at <http://www.computerworld.com/printthis/2002/0,4814,71382,00.html>.

May 2000 that it was dropping the incorporation of unique identifiers in its next-generation computer processors following a consumer boycott.[2000]

Several industry spokespeople, including Intel's Chairman Andrew Grove, have been supportive of federal Internet privacy legislation in order to stave off the states' recent efforts to enact such protections on their own.[2001]

The United States Department of Commerce and the European Commission in June 2000 announced that they had reached an agreement on the Safe Harbor negotiations that would allow United States companies to continue to receive data from Europe. The European Parliament adopted a resolution in early July seeking greater privacy protections from the arrangement.[2002] The Commission announced that it was going to continue with the agreement without changes. Over 200 companies have joined the Safe Harbor.[2003]

Surveillance of wire, oral and electronic communications for criminal investigations is governed by the Omnibus Safe Streets and Crime Control Act of 1968 and the Electronic Communications Privacy Act of 1986.[2004] Police are required to obtain a court order based on a number of legal requirements before capturing the content of a communication. Surveillance for national security purposes is governed by the Foreign Intelligence Surveillance Act that has less rigorous requirements.[2005] The use of electronic surveillance has more than tripled in the last ten years. In 2001, a total of 1,491 federal and state wiretaps were authorized. No wiretap applications were denied during the year. The vast majority of the wiretaps, 78 percent, were authorized for narcotics investigations. 68 percent of wiretaps were directed at portable devices such as cellular phones and pagers. Law enforcement encountered encryption in 16 of the wiretaps, however, police were able to access the plaintext of the communications in all cases.[2006] The question of police decryption methods has recently been raised in the case of *United States v Nicodemo Scarfo*. In this case, the FBI surreptitiously installed a key logger device on the defendant's computer in order to capture his PGP encryption passphrase. The defense successfully argued before a federal

---

[2000] See <http://www.bigbrotherinside.org>.

[2001] "Gates, Grove Differ on Net Privacy Laws," Industry Standard, June 6, 2000.

[2002] European Parliament, Doubts over security personal data in United States "Safe Harbors," available at <http://www.europarl.eu.int/dg3/sdp/brief/en/br000703_ens.htm#9>.

[2003] Safe Harbor List <http://web.ita.doc.gov/safeharbor/shlist.nsf/webPages/safe+harbor+list>.

[2004] 18 USC secs. 2510, et seq.; 18 USC 2701 et seq., available at <http://www.law.cornell.edu:80/uscode/18/ch119.html>.

[2005] Foreign Intelligence Surveillance Act of 1978, 50 USC 1801.

[2006] Wiretaps Increased in 2001, With Majority Tied to Drug-Related Investigations, Administrative Offices of the United States Courts, May 23, 2002, available at <http://www.uscourts.gov/Press_Releases/wiretap01.pdf>.

court in New Jersey that it should be granted access to the details of the key logger technique, in order to determine the legality of the search. The judge directed the government to produce a report "detailing how the key logger device functions" by August 31, 2001.[2007] In December 2001, the judge upheld the legality of the key logger device, and ruled that further exposure of its workings "would cause identifiable damage to the national security of the United States."[2008]

In December 2001, the U.S. FBI confirmed the existence of a technique called "Magic Lantern."[2009] This device would reportedly allow the agency to plant a Trojan horse keystroke logger on a target's computer by sending a computer virus over the Internet; rather than require physical access to the computer as is now the case. Controversy arose surrounding this announcement, as anti-virus companies argued that they could not leave a hole in their protection software to allow for Magic Lantern's surreptitious placement on computers. Doing so, they argued, would create a conflict of interests. Moreover if each country's law enforcement agency developed a similar form of virus, each virus would have to be excluded from anti-virus companies' products: translating the purpose of the software, and affecting consumer trust.

The federal wiretap laws were amended by the Communications Assistance to Law Enforcement Act in 1994 that required telephone companies to redesign their equipment to facilitate electronic surveillance.[2010] The Federal Communications Commission issued regulations in November 1998 implementing the law.[2011] The regulations include several additional provisions including requiring that all mobile phone companies facilitate location tracking of users. Privacy groups challenged the implementation of the law in federal court and telecommunications companies, who argued that the regulations give the government more power than authorized under the law and the Constitution.[2012] In August 2000, the United States Court of Appeals for the D.C.

[2007] Selected court documents on the Scarfo case are available at <http://www.epic.org/crypto/scarfo.html>.

[2008] United States v. Nicodemo S. Scarfo, et al., No. 00-404 (NHP) (D. N.J. 2001) (Opinion and Order of Dec. 26, 2001), available at <http://www.epic.org/crypto/scarfo/opinion.html>.

[2009] Elinor Mills Abreu, "FBI Confirms 'Magic Lantern' Project Exists," Reuters, December 12, 2001.

[2010] Communications Assistance for Law Enforcement Act of 1994, PL 103-411 <http://www.epic.org/privacy/wiretap/calea/calea_law.html>.

[2011] Federal Communications Commission, In the Matter of the Communications Assistance for Law Enforcement Act, CC Docket No. 97-213, November 5, 1998, available at <http://www.epic.org/privacy/wiretap/calea/fnprm.html>.

[2012] United States Telecom Association, et al., v. Federal Communications Commission and United States of America, No. 99-1442.

Circuit ruled that law enforcement agencies must meet the highest legal standard before using these new surveillance capabilities.

The intelligence agencies have also pushed for more authority and funding to conduct surveillance of Internet communications, arguing that this is necessary to protect the nation's infrastructure from "information warfare." In July 2000, it was revealed that the FBI has developed a system called "Carnivore" that is placed at an Internet Service Provider's offices and can monitor all traffic about a user including email and browsing.[2013] Earthlink, a major ISP, announced that it refused to install the system in its network.[2014] After the system was discovered, Attorney General Reno promised to conduct a review of its privacy protections.[2015] In the fall of 2000, the Justice Department commissioned a team of experts at the IIT Research Institute and the Illinois Institute of Technology Chicago-Kent College of Law (IITRI) to undertake an independent review of the carnivore system. The IITRI group issued its final report on Carnivore in December 2000 and made several recommendations for changes to the system.[2016] These recommendations have not yet been implemented by the Justice Department and the system remains in use today. In May 2002, EPIC obtained FOIA documents on Carnivore that indicated that the program may have hindered the government's anti-terrorism investigation by overcollecting data in violation of wiretapping laws.[2017]

The USA PATRIOT Act, which passed in the wake of the September 11, 2001 attacks, significantly weakened privacy protections in federal wiretapping statutes.[2018] The Act extended the "pen register" portions of federal wiretapping law, allowing Carnivore to be used to collect traffic data based on a mere certification of a prosecutor that it would collect information relevant to an ongoing investigation.[2019] The bill made computer crimes and terrorism predicate offenses for initiation of a federal wiretap.[2020] The bill authorizes national

---

[2013] Testimony of Robert Corn-Revere, before the Subcommittee on the Constitution of the Committee on the Judiciary, United States House of Representatives, The Fourth Amendment and the Internet, April 6, 2000, available at <http://www.house.gov/judiciary/corn0406.htm>.

[2014] "EarthLink Says It Refuses to Install FBI's Carnivore Surveillance Device," Wall Street Journal, July 14, 2000.

[2015] Reno to double-check Carnivore's bite, Reuters, July 13, 2000.

[2016] IITRI, Independent Technical Review of the Carnivore System, Final Report, 8 December 2000 <http://www.epic.org/privacy/carnivore/carniv_final.pdf>.

[2017] FBI Memo on "FISA Mistakes," available at <http://www.epic.org/privacy/carnivore/fisa.html>.

[2018] H.R. 3162, Uniting and Strengthening America by Providing Appropriate Tools Required to Intercept and Obstruct Terrorism (USA PATRIOT ACT) Act of 2001, P.L. 107-56, available at <http://thomas.loc.gov/cgi-bin/bdquery/z?d107:h.r.03162>.

[2019] Id. at § 216.

[2020] Id. at §201-2.

application of a wiretap order, that is, a court in one jurisdiction can issue a warrant that could apply anywhere in the country.[2021] Courts can issue roving wiretaps, giving law enforcement the ability to monitor many different devices that a suspect may use.[2022] Although supporters of the PATRIOT Act claimed that a sunset provision in the bill would limit police power, only some of the new surveillance authority will expire. Also, several states followed suit by passing state legislation that loosens protections against wiretaps.[2023] Additionally, at the time of publication, Congress is considering the creation of an official Homeland Security Agency[2024] and private-sector corporations are collaborating to use commercial marketing data for terrorism profiling.[2025]

The past year has seen a new trend towards the increased use of video surveillance cameras linked with facial recognition software in public places.[2026] This kind of technology was first used at the 2001 Super Bowl in Tampa, Florida to compare the faces of attendees to faces in a database of mug shots. Public usage of the technology then spread to the Ybor City district of Tampa, where the technology encountered much public opposition. In August 2001, the Tampa City Council held a vote on whether they should terminate their contract with Visionics, but they narrowly decided to keep using the software. Virginia Beach, Virginia, received funding in 2001 from the Virginia Department of Criminal Justice Services to install a system that can scan and process the facial images of tourists visiting the town. Face recognition technology is still not reliable and remain unregulated by United States laws. Studies sponsored by the Defense Department have also shown the system is right only 54% of the time and can be significantly compromised by changes in lighting, weight, hair, sunglasses, subject cooperation, and other factors.[2027] Tests on the face recognition systems

[2021] Id. at §§216, 220.

[2022] Id. at § 206.

[2023] National Review of State Surveillance Responses to September 11 Attacks, Constitution Project, April 8, 2002, available at <http://constitutionproject.org/ls/50statesummary.doc>.

[2024] H.R. 5005, Homeland Security Act of 2002, available at <http://thomas.loc.gov/cgi-bin/bdquery/z?d107:h.r.05005:>.

[2025] See Letter from the Center for Information Policy Leadership to Interested Parties, 2002, available at <http://www.epic.org/privacy/profiling/authcom.pdf>.

[2026] Robert O'Harrow, "Matching Faces with Mugshots: Software for Police, Others Stir Privacy Concerns," Washington Post, July 31, 2001 at A1. See also EPIC's page on Face Recognition <http://www.epic.org/privacy/facerecognition/>.

[2027] Declan McCullagh and Robert Zarate, "Scanning Tech a Blurry Picture", Wired News, February 16, 2002, available at <http://www.wired.com/news/print/0,1294,50470,00.html>.

in operation at Palm Beach Airport in Florida,[2028] and Boston Logan Airport have also shown the technology to be ineffective and error-ridden.[2029]

There have been a number of proposals to create a National ID in the wake of the September terrorist attacks.[2030] Most of these efforts have sought the creation of a national identification system through the standardization of state driver's licenses.[2031] A bill to create a National ID has been introduced in the House, but a companion bill has yet to be introduced in the Senate.[2032] There are also more limited attempts to create national identification systems through "enhanced visa" documents and "trusted traveler" programs.

In the summer of 2001 privacy and consumer organizations, led by the Electronic Privacy Information Center (EPIC), filed a complaint at the Federal Trade Commission alleging that Microsoft Passport and associated services, in the collection and use of personal information, constituted an "unfair and deceptive trade practice," in violation of Section 5 of the FTC Act. The FTC replied on August 7, 2001.[2033] The organizations filed a supplemental complaint on August 15, 2001, containing additional allegations.[2034]

The Freedom of Information Act was enacted in 1966 and has been amended several times.[2035] It allows for access to federal government records by any requestor, except those held by the courts or the White House. However, there are numerous exceptions, long delays at many agencies, and little oversight unless a requestor files a lawsuit to enforce its rights. It was amended in 1996 by the Electronic Freedom of Information Act to specifically provide access to

---

[2028] American Civil Liberties Union Press Release, "Data on Face-Recognition Test at Palm Beach Airport Further Demonstrates Systems' Fatal Flaws," May 14, 2002, available at <http://www.aclu.org/news/2002/n051402b.html>.

[2029] Hiawatha Bray, "'Face Testing' at Logan is Found Lacking," Boston Globe, July 17, 2002, available at <http://www.boston.com/dailyglobe2/198/metro/_Face_testing_at_Logan_is_found_lacking+.shtml>.

[2030] IDs -- Not That Easy: Questions About Nationwide Identity Systems, Stephen Y. Kent and Lynette I. Millett, Editors, Committee on Authentication Technologies and Their Privacy Implications, National Research Council, 2002, available at <http://www.nap.edu/catalog/10346.html?onpi_topnews_041102>.

[2031] Your Papers Please: From A State Driver's License to a System of National Identification, EPIC Report, February 2002, available at <http://www.epic.org/privacy/id_cards/yourpapersplease.pdf>.

[2032] H.R. 4633, the Driver's License Modernization Act of 2002, available at <http://thomas.loc.gov/cgi-bin/bdquery/z?d107:h.r.04633:>.

[2033] In the Matter of Microsoft, Complaint and Request for Injunction, Request for Investigation, and for Other Relief, filed with the Federal Trade Commission, July 26, 2001, available at <http://www.epic.org/privacy/consumer/MS_complaint.pdf>.

[2034] In the Matter of Microsoft, Supplemental Materials in Support of Pending Complaint and Request for Injunction, Request for Investigation, and for Other Relief, filed with the Federal Trade Commission, August 15, 2001, available at <http://www.epic.org/privacy/consumer/MS_complaint2.pdf>.

[2035] Freedom of Information Act, Pub. L. No. (1966), codified at 5 § USC 552, available at <http://www.epic.org/open_gov/foia/us_foia_act.html>.

---

records in electronic form.[2036] Most recently, the Congress has considered a "critical infrastructure exemption" to the FOIA. This exemption would shield information voluntarily provided to the government by private entities on security information from the FOIA.[2037] There are also laws in all states on providing access to government records.[2038]

[2036] Electronic Freedom of Information Act Amendments of 1996, available at
<http://www.epic.org/open_gov/efoia.html>.

[2037] Testimony of David L. Sobel before the House Committee on Energy and Commerce Subcommittee on Oversight and Investigations, Hearing on Creating the Department of Homeland Security: Consideration of the Administration's Proposal, July 9, 2002, available at
<http://www.epic.org/security/infowar/07_02_testimony.html>.

[2038] See Tapping Officials' Secrets, Reporters Committee for Freedom of the Press, available at
<http://www.reporterscommittee.org/tapping2001/index.cgi>.

INFORMATION & PRIVACY LAW
EPIC Publications 2002

Privacy Law Sourcebook 2002: United States Law, International Law, and Recent Developments.
ISBN 1-893044-15-7. $40.

The Privacy Law Sourcebook is the leading resource for students, attorneys, researchers and journalists interested in privacy law in the United States and around the world. Includes the full texts of major United States privacy laws and directives, as well as European Union Directives for both Data Protection and Telecommunications and a fully up-to-date section on recent developments. Also included is an extensive section on privacy resources with useful web sites and contact information for privacy agencies, organizations, and publications.

Privacy & Human Rights 2002: An International Survey of Privacy Laws and Developments.
ISBN 1-893044-16-5. $25.

This annual report by EPIC and Privacy International reviews the state of privacy in over 50 countries around the world, outlining legal protections for privacy and summarizing relevant issues and events. The 2002 report documents numerous anti-terrorism and security measures that have been implemented or proposed in response to the events of September 11, 2001. The report finds a number of quickly enacted common trends, including increased communications surveillance and search and seizure powers, weakening of data protection regimes, increased data sharing, and increased profiling and identification.

Litigation Under the Federal Open Government Laws (FOIA), 21st Edition.
ISBN 1-893044-17-3. $40.

Litigation Under the Federal Open Government Laws, published by EPIC and the James Madison Project, is the standard reference work covering all aspects of the Freedom of Information Act, the Privacy Act, the Government in the Sunshine Act, and the Federal Advisory Committee Act. Now in its 21st edition, the book is edited by Harry Hammitt of *Access Reports* and it draws upon the expertise of practicing attorneys who are recognized experts in the field. Appendixes include the text of the relevant acts, and sample pleadings for litigators. A comprehensive guide, essential for anyone interested in open access laws.

* Special Package Offer *
All 3 above titles, plus free shipping/handling: $100.

EPIC Publications Order Form

Privacy Law Sourcebook 2002 : $40.   Quantity: ___   Total Cost: _____

Privacy & Human Rights 2002: $25.   Quantity: ___   Total Cost: _____

FOIA, 21ˢᵗ Ed.: $40.   Quantity: ___   Total Cost: _____

All 3 above titles, free shipping: $100.   Quantity: ___   Total Cost: _____

                                                             Subtotal: $_____

Domestic Shipping: $3 per book.   Quantity: ___   Total Cost: _____

International:

    Surface Mail: $5 per book.   Quantity: ___   Total Cost: _____

    Air Mail: $10 per book.   Quantity: ___   Total Cost: _____

                                                             Subtotal: $_____

Add **Subtotal** fields together to determine your **Grand Total**: $_____

Payment Information

__Visa   __MasterCard   __American Express   __Check/Money Order

Card Number: _____   Exp. Date: _____

Name on Card: _____   Signature: _____

Address Line 1: _____

Address Line 2: _____   City: _____

State: _____   Zip/Postal Code: _____   Country: _____

Cut out this page and remit to:

EPIC - Publications
1718 Connecticut Ave. NW, Suite 200
Washington, DC 20009

Questions? Phone: 1.202.483.1140 or e-mail: bookstore@epic.org

EPIC Bookstore — bookstore.epic.org